STEVE RICH '95

1900

The Saugus River then.

—

2005

The Saugus River now.

Of Time and the River

Of Time and the River

Saugus

1900 - 2005

edited by
John J. Burns
Thomas F. Sheehan
Robert P. Wentworth

This edition is published by a joint effort of Jostens Printing and
Publishing and Saugus.net with Tom Keeley acting as liaison.

Jostens Printing and Publishing
4000 South Adams Road
Topeka, Kansas 66609

Tom Keeley
Publishers Representative
27 Brackenbury Lane
Beverly, MA 01915

Saugus.net
http://www.saugus.net
781-231-2621

ISBN 0-9703141-1-6

Acknowledgments

Co-Editors: John J. Burns, Thomas F. Sheehan, and Robert P. Wentworth

The Millennium Book Associates General Committee: Judi Alabiso, Jeanne Barrett, Eric W. Brown, David Burns, Stephen Carlson, Stanley Green, James Harrington, Betsy Hatfield, Neil Howland, Janice Jarosz, Wallace McKenzie, Jr., Richard Provenzano, Jean Raymond, Stephen Rich, Peter Rossetti, Jr., Robert Sacco, Clayton Trefry.

We were fortunate and privileged to continue our association with this dedicated and enthusiastic staff, most of whom were members of our former committee who so successfully helped guide *A Gathering of Memories* to publication.

Individually they brought with them a vast personal knowledge of Saugus' 20th Century, introducing a distinctive perspective, which was instrumental in maintaining our focus on the purpose and direction of this history.

We were blessed with the special efforts of some of these committee members, Jeanne Barrett, Ellen Burns, Betsy Hatfield, and Jean Raymond, who have given generously of their time on numerous occasions preparing this book for publication.

We thank them all, with special thanks to William Maloney, nationally known artist, who once again bestowed upon us, for our cover, this marvelous theme painting depicting a section of the Saugus River. Bill, a man of many talents, as well as a man of few words, when asked to be our cover artist, responded simply, "Of course;" to David Burns, who generously gave of his time and computer skills converting most of these stories to a computer-ready form; to Fred Brooks, who searched through the Saugus Historical Society photograph collection for us; to James Harrington, who offered unlimited use of his photo treasury and served so capably as our pictorial maven; and finally to Eric Brown, our computer virtuoso whose workplace became the final (before printing) destination of all material submitted. Eric spent countless hours at his computer standardizing and formatting all text and photos into the form so magnificently displayed herein. Thank you, Eric, and *bravo*.

Remembering with Heartfelt Thanks:

Once again we express our grateful appreciation to those listed below who so generously supported our original fund-raising effort when publishing, *A Gathering of Memories, Saugus 1900-2000.*

These generous donations, when added to the after-cost proceeds from the sale of the book, enabled us to establish the John J. Burns Millennium Book Associates College Scholarship Program, awarded annually to a Saugus High School senior. This fund also provided seed money for the publishing of this new book, *Of Time and the River*, making it unnecessary to launch another drive for additional monies.

An added bonus came our way when in 2006 Benson and Norma Shapiro, two loyal and ardent supporters, strengthened this fund with another generous contribution. They were joined shortly thereafter by Roger Howland. We are so fortunate to have their continued support.

A tributary of the Saugus River.

Corporate / Organization Donors:

- Aggregate Industries, Northeast Region
- Amicone Auto Body
- Continental Restaurant of Saugus
- East Boston Savings Bank
- Eastern Tool and Stamping Company
- G.B.A., Inc.
- Kane's Doughnut House
- Libra Carpets
- Moynihan Lumber Company of Beverly, MA
- Porcella Funeral Services, Inc.
- Prince Italian Foods – Saugus, Inc.
- Refuse Energy Systems Co. – RESCO Wheelabrator Technologies, Inc.
- Russo's Candy House
- Saugus Cultural Commission
- Saugus High School, Class of 1945
- Sawyer, Donaldson, Hollett Insurance Agency
- Town of Saugus Millennium Committee
- White Hen Pantry

Individual Donors:

- Blood, Russell L.
- Bond, Mr. and Mrs. Frank
- Bright, Mr. and Mrs. William
- Bucchiere, John J. Jr., M.D.
- Burns, John, Ellen and David
- Cunningham, C. Carroll, Maurice, Brian, Charlene Thompson
- D'Amico, Phyllis
- DeFronzo, Rose Scire
- Diamond, Allen
- Egan-McKenzie Family
- Everitt, Harold
- Falzone, Mark
- French, Sylvia
- Graves Family, Memory of Herbert, Ethel, Marion (Mugar), Helen (Davis) and Marleah
- Heffernan, Paul and Jodi
- Hoffman, Robert
- Hollett, Kathryn C.
- Howland, Roger
- Junkins, Donald
- Kelly, Carlene
- Kochakian, Miriam
- LaFerla, John M.D.
- Leahy, Mary
- Leone, Mr. and Mrs. Victor, Jr.
- Leuci, Janet M.
- Lockwood, Douglas
- MacDonald, Carol P.
- Maes, Raymond
- Magarian, Kathleen and William
- McAdoo, William
- Moorehouse, Elizabeth
- Natola, June
- Pastan, Mr. and Mrs. Harvey
- Polese, Mr. and Mrs. Albert
- Rohrbacher, Richard P.
- Ross, Cynthia
- Sargent, Lerlean
- Scire, Anthony
- Seelley, Mr. and Mrs. Robert
- Shapiro, Benson P. and Norma L. Charitable Gift Fund
- Valeri, David and Jeanne
- Wentworth, Robert and Barbara

First Benefactor

President and CEO of Saugusbank

by

Thomas Sheehan

Quite early in the generation of *A Gathering of Memories: Saugus 1900-2000*, before the book was even written, our committee realized the need for a large sum of money to get the book printed. In that pursuit, we prepared a nine-page proposal outlining our schedules, planned time lines of achievement, publicity programs, potential sales markets, etc.

With the proposal neatly prepared, bound under acetate cover, we proposed that it be read, or studied, by John M. Dean, President and CEO of Saugusbank, a co-operative bank.

We were looking for about $60,000 to print 2,000 copies of a fairly large book.

We left the proposal with John Dean.

We came back a week later.

As we entered his office (John Burns, Bob Wentworth, Tom Sheehan, and the printer's representative, Tom Keeley), John Dean looked up, stood up, raised his hands, and said, in one of the momentous lines dealing with our proposed book, "You've got your money."

He was declaring his interest in Saugus.

As we crossed Lincoln Avenue a short while later, John Burns, in complete honesty, said, "Did I really hear what I just heard?"

We were on our way, thanks to John Dean and Saugusbank.

John M. Dean

by

Theresa Kelley

John M. Dean, President and Chief Executive Officer, has been with Saugusbank since 1992. Mr. Dean plans, organizes and exercises control over all operations for the Bank. With nearly 40 years of banking and financial experience, he has been instrumental in the addition of new products and procedures at Saugusbank.

A graduate of Boston College and Brown University's Graduate School of Banking, Mr. Dean continues to broaden his knowledge of bank systems and operations by attending several financial-related courses every year. In addition to his position as President and CEO, he also serves as a member of the bank's Board of Directors. His activity in the Town of Saugus includes membership in the Saugus Rotary Club and has served as its President. Mr. Dean has also been a member of the Board of Directors for the Saugus Chamber of Commerce. Currently, Mr. Dean serves on the Board of Directors for the Co-operative Banks Employee Retirement Board.

Being an integral component of Saugus and its surrounding communities, Saugusbank strives to provide individuals and business with financial products and services to meet their needs, delivering excellent customer service through valued and knowledgeable employees, while supporting its community. To that end, a Branch Office was opened at One Hamilton Street, Saugus Center in May of 1988 and a new Loan Center at 481 Lincoln Avenue in Cliftondale Square was opened in April of 2005.

Editor's Note

Mr. Dean, subsequent to the writing of this tribute, announced his impending retirement effective August 31, 2006.

John Dean has been at the helm for the past fourteen years. Durng his tenure the bank has grown from 53 million to 174 million in assets.

It was announced that Kevin M. Tierney Sr. will replace John Dean as the new president. Mr. Dean will remain with the bank to assist in the transistion.

We wish John a very happy and healthy retirement, and once again thank him for all of his support.

Looking over the river.

Table of Contents

Prelude

A beginning is a very delicate time.

— Princess Irulan
from the David Lynch version of Dune by Frank Herbert

Prologue

by
John Burns

Memories as much as we cherish them do not have an easy time in this hard scrabble world. Life imposes daunting challenges on us, relentless demands on our time and our attention, distracting us from the sentimental impulses we feel. This is unfortunate, curbing our instinct to remember the moments we have cherished and the people we have admired and loved. Who can dispute that, in the process of forgetting, we do a disservice to the value of a life or of life itself? Sadly we acknowledge that what has been forgotten truly has no existence.

Marcus Aurelius, Roman emperor and philosopher, assures us that this is inevitable that "no sooner is a thing brought to life than it is swept away and another takes its place and this too will be swept away."

But we do not surrender. We keep our family scrapbooks and establish presidential libraries and national archives to serve memory against the ravages of time.

In that spirit, we offer this book.

Prelude

by
John Burns

Of Time and the River: Saugus 1900-2005, has been written at the urging of those who had read and enjoyed *A Gathering of Memories*.

A Gathering was working with a blank canvas, giving us freedom to choose whatever design or structure we wanted in developing a comprehensive picture of Saugus of that century.

The blank canvas was not there for us to use in producing *Of Time and the River* to play its role in supporting the joint effort of the two publications. We elected to concentrate on the men and women of Saugus in that century, but we have not confined ourselves exclusively to that. As submissions came in, in response to our invitation, we found them to be unpredictable, diverse and revealing. Inevitably they influenced the shape and spirit of our book. We are happy with the results.

Of Time and the River, a vehicle for these Saugonians and ex-Saugonians whose submissions make up this book,

regards itself not as a separate book in a series, but as a companion caught up in the spirit and objective of *A Gathering*. Companions who will sit on your bookshelf, joined in their objective – to leave for future generations the fullest picture we would create of Saugus as it was in the 20th Century.

Saugus 1900-2005

In *Of Time and The River* those men and women whom we recognize and honor; we join with those men and women whom we list here who were recognized and honored in *A Gathering of Memories*.

Snowing over the river.

Our Book is Dedicated to Tony Scire

In writing the *Gathering of Memories* in 1998 we were joined by a *blithe spirit* who left his mark on our book, and on us. You could not miss the enchantment life had for him, both the sublime and the commonplace. There was reverence in his account of what he witnessed, but humor too.

Tony Scire.

He did not mingle, he shunned meetings, but he had his own way of communicating. While he seemed to keep his distance, in reality, he was uniquely generous and open in sharing what was going on in his heart and mind with those who had won his respect and regard. Being his friend took on a special aura.

He died last year.

We are dedicating this book to him, Tony Scire.

In doing this we will be drawing on our memory of him as a means of imparting his spirit and his convictions to this book. As one who shared our intentions, he will hold us to our continued pursuit of giving honor to a portion of our past, to those men and women who made up the Saugus of 1900-2005.

We are offering with this dedication several selections of his writings and his paintings, which give a glimpse of this warm and unassuming man, with his appetite for life and a style all his own for conveying what he witnessed and how it touched him.

Looking Back

by
Tony Scire

My years have been notable for their unspectacular achievements. I've never shown prominence or expertise in any field. I've never enjoyed a *Great Victory* like some of the media-acknowledged giants of the political, artistic or scientific community.

I'm sure, to rationalize this point, that these super-achievers did not, could not, sustain this high level of performance.

But like a maverick wave that breaks suddenly and violently on the scene only to modulate, and level off to ripples, so do the aforementioned giants become compromised and slowed down by the influence of their daily lives. I guess what I'm trying to say is that the great and the not-so-great survive on hope. This usually manifests itself in a series of "small victories."

I will never reach "Tsunami" level. Mine will be a series of ripples, with an occasional swell. There was a point in time when I wanted to paint in oils – and I painted. I wanted to create interesting pieces from driftwood – and I did so.

And lastly, I wanted to write: about my old neighborhood, about my family, about my experiences – and I have written. These have been my "little victories."

My portfolio is not designed for the public. It is primarily my effort to give expression to my feelings and to record the imperfect life of a man seeking some relevance and truth in my remaining days.

"1988"

A Tale of Two Tails

by
Tony Scire

It was a most idyllic scene
To watch the horses graze
They seemed to move in unison
In the early morning haze.

Occasionally, you'd see but one
The larger of the two
But as they turned in tandem
The two came into view.

They met a-field one autumn day
Not quite the well-matched pair.
For he was four hands taller
With a tail both bobbed and bare.

The smaller horse was brown and white
More pony-size than he
Her golden tail was extra long
To ensure her fly-pest free.

Now whether it was natural
Or by some grand design
And whether it was his sire's frame
Or his greater bulk behind.

For soon as the sun broke through the haze
And drank the morning dew
You'd find him shading his little friend
As though it were by cue.

Each afternoon at late day's light
You'd find her circling left, then right
She'd move about a peripheral track
As she flipped and swatted
His fly-filled back.

Her golden tail coiled up so tight
Attacked the hordes of flying mites
Like birds at rest who are set upon
The flying hordes were soon long gone.

And steady as a thresher's flail
She screened his hide with her golden tail.

These horsey affectations
Just suited them to a "tee"
The one with tail
And the one without
Now grazed in harmony.

Pony pals.

The Joy of Growing Up Italian

by
Tony Scire

I was well into adulthood before I realized that I was an American. Of course, I had been born in America and had lived here all my life, but, somehow, it never occurred to me that just being a citizen of the United States meant I was an American. Americans were people who ate peanut butter and jelly on mushy white bread that came out of plastic packages. Me? I WAS ITALIAN.

For me, I am sure that for most second generation Italian-American children who grew up in the '40s and '50s, there was a definite distinction drawn between US and THEM. We were ITALIANS! Everybody else – the Irish, German, Polish, Jewish - they were the "MED-E-GONES." There was no animosity involved in that distinction, no prejudice, no hard feelings, just – well we were sure ours was the better way. For instance, we had a bread man, a coal and ice man, a fruit and vegetable man, a watermelon man, and a fish man; we even had a man who sharpened knives and scissors who came right to our homes, or at least right outside our homes. They were the many peddlers who plied the Italian neighborhoods. We would wait for their call, their yell, their individual distinctive sound. We knew them all and they knew us. Americans went to the stores for most of their foods – what a waste.

Truly, I pitied their loss. They never knew the pleasure of waking up every morning to find a hot, crisp loaf of Italian bread waiting behind the screen door. And, instead of being able to climb up on back of the peddler's truck a couple of times a week just to hitch a ride, most of my "MED-E-GONE" friends had to be satisfied going to the A&P. When it came to food, it always amazed me that my American friends or classmates only ate turkey on Thanksgiving or Christmas. Or rather, that they ate ONLY turkey, stuffing, mashed potatoes and cranberry sauce. Now – WE ITALIANS – we also had turkey, stuffing, mashed potatoes and cranberry sauce but – only AFTER WE HAD FINISHED the antipasto, soup, lasagna, meatballs, salad and whatever else mamma thought might be appropriate for that particular holiday. This turkey was usually accompanied by a roast of some kind (just in case somebody walked in who didn't like turkey) and was followed by an assortment of fruits, nuts, pastries, cakes, and, of course, homemade cookies. No holiday was complete without some home baking, none of that store-bought stuff for us. This is where you learned to eat a seven-course meal between noon and 4 PM, how to handle hot chestnuts and put tangerine wedges in red wine. I truly believe Italians live a romance with food.

Speaking of food – Sunday was truly the big day of the week! That was the day you'd wake up to the smell of garlic and onions frying in olive oil. As you lay in bed, you could hear the hiss as tomatoes were dropped into a pan. Sunday, we always had gravy (the "MED-E-GONES" called it sauce) and macaroni (they called it PASTA). Sunday would not be Sunday without going to mass. Of course, you couldn't eat before mass because you had to fast before receiving communion. But, the good part was, we knew when we got home we'd find hot meatballs frying and nothing tastes better than newly fried meatballs and crisp bread dipped into a pot of gravy.

There was another difference between US and THEM. We had gardens, not just flower gardens, but huge gardens where we grew tomatoes, tomatoes and more tomatoes. We ate them, cooked them, jarred them. Of course, we also grew peppers, basil, lettuce and squash. Everybody had a grapevine, a fig tree, and in the fall, everybody made homemade wine, lots of it. Of course, those gardens thrived so because we also had something else it seems our American friends didn't seem to have. We had a GRAND-FATHER! It's not that they didn't have grandfathers, it's just that they didn't live in the same house or on the same block. They visited their grandfathers. We ate with ours and God forbid, if we didn't see him at least once a day. I can still remember my grandfather telling me about how he came to America as a young man "on a boat." How the family lived in a rented tenement and took in boarders in order to help make ends meet, how he decided he didn't want his children – five sons and two daughters – to grow up in that environment. All of this, of course, in his own version of Italian/English, which I soon learned to under-stand quite well.

So, when he saved enough, and I could never figure out how, he bought a house. That house served as the family head-quarters for the next 40 years. I remember how he hated to leave; he would rather sit on the back porch and watch his garden grow and when he did leave for some special occasion he had to return as quickly as possible. After all, "Nobody's watching the house." I also remember the holidays when all the relatives would gather at my grandfa-ther's house and there'd be tables full of food and homemade wine and music. Women in the kitchen, men in the living room, and kids – kids everywhere. I must have a half million cousins, first and second, and some who aren't even related, but what did it matter. And, my grandfather, his pipe in his mouth and his fine mustache trimmed, would sit in the middle of it all grinning his mischievous smile, his dark eyes twinkling, surveying his domain, proud of his family and how well his children had done. One was a cop, one was a fireman, one had his trade, and, of course, there was always the rogue. And the girls, they had all married well and had fine husbands and healthy children and everyone knew RESPECT.

He had achieved his goal in coming to America and to New York and now his children and their children were achieving the same goals that were available to them in this great country because they were Americans. When my grandfa-ther died years ago at the age of 76, things began to change. Slowly at first, but then uncles and aunts eventually began to cut down on their visits. Family gatherings were fewer and something seemed to be missing, although when we did get together, usually at my mother's house now, I always had the feeling he was there somehow. It was understandable,

of course. Everyone now had families of their own and grandchildren of their own. Today they visit once or twice a year. Today we meet at weddings and wakes.

Lots of other things have changed, too. The old house my grandfather bought is now covered with aluminum siding, although my uncle still lives there and, of course, my grand-father's garden is gone. The last of the homemade wine had long since been drunk and nobody covers the fig tree in the fall anymore. For a while we would make the rounds on the holidays, visiting family. Now, we occasionally visit the cemetery. A lot of them are there – grandparents, uncles, aunts, and even my own father.

The holidays have changed, too. The great quantity of food we once consumed without any ill effects is no good for us anymore. Too much starch, too much cholesterol, too many calories. And, nobody bothers to bake anymore – too busy. And, it's easier to buy it now and too much is no good for you. We meet at my house now – at least my family does – but, IT'S NOT THE SAME.

The difference between US and THEM isn't so easily defined anymore, and I guess that's good. My grandparents were Italian Italians, my parents were Italian Americans, I'm an American Italian, and my children are American Americans. Oh, I'm an American all right and proud of it, just as my grandfather would want me to be. We are all American now – the Irish, Germans, Poles and Jews – U.S. citizens all – but somehow I still feel a little bit Italian. Call it culture, call it tradition, call it roots, I'm really not sure what it is. All I do know is that my children have been cheated out of wonderful piece of their heritage. They never knew my grandfather.

GOD BLESS…

A Song for Him Who Rose Early with Purpose

(for Anthony Scire)

by
Tom Sheehan

I did not know her, years abed
by a window, who drew but smiles
from her husband-nurse. He catered

to odd twists and turns, last-bent arch,
and watched her clutch at agony,
grain-fed birds, gay children scattered

in quick's playground across the square,
dreams leaping with thinned shadow leaves,
pious lips whose last kiss shattered

his lips, lay broken yet, whose eyes
saw his work before sun was due.
By dreadnought germ his heart was battered.

No words would he have scribed for him,
no testament to care, hands caught
of excrement. By his tears it mattered,

who saw long years in clockface pass,
degrees of dying in her bed,
 fed birds, the schoolyard chattered

parts of noon, recess breaks, bouncing
balls, seesaw squeaks, voices leaping
like some loosely maddened hatter.

He did not know she saw his face
on glass, in autumn's last leaf cling,
flowered first in morning's chatter,

on the mantel without a frame
in dismals of her wasting nights;
it was only her who mattered.

A stroll through a Chinese garden with Wun-Sung Ho. The
Chinese in the corner can be loosely translated as "I can
smell Kane's Donuts from here."

The River

The mark of a successful man is one that has spent an entire day on the bank of a river without feeling guilty about it.

— Chinese Proverb

The Britt Brothers Boatbuilders 1902-1941

The Pinnacle of Boatbuilding as Art

by
Andrew Britt, Jr.
(*Wooden Boat Magazine* #167, August 2002)

There's no doubt that the Britt Brothers' accomplishments are unique in the annals of boat building. Their business achieved incredible traction, largely as a result of their interpretation of the works of great designers, and the sheer number of great boats they built. But was their operation the pinnacle?

Did the Britt Brothers tower over their contemporary colleagues? Do their accomplishments stand above those of today's builders who turn out both new work and restorations at least on par with those of the pre-World War II era? Were the Britts the highest point? The culmination? The apex? No, they were not. But the brothers Britt were indeed standing on a summit, and they could look across and see eye-to-eye with the best of wooden boat artisans. At the height of it, they could see forever.

— Matthew Murphy, Editor, *Wooden Boat*

In 1902, two brothers whose name was Britt came down from Maine to West Lynn, where they bought a house on a lot of land sloping down to the Saugus River. The Britts lost no time in putting in skidways and starting to build.

In the next 39 years to 1941, when they built their last boat, they launched 121 confirmed boats with others unconfirmed. [updated as of 2005]

1937 *Yankee* one-design at Britt Brothers Shop.
© Mystic Seaport, Photography Collection, #1997.153.156

At least seventeen, thanks to a combination of fine design, workmanship and tender loving care, were in service for 50 or more years; some are still going.

In the last year of their business, and for the first time ever, the Britt Brothers built a boat on speculation, a 36' motor-sailer, ADELE, owned by Joseph E. Lamm. Mr. Lamm, also a boat carpenter, was quoted as saying: "What you are looking at is one of the examples of the *pinnacle of boat-building craft as an art.*"

The Britt Chronicle

Chester Britt (born in 1866) moved from Maine to Lynn in 1883. Andrew Britt (born in 1870) followed Chester in a move to Lynn soon after the Lynn fire of 1889. They made the move from Maine in search of job opportunities. They both worked as carpenters until 1902, by which time they had acquired sufficient capital to open a boat shop in West Lynn. They built dories for fishermen, as their father had, until a Lynn man, Dana Durgin, ordered a 40' motor yacht. The shop was enlarged to accommodate this project, more orders followed, employees were hired, and Britt Brothers Yacht Builders was in business.

Both brothers were "bib-overall" builders; their office was a small bump-out from the side of the shop with barely room for a desk, a secretary and a table. Andrew lived there in a room with a double bunk. From 1903 to 1913 the brothers built at least 38 boats – 22 of their own design. In later years, Chester assumed more of the running of the business end and Andrew more of the hands-on work as shop foreman.

In the middle years of their careers, from 1914 to 1925, the Britt Brothers built at least 32 boats.

Neighborhood children spent countless hours climbing over the oak and teak planks in the boatyard. The planks came in by rail, then by two-horse teams to the yard. About 1926, trucks began to bring the lumber. When a yacht was finished it was a big day for the neighborhood, everyone turned out to watch.

1936 was a test of courage. Andrew Jr. was in the seventh grade when the fire that totally destroyed the boat shop occurred. His recollection was that all the boats were insured, but the wooden-frame buildings, dating back to 1903 and 1920, were uninsurable. On July 27, 1936, the Britt Brothers announced that on October 1, 1936, they would be back in business at 3 Ballard Street, Saugus, Massachusetts, building larger boats and in better water facilities.

There was no business in the summer of 1939. In August of 1940 there was still no work at the shop, and it didn't look as though any would be forthcoming. Their skilled workers had gone elsewhere where they could earn a pay check.

Andy Britt still has a vivid memory of an August evening in 1941 when his dad at the kitchen table was reading the two-page telegram from the Navy Department asking if the Britt Brothers could build sub-chasers for the Navy. It was out of the question, for there was no work force.

Andrew, a student at the University of Maine in 1941, was at home during the Thanksgiving weekend when his father developed a blood clot in the brain and died three days later. The shop was sold soon after. (Andrew's uncle Chester died in 1945 at age 79.)

Andrew offered to leave school and return home to work. His mother Iona Britt rejected this idea and she went to work as a substitute teacher and finally became a regular teacher in the Saugus school system.

Mrs. Britt taught second grade in the old Sweetser School in 1958. A former student commented, "I loved Mrs. Britt, she was the best teacher I ever had."

The Ballard Street building built by the Britt Brothers to which they moved after the 1936 West Lynn fire, has continued, to this day, to be an important part of the Saugus industrial community. The Josephson and Thompson families, founders of The Eastern Tool and Stamping Company (ETASCO) and Ballard Street neighbors of the boatbuilders, purchased the building, circa 1941. Ownership in later years passed to the Josephsons' grandchildren, the Howland brothers, Ray Jr., Neil and Roger, then principals in the ETASCO business, where they established a limited light manufacturing and quality control operation for ETASCO until about 1960, when the building was again sold.

The building still exists at Lavoie's Landing, housing the Ballard Seafood Marketing.

A Britt-built Patrol Boat. A privately funded five-boat Naval Fleet launched in 1916.
© Mystic Seaport, Photography Collection, #1997.153.261

Among the Notable Launchings

The 50' schooner JOANN was launched in 1924. The JOANN was the first true sailing yacht built by the Britt Brothers. Surprisingly, they were awarded the contract with no notable history of sailing vessel construction. It is believed that their building of the five Patrol Squadron boats and their reputation for quality work had an influence on this decision.

Andrew Jr. (on the left) Adrew Sr. (on the right)
© Mystic Seaport, Photography Collection, #1997.153.255

PANCHARA II was described as a noteworthy houseboat of the Roaring Twenties. Ruggedly built in 1925 by Britt Brothers... she was first owned by Ledyard W. Sargent of the Sargent School, now a part of Boston University. PANCHARA II, 52' power cruiser saw wartime service in Lloyd's Harbor, New York, as a Coast Guard sick bay. (From the book *John G. Alden and His Yacht Designs*.)

SIVA, the largest boat built by the Britts, launched in 1928, measured 90' 11" overall, 15' 6" at the beam.

A 1929 newspaper article titled "Great Revival of Boat Building Industry at West Lynn Yard: Speedboats and Cabin Cruisers in Demand, Say the Britt Brothers Builders" noted that, "Every available inch of space is occupied by small craft in various stages of construction. Five substantial high powered motor boats will slide down the ways into the tidal waters of the Saugus River during the next few weeks."

When asked if the popularity of the motor vehicle had weaned many of their patrons away from sail and motor launch, they replied that, "the demands for high class small craft of the type they specialize in is even greater than before."

Britt Brothers has more than doubled in capacity and output in the last 25 years... They are not the only boat builders in Lynn and seldom engaged on anything other than new construction... with fifteen skilled men employed, they have had no indication of a slack period...

This article was written before the market crash in October 1929, yet three more "builds" occurred in 1930.

The economy finally caught up with the yard in 1931. That was a lean year with only one new boat.

In 1937, the Britt Brothers were selected to build the first hull of the new Yankee One-Design class. The names associated with the creation of this subtly beautiful design read like a Who's Who of New England yachting.

The YANKEE, an R-class sloop, launched in 1925, is believed to be a portent of the present generation of racing (and most cruising) boats. Britt Brothers built this boat.

YANKEE piled up an enviable record. She raced off Newport in 1926 for the New York Yacht Club. It was quite rough; she won seven Firsts out of seven starts against a field of about a dozen other in her class. She also won the Manhasset Bay Challenge Cup and the Greenwich Cup.

Live Yankee hauled out for repairs.
© Mystic Seaport, L.F. Herreshoff Collection, #73-3-456

In 1927, the significantly more radical R-boat LIVE YANKEE was commissioned. A newspaper clipping of the day stated, "Two of the most unusual yachts were built this winter by Britt Brothers at West Lynn for Rear Commodore Charles Welch of the Corinthian Yacht Club of Marblehead. One of these being the sensational LIVE YANKEE."

LIVE YANKEE was sailing on the West Coast by 1935 and won the Isherwood Trophy.

LIVE YANKEE participated in most races around Marblehead, and always beat the other boats and particularly the New York boats. A fleet of five New York area boats challenged Mr. O-Lie-Nielsen and the LIVE YANKEE at Newport, Rhode Island. She beat the whole fleet of five in a series of races.

A Britt-Built Patrol Boat Fleet

by
Andrew Britt, Jr.
(*The Rudder*, June 1916)

Assistant Secretary of the Navy, Franklin D. Roosevelt, reviewed the Volunteer Patrol Squadron in Boston Harbor on April 28, 1916, under conditions that would tend to dampen the ardor of the most enthusiastic, but which made the vessels of this squadron look grim and businesslike.

The five boats built by Britt Brothers were 40' long, 8' 9" at the beam. The boats were reportedly capable of speeds of 25 miles an hour. The boats were described as "plain, but intensely practical," and ready for scout service, coast patrol, submarine chasing or any other naval duties they may be called upon to perform in the time of war.

Mr. Roosevelt was highly pleased with the performance, while the weather made speed out of the question, the precision and certainty with which each boat executed its movements, showed the results of much careful study.

"Gad, that's bully," Mr. Roosevelt yelled as the five boats slowed simultaneously in observance of a flagship protocol.

Each of the boats is constructed for mounting a machine gun capable of 800 shots a minute. Because of their small size and ease with which they can be maneuvered, they make a difficult target for an enemy's guns while their speed enables them to easily overhaul a submersible.

About the Author, Andrew Britt, Jr.

Andrew Britt, son of Andrew and nephew of Chester of the Britt Brothers Boatbuilders was a 1941 Saugus High School graduate.

The *Saugus Advertiser*, announcing Andrew's 1943 enlistment in the United States Marine Corps, listed Andrew's family residence as 201 Lincoln Avenue, Saugus.

When Andy was in grade school, he would walk down Lincoln Avenue after his classes, across the bridge, over the Saugus River and down the railroad tracks to Raddin Station and to the shop; later to ride home with his dad. He has many fond memories of those afternoons in the shop watching the artisans, the machinery and browsing through the trade journals.

Andy currently lives with Phyllis, his wife since June 1948, in Penfield, New York. He retired from Eastman Kodak after 33 years in manufacturing engineering. He has a lifelong love affair with wood, restoration of antique furniture, whittling, carving and sculpting.

Andrew Sr. (left) Chester (right)
© Mystic Seaport, L.F. Herreshoff Collection, #84-8-108

Down the Saugus River

by
Tom Sheehan

When the moon splatters the heart of Saugus,
when I retreat before the coming dawn

to the still carriage of my room, voyage-maker,
all the town comes with me; the lost marquees,

the "paper streets," people who don't live here
anymore. What's missing is what's missed,

a bulletin indiscriminately issued, tossed.
The river here argues against its banks

like an old man getting into his tall bed.
I've seen him at nursing homes, unknown

to more than the orderly, the fatigues of nursing,
a doctor perhaps every third Thursday.

It's as though he doesn't live there anymore.
If he's really missing, does someone look?

The cat o' nines, brown as Irish setters,
stand taller than weeds, wave ominously

with groundswells the Caribbean throws
our way this September time of the year.

Leaves blur stones at Riverside Cemetery;
wet, they paste veined hands over carved names,

and the missing get more lost. I see them moving
within the secrets of a midnight moon,

time's shadows, mere names now spilling
out of a nonsense of all our histories.

I discovered, late one night, my whole town
is disappearing down the river, soundless,

a mote at a time. I'm with it, me and all
the other baggage, ready or not.

In the still carriage of my room the wheels
turn silently on and on. I am footman,

and driver, counting names and Septembers.
From here, I say, you can hear the river run,

or see where its water becomes the waves.

Still water, on the Saugus River.

Life on the River

by
Gini Pariseau

[A Saugus native who grew up along the river, offers her very interesting perspective on the Saugus River.]

Growing up on the Saugus River was such a unique experience (not that we knew it at the time). The neighborhood consisting of Spencer and Houston Avenues and side streets off those were our playground.

Across the river, to Lynn.

Lawn ornaments back then consisted mostly of lobster traps that were piled to the sky in the winter. Earl and Louise Allen lived a couple of houses away. Earl was Heck Allen's brother and was a lobsterman. Once in a while he would let a couple of us kids in the neighborhood get up really, really early in the morning and go out on his boat for the morning. Can you imagine a mother allowing that these days? I only went out once but I remember it vividly. Louise Allen's niece was visiting and the two of us went out on Earl's boat. I was never sure which made me more sick, the rocking of the boat or the smell of the bait. Anyway, it didn't matter out on the water; no one had any time for holding my hand. The three men on the boat were like a well-oiled machine. I was amazed that they could know exactly where to go and stop the engine and pull up a trap. They had to measure each lobster and they ended up throwing many of them back into the water. But there were a couple that we cooked while we were out there and sat and ate on the front of the boat. I seem to remember a steam pipe or something that cooked them. My memory fails me a little on that. I was always amazed at what hard work lobster trapping was. It certainly wasn't glamorous and I never knew anyone who got rich doing it. The lucky ones were those who made enough money during the season to survive in the off-season. I always assumed from the traps piled in so many of the other yards in the neighborhood that the men who lived there were lobstermen. I don't remember seeing very many of them. (There were other men in the neighborhood that had a couple of traps and lobstered as a hobby.) It wasn't a time when fathers were out front playing ball with their kids…kids kind of blended in with the landscape. Actually, the landscape was our playground. Occasionally we would row our boats over to the bridge near Heck Allen's and get some fried clams. Heck Allen's then was a small diner-like place with about four booths.

I know that whenever we had steamed clams in a pit lined with seaweed at my grandmother's house my uncles would be the ones who went out that morning and dug the clams. Everything was plentiful and we could have as much as we wanted whether it be lobsters or clams.

The marshes at the end of Spencer and Houston were places we drifted to for fun and would spend hours wandering out to the end where the river came in. We would jump over the little inlets that were all over the marsh. In today's world, it would be a very dangerous place to be as a child, but our mothers never seemed to worry and we always came home. We all knew the timing of the tides…it was as important as knowing what time your mom had supper on the table.

The river itself adjacent to Spencer Avenue wound itself around the island in the middle and went down the other side on Johnson Street. My uncle, Connie Freitag, lived on Johnson and would swim across to Spencer to visit my grandparents and us. We always thought he was such an awesome swimmer. This portion of the river was dotted all around with rafts that were made mostly out of old oil barrels to keep them afloat. Lots of people had rowboats and I remember how proud I was when I learned how to make the boat swirl around using the oars.

Another fun pastime was getting a basket, walking along the river's edge, and collecting horseshoe crabs. We would get a big basket full and then threw them back into the river. I remember having to always keep an eye for them when we went swimming because their tails would stand up straight and expose us to the risk of stepping on one of them.

Low tide on the river.

Another pastime was fishing. It is difficult for me to imagine worms and putting one on a hook but we all did it. There was a portion of Houston Avenue called The Boatyard that had a pier that we would fish off. I only remember catching eels but there were other fish too. The kids would always bring them over to my father because he would eat any kind of fish. The eels that continued to move even in pieces in the boiling water always intrigued us.

The Boatyard was also our favorite place to play hide and seek, especially in the fall and early winter when all the boats were brought in off the water.

I don't remember anyone ever getting lost or hurt in any of our escapades. Nature was our friend and playmate. It wasn't that we especially knew we should respect this environment necessarily. It was just a time when we were equals. It didn't hurt us and we didn't hurt it.

Sad Decline of the Great Lobster Fleet

(or, "I Could Have Been A Doctor," Dick Melanson, Lobsterman)

by
John Burns and Tom Sheehan

An afternoon with Bill Robinson and Ron Fisher, lifelong pals and lobster fishermen, is a grand revelation, a movie in reverse, an epic. We met at the Fox Hill Yacht Club, their dry land, onshore daily venue for the men of the Saugus lobster fleet. It exists as a social entity... there beside the river, between the sea and home. With storyteller's delight they spin yarns and memories that have undeniably enriched their lives. You get a taste of the adventures, the love of the chase, the love of the sea where they ply their trade, oft beset by the harshest of labor and the shortest return. The sea, big as it is, is not the sole enemy. These old friends tell of their life on the river, at sea, at lobstering; what it has meant to them, to their fathers, how it fostered their heritage, what memories it solidifies and cements in place. It also fast-forwards what the future holds for the industry where Saugus once boasted of harboring, on its river along Ballard Street, at the Saugus Landing, the largest lobster fleet in the state, even in New England.

Names drop from their lips, old Nova Scotia names, Down Maine names, lobstering names, the legends still coming in on the misty tides, coming up-river past the Rumney Marshes and the General Electric Plant, in under the Belden Bly Bridge once the Fox Hill Bridge with no hill in site, to harbor alongside Ballard Street in Saugus and the Fox Hill Yacht Club and the Officer Harold Louis Vitale Memorial Park where their lobstering facilities are located, for refrigeration, bait care, etc. These men love the sea and being out on it. Once, in their gloried past, there were more than 68 boats in the Saugus lobster fleet, somewhere in the mid '80s,

now there are a mere handful of 20 full time commercial lobster boats.

Ivan Allen and poker buddies.

Time runs about the fleet, and falls at their feet, in their search for homarus americanus.

In the heritage that belongs to lobstering, Bill Robinson started on the river at age 14, cleaning cabins on lobster boats for $1.00 each and from 12-14 years of age went out on trips with his father and others... out as far as the Old Light Ship, en route learning the river, the sea, the lure and lore of the prize, the catch, and the natural order of things. That natural order is work hard, get a day's pay, and carry on.

Lobster boats at rest.

It has been seemingly forever that a lobster license passes from father to son, or somehow stays in the family, and can only be sold once, and then it is gone... part of the controls imposed on lobstering by government regulations.

Bill Robinson has had his license for 35 years, but now, in the lean years with the vicissitudes that have befallen the industry, he has had to work extra jobs, at the Boston Globe as a security guard, as a bartender, and at other commercial-type fishing, such as chasing the giant tuna for far eastern markets.

There was the time, not too long ago, and the light shining in his eyes says so, when he loved to go to sea, could not wait to pass under the span of the Belden Bly Bridge, and be on the way out! He used to love to go out; now can't wait to get back in. For truth, there are more hours worked now and less money coming in. To keep plying this trade, you have to love what you're doing at sea.

Bill Robinson was 21 when he bought his first boat from Edmund Boudreau, a 38-footer. He had been taken under Boudreau's wing because that old fisherman had no sons to pass his deeds or his license on to, having but five daughters.

Fred Penney.

Bill and Ron, in their time in the fleet, have fished with Lollie LeBlanc, Kashie, Luke Zim and the legendary Allens... Ivan, Earl, Heck, Harry and Mike, the names solidified in river lore. And there was club-footed Gus Hubbard, another legendary lobsterman, and the Melansons, and many others who had come down from Nova Scotia and Maine; with names like Joe Tichi, Jack Loserf, Butch Thompson, Dave Penney, the Greens, Arthur Pop De'On, Fred Wortman, Clayton Boudreau. Also, there were the Crowells... Fred and Ron and Enos. Back then, in honor and homage to family heritage, the fishing rights to areas of the ocean were territorial, and protected.

Though there is no season on lobstering, these men usually stop just after the Christmas demand for lobsters and start back out in April. February and March are the toughest months to be out there on the deep, lobsters not moving in the cold water, the weather often abysmal.

What Happened?

Once there were 68 commercial lobster boats in the Saugus fleet, in the mid-80s, the heyday of lobstering, but things happened, impacts on the trade grew... federal and state laws and regulations were enacted, chlorine in waste dumped to the sea increased, safety requirements demanded breakaway lines and biodegradable rings on lobster traps. The regulations then said lobstermen needed to have EPERB (an Electronic Positioning Emergency Radio Beacon), a location device mounted on their mast, or they can be fined as much as $3500. The lobstermen lost bait to

protected seals, for seals often steal bait by diving where a lobster buoy floats to mark a trap location and ripping open the bait sack in the trap and feeding on the bait, and cormorants feast daily on newly-hatched lobsters.

RESCO across the river, sunken boat in foreground.

They must watch the weather forecasts endlessly, for when storms promise to imperil their traps, they have to go out and move them, get the traps into less perilous areas of the sea.

Finally, the V-notch law was enacted, for identifying pregnant female lobsters. All pregnant lobsters had to be V-punched on the second fin on the tail (and woe if a lobsterman is caught with a lobster that's V punched, even if the eggs have been cast off or deposited). Then there came a No Tolerance rule, the Department of Marine Fisheries saying, "If it looks like a V, it is a V, and subject to a fine."

Heading home.

At one time these men might retrieve 800-1000 pounds in a day, their storied past. Those were days when the catch was great. Now they are lucky to get 100 pounds a day, and are limited to 800 traps equipped with tags (and a ten per center factor for losses). And every trap in use has to have a tag on it!

Bill Robinson and Ron Fisher, in quick unison, say they are not "tree huggers" but have always believed in conservation of the supply... and the lobsterman's adage... Work hard, get a day's pay and don't try to make a million bucks in short order; leave something for tomorrow.

Facts come hard and true from their experience: A lobster boat needs a hard-working and loyal stern man for loading bait, carting gear, and a boat captain... fuel is costly... no new lobstermen of the old devotion are coming along, like the paralysis in many other trades or careers. In 50 years, they believe, the trade will be gone... for there will be few lobsters left, perhaps none. And in another 50 years, the lobster fleet will have disappeared.

Dick Melanson's saying, after a little productive but hard-working day at sea, "I'm going home to beat up my mother for not making me become a doctor," is a mark of the times.

They are not idealists, but realists, and unknown adventures continually dance in their eyes, like they know something else the rest of us have not experienced, but are vaguely aware of.

Spuds, at the left, on Lincoln Ave.

Poling the Marshes

by
Neil Bradford Olson

Now I understand that, within time, there is always the possibility
That Allen and I are still out on the salt marshes poling our slim skiff like
Young Prince Valiant out on the Cambrian fen, I mean, the history
Happening all-at-once theory, the timeless-time thing that God only knows.

If this is so, then we must agelessly, youthfully, be doing the same
Old routine; weaving around the trails off Lincoln Avenue, slipping past
The greenhouses in the shadow of the standpipe's rust-steel marbling,
Finding the old skiff hidden carefully in the marsh reeds half-waterlogged.

The poles were a variety of what was at hand, long, thin and strong
For the push off into the grid of drainage ditches reaching out into the marshes
Over the green rise of the Italian gardens and vineyards of what
Charlie, the Cliftondale barber, called Calabrian Revere. Where shall our inches-
High draft and glide over grass and high-tidal bracken lead us today?

Doubtlessly, like any other day, to curve of creeks hiding quicksand
Crescents, or the round, depthless sink-holes where we were assured gangsters
From Lynn and East Boston drove their heavy black sedans, with rivals
Bound within, down to the endless depths where, wearing their jaunty straw-hats,
They shall await the call of angels, or judgment from eternal mother church.

The rotting smell of the creek banks and the trickle up of rain-bowed
Motor-oil were a sure indication of rotting corpses and rusting Duesenbergs below;
(In my college year's Geology, I learned of Limonite bog-iron coloring
The waters, and spin of glacial sinkholes, deep to the bedrock's span, with limited
Number of thugs resting therein) but never matched the smell of the

Marshes in spring, running from the greening of grass to salt, seashell
Muck and the rust-iron taste of the square, burnt-out wrecks off the sandy, back-marsh
Roads, squat in the biting buzz of new marsh mosquitoes. This was our
Flat savanna out of darkest Africa, and we were keen to its juvenile exploration.

Once, we made it to the edge of the grass of the Revere Airport runway,
But never made it to the seaplane tidal pool under the sound of Rowe's stone-crusher.
In the end, it was the firemen that drove us off the marshes. They said,
It was too dangerous there, after two infant idiots, a year ahead of us in Ballard

School, set the marsh ablaze, burning out the old straw and the rotted staddle
Posts left from salt-hay farming. Dangerous! Of course it was dangerous, that was
The point of it. What adventures, later in life, could ever compare with the
First thrill of fear in chances taken on the fast tide, of storm, fire on the marshes,

The beginning of a youthful conquest of fear, and afterwards, the untying of the
Knot in your stomach, and the slight swelling in your chest; the look on Allen's face,
And the voice in the back of your mind, saying, "We have made it home safely,
And God, I feel so alive!"

Ties that Bind

One day I shall come back. Yes, I shall come back. Until then, there must be no regrets, no tears, no anxieties. Just go forward in all your beliefs, and prove to me that I am not mistaken in mine.

— The First Doctor

Saugus Town

by

Tom Sheehan

It is all my center of town is,
a white line on a street
talking to traffic and bending
around the one mean statuary,
a stone with a man's arm
and a woman's body, a hermaphroditic
salute to the wonders of pain and loss.
Once a year bugled Taps spills out
of an alley and floats lazy as blue smoke
over a cemetery the road infringed on.
The rest of the year a hole fills that air.

It is a hole where my old school
sat its red brickness before fire
shocked it redder and shucked it down;
and yet leaves what it meant it was for,
someone like me looking at a hole
from a passing car thirty years later
and feeling under the ball of my foot
old floors swelling with spring
and a carpentered grid work
down hallways four years long.

So, this school closed when I left it.
I have not been back to what there is
no going back to, or for or in.
It just came away with me, all the redness
when a meek boy burned it down one night.
Yet it was gone before its going then.
It came away that lost spring night
blazoned with mottos and insignia,
and I have it here with me, right now;
every odor that worked its way through
the slabbed tons of varnish summer people
tongued over woodwork already dark
in its deep coring and slightly warm;
the back of a study hall seat across my back
I later felt only once in a truck in Korea
as I sat stiffly dreaming on a dirt road
thick with corpses of burned-away visions;
perfume a girl wore on a May day of open
windows pushing lilacs, ball fields,
soon-stars working eye corners and fingertips,
with all my daring dried in the back
of my throat. There is no going back to her
who is not or the school that is not
or to the me who is not for having been
what I was in a school that nevermore is.

It is all my center of town is,
a white line down a wide street

leading to a pond that that no longer
sits its saucer in a green basketing
where stars cannot fall like rocks
into what has gone out of its middle,
nor moon drop its bucket of gold
into soft bluing of June or white nights
of December spreading a cool cake frosting
from brushed edge to brushed edge.

Some wizardry of politics and clutch
stole the pond away that was a pond
and left a hole that cannot catch up
all that it caught before its fullness fled.

Once, oh once, a January skater could sail
to musicless quodlibets and words the stars
held back, could ride the freewheeling
and lusty winds and bitter chills that
sweet sweat brought on, have a star
for companion shoulder high, wear him
into a new day in the free fall flighting
only ice can work up to, and die as ponds die,
as oceans die, from filth, mercury, sludge,
the fallout of acid rains. Things become
what they were not and only meant to be.

I sit, measureless me, measuring holes
in my town of things that cannot be but were,
and whatever was is and whatever is was,
but the cannot be is and the is not cannot be,
but mostly with holes the cannot be cannot be not.

It is all my center of town is,
a white line down a main street,
one half a cross, almost holy but not.

Founders' Day

by

Tom Sheehan

Founders' Day, the second Saturday in every September, is the day when thousands gather in Saugus Center to celebrate who and what we are. So, it is here every year, an illustrious day, a raucous and joyous day in Saugus. We've never had rain for the occasion, the gods being with us for 20 years, as founder Donna Gould has a direct connection overhead. Streets going past the Town Hall, the library, the gas station and the package store, two churches, two schools, another town building, are blocked off, vehicle traffic routed other ways. Hundreds of tables and booths are spread throughout the Center and up side streets; art, crafts, food and books are for sale, all kinds of vendors spread among the selections. Yard sales leap up on homeowners' lawns. The church lawns and parking areas are covered with booths and foot traffic. People in the crowd push at each other, coming in an out and through every conceivable entryway, looking all the while for old friends, classmates, teammates. They are around, you can count on that.

Typical Founders' Day crowds; taken in 2003.

Meanwhile, odors rise rich and pungent from innumerable grills, stoves and warming plates; sausages, subs, pizzas, hot dogs, Chinese and Vietnamese food and delicacies, you name it and it's there, for everything turns upward in steam, smoke, vapors rich and ruddy. Runners flash by in the annual road race, hundreds of runners, the young and the aged, huffing and puffing or in marathon style, their ID numbers flapping through the Center and up Main Street, some runners an hour behind others. Every other year the high school first football game of the new season is played at nearby Stackpole Field. Huge, inflated games and water games and pony rides are available for kids. Old friends are met, relocated Saugonians coming back for the whole day, visitors from nearby towns; and lots of handshaking and backslapping welcomes are made, smiles going electric across the crowd as old classmates or teammates are spotted, and an old girlfriend, toting a grandchild or two, sending off a smile for the yesteryear.

As always, in some corner of Saugus, there is an energy waiting to be tapped. We believe there are no holes and vacuums in our thoughts for this grand day. That is what brought Saugus to the event in the first place. It is most difficult to let go what is precious, a good memory, even when it threatens to slide off by itself into a gray and uneventful place, as if something concrete can suddenly dissipate like a summer cloud at a fresh breeze. But everyone here, every single person seen for one bright moment at Founders' Day, becomes representative of each and every part of Saugus, all that which has had its way in helping to form our memories, letting us become what we have become.

So, as this new Saugus book that you're now reading gathered toward publication and the 2005 issue of Founders' Day drew to an end, another day of elaborate

sunshine passed on, with the crowd banging shoulders and elbows all day long, and co-editor of *A Gathering of Memories*, and *Of Time and the River*, John Burns, 63 years in the Saugus High School teaching corps, was named Saugus' Man of the Year. It was a fitting triumph to another sparkler, this day of days, this celebration of what a community means to itself.

In the crowd were noted former winners and former Saugonians moved on. From Florida they had come, from Maine in all corners, from Georgia and New Jersey, from Rhode Island and Kentucky and New Hampshire, from all over, coming to remember and be remembered. Widows and widowers and children and grandchildren and former spouses and ex-officials and friends and teammates and classmates came ahunting in the crowd for old faces, old pals, warm memories. It was illustrious once again.

At 9 PM of Founders' Day night, as is the case every year, the roads are open again, the debris picked up and carted off, the visitors gone, the quiet middle of Saugus leaning into next year, looking ahead to the next Founders' Day. It will be here before we know it, a slam-bang day, an exalting day, a day for all Saugus folks no matter where they are.

The Hammersmith Stroll

by
Tom Sheehan

Great festive events, those chock full of gaiety and a sense of the spiritual, occur when all private and community organizations combine their resources to sponsor or participate in the event. One of the most heartening and enjoyable is the annual Hammersmith Christmas Stroll. This yearly activity has drawn the support of manifold organizations, merchants and churches and the municipal offices and associations within the total community. The support is magnificent and The Stroll comes off each year as if scripted by hard work, dedication and a fair bit of ingenuity at every level and at every reach of activity.

The range of support has been town-wide for years and stretches through all the churches, the municipal buildings, civic and fraternal and community-involvement organizations. Town Hall, police and fire stations, library and other community structures are thrown open for the enjoyment of townsfolk. Merchants, too, open their doors, associations and town organizations lend a hand or participate in a hundred different ways to make The Stroll one that all people look to. The crowds waiting at special pick-up and drop-off locations are merry and noisy and fully expectant or, in turn, thoroughly pleased at the rides they've been given to festive places along The Stroll routes. There are the famous trolley rides riding through the centers of town and a great assortment of wagon and carriage rides, and pony rides, all generating great enjoyment for people participating. There are many other festivities such as pie-eating contests, musical plays and choral group presentations livening the day, and hosts upon host of costumed cartoon characters directing the way to other supporting events and open facilities.

The list is amazing! And one cannot pretend to cover everything, fearing one name or organization will be left out, but we attempt to salute the many groups and infrastructures that have made The Hammersmith Stroll one of the most widely hailed activities in Saugus:

All our churches.

The National Park Service's First Iron Works in America.

All the civic, fraternal and historical organizations and associations, such as Saugus Band Parents, Millennium Book Associates, Friends of Breakheart Reservation, Little League, Pop Warner, Friends of Town Hall, Saugus Historical Society, Boy Scout Troops, American Legion and Veterans of Foreign Wars, Gardening Club, and SAVE.

All municipal buildings, just about every one of them from the Town Hall to the Public Safety Building to the Library and the Senior Center to the Essex Street Fire Station.

All municipal functions including Police and Fire Departments, Public Works, Public Library and deep commitment to activities by all our school principals and teachers.

Our realtors, our banks, our shopkeepers and merchants of every nature, and so many personal and individual inputs and participations that they are impossible to mention for fear of running out of space.

One of the Hammersmith Stroll's trolley buses stopping in Saugus Center during the 2001 Stroll.

Finally, Saugus.net and Saugus Photos Online and newspapers like *The Saugonian* and *The Saugus Advocate* and *The Saugus Advertiser* that generate specific and dedicated before-and-after coverage of the event.

To be sure, every time out The Hammersmith Stroll mirrors a great community in the reflection of its interests and continuity of spirit.

May Day

by
Tom Sheehan

It was a vital spring day in 1937 or 1938 when students of the Cliftondale School journeyed to the Boston Commons, out in front of the State Capitol building, to celebrate May Day. May Day, of course, is an old rite of spring championing the coming arrival of summer. The celebration extends long into our past and also into that of many European countries.

Teachers of the school at that time included Marleah Graves, Edith Stone and Myra Beckman, each memorable in their own right. Myra Beckman, fourth grade teacher, was the principal of the school on Essex Street, just outside of Cliftondale Square. Today that building stands in a silent tribute to the long teaching career of Marleah Graves.

The Commons that day was alive with people, pigeons and squirrels, and many other school groups that had come to honor the summer invocation. Long before, as part of old celebrations, the Maypole, a tree of life symbol, was placed in the center of many villages and decorated with bunting, flags, or colored paper, such as crepe paper. And so, in our festive day, did we also decorate the pole with bright crepe paper, ribbons and other adornments.

Normally, in such celebrations, a king and queen of the May Procession were selected, to make the day more festive in its salute to summer. And our king and queen, classmates, were crowned with tiaras carefully scissored from colored card stock. In addition, highly decorated baskets were carried by some of the participants from the Cliftondale School, as well as by those in other groups gathered on the Commons, all giving the day a splendid and colorful salute to summer.

The classmates in attendance included Theresa Nagle, Eileen Hayes, Dorothy Shepherd, Donald Gearty, Buddy Tottingham, Charlie Flynn, Kelly Reehill, John O'Neil, Ethel Bambury, Pauline Cabral, Arthur Laura, Barbara Ludwig, George Oxley, Grover Parsons, Patricia Sheehan, Gertrude Pitman, Constance Thulin, Ruth Cassey, Janet MacLeod, Gertrude Pitman, Donald Henshel, Alden Neal,

Ties that Bind

Donald LeBlanc, Jacqueline Ellis, Elizabeth Brougham, Robert Stahler, Ada Sweezey, Billy Callahan, Bayley Mason, Dorothy Biggart, Leonora Aucella, Vail Wilkinson, Marilyn Mclean, Florence Townsend, Natalaie MacAdoo, June Callaway, Agnes Chuck, Thomas Sheehan, Margaret Carbone and Jack Sampson.

We danced and pranced about the Maypole making the day somewhat brighter than it really was and, in the long shadows finally announcing the end of a day away from school, we folded up our meager decorations and headed home. On the horizon sat the promise of summer and nearly three months of school vacation.

Al Day as Mr. Saugus, 325th Anniversary, 1954.

Get Off My Back, Saugus

by
Tom Sheehan

Hey, Saugus, get off my back!
Get off my back, Saugus.
You, yes you, who preaches from Appleton's Pulpit,

you ranter and raver, you extraordinary tongue wielder,
you who yells in chorus from Stackpole Field when wind
brings from the banks of the lost pond voices forgotten
except by you, a goodly chorus of faces and spirited ones
how many times fallow for a quick generation of yells.
Take back your yelling, Oh Saugus, and your cries.
Get off my back, Saugus!
Saugus, get off my back!

You who hastily harangue from the Town Hall floor
a bending of principles and fundamental yields
your seeded and spirited politics have given the ages;
or your echoes, oh echoes of told timbre and tonic
Riverside throws up for grabs the one day trumpets
cut to the quick of small argument advancing outward,
when one falling leaf, nurtured by one, one old friend,
comes, October's breath and daring, to my footed path,
saying his name to me, her name to me, saying we to me.
Get off my back, Saugus!
Saugus, get off my back!

That trail over there, pond-sided, a boy once knew;
new here, that boy, brought to duck and carp and fox,
summer's sweet immersion, winter's scissored ice,
brought to this place out of all places, brought to you,
to be layered on, to be imposed, scribed and etched,
by what makes you what you are, and that boy,
that boy lured here to the burned edge of the pond,
which lingers in the mind one second longer than all.
Get off my back, Saugus!
Saugus, get off my back!

You do not come at me softly except night-shaded
where the wetted, youthful, endless kiss ends sixty
years later when her last picture is delivered
to New Jersey, to another, an older flaming moth
who knows you inside so deeply the ache is read;
who knew your waters blessed us, pond, stream,
river bend by bridge, marshy pools' awesome pair
wearing summer's threatening horseshoe crabs
down back of Sim's farm's wide spread of glass,
and sticks for miles and miles of reeds promising
fire, and antennae-slick worms marsh-dug for
a nickel apiece, for Atlantic bait, bye the bye.
Get off my back, Saugus!
Saugus, get off my back!

You take me past Eileen's house full of ache
I can still feel, the way her soft words flinched,
or Honest Lawyer's sign saying I'm almost home,
or where a rumble under stone is but the one voice
first comforted me, and my brother too, good lady
of iron who talks from under granite these days
of settled touch, who, landing here from Cork's land
and loving this place of yours, stays now forever.
Get off my back, Saugus!
Saugus, get off my back.

Today, trekking on you, you make me think of
a man I haven't seen in fifty years, or heard,
his coming out of your cut century of shadow
and of shine, A's and Cornet's old-time catcher,
big-mitted Sam Parker, died on Hopper's masterpiece device. Every day you do the same thing
taking me back, grasping, clutching, your claws
wrenching soul, letting me know you're all about,
on Pirates' Hill, Standpipe Hill, Catamount Cove,
where Charley's Pond used to be, the Pit, easterly
where our river runs dim and crooked to the sea,
and on all the artifacts of being, illustrious bones,
tossing them up, Saugus, oh one by one tossing
them up.

Ah, Saugus,
will you never
let go?

The Saugus Halloween
Writing Contest

by
John Burns

The Saugus.net Halloween Writing Contest, initiated by
Eric Brown and off to a humble start in 1998, is now in 2005
recognized internationally by Google as one of the biggest
(if not the biggest) contests of this kind.

As a person who holds himself and others to high standards
of writing and immersed as he is in the computer world,
Eric was struck by the fact that as the volume of on-line
communication grew, there was disquieting evidence of a
decline in the quality of writing. Some good writing, even
excellent, but a flood of bad.

Eric undertook this writing contest to encourage writing and
to observe and study growth patterns and tendencies at the
elementary, middle school, and high school levels and in the
adult population.

But why Halloween as a topic?

As a judge in this program since its beginning, I have
become somewhat familiar with the history of Halloween,
born as Samhein in the world of the Celtics of Ireland, when
on this day the world of the living was visited by the ghosts
of the dead returning to earth. Centuries later, with the
growth of Christianity in the Celtic world, November 1
became a day honoring the dead and was designated as All
Saints Day. The nature of this celebration, however, had
much in common with the pagan rite of Samhein.

But in our time, particularly in Ireland, the United
Kingdom, Canada and the United States, the menacing
spirit of the pagan era and the modified tone of the early
Christian era have changed radically in the celebration of
Halloween as a night now given over to the children, to
something "menacing," but playfully so, garish costumes
and to "trick or treat."

There is in the air that night
much to invite ghost
stories, haunted houses,
and visitations of phantom
hitchhikers, doppelgangers
and poltergeists.

The contest's "mascot".

There is much in the spirit
of this night to appeal to
Eric, to his nature and to his
taste in reading. Why
would I be surprised that
Eric, as a devotee of H.P.
Lovecraft and his tales of
horror and madness, would
prefer Halloween as a
subject to, say, Columbus
Day or Valentine's Day?

So the program began. A discouraging start in 1998, a
couple dozen entries, few from the school levels. One
encouraging note was that a few of the submissions were
from published authors.

In the next four years, school participation grew, with a
dramatic increase in 2001. School participation, in terms of
number, has declined since that date, but as a judge I have
observed a growth in quality in these ensuing years.

From 2002, there has been a steady increase in adult entries,
and the first emergence of out-of-state winners. Indeed in
2003 all the adult winners came from out-of-state. This
trend has continued, with 2004 witnessing the first out-of-
country top winners at both the high school and adult levels.

I don't know how much can be discerned about growth in
writing skills with no constant body of writers to observe.
More skill is observable, more skillful writers are participating but from a rapidly extended body of writers,
including more and more published authors.

By now adult writers from 47 states have participated in this
program, as well as representatives from 8 or 10 foreign
countries, including Afghanistan and Nigeria. There has
been one winner from the United Kingdom.

If babble being spewed out in on-line computers communication stirred Eric into sponsoring this writing contest to
counteract it, I think Eric must feel rewarded by the quality

of the submissions he is receiving and by the fact that the level of quality is rising each year.

The care, attention to detail and enthusiasm Eric has brought to this program have caused it to grow and prosper, and to be widely recognized throughout the country.

Further information about the contest (as well as all past winners) can be found online at:

http://www.saugus.net/Contests/Halloween/

The Historic Saugus Calendar

by
Darren J. Brown

The annual release of the Saugus Historical Society sponsored calendar is one of the most anticipated events of the year in the town. It is quite possible that there may be an image of any resident, house or municipal building past or present. The entire process of creating the calendar is truly a labor of love for the Saugus Historical Society's calendar committee and volunteers. The reception by the community every year is what makes this time extensive project worth while. The following is a brief history of the calendar and how close this very popular item came to being a thing of the past.

The first calendar containing images of the Town of Saugus was put together by the Town of Saugus in the mid 1990s. The origin of this endeavor was to produce something that most of the townsfolk would be interested in while raising revenue for the community at the same time. This town-run operation was for the most part done locally, including the printing at Park Press. The calendar endeavor wound up being more costly than originally envisioned. The entire process of creating the approximate five thousand calendars eventually moved completely out of Saugus with the exception of photograph selection and caption writing.

The 1999 edition of the Town of Saugus calendar was quite different from any other printed before or since. There was a slight decrease in size and additional sponsor advertisements placed within the days of the months. This was a result of the Town Manager working to reduce expenses and increase advertising revenue. This installment was not well received through the community. The Town decided that future calendars might be an ideal fund-raising opportunity for one of the local non-profit organizations. The Saugus Historical Society was approached to carry on the tradition and after much discussion, decided to do so.

The Saugus Historical Society is a volunteer organization with, up until then, no experience creating a calendar. Therefore, the Society decided to continue usage of the Town's existing framework. The only difference the first year was a return to the pre-1999 format. A marketing firm in Wakefield was recommended and they made the suggestion of requesting a dollar donation per calendar. The calendar would serve as both a fund-raiser and as a means of conveying the Society's relevance to the community. The calendar had been available in its early years only at the Town Hall. The Society decided that it would be good for all of the sponsoring businesses if the calendars were available at their locations. They were now also made available at other municipal buildings, including the Public Library. The product was better received than the previous year, but there was a problem. The stream of revenue predicted by the marketing firm was not there. The Society lost thousands of dollars, with the following year yielding the same results.

The Saugus Historical Society's Board of Directors was on the verge of killing the calendar project. The only way that it could be continued would be to reduce expenses and offer the calendar as the Town had, for free. A calendar committee led by Society President Darren J. Brown, was determined that the 2002 edition would be a success. The Society would have to give up this project if money was lost again. The image processing, layout and computer work were brought to Saugus.net. The printing was moved back to Park Press. This was the first year in the history of the calendar that it was created completely in Saugus. The expenses were cut by more than two-thirds, and even though no money was collected for individual calendars, the Society managed to come out slightly ahead of breaking even. This edition was released to the public for the first time on the night of the tree lighting and the subsequent day's Hammersmith Stroll.

The following year there was a slight decrease in sponsor advertisements; however the calendar was able to stay afloat. 2004 and 2005 have been very similar in that events outside the control of the Society have thrown obstacles in the way, but the calendar has continued on. George Brown, Harry Surabian and Russell Blood managed to make the calendar sucessful in 2004, thanks to their door-to-door fund-raising effort. George Brown decided to take on this task single-handedly in 2005. The selection of the photographs, the writing of captions, the deliveries to all of the distribution locations, and the solicitation of sponsors have all been done exclusilvely by volunteers since 2002. The Society has been blessed with many devoted volunteers who have made it their mission to ensure the continued success of the annual calendar. The following is a list of the people who have served on the calendar committee: Russell Blood, Darren Brown, Eric Brown, George Brown, Richard Provenzano, Harry Surabian, Dave Berkowitch, Janice

Jarosz, Steve Neth, Laura Eisener, Paul Kenworthy, Phyllis Brown, and Ed Patterson, Jr.

Friendly Festival

by
Eric W. Brown
(with material from Joe Chaves)

In the course of a year, Saugus has many celebrations; including numerous widespread traditional holidays, like Independence Day and Memorial Day, and numerous local celebrations like Hammersmith and Founders Day.

One major Saugus event often gets overlooked. It now gets over a couple thousand attendees each year; they come from not just Saugus, but from all over New England and even southeastern Canada. It has been held annually since 1927.

This event is officially called the *Festa do Espírito Santo*, but locally is known more commonly as the Portuguese Festival or even the Portuguese Picnic. The first few years it was held on Gilway Street, but it quickly outgrew that location and was moved to Mariense Field (*Campo Mariense* in Portuguese, or the local nickname "Portuguese Picnic Area") on the Lynn Fells Parkway. The first year it was held it was actually in part a community celebration of the sudden (and nigh miraculous) recovery of Saugonian Antonio Chaves, who had been deadly ill with little hope of recovery. There is, however, more to it than that.

At its heart it is a Christian religious celebration; *Festa do Espírito Santo* roughly translates to the Feast of the Holy Spirit, a feast day (also known as Pentecost Sunday) that commemorates the descent of the Holy Spirit onto Jesus' followers seven weeks after Easter.

It also takes flavor from its Portuguese roots. The founders of the *Campo Mariense do Espírito Santo*[1] all came from the Azorean island of Santa Maria, a 38 square mile dot of

---

1. The original members of the Campo Mariense do Espírito Santo of Saugus Association include the following: Manuel Bairos, Antonio Braga, Jacinto Braga, Peter Braga, José Coelho, Frank Camara, Antonio Chaves, Antonio A. Chaves, José Andrade Chaves, Manuel Andrade Chaves, José Farapelha, José Farapelha, Jr., George Farapelha, José Ferriera, Antonio Figueiredo, Antonio Freitas, José Freitas, Mariando d'Freitas, Manuel Garna, José M. Pacheco, Manuel Pahceco, Jr., Antonio Rezendes, Amanço Souza, Antonio Souza, João Souza, João Tavares, and Frank Xavier.

land approximately 2,500 miles due east of Saugus. The *Festa do Espírito Santo* is a major holiday in the Azores; each village parish (or *Império* – the attendees of the festival in Saugus are all loosely members of *Império Mariense*) has its own specific traditions, but there are a few common threads. The most important of these is charity for the poor and the hungry – the core idea is that even the poorest among us should be able to get meat in their diets once a year, and it is provided in the form of a hearty beef soup (*sopas do Espírito Santo*) poured over a delicious sweet bread (*massa sovada*) freely provided to all whom attend. It is interesting to note too that different villages tend to celebrate the holiday on different weeks, so in the Azores the needy can actually enjoy multiple feasts. Other common traditions include a "Queen for a Day" and fireworks.

In Saugus the festival tends to be held on a Sunday right around the beginning of July. The Queen for a Day is given special recognition and allowed to eat first. Traditional music is played. All who attend are given servings of the traditional beef soup and sweet bread, and even strangers are welcomed as if they were old friends. The atmosphere is warm and friendly, and I am certain Saugus' version of the festival would make the traditional celebrants in the Azores proud. It is not too surprising that some even fondly refer to this area as the "Tenth Island" of the Azores.

An ox-cart bringing in food and wine for the celebration.

Saugus, Here I Come and What Brings Me Here

(A note to local editors by Guillaume Destot, from Paris)

Dear Editor:

I leave Paris, France, tomorrow, for Houston, Texas, and in a few days from now, I shall be in Saugus, a town that has become somehow familiar to me, even though it will be my first visit.

I *met* Tom Sheehan a few years ago, when, working as assistant editor for the webzine `http://3ammagazine.com`, I received one of Tom's short stories and fell immediately under his spell. Tom's talent is immediately recognized by those who encounter his stories and poems, widely published across the web and on paper. Yet the project Tom always seemed the proudest about was not so much personal as collective: *A Gathering of Memories*, edited and published independently by him and John Burns, helped along by donators and, even more importantly, by an impressive array of local inhabitants of Saugus who contributed their own pieces to this impressive treasure trove of local history (find more about it on `http://www.saugus.net`).

I was not surprised to learn that the venture was a commercially successful one. It is sometimes hard, especially from abroad, to fully understand the relationship that America entertains with its past, to comprehend what roots an American finds in his soil. Yet here was, from a European perspective, a very striking example of the uniquely American talent for appropriating history, for deciding, in fact, what is history, what it's made of. It is very uplifting to see a community so enthusiastically agreeing that their past, their lives, private and shared moments, are worth writing, telling, reading about. It is popular history in the very best sense.

And beyond all this, as I leafed through *A Gathering of Memories*, Saugus, filtered through Burns's, Sheehan's and all the passionate contributors' literary prisms, seemed more and more like a *real* piece of America I just had to see one day, a place beyond the usual tourist sights, closer, perhaps, to the heart of this country. "Don't be deluded," I thought, "Norman Rockwell's America no longer exists; perhaps it never has." Yet, as I read those pages and dreamed about Saugus, its ponds, its groves and its hills, I mused how sweet it would be to walk the streets and places mentioned by those love-struck denizens. To dip my toes in Lily Pond – or is it Pranker's Pond? – and have a thought for the great horse Titanic, who sunk there under the ice a long time ago. To climb Baker Hill and Vinegar hill, go down again and see if it is actually possible that a house was once sawn in two after a family quarrel. To find out about the celebrated Iron Works, decide if there's anything heartbreaking about Breakheart Reservation. To stand on "Busy Corner" where Jack Winters' house once stood, and where he passed many a cold, lonely, miserable winter. To imagine how red Sim's disappeared carnations must have been.

Then, in the same grasp and chance, to see the ground where Tom's *A Collection of Friends*, sprang from his heart to his pen, where it has been duly praised in Tryst Magazine: "And as Johnny Igoe, the author's grandfather once

left his beloved Ireland to forge ahead into the New World thus carrying Ireland with him, Tom Sheehan carries Saugus wherever he goes. *Collection* will fill you with its rich details, its insight, its loving portrayal of childhood, boyhood and friendship. Pick up this book today and know that there will be few books in your life that will embrace you, or you will embrace them, as deeply as *Collection*."
~Tryst Editor

Or Steve Hansen, in Small Spiral Notebook says: "Akin to Sherwood Anderson's *Winesburg, Ohio*, Tom Sheehan's hometown of Saugus, Mass., plays a critical role in his brilliant memoir, *A Collection of Friends*. Whether it's down by the great wall of manure in a field in West Peabody, or the frozen expanse of Lily Pond – a hockey player's dream – a past generation's landmarks (long gone but for these venerable pages) live and breathe and stink and steam."

Finally, I thought how lucky Saugonians are to have these monuments of books to celebrate the legend of a town. How lucky Saugonians are to have each other, to have a past they can evoke together, a deep, friendly, rich soil to root their future in! I live in Paris, a city much visited by tourists from around the world. I know its charms, and its scars too. And much though I like that great capital, what a breath of fresh air it will be to visit Saugus this summer and imagine for a few days – who could blame me? – that it's my hometown too!

Looking ahead to our visit with *bon amis*,

Guillaume Destot and wife Kim

PS: And now I hear there is *A Gathering* sequel afoot, *Of Time and the River*. Time enough for Saugus to grab me again, to ultimately place that copy into The National Library in Paris where my copy of *A Gathering of Memories, Saugus 1900-2000* is now enshrined.

Memorable Words or Quotes from Saugonians or Those Afar about Saugus

The words will come! The words will come!

— Albert Moylan
SHS teacher to a student with writing
aspirations, 1945.

We may have broken noses, and we may have broken collarbones, and we may have broken legs, but we haven't got broken hearts! Let's go!

— Coach Dave Lucey
in the halftime SHS locker room at
Amesbury High School, 1946.

I want to thank those responsible for this momentous occasion.

— Belden Bly
Honest Lawyer, coach, athletic director, state representative, at his 88th birthday celebration and other auspicious events he was featured in or at.

Unaccustomed as I am to public speaking...

— C.F. Nelson Pratt
Town servant, county commissioner.

Time to put up or shut up, gentlemen.

— Eddie Smiledge
Houseman, The Rathole, 1952.

You can never tell from where you sit, where the guy in the balcony's going to spit.

— Welcome McCullough
SHS US History, circa 1958.

I have only but a minute,
only sixty seconds in it.

Forced upon me can't refuse it,
didn't seek it, didn't choose it,
but it's up to me to use it.

I must suffer if I lose it,
give account if I abuse it.

Just a tiny little minute,
but eternity is in it.

— Welcome McCullough
also, in every class every year of his long tenure.

Lady, you stay away from my bench and I'll stay out of your kitchen.

— Mike Annese
Babe Ruth baseball coach (to a mother who came screaming at his bench about her son's lack of playing time).

Homesickness (From one who hasn't been home for 50 years)

This is not exactly nostalgia (with apologies to Proust, more like "Remembrances of the Past"), but is inspired by the writings of and correspondence with Tom Sheehan, back in time to 1950: the Century's exact mid-point five decades past!

People, some gone but not forgotten: teachers, mentors, lifelong influences — names insufficient but all pervading now: Burns / Fox / Young / Pearce / Bly / Bradbury / Watson / Moylan / Gibbs / Mitchell / Germain. Friends, acquaintances, shared adolescent dreams, fantasies or objects of the same: Hogle / Nicolo(s) / Favuzza / Woodell / Brostrum / McTighe / Cook / Delaney / Constantine / Duffy / The Band / the entire 1949 Saugus High School football squad!

Tom has fixed the sense of place anchored in continuity and maturity and shared, aided, started the chain reaction of names. Like an astronomer looking back in time for me, the names, faces, words, gestures are frozen in permanent youth. A good thing— a good place, my hometown.

— Jim Smith
Waldwick, NJ, SHS 1950.

Postscripts to
A Gathering of Memories:
Saugus 1900-2000

I love America. I love Saugus. I love what you have done for our town.

— B. Merrithew, Saugus.

On advice, my wife and I purchased two copies, to prevent bloodshed at reading time. To date, our favorite line is, "I had a bad posture, a bad perm, and a soft-spoken voice." It was great over our morning coffee and the book. The book is marvelous. Carol and I have enjoyed it tremendously. It makes you feel as though you know the characters as you are reading. It also prompts a recall of our own personal experiences and aside of making us aware how long ago some of these things occurred, it generates a lot of memorable joy.

Ties that Bind

— Bill Jenkins, Orlando, FL (never been to Saugus).

The copy, the *Book*, arrived yesterday and I have been turning pages in wonderment ever since. Fantastic!! The work that went into it!! Kudos all around especially to you and John Burns and most flattered by your signing same. Much more to say later, but for now, Congratulations! Big time. — like the Bible — can open the book at random and start a chain reaction of memories with almost any page or occasional photo. So it goes — on and on — one memory after another, "Not docile, helpless objects, for indeed, they respond as they are being gathered and leave their marks on those who choose to gather them."

— James Smith, Waldwick, NJ.

A masterpiece. A classic. Must reading even for our carpetbaggers.

— Belden Bly, Honest Lawyer.

I received my copy yesterday. It is a masterpiece. I sat to spend a few minutes thumbing through it and was entranced hours later. I love the way it's organized and each vignette reaches out and touches the reader personally. I can hardly wait to spend a little time each day reading it and want the pleasure to last as long as possible. I think it is a magnificent job. It stands as tribute not only to Saugus but to all the hard work of John, Tom and the others.

— Bart Brady Ciampa, Vancouver, WA.

My eagerly awaited book-of-the-year came on Friday at 9 P.M. and kept me up until the wee hours reading bits of memories of the various contributors. We are mighty proud of you two and your committee.

— Bill Bright, Wilsonville, OR.

I sit here, late into the night, cradling the book in my arms like a baby. It is riveting.

— Tim Churchard, West Lebanon, ME.

What a piece of work you (John) and Tom and your gifted staff of historians and writers have wrought. What a monumental piece of work! I was first taken aback by the weight of the package that arrived at my door. Then I opened the box and found a beautifully jacketed tome, very much unlike the usual town histories I have seen in austere brown and green covers, housing pages of statistics and wax-museum people. It all started with "Saugus, I love the sound of that word. It has a magnetic field around it. It draws in the jesters, the curious, the puzzled."

This is a book of people first, living, breathing, flesh and bone people—with all their distinctions and disparities, each with a story, each with a place – a few rogues among the many angels. The names are legion. They crowd the pages in unbelievable numbers, but they retain their faces. This book supports my belief. How can such a small town house so many different places – so much beauty – so many landscapes. I feel as though I have been on a long trip to every neighborhood in town and have met nearly every person in town. As impressed as I find the magnitude and scope of this book, I find it even more impressive that you and Tom were able to attract so many writers with talent and memory to this project. How did one small town produce this abundance of literary talent?

Finally, thank you for dedicating this book "To all who were ever here in Saugus and to all who ever will be." Those words give me boldness to say at last, "My Saugus too! Thank you for letting me in."

— Miriam Kochakian, Methuen.

I can't wait to read cover to cover and reflect on the memories contained this winter in my easy chair with a warm fire in the fireplace.

— Unsigned.

It was as if I were reliving my childhood and my early adult years.

— Jessie Halpin, NH.

The whole book shouts "quality."

— Paul Heffernan, Ipswich.

Tom, now I know what you were talking about, 50 years ago in Korea.

— Frank Mitman, Bethlehem.

Growing Up in Saugus
Part 1

Too many people grow up. That's the real trouble with the world, too many people grow up. They forget. They don't remember what it's like to be twelve years old. They patronize, they treat children as inferiors. Well I won't do that.

— Walt Disney

The Summer Street Gang

by
Alden Trenholm

Auburn Court runs from Wilson Court to Pleasant Street. Not a very long street and today Greystone Road runs into it. When my father, George H. Trenholm, built our house at #5 back in 1935 or 1936, the road was quite a bit different than now. At the corner of Auburn and Wilson was #12 and Herb and Grace Barrett lived there and the only other house and barn that faced our house was unoccupied until the Reed family moved in a couple years later.

To the left of our place was a field and peach orchard owned by the Quarmbys and that bordered on Pleasant Street. To the right and rear of our house was farmland owned by Stazinskis and that stretched all the way to Central Street where the Iron Works restoration is now. To the right the field abutted "The Pit." That was the water-filled remnant where Scotch prisoners, captured by Cromwell in the Border Wars between England and Scotland, came to dig iron ore used at the Old Iron Works. That was in the 1600s.

My brother Bruce was four years older than I and except for Tykie and Shirley Westendarp, who lived on Pleasant Street, was probably my only playmate until the Reeds moved in. Until we started school in 1940, Shirley Westendarp and I busied ourselves catching garter snakes in Quarmby's field. I guess no one taught us how to paint doilies or organize preschool activities. The snakes must have liked us because I can't remember either of us getting bit. They would not have to worry about me now.

Then the Reeds moved into the "Haunted House." That was our salvation. There were five boys; John, Don, Sammy, Malcolm, and Georgie. The three girls were Sadie, Dot, and Betty. Lorraine came along later. Bruce got to play with the "Big Kids"; Don and Sam and I hooked up with Malcolm, my age, four or five; and George "Hit" was a year younger. No more playing with girls!

After a hard day of playing and getting dirty, we all might sit out on our front steps to watch Herb Barrett, the policeman, walking home from work. Mr. Barrett was also a hunter and the first thing he would do is stand out on his front porch and "Gee Yup" his fox hounds home from wherever they might be getting into trash or garbage. They could hear him if they were down to Saugus Center. It wasn't unusual, on a weekend, to see our "Lawman" walking home with his shoes, shotgun and a foxtail hanging out of the same pocket of his hunting coat. I believe Herb was also Saugus' first motorcycle cop, if it wasn't Jim Sullivan.

Our street was not paved at the time and sometimes a winter snow storm could pose problems. More than once we had our milk delivered by "Tabby" Barrett, using his horse-drawn sled or pung. At times we would all get together to shovel out the street, the plows being busy elsewhere.

Barrett and Berrett seemed to be the predominant names in that area back then. Tabby lived at the farm on the end of Summer Court where they still plowed with horses and if you happened to stop by at milking time you might get a squirt of warm milk in the face. There were at least four other families of them, two on Pleasant Street and two on Wilson Court.

Most everyone around that area raised chickens for eggs and meat. It was not uncommon, especially in early spring or fall, to be sitting at the supper table and hear a loud crack or kapow. That would usually turn out to be Herb Barrett taking a shot, from his front steps, at a rat crossing from the Pit over the open field to our chicken coop, looking for a free meal of chicken mash. Don't know if he ever hit one, but I wouldn't have wanted to be traveling up Central Street at the time.

Mr. Love was our mailman, and always on foot. Usually once a week, we'd hear a horn tooting to announce that Cap'n Quint was in the area with his fish truck. If you had an ice chest, you'd have a sign in the window and Mr. Fiske would know how much ice to leave. After Greystone Road and "the new section" went in, we got our milk from McAdams Creamery and our pastries from Mr. Gallant in his Blood's Bakery truck. We didn't have to make many trips to the A & P grocery store down town, at least in the summer, because most everyone had their own vegetable gardens, chickens and preserves.

If my mother sent me to the store, she would give me a list of what she wanted. I'd hand it to Mr. Graham and he would fill up the bag and grind the coffee. I don't remember carrying any money, so Mom and Dad must have had to ante up later. Amazingly, people trusted each other back then, even during the Depression.

If we got a few cents ahead, we kids would head for the Pioneer Store on Central Street and buy some penny candy from Mr. Benoit or later on from Joe LoPresti. If somehow we were flush, we would head down to Sanborn's paper store for some "tonic" and chips from Ben, or Joe, or Mrs. Pearce.

Another familiar sound back then was the metal to metal noise of old Mr. Guy turning out door hinges, horseshoes or whatever. He still ran a blacksmith shop at the side of Stazinski's farm or what is now the Ironmaster's house. The Reed kids and I would go down to watch him sometimes, but I don't think he was too thrilled with us hanging around.

For a while after the WPA built Stackpole Field, the new clubhouse became a kindergarten, Ms. Easter presiding. That started to broaden our horizons and we got to meet kids from the outer world. We met other humans from Summer Street, Appleton Street, Prospect Street, etc. I became mortified when they also opened up a tap dancing school and my mother wanted me to attend. With girls? And other boys could watch us? I don't think so!

Shirley Westendarp, Alden Trenholm and Janice Popp, ready for first day at Roby School where they will greet teacher Julia Nourse.

Finally, in September 1940, we started going to real school, to the Roby School with the big kids, although my mother still had to tie my shoes. Maybe that's why I wasn't destined for higher education.

Ms. Julia Nourse was my first grade teacher. Nobody rode school buses to the Roby School. You got there the best way you could, fair weather, rain or snow. When we left, however, we went in groups and by group. Our group was #7 and we were from first to sixth grade. Our group centered and left by the back door. I can't remember ever going in or out the front door.

So out the back door went Group 7, across Taylor Street, turn left, then right up Summer Street. At Parker Street, the first right beyond Taylor, the grade schoolers started peeling off. Over those years there would be Charlie Green, Bobby

Francis, Donna Julien, Carroll Cunningham. Across from Parker Street was the cabbage field of Alkides Farm.

Before Prospect Street, Mike and Harriet Graham would cross Summer Street, then Paul, Jerky and Audrey Spencer. Pleasant Street would take half the group. Betty, Norma, Jake and later Georgie Hull, Dick and Donald Gabry, Everett "Sunny" Deland, Brother Bruce and I, plus Don, Sammy, Dot, Batty, Malcolm and George Reed would head down Auburn Court while Tykie and Shirley Westendarp, Harriet Quarmby, Randy, Carol and Janice, along with cousin Stanley Popp, would finish off Pleasant Street.

As the main group continued up Summer Street, Don and Bill Conrad would cross, as would Dick Hussey, Ed and Evelyn Claflin and Cynthia Hecht. At that time George and Don "Lewie" Parker, then Joe and Kay Seely, would bail out before Wilson Court. Joe's dog "Shadow" would be waiting for him behind their picket fence if she wasn't busy fighting with Barrett's dog, Bozo, who would later join the Army's K-9 Corps.

Willard Wallace (Willy Plunkett) and Barbara and Dick Eastman weren't in the neighborhood yet, so the next to go were Louise Mills and Dicky Maher down Fiske Road, then Donald Dick Emmet. Walter Alukonis crossed just before Edna Winslow's house. If Edna was home, she was sure to say hi to Gordon, Jack and Charlie Prentice and Roy Roberts as they passed. There were also Boissoneaus, Swansons, Brookses and others, but the years take a toll on memories.

After getting home from school the serious business started; change out of our knickers and go out to play. During the '60s the cry was, "Don't trust anyone over 30!" I always said, "Don't trust anyone who never wore knickers to school or wore long pants before seventh grade!"

After playing or delivering newspaper or shoveling snow or reading comic books, it was imperative to listen to the latest episode of *Jack Armstrong and the All-American Boys* (Wheaties), *Little Orphan Annie* (Ovaltine), *Tom Mix* (Ralston), *The Shadow, On Sundays* (Anthracite Coal), *Captain Midnight, Don Winslow, Tennessee Jed,* or *Terry and the Pirates.*

At night, after supper, don't miss the next exciting episode of *The Lone Ranger, I Love a Mystery with Jack, Dock and Reggie, Inner Sanctum, Judy Cannova, Jack Benny* (LS/MFT) *Fred Allen, The Great Gildersleeve, Kay Kayser and His College of Musical Knowledge* or *Les Brown and His Band of Renown. Lux Radio Theatre* was another one you didn't want to miss or you'd have nothing to talk about at school the next day. What was little known on some big radio shows was the word "Television."

Ahh, second grade. Miss Chase. This time we were like upper classmen. Little kids, like George Reed, were just starting first grade with the other "youngsters," but now we were old hands who knew the ropes. We knew our group #7 by heart and were used to smelling the burning leaf piles on our way home in the fall. I think I even knew how to tie my own shoes!

Brother Bruce and I had probably spent a couple of weeks up to Grandfather's camp in Northwood, New Hampshire, during the previous summer. It took about 1½ hours to get there by car, it being about 60 miles away. Sometimes the Westendarps would stop by on their way to Newfound Lake. I wasn't really sure if the world extended beyond those points at the time, not knowing anyone who had been farther away. The Reed kids used to mention a place called Nova Scotia, wherever that was.

Anyway, after school was still pretty much routine. No homework yet, so get home, change out of your knickers, (hated corduroy 'nicks, made too much noise), then out to play. Maybe watch Stazinskis harvesting potatoes, or haying with their scythes. Once their blind draft horse got stuck in the mud at the Pit and the fire truck had to come to pull him out. That was pretty exciting!

I think the ice cream man, "Mike," was still coming around and would park his truck across the street from Delanos and ring his bell. We kids came running from all directions to get popsicles, fudgesicles, orange creamsicles, push-ups or Dixie cups with the blue and red dots on the cup and movie stars' pictures on the inside of the cover. Barbara Delano always got them, more for the pictures than the ice cream, I think.

—WHO WERE THEY?—

"Us kids came running from all directions for popsicles, fudgesicles, orange creamsicles, push-ups or *Dixie* cups with blue and red dots on the cup and movie stars' pictures on the inside of the cover. (some)... got them more for the pictures than the ice-cream, I think."
—Alden Trenholm

1. 2. 3. 4.

RING! RING!

MIKE'S ICE CREAM

DIX

1 CLAUDETTE COLBERT 2. BING CROSBY (of course) 3. INGRID BERGMAN (Ilya in "Saam") 4. SABU of INDIA

Bob Saccu '06

One Sunday, while Bruce was probably ice skating over at the Pit, I was home listening to *The Shadow* and some guy broke in on the program and announced that the Japanese had bombed Pearl Harbor. I wasn't too pleased with the interruption and felt a note of somberness at supper. Before going to sleep that night, I asked Bruce what a Japanese was. "Oh, they're big hairy things with big, sharp teeth and they eat people." Oh? "Well where is Pearl Harbor?" "Uhh," he says, "I think it's somewhere up around Lily Pond." I couldn't even cry myself to sleep that night. A Frankenstein movie would have been easier to accept.

War! What's war anyway? The most traumatic thing that had ever happened in my seven years was almost having to take tap dancing lessons with girls. How come we have to keep the windows covered at night? Well, that's so the German bombers can't see us and if Mr. Boyd Barrett, the Air Raid Warden, sees my light, he'll knock on our door and tell us to cover better.

Mom, being a registered nurse, got to teach a lot of the neighborhood ladies first-aid at night in our living room. Dad was working nights at the West Lynn G.E. Bruce and I did our part by becoming "Junior Commandos" along with some other kids. We even got to wear armbands telling what our jobs were, but we mostly hunted for spies. Funny, we never caught any, but we probably scared a lot away!

One day, Mrs. Doris Westendarp took a bunch of us all the way into *The Boston Globe* for a Junior Commando rally. There were some real soldiers and sailors there along with Governor Saltonstall. Beatrice Kay sang "Take Me Out to the Ball Game," and we all sang "Praise the Lord and Pass the Ammunition" with her. Buck Jones, the cowboy movie star, was there, too, and we heard later that he died in the Cocoanut Grove fire. Don Parker got carsick in the Sumner Tunnel on the way home. Anyway, I had been all the way to Boston!

On warm summer nights not even the threat of air raids could keep us from sleeping out in our screened-in porch. The only problem was on Sunday mornings we would get woken up way too early by Randy Popp. He would be delivering the Sunday papers out of his rickety, green, three wheeled-cart and whistling as loud as he could. Usually the songs were "I Wonder," "My Dreams are Getting Better All the Time," or anything else that was worth loud whistling.

Our paper was the *Boston Sunday Post*. Dad got the front pages, Bruce the sports page, and I started and ended with the funnies. *Prince Valiant*, *Fritzy Ritz*, *Brenda Starr*, *Red Ryder* with Little Beaver and the Duchess. Then there was *Smilin' Jack* and his fat side-kick whose shirt button was always popping off into the waiting chicken's mouth. Made my day!

Small white flags with a red border and blue star in the center started appearing in the front windows of some houses in the neighborhood. Buck and later Donald Reed were with the merchant marine, Leonard Popp in the navy, Marshy Berrett in the marines, Charlie "Brother" Parker in the army. Larry and George Cronin were also serving. "Red Barrett had to shut the boxing ring in his barn down for the "duration."

My dad had served on the Mexican Border with the army in 1916 and on a troopship in the navy during World War I, so it was up to me and Bruce to don uniforms in this one. Bruce was in Troop 64 of the Boy Scouts and me in Pack 60 Den 3 of the Mighty Cub Scouts. Mom was also in uniform as our Den Mother. No blue stars in our window, though.

Scouts, from Troop 64 and Pack 60.
(l-r): Dick Gabry, Tykie Westendarp, Stanley Popp, Clyde Allen, Alden Trenholm, Malcolm Reed, Dick Emmet, and Dick Eastman.

When the Boy Scouts weren't learning to tie knots or earning merit badges at Camp Nihan up in North Saugus, they got to go around in trucks on scrap and paper drives for the war effort. The Parkers, Gabrys, Jack and Charlie Prentice, Bruce and others were under the direction of Cap'n Parker and Ray Knox.

We Cub Scouts had our work cut out for us too, or actually we did the cutting. We would cut cartoons out of *The Saturday Evening Post* and other magazines to paste in scrap books to send to the boys "over there." Besides my mother, Ray Knox and Dick Gabry helped out and saw that we stuck to our business. I would rather have gone on scrap and paper drives with the Boy Scouts. The redeeming factor is if anybody asked, "Where were you in '42?" I could truthfully say I was in uniform. The rest of the "outfit" consisted of Tykie Westendarp, Stanley Popp, Dick Emmett, Malcolm Reed, Dick Eastman, Clyde Allen and Richard Campbell.

There were a lot of new things to get used to then. Besides the usual fire drills at school, we started having air raid drills. A lot of everyday things became scarce, like real butter, sugar, coffee and bananas. A lot of foods and gas

were rationed, you had to have ration stamps, and prices were regulated by the D.P.A. and a store owner better not cheat. Drivers had to really baby their tires because new ones were not to be had.

One thing that baffled me was, on the radio, the *Green Hornet* had always had a faithful Japanese valet named Kato. After the war started, Kato suddenly became a faithful Filipino valet. That must have been quite a trick.

At school, once a week you could buy either a 10¢ or 25¢ savings stamp which you pasted into a little book for that denomination. When you had $18.75 worth, you turned them in for a $25.00 War Bond. I was sure proud of my first bond and eventually ended up with three.

To earn money for the savings stamps, I hired out to my brother, helping out on his paper route. I only delivered eleven papers but that was six afternoons a week. Most of the people took either *The Lynn Item*, *The Lynn Telegram*, or *The Record American*, plus *The Saturday Evening Post* magazine. I usually made enough money to buy my weekly stamp and have enough leftover for the Saturday afternoon matinee at the State Theatre.

Sometimes you didn't have to pay to get into the movies. If they were having a "scrap drive," all you had to do was turn in enough brass, copper or aluminum and get a free ticket. The Saturday matinee was a *must* because that was when they showed the serials, and you had to see how *Deadwood Dick* or *Terry and the Pirate* or *Charlie Chan* would escape the peril they were left in the week before.

I wonder how many mothers' aluminum pots and pans were sacrificed, known and unknown, to find out how Deadwood Dick survived being thrown off a cliff or some such other dilemma.

In the winter, after a decent snowfall, the only thing to do was get your sled or skis or barrel staves or even a sheet of corrugated tin and go to Barrett's Hill on Summer Court. Some kids even had Flexible Flyers that could hold four or five bodies at a time, although somebody usually fell off halfway down the hill. We would slide all afternoon until it got dark. Then it was time to head home for supper.

After eating and before we could listen to *Baby Snooks*, *The Great Gildersleeve*, or *Fibber McGee and Molly*, the older folks had to catch up on the news. I think the most prominent commentators were Edward R. Murrows, E.G. Kaltenborn, Lowell Thomas, and Walter "Good evening Mr. & Mrs. America and all the ships at sea, let's go to press" Winchell.

What a lesson in geography World War II was. Who, in the general population of the United States, had ever heard of places like Bataan, Corregidor, Guadalcanal, the Savu or Coral Seas, Oran or the Kasserine Pass? Even with a globe, who could point out Midway or Wake Islands, Murmansk, Stalingrad, Anzio, or Salerno? The world surely did get big for this little boy!

I still didn't know what the knob on the radio that was labeled "television" meant. The only "visuals" I ever saw were at the movies when the Pathe News, "The eyes and ears of the world," was shown. Some film clips were about what was going on and where. More names like Tarawa, Saipan, Normandy, St. Lo, Cherbourg, Iwo Jima, Bastogne and Okinawa.

Then came VE Day and all eyes turned to the Asiatic-Pacific campaign. Things still went on in Saugus, though, and the town decided to resurface Pleasant Street just a couple days before I was to start in Mrs. Gibson's sixth grade. A big truck showed up and started spewing the black, sticky liquid, starting from Summer Street. As it went by Westendarps' house, where a bunch of us kids had gathered to watch, Tykie decided to give chase on his scooter.

He hadn't gone more than forty feet behind the truck when Mrs. W. stepped out her front door and yelled, "It's over. The war is over!" Everyone turned to look at her, including Tykie, and that's when he went down into the gooey mess. Talk about a "tar baby." He was made to take his clothes off in the garage before he could clean up.

I think everyone who had managed to hoard a few shotgun shells popped off a few that day. There may have been dancing in the streets in some places, but for me, my most ingrained memory would be of Tykie looking like Al Jolson. I don't think we heard about Hiroshima, Nagasaki, and the A-Bomb until later.

Things slowly started getting back to normal. As our neighbors, uncles, brothers and cousins began to return, we finally found out where they had been and what they were doing. I only knew of one from our area who didn't make it back. Some of the young guys were disappointed that it was over before they could go, little knowing their time would come sooner than expected.

Although the dance hall at Lily Pond had burned down earlier, MacGilvary's boathouse was still in operation. Overseen by Mr. Roy Roberts and his son, Roy Jr., row boats and canoes could still be rented. Bus loads of people from Boston would arrive on Sundays to picnic, swim or use the boats. The boat house was located beside Sawyer's Ice House, which was torn down around 1946. Sweezey's Screen Shop is in that location now.

Lily Pond was our realm, along with Barrett's Woods. It was everything a kid could ask for and all for free. We built camps in the woods and rafts for the pond. There was ice-skating, ice-fishing, sled sailing and hockey in the winter when the ice houses weren't in operation. There were three of them at that time. Sawyer's on Appleton Street, Fiske's on Cliff Road, and Rippon's, down by the dam. Rippon's became a mushroom factory while the other two were torn down.

Our fishing season usually started with the early spring alewife run up the Saugus River. We called them l-y's and they were a type of herring that came up river from the ocean to spawn in Lily Pond. Behind Salter's Mill on Central Street, there were small locks that they would climb to get up river. Charlie Tura would station himself with hip boots and a net in the shallows and had more success than we did generally. Us guys, along with Charlie's brother, Joe, would try to catch them by hand as they went up the pools in the locks. The ones we caught were used mostly for fertilizer in our "Victory Gardens." Put one under a tomato plant and watch it grow, and the tomatoes didn't taste fishy!

CATCHING "Alewife" (A TYPE OF HERRING) USED AS TOMATO PLANT FERTILIZER

PERHAPS TAKING A CUE FROM BEARS SNARING SALMON IN THE PACIFIC NORTHWEST ?? —Bob Sacco

"Us guys... would try to catch them (ALEWIFE "ly's") BY HAND AS THEY WENT UP THE POOLS IN THE LOCKS TO SPAWN IN LILY POND..." —Alden Trenholm

CHARLIE TURA IN HIP BOOTS AND WITH A NET

During the war, there had been a small army camp at the entrance to Breakheart Reservation. It was primarily a military police unit, and they guarded some Italian prisoners that had been taken in North Africa. The camp was disbanded shortly after the war, so we had access to the upper and lower ponds again.

Generally, at least once or twice in the spring, we would mount an expedition to the lower pond in quest of a type of fish we called "suckers." They were about the size and shape of two-pound bass but would not take bait. Their diet consisted of the algae they would suck off rocks, etc., in the water. The only way we knew to catch them was by spearing. We would cut our own spears along the way, so we would look for eight to nine foot saplings no more than one inch at the butt.

When spearing, you had to allow for water deflection and some got pretty good at it. The group usually consisted of Ed Claflin, Don Parker, Dick Hussey, Joe Seeley, Stan Popp, Bruce and myself. We passed the hiking time by telling the latest "moron" or "knock knock" jokes. Again, suckers were a soft meat fish that would end up in the garden. The "skill fishing" came later in the summer.

Stan Popp and
over 8 pounds of bass.

During the dog days of summer, the section of Lily Pond along Cliff Road would become encrusted on the surface with a thick layer of green "duck weed." That used to mean the end of fishing because cast out bait would just lie on the weed and fry in the sun. That was until someone came up with the idea of casting out and reeling back a "Johnson Weedless Silver Minnow." The large mouth bass must have thought it was a frog hopping across the weed and would come right up through it. Only the bigger ones, and some weighing over six pounds, were caught. The problem lay in reeling them in with half a ton of duckweed dragging along.

I guess I wasn't destined to be athletic. After some embarrassing attempts at baseball and a broken leg playing football, also wearing out my ankles trying to ice-skate, I figured the safest place for me was in the woods and waters. Eddie Claflin was the same way, so we became natural buddies. Ed's sister, Evelyn, used to call me "Ed's shadow," because if you saw him, I wasn't far away. Ed was four

years older than me, but it didn't seem to matter, where we shared the same interest of fishing, hunting and some trapping.

One summer evening, the usual bunch of us were up fishing along the extension of Cliff Road, which meandered out to Route 1 (the Turnpike). I think Ed, Dick Hussey, and Walter Alukonis were beyond me, and Stan Popp and Mike Graham were at the Fiske's ice-house side. Probably Edna Winslow and Charlie Austen were along as observers, until the mosquitoes got too thick. We were all fishing for bass at first.

I happened to have some worms and spotted an opening in the weed. I managed to plop a hooked worm into the hole and caught a good-sized horned pout (catfish) right off. Then I got another and decided to dress them out right there. My grandfather had taught me the easiest and cleanest way to skin them, but while I was busy doing that, Walter moved into the spot and took three or four more beauties, cleaning out the hole. He even talked me into skinning the ones he caught in my hole, for him. Talk about "falling off the turnip truck"! Ouch!

If you were to continue along the Cliff Road "extension," as I call it, it ran through what we called "Pollywog Pond." It wasn't a pond at all but a series of pools spaced amidst thick brush and saplings. The pools contained pollywogs, water snakes, turtles, etc. and the sandy bankings were covered with empty, curled up white shells left over from hatched turtles. It was kind of a spooky area, but Miss Louise Hawkes used to walk through there every day on her way to and from work at the town hall. She lived across Route 1, just up the hill from the Parkway Golf Driving Range at the beginning of the Lynn Fells Parkway.

The Hawkes property was one of the Bruce's mowing "accounts." A big yard, and hilly, he would sometimes recruit me to help. We rode up there, double, on his Elgin bicycle. He would pedal, and it was my job to hold onto our lunches and Boy Scout canteen of Kool-Ade. It would take a good part of the day to mow the grass or to stack their firewood at 25¢ an hour. We also did Mrs. Fisher's on Prospect Street and the Universalist Church. Shoveled snow, too, all at the same price and then did our paper routes. We did a lot of walking back then. Sometimes on a Sunday afternoon, a group of us kids, and usually Ray Knox and Edna Winslow, would set out for "nowhere-in-particular." We might go up Cliff Road, through Pollywog to the Pike. Crossing over the Open Air Theatre, we would proceed up the Fellsway. Sometimes we would go straight, through Melrose, all the way to Spot Pond Zoo in Stoneham and still be home before dark. Other times, we would hang a right at Squash Corner onto upper Main Street, past Veneziano's on the right, Berthold's farm and lumber yard on the left, then the Castle Rock Bottling Company on the right until we got to Castle Rock itself. We'd play around there for awhile then cut through the woods to Breakheart and retrace our steps home from there.

Later, Ed and I discovered that across the road from Castle Rock, towards Golden Hills, was some of the best rabbit hunting we ever had; it was a long walk for us, though. Also, and I hope there is a statute of limitations on this, we – Eddie, Mike Graham, Dick Hussey and Stanley P. – used to hike to the reservoirs to go fishing. Birch Brook in Lynnhurst and Hawkes Pond in North Saugus. Strictly illegal, but good fishing!

The Parkway Golf Range, owned and operated by Mr. Cronin and his sons Larry and George, provided after-school employment to several of our neighborhood kids: Bruce, Don Parker, Charlie Prentice and Mel Gurney to name a few. They worked from 6 P.M. until cleanup, for around $9.00 a week until they pulled a "wildcat strike" and got bumped to $13.00 a week. Dick Hussey and I used to pick up wooden tees during the daytime for 10¢ a bucket. Between shifts out on the field, picking up the golf balls with short-handled scoops, the guys would sit in a big chicken wire cage while being devoured by mosquitoes. However, they got to watch the movie over at the Saugus Drive-In Theatre, and if the wind was right, they could even hear it. Otherwise, you had to learn to read lips.

Just to the side of the Parkway's Club House and at the foot of the road that went up the Hawkes' house, was the Kelly residence. The kids were Foster, Big Bob, "Leadfoot Louie," Paul and Little Patsy. Later, when I was in high school, I worked there with "Big" Bob Kelly and "Little" Bob Kelly who lived up by Corbett's Corner on Water Street. That was after returning from "the big move."

1946 – Junior High School. A lot farther to walk, but no more corduroy knickers. New kids to meet from all over Saugus. Tom Virnelli and Oren Bentley and other North Saugus guys got to ride on a school bus. Carl Walker, Terry Smith and John Roby from "over river" still had to walk as did Billy Peach and Johnny Saunders from Cliftondale. I think Phil Veneziano from Oaklandvale got to ride with the Golden Hills people, but I'm not sure about the East Saugus or Lynnhurst kids like Harry Paine and Lillian South.

Seventh grade was also, for most of us, our first introduction to a male teacher. Mr. Horace Ezekiel Shuff was our math instructor, and we soon learned you didn't mess around in his class. I think everyone liked him, though, even after he threatened to throw Bill Peach out of the second story window!

Shortly after starting in seventh grade, I broke my leg in a "pick up" football game, so I was confined to bed for awhile. One afternoon I had two "sympathetic" visitors in the persons of Shirley Westendarp and Janice Popp. Thinking back, Janice was probably there to gloat! Just

before leaving 6th grade, our class had a "field day" at Stackpole Field. Janice proved to me, beyond a doubt, that I was not athlete material by consistently out-distancing me in the baseball throw. She could probably outrun Paul Sawyer, who was our star athlete at Roby School. It was about that time that Johnny Pesky held on to a ball just long enough for the Red Sox to lose another World Series, so we can't all be perfect!

Being an athletic flop wasn't my only drawback. In looking at my eighth grade report card, it is obvious that I had a very definite lack of "intelligentsia" back then. I can see no known reason why I was allowed to graduate, unless it was just to make me go away! However, 1948 was to become a very big year for my family as well as for other members of the "Summer Street Gang."

In the senior graduating class that year were Bruce, Ed Claflin, Don Parker, Randy Popp, Donald Gabry, Norma Hull and Lorraine Boissoneau. The beginning of the end of our old area as we knew it. There were a lot more changes to come and sooner than expected.

The winter of '47-'48 was a bad one, and we seemed to get major snowfalls almost every weekend. It did a number on my father, and he went down with a serious bout of pneumonia. He eventually recovered, but Dr. Joe Ward felt that change of climate might be in order. I had just started my freshman year, when I was informed of the impending move. With relatives in various parts of California, that was to be our destination.

This was to be a permanent move, so the house and furniture were sold and personal items were put into storage to be sent for when we settled. Even our cat, Rusty, was given away. After a few good-byes, we struck out on November 11, 1948, in our 1937 Oldsmobile. My father instructed us that anything we wanted to stop and see, just speak up because we would likely never have an opportunity to see the country again. That sounded pretty final.

Being the brat that I was, I just withdrew into my shell and don't think I said a word the whole trip. All I could think of was all the friends and places I would miss so badly. There would be no more Lily Pond, the Island, Evans Beach, and watching Sis Prideaux doing her "half gainers" off the diving board, or watching Marie Morrison rowing around the pond.

No more Barrett's Woods with Lookout Rock, Spencer's Field, Ace Welding, Austen's Hill or Siaglo's pig farm. Picking up our papers at Sanborn's to deliver, Walter O'Grady's barbershop, the 5&10 cent store, the Pythian Hall. Walking home from the State Theatre at night and being afraid to take the short-cut between the old Roby School and the Legion Hall because Skink Hanson or Gus Crilley might be lurking in the darkness.

Growing Up in Saugus

I wondered if they had football fields in California, and if they did, I'll bet their teams weren't as good as Saugus'. They definitely couldn't have bands and twirlers and cheerleaders like ours. They probably didn't even have mascots like Skippy Harvey. You probably have to be really smart to go to school there, but who cares? I'll likely run away anyway!

After fifteen days of riding in the car, we had developed mighty sore backsides and were thankful the trip was almost over. Ironically, we arrived in Tracy, California, on Thanksgiving Day, and celebrated by having hamburgers at a "greasy spoon" diner. So this is the great state of California. I bet they don't even know how to make codfish cakes and beans. Even Herb White could serve them back in Saugus.

After spending a couple of weeks with relatives in San Leandro, near Oakland, we headed south to Temple City, outside of L.A., and stayed a while with kin there, but still no work or school. About the only thing that happened there was Bruce turned 18, so he had to register for the draft in Alhambra. A distant uncle was the "head electrician" at the Lincoln-Mercury plant in Long Beach, so we headed there in hopes of work.

I was finally entered into Lindberg Junior High in North Long Beach in January, 1949. I was kind of glad I hadn't run away because for the only time in my life, I shined as a student. They were just starting long division in my class, and had never heard of fractions or equations. They must have thought I had just matriculated from M.I.T. I even looked good in English.

Oddly, I never met a native Californian at that school. Most of the kids were transplants from the Oklahoma dust bowl or were Idaho potato farmers. Surprisingly, none of them had ever heard of Saugus, MA! My time as a "whiz kid" lasted only about two months.

California had its "hey day" during World War II when there was plenty of shipbuilding and aircraft defense work going on. It was at that time, still in the process of post-war demobilizing, that little work was to be had and plenty of young veterans were around to take what work came available.

My folks finally "threw in the towel" and on March 8, 1949, we headed back across the country that we thought we'd never see again. I know they were heart-broken and now kind of poor, but I couldn't have been happier. After arriving back in Massachusetts, we spent a few miserable weeks at Provincetown on the Cape, eating clam chowder three times a day, it was cheap then, but we finally made our way back to **Saugus**!

Bruce and I were "farmed out" to the Archibalds' at the corner of Central and Taylor Streets across from the town hall. I started back to school in April, and, fortunately, one

of my father's first jobs was painting Mr. John A.W. Pearce's house. Mr. Pearce, being the high school principal, Dad explained to him that the school uniform in California was dungarees and that was all I had at the time, so might I be admitted back "as is." I may have the distinction of being the first person allowed to wear dungarees at Saugus High. My math teacher, Mr. Scarborough, being from Texas, thought it was about time. I'll bet some of the mothers weren't so pleased.

Before the summer of '49 was over, my folks had acquired the old house of Herb and Grace Barrett. They had moved to Maine, and the Grahams (Mike, Harriett, and their mother, Marion, who had been living there), moved to Vermont. We finally had a place to call home again and even our old cat, Rusty, found his way back.

Dad converted the old fox hound pens into a chicken coop, and we had twenty-five laying hens. Many times on my way home from school, I would have to stop into Comfort's Hay and Grain, down by the train station, and carry home a sack of chicken feed or grit. The grain bags at that time had prints on them, and Mom would use them to make shirts for me. The Reed kids, who still lived next door, wore those kinds of shirts, too.

Some of the changes were the following: my father was working as a house painter, my mother became Dr. John Silver's dental assistant, and Bruce went to work at a welding rod plant in Malden. A few faces were missing from the neighborhood, too. Randy Popp and Dick Gabry were off with the navy, while Don Parker and my best friend and partner, Ed Claflin, were away in the army. Carl Walker went in with them, but got sent home when they discovered he was only sixteen!

There were some new faces hanging around Summer Street, too. John "Buzz" Favara, Mel Gurney, Kenny Richards, Paul Lally and Roger the Russian, all from "The Center." Vernon Owens, Monk, George "Juddy" and Albee Couturier from "over the river," and Carl Walker 'til he turned seventeen and went back in the army. All nice guys and some were good additions to the sandlot baseball team.

"Buzz" was a natural comedian, and a good pitcher, and it was common to see him get a batter laughing so hard he could throw three strikes by him without a swing of the bat. With him, the Prentice brothers, Dick Hussey, Dickie Maher, Mel Gurney and others, Summer Street was a hard team to beat. I wish I could have contributed something, but they were fun to watch anyway. Edna Winslow was always there with coaching pointers.

Roger (Wasile Bereshny) the Russian, was actually a Ukrainian D.P. (displaced person) who had survived the concentration camps in Europe and was sponsored to come over here by the Morses on Columbus Avenue. At the time his

English was very limited, but we kind of took him "under our wing," and he progressed to the point where he got a job working at the Old Ironworks Restoration. He had to sift every shovel full of gravel to look for old artifacts like Pine Tree shillings and the clay pipes the Scotch laborers smoked.

In the winter, when neither of us were working, he used to like to tag along with me while I checked my muskrat traps at Lily Pond. One cold day Roger was skating around while I chopped through the ice along the shoreline to look at the traps. After chopping one hole and reaching into the water with my bare hand and arm to check the trap, I heard Roger yell. Looking around, all I could see was his head and his arms flailing in the water!

Three things happened that day that pretty much made me a believer. First, I didn't have skates on, which made the second possible. I was able to run into the woods and immediately find or possibly tear out a suitable long sapling. With that I was able to crawl to him on my stomach and, between the two of us, got him out of the water and onto shore. That's where the third came into the picture.

I think most people who spend a lot of time around the water inadvertently fall in at some time. With that in mind, my friend, Malcolm Reed, and I devised a waterproof, instant torch which was easy to carry in our pocket. By the time we reached shore, far from any houses, we were so wet and numb we never could have lit a match. Fortunately, I had my "wonder torch" with me and soon had a large fire going, no snow and plenty of dry kindling around. Roger was able to strip down to his underwear and in about an hour could put his dry clothes on and we both headed home. I don't think he even caught a cold.

That section of Lily Pond was kind of narrow and marshy and extended up to Route 1. In the fall it provided really great duck hunting just before dark set in. On the left bank, looking toward Route 1, you would usually find the Lynnhurst boys, Jimmy Kusch, Lee Johnson, the Walrus, etc. On the right, what used to be Pollywog Pond was now just a big clearing, and you could usually find Walter Alukonis, Malcolm Reed, Willy Plunkett and, sometimes, if the football players got out of practice early enough, some of them would show up, too.

We were all, always, very safety conscious. One evening, after it got too dark to shoot, we all unloaded and headed for home. It just happened that Paul Lally and I were in the lead, when we came up to the first lamp post at Cliff Road. As we approached it, two rabbits jumped up and ran into a small corn field that was now just stubble. We both bolted after them loading as we ran. At the field, Paul kicked up both rabbits, but when he tried to fire, there was a just a "click." He pulled back the hammer and tried again. Another "click"! Needless to say, the rabbits got away.

Paul wasn't happy and back at the lamp post, I unloaded my unused shell. Paul unloaded a slightly used roll of pepper-mint lifesavers!

I sometimes wonder what the reaction would be now if somebody was driving up Summer Street, and saw from six to a dozen teenagers walking along with shotguns. Especially just after dark!

One June morning, I woke up to strange noises coming from downstairs. On investigating, I found a puppy tied to the leg of the old washing machine in the kitchen. It turned out that Bruce had acquired it from the Cronins on Summer Street. They had a collie dog that was missing for awhile and searching around, they found her in Barrett's Woods nursing a litter. Next to Cronin's house was a barn where Freddy Crafts kept his dray horses that he used at the Topsfield Fair pulling contests. Fred also had two big malamute dogs known as Major and Minor. Either of them was the suspected sire of "Smoky," our new dog, who became my second best friend.

Just about that time, the headline one day in the paper said, "Reds Invade South Korea." Here we go again with "Faraway Places with Strange Sounding Names," to quote a song of the time. Many more changes were about to occur in the neighborhood as a result of those headlines.

Carl Walker (left) and Malcolm Reed holding a mink.

As it was, Ed Claflin and Don Parker were both stationed in Japan when the "Police Action" broke out. Don, or "Louie" as we called him, went in almost immediately with the 24th Division, and Ed was not far behind with the 1st Cavalry Division. Both were backed into the "Pusan Perimeter" when "Buzz" Favara showed up with the Marine Expeditionary Force. He had joined up shortly after graduating in '49 and had been stationed at Camp Pendleton, California.

Shortly after arriving there, "Buzz" sent a letter to Ken Richards telling of being wounded by shrapnel at Masan but was not evacuated. He went on to participate in the Inchon Invasion and the "30 below zero withdrawal" from the Chosen Reservoir. I often wondered at the time, if, as in his baseball days, he made the Chinese laugh so hard they couldn't shoot straight. Fortunately, all three of our Summer Street representatives made it home all right, though Louie was hospitalized with malaria for awhile.

Familiar faces started disappearing fast then. Dick Gabry and Randy Popp were already in the navy and were followed shortly by Charlie Green, Mike Richards, the Prentice brothers, and Donald Gabry. Dick Hussey went to the air force and in April, '51, Bruce got his "greetings" from the Alhambra, California draft board. Shortly after that, Roy Roberts, Vernon Owens, and Sonny Delano were drafted into the Marine Corps. They needed a "few good men" and got them. Paul Spencer went to the air force while his brother, Jerry, Tykie Westendarp and Danny Silver were "greeted' into the army. Not much left of the old baseball team!

In both summers of '50 and '51, I worked at the Parkway Golf Range with Big and Little Bob Kelly, Johnny Graham and sometimes Wally Green. Wally's father was a ranger at Breakheart Reservation, and they lived in a house right at the entrance. Wally was a pretty rugged kid and had spent some time at a juvenile "work farm."

One night, we went to the State Theatre together and saw the movie *Jim Thorpe – All American*. A good movie, and afterward we stopped into Herb White's diner for a cup of coffee. We talked a bit about Korea, and he said he had a brother that was over there. We left the diner and at my house said "so long," as he started his walk through the woods to Breakheart. I have never seen or heard from him since! His father called and said he never came home and did he stay at my house? I scoured the woods for weeks and never found a trace. Does anybody know anything about it?

In August of 1951, George "Whitey" Walker, a schoolmate, talked me into going down to the Lynn Armory and joining the National Guard Company 101st Combat Engineers. Whitey's brother-in-law, Herb Dever, was the first sergeant, and a couple of Jackson brothers from East Saugus were also members. Gene Somerby from Greystone Road was in Company C. Drill night was on Thursday, which was my only night off from the Driving Range, so it didn't leave much time for socializing or homework.

One bitter cold night in January, 1952, my mother was walking home in the dark from Dr. Silver's office, when at the corner of Summer and Pleasant Street, she had a stroke. It was only 9 degrees above zero, but somehow she crawled through the snow to the foundation of Norman Hull's house. Not much stirring at that time of night, but it happened that

Edna Winslow's brother, Arthur, was walking home from the bus stop after a six month absence. He spotted her and got her into Hull's house before she froze.

They called my father and the ambulance, and she was in the Saugus General Hospital in time to save her. Thank God for Arthur Winslow and Hull's fast reaction, or she would have frozen to death in a short time. The Red Cross got Bruce home for a few days leave from Fort Hood, Texas, and that perked her up some, although she never did regain the use of her left side.

That all took place during my senior year in high school, so with Mom's condition, work, and the Guard, it was pretty hard to concentrate on school work. However, on June 5, 1952, I, wearing the same suit that Bruce did when he graduated, was handed my diploma. Under the circumstances, no one in my family was able to attend, so not having a car or driver's license, I celebrated by walking up to Howard Johnson's on Route 1 with John Graham and Genny Legget and sprang for ice cream sodas.

On the Monday after graduation, I went to work roofing, side-walling, and painting for Sammy Reed and his brother, Malcolm. We worked mostly in Revere and Lynn, but also did the house directly behind the Rexall Drug Store in Saugus Center. Dick Eastman worked at the soda fountain at the store. Malcolm had just got out of the air force on a hardship discharge. He had enlisted the year before Mel Gurney and Willy Plunket.

After the annual two week encampment at Camp Drum, N.Y., I decided it was time for me to go full-time, so I left Sam and Mal and joined up. In my three years in the army, I never met another Saugonian until just before discharge.

I think one of my biggest thrills, at the culmination of my return trip across "The Big Pond," was sailing under the Golden Gate Bridge into San Francisco Bay. I told some of the guys, in a bragging way, that I had been across that bridge in a car a few years before. Ironically, we landed in Oakland on Thanksgiving Day, just as I had a few years earlier.

Saugus Café, Saugus, California.

A lot of us boarded a train that night and slept as we headed south for Los Angeles. After waking up and having breakfast, the train slowed down and stopped. Down the train I heard someone shouting, "Hey! We're in Saugus, my hometown." Looking out the window, I saw a building with cars in front and a big sign that said "Saugus Café." Well, it was only Saugus, California, but I got my camera and took a picture, knowing I'd be in the real place soon. The soldier that had shouted out was Johnny Graham's older brother, Tom, whom I knew slightly from high school.

After coming home, I worked for a while as a laborer in Wakefield with Little Bob Kelly, then got hired by NET&T. At times, I worked with old friends and schoolmates like Bill Peach, Ben MacGlashin, Mel Gurney, Danny McCullough, Gordon Taylor and Don Deveau. Sometimes I would run into other friends at Romeo's, the old Keogh's Dugout, on the Pike, until I left Saugus in 1960.

To me, growing up in Saugus was the most ideal setting possible. The friends, the ponds, the woods, and even the schools and teachers were what you'd read about in storybooks. It broke my heart when they drained Lily Pond, but I can still remember it as it was.

This is in no way supposed to be a story about me. Only a bit of nostalgia about the people and places that were.

God bless Saugus!

Shirley Westendarp, Alden Trenholm
and Janice Popp, 2004

Saugus, America

I only actually lived in Saugus for about 23 years, from the mid-'30s to the late '50s, which to me were good years. Those were my formative years when I had my views and values ingrained in me and which I carry to this day.

I'm sure I learned a lot more by example than by having thoughts and ideas pounded into me. Having outstanding, loyal, honest, hardworking parents who were always there for us was certainly a plus. Until I was a teenager, I can never remember my mother not being there when I got home from school.

Work ethics also came by example, from parents, friends, and neighbors. I, personally, at that time, never witnessed anyone who expended more energy trying to duck a job than by just doing the work and being done with it!

Pledging our allegiance to our flag and country every morning before school was never considered by me to be a chore. Marching in or observing the Memorial Day Parade was never debated; it was a privilege we cherished. As it was, when the country called on us we turned to and served to the best of our abilities.

Maybe I had my head under a blanket in those times, but I can never remember an incident of bigotry or prejudice. Maybe some jealousy over someone's looks, job or athletic ability, but never about religion or ethnic background. There were always too many other things to think about than wasting time trying to belittle someone else.

I also still believe in "ladies first." In those days, if a male cussed in front of or showed disrespect to a female, at least in my neighborhood, he had best head for parts unknown. This is still a part of my Saugus make-up.

For all the years I have spent elsewhere, the 23 years I spent in Saugus have left their mark on me. Saugus will always be my "home town." Proud to be a Sachem!

— Alden Trenholm

Business

The business of America is business.

— Calvin Coolidge

George's Barbershop

founded in 1902
By George, they've still got it

by
Stephanie Southworth
(*Saugus Advertiser*, September 9, 2004, entitled
"Celebrating Business, The Top 10 Oldest
Businesses in Saugus")

Tucked in a corner on Jackson Street, nestled next to the cable company and a parking lot, stands the oldest barbershop in Massachusetts – and the oldest business in Saugus. Walking into George's Barbershop, which was founded in 1902, you can almost see what it must have been like in days past – door open, the sound of razors and chatter filling the white-walled, black-and-white checker-floored room.

The addition, as a sign of the times, are the television sets hung in each corner of the room, adding a different sort of buzz to the friendly and homey atmosphere.

George R. Moriello, second generation, 1932.

Four men stand around the room; one is using the razor to *fade* a customer's hair, another is chatting with the customer leaning on the counter in front of him. The third man is sweeping the fallen hair on the floor into a dust pan and the fourth, George Moriello III, has taken a few moments out of his busy day to speak to a reporter from the Advertiser.

This past week has been busy, he says – school starts next week and everyone is coming in for a haircut. A line of 20 people out the door has been a constant. Moriello likens the line to that of a deli – they take a number and wait their turn until their number is called.

Not many barbershops have number ticket machines. But not all barbershops would need one. George's does.

Started by George's grandfather, also named George, who moved over to the United States from Italy, the barbershop has had five or six locations in Cliftondale Square but has made its current home on Jackson Street permanent.

"My father bought and built this place in 1960 and this is where we'll stay." Moriello said.

Six months ago George's Barbershop was featured on the TV program "Chronicle," honoring the shop's stature as the oldest in the state.

"It feels weird. I didn't think much of it before. All my life it's just been a barbershop," Moriello said.

Other people also began to take notice when the barbershop reached the centennial mark, but all along it's been the Saugus residents, Moriello said, who have made the shop what it is. And because of that Moriello feels it's important for the business to give back to the community.

Over the years the barbershop has given donations to the Saugus High School Hockey team and the Saugus American Little League All-Star team. Adorning the walls of the barbershop are a home plate plaque from the Little League and a framed SHS hockey jersey, gifts of thanks from the teams.

Moriello himself spent fifteen years with the National Little League and nine years on the Board of Directors of the Kasabuski Rink. He was an original member of the board that helped secure the purchase of the rink from the MDC.

The barbershop hasn't changed much since 1902 and that's part of the reason why so many people keep coming back, said Michael Moriello, George's son.

Michael Moriello also works at the barbershop full-time and has been there for eleven years, having started when he was just nineteen years old.

In the '70s Moriello said the barbershop had a little bit of trouble because in the era of "peace, love and understanding," the freedom-loving "hippies" weren't that into getting their hair cut. But, the shop got through that, Moriello said, and everything's back together now.

"That's all thanks to the people of Saugus," he said.

Customers at George's Barbershop are from all generations and are often descendants of past customers. Whole families come to George's for a hair cut, a shave and a friendly talk. The great thing about George's, Moriello said, is that when someone leaves they know they can finish the conversation they were having the next time around.

"There's always the same four guys here," Michael Moriello said.

For the younger customers, George's has a certificate for a baby's first haircut. The baby's name is written on the certificate and a lock of hair is included. Mothers can frame it and use it as a keepsake.

"The mothers love this," Moriello said.

Recently, George's Barbershop was given two American flags from soldiers from Saugus who had been fighting in Iraq and Afghanistan. Gary Sacco, who was serving in Afghanistan, sent a flag to the store and Moriello has it hanging along with the certificate on the wall.

The second flag, which he just received, is from Michael Pietrantonio, who served in Iraq. Moriello is working on getting a frame so he can mount that one too.

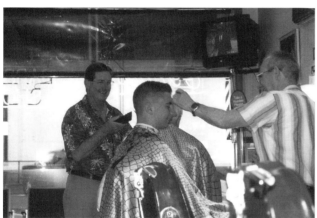
George Moriello, third generation, 2005.

"They think enough of this place to bring these back with them and give them to the shop. I don't know why," Moriello said shaking his head. "These kids came here when they were little and now when they've been putting their lives on the line, they've been thinking of sending these flags here."

It seems Moriello is as touched by his customers as they are by him and what his establishment has given their lives and their childhoods.

Closing time is upon these four men and the work day has finally wound down to a stillness they haven't seen all day. When asked how long he's worked there, Dick Robbins says fifteen years. Does he like it?

"Well, I haven't quit yet," he laughs.

Jim Fleming has worked there for thirteen years and Moriello's brother Ted is back working part-time, although he's not here on this night. A younger cousin is currently going to barbershop school, learning the ropes, readying to join the family business.

So you're still going to have to take a number the next time you go to George's Barbershop. It's a popular place.

H. Dwight Bisbee

A Saugus Name for 34 Years

by
Vera Bisbee Underhill

H. Dwight Bisbee was born October 30, 1874, in East Wareham, MA. His early childhood was spent at the old family homestead in North Rochester, MA, with his parents and grandparents. A family dispute arose and caused his father Augustine to pick up stakes and move to Falmouth, MA. Dwight graduated from Lawrence High School in Falmouth. He then enrolled in the Rounard Institute in New York where he received his training as a mortician. He wanted to be a doctor but did not have the financial means to go to medical school. Dwight had his first office and funeral business in Orange, MA, in 1893. The business was for sale and he felt it would give him a good start to buy a business that was already established. Eventually he moved to Saugus and transported the wagons, horses and equipment when he set up his business there.

H. Dwight Bisbee.

Dwight was a Mason and in 1904, he made the trip to San Francisco, California, to attend the 29th Triennial Conclave. I do not know, but I believe he met Joe Quint from Saugus and it was Joe who talked him into starting a business in Saugus as there was no undertaker at that time in town. Dwight had planned to start his business in Middleboro, MA, and live at the Rochester homestead. However, he made the decision to move to Saugus in 1904 and established his office and business in the Cliftondale section of the town. He purchased the land at 549 Lincoln Avenue with a small house that had two rooms downstairs and two rooms upstairs. He used the front room for his office. Back in those days, most funerals were held in the home or church and funeral parlors were not needed. After moving to Cliftondale, he needed a barn for the horses, wagons and equipment. On the corner of Myrtle Street and Lincoln Avenue was a large barn belonging to the Kent family who lived on the opposite corner of Myrtle Street. My father was able to buy the barn and because it was so large he had it cut in half and moved over to the lot on Lincoln Avenue. The barn had three floors and Dad added a building on the right end of the barn for the morgue. On the second floor, he had a number of small rooms, some of which he used and rented out the others for storage. On the left side of the barn were the stalls for the horses. I understood he had eight horses at one time.

Bisbee home and office; morgue is on right side of barn.

In 1907, my father married my mother, Sarah Faulkner Mosher from Nova Scotia. Sarah had come to Boston to stay with her uncle, Jeremiah Mosher, who was a captain in the Boston police force. She started her training as a nurse at a Boston hospital and that is where my father met her when he came to pick up a body. Mother wasn't happy with training to be a nurse so she enrolled at the Boston Conservatory of Music. Before she moved to Massachusetts, she had been a piano teacher in her home in Nova Scotia. After my parents were married, they lived in the little house on Lincoln Avenue. My sister Reta was born there in 1910. Dad bought a building on the Saugus / Revere line and had it moved up to 549 Lincoln Avenue and had it placed on the lot in front of the barn. He moved his office to that building. Later on, he added a back room, which became the funeral parlor. He then bought the house at 8 Myrtle Street and moved his family there and eventually there were four children, Reta, Vera, Malcolm and Freda. He rented the little house to Peter Howland, who became his hired hand. Peter took care of the horses and the many chores connected with the business. Across the street from the office was the fire station with the large fire bell on the top of the tower. Later it became a garage. My father told us the story of how he trained his dog to recognize that when the fire bell rang the dog was to rush to lower the rope across the stalls and back the horses down the ramp to the barn door, and wait for Peter or my father to hitch the horses up to the horse-drawn ambulance and away they would go! My brother Malcolm

reported in the Saugus Advertiser in 1982 that the horses at the fire station would run out if they could and if they couldn't, the firemen would have to let them out and they would run to the "hose house," as it was called, and be backed into position. The harnesses would then be dropped down on them and away they would go! Eventually the horses and wagons were replaced by fire engines. Most of the wagons and funeral coaches were transported to the barn and carriage house in North Rochester. My husband tore down the carriage house, over my strong objections, and, as there was no room in the barn for all the wagons, I had to sell a few of them.

Dwight soon became interested in Saugus town government affairs. He served as a Town Treasurer from 1912-1921 and several times, he served as a member of the Finance Committee, Sealer of Weights and Measures, and as a member of the Planning Board. He was active in the affairs of the Cliftondale Congregational Church, serving for many years as its clerk and a member of the Board of Trustees. He was a 32nd degree Mason, a member of the William Sulton Lodge A.M. & F.M., The Aleppo Temples of Boston, Commandery of the Knight Templers, Moswetuset Tribe 61, I.O.R.M. Saugus Knights of Pythians, and Past Noble Grand of the Cliftondale Lodge #193.

H. D. Bisbee at reins of horse-drawn hearse.

My father had very strong opinions on many things. He strongly opposed the government telling him what he could or couldn't do. One example happened when I was learning to drive the car. At that time in the early 1930s they were just installing stoplights at the intersections. I was driving back to the Framingham College one Sunday night when I came to a stop light. I proceeded to stop but Dad said "Don't bother to stop; just keep going." I knew it was wrong but Dad insisted and I knew better than to not obey him, so I proceeded across the intersection and wouldn't you know a cop was waiting for me and stopped me. Dad just sat there not saying a word and chuckling to himself as I tried to explain to the officer why I didn't stop. Dad thought it was funny; I didn't!

I have so many memories of the barn on Lincoln Avenue. I spent a lot of time there because I loved being around the horses. There was a large opening on the second floor above the barn door with a long pulley attached overhead. We used to grab the rope and swing out and then slide down to the ground. Dad even kept pigs under the barn door. In the spring, there would be piglets. It was fun for us to go over to the barn and watch the Italian women from Revere come up to the barn to buy the piglets. Dad had small wooden crates made to put the piglets in and he lined them up in front of the barn. The Italian women spoke in the native Italian, and although we couldn't understand them, it was fun to watch them as they tried to decide which piglets to buy.

During World War I, a flu epidemic spread across the country. My father was very ill with the flu and my mother and little sister Freda were also ill. We had a wonderful nurse that came and took care of the sick, and a wonderful lady that came and did the cooking and laundry and took care of us kids. Dad needed something from the morgue and sent me over to fetch it. I was only seven or eight years old and I remember how scared I was to open that door and go inside, as there were dead bodies everywhere. Because of the flu epidemic, they were unable to bury the dead.

Growing up on the Cape, Dwight loved all kinds of shellfish and especially he loved quahog or clam chowder and he was an expert at making clam chowder. When one of the lodges he belonged to would have a supper they had Dad make the chowder with help from the lodge members. About six lodge members would invade our kitchen on Myrtle Street and Dad would supervise the making of the chowder. There were onions and potatoes to cut up, clams and quahogs to open, and suet to render for the onions with large quantities of milk and cream. Once the chowder was ready, the men filled the large pots and carried it to the hall where the supper was being held. I believe it was in Cliftondale Square in the Odd Fellows building (if I remember correctly); everyone said it was the best chowder they ever tasted. Dad took a lot of pride in making sure it was the best.

My father told this story, which I thought was quite extreme. He strongly opposed liquor and never allowed any in our home. At times, he hired a young man to help around the barn. One night Dad found the young man dead drunk and out cold on the barn floor. He got Peter to help him put the young man in a casket, lighted candles around the coffin and waited. When the young man came to and realized where he was, Dad said "you never saw anyone move so fast." Dad never saw him again but he did hear that the young man was so scared that he never touched a drop of liquor after that.

Dad liked to collect many things. On one wall of the barn, he had a large collection of horsewhips. On another wall, he had a collection of old automobile license plates. After Dad died in 1938, both of these collections disappeared. Someone wanted both collections badly enough to steal them. No one ever locked the barn doors in those days. After Dad died, Malcolm took license plate 6659 and I took 6656, which my son has now, almost 80 years later.

My father told the story of going to Maine to pick up a body. On the trip back he noticed a police car following him. They finally stopped him and wanted to know what he was carrying in the hearse. He replied, "What I always carry, a dead body." Well they made him open up the casket containing the dead body. Satisfied they let him go on his way. It was prohibition time, and people were using hearses to deliver liquor and the police made sure he was not one of them.

H. D. Bisbee, Grand Marshall of a Saugus parade.

My father knew a great deal about horses; he had taken care of them a good part of his life. One day I went into Walkey's Store in Cliftondale Square. Mr. Walkey said, "Vera, I've just bought a horse for my daughter who is away at college; you may take him out for a ride anytime." I raced home to tell my parents and Dad just looked at me and said, "Young lady, you stay off that horse!" Well I didn't like his orders and I thought if Mr. Walkey said I could ride that horse then that was what I was going to do. So a few days later I went down to the farm, saddled up the horse, and led him down to the Saugus / Revere line, where there used to be an old racetrack. Suddenly, the horse stopped and turned and galloped out onto Lincoln Avenue through Cliftondale Square down Essex Street to Mt. Vernon Street. I stood up in the stirrups and pulled as hard as I could on the reins, and as quick as he could, he upped with his hind legs and threw me to the ground. He took off for the barn and I got up and walked home. My father was waiting for me. Mr. Walkey had seen us galloping past his store and called my father. Dad said, "I told you not to ride that horse; I knew all about him. He has a very hard mouth and is difficult to control and he never has had a woman on his back." "Well," I thought, "Why didn't you tell me that?" But I knew better than to talk back to my father. I have often wondered what went on at that old racetrack that scared that horse. He knew something that I didn't.

Dwight Bisbee was well respected by most people in Saugus, but you always make some enemies if you are in the public arena. There was never anyone who could conduct a funeral better than Dwight Bisbee. He was always dignified and compassionate. He cared about the bereaved family and many times even lent them money if they were in need. Whenever he had a newborn baby to bury he never would charge the family a penny for his services. He took great pains to see that every detail was taken care of and to help the bereaved family if he could. Once a man was reported as saying, "I never really liked Bisbee, but by God he could conduct a funeral better than anyone I ever saw." When he dressed for a funeral, he made a striking figure in his black suit with the long coat tails, a stiff white shirt with a black bow tie, one of his gold stick-pins below the tie, his vest with his gold watch and chain and his tall silk hat.

Dwight Bisbee was above all else an honest man. He willingly gave of his time and knowledge over the years to anyone in Saugus who needed help.

Paul Ciccarelli, who now owns the Bisbee-Porcella Funeral Home, has transformed the establishment into a beautiful quiet peaceful place for funerals. H. Dwight Bisbee would have been more than proud of what Paul has done for the name of the Bisbee-Porcella Funeral Home.

The Hart Bus Lines

by
Patricia Rockhill Woodbury

William S. Rockhill.

That was my dad. He was a very private man. I don't recall having had a serious conversation with him during my entire life. However, I do have fond memories of the many special times we shared. Now, in my own later, and hopefully "wiser" years, with grandchildren and great grandchildren, I realize the value of the quiet time spent with my dad.

There are a few things of his left to me. One large and significant one is his Governor Winthrop desk, no doubt an antique by now. I can still see him sitting at it handling family finances. In addition, he conducted some of the business of his role as vice-president of the local bus company, Rapid Transit, Inc., there.

My mother liked to tell the story of how Dad came to pursue his dream of owning that company. Dad was a bus driver for the Hart Bus Line. He asked Mr. Hart if he could take the day after his wedding off. Mr. Hart refused his request. Dad replied, "Mr. Hart, I'll own this bus line some day!" And he did. Wisely, he selected two excellent business partners, Judge Charles Flynn and James Conway. With only an eighth grade education, Dad became a partner in what became the Rapid Transit, Inc.

Bill Rockhill, after WW I.

The company provided transportation for many citizens from Saugus Center to Malden Square and Winthrop. In addition, schoolchildren in outlying areas were safely carried to school. The town of Saugus also received the benefit of snow plowing of the various routes served by the bus company.

A Rapid Transit Co. bus.

Dad was active in many organizations, including the Masonic Lodge and the Lions' Club. He was an honorary member of the Police Chiefs of Massachusetts. The one of which he was most proud was The American Legion, having served as commander at one time. When he passed away, I was privileged to plan the services for his burial. It would have pleased him to know that members of the local American Legion conducted the graveside ceremony with great dignity. A stirring rendition of "Taps" was played by a high school band member.

As I said, Dad was a very private man. Because of that I never heard first hand of his life experiences, including the several years in the U. S. Army during World War I; a lot of what I know came to me from his younger brother, Herbert.

The greatest gift I received from both my dad, William S. Rockhill, and my mother, Helen Lundholm Rockhill, was their love of and dedication to their family and friends.

The Saugus Grain Company

Webb Place, Saugus Center
Charles and Dorothy Comfort - Proprietors

(The following story is in Mrs. Comfort's own words as told to Mr. Richard G. Provenzano)

The Forecast calls for grain

by
Richard G. Provenzano
(*Saugus Advertiser*, June 2, 1994)

How did Charlie and I get into the grain store business? Well, as I said, my husband worked in the Cliftondale post office along with Mr. Townsend who lived next door to us. They would drive to work after picking up Frank Hall; Charlie was the only one who had a car.

One day Frank called and said that he thought they were going to sell the Grand Army Hall. He was an official in the Grand Army, you see. All the men were getting old and dying off, he said, and they decided to sell the building. Charlie came home one day and said, "What do you suppose? I bought the Grand Army Hall!"

"You what?" I said. "What do you want that old building for?" And he replied that he's found a use for it. Charlie always wanted to get out of the letter-carrying job. He had a wonderful head for figures and always wanted to get into business. A friend of his named Andy who lived near the top of Baker Hill told him that Saugus badly needed a grain store as he had to drive all of the way to Danvers to buy grain for his 100 or so chickens. This was around 1937.

Charlie decided to open a grain store and have Andy help him. They partitioned the first floor off and they left a big area in back for storage. The store itself was in front and they had a smaller area partitioned off for an office. It was slow at first; it really takes five years to get that kind of a business going. Andy was a good fellow and as honest as the day is long, but he was no salesman. He stayed for several months and then when he could see that he wasn't making it, he quit. Charlie got other boys and men to work for him, but they didn't work out too well either.

One day Charlie met a man on his mail route, a Mr. Peters from Palmer Avenue. He was a retired policeman living with his wife and daughter. Charlie explained that he couldn't pay much but Mr. Peters wanted the job anyway. He was hired and the business began to grow. He made signs and put them up in front of the bins filled with corn, grits and things like that, and the customers liked him a lot.

When the Second World War came, everyone in Saugus, it seemed, raised chickens and of course, they all needed to buy grain. It seemed that we didn't have a minute to sit down. Some customers even had chickens living in their houses. We had one who had a new house on Burrill Street and they had chicks running around on their nice oak floor in a bedroom. We had customers on Highland Avenue, one of the nicest streets in town, and they had a pig.

It was all part of the war effort then, you see, and these people all needed grain for the chickens and all of the other animals they raised. We had people coming from all over, buying 100-pound bags of chicken feed because they had a printed design on them so that you could cut up the empty bag and make some kind of clothing out of it. They made dresses, aprons, curtains, everything out of them. Nothing went to waste during the war!

We had the grain store 27 years. We sold it three times but bought it back twice. Why did we buy it back? Well, we sold it to young fellows who saw it was a good business. Charlie would work for them for a while to show them the business, but after a while the new owners would get lazy and not put the effort into the business the way that Charlie did. They wouldn't accommodate the customers even to breaking up a bag of grain. When Charlie asked a new owner why he wouldn't do it, the answer was that it was too much trouble. Of course, you understand that keeping the customer happy is part of running a good business.

After we bought the business back, it continued to grow. We got greyhound owners; they used to buy cases of things. The dog men would buy cases of vegetables and fruit, cod liver oil, anything they wanted, Charlie would get it for them. Sometimes he'd go to the Boston and Albany auction and buy cases of things that had been a little damaged. Sometimes he'd bid on anything he thought he could sell. One time it was cases and cases of crabmeat at a good price.

Charlie was a good businessman. People didn't realize the amount of business we did in that store. I enjoyed working there and talking to people. The store was hard to keep clean, but we had some lovely customers and I have some wonderful memories of the place even now.

A Few Random Thoughts

by
Beverly Comfort Barrish

Some names of boys who, in high school, worked in the grain store over the years come to mind: Dickie Evans, Freddie Landry, Jimmie Blundell, Earle Dudman, Bruce Davis, Harold "Hank" Waitt, "Bo" Parrott and Frank Breyer.

Something that the customers of the Saugus Grain Company will remember, I am sure, is the pot belly stove in the middle of the retail part of the store. In the winter, my father always kept a fire going in it, and so many people enjoyed the warmth from that stove.

During World War II, when meat was rationed, many people in Saugus started raising their own chickens. That is when business at the grain store really picked up and the business prospered. There was such a huge demand for grain that my father was getting one, sometimes two, carloads of 100 lb. bags of grain by train a week. They would arrive someplace over by Adams Avenue, or was it Denver Street? He and the young high school boys would unload those carloads of bags of grain onto a truck and then unload the bags from the truck into the back of the grain store. Old-fashioned weight-lifting!

A multi-level chick incubator was in evidence in the store every spring. Each level of the incubator would be filled with baby chicks. Again, due to the rationing of meat, the appearance of these baby chicks was an anticipated event and created many sales and customers for the store.

It's interesting to note that today's strict store hours of business was something that my father knew nothing about. If he had customers in the store after 6:00 p.m., he would stay right there and take care of their needs.

Paper Route

by
Ed Murray

What experiences of youth help to form our later lives? In my case, it was a stack of newspapers and a shoulder bag to carry them. I delivered papers for about five years, from 1955-1960.

There were three types of routes: morning, evening and Sunday. I had a morning and a Sunday route.

I usually rose at about 5 AM for the mile walk to Saugus Center. It was a hard way to wake up on winter mornings with the wind howling across Riverside Cemetery. It found ways to creep through the many layers I had hoped would keep me warm.

On some mornings, the driver of the Eastern Mass Street Railway bus would stop and give me a lift and other days the bus would roar on by. You were thankful when he stopped, and accepted it without complaint when he didn't. I always imagined that the driver who stopped had once been a paperboy.

At the end of that walk, Sanborn's shone like a lighthouse beacon in those predawn hours. Nothing else was open, nor was there much traffic in those days. Those of us who came through the front door in the early morning darkness knew little of the men who waited for the bus ride to work in the little waiting area at the front of the store. But we were a fraternity of sorts, older and younger members, mostly silent, or at the most nodding to one another. I cannot remember ever seeing a woman at that hour in those pre-liberation days.

Sanborn's Store.

The tobacco-fragrant interior of the store contained a rack of magazines down the center and newspapers piled high on the counter or stacked along the wall in piles for us to gather up into our bags and deliver to our yet to wake customers. It was a far cry from modern convenience stores. Cigars, ciga-rettes, penny candy, snacks, and, of course, newspapers and magazines.

Presiding over the store on alternate mornings was either Ben or Joe Sanborn. Two brothers who were as different as could be. Joe, with a full head of hair and a ready smile and Ben, bald and cigar smoking with the appearance of a "grumpy old man," but in reality not as grumpy as he would have you believe. Once Ben grew to know and trust me, he would ask me to fill in for a few minutes behind the counter before starting my route so that he could attend to other business. My payment was a Coke or a candy bar, and that seemed fair to me. To the best of my knowledge, they never took a vacation or a day off. They were hard working role models who had their rules. We had to live by them, but I can never remember anyone treating them with anything but respect. To this day I cannot enter that much-loved store without seeing them there.

One of the oddities of those days was a "free range" dog. Canine companions joined many of us on our routes. Never on leashes, and not a purebred in the lot, but attached to us by that invisible bond known only to boys and dogs. Returning to our side with only a whistle. Many mornings my dog would slip off to Herb White's Iron Pot restaurant while I gathered my papers, and I would stop there to call him, usually finding him sitting in Herb's back booth "office," being hand fed toast. His loyalty to me was never in question though, for at the sight of me he would be out the door in a flash, and off we would go, up and down the hills along Winter Street, delivering the morning *Globe*, the *Record*, as it was known then, the morning *Herald*, and the *Boston Post*, which was in and out of publication as it died a slow death.

My Sunday route took me along the length of Central Street to Hurd Avenue pushing a high-wheeled green wagon, and in snow, a similar version with runners. It was hard work by today's standards, but with the legs of youth. Shortly after graduation, when I traded civilian clothes for an all green wardrobe and a rifle, long walks were not as much of an issue to me as they were for some recruits. I had done my "basic training" on the hills of Saugus.

Sunday work involved even earlier rising, as Wayne Gautreau and I also assembled all the newspaper sections for Sunday delivery and store sales. It meant extra money, and jobs were not all that plentiful in those days.

I have often wondered how many of us were better prepared for life because we were out in all kinds of weather, learning the meaning of dependability, managing money, and sales-manship. Ben and Joe gave many of us that first opportunity. I wonder how many of us know what a great gift that was.

Tommy Maher, Jimmy Sacco, and The Ace Welding

by
Richard Maher

Ace Welding began in the late 1930s. It was started by Tommy Maher, a resident of Lynn, Massachusetts. Many of his friends referred to him as "Ace," and therefore, the name Ace Welding. While working as a welder at the Charlestown Naval Shipyard, he purchased a welding machine and started a welding school on the hill located at the top of Woodbury Avenue in Lynn. Tom Maher was a tireless and ambitious young man, but was no mechanic. My father told me that after a few lessons all his students could weld better than he could, but he never let them know it.

Tommy Maher at the office, Ace Welding.

Tommy Maher had the Irish gift of gab and could sell ice cubes to the Eskimos, but lacked mechanical ability to read blueprints or break them down for manufacturing. He needed someone with that knowledge to complement his sales ability. While working at the shipyard, my father met an engineer named Jimmy Sacco from Everett. They became friends and soon became partners and formed the Ace Welding Service, Inc. The welding school closed and they rented a small shop on Marion Street in Lynn, where they did general welding and started to fabricate oil tankers that fit on the trucks for oil deliveries to homes in the area. They had great success with the oil tankers, which became their main product until its closure in the 1970s. The company soon outgrew the Marion Street facility and, in 1941, a new and larger facility was located in Saugus at 12 Newhall Avenue where the company moved, expanded over and over and prospered.

World War II began and Ace Welding became a supplier of a variety of manufactured goods for the war effort. The firm continued to make its main product, the oil tankers, but received many contracts and sub-contracts to produce items for the U.S. Government, mainly the US Navy. The workforce expanded as new orders for war material came pouring in. In addition, new construction was necessary as more and more manufacturing space was needed. Bay after bay was added. In addition to enlarging the welding shop, a machine shop was added, a sheet metal shop, and a larger fabricating and assembly area was needed. Larger and larger equipment was added and Ace Welding had the ability to manufacturer large fabrications.

Workers at Ace Welding shop.

Palmer Electric, a company located in Wakefield, was loaded with government contracts and unable to complete them. They needed help, and Ace gave it to them. They subcontracted all sorts of orders to Ace Welding. In addition, they supplied Ace Welding, with the help of the Navy, new and larger machinery used to make more complex parts. Palmer also provided the engineering and manufacturing "know how." This gave Ace Welding the ability to compete with other firms in the area that made large fabricated items.

Tommy Maher handled the sales and administration while Jimmy did the bidding and was in charge of the manufacturing. They did, indeed complement each other.

Ace Welding shop, 1944.

Many of the young men who worked at Ace were later drafted or joined the armed forces. My father and Jimmy received a deferment, because the government needed them to make products used in the war effort. While most citizens were under gasoline rationing, Tommy and Jimmy were exempt because of their position as government contractors. I remember that my father let many of his former employees, home on leave from the military, use his

1941 Plymouth convertible, and I'm sure Jimmy did the same with his car.

Tom Maher moved to Saugus in 1942 and resided at 6 Fiske Road and Jimmy moved to Saugus about the same time and purchased one of the largest and most beautiful homes in the town on Essex Street.

An area above Ace Welding was groomed and turned into a picnic area. It was large enough for a softball diamond. Later, an area for horseshoes was added. The employees and their families spent many Sundays playing softball or horseshoes. Others just plain socialized with one another. But the best part was the food provided by Mrs. Sacco, Jimmy's mother. She was the cook. It was an Italian feast. She provided the group with all they could eat. It consisted of spaghetti, corn on the cob, salads, and all sorts of great food. All had a wonderful time.

The business prospered during the period 1942-1945. The partners expanded and purchased a restaurant located in Saugus Center which later became the Iron Pot. It was later sold to Herb White. They also started a "shoe factory" located off Jasper Street next to the railroad tracks. It burned down one night, and I'm sure, was one of the largest fires ever in the Town of Saugus. They also obtained a Ford dealership.

Working at the Ace Welding shop.

After the war, the partnership became strained, and the two men decided to go their own way. Jimmy kept the Ace Welding and my father took over the Ford dealership. He named it Maher Motor Sales and the dealership was located at the corner of Route One and Main Street. It is now an empty building.

Jimmy's brothers returned from the war and went to work helping Jimmy run the plant. Vic became the superinten-

dent, Ernie was in charge of manufacturing and Fiore became the sales manager.

Jimmy Sacco at the office, Ace Welding.

The two ex-partners maintained a cordial relationship after the breakup and, years later, my father went back to work as a salesman for Ace Welding. He had sold the Ford dealership and was in between businesses. He worked for Ace for several years and Jimmy even gave me a job at the plant. While working at Ace Welding, Tom met Larry Travis, an engineer, who spoke to my father about going into a "metal spinning" business. In 1953, he, Larry Travis, Billy, Bob, and Norman Gustafson all formed a business named Precise Metal. In 1957, they located the business in Saugus on the Route One Turnpike. My father once told me that he had never heard of "metal spinning," but after a month in the business, "people thought he invented it." That was the Irish in him.

Ace Welding is gone now. It has been replaced by the Saugus Commons. But over the years, hundreds of men and women were employed there. It was a vital firm. During its existence, it made an assortment of products for the military including the shell for mines used by the Navy. But always the mainstay of its business was the oil tanker. When Gibbs Oil delivered oil to your home, it's a "good bet" that the tanker containing the oil was made at the Ace Welding.

Helmer G. Josephson & Eastern Tool

by
Neil Howland

Helmer G. Josephson was all man and a yard wide. He was definitely larger than life. I can say that with some confidence since I am his number two grandson and I bear his middle name.

Although Helmer Josephson was a highly regarded figure in Saugus, he was an immigrant from Sweden around the turn of the last century, a live example of the word "charisma."

The cliché becomes a cliché because it comes to represent an established truth. Sure, if you deploy it a lot in everyday use to illustrate a point, it becomes weary and worn out, but nonetheless still true. There are a number of clichés about immigration that remain truisms, with the most popular and persistent and accurate being that the good old USA is a "melting pot." Our welcoming open-arms symbol of opportunity and freedom has resulted in tides of immigration that have ebbed and flowed to our shores from all over the world. It seems to be without question that one of the true strengths of our social and cultural fabric is the enormous pulsating energy of those plucky immigrants who sense so clearly that our great land is, indeed, the land of opportunity, the land where anything is possible.

Poll after poll after poll confirm that Americans: 1) approve of immigration as a fundamental and profound cornerstone of our nationhood; 2) believe that breathing-spell periods of assimilation are necessary every 35 – 40 years; 3) resent those foreign arrivals for whom the only magnet of our beloved country is the welfare dole.

Now in mid-2005, the delicate concept of immigration is wrenching the national psyche. Clearly the system needs to be regularized, uniform and enforced. A highly charged political football.

A recent popular sociological treatise decried in its title; "The Death of Common Sense." The root lunacy of those who endlessly pander for votes confirms the veracity of the book's thesis, as politicians now debate – with a straight face – the extent to which we must grant security blanket benefits to – are you sitting down? – illegal immigrants. God save our great land – and, mostly from ourselves.

This frenzied political debate, however, is not an abstract dilemma. Almost everyone I know has, within their living memory, immigrant forebears, and so we all indeed share a mostly favorable view of immigration as a common, accepted and wonderful underpinning of our national and cultural fabric.

I love both of my Swedish grandparents. Although now dead for 50 years, I never employ the past tense "loved," because they are as vivid a presence in my life today as they were 50 and 60 years ago. Much of whatever may be good in me is a reflection of them. What sturdiness of character, of integrity, of decency, of energy, and of absolutely total devotion to their adopted country and all that it then stood for, now sadly, though not wholly, diluted.

Helmer Gustave Josephson and Anna Otelia Hoeglin (isn't "Otelia" solid?) came to the United States from Sweden just at the turn of the 19th Century to the 20th. Part of the great tide of late 19th Century migration from Northern European Christendom, they placed their trust in liberty and opportunity, and dreamed that just maybe the streets of America were paved with gold. That turned out to be the case for them, but only after years of sacrifice and dedication, and, of course, hard work.

My grandfather was the son of a rather grandiloquently named Solomon Oskar Josephson and Matilda Andersdotter, and the youngest of three children. His brother, Karl, and sister, Anna, chose to remain in Sweden, working close to the land that in significant measure had spurred my grandfather's exodus to "The New Land." Both Karl and Anna lived beyond the age of 90, all in good health and serene simplicity. My grandparents returned for visits on two occasions, once crossing on a liner with the enigmatic film icon Greta Garbo. My mother visited Great Aunt Anna in Sweden some years after my grandparents' deaths in the mid-'50s. Aunt Anna, who had remained unmarried, had a charming, doll-size, very spic-and-span cottage and as Anna warmly greeted her American niece, the first thing that caught my mother's glance was my high school graduation picture adorning the snug mantelpiece, a little piece of Saugus in far-off Sweden.

It's somewhat odd, given the fact that I was so close in my relationships with both my grandparents, that my grandfather never engaged me with stories of childhood derring-do involving him, Karl and Anna.

Neither did he ever talk with me about his parents, and over time, picking up bits and pieces here and there from my mother and others, I came intuitively to the belief that a falling out had developed over his determination to emigrate to America. Upon attaining a certain measure of wealth in Saugus, he regularly sent money to his sister, Anna, that generosity being so typical of him.

My grandmother's only sister, Hilma, had come to America – and then to Lynn – with her, and in a colossal mismatch of a marriage, hooked up with a spare, eccentric old Yankee, Rufus Breed. So I would see my Aunt Hilma with some regularity as part of the family.

Helmer Josephson came off a hardscrabble farm in a little town in South Central Sweden called Ulricehamn (pronounced "oo-rah-sah-hahm," accent on the last syllable, all together now...), and our Nana, "Annie" Otelia from a small city, Motala, on the great canal that cuts diagonally across Sweden from the Baltic Sea down to Gotesberg on the west coast.

Only lingering remnants remain in Manchester, New Hampshire, of what was a sizable Swedish community during the early decades of the 20th Century. I use the word "community" with apt propriety. The community of immigrant

Swedes was not clannish, or purposefully aloof – but really were simply supportive of one another, and constantly on the lookout for possible opportunities for advancement.

My grandfather must have had relatively little formal education in the old country and none in the USA, and it's not clear to me if that education had any specific focus beyond the fundamentals of the "three R's," but he was infinitely graced by God with astonishing intellectual talent as a mechanical engineering theoretician, **and**, he had that unquenchable fire-in-the-belly, that undeniable fervor to succeed.

He began work in the Manchester, New Hampshire, locomotive yards for $3.00 a week, before moving on to Lynn and the lure of G.E., where he excelled in their highly praised Apprentice Program for tool-and-die makers. He first began to acquire minor celebrity status when, as Night Superintendent at Worcester Pressed Steel during the First World War, he redesigned the tooling for munitions shell casings, which effectively doubled the plant's productive output. Some thirty years later, the company he founded in 1919 on Ballard Street, Eastern Tool & Stamping Co., was singled out by the War Department for the prestigious ARMY-NAVY "E AWARD" recognizing the outstanding contributions by the Company and all of its employees to the heroic efforts of WW II.

The Award ceremony banquet was held in the Town Hall, and my grandfather was bursting with unrestrained pride. It was a true pinnacle in his life – an immigrant lad of 20, incapable of uttering a single syllable in English when he stepped off the boat, was now being heartily praised by a coterie of high-ranking military officers, the Town Fathers, and his fellow Saugus citizens, for his singular achievements. Reminds me of the wisdom of another old and hoary cliché, "Only in America."

The Eastern Tool 1933 Christmas Party.
Helmer Josephson is the rightmost man in the front row.

My mother called her father "Pa" so his three grandsons naturally followed suit, although once involved in the workplace environment as young adults, in public we referred to him mostly as "Joe" or "Boss." Almost a cliché is the characterization of someone being "larger than life," that characterization aptly fitting my grandfather in every sense. He was one of the most intelligent people I've ever known. Lacking in formal education, he was, nonetheless, one of the most educated people I have ever known, constantly absorbing that which came into his orbit. A Ph.D. from the College of Life.

And, as a business owner he was a throwback to the paternalistic autocrat that more nearly typified the approach of 19th Century moguls. Generous to a fault, tough, and tough-minded, authoritarian yet loving, mildly vindictive when crossed, hugely loyal to friends, and implacable with those identified as foes, perceptive with an enormous gusto for dining at the banquet of life. He was in a quite self-assured way a prototypical patriarchal figure. His demeanor, and his own sense of natural command earned respect from all with whom he came in contact. But his earthy sense of humor, and that head-thrown-back roar of laughter, enabled him to put all with whom he came in contact at ease, commoners and kings alike. I count every hour I spent with him as a treasure in my memory bank – that natural love and regard, which vibrated so easily between us, will nourish me until we meet again. As a skinny, little teenager, I thought I was a hotshot baseball player. Baseball was not part of Pa's ethnic heritage, and, although it's a game many people could take to secondhand, I am sure it didn't occupy much of his attention. Nonetheless, he gathered enough awareness about the game to be able to talk knowledgeably with me about my miniature heroics. What a guy. A real man and never a cliché in thought or deed.

But for me as a kid growing up, the marvelous experiences of being around my immigrant grandparents almost daily transformed my life with joy, and wonder, and memories evergreen 60 years later. Clearly an underlying benefit of immigration is the constant interplay of contrasting cultures, and the homely pleasures of ethnic food and foreign tongue. Although Swedish cuisine is not normally regarded as bellwether cookery, you've got to believe me, my Nana could create pure magic out of pretty ordinary stuff. She was a master at making the Swedish coffee roll called "bulla" that traded on the seductive hint of cardamom to addict me for a lifetime.

Since we grandkids lived near at hand to their 77 Winter Street home, I started the habit of eating Sunday breakfast with my grandparents at an early age, part of the attraction being the Sunday comic strips, which we always then called "funnies." Nana would make Pa and me a huge batch of silver-dollar sized Swedish pancakes, called "pletta," with crisp sausage and coffee, and this treasured ritual of food and loving conversations spun out over a dozen years.

When it came time for them to meet my fiancée, Kellie Reehill (from Saugus too, and herself the daughter of Irish immigrants) it was over the Sunday morning breakfast table.

Inasmuch as I would frequently either walk over to visit, or stay overnight, I was exposed often to the warm camaraderie of impromptu and informal gatherings in Nana's kitchen of other immigrant Swedes who looked, as I did, to my grandfather as an ideal role model. The wholesome but boisterous kinship of Axel Brostrom, Clara Johnson, Victor Bok, the Nygaards, etc., around the kitchen table marked the only occasions in which they would lapse into their native language. Without exception they were all determined to master English, and, partly as a consequence of that determination, a stubborn regret for me is that I never learned more than a handful of Swedish words.

Imparting the true values of life came naturally to my grandparents, both by their conduct and words. Occasionally their love for me would collide with an object lesson at hand. Pa had a garden plot out back of the house for summer vegetables, and hanging around with him one hot Saturday in August, when I was about nine or ten, he commissioned me to pull weeds, at ten cents an hour. I went at it with enthusiasm – briefly – but laboring under the August sun soon lost its luster as I recalled that Pa gave me an allowance of 25 cents a week anyway, and, thus, his incentive program, not yet clearly perceived by me at age nine, quickly waned.

In June 1955, brother Roger graduated from Harvard College, and I from its Law School, together, and with his typical tenacity and love, my grandfather, in excruciating pain from inoperable stomach cancer that would claim him in six more weeks, came to witness for himself one final compelling attainment in a lifetime of achievement.

Recent Changes

by
Eric W. Brown

The past decade has been a particularly turbulent time for Saugus businesses. There have been several cases of long-established Saugus businesses moving, downsizing, or even completely closing up shop. Following you will find a few photographs of just three of these businesses; while hardly complete (or even representative) they'll be familiar to most Saugonians.

Cliftondale Woodworking departs.

Russo's Candy downsizes and moves to Oaklandvale.

Eastern Tool shuts its doors completely.

Alwinol

by
Joyce Cook Evans Barry

My father-in-law, Frank Evans, Jr., developed a multi-purpose liquid cleaner called "Alwinol" in the late '40s – early '50s. He first started bottling this product in the basement of his home on Lincoln Avenue and called his business The Alwin Color & Chemical Co., Inc. named after his youngest son, Alwin. Later, as the popularity of this amazing cleaner increased, Mr. Evans moved his business to a building near Cliftondale Square. He was the typical super-salesman of his day – friendly, gregarious, and quite a talker. His motto was "You can do it all with Alwinol" and to demonstrate this, he would rent a booth at the Topsfield Fair every fall. His claim was that the cleaner was strong enough to soften a hardened paint brush, which he would duly demonstrate while also being gentle enough to clean one's false teeth. And to the amazement of onlookers he would drop his dentures into a glass of Alwinol. Needless to say, the sales rose rapidly. Two of his sons, Alwin and Dick worked part-time as salesmen for him, selling to hardware stores throughout the greater Boston and Northeast areas. After Mr. Evans' death in 1961 his son, Alwin, took over the business until it became too difficult to compete with the larger companies, such as Proctor & Gamble, etc. It was great while it lasted, though – a true "home-grown" product of Saugus.

Fire & Police

Every society gets the kind of criminal it deserves. What is equally true is that every community gets the kind of law enforcement it insists on.

— Robert F. Kennedy

"Bud" Courtis

by
James Blanchard
(Chief of the Saugus Fire Department)

Robert Lawrence Courtis was born on March 12, 1924, at 35 Taylor Street, Saugus, Massachusetts. Robert was the only child of Leonard August Courtis and Dorothy (Dottie) Pratt. The home at 35 Taylor Street belonged to Mr. George Herbert Pratt, who was Robert's mother's dad. George's wife, Robert's grandmother, was a "Hawkes," a direct descendent of the founding family of Saugus.

George H. Pratt owned a stout team of horses and he used them to haul hay and grain throughout the local area. The team was kept in a barn at what is now 37 Taylor Street. In addition to hauling freight George Pratt also used his team to pull the Saugus Fire Department apparatus. Whenever a firm alarm occurred, the bell in the steeple of the Congregational Church in Saugus Center would ring. George Pratt would stop whatever he was doing and respond to the Central Fire Station with his team. An alarm occurring after midnight required that Mr. Pratt run out of the barn, place his team in a hitch and walk them down the street to the firehouse. These horses quickly recognized the fire bell. When Mr. Pratt entered the barn the team would be raring to go. They would march themselves out of their stalls and stand under the "quick hitch." George would pull the rope and the hitch would fall onto their backs. Once the belly strap was fastened and the door opened, George grasped the reins. Feeling George at the reins set these fire horses into a gallop.

Neighbors would love to see George leaving his barn for the firehouse. They claimed his feet never touched the ground all the way to the station. This so-called walk of the fire team was the closest thing to flying that George ever did.

That church bell soon had one person up and alert every time it sounded. A little boy watched in fascination, his face pressed against the window on the second floor of 35 Taylor Street, watching his grandfather race with the fire horses to another alarm. George was a teetotaler but his language, especially when angered, was very colorful. A young Robert Courtis listened more than once to his grandfather vehemently complain about being abandoned by his team.

At an address up on Newhall Avenue, George had gone into a building to make a delivery. When he came out his team and wagon were gone. The horses heard the church bell sound an alarm, and they bolted for the fire station. Escapades like this caused George considerable extra work. He had to pick up the scattered hay and grain deposited all along Main Street. Robert often played in the barn and remembers that one of the fire horses was named Major. He

has a photograph of him sitting on his horse, but he hasn't been able to find it.

George H. Pratt sold the piece of land his barn had been on to his daughter and son-in-law. Leonard August Courtis and his wife Dorothy built a house on this property which is 37 Taylor Street. Robert still lives there today.

July 29, 1935, Robert was eleven years old. He was visiting his grandparents who lived in an apartment opposite the old police station. Robert loved to go there because he was that much closer to the firehouse, a location he had already begun visiting on a regular basis. He was sitting on the front porch anxiously watching smoke rise up from a building fire at what is now the new fire station. Robert pleaded with his mother to let him go to the fire but she refused to let him off the porch. Suddenly an explosion rocked the neighborhood. An acetylene tank, located inside the burning building, had ruptured, emitting a large fire-ball. The explosion and fire proved fatal to Saugus Fire Chief Mellen Joy who succumbed to his injuries several days later. Firefighters Warren Newhall and Norman Hull, who were with Chief Joy on the first hand line in, were critically burned. Both men eventually recovered and continued with their careers.

"Bud," a nickname Robert picked up early in his life, attended grades one through six at the Roby School, just across the street from his home. He had already begun visiting the fire station on a regular basis and knew all the firemen and the location of all the alarm boxes. Bud's sixth grade teacher, Mrs. Peckham, was a fire buff herself. The classroom faced Main Street and whenever an engine passed by on the way to an alarm Mrs. Peckham would go to the window. Coincidentally Bud's seat in the classroom afforded him an excellent view of the Main Street and he never missed a passing engine. If several engines passed by, or if Mrs. Peckham could see smoke off in the distance, she would call Bud up to her desk and discreetly ask him to call the station and find out where the fire was. Mrs. Peckham was easily one of Bud's favorite teachers ever.

Through junior high and high school, Bud developed a love of music and took up the trumpet. He quickly learned how to play the instrument well enough to become a member of the Saugus High School band. If Bud has a second love in his life, it is the Saugus High Band. He is an ardent supporter; a few years ago he personally bought all new uniforms for the entire organization. At the same time, Bud was a staple at the fire station. He spent all his available time helping out wherever he could. A quick learner, Bud was given more and more responsibility, and soon he was responding on the engine with the firefighters.

Bud graduated from Saugus High School in 1942. He went to work for General Electric in West Lynn. Bud worked in the tool and die office. His interest in firefighting never waned; he spent his lunch time in Lynn Ladder Two on Federal Street. Captain Evans was the captain in charge. Bud left G.E. in 1943 to enlist in the navy. He was sent to Newport, Rhode Island, for boot camp. While he was at Newport the Navy asked if anyone has any experience playing a trumpet. Several personnel volunteered and auditions were conducted. Seaman Courtis made the cut and became a navy bugler.

Graduating from boot camp, Bud was stationed at Cottington Point, Rhode Island, not far from where he attended boot camp. Buglers had to learn all the calls and at the beginning, there were many buglers in Bud's outfit. As the war raged on many of these buglers were deployed to the Pacific Theatre as replacements. Bud's main assignment was as a member of a funeral color guard. He played taps at the graves of sailors and marines who were killed in action. Even today Bud chokes up thinking of the faces of the countless

Buster Courtis, U.S. Navy, 1943.

mothers, wives, and children he saw while playing taps at the gravesites. Bud came home as often as he could. A quick change of clothes and he was back at the fire station. He recalls being at a large woods fire up behind what is now Caruso's. It was a Sunday and he had forgotten the time. His father showed up and reminded him he was going to miss the last train back to Newport if he didn't leave right away. Bud didn't even have time to clean up. He threw on his uniform and with a dash at the station made the last train. The lady in the seat beside him kept sniffing the air and looking at him with a puzzled look.

Bud managed to swap weekend duty with another sailor who was billeted in Barracks B with him. This was not sanctioned by Navy regulations and a sailor could get in trouble if caught participating in this type of swap. Bud returned to Newport late on Sunday after swapping with another sailor only to learn Barracks B had sustained a terrible fire. Four sailors perished in this blaze. Bud was sent to Barracks C where he blended in with the other sailors until he found the sailor he had swapped with. The man was not injured and with all the confusion, the Navy never learned that Bugler Third Class Courtis had not been aboard the night of the fire.

Bugler Courtis was instructed by his chief that a large ceremony involving the entire complement of personnel was

to occur the next day. More importantly he was going to be the bugler for the entire ceremony. Bud had never seen so many sailors all in one place. All Bud knew was that it was a review by visiting British Royalty. He sounded calls all morning on his bugle. When the ceremony was over, bugler Courtis was still standing at attention when a very properly dignified British lady strode up to him. With a thick British accent she said, "You did a fine job, bugler." Bud later learned that this lady was the Crown Princess of England. Her name is Elizabeth; today we refer to her as the Queen of England. The young man from Taylor Street, who learned to play the trumpet as a member of the Saugus High School Band, had played for and spoken to the Queen of England.

Bud returned to his job at General Electric after the war. He continued his love of firefighting and spent every spare moment at the station. Bud was appointed a call fire fighter in 1955, which meant he could officially ride on the apparatus and would receive a stipend for his service. In 1957 Bud left the GE to accept the job of "permanent intermittent" firefighter. In this capacity Bud worked a regular shift and in 1961 Robert Lawrence Courtis realized his dream and was appointed a permanent Saugus firefighter. Bud has the distinction of being the last call fireman appointed as a permanent firefighter. The job was everything he had hoped for and he loved the challenge. It did come with several downsides, however. Bud was injured several times; the most serious injury occurred at a house fire at 17 Whitney Street on January 21, 1962. Bud was attempting to move a 35-foot extension ladder from the structure. Due to the subzero temperatures this became a very arduous task. A Lynn firefighter, Killiam Brady, was assisting Bud with the ladder. Suddenly the entire cornice came crashing down. Bud's ice encrusted mitten was frozen. Bud's mitten, frozen to the rope, catapulted him along with the ladder. Lynn firefighter Killiam Brady was not as fortunate. He was burned by the falling cornice and critically injured. Firefighter Brady survived but never recovered from his injuries and was forced to retire. Bud suffered serious knee and back injuries but eventually returned to duty.

Bud became the chief's aide and handled all of the department's paperwork including payroll. He liked this job because in addition to his office duties he had to respond to all fires and assist the chief. In 1969 Bud was appointed Town Constable by then Town Manager Clarence Wilkinson. He delivered court orders to persons all over town. He also served notice on the fire chief, more than once, in regard to labor disputes. One of Bud's proudest achievements was the development of a firefighter memorial that stands on the Saugus Firefighters plot at Riverside Cemetery. It is a granite statue of a Saugus firefighter descending a ladder holding a child. All deceased members' names are inscribed on this stone. Bud accomplished this while serving as an officer on the board of the Saugus Firefighters Relief Association. Bud spearheaded the drive, designed the memorial, acquired the plot and even the drive, designed the memorial, acquired the plot and even solicited the funding. The annual firefighter memorial Sunday begins with a service at this beautiful memorial.

Robert L. Courtis retired in 1987. Bud had reached the maximum age allowable for firefighters, 65. Although officially retired and out of the firefighter uniform he loved so much, Bud continued to arrive at work every day, a tradition he maintains to this day. He arrives at 7:45 and has a cup of coffee in the fire house kitchen with the oncoming shift. After swapping several fire stories and giving and taking several well-aimed barbs, Bud takes his place in the office. He has a table and chair near the window on the first floor. He collects and catalogs all the runs from the previous night. He arranges the runs in the various categories: medical aids, hazardous material, outside fires, vehicle fires, building fires and auto accidents. Bud makes a monthly report of the various alarms, by category and thereby assists me in recognizing trends and areas that need more training, equipment or manpower. Although he is now in his eighties, Bud lives in the same spot he has lived in his whole life. Bud continues to do what has made him the happiest. He comes to the fire station ever day, interacts with the firefighters and shares fire stories, all the way back to horsedrawn days.

Buster Courtis, Saugus Fire Department.

An Officer and a Gentleman

by
Chris Danahy

My family moved to Saugus when I was three years old and I lived in town until just after I graduated from high school in 1968. I left town in January of 1969 to go to college in Kansas. It was tough leaving Saugus after spending my previous fifteen years there and Mother realized it so she had the *Boston Globe* delivered to me in Kansas on a daily basis. This was well before the days of the internet so I had to wait three days before the paper arrived. The *Globe* wasn't going to keep me up on what was going on in Saugus but I was happy to get it so I could read the articles on the big, bad Bruins. Bobby Orr was in the prime of his career and the Bruins were the hottest thing in Boston. It was tough enough not being able to watch the games on TV because hockey didn't get any coverage in Kansas and there was no such thing as cable TV. It's hard to explain today but before cable TV and the internet if you were far from home the only way you could find out what was going on at home was through a letter, a phone call or yesterday's papers.

I was homesick when I first got to Kansas so one of the first things I'd do each day would be pick my mail. E-mails hadn't arrived yet so people actually wrote letters to one another to keep in touch. Being homesick, I wrote a lot of letters and quickly learned that the only people who wrote back were girls, which was fine with me. I wasn't going steady with any particular girl at home so I wrote to a lot of them and most of them wrote back to me. It was nice to know that I'd at least have the *Boston Globe* waiting for me when I went to my mailbox but I actually got a lot of mail. Those were the days when getting mail was very enjoyable because there was no junk mail and I was too young to have any bills. Only good things came in the mail when I was nineteen years old.

Not long after I arrived in Kansas the headlines in the *Boston Globe* brought me some disturbing news. The Ocean House in Swampscott had burned to the ground and that only made me more homesick. I had no attachment to the Ocean House except for the fact that my high school senior prom was held there the previous May. It just got me thinking of that night and the great time that I had there with my friends.

A few weeks later I saw a headline that stopped me in my tracks. I had a letter from Nancy Conrad that day and I'd normally go right to the letter and read the paper later. Saugus had made the headlines of the *Boston Globe*, which is never good news but this news was the worst. Officer Gus Belmonte of the Saugus Police Department was killed in a shootout at the Red Coach Grill on Route One. He wasn't on duty but he heard of a robbery in progress on his police radio and responded in plain clothes. There was gunfire in the parking lot and Gus was shot and killed. I call him Gus because that's what he insisted that all kids in Saugus call him.

Saugus Fire Department pumper.

Saugus Police Department, 1904, l-r, top to bottom rows:

Francis W. Clark (later Essex County Agent for the Society for Prevention to Cruelty to Animals); J. Henry Williams (later Captain of Saugus Fire Dept.); Levi Florence, Edwin P. Burnham.

Peter A. Flaherty (first Irish policeman appointed in Saugus); Roland L. Mansfield (later Saugus Police Chief, founder of Saugus Police Relief Association); Chief Charles O. Thompson; Walter A. Pratt (uncle of C.F. Nelson Pratt, son of James F. Pratt); Frank W. Joy (was former Chief of Police in Saugus in the 1890s, 44 years a patrolman).

Carrie Mansfield (matron of the Saugus Town Hall, wife of Justin Mansfield); Charles E. Torrey; Charles F. Clark: Joseph R. Gillan: Justin E. Mansfield ("keeper of the lockup" and janitor of Saugus Town Hall).

Gus Belmonte was an officer and a gentleman. He was far and away the most popular member of the Saugus Police Department to the kids of Saugus. He commanded our respect simply by being our friend. I don't remember going to a dance while I was in high school that Gus wasn't at. I think that he volunteered for the detail because he loved being around us and that didn't bother us because we loved having him around. We didn't have to worry about Gus dragging us down to the police station if he smelled alcohol on our breath because he didn't want us to get into trouble. He understood that kids will be kids and he was more interested in looking out for us than he was in seeing us get into trouble. If you were a kid who was arrested by Gus

Belmonte, you were considered a jerk and you had some serious explaining to do.

I didn't know Gus any better than most kids from Saugus did, but I did get to spend a little more time alone with him. I worked at Star Market during my junior and senior years of high school and many times I had to walk home from work if I didn't have any wheels. The only time I had wheels was when my brother Billy let me use his car, which was quite a bit, but I still did a fair amount of walking. One night I was walking down Forest Street on the long trek to Second Street where I lived when Gus pulled up beside me in his cruiser and asked me where I was going. When I told him that I was walking home from work he told me to jump in and he'd give me a ride. Gus knew me as a friend of his nephew, Tommy Belmonte, but that's not the reason that he picked me up. Gus would have picked up any kid walking alone after ten o'clock but he wouldn't bother a group of kids walking around. I appreciated that ride because I did a fair amount of walking on my job at Star Market and I was tired by the end of the day. I could usually get a ride home from one of the many kids who worked at Star but I stayed as late as I could to earn more money if I had the chance, while most kids wanted to bolt as soon as the store closed.

A few weeks later I was walking home from work again when Gus pulled up beside me on Forest Street and told me to hop in. I didn't think that it was only by chance that his happened and that was confirmed when he picked me up a few weeks later at around the same spot. I can't say for sure that Gus drove down Forest Street at about 10:30 every night that he was on duty but I'll bet that he did as many nights as he could. If Gus knew there was a chance a kid was walking home alone he would make an effort to drive by and give him a ride.

This is only one example of the way Gus would go out of his way to help kids. I developed a nice relationship with him during those rides home, so much so that many times, I felt like refusing a ride home from my co-workers and walking to Forest Street knowing Gus would be there. My heart was broken as I read the news of Gus's death from fifteen hundred miles away. I kept looking at the picture of the Red Coach Grill in the newspaper realizing that it was only a few hundred yards from the spot on Forest Street where Gus first picked me up. I had experienced the deaths of people in the past year who were young and closer to me than Gus Belmonte was, but Gus's death hurt just as much. I felt sorry for everyone in Saugus and wished I could have been there to say goodbye to Gus. I felt bad for Gus's family but I really felt bad for the kids from Saugus who were not going to have the chance to go through high school with Gus Belmonte. Gus might have been on the Saugus Police Force but he went through high school with me and I'm sure he did the same with thousands of kids before me. I was pleased to learn that the new middle school in Saugus was going to be named after Gus but it's too bad they couldn't have named the high school after him because high school aged kids seemed to be Gus's specialty. Gus Belmonte was an officer and a gentleman but he was a great person and must have been a great kid himself. I know he was because I knew him as a kid even though he was probably twenty years older than me. He had the ability to relate to teenagers as if he were one himself but everyone respected the badge on his chest. It's not fair that Gus died at the wrong end of a gun, but it didn't really surprise me because Gus wouldn't fire his at anyone unless he really felt that his life was in jeopardy. It was in jeopardy that night, but Gus didn't know it because he had just arrived on the scene and caught a bullet before he knew what hit him. Gus never would have fired first.

Officer W.A. Pratt

by
Hugh Somers

Walter Andrew Pratt was born in Saugus in 1868, the second son of James F. and Elizabeth Pratt. He worked alongside Roland L. Mansfield and Frank W. Joy, and all three served as "Regular Officers" in the Saugus Police Department. He served under Chief Charles O. Thompson until about 1904. Walter's salary for the year 1897 was $748.65.

Officer Walter Pratt.

Although physically imposing at over 6'4", he had a quiet reserve and was able to command respect with few words. He was known by his family to successfully practice the ancient art of water divining. A natural spring well he found in the 1920s with this talent was still being used until recently. He lived with his wife, Minnie, and children, Freda and Walter L., on Summer Street in Saugus.

Officer Ken Shaw

by
Eric W. Brown
(*Saugus.net*, October 1998)

You could say Kenny Shaw was a well known local figure. A veteran of both the Saugus and Boston police departments, Ken's personality, jokes, and stories never failed to charm and entertain everyone he met. Born in Lynn (the oldest of five), and a graduate of Lynn Trade High, Ken moved to Saugus in 1958. He was happily married and had two daughters and two sons.

Ken Shaw had a variety of different experiences. He served a tour of duty off of Vietnam on the U.S.S. *Ranger*, a Navy aircraft carrier. After his honorable discharge in 1964, he worked as a stationary fireman in the Lynn Hospital and soon earned his second class fireman's license.

His life's goal though was to be a police officer. In 1965 he got onto the reserve list for the Saugus Police, and on April Fools' Day of 1966 he got his long standing wish and became a regular patrolman.

His time with the Saugus Police was eventful. He managed to apprehend the man who had robbed the Robert Hall Store in Chelsea after a car chase and gun battle, he was one of the first officers on the scene when the ape was running loose in the Golden Hills, and in 1967 he became the president of the Saugus Brotherhood of Police.

In 1970 he joined the Boston Police Department. He went through the intense FBI certification course for finger-printing in Quantico, Virginia and eventually became a detective. He worked on numerous high-profile cases (such as the Charles Stuart case), and in his spare time started a program fingerprinting kids and providing their parents with ID cards for emergency use. His program started in Clifton-dale, but quickly expanded beyond Saugus into Boston with sponsorship from Bank of Boston. In the end, his team handed out ID cards to the parents of approximately 80,000 kids.

His official work in the Police Department involved searching crime scenes for evidence, fingerprinting, and the processing of blood and blood related products; he started this work well before rubber gloves and other modern precautions were manditory. While assigned to this position, Ken was diagnosed with hepatitis C, a blood-borne viral disease, which ultimately led to the failure of his liver.

As a direct result of his failing health, Ken was forced to retire from the job he loved at the end of 1997. Although he'd always been dextrous and skilled in his hobbies of stained glass and ceramics, the hepatitis C made his hands too shaky for such detailed work – it was difficult for him to even write.

Ken had a successful liver transplant, but complications afterwards caused him to go into a coma and he passed away in the afternoon of December 23, 1998.

Growing Up in Saugus
Part 2

There are few successful adults who were not first successful children.

— Alexander Chase

Boyhood Baseball and Other Adventures

by
Jay Nelson

Growing up in Saugus Center in the years just after World War II, my boyhood pals and I had some wonderful adventures. Of course I'm biased, but I believe that the town offered then (and still does) an unusually rich variety of striking physical settings – natural and man-made – for the unfolding of childhood adventures. How about, just to mention some of the most obvious, Route 1, a major national highway; the Saugus River emptying into the Atlantic Ocean; the Iron Works; Breakheart Reservation; the Reservoir; and the East Saugus marshlands! The time, too, 1948-1956 (my ages 7-15), was an unusual period in American history – a time when Americans were still basking in the post-war glow of American "triumphalism" and exceptionalism as trumpeted in the media and in our textbooks with very little dissent.

It was also a time when a kid living in a suburban setting with rural elements, as Saugus was then – and much less traffic than today, especially in the Center – could typically ride a bike in safety almost anywhere, anywhere your parents would allow, that is. Oddly enough the "short leash" that my parents, Mary and John, and my grand-mother kept me on, not unusual for the times, contributed to a thrilling feeling of "Boy, I'm really exploring now," during an adventure which might seem provincial, even childish, to similarly-aged young boys today. I mean, a bike ride up Central Street to faraway Cliftondale with Brian Cunningham after school on a beautiful day in May of my sixth grade, fifth for him, to visit his grandmother (great aunt?) and get a snack was a Big Deal, a Major Adventure for both of us.

Many of my teachers in Saugus, often simply by listening attentively to our animated accounts, encouraged a sense of adventure, a taste for novelty and surprise, most notably Miss (Helen) Long, fourth grade at Roby; Mrs. (Florence) Gibson, sixth grade at Roby; Miss Hayward, seventh, at the old High School; and Mr. (Paul) O'Brien, eighth. And my next-door neighbor, the fabulous teller of sports and war stories and my baseball mentor, Bill Harrington, passed on his relish of adventure.

Life was not all ice cream and chocolate cake in those years for any of us kids, and I don't mean to imply that it was. We all knew fear and sadness and pain in our lives. But those adventures in Saugus, it seems to me, nurtured our sensi-tivity, our receptivity to surprise and mysteries, to wonders and to natural beauty. I am very grateful for that.

I apologize in advance for any errors of inclusion or omission regarding the names of other kids involved in these anecdotes.

Spring Training

Early March of 1949 or 1950, before there was Little League baseball (arrived 1952) in Saugus, one of those fluke late-winter 65-70 degree days a short while after a snowfall. Spring training in the Major Leagues had already started, so the papers already carried accounts of our Boston Red Sox and Boston Braves heroes down South (yes, the Braves(!), with us until the '53 season), but we kids in Saugus were reconciled to the fact that our own baseball games were a good month to six weeks away, and probably in miserable weather at that. Then, waking up one day, greeted by a veri-table "heat wave," which we were immediately informed by "the adults," would be short-lived: "It's supposed to get cold again tomorrow." After school, either Mrs. Pfuntener's or Miss Nicholson's class, I was outside, wearing a sweater – goes with the short leash – contentedly tossing a ball up in the air in the sunshine in our driveway, catching it in my "Warren Spahn" (never mind that he was a lefty and the glove a righty's) and avoiding the melting snow islands on the pavement and the grass. A gentle breeze added to the magic. Suddenly, Jackie Mitchell, Eddie Beaton, and Kenny Greene appeared with amazing news: there was going to be a ball game behind the new Catholic Church construction site on Summer Street near the end of my street, Parker.

The church construction area was set out close to Summer between Parker and Taylor at the top of a slight rise – I don't think much building of the Blessed Sacrament had actually taken place. Beyond the rise a broad field declined gradu-ally to a small stream running parallel to Summer Street about halfway to the Ace Welding shop and yard on Newhall Avenue. The field, which, in service of the church construction, had been cleared the previous fall down to the near bank of the stream of essentially all the shrubs and bushes and even vines that had rendered it unplayable for baseball in the past – though not for wandering about – now practically demanded that we stake out a (muddy) baseball field. It almost looked like farmland primed for planting, except for the snow patches. The sun shone down gamely in the cloudless winter sky when we arrived, although, the time being probably 3:00 or so when we got started, it was already well down from its noontime peak and on its way to the horizon in the west behind the Ace Welding. Tall, leafless trees from Summer and Main Streets and from the woods at the northern end of the field swayed slightly from time to time at the edge of our consciousness. For the game we would probably have been joined by, or perhaps ourselves joined, some number of Cunninghams, Standishes, Kellehers, Robertses, and Regans, and maybe

Benson Shapiro, Gerald Moynihan, Dave Huggins, Bobby Gallant and Bobby Stahler.

About the baseball itself – I played outfield on defense – I remember only that fly balls and would-be line drives didn't carry very far (muddy ball / heavy ball), landed and bounced once or twice, if you could call it a bounce, and then just sort of adhered, while grounders, however hard hit, bounced exactly twice before suffering a similar fate. All of which delighted us tremendously, occasioning great yelps and misplays and unplanned slides and finger pointing – "Look at that!" – by confounding our already programmed expectations of a batted baseball's proper behavior and in the process reminding us over and over again that we had stolen some baseball time from Old Man Winter. I'm sure birds whipped around over our heads that day – they usually did in the skies everywhere else over Saugus Center – though I can't picture any in memory. Waiting to bat, we clustered right next to the stream – "Make sure the ball doesn't go in!" – which paralleled the third base line. With all the snow melting on and around its banks not only where we stood but presumably for the length of its course, the stream, which we had barely noticed in the past, was quite vital now, coursing determinedly along, demanding a measure of respect, and, could it be, seemingly rising – Jeez, would it overflow its banks? A flood! We certainly hoped so, get ready to run! Every once in a while the sweet realization would settle down upon us through our senses and then radiate out in our emotions: here we were playing ball, in the sun – it was probably still 60 degrees at this point – and yesterday it had been winter.

And then, between 5:00 and 5:30, we had to go home for supper, knowing that our ball-playing was done for many weeks. I remember walking carefully up the incline to where the church is today, avoiding the worst of the mud as best I could, and, on a dry spot near the top, turning to look back down to the west, out and over our "field" and the stream and the shrinking snow patches to the setting sun behind the now dim outline of Ace Welding. Our day of spring training.

March of Dimes – What Is Junk After All?

In the fifth or sixth grade, we had a four-team March of Dimes contest to see who could collect the most money for the Fund, then dedicated to finding a vaccine against infantile polio (which Dr. Salk soon did). We had all seen the pictures of kids in iron lungs. Armed with canisters we rang doorbells after school soliciting cash – almost everyone gave – but also let it be known that we were on the lookout for old newspapers and magazines, rags and even any scrap metal which might be sitting around. We'd often be invited to go into cellars and garages to root around, as long as we then showed our finds to, almost always, the woman of the house. We sold the materials for cash to a man who at the

time was known, with '50s literalness about jobs, as "the junkman." He'd weigh everything with a hook-type scale, typically in the garage of one of the group members, often mine, as we watched eagerly, and then he'd pay us the appropriate amount of money. We were very gung-ho.

I can reveal here for the first time publicly that my team, which finished second to Jackie Pike's despite our most creative efforts, had its greatest success in terms of cash receipts with the "scrap" metals of various kinds we carted off from the DPW's hillside inventory storage dump just off Hamilton Street near the Center. Imbued with the innocence of ignorance, we took the metal quite openly – well, it was during winter, often bitterly cold, and almost always at dusk, so there was usually no one around outside, and who, I ask, would have had the sheer imagination to suspect us even as they saw us lug our fully-laden carts along Hamilton past the Fire and Police Stations anyway? We assumed that the metal had been discarded, thrown away, and of course our cause (the March of Dimes, after all!) was just. Finally, someone from the DPW came out while we were at work stripping their inventory, and, flabbergasted more than anything else, yelled plaintively, "Hey, what the heck are you kids doing? You can't do that!" I replied that we were "collectin' for the March of Dimes." He just shook his head in disbelief. We quickly came to a full understanding of our position, unloaded our carts and scurried off, none the worse for wear. We had been completely unaware that we were doing anything wrong; who knows, maybe we weren't.

About midway through our highly-successful DPW-to-March of Dimes caper, which extended over several days, it hit me that Ace Welding might prove another rich source of indirect contributions to the Fund. I was again convinced that "they throw that stuff away," that stuff being anything lying around on the ground outside the shop which we could cart away. Well, we didn't get very far – "Giddahdaheah!" – and casting self-righteous, aggrieved looks back in the direction of the shop, we retreated empty-carted.

But what a shop it was to a young kid, the Ace Welding, a weighty, mysterious presence to my eyes from my vantage point at the corner of Summer and Parker – especially before the construction of the Blessed Sacrament but after as well – out there beyond that little stream and beyond that overgrown and unkempt field. It seemed to represent the world of serious, adult, above all industrial men – Ace Welding! Clang! – and there it was, every day, looming, unlike the General Electric, where my father worked, which was in Lynn, not in plain sight just up the street. A second recollection regarding Ace Welding, which seems absolutely bizarre, is going blueberry picking near there with my father once. Blueberry picking just past the mighty Ace Welding? Am I dreaming?

The Pasture

Up Summer Street toward Stackpole Field and on the same side of the street was the primary baseball (and winter sledding) venue of those pre-Little League years for us Saugus Center kids: the Pasture. Wait, there was also Ronnie Meagher's one-of-a-kind backyard baseball field off Fiske Road near the entrance to the Pasture. A stand of tall, leafy trees on an incline formed right and right-center fields in Ronnie's backyard and were in play(!) – imagine, as a fielder, waiting for the ball to pinball its way down unseen through the branches as the runners circled the bases. A white picket fence parallel to Summer formed the left field line – and, to minimize downtime, a batted ball over the fence made the batter automatically out. (No wonder I was never a pull hitter.) Finally, I well remember the dense, yellow jacket-laden bushes of the backing house from Summer Court behind the picket fence in center, over which a batted ball, the good news!, was a homer, but the ball, the *bad*!, had to be retrieved by the batter.

Back to the Pasture, up the street. The Pasture ran roughly north-south for what I'd guess was 150 yards beginning just south of Fiske – Stackpole Field was plainly visible to the north – and extending past the western end of Summer court. The Pasture was about 55-65 yards wide east-to-west, bordered on its western side by woods for its entire length. On the east side, near Fiske Road, was a rocky slope – great as a take-off point in winter for sledding down and out into the Pasture – and where the Pasture met Summer Court a barn, complete with a couple of horses, in summer at least. (I personally never saw the horses out of the barn.) There were six or seven crab apple trees roughly opposite the barn – just too far for a batted ball to carry – and beyond them heading south, more open field until more woods were reached. In short, the Pasture encompassed roughly what is now Summer Drive. The land belonged to Bobby Gallant's grandfather, I believe, and he allowed us kids unrestricted access.

On any given summer Saturday the scene at The Pasture was straight out of Norman Rockwell, or, more accurately, it was the kind of reality from which Rockwell created his romanticized versions of small town life. It was not uncommon for 20-22 kids to show up for a game on a sunny Saturday morning at 10:00 in June or July, meaning, since everyone who showed got to play, that not everyone played the entire game of (usually) seven innings. (Does anyone remember the concept of the call of "guaranteed last at-bats," i.e., even if the home team is ahead, it gets to take its last turn at bat? Very important to stipulate if you've been designated a late sub for the home team. Usually granted, alas, not always implemented.) My recollection is that Bobby Tenaglia and Billy Regan would often be the two captains and would "toss the bat" to choose sides. The competitive aspects of the game would be treated very seri-ously for about three innings, after which attention would gradually start to wander, and how could it not in that lovely setting. The woods and the crab apple trees – crab apples can be thrown like baseballs, or rocks, they hurt! – and Stackpole and the rocky slope would siphon off attention, and by the fourth or fifth inning the first kids, maybe those who had already been subbed for, would just wander off, often into the woods along a rising and winding path at the northwest corner of the field.

Waiting to hit, we would either stand and practice our swings or gossip or goof around or just loll around on the grass. Bikes and baseball gloves were strewn everywhere, and there'd be five or six little kids – boys and girls – trying to make sense of things, for a few seconds at a time anyway, and then give way to just running and jumping around. Somebody would hike off with a milk bottle or two to a near-by house's hose faucet for water, and the careful monitoring of gulps – two to a customer! – would ensue. After the game, several of us who had stayed for the duration might join the trek into the woods, just to wander around amongst the dense trees and the bushes, trying I suppose to get slightly "lost," to find a new path, a new stream bed, even if a dried up one. Then, we'd bike home down Fiske or walk down Summer Court with the memories of the plays we'd made, edited somewhat perhaps, still in our heads.

The Trip to a Big Game

The Saugus Center vs. East Saugus ball game of July 1951 was quite an event. School had been out for only a short while when the word went forth that we Center kids would be hosted on the upcoming Saturday morning at 10:00 at Stocker ("Stocka" to one and all) by the boys from East Saugus. The kids who organized the game were at least a year, possibly two, older than me and my peers, so we were no more than "allowed" to come. I loved the "official" nature of the game, the competition, not just another pick-up game with sides chosen at the field, but two teams, representing their neighborhoods even if the neighborhoods, except for our parents and selected siblings – such as my sister, Betsy – didn't know that they had champions. We were to ride our bikes down to Stocker, leaving at 9:00, which would leave plenty of time for travel and warm-ups (and presumably sizing up the kids of the opposition). For the first time in my life I was too excited to sleep more than three to four hours; I kept waking up and wishing it were light outside. The surprise of my agitation just added to my sense that something big had been set in motion.

The next thing I remember was assembling at the Monument at 9:00. Our team was probably made up of Maury and Brian Cunningham, Sonny and Dougie Roberts, Johnny Standish, Billy Regan, Jackie Mitchell, Jimmy and Freddie Kelleher, Eddie Beaton, Bobby Stahler, Bobby Tenaglia, Kenny Greene, Benson Shapiro, Dave Huggins,

Richie Rohrbacher, Paul Mahoney, Dave Lucey, Richie Gibbs, and perhaps one of the Stead boys. The East Saugus kids included, in all likelihood, Jeff Smith, Alan Bloom, Tommy Sullo, perhaps Neil Jackson, Tommy Warner, Glenn Evans, and maybe Dave Soper.

I don't recall any details of the game itself beyond the fact that I popped out to second in one at-bat and didn't make an error because nothing was hit my way in the outfield. But the ride up Winter Street – yes, I know, we were going *down* to Stocker by going *up* Winter – and the layout of the field at Stocker Playground, were what made the lasting impression.

I was nine and had never ridden my bike up Winter past what was then the Saugus High School, if that far, though I had certainly been driven along its full course in my parent's car and in public buses. I and some of the pack stayed on the sidewalk all the way, while some of the older kids rode out in the street. We all had our baseball gloves securely snapped onto our handlebars; I think I rode a 24" Schwinn. Winding past the Riverside Cemetery on Winter on the sidewalk, I was drawn in by the beauty of the sunlit landscape, by the green and the gravestones, and the latticed road and pathways. A few people were already walking around in small groups, heads down, some arm-and-arm, in the cemetery, along with a couple of landscape gardeners at work near their trucks. The cemetery sloped gradually down to the River marshes from the sidewalk, from which it was separated by a four to five foot stone wall. Winter street, and therefore we on our bikes, was mainly in the shade of the many trees along that part of the route, but the sun broke through the leaves onto the road and the sidewalk at a few places, and most of the cemetery itself was brightly lit by the sun. It probably took us only two or three minutes to pass it. But that was just the beginning.

When we got past Howell Street a ways, still on the sidewalk, we were met by stunning, unimpeded and broad views of the Saugus River and the surrounding marshlands. The marsh grasses were a vibrant green, in gleaming sunshine down below and out beyond a field cultivated with some kind of green crop (corn stalks?) which extended right up to the sidewalk but was set well below it. I had never seen such a sight up close, had never paid it any attention at any rate, and just gazed as it, to the extent that I could. I say that because in places the sidewalk wasn't the safest I've ever encountered – the fence protecting us from a tumble down onto the field was more air than wood, just a hand rail in places – but there were enough secure stretches on the route that we could cast glances of three-four seconds duration riverward for the rest of the trip down to Stocker. A thrilling trip with that panoramic view down the hillside and out to the far banks of the River below Hamilton Street. I recently read that Ansel Adams wrote once that it was his ambition to photograph "the,,, light {that} turned every blade of grass... into a luminous metallic splendor." The greens I

saw that morning biking down Winter had exactly that, a "luminous metallic splendor."

The field at Stocker was, to my surprise, sandy in places. Still, I recall that someone (a parent, up early?) had nonetheless "lined" off foul lines with some kind of white substance (lime?). Nice and "official" in my view. (I always like stone-"chalked" baselines, all the way around, when we played baseball – with a tennis ball – in the middle of Parker Street. Official.) While we were playing – even for the team in the field, baseball has so many pauses – we could gaze out beyond the playing field past (and through) the playground's gazebo-like shelter, where all the little kids had gathered with their playground instructor (Clue? Story-telling?), to take in the nearby river scene. And there was one more amazing feature of Stocker Playground: the ballpark was in effect sunken; sandy cliffs stood back in foul territory from behind left field all the way around to first base. A foul ball would hit halfway up the cliffs, maybe fifteen feet above the ground, and hesitate for a second before rolling back down. So there we were beside the Saugus River and surrounded by cliffs – we'd had to bike a fair distance from the entrance off Winter down and into the playground before we reached the ballfield – on which were perched houses and little kids outside them peering down on the scene below. I know for a fact that we lost the game that day to the East Saugus boys, but as I rode back along Winter to Central and then up Parker, my disappointment at our loss quickly gave way to something akin to awe, the feeling that I had just been a part of something big.

A Late Saturday Afternoon in February 1955 on Lily Pond

I was always a mediocre skater. I had weak ankles, I started skating a year later than my peers due to a winter of sore throats (short leash again), and I had an intuitive preference for basketball, or, "bouncy-bouncy" as my ice-skating father once dismissively called it, before spending two weeks of evenings building me a hoop-and-stanchion apparatus for the driveway and, later, taking me to Bill Russell's first game (!) as a Celtic in 1956. Unlike me, many of my pals in the Saugus Center area developed quickly into excellent skaters and, later, committed hockey players. Until the eight grade I generally took a pass on Lily Pond except for the occasional Saturday lace-up with my father when I was younger. I confined my skating to weekday afternoons at The Pit behind Billy Regan's house on Greystone Road where the talent level among us regulars was, in most cases – certainly in mine – a cut below that of our peers who skated mainly on Lily Pond. We did have fun playing hockey, usually 3-on-3 at best, at The Pit after school for a couple of hours in the late afternoon grayness up to and into the dark – except for the house lights from Greystone and the streetlights from Marion and Juliette – and usually in the bitter cold (which, after a few dashes around the "rink," was no longer an issue) and always amongst leafless trees and bushes held fast in the ice. In particular I remember Ray Smith and Buddy and Roberta Regan – all better skaters than me – from those afternoons. (Billy Regan, Bobbie Gallant and Jackie Mitchell from nearby Juliette Road and others of my friends would have been playing hockey at Lily Pond.) Usually I just sat out the weekends, when the skill level of the games at "The Pit" jumped a notch.

And then, somehow, in the eighth grade during the week off school bookended by Lincoln's and Washington's birthdays, i.e., February 1955, I suddenly discovered hockey on Lily Pond and with a vengeance. I think I played there all morning and, after a short lunch at home, all afternoon for six straight days. I was obsessed, could think of nothing else. However, just as at The Pit after school, this wasn't a game for the hockey stars around town, it was a sort of self-organized hockey "minor league," basically allowing kids like me to shine, or at least shine relatively. To be painfully honest about it, I think a lot of the kids in this game were a year or even two younger than me. The ice we played on was at the far end of the eastern loop of the pond, where it actually heads back toward Appleton Street, in short pretty far away from the more serious action which Lily Pond hosted.

I had a wonderful time playing hockey that week, the only time in my life when I was really hooked on that wonderful game, when I came close to sensing its essence. But it was a return trip on Saturday from our little place around the corner to the front lacing-up area right off Appleton where Summer ends just before dark that has stayed in my mind all these years.

"THE ORANGE CRUSHER" (or SQUEEZER)

APPLETON'S PULPIT

"EASY AT FIRST, THEN A LITTLE TOUGHER, ROCK WALLS ALL AROUND AND THEN ... 'I WAS STUCK!'"
– Jay Nelson

It was still light enough to see OK but it was a bleak gray. I distinctly remember that on several other days of that vacation, the sun had shone brightly, and the ice had even gotten a bit slushy, but on this day it had been cloudy and now it was cold and bleak. Bare trees lined the shore, near and far. I skated at a leisurely pace. Suddenly I was struck by the number and variety of groupings of skaters I was passing, some nearby, some in the middle distance and some quite far away, all these different stories unfolding at the same

time. There were two or three different hockey games in progress, announced by the shouting – "Over here!", "Dave, Dave!", "Aww!," "Nice shot, Jimmy!", "No lifting we said!" – and the thwack of stick-against-stick and stick-against puck. Elsewhere, a pair of parents were trying to teach their young daughter how to skate, half-holding her up and escorting her as she splay-footed her way along the ice– "That's it, that's it, ohh! Try it again, Linda, just keep trying, you'll get it. I'm right here." I couldn't see any details of their faces. A group of teenage girls worked on their pirouettes together, not unhappy to be interrupted by some boys sending the chips flying with a series of abrupt stops only a few yards away. A lone old man, bundled up in a woolen hat and scarf, skated along with hands linked behind his back. There was a fire burning somewhere on distant ice. And more, for the entire trip back.

It wouldn't have been at all the same if I had been simply walking past these very same groups doing the very same things. It was the compression of time. Somehow, my being on skates, by speeding up the succession of my various encounters – onset, duration, fade-out – created a qualitatively different experience, almost cinematic. I couldn't quite comprehend everything, get my arms around things. Narrative overload? Just a few seconds and then, bang! another group, only to be replaced in a few seconds by yet another, or maybe two at once. Look to the left and there's something else going on, and way out there, what is that? Each group seemed significant, eye-catching, and yet, because they were gone so soon from immediate sensory awareness and because I couldn't make out facial detail at all, also abstract and, hence, oddly, permanent. I played basketball competitively the next winter, and I can't remember ever skating on Lily Pond again.

Getting Through the Orange Crusher – A Mixed Blessing

And then there was the Orange Crusher – Appleton's Pulpit on Appleton Street down just a bit from the lace-up area at Lily Pond. That huge boulder outcropping backed by a rocky cliff with the mysteriously modern house way up on top, only partially visible. The plaque explaining Major Appleton's courage in defiance of the tyrannical British Governor Edmund Andros more than 250 years before, and prefiguring the Revolution by almost a century, was one of several historical icons around town – the Iron Works being the most notable – which lent Saugus weight, roots. We kids, I'll speak for myself here, while not dwelling on Saugus's long history, certainly appreciated that it was a neat thing to live in a town which had deep historical roots, and deep pre-Revolutionary American roots at that. Some of that rubbed off on us, we figured. But the rock not as Major Appleton's pulpit, but as the Orange Crusher – as we called it, I think, though it may have been the Orange

Squeezer – is what sticks in my mind, I guess because I got stuck in it.

I think it was a pleasant day in October, after school, probably 1953 or 1954, and we were just wandering around. When we got to the Crusher, the gauntlet was soon laid down. Didn't bother me, I was sure I could get through without a problem. A couple guys went through, with a little more difficulty than I expected. Then me. Easy at first, then a little tougher, rocky walls all around, and then... I was struck. At first amusing and finally, amidst much laughter from my pals – I'm sure I would have done the same if the tables were turned – a full-blown panic anxiety attack. I was too scared to cry, my emergency systems had all kicked in, but of course the harder I fought it, the more impossible the task of extrication became. I was stuck, mute, for a good 45 seconds in a very narrow and very dark space with almost no freedom of movement, staring rock in the face from about a foot's distance.

Finally, the kid who had preceded me, and made it through with only minor incident (Hey, you don't suppose he had done this before, practiced even – no, no sane person would voluntarily practice at the Crusher!) and was peering back in from a ledge outside the Crusher said something like "C'mon, will ya,' Nelson, ya' just have to bend down your shoulder, not that one, the other one, so it's under that thing sticking out." That did the trick and I was soon out. What relief! One way or another I had passed the Orange Crusher test. However, full disclosure requires that I admit to a suspicion that that experience at the Crusher was a major contributor to a fairly powerful subsequent tendency to claustrophobia – I will never be found, at least not conscious, in a full-body MRI – a phobia which I believe had not been previously evident. Anyone who knows that feeling would probably say it was a bad bargain, submitting to the Orange Crusher test. I honestly don't know.

Saugus Bayous

Two afternoons of spring snowmelt-cum-rain floodings, very similar experiences, one behind the home which faces the Cunningham's on Summer with the beautiful willow tree on the side, and the other off Central behind both the Rat Hole and the State Theater, i.e., on both sides of the train tracks, allowed us at ages twelve or thirteen to slosh around for a couple hours in a swampy "bayou" setting. We hurried home from school the day after the rains (two or three days' worth in late March or early April) had stopped, got out our fathers' hiplength boots – I was amazed to learn that my father even owned a pair – and soon, surrounded by woods, with the temperature around 55 degrees, were in water up over our knees. Quite unlike anything else I had ever (or since) experienced in town. It made us feel part of some sort of rescue team – only the rescuees were missing – through occasionally, cut off from any sight of dry land on

all sides and with water within a couple inches of the top of the boots, we'd think "OK, now I wouldn't mind seeing some dry land." And when, as we waded on, dry land didn't appear, just the slightest feeling of having gotten in a little deeper than we wanted to, a little bit of danger. Which was of course our secret goal all along: danger, but not too much. When finally we did emerge from the water somewhere "deep" in the woods – I suppose I could look at a map now and figure out almost exactly where – I can remember that it felt so exotic that it might as well have been Kentucky. After a bit of wandering in the "strange" woods, however, someone, near the State Theater, stumbled onto the sight of the Boston-and-Maine tracks, or up on Summer Street, someone else onto the southern tip of The Pasture and the adventures were over. But the memory, and the taste for adventure, stuck.

A Highland Scene

One more absolutely delightful landscape. For a brief period I found myself part of a group from the Center which palled around with the Wolfes and Richie Rainsford and Pete Dixon on and around the Highland Avenue area. R. K. Smith was probably with us. Bruce Wolfe had been the star pitcher for our Saugus Little League Red Sox in the league's first year, 1952, and a couple of us had been on that team. I think his younger brother Jerry played for the Giants. Richie Rainsford had, amazingly, designed and sewn by himself an authentic-appearing (major league) Red Sox uniform top with a bright red number eight on a lush white background. I might add that Highland Avenue was also home to the pretty Merilyn Meeker, a possible sighting of whom may have added to the appeal of a bike ride after school in May or June to meet up with the boys on that street. In any event, the view I have in mind involves the property on the northeastern corner of Highland, where it meets Vine. A house was set back on a rise from which a spacious green lawn gently spread out down to Highland and to Vine. A stream bordered the lawn on the north and then along Vine and then, though I didn't make the connection at the time, flowed eastward all the way down under Central at the train tracks to empty into the Saugus River off Winter Street.

On the banks of that stream, where it widened for a stretch down twenty yards or so from the house, stood an imposing weeping willow tree. Sometimes, on the way home for supper, as if drawn by a magnet, we would abandon our bikes in the gutter on Highland and walk, eyes and ears alert to any possible objection coming from the house on the hill, over the lawn – nobody in the house ever said a word – to the stream. We would just stand under the willow by the stream, or toss a stone or two into the stream, or pretend to try to push one another in. The late afternoon sun created a dappled effect under the tree where we stood, mesmerized by the flowing water of the stream next to the green lawn.

This, 200 yards from the rush-hour car and truck traffic on Route 1 and 200 yards from the arc lights of Ace Welding.

The Views From Donkey Hill

Donkey Hill, which we Saugus Center kids usually approached from the western end of Emory Street – where Emory was crossed by that same little stream from Highland Avenue – was another memorable kids' baseball venue and all-round good place to wander about. We of course usually played there in dry weather, but we once played a game there in a warm, unremitting summer downpour on a nearly flooded clay field. Rather than run for cover or head home, however, on this day we all stayed and played on because, after a short while, we were all soaked (but not cold) anyway and having too much fun but more importantly, I think, because someone had brought a souped-up, rubber-coated ball which carried about 30% further than a normal ball, even in the rain, and made us all feel like Ted Williams! Absolutely soaring fly balls, splashing down in small lakes. More typically, when the sun was shining in those summer days, the post-game, late-afternoon panoramic views from the cliffs of Donkey Hill – and no matter how often we enjoyed them, they always seemed to appear abruptly and unexpectedly in the midst of our wanderings – down and out over the railroad tracks and Denver Street, beautiful and somehow reassuring.

The Clay Pits, Winter Street.

In addition to the settings involved in my personal adventures, all of us Saugus kids, I want to say again, carried with us the knowledge based on the evidence of our own eyes and ears, that our town – and how many other towns of 18,000 people or so in the country could make such a claim? – contained within its borders: one of the longest highways in the entire United States, Route 1, or the "Turnpike," as we all know a huge presence in almost all Saugonians' consciousness for a myriad of reasons, only one (two?) of which was the Adventure (!) Car Hop; a river bearing our town's name which flowed into an ocean; the amazing Breakheart Reservation; our own Reservoir (shared, I guess we must admit, with Lynn); our own public (!) golf course,

Cedar Glen in North Saugus, where I and my mates – including Timmy Churchard, Jon Spencer, Brian Cunningham, and later, Richie Stevens, Dave Huggins, Billy Regan, Bob Tibbetts, Kelvin Hecht, and a real golfer, Bruce Weyler – played many times beginning at age eleven or so; and the amazing marshlands beyond Eastern Avenue in East Saugus.

Little League – And We Thought Beating East Lynn Was A Big Deal

Because of the way the first Little League field was laid out in 1952 at the Poor Farm between what is now Pearce Memorial Drive and Route 1 – the right field foul line ran south-to-north from home plate parallel to Pearce and the left field foul line east-to-west in the direction of Route 1 – weekday twilight games had to be suspended for fifteen minutes or so at around 7:30. Play couldn't resume until the setting sun behind center field and Route 1 got low enough and weak enough to no longer shine distractingly into the eyes of a batter at home plate while still providing sufficient light to play by. Consider: in effect we were virtually forced to take time out and contemplate sunsets for around 15 minutes two or three times a week for about ten weeks! Not the worst practice to be introduced to at ages ten to twelve. I remember Robin and Jonny Eisenhaur, Norm Peach, Terry McDermott, Sammy Amabile, Dave Mathews, Donnie Barrett, Pete Orlando, Lee Wilson, Bobby Anderson, Eddie Shipulski, Ronnie Ellis, Red Hanlon, Joe Bartow and coaches Ed Caffarella, Jack Burt, Bill McKinney, Don Reiniger, John Quinlan, and the great, gravel-voiced Mr. Jackson as home plate umpire, in addition to names mentioned previously.

Little League itself was a wonderful experience for most of us, the pluses far more than offsetting the minuses. The uniforms, the competition, getting better at the game, seeing your name in the paper, becoming aware that even some of your teachers and neighbors were aware of the games, it was great. And playing other towns in the all-star games at the end of the season was exciting. We only had one win in my three years – the format then was single elimination – but it was a doozy, 3-1 in eight innings in the hot afternoon sun in July 1953 with Route 1 as backdrop over a heavily-favored East Lynn team, which could boast future Major Leaguer Mike Hegan. We bunted our way to victory in the eighth! In 1954, the Saugus Little League realized that there were too many kids wanting to play for one league and split into the Saugus National – I had to turn in my Red Sox uniform for a Pirates one – and Saugus American Leagues. Fifty-one years after my and the town's first Little League season, I was channel-surfing one night in my apartment in New York City when I heard an announcer on ESPN 2 say, "So it'll be Augusta West of Maine versus Saugus American of Massachusetts for the New England Regional Championship." This was my first inkling of what was unfolding for

the Saugus American kids and the whole town. Talk about
an adventure!

Military

I do not love the bright sword for it's sharpness, nor the arrow for its swiftness, nor the warrior for his glory. I love only that which they defend.

— J.R.R. Tolkien

James F. Pratt

by
Hugh D. Somers

My great-great grandfather, James Franklin Pratt, was born in Lynn on January 13, 1844. At an early age, he moved to Saugus. On July 25, 1862, at age eighteen, he enlisted and joined the 1st Massachusetts Heavy Artillery Company C. (His father Andrew was simultaneously serving with the 38th Mass. Regiment). Over the course of his two-year service, he took part in many engagements: Spotsylvania, Cold Harbor, and North Anna River, to name a few. He was held in reserve for the battle of Gettysburg. James was wounded on June 16, 1864, at the beginning of the siege of Petersburg, Virginia. He was initially treated at the 1st Field Hospital, Lincoln Hospital, Washington DC, and later moved to Satterlee Hospital in Philadelphia before being honorably discharged on July 8, 1864. It was during his military service that a family legend was born. In later years, James would proclaim, "Shake the hand that shook the hand of Abraham Lincoln."

His great-grandson, Dr. George J. Gottwald, recently made some observations about James's wound. "Petersburg was a siege, characterized by trench warfare. Snipers on both sides were used and caused many casualties. Snipers used newly developed rifles which featured a rifled barrel that imparted spin on a steel bullet. This permitted accuracy over great distances. The lead minie ball was used by regular troops and was a low-velocity weapon. The spores of tetanus and gas gangrene, both anaerobic organisms, could ride easily on low speed and penetrate deep into oxygen-free deep tissue which was ideal for these killer organisms and that is why there was such a high death rate among the wounded in the Civil War. The high velocity sniper bullet on the other hand burned up these spores by air friction in transit to the target."

His ancestors gratefully remembered this as contributing to James's surviving the war.

After the war, he returned to Saugus and soon after married Elizabeth Brown. Elizabeth was the daughter of Thomas Brown, a close friend and comrade from Company C who was also wounded at Petersburg. The couple settled in Saugus and went on to have four sons and a daughter. Elizabeth was said to be close to 6 feet tall, compared to James at 5 foot 7.

Although partially disabled as a result of his military service, James was still a very active member of the community. For many years, he held the position of Sealer of Weights and Measures. He was also listed in the Saugus Annual Reports (of 1910-1917) as a "Special Officer" on the Saugus Police Force.

On February 9, 1883, he joined General E. W. Hinks Post 95 Saugus Grand Army of the Republic. He enjoyed his membership in this organization and when he died in 1918 was serving his fifth consecutive elected term as commander of the post, a position which he cherished above all others. Over the course of his 35-year membership, he held many offices within the organization: Junior Vice-Commander in 1884 and for nine months in 1885, Sergeant Major for three months in 1885, Senior Vice-Commander in 1886, Commander in 1887, Senior Vice-Commander in 1890, Sergeant Major in 1893, Adjutant in 1894, Office of the Day in 1896, Commander in 1897, Delegate in 1898, Commander in 1912-1913, 1914-1915, 1916-1918. He was a very active member and attended many Grand Army of the Republic encampments, including the 50th anniversary of The Battle of Gettysburg in 1913. This was held at the battlefield and attended by 54,000 fellow veterans. He was one of five members of his original Company C to attend the reunion.

James F. Pratt, G.A.R. Commander.

He was a fiercely patriotic man, and proud of his military service. Every Memorial Day he would walk from his home at 6 Columbus Avenue over to the Old Burying Ground on Main Street. There, usually accompanied by one of his grandchildren, he would place a flag on the grave of his own great-great-grandfather, Amos Pratt, who answered the alarm on April 19, 1775. In 1913 as newly elected G.A.R. Commander, he carried the tradition over by conceiving the idea of having the local school children participate in the town's Memorial Day Parade and assist in decorating the veterans' graves with flags and garlands of flowers. He thought it would teach the children "a valuable lesson in patriotism."

James was a tough, no-nonsense character, with an independent streak. His granddaughter Freda did some housekeeping for him when she was about 14. She remembered his arm wound would ache any time the weather was about to change. In a 1969 letter, his grandson Les recalled an incident from World War I which best describes him. "My grandfather was quite a guy. When he died, he still had a 'reb' bullet in his left arm. Before we shipped out overseas, he came riding on the rear seat of my motorcycle to Westfield, MA, where the Yankee Division was stationed, to bid me goodbye.

"He raised hell with the captain of my company, because visitors were ordered off grounds at a certain hour. Lucky for me the captain was a good scout, because I still remember Gramp told him it could be the last time he probably would see me (and it was, he died before I got home), and he would stay as long as he wanted to that he had been fighting in a war before the captain was born. Well I finally talked him out of it and he left. I will never forget him. He was quite a swinger, liked his grog. I think and hope I took after him."

Elizabeth Pratt died in 1896, and James remarried a local widow, Margaret (Coates) Rhodes in 1908. Margaret was very active herself in the Saugus G.A.R. (her father, Benjamin, having been a long-standing member). In the early 1920s, as membership dwindled, she was appointed the only female adjutant of Post 95. She held this position for six years, until her death.

Bert Butler leading Sons of the G.A.R. in parade.

James became Superintendent of the Saugus Fire Alarm system in 1913. While conducting his duties, he became sick and shortly thereafter died at the Chelsea Soldiers' Hospital on September 30, 1918. Veterans of the Civil War, town officials, associates in the fire department and members of the kindred organizations of the G.A.R., together with a host of townspeople attended his funeral at

his home on Columbus Avenue. A silk American flag from General E.W. Hinks Post 95 covered his casket. He was buried with full honors in the Riverside Cemetery.

The Slow Sleep, The Time of War

by
Tom Sheehan

A time of nervous commerce in '43, reclaiming
lost Fords, Chevies gone astray with rusting,

Desotos and Hudsons and Packards before
they merged with Reos and Grahams waiting

on them. We lacerated seat cushions for cotton
batting and lost coins, tearing our finger flesh

on inner springs, drawing good American
the way newsreels would not show, piling

the white matter for conversion to olive drab
fatigues, bell bottom blues my brother wore,

costumes children donned those days of infamy.
On June mornings, covers slipped from our sleep,

stretching out our lost sunshine, hearing pigeons
in the last eaves of departing darkness, forgetting

the mail that had not come the day earlier, unknown
what the fires of hell were on what island sands,

whose brothers were with whom where, we rose,
made our skimpy lunches for brown bags

and went to war on old car cushions. Salvagers!
Into ranks we went, Salvagers! Marching off we went,

through Saugus Center chilled and quiet and gray,
down behind Riverside Cemetery our ghostly

column of the day. Salvagers en route, massed,
we young infantry of someone's brothers,

out of mother's linen, out of young hands at crotch
before those thin hairs began to curl, out of touch

with the slow, languorous sleep given over
to the voice of the enemy, his picture at newsreels,

the odd face, the strange misshapen helmet he wore,
that godawful bayonet raised a bloody Lucifer sword.

Christ! How we'd rip and tear at cotton tough as roots,
pile dense handfuls for the mill's penultimate loom,

dig out Liberty dimes old pockets gave up, picture
our brothers all suited up, scarred but coming home,

all across the Pacific the parade coming the other way.

Medal of Honor Rights and Privileges

by
Tom Sheehan
(summarized from various sources)

Staff Sergeant Arthur F. DeFranzo[1]

Citation:

S/Sgt. Arthur F. DeFranzo

Rank and organization: Staff Sergeant, U.S. Army, 1st Infantry Division. Place and date: Near Vaubadon, France, 10 June 1944. Entered service at: Saugus, Mass. Birth: Saugus, Mass. G.O. No.: 1, 4 January 1945. Citation: For conspicuous gallantry and intrepidity at the risk of his life, above and beyond the call of duty, on 10 June 1944, near Vaubadon, France. As scouts were advancing across an open field, the enemy suddenly opened fire with several machineguns and hit one of the men. S/Sgt. DeFranzo courageously moved out in the open to the aid of the wounded scout and was himself wounded but brought the man to safety. Refusing aid, S/Sgt. DeFranzo reentered the open field and led the advance upon the enemy. There were always at least two machine guns bringing unrelenting fire upon him, but S/Sgt. DeFranzo kept going forward, firing into the enemy and one by one the enemy emplacements became silent. While advancing he was again wounded, but continued on until he was within 100 yards of the enemy position and even as he

fell, he kept firing his rifle and waving his men forward. When his company came up behind him, S/Sgt. DeFranzo, despite his many severe wounds, suddenly raised himself and once more moved forward in the lead of his men until he was again hit by enemy fire. In a final gesture of indomitable courage, he threw several grenades at the enemy machinegun position and completely destroyed the gun. In this action, S/Sgt. DeFranzo lost his life, but by bearing the brunt of the enemy fire in leading the attack, he prevented a delay in the assault which would have been of considerable benefit to the foe, and he made possible his company's advance with a minimum of casualties. The extraordinary heroism and magnificent devotion to duty displayed by S/Sgt. DeFranzo was a great inspiration to all about him, and is in keeping with the highest traditions of the armed forces.

Notes:

If a veteran wearing a Medal of Honor enters a military gate on any base for any branch of service, the sentries are required to render salutes!

Who said, I would rather have the blue band of the Medal of Honor around my neck than be president?

President Harry S. Truman.

Each Medal of Honor awardee may have his name entered on the Medal of Honor Roll. Each person whose name is placed on the Roll is certified to the Veterans' Administration as being entitled to receive a special pension of $100 per month for life, payable monthly by that agency. The payment of this special pension is in addition to, and does not deprive the pensioner of any other pension, benefit, right, or privilege to which he is or may thereafter be entitled. A written application must be made by the awardee to have his name placed on the Medal of Honor Roll and to receive the special pension. For Army personnel, proper blanks and instructions shall be furnished without charge upon request to The Adjutant General, Department of the Army, Washington, DC 20314, Attention: AGPB-AC. The application must bear the full personal signature of the applicant.

(d) Additional benefits.

1. Air transportation: See AR 96-20 (Army Regulations pertaining to Air Transportation).

2. Sons of winners of the Medal of Honor, otherwise qualified for admission to the United States Military Academy, will not be subject to quota requirements (see annual catalog, United States Military Academy).

The Medal of Honor is one of only two United States military decorations which are presented as neck orders.

---

1. **N.B**. An asterisk in the citation indicates that the award was given posthumously.

The other is the Commander's Degree of the Legion of Merit.

The Medal of Honor confers special privileges on its recipients both by tradition and by law. By tradition, all other soldiers, sailors, and airmen, even higher-ranking officers, initiate the salute.

Recipients of the Medal of Honor receive $1,000 per month for life, a right to burial at Arlington National Cemetery, admission for them or their children to a service academy (if they qualify and quotas permit), and free travel on government aircraft to almost anywhere in the world, on a space-available basis.

The grade, name, and organization of the awardee are engraved on the reverse of the Medal of Honor. The name only of the awardee is engraved on the reverse of every other decoration and the Good Conduct Medal. Normally, engraving will be accomplished prior to presentation. When this is impractical, the awardee will be informed that he or she may mail the decoration (or Good Conduct Medal) to the Commander, U.S. Army Support Activity, Philadelphia, 2800 South 20th Street, Philadelphia, PA 19101-3460, for engraving at Government expense.

- Each Medal of Honor awardee may have his name entered on the Medal of Honor Roll (38 U.S.C. § 1560). Each person whose name is placed on the Medal of Honor Roll is certified to the United States Department of Veterans Affairs as being entitled to receive the special pension of $1,027 per month. As of December 1, 2004, the pension is subject to cost of living increases.

- Enlisted recipients of the Medal of Honor are entitled to a supplemental uniform allowance.

- Recipients receive special entitlements to air transportation under the provisions of DOD Regulation 4515.13-R.

- Special identification cards and commissary and exchange privileges are provided for Medal of Honor recipients and their eligible dependents.

- Children of recipients are eligible for admission to the United States military academies without regard to the quota requirements.

- Recipients get a ten percent increase in retired pay under 10 U.S.C. § 3991, subject to the 75% limit on total retired pay.

- Those awarded the Medal after October 23, 2002 also receive a Medal of Honor Flag. The law also specifies that all 143 living Medal of Honor recipients receive the flag also along with all future MOH recipients.(14 U.S.C. § 505).

On a ribbon bar, the Medal of Honor ribbon is the first ribbon placed on the bar (top left when seen on the uniform). The ribbon bar's design is the same blue as the neck ribbon, and it includes five white stars, pointed upwards, in the shape of an "M." For civilian wear, a rosette is issued instead of a miniature lapel pin (which usually shows the ribbon bar). The rosette is the same blue as the neck ribbon and also includes white stars. The ribbon bar and rosette are presented at the same time as the neck ribbon. On special occasions, the medal itself can be worn on civilian attire.

The Medal of Honor is the only service decoration that cannot be privately bought, traded, or sold. All Medals of Honor are issued in the original only, by the Department of Defense, to a recipient. Misuse of the medal, including unauthorized manufacture or wear, is punishable by fine and imprisonment pursuant to 18USC704(b).

After the Army redesigned their medal in 1903, a patent was issued (United States Patent #D37,236) to legally prevent others from making the medal. When the patent expired, the Federal government enacted a law making it illegal to produce, wear, or distribute the Medal of Honor without proper authority.

Violators of this law have been prosecuted. In 2003, two persons, Edward and Gisela Fedora, were charged with violating 18USC704(b) - Unlawful Sale of a Medal of Honor. They sold medals awarded to US Navy Seaman Robert Blume (for action during the Spanish-American War) and to US Army First Sergeant George Washington Roosevelt (for action during the Civil War) to an FBI agent.

Walter Daniels

by
Janice Jarosz

In 1993, singer David Bowie wrote a song about wanting to become a hero "just for one day." He sang, "We can be heroes if just for one day."

The late Walter Daniels, of Saugus, was a genuine hero for most of his life to those who knew him, but it was only recently that his family became aware of his war record as a pilot for the famous "Flying Tigers."

A dedicated family man, community leader, and loyal friend to many, Walter's family thought they knew all about him.

They knew that he had served during World War II, but he never shared with them the true extent of his "career."

Walter was born at home, in the Cliftondale section of town, into a large family of eleven children. His siblings were Frank, Bill, John, Laurence, Charles, Carol, Dorothy, Gert, Millie, and Alice.

His younger years were spent much the same as most of ours. He helped in the care of his brothers and sisters, played football for Saugus High, and graduated in 1931.

Walter Daniels of the Flying Tigers.

After high school, he worked at various jobs for several years and eventually enlisted into the Army Air Force on January 16, 1942. He received his wings in Texas and underwent extensive combat training in Kracki, India.

After his tour of duty, Walter was discharged from the service on November 30, 1945, and went home to Saugus. The war had ended and Walter was ready to begin a new life.

At approximately the same time in another part of the world, Virginia Linehan, a young and beautiful girl who was soon to be married, was concerned for her girlfriend, who was going through an engagement breakup. Virginia suggested that they go out for the evening in the hopes of cheering up her heartbroken friend.

Virginia took her to the Oceanview Ballroom in Revere, which is now known as Wonderland Ballroom. In the '40s the most popular form of entertainment and the best way to spend time was dancing, and both girls loved to dance.

To this day Virginia still can feel the "tap" on her shoulder as she sat watching couples dance by. It was when she turned to see who it was that she first laid eyes on her soon-to-be-husband, Walter. He was handsome, a great dancer and, as Virginia tells it, he just literally swept her off her feet.

Within two years they were married and eventually settled in Saugus. Several years later the family purchased a home on Pleasant Street and three children, Walter, Laurence, and Susan, completed the family.

Unfortunately, a terrible tragedy struck the family when their 4-year-old son, Laurence, was killed in an accident.

Young Laurence had been named in memory of Walter's brother who was killed during World War II at age 19.

For approximately six years, Walter served as an MDC policeman. He eventually took the civil service exam for the position of Building Inspector in the Town of Saugus, and after he topped the list Town Manager Stinson appointed him to the position.

Mr. Daniels served as the town's building inspector for ten years. During his tenure the town was hit with several large fires, one being the former high school in Saugus Center. Mr. Daniels coordinated dealing with the disaster, was in charge of the cleanup, and oversaw the renovation of the portion of the building that the fire hadn't ravaged.

The main building was demolished, but within weeks the school children were able to resume their schedules.

All this was accomplished by Mr. Daniels without much fanfare, but the stress of the job took its toll. In 1963 he suffered a heart attack and was advised to scale back some of his responsibilities.

Eventually he left the town job and became a state building inspector until he was forced to retire due to ill health.

He passed away at the age of 61 after a lengthy illness. In his obituary it stated that he also served as a town meeting member for several years, was a member of the VFW Post and a longtime Lions Club member.

Anyone who knew Walter during his lifetime knew that he was a good family man, a dedicated town official, and had served his country well. But it wasn't until years after his death that the true depth of his character, together with an impressive war record, came to light.

Several family members, his nephews, Peter Daniels and Eddie Moore, along with Ed's son, Walter, were invited to attend a reunion of their uncle's war buddies and it was at this reunion that the family discovered another side of their uncle.

The family learned that there were books written about him, that he saved many fellow pilots during combat, and that he had flown over 100 missions for the Flying Tigers.

According to a book written by Donald S. Lopez entitled *Into the Teeth of the Tiger*, Walter was a member of the Flying Tiger Squad of pilots who participated in one of the most remarkable air campaigns of World War II in the war against the Japanese in China.

God Is My Copilot, written by Col. Robert L. Scott, tells of the American Volunteer Group (AVG) also known as The Flying Tigers under the direction of General Clair L. Chennault. The tactics that General Chennault taught were so successful against the Japanese that the Flying Tigers became a legend. July of 1944 was the second anniversary of the formation of the 23rd Fighter Group from the disbanded AVG. Although the American Volunteer Group was in combat for only six months, its record was amazing: 299 Japanese aircraft were destroyed in the air, with the loss of only eight P-40s in combat.

Even more important than the numbers was the defeat of the up-to-then invincible Japanese Zeros.

According to fellow pilots, Walter Daniels was one of the bravest. He was an expert aviator in the cockpit using the strength of the P-40's diving speed and rugged construction, to overcome the maneuverability of the Zeros and Oscars. Taught by Brig. General Chennault, the Flying Tigers were instructed to keep up their speed and never try to out turn a Japanese fighter. If one attempted to evade with a right turn, the pilots were taught to keep diving, then climb up to attack again. The Tigers earned their reputation for being fearless and deadly.

Although glamorized in movies, the fighter pilots lived a precarious existence in a remote sector of the war. Intense air action over enemy territory alternated with long interludes of boredom and inactivity. Life was austere, with poor food, bouts of dysentery, rat-infested barracks, and irregular mail deliveries. Heavily-laden C-47's and C-46's kept the Fourteenth Air Force going by flying supplies over the Hump (the Himalayas) from India.

In *Into the Teeth of the Tiger*, by Lieutenant Lopez, there is the following story about Major Daniels.

> Lieutenant Lopez reported that "Oscars" (enemy planes) littered the sky and, according to Chinese intelligence, there was also a lot of ground activity. Three flights of P-40s were being readied for a strafing mission in the Puchi Bridge area.
>
> When the plans reached the target area, they spotted large truck convoys. Two flights went down to strafe and one stayed up as top cover, but at only 3,000 feet because of the clouds. Suddenly they were jumped by 15 to 20 Oscars and Tojos. Earl Green, my roommate, was shot down in flames and bailed out, as did Moose Elker. Flash Segura shot one Oscar off Curt Scoville's tail and damaged another. "Danny" Daniels, [Walter's nickname in the service] had dived away from the first attack, but looking back he thought he saw two Japanese attacking a P-40. He turned back to help. When he attacked he found that all three were Oscars. His airplane was clobbered, but he managed to break away and head for home.

At Hengyang we were told by the net that four P-40s were coming back followed by a gaggle of Zeros. I was in the alert flight, so we jumped into the cockpits to intercept the Japanese. As we were starting our engines, Daniels' P-40 came into view from the north, trailing a heavy stream of smoke. He came right in without lowering his wheels – his hydraulic system was shot out and he bellied it in. The plane slid right past our flight, and Daniels dived out onto the wing and rolled off as the P-40 slowed to a stop. We took off immediately and headed north, but the Japanese had turned back well short of Hengyang. We returned to land, anxious to see how Danny had fared.

We found that he was okay except for a cut on his head where it had banged the gunsight. He said that he was getting ready to bail out, but decided he could make the field, not knowing that the hydraulics were gone. Later, the parachute rigger came into the alert shack to show us Danny's chute. He said, "It's lucky you didn't try to bail out, Lieutenant Daniels, your chute was hit by an incendiary bullet that came up through the seat." Most of the silk was burned or charred and had he jumped he would have been killed. Luck was with him.

Lopez's book is filled with excerpts of bravery, dedication and heroism by the Flying Tigers and he depicted Walter Daniels as being one of the finest.

Walter Daniels,
Army Air Force, 1945

A large retirement party was given him in honor of his service to the Town of Saugus, and at his death, Town Meeting stood in moment of silence to honor his memory as a public servant.

During his last years, he did attend a few reunions of the 23rd Fighter Group, 75th Fighter Squadron, and 14th Air Force. As a fighter pilot with General Clair Chennault's Flying Tigers in the China-Burma-India Theater, his acts of heroism became well known among fellow pilots and some of these stories finally made their way to family members.

During his military careers he earned two Purple Hearts, the Distinguished Service Medal, the Distinguished Flying Cross, and the Air Medal.

To the family of Walter Daniels, he was already a hero, but learning of his fearless exploits and daring rescues of many of his fellow soldiers only added to their respect for him.

Walter gave so much to his town, his family, and his country as matter of course. He never considered himself a hero.

Walter died in Lynn Hospital on Saturday, December 10, 1977, and is buried alongside his son at Riverside Cemetery, in Saugus.

David Bowie asked to be a hero "for only one day," but Walter Daniels will live on as a hero for an eternity.

Memories of WWII Link Generations

by
Janice K. Jarosz

During this past year, many of us have paused to remember the 60th anniversary of World War II. The recent talk of sending troops into other parts of the world stirs other memories of Vietnam and Korea, especially for baby boomers. But no matter where we are on the generation scale, when our young men and women are being sent off to foreign soil, we all "connect" again in some way.

It was not until I went through some of my grandmother's old pictures that I learned the reason why I feel such emotional ties to World War II and why a Veterans' Day Parade can rekindle those emotions.

All of my uncles, on both sides, served in World War II. Uncle Jack Penney landed on Normandy Beach, was twice wounded, and received two Purple Hearts; Uncle Frank Penney served in the South Pacific and was missing in action for several months. Uncle Harry Penney, although too old (39) to serve on the front lines, signed up to be a cook at Fort Devens, and my father, Ralph Penney, served in the Merchant Marines.

On my mother's side, my Nana Murphy made the front page of the *Saugus Herald* the day all six or her sons registered for the draft. My uncles Frank, Edmund, and Charlie all served and my Uncle Harold tried to but was disqualified because of a physical condition.

When her sons came home for good, my grandmother Penney would take out the big, black camera of hers, the kind you look down into, and take pictures out on the front lawn. Invariably, I would try to get in the picture too, most times in the background but sometimes in the arms of one of my handsome uncles. I cannot consciously remember those moments, but a connection lingers.

I remember in later years going up to the attic and finding the uniforms, medals, letters and photographs that went back and forth to family members. Little pieces of paper with vague messages filled with longings for home.

Ralph Penney, Frank Penney, Harry Whyte, WW II.

I loved the stories.

My Uncle Jack was shipped to England to recover from his injuries. My father, who was 20 at the time was stationed on a merchant ship in the English Channel. Upon hearing that his brother was in a hospital in London, he left his ship and walked all over London trying to find him. He finally gave up when darkness came and he had no choice but to get back to the ship. Before he gave up completely, he wrapped a package of Baby Ruth candy bars and left it with someone at one of the bases. On the envelope, he wrote that if the package could not be delivered to brother Jack, then it was to be delivered to brother-in-law, Edmund Murphy, who was also stationed in London as a medic. Needless to say, my Uncle Jack never got over the fact that Uncle Ed received the candy and he didn't.

Uncle Frank joined the Army in the hopes of becoming a pilot. Just when his schooling was almost completed, he was shipped to Okinawa, where he soon contracted malaria. It was almost Christmas time when he turned over his PX keys and told the soldiers to help themselves. He watched them for a while, then walked into the jungle and wasn't found for three months. That very same night that he walked away from his unit, my grandmother woke out of a sound sleep, knowing that something had happened to her son.

Uncle Frank was eventually found by his platoon, suffering from malaria, and they shipped him home for treatment at a hospital in the States. For the next few months he was in a semicoma.

Eventually, when he came out of the coma, he sat up in bed and asked a nurse, "Where am I?"

"Babylon," she answered.

"God," he said, "Babylon, did you say? You mean I'm in Heaven?"

"Not *that* Babylon," she said, "you're in Babylon, New York."

Shortly after, fully recovered, he came home to Saugus.

Stories like these were happening to families all over the country. Young men and women were leaving their loved ones to fight in a war they probably knew little about.

In Saugus, prior to the declaration of war, residents were gearing up for what was to be the inevitable. On October 17, 1940, 1,322 men from the town of Saugus registered for the draft.

On October 31, 1940, Norman Yeo, No. 158, 23 Acadia Avenue, was the first Saugonian to receive a questionnaire as a preliminary step to a year's service in Uncle Sam's army. The second number, drawn from the large fish bowl in Washington, DC, was 192, Edwin Maurice Westendarp, 25 Highland Avenue. The third number, 105, was assigned to Joseph Sciacca, 12 Harlow Street. The next local was Robert Adams Graham, 75 Fairmount Avenue, No. 188; and Robert Culbert Baby, 20 Clark Street, followed with No. 120.

Others in the first group of 25 local men whose numbers were drawn in the first hour of the national lottery included the following: Donald B. Forrest, 8 Fairview Avenue; Raymond A. Firth, 9 Dale Street; Orlando A. Smith, 185 Essex Street; Edmund W. Torrance, 43 Denver Street; Charles Clinton, no street address could be found; Lewis Brougham, 23 Maple Street; Russell S. Smith, 177 Essex Street; Arthur W. Fairchild, 64 Palmetto Street; Charles E.

Lambes, 9 Liberty Street; Warren B. DiPietro, 21 Fairmount Place; Nathaniel Diamond, 4 Dreeme Street; Arthur Dearing, 78 Clifton Avenue; William J. Burke, 200 Hesper Street; Matthew P. Mirabella, 17 Waverly Avenue; William R. Larrabee, 10 Laconia Avenue; Alexander G. Ferguson, 83 Winter Street; Chester H. Cook, 8 Morton Avenue; William F. Vater, 6 Clifton Avenue; and Stanley M. Uscilka, 56 Bristow Street.

On November 21, 1940, it was announced that volunteers Dana Bradford Lewis, 73 Lincoln Avenue, and Arthur DeFranzo, 16 Prospect Street, two of the five volunteers, left on the 8:16 train Wednesday for Irvington State Armory and then to Fort Devens, where they were assigned to their units. Both soldiers received watches from the town.

On January 9, 1941, a delegation of high school students, parents, and friends crowded the Saugus Center Station on a cold Tuesday morning to witness Saugus' second quota of draftees for the selective military service leave for Camp Devens.

Attorney Laurence Davis and Alfred H. Woodward, Secretary of the Civil Defense, were also there to bid the boys an official farewell. They presented them with wristwatches from the town.

In the group were Arthur W. Rand, Jr., 11 Henry Street; and Walter H. Fuller, 7 Warren Avenue; Angelo Calcagno, 53 Howard Street; Edmund Torrance, 43 Denver Street; and Russell Smith, 177 Essex Street; who joined Company E of the 182nd Infantry of the National Guard; and Norman R. Yeo, whose number was the first drawn.

I remember the excitement among family and neighbors when soldiers finally arrived home safely. I also remember overhearing the grownups talk about "young Billy McCarthy," who was among the missing in action, and of Philip McCullough being taken prisoner by the Germans.

It was a time of sacrifice, of patriotism, and of idealism and, when I hear talk of our country sending American troops to a strange land, I feel "connected" all over again.

The Daring Life of a Saugus Private

by
Janice K. Jarosz

Saugus has had more than its share of war heroes over the years and Pvt. Joseph Barressi, late of Bristow Street, was no exception.

Operating with General Mark Clark's 5th Army during the early '40s in Europe, Paratrooper Baressi and his outfit of 51 other selected men were ordered to relieve the tension at Cassino, Italy, by attacking the Germans in a rear guard action. Taking off after midnight, they landed 40 miles behind the enemy lines and for fourteen days carried out their orders to destroy the enemy.

Joseph Barressi in the fold of his family.

Not making any inroads against the Germans, the outfit was then ordered to blow up a bridge nearby as they had heard the Huns were sending in reinforcements. Thirty of the men planted explosives and then hid on the opposite side of the road. A short while later a German motor column appeared and, just as the first truck reached the crossing, the charges went off. The truck blew up along with the bridge. The rest of the German convoy came to a halt. The Americans opened fire with machine guns and mortars, but being outnumbered, the soldiers retreated to the hills to rejoin their outfit.

Upon reaching their original unit, the soldiers learned that food and ammunitions were almost depleted. The unit found themselves wedged into a hill, surrounded by Germans and with no way to replenish their food or weapons. Something had to be done or they faced starvation or being taken prisoners. The major in command asked for a volunteer to sneak through enemy lines in the hopes of reaching the Americans camp to seek help.

Joseph Barressi volunteered for the assignment. He knew that, with his beard and his ability to speak the Italian language, he among all of them had the best chance of making it through enemy territory.

Dressed as an Italian peasant and carrying a cane, the 23-year-old from Saugus, Massachusetts, started out on a 40-mile trek through terrain full of Germans. At one point, he came within 50 feet of a German contingent.

On the fourth day of his mission, he finally reached the American lines. However, dressed as he was, it took him

close to six hours of interrogation to convince the allies that he was an American soldier. Once the commanding officer realized Barressi was telling the truth, 2,000 infantrymen were dispatched to the location of where his men were. Because of Pvt. Barressi's bravery, all 51 soldiers were saved.

In other battles during his service, he was wounded several times and became deaf in one ear because of a land mine at Anzio. Barressi was also held prisoner by the Spanish government for 94 days when found after bailing out of a plane over Morocco, North Africa due to engine trouble while on another mission.

He was awarded the Purple Heart, the Combat Infantryman's Badge, seven Battle Stars, the Presidential Citation and General Clark's unit citation to show for his 22 months overseas.

Several years ago, *Saving Pvt. Ryan*, a movie about World War II, was released. The film graphically describes the horrors of the war and what American soldiers endured. If you happen to catch the movie, look carefully during the blowing up of the bridge scene, you might just see a facsimile of Pvt. Joseph Barressi, of Bristow Street, Saugus.

Absolution

(for PFC Hugh Menzies)
187th Inf. Korea April, 1951

by
Tom Sheehan

You think I don't remember you.
Your nose was red, ears outsized,
you moved lanky in your lanky way,
you had blue eyes, your cheeks red.

In front of the State Theater on Sat-
urday matinees you towered over us.
But I do remember you, Hughie. I do!
Your hair was tall in front, dark;

your arms were long, your nose English
like mine's Irish but mostly for word music.
You wore dark blue denim dungarees;
once a blue jacket with red sleeves.

You didn't skate with us, but I remember
your picking leaves, watching the sun
fall all the way through the filaments.
I saw you Saturdays, later on, watching

us play football at the stadium. Then,
how Time plays tricks on all of us,
we were in Asia, carrying carbines
in the Land of the Morning Calm.

That far Asia's sun set down on you,
Hughie, but I walked free of that hole.
Each morning now, on my way to work,
old shells echo, shy infiltrator eyes me,

cursed land mine sits a maimed turtle
in my path, dark clouds grow darker,
dread rain becomes yellow madness,
deep earth opens its welcome arms,

and your name flies its black letters
on a gray cast iron sign in East Saugus.
Once, when I was late for work, snow
on the hillside, flowers rimmed the pole.

I keep wondering for you, Hughie,
Who put the flowers out in January?
Is there a friend with long memory?
A girl who dreams? Did you visit?

In His Short Life, Vietnam Veteran Touched Many Lives

by
Janice Jarosz

The Clarence Egan family, well-known residents of Main Street, Saugus, for many years, has been very generous in "giving back" to the community in many, many ways. As young parents trying to raise three growing boys during the '50s, they still found the time to volunteer as Sunday school teachers and Boy Scout leaders. They were two of the original founders of the Mid-town Betterment Association, a grass roots civic group organized to represent the upper Main Street youth and to improve representation in town politics.

Their three sons, James, George, and Stanley, followed in their footsteps by graciously giving their time and energy outside of their own personal lives to Boy Scout programs, and by serving as altar boys in their local parish. And as generous as they all were, it was Stanley who gave the most.

Born in 1949, Stanley was a fun-loving, happy-go-lucky kid who loved life and just about everyone he met. He loved playing all kinds of sports and fixing up old cars, but, as family and friends discovered over the years, there was always something more to Stanley than just his endearing

ways and gentle smile. Young Stanley also possessed a very special nature – a special grace not often found.

He was born with a natural curiosity about life and always wanted to know more about everything, especially about God. Sometimes the questions he asked were too deep for even his family to answer.

Stanley's mother remembers the "testing" that often occurred between her and her son. Mrs. Egan always insisted that Stanley dress properly when serving mass – it was one of the rules of the house. Stanley didn't think clothes mattered, particularly in front of God, and every once in a while he would send that message to his mother in a very clever way.

"Sometimes he would sneak by me Sunday mornings wearing his favorite black high-top sneakers unbeknownst to me," said his mother. "At mass, when he knelt before the altar, I could see those sneakers beneath his church garb. It was as if he were saying, 'See Ma, God loves me no matter what I wear.'"

When not in school, Stanley spent most of his off-time playing sandlot baseball or pond hockey, whatever the season. He and his best friends, John Faragi, Rich Salsman, and Andy Penney never missed an opportunity to get a game together just for the fun of it. My brother, Ralph, who was several years younger than Stanley, remembers how Stanley would always include the younger kids who were standing on the sidelines, and invite them to play – regardless of age or talent – always insisting that everyone should have "their turn." Ralph never forgot that act of kindness.

Susan Campbell, a cousin and next door neighbor, felt the same way about Stanley. Susan credits her cousin for teaching her how to play ice hockey. Years ago the property next to the Egan home contained a brook and in the winter time it made for great skating. Susan's mother was not too keen on allowing Susan to skate as she was quite young, but that didn't stop Stanley. He found some skates for her and spent hours upon hours showing her how to skate, play hockey and shoot the puck.

He taught her so well that, in 1974, Susan was picked as a member of the U.S. Ice Hockey team of the Olympics. Unfortunately, it was the year the Olympic Games were boycotted and the team never got the chance to participate. But she believes that it was Stanley who got her that far.

Susan describes her cousin as being full of life and goodness and a true friend who was always there for her. She remembers him for his love of friends and family and his love of God.

"Stanley believed that each of us should live life to the fullest – to have fun while we're doing it and be kind to one another and that's what he left with me – those values."

Andy Penney met him on the bus going to the Oaklandvale School one day and they remained friends for life.

"Not only did he know how to laugh and have fun – he was also a hell raiser just like the rest of us and it was all innocent fun," said Andy.

Andy remembers the time he and Stanley snuck into the golf driving range next to Russo's Candy House. They started filling their pockets with golf balls but before they realized it someone spotted them and took up the chase. The boys had confiscated so many balls in their pants that the pants started to fall down as they tried to run. They were eventually caught and turned over to their parents, not without receiving the required lecture and punishment.

After high school Stanley thought he might like to become a sports announcer so he enrolled in Graham Jr. College. Several weeks into his studies, he was given the assignment to interview a mother who had recently lost her son, in the hopes of finding out what she had to say. His reply to his professor was, "What do you think she would say?" He left the school after that.

Shortly after he left college, some of his friends decided to join the reserves and suggested to Stanley that he should do the same. The war in Vietnam was taking its toll, and there was a great deal of unrest throughout the nation. Stanley, however, preferred to take his chances with the draft like his older brother George. On May 6, 1969, he received his orders. He was able to spend his last time at home on a 30 day leave before being sent to Cambodia. His friend, John Faragi, was getting married and Stanley was happy to be able to attend his friend's wedding just prior to being shipped out.

Andy Penney remembers talking with him the night before he had to leave. Stanley told him that, for some strange reason, he was concerned about his legs, but he didn't know why. Andy will never forget that conversation. And as he kissed his mother goodbye the next morning, he told her he didn't think he would ever see her magnolia tree blossom again. His mother will never forgot that conversation either.

Sadly, those premonitions came true when, within a month of being in Cambodia, Stanley walked into a land mine that was set along two trees. He lived for several weeks, but died on November 23, 1969, from the injuries he sustained. His life ended at the young age of twenty, but not his spirit. While his passing was a tragic loss to this family and friends, his spirit remains with all who knew him.

His friend Andy still dreams of Stanley and remembers the lessons and examples Stanley taught him. Andy believes that his best friend is still by his side whispering support and encouragement.

Stanley's cousin Susan has spent the last several years setting up and operating a private home for dozens of Vietnam veterans to live in peace and dignity. Stanley's spirit lives in that home.

Several visitors to The Wall in Washington, DC, some who never knew him personally, have rubbed his name on a transfer and left copies in the family mailbox on Main Street in the spirit of Stanley's memory.

His spirit was with John Faragi when, 18 years after Stanley's death, it was discovered that John needed a heart transplant. Such an operation was not done in Massachusetts at the time, so family and friends raised enough money to send him to California where they were doing experimental transplant surgery.

John waited almost two weeks and in that time he grew weak and discouraged. On Sunday afternoon when he was at his lowest, the spirit of Stanley appeared. John spoke to Stanley just as he always did, telling him he was tired and wanted to go home.

Stanley told him no, it wasn't his time and promised him that a heart would be there that evening. Several hours later a nineteen year old motorcyclist was killed and his family donated the perfectly matched heart to John. The successful surgery was performed that night. John lived for many healthy years after the transplant, only to pass away recently.

Stanley's spirit can also be found at the memorial on Main and Howard Streets. The beautiful tribute to him stands as a quiet and constant reminder to all those who pass by of what he so freely gave to his family, his friend and his country.

And the spirit of Stanley Egan is alive and well with all those he touched during his lifetime, and even those who are just learning about him. The lessons and examples he left with us during his short time on earth are the presents he continues to give us through his spirit today. The lessons of love and brotherhood – of loyalty and kindness – are the gifts he sends to all of us – not just at Memorial Day, but all year through.

Rubbing Elbows with "Papa"

by
Frank L. Currier

Frank L Currier wrote the following regarding the note shown above:

"On 06 June 1944, during the allied invasion of Normandy, France, at approximately 0600 hours, Ernest Hemingway, who was a war correspondent for Collier's Magazine, was one of my passengers on No. 16 LCVP (Landing Craft Vehicle Personnel).

"After returning to the starboard side at Number 6 hold of the U.S.S. *Dorothea Dix*, APA #64, (Attack Transport) at approximately 1600 hours, Ernest Hemingway presented me with a Ten Shillings note. The inscription reads 'Good Luck to Frank L. Currier, from his shipmate, Ernest Hemingway.' This was written in pencil, and as an afterthought, he asked for a pen and then placed his signature on the right margin."

Frank L. Currier

Born, 4/27/1925 – Served, United States Navy 4/1943-3/1946 – Rank, Cox

Significant Duty Stations

- NTS *Newport, RI*
- USS *Dorothea L. Dix AP-67*
- Kerama Retto Boat Pool SLCU-40
- WAIPIO AMPHIB. Operating Base
- Naval Torpedo Station, Newport, RI

Significant Awards

- American Campaign Medal
- European African Middle Eastern Campaign Medal with two Stars
- Asiatic Pacific Campaign Medal with Star
- World War II Victory Medal

The Dog of War

A Saugus canine did his part during WWII

by
Christine MacKinnon
(*Saugus Advertiser*, October, 15, 1998)

When Theresa "Tootie" Demaso O'Leary was a teenager, growing up on Knowles Avenue in Saugus, the country's focus was on the Second World War and the activities of the Allies overseas.

"It was so different then," she said. "Everyone was so patriotic."

So when popular radio personality Lowell Thomas told his audience about the government's new "Dogs for Defense" program, O'Leary wrote to him immediately.

"My brother was in the Navy and my sister was a WAVE," O'Leary said. "I was only 17, and I was too young. My parents wouldn't let me go, so I sent my dog."

On March 13, 1942, Major General Edmund B. Gregory, the Quartermaster General of the Army, granted a franchise to Dogs for Defense, Inc. The agency coordinated the procurement of dogs to be trained by the military for sentry, pack, messenger, and other war work.

It was the first time in U.S. history that dogs were given official recognition by the War Department.

Rex, a mixed-breed shepherd, was six months old when O'Leary and her father brought him into their family.

"Someone in Saugus had a pure bred shepherd with too many puppies," O'Leary said. "Pa took one look at him and said, 'His name is Rex.'"

Rex enlisted in the service in May, 1943 and was returned safely to his young mistress in December, 1945.

The Army did not favor any one breed; they only asked the dogs be at least 20 inches tall and weigh a minimum of 50 pounds. O'Leary was asked to verify that Rex met these requirements and to also to furnish a photograph of the dog.

Once he was approved, O'Leary waited for Army personnel to come and collect him.

"They came on a Sunday," she said. "They had to test him for gun-shyness. They fired a starter pistol right next to his head, and he didn't even flinch."

Rex left with the officers that same day.

While Rex was at the front, O'Leary received only periodic updates.

"Rex received his training at Front Royal, Virginia, and should now be somewhere on active duty," one letter said. "Military regulations do not permit us to give his present location... We are extremely sorry that we cannot give you more definite information about Rex."[1]

Rex's mother was also part of Dogs for Defense. O'Leary said she was killed in the war.

"The Army called him 'Red' – it was a typo," O'Leary said. "He was a sentry and a scout."

The Army sent O'Leary a paw print to place in the window of her home, similar to the white stars that signified a family member's enrollment in the military.

After Rex completed his tour of duty, he was "subjected to a reprocessing course of training designed to rehabilitate and adjust [him] for return to civilian life," according to a letter from the Army.

"He had to be debriefed," O'Leary said.

When he came home, Rex was hailed as a hero.

"It was written up in the newspaper – 'Rex comes home from the war,'" she said. "One of the neighbors baked him a dog biscuit cake, and another brought him over a brush."

Rex became a well-known figure in Saugus and in nearby communities. O'Leary's father took him to his favorite club in Revere, and O'Leary took him shopping with her.

Rex was a frequent visitor to the high school, then located at the corner of Central and Winter Streets, and O'Leary said the bus driver would pick him up and drop him off at the end of Knowles Avenue.

"He'd come home with mustard all over his face from the high school kids feeding him," she said.

In those days, O'Leary said, there was no leash law, and Rex had free rein of the neighborhood.

In 1947, Rex was hit by a drunken driver–who was, ironically, a serviceman home on leave.

"Rex was at fault and so were we," O'Leary said. "He liked to chase cars."

Rex stayed in the hospital for two months. He came home on Christmas Eve, the same day O'Leary became engaged.

"Instead of spending time with my future husband, I was taking care of the dog," she said.

Rex, the Dog of War, at peace.

Rex never fully recovered from his injuries and died in 1948.

Over the years, O'Leary has kept Rex's memory alive. Other pets in her family, she said, have been named for Rex, including another dog, a cat, and a piranha.

O'Leary has also saved money to buy Rex a brick in the new War Memorial.

Rex entered the service only three months after he became O'Leary's dog; when asked if that was difficult for her, she laughed.

"Are you kidding me? I was so proud," she said. "Everyone, everything, was for the war."

---

1. It was later learned that Rex served as a scout dog in the China, Burma, and India areas. Rex's mother was killed in action in the European Theater of Operations.

Military

I Remember Joe Pace and Pearl Harbor

by
Richard C. Howland

Joseph W. Pace, a 1936 Saugus High School graduate and the first Saugus serviceman killed in World War II, is remembered in the following excerpt from an article titled "Eulogies for Two Sailors" that appeared in the *Boston Globe* dated November 15, 1987 written by Richard C. Howland. Joseph Pace was 24 years old when he died in 1941.

Joe Pace.

... And I, a retired English teacher and high school principal, remember a eulogy I gave 45 years ago in the East Saugus Methodist Church for a good friend, Joe Pace, who was mortally wounded aboard the USS Pennsylvania at Pearl Harbor. He was a radioman and the first Saugus casualty of World War II.

Joe enlisted when we were technically at peace. But England was in the war, and our armed forces were recruiting. Hard times still prevailed throughout much of the country. Like thousands of others, Joe enlisted for personal, patriotic and, certainly, economic reasons. He had no technical training, no prospects, no money.

However, Joe took his "everybody's brother" personality and an easy, unbeatable smile with him into the Navy. He had to leave his violin at home though. Joe insisted he was a compulsive fiddler, not a violinist. So the fiddler played everywhere–in church, with a pick-up band on the North Shore, at a picnic, around a fireplace.

What were those times really like for Joe and his contemporaries? Looking back, surely there were innocence, romance, hope, at conviction of "can do."... I remember Joe Pace and Pearl Harbor.

Corporal Scott J. Procopio, USMC

August 30, 1985 – April 2, 2006

by
Robert Wentworth

Corporal Scott J. Procopio, Unites States Marine Corps, age 20, married only a few months before and serving his second tour of duty in Iraq, was killed on April 2, 2006, by a roadside bomb in Ramadi, Iraq.

The funeral, believed to be the largest ever in Saugus, was held in the gymnasium at the Veterans Memorial Elementary School, April 11, 2006. All public schools and town buildings were closed and many businesses shut down during the service.

Scott Procopio and wife Kristal.

The hearse, escorted by Marines, led the walking cortege from the school along Central Street, where hundreds more townspeople lined the one mile route in respectful silence, to Riverside Cemetery where Scott was laid to rest by a Marine honor guard.

Saugus was again confronted with the dreaded ravages of war with the loss of another native son.

A Saugus Resident Reflects on the Passing of Scott Procopio

by
Al DiNardo
(*The Saugonian*, April 6, 2006)

As the debate of the annual Town Meeting is about to open, our town mourns its great loss in the passing of Scott Procopio. It was just last month while driving back from Florida that I stopped in Washington, D.C. and while standing in a vast sea of white crosses at Arlington National

Cemetery I asked myself, "Where do we find such men and women?"

It's like two worlds, our world here of daily life, work, errands, bills, and obligations and then the life of those men and women that stop all those very things we did today and decide to do something else. To go beyond themselves, to a place of selflessness and total dedication to a cause. Hoping for a better place, a new day of peace, kindness and LOVE in a broken world, and at times it takes a flight to get there.

In the coming debate at the Annual Town Meeting we will hear about the issues facing Saugus, the budget battles for monies, and the call for more money to make Saugus a better place. However, it's people like Scott that make Saugus great.

I didn't know Scott, nor did most of you. But he knew us. He knew we need such people as him in life. People that would stop what life has handed them and step out in faith for a cause to help set people free. It's happened before, Lincoln, Kennedy, King, Christ and now Scott. Each gave his life, an act of LOVE, hoping, dreaming for a better place beyond today, beyond what we see. Don't we all dream that? But so few follow the call. But Scott said yes.

Where do we find such men and women? In Saugus, Massachusetts, in Scott Procopio, a young man to be honored for his mission for GOD and Country. A young man's act of LOVE for those he did not know, he was willing to fight for peace and love. Let's choose LOVE today and every day. If Scott can, we can too... Thank you, Scott.

A Soldier Through and Through

by
Janice K. Jarosz

Webster defines the word "soldier" as an enlisted man or woman engaged in military service, of military skills and dedicated to a cause. William Bilton, late of Saugus, was just that sort of man.

Perhaps you too noticed him on past Memorial or Veterans Days when he marched in the parades honoring those who served their country.

He was the soldier in the black uniform, with a chock-full of medals and a rifle resting on his shoulder. He was the soldier that stood the tallest and who marched with an air of pride and respect. He was the one who, despite his aging body in later years, kept up with the best of them, and when a palsy took hold of him he ignored it and continued to march with the same pride and honor to the very end. No one who ever watched the local parades could help but notice how proudly he wore his uniform and how he displayed his love of his country with every step.

William Bilton was more than just a member of a contingent or a group when he marched in those hometown parades. He demonstrated by his very being how proud he was to be an American. He stood as straight as a string in the best and worst of weather never missing a parade in 52 years. The manner in which he held his body erect and his head so high never ceased to inspire me. He put personal pain, discomfort and inconvenience aside on those very special days, to show the world how important it was to respect our country and honor those who gave so much.

Several years ago, Mr. Bilton was to be recognized for his dedication by serving as the grand marshal for the Memorial Day parade in May of 1999. Unfortunately, he never got that opportunity as he passed away Feb. 19, 1999, just a few months away from the Memorial Day festivities that would have honored him.

According to his family, he had three great loves in his life and all were equally important. His first love was of his country – he enlisted as soon as he was able to when World War II broke out. He wound up in the mountains of Italy because of his expertise with horses and mules. He spent four years in combat as a member of his beloved Tenth Mountain Division.

Secondly, he was a cowboy. He respected the land, loved horses and all kinds of wildlife, and taught his children to appreciate nature in all its splendor.

And thirdly, he was a loving, compassionate husband and father. He instilled in his children a deep sense of respect and responsibility for others. He spent time with them showing them that he had learned as a child – always with a kindly patience and respect. For many years, he volunteered his time as a baseball coach and a Boy Scout leader, always contributing to the growth of the youngsters.

His grandson, Jeff Kent, read the following poem, author unknown, at Mr. Bilton's funeral, that perhaps best describes his beloved grandfather.

I was that which others did not want to be;
I went where others feared to go, and did what others failed to do.
I asked nothing from those who gave nothing, and reluctantly
Accepted the thought of Eternal loneliness... should I fail.
I have seen the face of terror; felt the stinging cold of fear; and

Have enjoyed the sweet taste of a moment's love.
I have cried, pained and hoped... but most of all,
I have lived times
Others would say were best forgotten.
At least someday, I will be able to say that I was
Proud of what I was...
A soldier.
And that he was.

One More Stone Pushover

by
Tom Sheehan

In the town square,
shadowed by Town Hall
and small beads of commerce,
a cold stone grays my old uniform:

vintage helmet with strap
dangled from one turned edge;
conclusive fatigue jacket, pocketed,
short-skirted, web-belted at the waist,

bandoleer and grenades
pendulous as after-thought
decorations across the breathless chest;
bulky fatigue pants, bloused into stone boots,

the pockets I bet still rich
with letters, pictures, a spoiling condom
making a circle the size of a silver dollar
on a soft leather wallet, a pair of brass knuckles

for weekend survival.
The sculptor did not dare
to grave the rifle free, chipped it closer
to the heart than it was meant. He should

have carved him armless,
walking into dreams, the firefight
passed into another valley, the last shot
beginning a final crusade, the walk up the grand

and glorious avenue of stares.
When the snow falls in silent employment
and buries the stone of his son, a father,
three wars wearied, jaw slack, forgets to breathe.

I feel a shiver
where the cold star lies,
and a heart beat, a heart beat.
All these acts wind down to their source.

Sports

What Little League team do you coach?

— Jimy Williams

Art Statuto

An Update on Art Statuto, Saugus High School 1943, of Notre Dame's Blue and Gold

by
Bud Maloney

Art Statuto always wanted to go to Notre Dame, and when he did, for two years during World War II and then, for two more years after service in the Navy, he created one of the most unusual stories in the school's colorful football history.

Statuto played on three national championship Notre Dame teams, in 1943, 1946, and 1947, but because of the wealth of talent on those Frank Leahy-coached elevens, Statuto never won a Notre Dame monogram.

Three years after his graduation, Statuto, who came to Notre Dame from Saugus, was the starting center for the Los Angeles Rams, who barely missed winning the NFL title when the Cleveland Brown's Lou Groza kicked a last-minute field goal.

From not being able to win a monogram in four years of college competition to playing prominently in the NFL's championship game – that's likely unparalleled in football history.

John Lujack and Art Statuto
at the 1945 Orange Bowl in Miami.

Statuto today, at the age of 79, has yet to retire. He stays busy with his own business, Empire Bearing and Transmission, in North Allendale, New Jersey, and retains an avid interest in former classmates as well as the elite group of former Leahy players who call themselves Leahy's Lads.

"I've made all of my class reunions," Statuto says, "and also the Leahy Lads reunions, but I've missed them both for the first time this year because my wife isn't in good health and I don't want to leave her alone." He and his wife, Frances, have been married for 57 years, have five children and eleven grandchildren.

Statuto grew up in the Boston suburb of Saugus, not much more than an outfield throw from Fenway Park and with Ted Williams and Jimmy Foxx as early heroes, he was as much into baseball as football. At Saugus High, he was talented enough to win four letters in football as well as two in baseball as a catcher.

Art Statuto.

His high school football coach was Hank Toczy-lowski, who had played quarterback for Leahy at Boston College and Toczy-lowski was able to arrange some financial help for Statuto at Boston University. But Toczylowski also talked to Ed McKeever, one of Leahy's assistants, and McKeever put it simply: "Get him on a train to South Bend."

So Statuto was a freshmen center at Notre Dame in the fall of 1943 when the Irish, stocked by tremendous Navy V-12 talent, were to win a national championship. Statuto was the third-team center, playing behind Herb Coleman and Frank Szymanski. It was ever to be thus. Johnny Ray came along to be the starter in 1944, backed up by Szymanski and Ralph Stewart who would play at Missouri after the war. After Navy service, Statuto came back to find George Stroh-meyer, Bill Walsh and Marty Wendell in his path in 1946, and Strohmeyer, Walsh and Walt Grothus there in 1947. Of all those centers, only Ray and Grothus did not play professional football.

Bill Fischer, a Notre Dame All-America guard in 1947 and 1948, who played with Statuto for two seasons, pointed out that in those days all centers were what today we call "long snappers." There were no specialists as there are today. "All the centers could center the ball," Fischer remembers. "Nobody was needed just to center it to the pointer and that limited Art's playing time."

Statuto never got in the 60 minutes needed to qualify for a monogram, but came the closest in 1944 when the Irish slaughtered Dartmouth, 64-0, in of all places, Fenway Park.

"We had several Massachusetts boys on the squad and after we were well ahead, McKeever (then the head coach), made sure all of us got in. I played better than a half." But he was on the field in only three other games and it didn't add up to the magic 60 minutes. Nevertheless, in the 1948 NFL draft, the Philadelphia Eagles saw fit to choose Statuto in a late round.

He chose, however, to go with the Buffalo Bills in the All-American Football Conference because the Bill's coach, Clem Crowe, had been the line coach under McKeever in 1944 and was well aware of Statuto's talent. "After our final game in '47 in Los Angeles, he came into the locker room, held out a contract, and I signed it," Statuto remembers.

Two years later, a similar coaching coincidence got Statuto to the Rams. Hamp Poole was an assistant to head coach Joe Stydahar in Los Angeles and Poole had been the coach of the Fort Pierce, Florida service team when Statuto played there in 1945. The Rams needed a center and Poole remembered his center at Fort Pierce so Statuto came to Los Angeles.

There he was surrounded by an incredible collection of football greats. Bob Waterfield and Norm Van Brocklin were the quarterbacks. Glenn Davis of West Point fame and Ed (Crazylegs) Hirsch were the running backs. Those were the big names, but the rest of the team was of equal quality.

"We have two other centers, Fred Naumetz from Boston College and Don Paul from UCLA," Statuto says, "but Stydahar wanted them to be linebackers so I was the center when we had the ball."

The Rams beat the Chicago Bears for the National Conference title, then went on to play the Browns in the championship game. "We were the champs for 59 and a half minutes," Statuto recalls with remarkable clarity, "but then came Groza." Los Angeles had gone ahead midway in the third quarter, but Groza's field goal with 28 seconds left to play gave Cleveland a 30-28 victory.

In the off-season, Statuto accepted a job with a company called Boston Gear, in North Quincy, MA. "I was only making $5,600 with the Rams. Pro football salaries weren't much in those days so I took the job to see how I'd like it. It turned out I liked it very much so I never went back to pro football."

Other than his trips to South Bend to see Notre Dame play, Statuto doesn't see much live football these days. "Most of the time I just watch TV. The crowds and all the screaming. It's just not my way to watch football."

The Notre Dame monogram winners have remained close over the years through their Monogram Club and from time to time award honorary monograms. Fischer, a past club president, has this to say about his old teammate:

"As soon as Art's name was brought up, there was no question about it. He was going to get his monogram." And so it was that in the early 1990s, Art Statuto finally got his "ND."

Honorary or whatever, perhaps no one has even been more deserving.

A Different Era of Football

by
Janice K. Jarosz
(*Saugus Advertiser* circa mid-1990s)

"Dave Lucey, who played with Hank Toczylowski at B.C., will be taking over the coaching position left by Ted Galligan. Galligan has been called up by the Navy. Lucey will make a good leader."

Wesley W. Gage first reported this news on the front page of the Saugus Advertiser, September 9, 1943. Mr. Gage, who later picked the football favorites as Professor Pigskin, couldn't have known at the time how true his prophecy would become.

Coach Dave Lucey.

In 1944, the Saugus High School football team, under the direction of Dave Lucey, succeeded in becoming the first Class B champions in Massachusetts. It was stated in a press release that "Coach Lucey was gifted with a virtual powerhouse of material, which he developed into one of the strongest teams in the state." That same year, eight players from the Saugus team made it to the North Shore All-Stars.

After reading such an impressive write up, I contacted former Coach Lucey in the hopes of learning how he did it. No Saugus team ever accomplished so much and some believe they never will again.

Mr. Lucey was very gracious and candid with me, but when I asked whether he had a practice schedule, I almost felt as if he had transposed himself back to Stackpole field, yelling out orders to his linemen.

"Practice? Did we practice?" (His voice was now like a voice from hell.) "We practiced seven days a week, sometimes twice a day. We even had 40-50 spectators through the week watching. The Waybright boys would scrimmage in the afternoons, walk home to Golden Hills for supper, and then walk back to the Rat Hole for a few games of pool and again walk back home. I worked their butts off. We would do the plays over and over again. Some called it Lucey's trained animal act. Most of the players wanted to punch me to shut me up, but none of them ever dared.

"In 1943 when I took over the team, Leon Young told me I might be interested in a talented kid by the name of Frank Pyzsko from East Saugus who had just quit school. I was told I could find him digging worms at the marsh. I got into my car, drove over there and, with my only pair of shoes, started walking the marsh looking for this "kid." When I finally caught up with Frank, I was able to convince him to get back into school and sign up for football. Any kid who was big came under serious question as to his masculinity if he didn't go out for football in those days."

Coach Lucey went on to explain the tenor of the town in the '40s. "The most important man in Saugus during the '40s was the football coach. After him came the band director followed by the politicians. Upwards of 10,000 people attended football games each week and the post-season game with Peabody saw over 22,000 fans spill out over Manning Bowl.

"Remember, the population of Saugus at that time was only 15,000. In an article in a 1944 Advertiser, the storekeepers were told to close their shops on Saturday afternoons because the football team would be playing and no one would be shopping. Cheerleaders were transported to games in hay wagons."

Leo Reardon served as the assistant coach and Belden Bly was faculty and equipment manager, along with being a teacher at the high school. "I made Bly what he is today," boomed the mighty coach. "He used to be more afraid of the principal than the entire freshman class. At one banquet I asked the MC to please call on him for a financial report. He reluctantly got up out of his chair and made his first speech. He hasn't stopped yapping since."

Already intimidated by this powerful legend, and not wanting him to know of my limited football knowledge, I asked him about his feelings for the boys that brought the town such pride and recognition. His voice changed – it became gentle. "My football kids were the greatest. '43 and '44 were great years for Saugus. The war was still going on, food was rationed, no one had much money, but what we did have was a lot of pride in our community. Football was the only bright light. No team can win a championship with only two or three good players. The entire squad was great."

Coach Lucey wanted to get back to the drilling of the team. "At practice I'd push them to the limit until I could see fire in their eyes. Most times they wanted to kill me; I'd scream at them, 'You can't win a game if you can't block or tackle,' and to aggravate them even further, I'd go after Pyzsko. 'Hey, Pyzsko, you're nothing but a dumb polack; why don't you go back to digging worms.' That really got him, and just to keep the fire blazing, I'd let Frank get away with answering back. It was sort of a little game we had between ourselves. He'd yell back at me, 'Yeah, well your kid is half-polack too; what do you say about that?' The rest of the team would hold their breath, but I'd let it go. It was part of the strategy."

I had one last question for the coach; what made them so great? Mr. Lucey didn't take long in answering. "It was before the auto. These kids walked. They were in good condition with plenty of stamina even before I got hold of them. They never spent time in front of a TV. They were either walking somewhere, shoveling snow, digging for worms, or practicing football. They were never cold; they never complained, and Frank actually played better when he was injured."

Mr. Lucey's last few words of wisdom were to wish the current Saugus High team the best of luck. "Go out on the field; take the game away from your opponent. Don't let anyone or anything beat you. Winning is everything, losing is for the birds."

Clifford George "Cushie" Harris

by
Tom Sheehan

Cushie was a four-year classmate and a four-year teammate on the Saugus High School football team, from 1943 to 1947. We were in many classes together and in just about every game for four years. He was a handsome, rugged kid who came out of Golden Hills with the likes of Doug and Bruce Waybright and Charlie Sampson, all of whom played illustrious parts on teams that were dubbed The Giant Killers, by a Boston sports reporter, and adopted by many local sportswriters.

Cushie was fiercely loyal to Saugus and to his teammates, bringing that ferocity with him onto the football field. I can see him now, those windmilling arms of his as he cut back into the line with the ball against Lowell High School in a spring game in April of 1943.

On the golden river.

The sun starts to set over the docks.

Fall foliage in Breakheart Reservation.

Prince Restaurant at night.

The Saugus Square One Mall at night.

Time elapsed view of Route One traffic at night.

The river at night.

The Kowloon Restaurant at night.

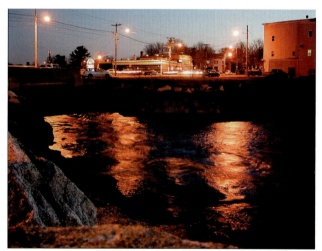

Another view of the river at night.

Sunset on the river.

The Private Devine Memorial at the Town Hall.

The Veterans Memorial at the Town Hall.

Boats on the river.

At the docks.

Industry on the river.

The Town Hall and Library.

Cliftondale Square in the winter.

The Iron Works in the winter.

The river in the winter.

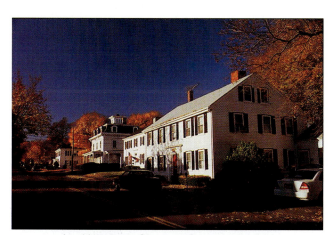
Looking down Chestnut Street in the fall.

The Iron Works in the fall.

River and rail, in East Saugus.

Spring on the river.

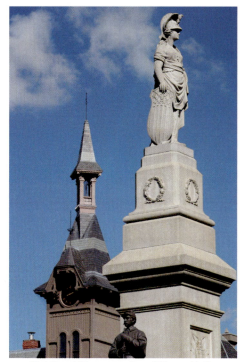

Soldiers' Monument and Town Hall.

Of Time and the River

He was in the eighth grade then and sprinted for more than 60 yards for a touchdown at Manning Bowl. Before the game he must have weighed in at about 125 pounds. It was a sign of things to come. In the next four years he might have added 30-35 pounds, but the tenacity rose exponentially, and the fierceness. Across the huddle it was his eyes that said, "Give me that ball. I can get the first down we need, or the touchdown." So right was he, scoring the winning touchdown in games against Lynn Classical with Harry Agganis in 1945, against Chelsea, Amesbury, Watertown, Swampscott, Newburyport, and a few others, I am sure.

What fades are yardage, linebacker tenacity, open field tackles, tearing into a tackle from Amesbury who outweighed him by over 100 pounds, and scoring the lone touchdown in the game. Those visions go the way of memories, slipping and sliding away, lost it seems when he lost his battle with life and the grasp of the dialysis machine for the angry and tough last year of his life. But he does not take all of them with him. For pure pleasure, for grit and determination, when I want some new Sachem to dig down for the last ounce, I bring back those moments when Cushie swept behind me, taking the ball from my hand-off in the 42-Reverse and aiming his drive at an opponent's mid-section. I've called him back in recent years at Stackpole, him and George Laskey and George Miles and Bruce Waybright and Dougie Waybright and a host of Giant Killers, to lend a hand to the new hands, the Ghosts of Stackpole Field digging deep for the new kids on the block, the new kids on the line.

Additionally, in 1946 we played on Saugus High's first hockey team in the old North Shore League. Cushie, Neil Howland and I were seniors, getting a first whiff of organized hockey, coming away from the incessant scrambling hockey on the ice at Lily Pond or one of the three lakes in Golden Hills. For us it was hockey first carried to some kind of perfection by the Prentice brothers that year and later on and, in the long run, most recently by Coach Jimmy Quinlan's two state championships (on top of Coach Lou Finocchiaro's 1999 championship) and their going eleven minutes into the overtime period at the Fleet Center when they fell short of their third straight state title in 2005.

In the classroom, Cushie was a good student, heady at writing, studious when he needed to be. His tour as an Air Force officer and his matriculation at the University of New Hampshire are both testaments to his intelligence and determination.

One of the other attributes that I recall with distinction is his ability to get a ride home, all the way home to Third Lake in Golden Hills late at night when we called our social graces to an end for the evening. Usually, it was a black and white police car that took home the fullback on the team, who for his four years worked his butt to the bone for SHS, only to see his senior year killed off by a severe knee injury that

brought him a few minutes of playing time in an unwieldy brace into his one, and only, game of the year.

To and from games on the bus, or in the locker room before and after games, what I remember most of that lost year, is his broken heart, not being able to look me in the eyes, saying, like he had so many times, "Give me the ball. I'll get that first down or that touchdown for you."

I still miss those promises.

We partied in our way, of course, had close friends and small romances, and began to grow as people, as individuals. Diversion and division naturally came upon us, and geography, and school, and the military, for Korea, breathing down our necks, had a relentless reach.

Over the years I read about some accomplishments of Cushie, but they were always overshadowed by memories of his tenacity, his willingness, and his courage.

Then I read his obituary. It did not take away what I treasure. I will always miss his promises: "Give me the ball. I'll get that first down or that touchdown for you."

Irving "Soupy" Campbell

May 21, 1928 - November 5, 1969

by
Tom Sheehan

Though he's been gone from us for more than 35 years, some vivid memories remain with me of Irving "Soupy" Campbell, classmate from Saugus High School in 1947, teammate on the football team the previous three seasons, and later a civic player in the management of our town.

The first recall is that Soupy's father was seriously hurt by enemy gas in World War I, suffered on his return from Europe, and that eventually Soupy and his sister lived, fatherless for all of their school years, with their mother on the corner of Vine Street and Essex Street in an apartment at the old Cheever Estate.

The second significant memory is Soupy's dedication to family welfare. After all those long afternoons and early evenings of football practice, he would somehow get by diverse means to the Palace of Sweets, a soda spa on the corner of Pleasant Street in Malden Square. He worked late evenings for those years, and before and after the football season, on his feet behind the counter until closing time. Then, after his long day, he had to get himself home, get to sleep, get to school, get to practice, and go back to work on another day.

During football games at Stackpole Field or Manning Bowl or out on the road, he was a high octane, enthusiastic tackle, playing both ways on the scrimmage line, offensively and defensively, as most players did in the years where they tabbed Saugus The Giant Killers. He was all of 165 pounds on his best day. Some of his linemates those years ring with the litany of great Saugus linemen: John Quinlan, George Miles, Bruce Waybright, Andy Forti, Dick Evans, Jim Blundell, George Winters, Wally LeBlanc, Les Woodbury and Gene Decareau. Soupy was a stalwart combatant in games where undefeated opponents (Melrose, Revere, Lynn Classical, Chelsea, for example) were on the march to spectacular seasons only to be ceremoniously knocked out of the undefeated category by the upstart team from little Saugus, in its own run to an undefeated State Championship Class B title in 1944.

Coach Dave Lucey often said, "Soupy Campbell not only has fire in his eyes, he has a fire in his belly." His whole life-style echoed those sentiments.

After high school, and cutting into his college days, Soupy's military service brought him to two separate hitches in England and Iceland wearing Air Force blue. The climate in those locales did nothing to hinder the oncoming onslaught of arthritis that soon thereafter seriously impaired his health, and which eventually, in great part, brought about his death. I can recall his stopping to give me a ride when he would not be able to turn his head to look at me as I got in the car, his body rigid and near immoveable. He'd swing his whole torso about, as he said, "Where you going?" Those days, Soupy was either the Town Accountant or the temporary Town Manager, which seemed to be a hat he put on at various times, as he was always at the call.

He was, for all these accounts, the handsomest guy in our class, a teammate, a worker and a warrior, a stalwart friend, a true community servant, and a most memorable personality.

Life for Soupy, as it flowed down the years, was fraught with much discomfort, pain and certain disabilities that would have crushed another man. But, to this day, he was the guy I remember most across the huddle from me, the fire leaping in his eyes, ready to jump back to the scrimmage line, ready to do whatever was bid of him.

And I used to think at times, in the middle of games, that he would leave us right after the game, celebrations notwithstanding, to go back to work. The thought still haunts me, though the revelation is that it was his way of life, really unconquered for longer than it might have been.

Three Views of George Laskey

Saugus High School – 1948

by
Bob Wentworth

In compiling this glimpse of the life of George Laskey, his widow, "Sis," provided the material that she feels best characterized some of the many aspects of his life.

One view is that of his legendary high school football career. The article by Curt Noyes is her favorite football story of George. She added to this segment her recollection of a difficult situation George faced as a result of his gridiron accomplishments.

The other two views are excerpts from eulogies delivered at George's funeral service. They describe George and their relationship to him as a friend and co-worker in one, and in the other as a beloved family member.

In whichever view you may have known George, you realize that he, as Sis often remarks, "was one great guy."

The Football View

George loved football for the fundamental skills involved: the athleticism, the competitiveness, the vigorous physical element, the team camaraderie. He was good, he excelled, as all of us who followed the sport during that era recall. He WAS NOT, however, comfortable with the fame he attained. He disliked, and was embarrassed, by the notoriety.

His feats were widely acclaimed, and offers of college football scholarships followed, creating a personal dilemma that began an unhappy period in his life.

His wife, "Sis," recounts his inner conflict at the time. He wanted to leave football behind after high school, and get on with his life. Some of his family and friends were urging him to continue, to take advantage of the opportunities being offered. His heart was not in it. However, he felt an obligation, out of a sense of loyalty, to heed their advice. He succumbed to the pressure and enrolled in a prep school to better prepare himself academically and athletically.

It wasn't long before he realized his mistake. This life wasn't for him. A few months later, being true to his character, he walked away from football and returned home to Saugus to begin a new life. He joined the Air Force, learning a trade that served as his life's career as an airline mechanic with Northeast Airlines, which later became Delta

Airlines. He married his high school girlfriend, Marion "Sis" Prideaux, built his home in the family neighborhood, with Sis, raised a family of three children – Brenna, Bryan and Blayne, and at last found the contentment he had sought since high school.

That's What The Lady Said

(A reprint from The Lynn Daily Evening Item, circa 1947 by Curt Noyes)

My wife, who is the smartest woman I know outside of Lassie, recently tipped me off to the fact that George Laskey of Saugus is a pretty fair halfback.

Said she, in her Marblehead dialect, "This guy Laskey is a *wham bam* of the first order, and he can do more things on a gridiron than a helicopter in a high wind. He can not only run like hell to his left but he can run equally well to his right. And when he puts his head down and pistons up the middle he can carry more men on his back than a Trojan horse."

"What stops him occasionally?" I asked her, and I should have known better.

"His own blockers," she replied, tossing a couple of high powered adjectives in ahead of the word blockers. "They get in his way. The first time I see Dave Lucey I'm going to tell him to let Laskey do his own blocking hereafter. And furthermore, if you don't put him on your all-star team I'll put him on for you, you dope."

"Can he beat Lynn Classical single-handed?" says I.

"No," says she, "but he'll give 'em a *heehawhell* of a battle." And darned if she wasn't right again, as I saw for myself last Friday evening at Manning Bowl.

Young Mr. Laskey is recuperating from a broken collarbone and was not at his peak. Yet against Classical, a fair ball club in some respects, Laskey carried the windbag 20 times for a net gain of 121 yards and an average of six yards per carry. Once he ripped off Classical's right side and raced for 40 yards before Agganis hauled him down. And a moment later he whirled and scooted off their left side for twelve more and a touchdown. And

George Laskey.

when he wasn't running with the ball he was bulldogging Classical backs as they whizzed and breezed through the Saugus line into the wide open spaces.

It was a busy evening for the convalescent Saugus cripple.

Meanwhile Classical went about their business and won the ball game by a top heavy score of 34 to 7. They had a system. Every time Laskey could be persuaded to give up the ball, Pike or Agganis or somebody would scamper for a touchdown.

And this had a dampening effect on everybody but Laskey, who apparently hadn't been told that he and his teammates were being massacred by a great ball club. At the finish Laskey had just punched out fourteen yards in two slaps at the Classical line; and he was up on his feet and ready for another crack at it when the whistle blew.

A great football team, Lynn Classical... a great halfback, George Laskey of Saugus.

The Friend and Co-Worker View

(An excerpt from a eulogy written and delivered at George's funeral service, March 1998, by his friend and co-worker Gary Swanson.)

When I was a young teenager, George Laskey became one of my first real-life heroes. I'll never forget the first time he pulled up in front of our house in a hot new red Mustang Fastback. This car came with everything including a great looking lady on the passenger side. He had my attention all right. I wanted to know more and more about him. My mom then told me he was a very talented guy – that he built his own house, that he fixed his own cars, that he was a mechanic for Northeast Airlines, and that he flew anywhere he wanted for nothing. I knew then that George was my kind of guy and all I wanted to know was, "Where do I sign up."

George was always very generous with his time and his talents. He would bail my brothers and me out time after time as we invested in one junk box (car) after another; and I know he did the same for many of you as well.

He had a deep sense of pride for his profession of 37 years and for Northeast and Delta. It was hard to get a job with the airlines way back then. Your timing had to be perfect and it helped a lot if you had someone already working there pulling for you. As opportunities presented themselves, George would bring home job applications and vouch for people like me and others here today who needed a break and needed a job.

I'll also never forget the first time George and I were working on the same plane together – it was on a midnight shift – he was doing all the important stuff in the cockpit while I was cleaning the lavatories. There I was working in the shadow of the great one – I knew then that I was well on my way.

George was also an inspirational leader for many of us here today:

- He led by example... he always did the right thing.

- He cared more about the people he worked with than any stockholder or so-called VIP. At his retirement party, most of the war stories had to do with how people pulled together, bent the rules to cover for each other, and yet always got the job done. As a foreman, George instilled this kind of behavior in the people he worked with. In conversation with mechanics at his retirement party, they volunteered that they would walk through fire if he asked them to.

- He was strong as an ox and he never took any guff from anyone.

- There wasn't a phony bone in the man's body.

- His integrity was beyond reproach and his attitude was totally *"gung ho"* – *"can do!"*

Believe me, when you're flying at 35,000 feet, traveling 600 miles an hour, this is the kind of guy you wanted making sure everything that needed to be done to your airplane got done.

As the old proverb goes – "They are not gone, those that live on within us."

George is alive and will live on in the hearts of those of us that he has touched with his love, his generosity, his friendship, and his inspirational leadership. . . .

The Family View

(An excerpt from the eulogy written and delivered at George's funeral service, March 1998, by his niece Melissa Goodwin.)

George Laskey is to be remembered today... remembered by each and every one of us.

As I began to think, the first word that came to my mind was PASSION.

I thought of how my uncle was passionate about so many things:

his wife, his children, his friends, his beliefs, his feelings... his life.

And then there are his toys – whether it was snowmobiles, airplanes, his boat... and of course his Harley.

He loved and enjoyed it all.

He grabbed hold of his life and lived it passionately.

My Uncle George was also a very committed and loving person:

to his best friend and wife... my Auntie Sis... to whom he was married for 46 years.

to taking great care and pride in his children – Brenna, Bryan and Blayne.

He loved them so much!

His love and commitment will always shine on in them.

We are all so lucky to have been touched by his love... charm... and charisma:

From being a young boy... with three sisters – they watched him raise homing pigeons, build model airplanes, always involved in sports – football is what he excelled in.

He loved to tinker around with anything mechanical and this blossomed when he joined the Air Force.

To... being a doting husband... loving father, and always providing for his family.

He was a kind and giving person... he was a good man.

If he wasn't snowblowing your driveway... he'd be helping you fix your car.

He loved to be surrounded by his friends and family... and an occasional Colt 45.

And then we saw the little boy again as he sat so high on top of his new "Harley."

Cruising around on his motorcycle... smiling... laughing... and living.

He just loved to be active... especially outdoors.

We've all been touched by such a special person.

So... how do you remember George Laskey?

I'm sure you all have some funny tales to tell.

Close your eyes... picture him doing something that made you smile... and hang on to that image.

Mine is that big grin . . .smiling wide... with his eyebrows bouncing up and down.

... he will always make me smile...

Bill Harrington

Teaching by Example

by
Jay Nelson

"O.K., Jay, just throw these guys a few curve balls and then we can hit."

I can still see his face and hear his voice — sort of a wirier version of Kirk Douglas with a little Danny Kaye thrown in – as he took the ball from Sonny Roberts, a pure fast-baller and the best pitcher we Saugus Little League All-Stars had on a stiflingly-hot day in July, 1953, and gave it to the second baseman/reliever, me. He spoke with that combination of amusement and cocky confidence, a certain disdain for the opponent — "these guys" — that I had seen so often before when it came to baseball.

"These guys" were the heavily-favored East Lynn All-Stars and they just happened to have loaded the bases with one out in the bottom of the sixth with the score tied 1-1. Well, it worked, his confidence and, yes, his disdain for the East Lynn hitters — he was after all a pitcher to his core-- came right along with that ball to me and we went on to beat them 3-1 in eight innings at the Poor Farm next to the Turnpike. It was a big win for us Saugus Little Leaguers in our second year of existence, the last year of

Bill Harrington.

a single league in town, and, I believe, for our manager, my next-door neighbor, Bill Harrington.

The Harringtons moved into 13 Parker Street, separated from the Nelsons at number 15 only by a narrow driveway, in 1949. Bill was 30, I was 8, my sister Betsy was 13 and

my parents, Mary and John, in their early '40s. I was already a baseball lover. Our family, like many Saugus families then and now, placed a very high value on sports. My maternal grandfather Gillespie had been a professional 'footballer' in Scotland and England for sixteen years around the turn of the century. And in American society as a whole at mid-century, baseball was the national pastime in name and in fact.

Now, out of nowhere I was living next door to an adult who, it very quickly turned out, had played baseball as a pitcher at a high level: semi-pro, high amateur, and in the army. And he was still really, really good, and he still loved to play catch and work on his pitches, including his famous dipsy-doodle (more about which later). And he had great baseball stories to tell! What a break for me! My father spent countless hours playing catch with me in my pre-Little League and Little League days, and even more importantly, "hitting them out," as we called it, at the Poor Farm: a bag of four or five balls, he'd pitch 'em (accurately and with speed), I'd hit 'em, we'd go get 'em and then we'd do it again. My father was a great and natural swimmer, and a great and natural skater, but I was mediocre, to put it in the most favorable possible light, at both. Baseball was it for me, and for Bill.

My contemporaries on and around Parker Street of course got some of the benefits of playing catch or hitting/throwing grounders or shagging flies with Bill—in my driveway or on the vacant lot on the other side of Bill's house, what was to become the Blatsos home—but I was right next door! He taught me how to throw a curve in the space of ten minutes when I had been working unsuccessfully on it for three months, and he taught me, by example, the value of control.

"Put your glove up, Jay."

"Where?"

"Anywhere." And, from a distance of, say, 40-60 feet, he'd come closer, more often, than anybody who no longer pitched regularly had a right to.

"How was that, Jay?"

"Hit the target." He could effortlessly catch a thrown ball behind his back, and, more remarkably, pitch, not throw, with speed and accuracy behind his back. "Think fast!" and I did. He would even throw a knuckle-ball behind his back, and do a little of what has come to be known as "hot-dogging" as the ball danced toward you.

He was very funny. "I'm 33. I would've been 35, but I was sick two years."

"I see in the Item that that kid *Penulty* gained 95 yards in the Saugus-Peabody game."

"Bill, I've never heard of him." Well, after 2-3 minutes of good-natured teasing, it turned out it was the "penalty" column of the two teams combined which amounted to 95 yards. Bill was a guy who, I'm sure, under different circumstances, could have been an impressionist or a stand-up comedian. He was a natural entertainer, like many people who at first come across as shy. But once they feel comfortable…

His dipsy-doodle, he explained, became a feature of his repertoire while he was playing army ball as a lieutenant in the Artillery in Burma in 1944 or '45 during WWII. Used only when there were two outs and he had two strikes on the hitter, it amounted to a slow, nearly-underhand — the motion almost like the pitcher's in modern softball — curve ball delivered just as Bill turned his attention away from home plate and began to walk off the mound toward the third base line, anticipating of course the third strike, whether called or swinging, in any case a sure thing. Now that's chutzpah! And that's fun!

Bill coached my team, the Red Sox, under manager Ed Caffarella, who was also liked very much by all the kids, in 1952, the first year of Little League in Saugus. Then he managed the Red Sox (and, as mentioned, the All-Stars) in 1953. Work and family obligations — six children eventually – made that his last year of Little League work / play. But for years after that, whether listening to Boston Red Sox games on radio in summer in one of our adjoining backyards while mowing the lawn or painting or just sunning — that, by the way, took loyalty bordering on devotion during the 1951-1966 Red Sox Dark Ages! – or playing catch in the driveway, or just standing around with our earflaps down throwing snowballs at trees in winter, we stayed in touch.

Bill Harrington.

I didn't play much baseball after high school, though when the chance for PFC Nelson to play on the post team at Fort Meade, MD, in the summer of 1963 arose, I jumped at it, and enjoyed a delightful two-month return to my youth. But I have played the sport of squash now for nearly 50 years and won some age-group national championships, the most recent one at age 62. I took up squash at Andover Academy, which I attended beginning in the 10th grade (Bill wrote one of the two non-teacher letters of recommendation to Andover for me at my mother's request.) I believe that Bill's open and joyful love of playing baseball as an adult — I stress, as an adult — helped to show me the possibility for a lifetime commitment to playing a sport, not just being a spectator, that I might otherwise not have imagined. He never said to me, "You know, you can keep playing sports actively after you've grown up and still have a lot of fun." His example said it all.

Squash – Jay Nelson

by
Betsy Nelson Hatfield

With 21 US Squash Racquets Association age-group national singles titles to his credit, the most recent in the 60-and-over category in Seattle in 2004, Jay Nelson can claim the second-highest age-group total in American squash history. His run of thirteen consecutive age-group titles was broken only this past March when he had the flu and couldn't play at the Championships at the Harvard courts in Cambridge. He hopes to be back in the winner's circle in March, 2006, in New Haven.

Jay's curiosity about squash was piqued during childhood "attic explorations" when he would see our father's vintage Wright and Ditson racquet--last used circa 1930--standing in a corner. Jay only took up the game, however, as a junior at Phillips Academy, Andover, in 1957. He quickly fell in love with the game's intricate geometry and intense physical demands, and competed interscholastically for two years for Andover.

Jay went on to play for perennial intercollegiate powerhouse Harvard under legendary coach Jack Barnaby, lettering twice but never playing higher than #5 on the nine-man varsity team. Following three years in the Army and two working in Boston, five years when he didn't so much as pick up a racquet, he began playing again in the Boston 'A' League during his second year at Harvard Business School.

In 1969 he moved with his family to New York, and, playing out of the Harvard Club of New York, he hit his stride. He soon won both the New York City and New York State Championships. He was ranked #2 at season's end twice in the 1970s in the US open amateur ranks. He captained the US team at the 1973 World Amateur Championships in Johannesburg in 1973. In 1975 he received the Eddie Standing Award "For Sportsmanship Combined With A High Level of Play" from the Metropolitan Squash Racquets Association of New York. He was featured in Sports Illustrated's "Faces in the Crowd" in 1987 for play during that season. In 1998, nine months after surgery for prostate cancer – Get your PSA checked, guys! – he won the 55-and-overs.

Rob Dinerman, a squash journalist, historian, and player wrote this in 2003: "[Jay] is by a large margin the remaining protagonist from an otherwise by-gone period of USSRA history who made the transition from the cold courts and gentlemanly atmosphere of the earlier era to the far more athletically demanding pitch of today's environment, an old-school product who is nevertheless thriving in the present climate and who, by virtue of his recent results and continuing enthusiasm for the game, may well be working his magic for years to come."

Today Jay says, "As a Saugus boy growing up in the late '40s and early '50s, I always dreamed of playing for the Red Sox. Unfortunately, I didn't get big enough young enough to excel in baseball in my mid- and late-teens. But I was lucky enough to find squash. What a game!"

Saugus Little League, 2003

by
Tom Sheehan

They were six innings away from the USA National Little League Championship after competing in and winning the most dramatic game any team from Saugus ever played in; the Saugus American Little League team, New England Champions and Regional Champions, victors over Richmond, TX (Southwest champions), in a game that several correspondents described as follows:

"I mean this was more entertaining than any baseball game I've seen in a while. It was Saugus, Massachusetts vs. Richmond, Texas... Massachusetts went out to a 10-2 lead, then in the sixth inning Texas came back with 6 runs to tie the game. It went to extra innings and Texas scored 3 more runs to go up 13-10. Then, in the bottom of the seventh inning, Massachusetts scored 4 runs to win the game, it was crazy." Final: Saugus 14-Texas 13.

"The win woke up the fans at Fenway at the P.A. announcement."

"Saugus wins the game of the year in any sport."

"Wow, Saugus and the BoSox even nailed the first two segments of ESPN's Sportscenter."

Little League parade, 2003.

It was a game that brought the Saugus Americans and their coaches to Los Angeles as one of the selections for ESPN's Best Game of the Year, where they made entrance on another national TV stage in almost winning another great competition, only to lose out to a Super Bowl game won by the Patriots, also representing New England.

The Texas game was a game that the old home town, much of Massachusetts and much of New England had watched. Indeed, as many reports surfaced, many people in the country watched.

I was glued to the TV watching it, spotting many Saugus folk in the stands who had journeyed down to Williamsport, PA for the Texas game and final game against Florida, the Southeast champions, witnessing one of the greatest Saugus finishes ever.

Three young heroes, 2003.

The names of team members are etched in the memorial stone at our new World Series Park at the Belmonte School.

Bob Davis

Our World Series Park

by
Tom Sheehan

If you were to track him with a heat-sensing GPS tracking satellite (Global Positioning System), plotting the red lines of his industry at work at the new World Series Park behind the Belmonte School, the result would not be a series of hen-scratches, or minor red trails in a scratchy pattern. It would be rather a solid red diagram of his efforts, a red blob without holidays in it or spaces or emptiness of any order. There'd be no white space, not for Bob Davis in his continual assault on volunteering for baseball talent abounding in Saugus.

World Series Park dedication with (l-r) Bob Davis,
David Fauci, Lennie Fauci

And there is no white space in a description of him. It flows in a continual motion. Bob Davis is groundskeeper, green thumb, earth leveler, fundraiser, general factotum of the art of maintenance. He has one speed. It's of the always in gear variety: continual, pre-game, game, and post game, a litany of mundane and specialized tasks that are time-consuming and legendary. These are words hardly fit for someone without observation and devotion, someone who a number of years ago realized the need of a new and special playing surface in town, and a need augmented by decisive memories of that exciting time a few years past when a bunch of Saugus youngsters wrapped this town and half the country to its bosom.

Minute glory succumbs to time, but memories have the deepest clutches. Bob Davis remembers how his heart was grabbed by a bunch of kids, before 2003 and after 2003. It made his work ethic endless; it made the need for a new field a raw necessity, one beyond dream and celebration.

Opening Day, Belmonte Park, 1995
dignitaries l-r are Joe Attubato, Janette Fasano, Guy Moley,
Tim Whyte (in back), Steve Angelo, Dick Barry, Anthony
Cogliano, Ed Collins, Chris Ciampa, Jon Bernard, George
Lasquade, and Mike Annese.

Follow him in his devotion for a day of games at World Series Park, and you'll smart with wonder, that all-tracking GPS in the sky getting itself dizzied, fluttering and oscillating in orbit. He goes from grass to dirt infield, to bases, to PA system, to mower maintenance, to supply control. Gas is needed, line paint is needed. When weather declares such need, he lays down tarpaulins or lifts them from placement. He stores them for next use. He lugs ice and pizza and drinks to the food wagon on this game day. He checks the foul lines and drags the metal nail mesh to smooth the infield for the liquid capture of ground balls by infielders. He hawks tournament T-shirts through the stands, his voice ringing out. Then, at the end, the crowd dissolved, broken down and moving away, he is at trash removal, the ultimate volunteer. A look at his volunteer work pants points that out; they have been worn to near tatters, the kind that a wife tries to throw out at an inconvenient time, only to be reclaimed by the faithful, by the pursuant.

World Series Park, game day.

Without his trying to do so, he can make you tired!

We all know the frenzy of volunteer activity when a new effort is activated, and how slowly but surely some of that promise and activity disappears. Generally it is a few men, or one man, like Bob Davis, who keep to the grindstone, head-manning the necessary operations that keep a thing in place, herding a minority of help, some constant, some not. Any long-standing organization has such a person or persons, like John Burns and Bob Wentworth for *A Gathering of Memories, Saugus 1900-2000* and this sequel, *Of Time and the River*, and Ronnie Barresi for years on end at the service of Babe Ruth baseball. You know who keeps things going for any activity. Often it is one man or a small core of people who carry the fever. See Harry Mazman and Bob Heffernan and Don Trainor selling split-the-pot tickets for years on end at SHS football games. They never miss. Scoutmasters do it, oftentimes for their whole adult lives. Coaches do it, when their own children have passed eligible age for their particular sport. You know them without stretching for names.

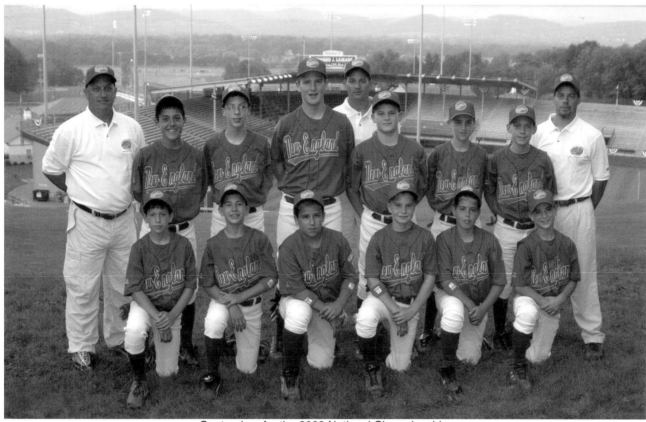

Contenders for the 2003 National Championship.
Front row, left to right: Craig Cole, Ryan Bateman, Sebastiano "Yano" Petruzzelli, Dario Pizzano, Mark Sacco and Michael Scuzzarella.
Back row, left to right: Coach Mike Ferreira, David Ferreira, Anthony DiSciscio, Matthew Muldoon, Coach Rob Calla, Tyler Calla, Tyler Grillo, Joe Kazabuski and Manager Rob Rochenski.

There were a few activists that hung together for the long run on the new field, for reason; there was a dire need for a classic baseball diamond for the kids of Saugus, a diamond to be proud of. Truth be known, Stackpole Field's diamond was entirely overworked, overscheduled, overwhelmed. Due to its sole being, many Babe Ruth games, in the next-step diamond for Little Leaguers, were played with every batter coming to the plate saddled with a one and one count on them before the first pitch. That was necessary to finish games before darkness set in, or to fulfill a schedule that included the high school team, the Legion team and the Saugus Braves.

Bob Davis and his son Glen inspected all potential sites. Belmonte was best and was chosen. And when the Saugus American Little League All-Stars captured the hearts of so many in 2003, their first really tangible gift, piled atop their many intangible "honors," was a new field, the World Series Park with their names etched forever in stone.

I heard a couple of recent college graduates, who had played at Fenway Park in College All-Star games, say at a recent Babe Ruth Tournament that the infield is as good as Fenway

Park. I'll bet Red Sox third baseman Mike Lowell would agree.

At bat, World Series Park.

Lucky Saugus. Lucky World Series Park. The ubiquitous, obviously ubiquitous, Bob Davis, like horse feathers and that other stuff, is all over the place. Often, as we know, it is the Bob Davises of the world who get it done.

Charlie Bilton

by
Tom Sheehan

I first saw his intensity from a spot along the outfield fence behind the Oaklandvale School where the Saugus National Little League major field was located at the time. To come from a day's work, take off the tie, get a coffee and a hamburger and sit in the sun in the Oaklandvale stands was Elysium. I loved those days. My son Matt was with the Braves and was constantly in contact with Charlie Bilton, the Mets manager. Charlie was noticeable: he was noisy, could yell without rancor, but could drop a solicitous and caring hand across the back of a boy who stumbled turning at third base or dropped a pop up outside first base. His instructions were acute and to the point, and boys learned the game of baseball under his direction.

He reminded me of an old coach of mine who was also an intense but caring man, Dave Lucey, whose memory is locked in place within me for all times that are mine. For a brief second of that glimpse they merged in one person, the new and the old, and I knew my sons would thrive at his hand, under that intensity. He was my kind of coach. Son Matt played for Charlie's All-Star team, as did son Jamie, who also played for Charlie for three years on the Mets. To this day they say he was the best baseball man they ever played for.

Charlie Bilton was in the game for every pitch, every inning, from the time he came to coaching with his father in the league… at age thirteen in the National Little League, in 1963. In 1967, at age eighteen, he had his own team in that league, the Cardinals. The intensity I had first seen, that desire to give kids the best chance of winning, never left him. In 2004, beset by health issues, he retired from the coaching and management of kid teams.

In between those dates hangs like a mural his illustrious career for the kids of Saugus: 25 years as manager of the Mets, service in the U.S. Navy during the Viet Nam War, coach of the National All-Stars in 1985 with Mario Coco and Jim Allen, and manager of the National All-Stars from 1986 to 1992. During one of those tournaments, not wanting to leave his team entirely, he talked to coaches by phone from his bed at Massachusetts General Hospital where illness had taken him.

When he left the National League in 1995, he was invited to the American League the very next day. He ran the American All-Star team practices from 1995 through 2003, when the Americans excited much of America with their play in Williamstown, PA (and they subsequently went on to the ESPN Awards Show in Los Angeles, losing the top award by a hair).

Another look at results reflects the image of a man truly devoted to kids and baseball:

His All-Star teams were three times District Champions, two times Bi-District Champions, and in 2003 were District, Sectional, State, New England Champions and first place in pool play. In one of the great moments of Little League baseball that team beat a Texas team on national television to advance them all the way to the ESPY Awards Show.

Background to that glorious run were mottos that Charlie Bilton coined for the team, helping to keep them at the task and in pursuit of the dream:

"Why not us?" and "We have a dream and nobody is taking it away from us."

I can still hear those words leading the national charge of a bunch of kids from Saugus that much of America took to its heart. My son Jamie and I were glued to the TV, and my son Matt, at Penn State University earning his way toward an MBA, brought a dozen classmates to each Saugus game at Williamsport's Little League World Series. To a man they wanted Matt to leave when Saugus went behind in the Texas game, figuring it was all over. Still exhibiting his sense of "Charlie Ball," Matt said, "Not until the final out." To a man they were all glad they remained to see the great finish.

A Green Stick Fracture in 1944

The Afternoon of the Post-Season Night Game at Manning Bowl in Lynn

by
Don Junkins

Ray carried me home in his arms from Mag's field
and I remember the bare November maple
branches overhead, the way they shielded
the once perfect sky with gnarly lines of scrambled
zigzag forms. I was dead weight in the fall
of my eighth grade year when Pyszko and Kane gave the town
what Blanchard and Davis gave West Point nation
while the war rumbled on. The Peabody game was all
that mattered in my world, and those maple branches
above Ray's head were black in the waning afternoon.
Ray carried me past Sewall's house in my gloom.
We had collided on an end-around where the chances
of a broken bone in a football game as such
were nil; it was only a game of one hand touch.

Sports

Jim Merrill

by
John Burns

Jim Merrill (AKA Jim Foley), a half dozen years older than I, was an early hero of mine.

Living in the Sunnyside Park area, close to my Stone Street residence, his prowess in every sport he engaged in, despite being one-armed as a result of an accident, put him up on a pedestal for me and my friends. He is presently, to the best of my knowledge, living in Colorado, looking back on an active, successful life, marked by the same gusto and confidence he brought to the playing field way back when.

Growing Up in Saugus
Part 3

Finally, don't forget to throw in distractions and sub-plots. This makes an unconventional story, long on situations which have to be faced sooner or later, short on chains of consequence and changes of heart or attitude.

— Graham Nelson

A View of Saugus from the Hill

by
Don Junkins

Once Upon A Time there was a town, eight miles north of Boston, and all the people I knew lived there, and because I loved them I loved the town—its Lynnhurst woods beyond the dirt back road (Fairmount Avenue) where we played with toy guns, and fished for hornpout in summer or ran winter buckeys on "Wormy," Mr. Wormstead's cow pond; Cleveland Avenue where we jumped rope between Frederickson's and Sewall's houses, and played hopscotch in front of Hammerstrom's house on the sidewalk put in by the W.P.A. in the 1930s, then later, touch football in the street after school and ring-a-leavy-o after dark; Barn Hill where we ran with our sleds and leapt upon them running and tried to make it as far as Johansen's house on Sherman Avenue, and when we were older, steep Washington hill ("Washy") which crossed the Lynn line before Shebelli's and Laurenti's houses and leveled out beside Cricket Field ("Cricky"); and Maes's Field across from Adrien's house where we played touch and sometimes tackle football; and Maes's horseshoe court up from Al Rippon's house; and maple trees that turned color as the seasons passed—and the seasons passed, and I went away.

When I came back, as if in a twinkling, all was changed. The former fields were full of houses, neighbors had died or moved away. The old Saugus High School was gone. Harry Bamford's pool hall was gone. Central Street in front of the Iron Works was gone. The State Theater was gone. The railroad tracks where my brother rode the train off to war were gone. Benny Fullerton's funeral home was gone. Walter O'Grady's barber shop was gone. Someone else was living in dentist Dr. Roos's house.

With those who have luck, however, their home towns abide through the years, and time neither scars nor dulls the poignancy of first things. In my mind, everything is just the way it was in the 1930s and 1940s.

Saturdays in Saugus in the fall are smoldering piles of leaves along Cleveland Avenue. The white pea beans that soaked all night in the bean pot are still in the oven, now molasses brown, filling the kitchen with their aroma. In the afternoon, the old wooden football stands at Stackpole Field are full of people and hundreds of cars are parked all down Summer and Appleton streets. The radio broadcaster Curt Noyes calls Saugonians the Brooklyn fans of football. On the kickoff, Harrington laterals the ball to Shipulski and runs interference for him up the sideline. After the game, I'm sitting at the round kitchen table with my mother and father, now eating those beans with frankfurters my mother fries in a round black iron skillet with a teaspoon of bacon fat. (My older sister is in the W.A.A.C.s at Camp Devens; my older brother is working the 3-11 shift at the River Works in Lynn before being drafted.) We're listening to *Bessa May Mucho* on the radio, the Tin Pan Alley show. Then we're riding in our second hand 1938 Buick to Lynn and the Warner Theater to see *The Third Man* with Joseph Cotton. After the show my father stops in Olympia Square and buys a *Sunday Boston Advertiser*, and as we pass street lights on the way home, in the back seat I get glimpses of Maggie & Jiggs on the front page of the funnies. Up in the left corner there's a drawing of a smiling blonde curly-headed child with a long trumpet and banner that says, "What fools these mortals be. – Puck." I didn't know until much later about Puck and *Midsummer Night's Dream*.

I begin again this brief reminiscence with quotes from two former Saugus athletes who have written poignantly about Saugus: quarterback Tom Sheehan, who grew up on Central Street, and left wing Neil Howland, who grew up between the old high school and East Saugus. Neil, in his Saugus memoir refers to "Lovely Lynnhurst"; Tom has written of the town, "I love her, this old flame of mine... walk with me if you would..." What follows is what occurs to me in the summer of my 73rd year from the December day I was born in the upstairs front room at 82 Cleveland Avenue in Lynnhurst.

My earliest memory is the summer sunlight coming through the living room curtains of our home almost at the end of Cleveland Avenue when I was four, and I remember the overpowering smell when my mother opened the front door to greet Mr. Hicks the mailman (who had walked up from the West Lynn post office), from the piggery below Tom Mahan's farm on Fairmount Avenue. After the piggery burned down — I didn't find out who set that fire until I was in my sixties — and the fire engines roared from Sherman Avenue across Cleveland and down Fairmount, I was hesitant for months to cross the street alone.

Then I was in the first grade, and I remember Carl Nelson teaching me how to catch crawfish under the shallow rocks along the shore of Birch Brook Reservoir. Later, Buddy and Kent Frederickson and I swam the dog paddle in the reservoir (the "Rezzy") across from Miss Bridgham's house on Walnut Street (our grammar school principal) where the pines to this day are still deepest. Later still, we swam the overhand crawl with Eddie Fairchild and "Butch" Bishop down in the coves where the ledges are hidden from Walnut Street and the old pond cop.

Before World War II, the State Theater cost 10 cents, and on Saturday afternoons in the summer or when there was no football game at Stackpole Field, we'd walk down Fairmount toward Blue Ridge, take the path beside old man Brault's house and cut through the woods, past the silver and black iron sign of the Massachusetts Historical

Commission denoting the original site of a stockade, to the top of Elm Street and then across the Saugus River bridge to Central Street, past the Iron Works, to Saugus Center. My mother kept the yellow Coming Attractions card in the top kitchen drawer beside the sink, and there were always two feature movies, news, a Loony Tunes cartoon and a serial. The serials were great: Jackie Cooper in *Scouts to the Rescue*, *Terry and the Pirates*, *The Green Hornet*, *Captain Marvel*, and *The Shadow*. Some of the movies scared me to death, especially *The Return of Doctor X* with Humphrey Bogart, and *The Cat and the Canary* with Bob Hope and Paulette Goddard. The ending of *Hurricane*, when the reunited lovers run into each other's arms after the storm, was a heart shattering moment in the love life of this correspondent, remembered to this day. When World War II began, the price of a child's State Theater ticket included a war tax, which pushed the price up to eleven cents.

The routes from Lynnhurst to Saugus Center were several, and coming home after the show in the fall when it was dark, at the top of Elm Street, instead of cutting through the woods, we could take the first right, past scoutmaster Thompson's house, then a left, then through Urquhart's yard, then another left past Kenney's house, and after a right on Fairmount, all the way home. The other route home on warm sunny days was to cross the Saugus River in the low area in front of the Iron Works, through a settlement of houses, and over Vinegar Hill past the west entrance to the valley and the path that led to Barn Hill on Fairmount, a few hundred yards from our block on Cleveland. That particular route holds a painful memory for this young lover.

There are two variants of the regret story: I Wish I Could Have Kissed Her, and I Should Have Slugged Him. For me they came together in the same event: May Day, 1944, the afternoon of my first date. I had invited my seventh grade classmate from Miss Hyland's room, Marion Gray, to go on a bus ride to Lynn beach, and I had persuaded my mother to let me wear my Sunday long-pants suit, the wool scratchy suit that, remembering almost seventy years later, still gives me the shivers. It felt like horsehair raw against my thighs and knees, and all my life I haven't been able to figure out why I agreed to that suit in Raymond's store in Boston ("Where You Bot the Hat"), on the day my mother and I rode the Eastern MA bus to Haymarket Square and walked over to Washington Street. When I tried it on and felt the raw threads like steel wool, we agreed that I would wear a pair of cotton long johns when I wore the suit in church, but on this day I was worried that Marion might discover when I sat down on the bus that I was wearing long underwear on May Day.

So on this warm spring day I entered the woods above Barn Hill and walked the crow flight route from home over Vinegar Hill that would take me to the Appleton Street bus stop. I didn't want anyone in Lynnhurst to see me walking around in that Sunday suit.   The only problematic moment

occurred when I passed a boy about my age, chopping wood in the Vinegar Hill neighborhood, and he called, "Hey, Fancypants!" I pretended I didn't hear him and increased my pace, looking back once to see if he was following me, but there was no one there. This should have been my warning not to return by the same route.

When I got to the river below the Iron Works, I climbed the last hill, sweating, and turned right on Central Street, past Tom Sheehan's house, and waited for the bus across from Evie Rodgers' house (later my ninth grade English teacher) across from the corner of Appleton and Central streets, up Appleton and down Summer to Saugus Center at the drugstore where Marion got on the bus. My feelings for her were obviously of a strong nature, and my mother, though baffled about the whole enterprise, had agreed to this adventure. For me, a walk along the boardwalk beside Lynn Beach (it was probably Nahant, for we could look straight out to Egg Rock) seemed a sophisticated thing to do. (We didn't use words like "neat" or "cool" then.) The thing I remember most about that "date" was how cool Marion looked all day in her white blouse, and how miserably my legs scratched and chafed against the rough wool.

In Lynn, in front of the shoe shops at the foot of Market Street, we changed buses for the next leg of the ride to the beach. (Later in the summers of my senior year in high school and first year of college, I pulled lasts and edged wedgie soles for the David Shoe Company.) Walking next to Marion along the hot, sandy sidewalk up from the beach, drops of sweat ran down my raw legs inside my horsehair pants. Marion could see that I was warm and convinced me to take off my suit coat and loosen my tie. She herself had a thin gleam of perspiration over her upper lip, and the tiny gap between her front teeth and barely the tinge of a lisp when she talked were quite special to me.

On the way home from the beach, the windows of the bus were open because of the heat, and Marion became a little nauseated from the incoming exhaust fumes. When we arrived at the Lynn line and crossed over the river into East Saugus and could smell the marsh and the ocean breeze, she seemed to recover. Marion got off the bus in Saugus Center and waved goodbye, and I continued to the Appleton Street stop, walked back up Central to the dirt road leading down to the Saugus River and up through the neighborhood at the foot of Vinegar Hill. I almost made it to the woods without attracting any attention. Suddenly the boy who had yelled "Hey, Fancypants!" was up ahead and I had to get by him. Within seconds another boy on a bicycle joined him, both blocking my way.

Here, adult regret supersedes all pacifist justifications and philosophies, and one who shies from his Vinegar Hill moment, wherever the geography or the instant in time, is stuck with it forever. Another boy appeared and suddenly I felt my hand burn and looked down and saw my burning cigarette. I weaseled and evaded, and meekly accepted the menacing threats not to come sashaying again through their neighborhood in my fancy clothes. I climbed Vinegar Hill, the sweet memory of Marion Gray and our walk by the ocean now gone with the salt breezes, and passed by my own valley through the woods and down Barn Hill, trudged head down up my driveway, and into my house. On the stoop landing before I climbed the four steps into the kitchen, I took off the horsehair pants, one month before D-Day and the Allied invasion of Normandy.

The seventh grade dandy in me had won out over the Lynnhurst flash. I brooded over the advertisements in the *Saturday Evening Post* that showed troublemakers at the beach kicking sand on your girlfriend's blanket, and sent away for Charles Atlas booklets that cost 25¢: *How To Put Inches on Your Chest Measurement*; *How To Develop Your Forearm Strength*, and sent away again for a ball to squeeze and toughen my hands. Up the street Ray Maes had a set of barbells, and soon afterward I started lifting them. Still later, I took boxing lessons from my neighbor in Lynnhurst, Red Hudland, who was an amateur fighter. He had told me the story of a couple of toughs in Lynn who shoved past his wife Ruthie and knocked her backwards in Olympia Square, and Red dispatched them with two quick jabs and two body punches and two right crosses. Such are the ways of boys who dream of beautiful girls, and who in dressing the part become distracted.

Selected Memories of the Thirties and Forties

- In 1937 I remember listening to the coronation of King George VI of England in Miss Bridgham's second story fifth and sixth grade room in the Lynnhurst School. She brought up Miss Reynolds with our first and second grade pupils, and Miss Wells with the third and fourth graders, and we stood along the back of the room and then down the aisle next to the garden beside Maeses' house, all her hanging plants before the windows, and we listened to the static and the somber radio broadcast from Westminster Abbey.

- I remember getting up before my parents on a spring Saturday morning in 1937 and flying my kite from the first big rock beyond Ahl's house, a couple hundred yards beyond the Lynn line:

- I remember sitting next to my older sister, Betty, during the 1939 post-season football game with Salem, and couldn't understand why Saugus lined up for the extra point without scoring a touchdown, then saw Johnnie Bucchiere kick a field goal wearing sneakers to win the game. Coach Buzz Harvey had ordered sneakers for his Saugus players for the second half so they could get better traction on the frozen field.

- I remember the September 1938 hurricane when in the late afternoon Mr. Frederickson was almost blown over coming out of his cellar door to his lawn next to the vacant lot from our house on Cleveland Avenue. My father and I were standing with Arthur Blood next to his house watching a U.S. Navy weather dirigible pass overhead, ropes dangling.

- I remember the Sunday School demonstration in the Dorr Memorial Methodist Church in Lynnhurst on the day after the Thanksgiving Day football game in 1940. On the previous Friday night some of the players had gone to the Old Howard striptease show in Scollay Square in Boston, and it was rumored that they had a few drinks that led to a less than topnotch Saturday afternoon performance. Sunday School Superintendent Andy Boynton poured some whiskey from a pint bottle into a frying pan, then broke an egg into it, turning the egg white, demonstrating how whiskey cooked the egg: a drama most mysterious and impressive.

- I remember riding through Marblehead in the car after the Saugus-Marblehead football game in 1940, and my older sister, Betty, calling out the open window to a group of Marblehead supporters, "Where was Soapy Waters?" and one of them calling back, "In the soup." A sports page headline the next day in the Boston Post read, "Harrington 14 – Marblehead 0." That was one of the golden years of Iron Mike Harrington and Ship-wreck Eddie Shipulski.

- In 1944, I remember watching in the Assembly Hall of the old Saugus High School the inauguration of Harry Truman after Franklin Roosevelt died in Warm Springs, Georgia. Principal John Pearce had ordered a black and white television set on the stage, and Harry Truman said, "The weight of the moon has fallen on my shoulders."

- I remember the Curt Noyes six o'clock radio show after the Monday football game in 1944 when Saugus beat undefeated Melrose 13-0, during which Curt played a Sousa march in honor of the Saugus team. And I remember the football assembly in the old Saugus High School in 1947 when the team presented Curt with a Saugus football letter.

- The highlight of my school day in 1944, when I was in junior high school, was watching Frank Pyzsko sitting on the top steps on the side of the high school assembly hall, eating his lunch. That was, in the praiseworthy language of the day, "the nuts."

- I remember my first year on the junior varsity in 1947 when Mike Harrington was my football coach. I played left halfback behind Sardi Nicolo, and when Sardi was called up to scrimmage against the varsity, Mike would call "Inside Tackle Power." We still ran the single wing offense then and it was the left halfback's call, and every time Mike called the play in the huddle I would take the direct snap from center and fumble as I hit the line. Mike would say, "Come on, Junk, hold onto the ball," and call the play again and again, until I held onto the ball.

- I remember setting pins in the Rat Hole (Bamford's Pool Hall) for five cents a string in 1948, until my mother called Eddy Smiledge on the telephone and blackballed me from descending the stairs into that friendly and comfortable place.

- Until I left in the fall of 1949 to play football at the University of Massachusetts in Amherst, these are the boys from Lynnhurst who played on the Saugus High School football team: Johnie Bucchiere, Duck Dean, Buddy Frederickson, Lee MacWilliams, Ray Maes, Al Mason, and Ranny St. Pierre.

Seven Poplars Along This Road

and a path to the high boulder
for king of the rock
or flying a kite. It is six-thirty on a Saturday morning
in October and I am eight. Up here
I can see the Atlantic on the horizon like a blue knife.
My kite is a red badge with a tail of fleece—
it glides and rattles like the Salvation Army;
my string smells of tar and brine; it is my father's
deep sea drop line. And my face is all sky
and all air.

Fly kite while you can.
Our house is still asleep.
Fly across Sunday while the leaves
burn. Flee the hurricane
and the bees in the cherry tree
and Jane the skinny. Fly kite,
fly through the wet beard
and come to my hand.

When I Was Twelve

I caught alewives
with my hands
in the concrete troughs
easing Lily Pond down

to the Saugus River,
and spread them
on the grass like knives
glistening in the sun

glistening in the kitchen light
on Saturday night
spread headless on the Lynn Item
bones and soft flesh

in the photograph,
knuckles on the trough slime
finger touch, the brush
of tail, the rush

of shadows gone.

Playing Glassies with Dickie Mallar

Alone in the garage, I work my hand
through the floppy top cloth of my marble
bag and squeeze whole hands full of little glass
balls, dribbling them on the pile
in the metallic dark. I know the crystal balls
by heart, swirls of cream and raspberries,
here a wine red, here a buttercup yellow streaked
with devil's grass. May: the marble season. I

carry the sugar bag around
the neighborhood after school, plopping
it in back yards, calling for takers. We
gouge holes with our heels in lawns,
scoop fists full of dirt with our hands,
pat the edges of our holes with our fingertips. Closest to the hold shoots first. Tucking
my thumb against my curved forefinger
I nub the sweet rolling glassies
into the hole, every one. I never lose. I
am Midas Junkins the glassy king. One

day, Dickie Mallar walks up from Blue
Ridge Rqad and stands in the street outside
my house: "You got any
glassies?"

"Sure."

"You want to play?"

He digs ten giant purees
out of his pocket: he'll roll against everything

in my bag. One by one he fingers them
in the late afternoon sun: blue bachelor-
buttons, orange poppies, copper green lily
pads—the colors are so rich my belly
churns with a lover's passion. Mallar
keeps throwing them: candle wax

black, burnt pumpkin belly
black, the black eyes of the new girl

on her back in the field staring
sideways—Mallar rolls them all

and loses every one.

When it is over, his risky
debonair ways puzzle me. "What's
a glassy?" he asks and walks
home in the dusk. I feel cheated. I
have everything in the bag.

I stash
my glassies in the garage. Behind
closed doors I finger them
in the dark.

Sliding on Barn Hill in the Dark of the Storm

We bite the ice balls off our mittens with our teeth,
run head starts and belly-bump our Flexible Flyers
down past suppertime. The snow turns to sleet, Keith
Berry cries "It's getting slipperier and slipperier!"
and races Rusty Hultzman to the McGann's front
steps. One more run, just one. Rusty is game:
sweaty, played out, on a dare he touches the blunt
of his tongue to his sled runner, a piece of skin comes
off but he's happy. "This is the nuts," he says
over and over, and soon, "I gotta go home." One
by one the ice-crusted players drift off in the dead
of the storm. I'm alone with Agnes McGann. "Fun,"
she says and breasts her sled before me down the hill,
and up and down again before I tackle her—
"Let me go," and I do, and run with my sled until
my ice-clogged overshoes drag me down. A blur
of icy wool shoves in my face, then against my naked throat
a winter wooly crab, ice pinching—I grasp
my frozen claws around her; "Let me go," our lobster coats
buckling: shedders in December, out of season in the rasp
of winter. I will not let her go as the sleet turns to hail
on little Barn Hill eight miles north of Boston in 1945.
Agnes,
I kiss you still, the ice pelts our foreheads blue snails,
waves of small round snails bouncing and rolling, alive
on the glassy crust, pelting our short quick kiss, our light
kiss, our melting icy kiss, and then I let you go—
and then I let you go. Down we crunch toward the bright
lights in the houses below and say "So long," "So
long," in the dark. I drag my sled past the high street
lamp at Sherman and Cleveland as the hail turns into sleet.

Running the Buckey on Wormstead's Pond

In the hollow below Wilfred South's house
we show up for hockey at "Wormy,"

the cow pond. The November ice is black
thin, no one dares skate,

then Buddy Frederickson starts across
edging and slipping, laughing that no
one else dare do it. Ralphie Romano
takes a head start from the low bank grass

on the cow road and runs past Buddy, white
cracks streaking tiny lightning in the dark
glass. I watch them form the line, light-
headed, holding my dog Pickles, barking,

I have ideas of my own: no black ice.
Wormy is my summer pond: I stocked
the hornpouts at the cold dark
bottom, spring handouts Paul Baldwin netted in Sluice

Pond for pickerel bait, slipped to me
when they outgrew his glass tank. (I
can see the five foot blacksnake writhing
on the surface, over and over: Charlie

Blood keeps flipping it back with a clothes pole
until it sinks.) "Let's go Ranny!" "Come on
Ray!" Arm in arm they stomp the coal
black ice over Wormy, whoop under the morning sun

and start back: four buckeyes before Charlie
Maes's foot goes through and they have
enough and stomp up Fairmount so Charlie
can change his shoes. The ice is still wavy. I

stare at the hole where Charlie's foot went through:
a pool is spreading on top of the crackle glaze,
the once black mirror that held like glue.
Am I safe on shore?—I see the white ice

turning dark again—can I get to the bottom
of it? I sit beside the golden tall November grass
watching after their young autumn ways
with my old summer eyes.

Childhood, the Glass Crystal

My yellow school, my yellow
childhood, my birches in the playground
my sea green swings, my stone
running place:

            Miss Bridgham
claps her hands on the school balcony
porch: recess over. The girls play
the field along Cleveland Avenue,
the boys play along Fairmount. No one
may enter the birch grove. Near

the swings, Dickie Mallar shows
me his glass crystal, fast, before we go
in, holds it above my wrist, holds
my wrist tight with his hand: Keep looking,
you'll be surprised,

                        the sun burns my skin. I
pull my hand, shake it, tears
in my eyes, You goddam
Mallar (laughing,
putting the crystal back in his pocket)
Miss Bridgham clapping, Come
girls, come boys. Years

later, walking home from the senior
play with senior Evelyn Kenney, my first
ninth grade high school date, we meet Mallar
at Elm and Blueridge. At the end
of Sterling he is in the middle, cocksure,

putting an arm around, saying something
in her ear: Evelyn
pulls away not tonight. At the beginning
of Fairmount goodnight boys she walks
the rest of the way alone.

             The next day
at band practice, Esther Gibbs tries
the baritone solo until Mr. St. Germaine tells
Mallar to play it. Dickie can really play
the baritone. He never missed a note.

Farming & Horticulture

Burn down your cities and leave our farms, and your cities will spring up again as if by magic; but destroy our farms and the grass will grow in the streets of every city in the country.

— William Jennings Bryan

Berthold Farm

by
Janice Jarosz

Saugus was once rich with farms and the upper Main Street/Oaklandvale section of town played host to many of them including the Berthold farm, one of the largest in the area and one of the last to go.

Konrad Berthold came to this country from Germany as a very young man. Born in 1866 and orphaned at an early age, he apprenticed as a cabinetmaker. When he had earned enough money, he and his only brother booked passage on a ship bound for America.

A fellow passenger advised him to head for Lawrence as there were many Germans there and work was plentiful. Konrad took the stranger's advice but his brother chose to head out West and the brothers never saw one another again.

Konrad was immediately hired to make spindle spools for knitting machines and time passed but he was lonesome. He had left his sweetheart, Celia Stahl, back home but as soon as enough funds were available he sent for her. Shortly after her arrival she gained employment as a chambermaid at a rooming house in Malden.

They were married in Wakefield in 1890. A daughter, Louise, was born to them in 1896. Frank decided that it was time for the family to have a permanent home and was able to find property in Saugus. A second child, Frank, was born and down through the years several other parcels of land were purchased and by 1914 the Berthold farm contained 25 acres, just enough to start a dairy farm.

Frank Berthold.

Konrad and Celia proudly became citizens as soon as they were able to and both became active in local affairs. Konrad served as a town meeting member for many years and as soon as his son Frank was able to walk, his father brought him to all the local meetings.

His dairy and produce business thrived. A vegetable stand was established in the front yard and daily specials were noted and tacked up on trees. Travelers along Main Street could purchase some of the freshest vegetables in Saugus and by bringing their own brown bags, were able to get a discount too. Eventually he decided to start up a lumber business on the same site. Customers could now drive up to the homestead, visit with Konrad, and purchase some 2x4s, milk, and fresh carrots at the same time.

As the businesses grew, more and more local men were hired to help in the fields. Young boys from state homes were transported to Saugus to help with the weeding. One young boy named Lester became a favorite and was eventually adopted by the family.

The dairy business was a demanding and precarious business. Rumors had started stating that raw milk was causing sickness and that the farmers in the Main/Howard Streets were not delivering fresh milk. Hearings were scheduled and the threat of a new regulation called "pasteurization" was being considered.

On August 3, 1928, Konrad Berthold appeared before the Malden Board of Health defending the use of raw milk. During his testimony he stated quite eloquently that, "raw milk was merely fresh, sweet milk, properly cooled and delivered to the customer within a few hours after it had been produced." He went on to state: "Pasteurized milk was milk that may be five or six days old before delivery!"

Mr. Berthold also claimed that it was a matter of record that the strongest and healthiest persons have thrived on raw milk and he defied the Malden inspector to show a single case of disease that was caused by the Berthold Farm milk.

Mr. Berthold succeeded only in prolonging the inevitable for a short while and by the 1930s most small dairies were put out of business because of not having the money to incorporate the new regulation. The argument prevails to this day as to the benefits of pasteurization.

During his entire lifetime Konrad Berthold never feared speaking out on issues and when agitated enough would quickly trade the pitchfork for a pen, and write scathing letters to the *Saugus Herald*.

In chastising the Planning Board on March 3, 1939, he wrote: "Let's hear what the Planning Board has done beside milking applicants by rezoning their property. I claim we do not need a Planning Board – at least not a one-sided, autocratic one as we have now. Next to a Lynn newspaper, I know of nothing else that has hurt the growth of Saugus as much as the Planning Board. The town could do without both of them!"

Konrad passed away on July 30, 1941, at 75 years of age. In his will drawn on November 7, 1931, he left his entire estate, home property, eight shares of the Saugus Bank and Trust Company, various other bank accounts, one bull and 18 cows to his wife, Celia.

Son Frank K. followed in his father's footsteps and carried on with the farm and lumber business in the same manner as his father. Konrad's daughter, Louise, moved to Connecticut, became a school teacher, married, and died at the age of 98.

Frank married Anna Roland of 6 Waverly Street, Melrose, in 1921, and brought her home to the farm. Four children were born to them: Carl, Bud (Frank David), a daughter who died shortly after birth, and Conrad. Bud died at the age of 48 and the K was changed to C in Conrad because as the family explained it, "It was 1941."

The exposure to politics at an early age drew Frank into the public spotlight just like his father before him. He served as a town meeting member for over 30 years and in 1959 was sworn in as a selectman, a position he held for ten years.

Known as the *no-nonsense* selectman, Mr. Berthold would always toss a little humor in to spice up the tedious board meetings. Colleagues valued his friendship and respected his integrity. His youngest son Conrad witnessed many a favor seeker coming to the house bearing gifts only to be turned away by his father.

It was written that Frank was "built like a bull, could lift large timbers, toss heavy bales of hay and work an eighteen hour day for most of his life."

Unfortunately, he expected the same kind of performance from all of his employees. A young worker approached him one afternoon complaining to him that he was cold. Frank replied, "Well if you can't work hard enough to keep warm you might as well go home."

In later years Frank was plagued with poor eyesight and two young out-of-town workers thought they could outfox the *old man*. After a day's weeding they stood in line to collect their pay. There were two rows of workers and they were first in both lines. Once paid they ran to the back of line hoping to collect again. Frank handed them another salary envelope and said "Boys, take your money but don't bother coming back again."

In an interview in 1977, Mr. Berthold complained of the "relentless incursions on farmland which residential subdivisions have subjected upon the town's land." He stubbornly held off sale of his property for such projects.

In 1979 his beloved wife Anna passed away and the loss was too much for him to bear. Within ten days of her passing, on January 14, 1979, he asked to be taken to the hospital where he died just moments after being admitted.

The late William Robinson, Town Clerk, stated in Frank's obituary the following: "Frank was one of the most respected and beloved political figures in the town's history

and he never had a bad word for anyone. He was the salt of the earth and everyone loved him."

The Berthold farm is no longer there, as a subdivision has taken its place. But if you look very closely at some of the old trees that were left and if you are so inclined, you still might see Frank out tending his crops, measuring up some lumber, or sitting on the porch with his beloved Anna.

William Sim

(1869-1940)

by
Roy Sim

William Sim, who was my father, was born June 18, 1869, in Fyvie, Scotland. This was during the Victorian Era and at the time of my father's advent into the world, Queen Victoria had passed the halfway mark of her long reign. This is mentioned because the customs of her times were now firmly established and they were influential in molding the early years of my father's life.

William Sim.

In keeping with those years, the families were large and the houses were small. Therefore, it was necessary as the younger ones came along for the older ones to make room for them by leaving. At the age of eleven my father was sent out to learn the trade of a gardener by serving an apprenticeship which would take seven years.

His father, Thomas Sim, was a photographer by profession but he was very fond of flowers and of gardening. This may account for my father's fondness of his trade, and for his being so partial to photographers. The learning of the trade of a gardener was indeed very thorough and covered about all aspects associated with the cultivation of the soil. During the course of learning his trade, my father was taught how to farm and to care for farm animals. His training included the growing of fruits and vegetables as well as grains, the main one being oats, which was a staple part of their diet in Scotland. Then came the outside work such as the growing of trees, shrubs, lawns, flowers, etc. After that came greenhouse culture. In my father's case, most of this was learned on the estate of a Scottish brewer.

My father had his trade learned when he was eighteen years old and, like many others, he came to America, then as now, the land of opportunity. His first job was on the Hornblower Estate in Arlington, Massachusetts, where he was employed as a gardener. It was during the second administration of President Grover Cleveland that my father became a citizen of the United States.

Sim Carnation Farm.

From Arlington, my father went to Nahant, Massachusetts, where he worked for Thomas Roland. It was while here that he met my mother. In 1896, my father and mother were married. For $12.50 a month, he hired a house and some greenhouses in the Cliftondale section of Saugus and went into business for himself. The first plants grown in this new venture were ivy. For this reason, I selected the ivy leaf design for both of my parents' grave memorials.

A Sim Farm truck.

In 1898, my father purchased some property on Morton Avenue, also in Saugus. It consisted of a new house and a large tract of land. The previously rented greenhouses were bought, dismantled and then assembled on the Morton Avenue property, forming the nucleus of his range. My father prospered from the outset and by 1906 he had eight greenhouses, which had a glass area of about 75,000 square feet. His specialties were violets, chrysanthemums, sweet peas, and tomatoes. The quality of these crops was superb. The sweet peas that he grew have in all probability never been equaled. Some had stems three feet long and won many prizes. As time went on, he added to his range and also grew primroses, cucumbers and had a house of roses. World War I changed everything, as wars do. The flowers that had been popular before the conflict involved the United States were not so popular when the post war era came. The growing of vegetables in greenhouses was also not profitable now. Times had changed and my father had to change with them, which he did.

For his new venture into these new times, he chose carnations. The rich soil, which had produced such bountiful crops in the past, was just what the new carnation liked. Some of them grew over six feet tall the first year, the foliage being that beautiful, lush, blue-green color. In his carnation hybridizing work, I would say that my father originated a thousand or more new carnations of consequence and, of this number one hundred or fewer were disseminated.

Most of my father's carnations did very well in Europe. His friend, Mr. Carl Engelmann, the English grower, used to keep my father informed as to how his carnations were doing abroad. I remember once his telling my father that his carnation, "Arctic," was still being grown in window boxes on the continent. Mr. Engelmann also told my father that his carnation, "My Love," was very popular in England and that Queen Mary, then the Queen Mother, admired this variety greatly at one of the English flower shows.

Sim Farm employees.

Before World War II, we enclosed a few cuttings of one of his new carnations named "Coronet," in an order destined for Sweden. This was a striking red, white and yellow flaked variety. After the war, I learned from a visiting Swedish grower that a carnation answering the identical description of "Coronet," was a sensation in that country. When Mr. Nehrling of the Massachusetts Horticultural Society needed a new carnation to honor some society matron, or debutant, or actress, he invariably put in a hurry up call to my father who never failed him. He not only produced the new carnation, but he was there for the presentation and to have his picture taken with the recipient. My father enjoyed these affairs and always made a fine appearance. My father passed away on Thanksgiving Day, November 28, 1940, in North Berwick, Maine, where he had lived the last four years of his life. He requested that his final resting place be Puritan Lawn Memorial Park in West Peabody, Massachusetts. And that is where he is among the green lawns, flowers, shrubs and trees which were so much a part of his life.

Metcalf's Farm

by
Janice K. Jarosz

Florence Metcalf, who was born during the late Thirties and raised in Saugus, still carries with her a lesson her father taught her at the very young age of five.

One day Mr. Metcalf took her out into the family field and, together, they walked the entire length of the property. Mr. Metcalf explained to his daughter that the stone walls surrounding his property represented the limits of his acreage and the beginnings of another. He told her that by crossing over the stone wall she would be "away from home" and if she stayed on her side of the property, she "would be home." He told her that property rights were to be respected and one was never to cross to another's land without permission.

Up until the late Fifties, the western part of Saugus was home to many farms. The Berthold, Spencer, Penney, Howard and Metcalf families made their living and supported their families mainly from farming and dairying.

Florence Metcalf's grandfather, George, who was originally from Vermont, came down by rail around the turn of the 19th century, to meet his employers, the Putnam family, who would take him, by horse and buggy, to work in the family business.

It wasn't long before Mr. and Mrs. Metcalf and their family grew tired of the commute and eventually decided to make Saugus their home. They purchased a parcel of land containing approximately 48 acres on Howard Street from the same Putnam family. George Metcalf built the main portion of the house first and then another section was moved in from another area and was attached to the new building. The finished dwelling was placed a few feet from the dirt road of Howard Street.

A Metcalf Farm advertisement.

Curtis, the second generation Metcalf, son of George, was born and raised in the Howard Street homestead. He stayed on the farm and followed in the family tradition by bringing his new wife, Addie, to the family homestead to live and raise their family.

Three children were born to them, Oscar, Florence, and Ernest Metcalf, who stayed on the farm and continued with the family business of operating a family-owned farm.

The farmhouse was situated to the right of what now is called Juniper Drive and behind the house, to the left, was a large wooden barn. The Metcalfs were gifted farmers and the gentle topography of the land was lush with rich soil. It wasn't long before Metcalf Farm produced some of the best vegetables in the area.

I remember seeing the entire front portion of the field covered with corn stalks during late summer seasons, just like a picture out of the movie, *Field of Dreams*. Mr. Metcalf would dare anyone to find a stray weed or a dry ear of corn in his prized fields. Tomatoes, squash, rhubarb, strawberries, cukes, parsnips, and potatoes were planted each season for family consumption first. The remainder of the harvest was sold for profit.

The Metcalf's vegetable stand was located right on the lawn, in front of the barn, and close to the street. Customers could ring the bell that was left at the stand for the convenience of the customers, holler, toot their horn and either Addie or Florence would run out in their housedresses and white aprons and wait on them. Freshly picked vegetables and other sundries were displayed on the wooden stand with a weighing scale, brown bags and a sharp pencil ready for business and bartering.

Henry J. Penney's farm, (my grandfather's) abutted the Metcalf Farm on Howard Street. The property was divided by fieldstone walls, which staked out the division of the land by owner. My grandfather told me years ago, that as long as he could remember, "old man Metcalf," who must have been George, would leave a tumbler by his well, which was in his front yard, so that thirsty travelers along Howard Street could stop and help themselves to a drink of cold well water.

Early one morning in 1972, a fire broke out in the barn and, within minutes, spread to the main house. There were no injuries, but the entire Metcalf home was burned to the ground, taking with it all the family possessions, furnishings, and worst of all, the family photos.

The reason my grandparents rented from the Metcalfs after their marriage, instead of moving in with either family, is a story in itself. My grandparents, Henry and Anna (Ebert) Penney, were married in the early winter (all farmers married in the wintertime) of 1904. Unfortunately, the news of the marriage was not well received as she was German Catholic and he English Baptist. Needing a place to live, the bride and groom set up housekeeping in the Metcalf home, renting two rooms in the second floor with kitchen privileges for $9.00 a month.

Eventually, both families accepted the union and the young family built their own home at 125 Howard Street, just down the street from the Metcalf family. The families, once good friends, now became good neighbors as well.

Saugus Farm Photographs

Largely from the Norm Down Collection

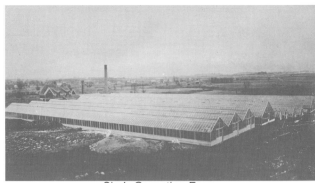
Sim's Carnation Farm.

Byron Hone Farm off Water Street in North Saugus; note the barn in the background – it was said to be the largest in the area at the time.

Stocker-Rutten Farm.

Hawkes' Farm in North Saugus.

Howlett's Farm in North Saugus.

Holmes Farm (on the Main Street side of Highland Avenue.)

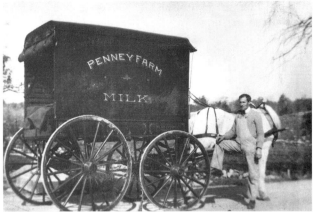

Henry Justin Penney and his milk wagon.

Fiske's Dairy Farm (on School Street).

Gordon's Pansy Farm (between Vine Street and Route One.)

Franklin Bennett Farm in Oaklandvale.

Civil Servants

As the happiness of the people is the sole end of government, so the consent of the people is the only foundation of it.

— John Adams

Albert Cornelius Day & Stanley Warren Day

A Father and Son's Civic Dedication to Saugus

by
Stephen L. Day

Albert was of the seventh generation descended from Anthony Day of Gloucester, who emigrated to America from England in 1635 aboard the Paule of London. Awareness of these early colonial ties instilled in both Albert and his son, Stanley, the sense of civic duty prevalent among their forefathers. Another genetic predisposition common to both men was an incredible mechanical aptitude which would tend to shape their public contributions to Saugus.

Al was born March 16, 1867, at Woburn to Thomas Day, a blacksmith and the son of a blacksmith, and Clara Melissa (Smith) Day. He was the twelfth of fifteen children born to Thomas, and was named, as was common in those days, after an older sibling who had died shortly after birth. In 1886 Albert married Margetta Dorherty by whom he was to father eight children.

Al Day.

Albert was quite an entrepreneur and inventor. Over his life he designed and built a plant for reducing bones to bone meal, manufactured covered wood heels for the Lynn shoe industry, was involved in a coal mining enterprise, drilled for oil in Wyoming and Texas, designed a "flying piston" for a two-cycle engine developed by the Giles Motor Company, built a power generating plant which ran on peat, dabbled in real estate, owned a jewelry, a piano, and a paper goods store. Unfortunately, Al was much better at starting businesses than making them profitable.

Around 1896, Al and family moved from Woburn to Saugus, eventually settling at 17 Emory Street. It was here that Stanley, the youngest of the eight children, was born on February 22, 1904, amidst a snow storm. Stanley's mind was even more acute than that of his father. From his earliest years he was rather a prodigy in things electrical. At age ten he built a spark gap radio telegraph in the attic of his father's home. He burned a hole through a pane in the attic window using acid, through which he strung an antenna wire. His broadcast was received in Key West, Florida. The Day family Christmas tree was the first to feature electric lights strung together by the boy genius. He built a working steam engine from pieces of scrap and smoked glass so that he and the other children on Emory Street could observe a solar eclipse. At age fourteen Stanley built a two-bay garage complete with sliding doors, a concrete floor, and a hip roof - all by himself. This garage is still standing after 85 years. It was from this garage that Stanley began a "Starting, Lighting, and Ignition" business for automobiles in 1918. This business would later be moved to 277 Lincoln Avenue in Cliftondale, next to the Post Office, and eventually to 9 Vine Street where it would be called A.C. Day & Sons. Like the garage, this shop is still standing.

Albert and Margetta Day.

What would be by today's medical standards a minor incident, in 1909, changed the course of Stan's life. It started when a child shoved a piece of paper in his ear and an elderly Civil War doctor was called upon to remove it. Using a rusty tweezers held in trembling hands he ruptured Stanley's eardrum, thus beginning a long series of ear infections which would, in adulthood, nearly cost Stan his life, and would terminate with mastoid surgery. There were no antibiotics in those days and the only relief came when Al would sit by his son's bed blowing hot tobacco smoke into his ear until the abscess broke. The lassitude caused by chronic ear pain was misinterpreted as a discipline problem by Stan's ninth grade teacher, causing him to quit school in 1918.

By age sixteen he was the chief trouble-man at Lynn Gas and Electric Company, which at that time generated power using reciprocating steam engines and 72 pole alternators. As part of his duties for LG&E he frequently visited the General Electric Company in Lynn. It was there that he was befriended by Charles Proteus Steinmetz. Steinmetz, a world renowned scientist known for his mathematical analysis of alternating current circuits, saw in young Stanley a thirst for knowledge and took the time to encourage that spark of genius. Nor was Steinmetz the only man of scientific renown Stan had the pleasure to meet. His interest in early radio gave him opportunity to meet Thomas Alva Edison. And, through his brother-in-law, a reporter for the Boston Post, he was invited to attend an interview with Albert Einstein.

Stanley and Anna Day on their wedding day.

On October 26, 1938, Stan went to the Tax Assessor's office to complain about an excise tax bill. The clerk listening to his complaint, Anna A. Swanson, would, in 1941, become his wife. Both Stan and Anna (better known by her middle name, Arvida) were Town Meeting members, Stan from

precinct 1, and Arvida from precinct 5. Stan would remain a Town Meeting member for some twenty-five years.

In 1946 both Albert and Stan served on the Water Committee. Albert, age seventy-nine, was the chairman of that committee. Both were convinced that Saugus' future interests would best be served by connecting to the Metropolitan District Commission's water system. It was largely due to their advocacy that Saugus enjoys the clean, abundant water supply it does. Their mutual zeal in this pursuit at times manifested itself in confrontations at Town Meetings. On May 26th Stan invited one of the Selectmen "outside" over differences around hooking up to the MDC. Albert too was well known for waving his cane in a threatening manner at his political antagonists.

Stan Day.

In 1940 Stan went to work for General Electric Company in their welding laboratory. Here he pioneered the spot welding of dissimilar metals, and won GE's coveted Coffin Award in Engineering for his work on thyratron controls, which contributed to the development of a more accurate bomber sight for the U.S. Army Air Force during WWII. Later in his career Stan would become a Registered Professional Engineer in the State of Massachusetts.

From 1952 to 1954 Albert served as a member of the Planning Board. In 1954, the year the new Saugus High School was being constructed and Hurricane Carol wreaked havoc in Saugus, the planning board recommended the passage of Article 6 which rezoned the old town farm on the west side of the Newburyport Turnpike, opposite the new high school, for light industry and commercial use. It was this action that opened the way for construction of Sears Shopping Center. At that time Albert, age 88, enjoyed the distinction of being the oldest living elected town meeting member in Massachusetts.

1954 was also special for its celebration of Saugus' 325th anniversary with its dedication of the Saugus Iron Works that summer. The cover of the town's 1954 annual report displays a photograph of Al Day as "Mr. Saugus" clothed in colonial garb with a three-cornered hat, flanked by steel executives from around the U.S. and by Christian Herter, the then governor of Massachusetts. [A photograph of Al Day as "Mr. Saugus" appears on page 23.] Four years later, in January 1958, Al passed away only two months short of his 91st birthday. One obituary concluded, "Al was an individualist, with the courage to express his deeply held convictions; he was considered an expert on the water problems of both Lynn and Saugus and was frequently called to give expert testimony in court cases. Saugus has lost a loyal, useful and devoted citizen in his death."

Stanley's service to Saugus would continue into the 1980s. In 1957 he was hired by the town to look into shoddy contractor wiring of the new high school. In 1963, in line with his empathy for the working man, he vociferously supported and voted for a 5% raise for town employees. In 1967 the town manager, John O. Stinson, came under heavy criticism by the Board of Selectmen. On March 7, 1967, amidst a political firestorm, Stan was appointed temporary town manager in Stinson's place.

Stanley's stint as town manager lasted about six months. But during that time he did battle with the power company over rates charged the town for street lighting and went to bat for the residents of East Saugus over health and environmental issues caused by DiMatteo's dump and incinerator. The dump was 28 feet above the grade level authorized at its founding. Stan led a battle against an array of opponents including sixteen surrounding cities who used that dump, the rubbish haulers, and the dump's owner. In the heat of battle he received threats of violence against himself as well as attempts at bribery. Nonetheless Stan held his ground, issued the order to DiMattio to "Cleanup or shutdown," and then joined Saugus residents in picketing the entrance to the dump. The dump issue wouldn't be resolved under his tenure, but the die was cast which would eventually bring relief to East Saugus.

In the ensuing years between 1968 and 1983 Stan worked to maintain the aging sewer pumping system. Many times he actually had to manufacture parts in his own cellar to repair obsolete equipment still critical to the proper operation of the pumping station. On June 23rd, 1983, at the tender age of 79, Stan took over as head of the Saugus DPW. He would hold this post through October of 1984. Like his father before him he was hailed as the oldest town official in Massachusetts.

In recognition of Stan Day's long service, on October 28, 1987, the Town of Saugus named its new East Saugus pumping station after him. And, on September 15th, 1989, Stan was honored by receiving the first ever "Annual Founder's Day Citizen's Award."

On February 22, 2004, Stan celebrated his 100th birthday at Longwood Place in Reading, where he and Anna resided. It was well attended by friends, family and present and former Saugus town officials. He received citations from President Bush, Governor Romney, both the Massachusetts House and Senate, and the Saugus Board of Selectmen. It proved to be his last tribute. On March 29th, 2004, with his grandson, Stephen and his granddaughter, Jessica, holding his hands and praying for him, Stanley breathed his last breath. He

was laid to rest with his father, grandfather and great-grandfather at Wildwood Cemetery, Wilmington.

On July 11, 2004, Stanley's faithful wife, Anna, passed on into eternity. Like Stan, two granddaughters, Heather and Elise, were at her bedside when she bade this world adieu. She was buried beside her husband of 63 years, there to await the Archangel's trumpet.

Frank B. Sloan

by
Russell Blood

Frank Sloan was born at Stanstead, Quebec, in 1873. He became a naturalized citizen later and graduated high school from Derby Academy in Derby Line, Vermont.

Friend Connie Putnam doesn't know when he came to Massachusetts but when he did he worked for a railroad (which one unknown) in Boston before coming to Saugus.

He had a real estate and insurance business in Cliftondale Square in the block where Hanson Chevrolet, Louie Gordon-Tailor, and Mr. Provenzano's Barbershop were located. He also had a gas pump outside where he sold and pumped gasoline. Later he moved to what we knew as the Solomita Building where he was also the Director of the Peabody Cooperative Bank.

From left to right: Mrs. Thompson, Frank Sloan, Constance Putnam, and retired Police Chief Thompson.

Mr. Sloan was the Director of Essex County Income Assessments from 1917 to 1928.

In the 1920s the following men started the Saugus Bank and Trust: Karl Norris, President; Frank Sloan, Vice President; and directors Judge Ludden, Arthur Hitchings, Henry Peckham, Janet Conway and Mr. Yanofsky. The bank opened for business in 1928. On March 4, 1933, a proclamation from the governor closed all banks in Massachusetts. This was during the Great Depression. On March 14th representatives of the bank were called to the Federal Reserve Office in Boston at 11:30 p.m. with their bank records for examination. At 5:50 a.m. they were granted a license to open, which they did at 8:00 a.m. that morning.

The bank was located in a small office along with other small business offices in what we know as the Eastern Bank today in Cliftondale Square. In the beginning it was a very small office and all of the equipment was second hand. Eventually they obtained all of that block.

They had three tellers: one Catholic, one Protestant, and one Jewish teller. There was no safe deposit box until 1955 so that meant you had to go out of town to get a safe deposit box. Mr. Norris died in 1930 and Frank Sloan became president of the bank.

Mr. Sloan was a selectman for many years, President of the Saugus Board of Trade in 1915, a member of the Saugus Finance Committee, past Master of the William Sutton Lodge of Masons, past Master of the 7th Masonic District, a 32nd degree Mason, past High Priest of the Henry Mills Royal Arch Chapter, a member of the Tontaquon Chapter, Order of the Eastern Star and the Scottish Rites Bodies of the 32nd degree in Boston.

Due to illness Mr. Sloan retired in the 1940s and sold the property to Hazel McKenney who I think had an insurance business there. He passed away in 1950.

As for the Sloan house decoration at Christmas time, Connie said they had candles in all of the front and side windows, colored lights outside on the trees and shrubs, and a Christmas scene on the front lawn that was changed every year. People came from all around to see the house for a number of years.

John J. Mullen

by
Clayton W. Trefry

John J. Mullen was one of the most colorful political figures of Eastern Massachusetts. During his long career he was a selectman and assessor in Saugus, a Boston City Councilor and an alderman and Mayor of Everett. A Boston native, he served on the city council with James Michael Curley in 1900-1902.

Mullen was a short, stocky man with a shock of long gray hair. As an elected assessor in the Great Depression period of the '30s, he prevailed upon members to raise the assessment on Saugus marsh land on Route 107. As a result, the town's tax rate dropped to an all-time low, and Mullen was

elected to the Board of Selectmen, where he served as chairman and continued to be controversial. In a few years, the State Appellate Tax Board reduced the assessments, the town tax rate went up and Mullen's elected career ended. He always maintained that the salvation of Saugus lay in the marshes and the increases which were imposed on them were justified. The owners disagreed and their refusal to pay caused the property to become tax title and it did not return to the tax rolls until after WW II.

For many years, Mullen conducted a real estate and insurance business in town and was chairman of the Democratic Town Committee when Saugus was largely Republican. When Curley ran for governor, John ran down the aisle of the Town Hall shouting, "Everyone up for the Governor." Of course, they all rose to their feet.

At one time, his business was conducted in a small building at the junction of Centennial Avenue and Central Street. It had a high facade and contained the name of John J. Mullen in large script letters. The building later burned.

He was a familiar figure at Saugus Town Meeting. Speaking in a loud and commanding voice, before the use of microphones, he demanded attention but seldom had much influence on the final vote.

He died in 1952 at the age of 76.

Frank P. Bennett, Jr.

1878 - 1965

by
Advertiser Staff
(*The Saugus Advertiser*, July 13, 1965)

Frank P. Bennett, Jr., a leading citizen of Saugus during the first half of the 20th century, represented this community as a member of state government as well as numerous town political bodies.

He served as Town Moderator, succeeding his father Frank P. Bennett, Sr., and served for 16 years, resigning in 1937. Many town officials remembered him as the most skillful town moderator ever in Saugus. He was acknowledged as one of the ablest parliamentarians in the Commonwealth.

Mr. Bennett represented the town in the Massachusetts House of Representatives from 1904-06, and was a state senator in 1910-12. He ran unsuccessfully for the United States House of Representatives from the 7th District in Massachusetts in 1912.

He was a member of the Saugus School Committee from 1921 to 1923. He also chaired the Republican Town Committee in 1913. Mr. Bennett earned a reputation as a gifted public speaker, always in demand, especially at area Republican political gatherings.

A native of Palermo, Maine, Mr. Bennett graduated from Harvard College, Class of 1900, after attending Everett High School. During his college years his family moved to Saugus where he met and married Irene (Willard) Bennett, and remained in Saugus until 1953.

The Bennett family farm was situated opposite the present Oaklandvale School. His parents were Mr. and Mrs. Frank Bennett Sr. The Frank P. Bennett Highway (Route C-1), beginning at the Felton Circle in Saugus, was named after the senior Bennett.

His wife was President of the Saugus Historical Society in 1912, and President of the Massachusetts Federation of Women's Clubs in 1953.

Mr. Bennett was the retired editor and publisher of *US Investor*, and associate publisher of *America's Textile Reporter*, both published in Boston. He also authored a book, *The Story of Mutual Savings Banks* in 1924.

After selling wool for the firm of Bennett and Williams during several summers, he entered the publishing business with the Frank P. Bennett and Co., Inc., founded by his father in 1887.

Because of his father's interest in the textile industry and sheep industry, Mr. Bennett also worked for a time in worsted mills in Lawrence, Massachusetts, to learn the business.

He was a trustee of the Boston Five Cents Saving Bank, and an original incorporator and director of the Saugus Trust Company, and a director and investment committee member of the Holyoke Mutual Fire Insurance company.

Mr. Bennett died in Flint, Michigan, where he had been residing with his son, the Reverend Franklin P. Bennett of St. Paul's Episcopal Church in Flint for the last twelve years of his life. His wife, Irene, predeceased him. At the time of his death, he was survived by his son, a brother, E. Howard Bennett, and three grandsons.

Services were held in St. Paul's Church in Flint and St. John's Episcopal Church in Saugus where he had been a longtime communicant.

Harold Dodge

by
Norman Down

Harold was born in Lynn in 1886 to Harriet and Herbert Dodge, the first of two sons. The family soon moved to Summer Street in Saugus. Harold was active in sports as a young man, playing baseball as a pitcher. He was good enough to attract an offer from the minor leagues, but he turned it down in order to stay home and help care for his ailing father.

As a boy he summered with his family at Northwood Lake in New Hampshire. Such a trip was a major expedition in those days. The family would pack enough food, bedding and provisions for a prolonged stay, take the train to Boston, board another train for Concord, New Hampshire, and complete the trip on a stagecoach from Concord to Northwood, a distance of about 20 miles. I have a picture of Harold riding next to the stage driver in Northwood.

After high school, he attended Burdette College in Lynn where he majored in Business. Circa 1908, he married Agnes B. Kennedy of Saugus. They had three children, a son Norman who died of diphtheria at age four, and two daughters, Phyllis and Thelma. In the early years Harold worked as a milkman for Frank P. Bennett who had a dairy farm in Oaklandvale. The Dodges lived in an apartment on the farm. Harold eventually went to work for the brokerage firm of Paine, Webber, Jackson and Curtis of Boston where he worked his way up to head teller, which position he held until his retirement in 1954.

As a Saugonian, he had a keen interest in civic affairs and began a long career in local politics. At various times he served on the Board of Selectmen (serving for a while as chairman), was Town Accountant and a member of the School Committee. In 1929, he was appointed Town Treasurer. All during the Depression, money was short, but Harold managed it in such a way that town employees never had a payless payday. He was a fiscal conservative. Having seen the Depression coming, he kept his own money out of the stock market and refrained from investing even after prosperity came. In 1939, he had the opportunity to buy a small unfinished summer cottage at his beloved Northwood Lake. The family has summered there ever since.

Harold was a man of rock solid honesty and integrity. His daughter Phyllis often told two stories that illustrate this. One involved a black family that was denied the use of the town ambulance. When Harold found out about it he faced the official responsible and threatened to call for his resignation if anything like that happened again. The other story involved a family in Golden Hills. Golden Hills had no town water, and every year the residents went to various officials to try to get relief. Many promised them that the water system would be extended to them, but it never happened. When they went to Harold, he told them, "I'm sorry but the town is not in a position to do it at this time." One of the people looked him in the eye and said, "Thank you, Mr. Dodge." Harold said, "Why are you thanking me? I've just told you I can't help you." The answer came back, "Because you have been honest with us. All the others promised and never delivered. From now on you can be sure of my vote."

In addition to his official positions in town government, Harold was a Town Meeting member for 40 years. He always had a knack for knowing just when to speak. Others would get up and make long speeches enunciating their point of view. Just when it seemed that debate had ended, Harold would ask to be recognized. If he hitched up his pants as he stood, those who knew him well knew that fireworks were in the offing. I saw a few of these performances in my early teenage years. They were impressive.

For many years, Saugus was run by the Board of Selectmen. As the population grew it became obvious that the government had to change. One of the proposed changes was to institute a Town Manager. Town Meeting was deadlocked on the issue. Vote after vote ended in a tie. Finally, he said to his wife, "I've got to break this deadlock." Even though he had misgivings about the Town Manager form of government, he changed his vote and the town's present form of government was passed by that one vote.

The Harold Dodge I knew was the private family man. He was "Gramp" or "Pappy." My grandfather was a kind, warm, deeply sensitive man with a rather gloomy outlook on life. I think he may have suffered from clinical depression, although I can never be sure. The death of his son affected him deeply. When I was born to Thelma, I was named for him. We lived across the street from my grandparents practically from my birth to his death. We spent every holiday together and summer vacations at Northwood, sleeping ten people in a tiny five-room camp. My grandfather once sat me on the edge of the lake while he bathed. As he bent to rinse his face, I fell in. When he looked up I was nowhere in sight. He spotted me at his feet and scooped me out. I spluttered and coughed until I caught my breath. I know he relived his son's death in those few moments. He was there when I learned to swim and row and fish. He taught me to shoot. He held me in his arms and sang lullabies to me when I was small. He helped arrange a grant for my college education. He was 6'2". To me he was 10' tall.

When my father developed tuberculosis, Gramp got him into the hospital, although there was a long waiting list. The doctors said it saved his life. When Dad got out, Gramp helped get him a new job and bought the house across the street so we would have an apartment. Later, he sold Dad the house. He helped John Bucchiere get his start in town

politics. He helped the Coglianos move their family store to the location on Lincoln Avenue.

He put sugar on beans, ate strong blue cheese, and enjoyed poker and a good drink. He was a good horseshoes player and had an accuracy with a gun that I have admired ever since. He was also a worry wart, possibly with a touch of what is now called OCD. When we left the camp to come home he would go back and forth between the front and back doors rattling the door knobs. In time they just sort of floated in their sockets.

When my grandmother died in February of 1959, he lost all will to live. He was fine for two weeks, then every day he would tell people he only wanted to die. That July, on the eve of his 73rd birthday, he got his wish. He was sitting in the living room at camp. I was getting ready to leave for home. I went up to him, shook hands as we always did, and went up the hill with the rest of my family to my car. I left, and the family came back down to the camp. They found him on his bed, dead of a heart attack. When word reached Saugus, town officials ordered flags flown at half-staff. One of their best was gone.

Frederick Bancroft Willis

Claiming Our Own
1904-1971

(Paraphrased from *The Lynn Daily Evening Item* (1971) and *The Saugus Advertiser*, circa 1940s)

Frederick B. Willis served as Speaker of the Massachusetts House of Representatives from 1945 to 1948 and as Counsel of the House from 1948 to 1969.

Fred Willis.

Mr. Willis, one of the most widely known Republicans in State affairs for more than 30 years, had played a leading part in key legislation for these three decades while serving as a representative, Speaker and House Counsel. A favorite with leaders and rank-and-file members of both major political parties, he was rated one of the most astute men in State House circles.

A native of Saugus, he began his career in public life in that town as a member and chairman of the School Committee.

Mr. Willis subsequently served as Acting Superintendent of Schools and later was elected Town Counsel and secretary to the Board of Assessors in Saugus.

His service to the Commonwealth began in 1936 when he was elected State Representative, a post he held for many years. He moved to Lynn in 1948 after being elected House Counsel.

After he retired in 1969, he was tendered a testimonial in Boston where he was commended by state officials, including Gov. Francis W. Sargent, in recognition of a long and distinguished public career. Also honored at the affair was his wife, Marguerite.

His ability and industry won him the confidence of three Speakers, who rewarded him with positions of trust and responsibility on committees of the Legislature.

During the 1937-38 session, Speaker Horace T. Cahill appointed Mr. Willis to the committee on Civil Service and Labor and Industries and to the special Commission on Taxation and Public Expenditures.

Under Speaker Christian A. Herter, later Governor and Secretary of State, he served as chairman of the Committee on Civil Service and as a member of the Committee on Legal Affairs.

He was also named by Speaker Herter as House Chairman of a Recess Commission set up in 1941 to study and revise the civil service laws of Massachusetts and was author of the Civil Service Reform Bill.

Under Speaker Rudolph F. King, Mr. Willis was appointed to his cabinet as Republican floor leader of the House and during recesses of the Legislature he held the vital post of House Chairman of the Special Commission on Post-War Rehabilitation.

A graduate of Saugus High and Northeastern University and Boston University School of Law, Mr. Willis was named Counsel of the House in 1948, a post he held until his retirement in May 1969.

He was chairman of the House Committee on Aeronautics that made Logan Airport a modern facility in the late 1940s and was also chairman of the Steamboat commission that established the Nantucket Island Steamship Authority.

Mr. Willis was also the author of the Town Manager Bill under which his native town of Saugus has been operating since the 1940s.

Mr. Willis was the 72nd Speaker of the House of Representatives. His election at age 40 gave the House the youngest officer in many years at that time. He had the distinction of being the first Greater Lynn legislator ever to be named Speaker of the House.

Among the many measures under his sponsorship during his first term were the following:

• A bill on labor and industries for the licensing of employees and employers connected with work manufactured in private homes. (Prevents the occurrence of "sweat-shop" conditions.)

• An act relieving the Town of Saugus and City of Lynn of the cost of maintenance of the General Edwards bridge.

• A bill to provide compensation for injured employees and with the right to sue third parties responsible for the injuries. (This bill was defeated in the Senate after passing the House due to intense lobbying of insurance companies.)

• An act preventing the discrimination in private industries because of age. (Age 45 and beyond.)

• A resolution for the study and investigation of the Civil Service Rules and Regulations. (A recodification of the Civil Service laws.)

• A bill requiring overnight camps to be licensed by local boards of health.

• A bill placing State House employees under Civil Service.

• Piloted a bill through both Houses appropriating $4,000 in State funds toward the purchase of Saugus' Old Ironworks House. This, together with similar sums from the Town of Saugus and Society for the Preservation of New England Antiquities, assured this landmark of remaining in Saugus.

An avid baseball fan, Mr. Willis entered a contest to name the Boston National League baseball team. His name was drawn and his winning entry resulted in naming the club the "Boston Bees."

Mr. Willis died on October 2, 1971, at Lynn Hospital after a lengthy illness. He was 67 years old and lived at 29 Greystone Park in a spacious home overlooking the Atlantic Ocean at Lynn Shore Drive. His wife, the former Marguerite Hennessey, predeceased him on June 1, 1971.

He was the son of the late Daniel W. and Clarissa (Bright) Willis. He left a son, Richard B. Willis of Lynn; a daughter, Mrs. Susan P. Simone of Metheun; a brother, Gordon Willis of Mashpee, Cape Cod; three sisters, Mrs. Phoebe Randall of Nahant, Mrs. Helen Condon of Saugus and Mrs. Dorothy Lewis of Florida and two grandchildren.

Services were held at the Central Congregational Church. Burial was in Riverside Cemetery, Saugus.

Mr. Willis was a charter member of Saugus Lodge of Elks, a life member of the Henry J. Mills Chapter of Masons and the William Sutton Lodge of Masons, and the Massachusetts Consistory. He was also a member of the Massachusetts Legislators' Association, the Volunteer Yacht Club of Lynn, Aleppo Temple of Boston and the Canopy and Knockers' Club of Boston.

On April 16, 1971, Mr. Willis was awarded *The Lynn Item*'s "Bouquet of the Week" in honor of his long and distinguished career.

A History of Charles Forest Nelson Pratt

by
Barbara Pratt Yohman

C. F. Nelson Pratt was born in Saugus on February 4, 1891. His mother, Agnes King, came down from Nova Scotia, met Charles Pratt, married and had four children of whom Nelson was the oldest. His mother's ancestors were descended from early settlers of Newfoundland and moved to Halifax in the 1830s. They were in the shipbuilding business and came to Lynn in the 1890s.

Nelson liked public speaking and was a good student and involved himself in baseball and football in high school where he exhibited the same combative spirit that marked his career in the years to come.

He was always very interested in public life and while still in school attended a Town Meeting one year where he rose to deliver his opinion of a standing piece of legislation. He was half way through the delivery when the Moderator recognized him as a non-voter and ordered him to be seated.

He went to work in a shoe factory upon graduation, vowing he would continue his education one day.

In 1916, he married Florence Shorey of E. Rochester, New Hampshire. He had commuted to New Hampshire to court her on weekends by motorcycle over the dirt road that is now Route 1. He was a devoted husband and they celebrated their 50th wedding anniversary in 1966. The had 4 children and 16 grandchildren.

He leaned towards Socialism in his early years, but finally adopted a line of progressive Republicanism.

He started his career in Saugus town politics – as rough an arena to be found anywhere. He served as Town Meeting member, Selectman, Town Moderator and School Committeeman, as well as State Representative. Frequently, he made his way to meetings of the Selectmen and Town Meeting sessions to let his views be heard loud and clear on Saugus issues. He was never afraid to take a stand.

In 1943, he was awarded a law degree from Boston University School of Law. This was after attending night school while working to support his family.

C.F. Nelson Pratt.

He made two unsuccessful bids for the Congress and Senate at one time. He served as County Commissioner of Essex County for 28 years. He was a public servant 24 hours a day – whether he was school committeeman, selectman, moderator, legislator or commissioner. He was one of the first members of the General Court to sponsor legislation to help the elderly and that was a long time ago.

He supported the labor unions, championed policemen and insisted in 1968 that in the redistricting by County's governing board that Saugus be allowed its own representative in the lower branch of the legislature. His efforts in behalf of the worker, the war veteran, the ailing and the underprivileged were constant and lifelong. Although he held office for 28 years on the Essex County level, he never failed to speak out on town matters. He was a Republican who supported labor long before FDR took office, a Republican who was a favorite of the Democrats, for Republicans nominated him and Democrats elected him.

He won praise from labor unions and introduced several bills which were described as having paved way for success of the trade union movement in Massachusetts.

During World War II, he served as an executive at the General Electric River Works. He left as soon as the war was over to make way for the veterans who would be going back to work. Despite the fact that he was a Republican, he had many Democratic friends as witnessed by the fact that he was able to win elections in years of Democratic landslides.

He was a member of the Masons of Saugus for more than 50 years and also the Cliftondale Lodge of Odd Fellows. Other groups of which he was a member were Saugus Republican Town Committee, Massachusetts & Essex County Selectmen's Association, County Commissioners and Sheriffs Associations, Saugus High School Alumni (where there is a scholarship in his name), Delta Theta Phi Law fraternity, Honorary Membership in the Massachusetts Police Chiefs Association.

The initials C. F. stood for "Cold Facts" as he liked to tell everyone and it often set the tone for whatever public business he was involved in at the time. He didn't need a microphone when he spoke on any issue. His voice literally blasted into the farthest corner of an auditorium with little effort. Even though sometimes the audience was determined not to applaud in agreement, they were swept along by that voice which shredded many an opponent. They just couldn't help it. Another favorite expression he frequently used when he was presiding over a meeting was, "Dignity, decorum and dispatch." Hammering his gavel to bring order to an overheated discussion, he would look ominously at his audience and announce the business at hand "must be conducted with dignity, decorum and dispatch." It almost never failed to bring an unruly meeting to order.

Nelson Pratt always thought big and was traffic minded. On October 26, 1971, the overpass at Lynn Fellsway over Route 1 was dedicated to him. It was a fitting tribute to him because he had fought for that and similar traffic measures along the Turnpike that bisected his home town. There is a plaque there in his name and also a memorial on a stone which stands at the Soldiers Monument in Saugus Center.

It was written of him, "Rank him no lower than a political servant, a powerful personality, a supreme debater with a thousand facts on his tongue tip and ten thousand at his fingertips."

It seems that if Nelson Pratt had to die, he died the way he would have chosen – on an election night in the midst of a hard fought campaign doing what he loved so well.

It was written in a newspaper at the time of his death, "It was a dramatic political 'last hurrah' as fate intervened to spare the warrior of numerous political frays the bitter taste of unaccustomed defeat."

Paul A. Haley

by
Cynthia Haley Draper

Paul A. Haley, civic leader, writer and historian, was born in Saugus in 1906. He was the son of Alfred C. and Bertha M. Haley. Paul worked on the high school monthly paper, *The Independent*, and was the editor-in-chief his senior year. Reading old issues is very interesting. Ashton Davis was a class editor, Francis Fox was sports editor and Vernon Evans was the faculty advisor. Paul also contributed articles to the *Saugus Herald* starting at about the time he was fifteen.

In their senior year, he and his future wife, Elsie Anderson, were in the cast of the musical *HMS Pinafore*, which was directed by Amy Hanson Jones.

Paul attended Boston University School of Business Administration and its School of Journalism. He left school to become the Saugus correspondent for the *Lynn Telegram News* and later for the *Lynn Item*.

An avid reader, he read several books a week throughout his adult life. He had the uncanny ability to paraphrase long passages of a book that interested him and could find the book and passages after long periods of elapsed time. Paul was a member of the Saugus Historical Society and compiled a chronology of Saugus, as well as many articles of local interest. His knowledge of local history and his ability as a story teller made him a popular speaker for North Shore organizations over many years.

Paul A. Haley.

Paul was very involved in his attempt to make Saugus a better place to live. He served the town government in one capacity or another for over 30 years. At 18 he was elected Clerk of the Board of Selectman, a post he held for 10 years. He served on the School Committee on two occasions. Once in the 1930s and again in the 1950s. He also served as a Town Meeting member and a member of the Republican Town Committee. An expert on parliamentary procedure, he served as Town Moderator for over four years.

He was on the building committee for the combined Police / Fire Station in the mid-1930s; he was on the building committee of the Junior High School located behind the old high school, and was Chairman of the Building Committee for the new high school on Route 1 in the 1950s.

Paul was also Chairman of the Town Finance Committee, member of the Saugus Iron Works Committee, and Chairman of the Saugus Board of Appeals. He was very proud of the fact that only one of the rulings that he was responsible for was turned down by the courts. It was later overturned by a higher court, so Paul would proudly tell you that his Appeal Board record was perfect.

Paul worked for 33 years at the *Lynn Item*. His work as a political columnist on state and national issues earned him recognition in the 1950s as the "Best Political Columnist in Massachusetts" by the *Boston Morning and Evening Globe*. During this period, Paul covered the State House and became a speech writer for Governor Christian Herter.

An interesting aside was that Paul and a few other people used to car-pool to the State House when the legislature was in session. One person in the car pool who was picked up along the way was a State Representative whose name was Tip O'Neill. Years later, when Paul went to Washington to work, Tip, who by then was a leader in the House of Representatives, very graciously gave Paul advice about living in Washington and took him on tours of government buildings that Paul would otherwise not have been able to see.

While in the Washington area, Paul worked for Secretary of Labor Mitchell as a speech writer during Eisenhower's second term, and later as the Associate Editor of the *Frederick Post* newspaper in Frederick, Maryland. There he received awards as "The Small Newspaper Editorialist of the Year" and received letters commenting on his editorials from then President Richard Nixon.

While working at the *Frederick Post*, Paul, being interested in Civil War history, worked with Congressman Goodloe E. Byron and Judge Edward S. Delaplane to get the Civil War Monocacy Battle Field set aside as an historic site.

Paul was active in his church, fraternal organizations, and the Sons of the American Revolution.

Paul passed away shortly after his retirement in 1976. He would have been proud had he known that his friend, Congressman Goodloe Byron, read a description of Paul's accomplishments into the Congressional Record to note Paul's demise.

At the time of his death, he was survived by his wife Elsie, a daughter, Cynthia Draper, and was predeceased by a daughter, Paula Abbott. Fulfilling his last wish, Paul was buried in the Riverside Cemetery in his beloved Saugus.

Laurence Frederic Davis

A Man Who Loved His Town

by
Gretchen Davis Hammer

My dad, Laurence Frederic Davis, known as Mike by his friends, was born on June 3, 1900, in Melrose, Massachusetts – the third child and second son of Ernest Carl and Jennie Pike Davis. He had an older brother Edward and an older sister Charlotte. The Davis family moved to 21 Columbus Avenue in Saugus Center when Mike was about three years old, and this remained the family home until both parents died. The three Davis siblings were very close throughout their lifetimes and were devoted to their parents. Both parents were active in church and town affairs, passing this legacy down to all three of the children.

According to my Grandmother, Mike was a very active child, participating in sports, church, singing in the choir – his boy soprano voice was enjoyed by all who heard it in his younger days – and other activities of the community. Being a boy of considerable size and strength for his age, he played on the Saugus High School football team as its center when he was in the eighth grade – Dad also ran track, at one time holding a school and state record for the 100-yard dash, as well as being a hurdler.

Laurence and Helen Davis.

Dad graduated from Saugus High School with the Class of 1917, during World War I. He and several others in his class enlisted in the Army, and left for boot camp prior to graduation. Upon completion of his time of service, he went to Boston University and its Law School, funding his education by being a member of the football coaching staff at Saugus High School. After passing the bar in 1924, Dad set up his law practice in the Security Trust Bank Building in Central Square in Lynn.

In 1924, while doing some legal business at the Saugus Town Clerk's office, he met again Helen R. Graves, who had graduated from Saugus High School two years after Mike did. He courted her – "the most beautiful girl I ever saw" – and they married in 1926. Since both loved the town of Saugus, they first rented an apartment on Central Street and in 1929 purchased their home at 13 Pearson Street, where they resided until his death.

Having established his law practice and started his family, Dad decided that it was time to become actively involved in Town affairs. He ran for and was elected to the School Board. He also ran for and was elected as a Town Meeting member, and shortly afterwards began serving as the Town Attorney. He found these most challenging, and when there was a need for a Town Moderator, Dad ran and was elected. He held this position for about twenty years, enjoying the people and the debates. In the late 1940s the Selectmen decided to present to the town for approval the Plan E form of governing. Dad spoke out firmly in opposition to this idea, believing that it placed an unnecessary layer of authority between the people and those governing. Plan E was voted in, however, and Dad was defeated at the polls at the next election. A year later the voters presented to him a petition with hundreds of signatures on it, so his name could appear on the ballot. It was my job to take it to the Town Clerk's office for filing – I forgot to do it, his name then did not appear on the ballot that year and he chose not to run again.

During World War II, Dad was offered the position – or volunteered, I am not sure which – as head of the Town's Civilian Defense. He was given an office at the Town Hall, where the air raid wardens were to check in during air raid practices. Dad refused this office space and instead built a blacked-out office / family room in the basement of our house. This way he could be with his family during these drills, and still have all the advantages of an office where the wardens could report in. My memories, therefore, of air raid drills during the war are of people coming and going, reporting the activities of their districts, while the four of us children played ping-pong and listened to our music. There were occasions, however, when I recall Dad saying that we had to stay in the dark, or almost-dark, and sit and wait for the all-clear – just as if a real air raid was happening. He was afraid that we might get too complacent and not know how to behave, should the real thing happen.

Around the middle of World War II Dad and others organized town activities which would show our support of our military and of our country. There were aluminum drives, with big bins on the Town Hall's front lawn where people would come and toss in their old pots and pans. He even taught school children how to peel the aluminum foil off gum wrappers, roll it up and save it in big balls…tossing it into the bins during these drives. All ages got into the act!

My mother had a huge vegetable garden – called a Victory Garden – raising most of our vegetables during the war. She and Ellery Metcalf used to talk "garden talk" a lot of the time, and decided to start a Victory Garden Club, where people could share their garden tips. This became bigger than they had thought would happen, with many, many residents starting gardens. In the mid-Forties – just after the war ended – during a discussion which happened around our dining-room table with Mr. Metcalf and my parents, it was decided to organize a Fair, where people could bring samples from their garden and compete for ribbons as prizes. This idea grew rapidly into the Victory Fairs, with amusement rides on the Town Hall lawn and garden and knitting / sewing / craft exhibits on the second floor of the building. The Fairs lasted three days and were hugely successful. The Governor of the State used to attend, and one year Senator Saltonstall came. It was a fun way for the town to come together to celebrate the end of that awful War.

Shortly after that, a group gathered to discuss restoring the Saugus Iron Works. A Saugus Iron Works Association was formally formed, with my dad doing a lot of the legal work around the project; my mother was the clerk of the Association. It is fascinating to read through her secretary's notes of those meetings. The formal completion and dedication was during my sophomore year in high school – either in the fall of 1949 or 1950. I recall that Senator Robert Taft was among the dignitaries attending.

Laurence Davis and "Duffy."

Church played a very important role in my parents' lives. My dad grew up in the Episcopal Church, attending St. John's on Central Street. He had a beautiful soprano voice, and sang in the choir throughout his childhood. After my parents married, and because they were living in Saugus Center, they both attended that same church. My dad served on the Vestry as well as later becoming Senior Warden of the church. My mother taught Sunday School, was a member of the Altar Guild and a member of the Vestry. All four of us children attended Sunday School, some of us sang in the choir, most of us attended youth group, and we all were part of various organizations which met at St. John's. My oldest brother gave his first sermon there after being ordained a deacon in the Church in June of 1954. Some of my parents' grandchildren were even baptized there in later years as well.

Family meant a great deal to Dad, and he would travel hours to get home in time to be with us all: when we were little to be there at bedtime, or to arrive in time to attend some event one of us was involved in when we were older. When we were little, we children often accompanied Dad on his almost daily early morning walk. Often, when I would go with him, we would walk up Main Street to Vine Street, and cut across Donkey Hill to get back to Central Street. Then we would hurry to the railroad station to wave good-bye to my dad's father, who would be taking the 7 a.m. train into Boston to work. Right after that we would dash down the street to Mr. McNaughton's donut shop (right beside Graham's Market) to pick up fresh donuts for breakfast. If we got there before he had put donuts in the window, I would get one of the warm, delicious donuts to eat on the way home. You can imagine how much I looked forward to that race each time!

We also would often stop in at Mr. Noretsky's tailor shop, which was right beside the donut shop, to say hello. Walking by Graham's Market, we would wave at Mike and Louie as they were putting out the fresh vegetables for the day. As we went down the street, Mrs. Woodbury would sometimes be heading over to her shop to prepare for her day. If we happened to go in the reverse direction, we would see Mr. Rogers putting the shoes in his shoe-shop window, and Mr. Adlington opening up the doors at his hardware store. I also recall going into Mr. Grady's Barber Shop for a gumball before the shop was officially opened for the day, and thinking that that was such a thrill. Dad would always insist that I wave and speak to everyone, telling me just how important each of these people was to the success of the town. At that young age I always felt he knew just about everyone – and in a way he did! He loved people, and imparted his appreciation of people on to his children.

The Fourth of July was a big family day. Dad would purchase a variety of fireworks, and after a big family picnic, the neighbors would all gather on our front steps for the big show. We all enjoyed home-churned ice cream, and tons of watermelon (complete with watermelon seed spitting contests), while we watched the fireworks. I do recall one night when one of the aerials went astray and landed on the roof of David Fisher's house, which was at the top of the hill on Pearson Street. Fortunately the fire department was less than a block away and quickly came to the rescue before there was any major damage.

Dad always enjoyed young people and was a big supporter of all the school events as well as of education in general. I remember his traveling home one night to attend a talent show I was in when I was in high school. It didn't matter that he had to drive two hours back the next morning to continue his meetings – it was important for him to be there to support me and the other students involved. I believe that he and my mother attended almost every home football game while I was growing up (and probably before I arrived on the scene). Football was his favorite sport, and he was always a coach, even when he wasn't a coach. He knew many of the boys playing, and even arranged for college football scouts to attend some games when SHS had an especially talented player. I recall a couple of players who received scholarships to college because of my dad's efforts, though I doubt that those players realized that my dad had been instrumental in that happening. He also helped more than a few through some minor scrapes with the police, taking responsibility for seeing that these young people did community service rather than pay a fine – this long before before minor offenses were dealt with by doing community service.

Dad did all these things because he had such a love for his community, a sense of responsibility to pay back to the community for all it had given to him---a safe place to grow up in, a nurturing environment where people cared for their fellow man, and a place where people came together for the common good of their town. Dad died suddenly and way too young, at age 59, still talking about plans for ways to help out the town he had already given so much to.

What's Cooking

Edward Gibbs Jr.

by
John Burns

Edward Gibbs Jr., a man of great energy, intelligence and strong convictions, was a dominant Saugus presence in the middle of the 1900s.

There were many sides to this complex man. *It is impossible* to overstate the firmness and competence he brought to the task in the various offices he held in serving the Town of Saugus, or to overstate the generous impulses which would distract him from his civic functions to give his attention to someone in need. There was no pattern to his acts of kindness, no qualifying conditions, at times, even, no logical explanation of what would move him to action – but always clear was his willingness to lend a helping hand, with no eye to the cost.

The public was familiar with Mr. Gibbs as Chairman of the Board of Selectmen, and as Chairman of the Finance Committee at whose meetings it was his practice to set up a "bed sheet" bulletin board on which he would display for the committee and the public in attendance the financial data critical to the evening's discourse.

Four generations of the Gibbs family.

They were familiar too with his service in his years as Town Accountant.

Less known were his various business enterprises: his CPA office in Boston, his acquisition of the Arthur Brown Woven Belt Company, and his ownership of the Tilton, NH Water Company.

And there was his life as a pull-no-punches journalist and the lasting impression of his "What's Cooking" opinion column which he wrote weekly for the *Saugus Advertiser*, owned jointly by him and Al Woodward. There was a special aura in Saugus on the day this paper came out, an air of speculation in the general public about who would be cooked that day, and a sense of trepidation among those who feared they might be served up as the fare for the day.

The remainder of this account touches on the other side of Mr. Gibbs' life, his family life, his life replete with acts of kindness and concern for those in need, for the light this "other side" casts on this man in the fullness of his being.

Mr. Gibbs and his wife Blanche bore and raised seven children: five sons, Edward III, Berthier, Walter, Ralph and Charles; and two daughters, Dorothy and Alice, all of whom went on to higher education and productive lives.

A large family, but there was always room for more. When the Anderson children, cousins to their children, were orphaned, it was typical of the nature of Ed and Blanche to invite into their home the four Anderson children, Marjorie, Laurie, George (Archy) and Ellen, to be part of their family.

It was only recently that I talked with a friend who gave me another enlightening view of Mr. Gibbs. As a high school graduate, with limited prospects of going to college, he

received unexpected help when he was assisted by Mr. Gibbs in being granted a full four-year scholarship at a college of his choice from a fund governed by the Belle Peabody Brown Foundation which provided scholarship assistance for students of merit whose grades did not qualify them for most scholarships. My friend, the beneficiary of this grant, went on to a successful college career and a successful career as a teacher.

A remarkable act of generosity! Perhaps it was the early emerging of ecumenism in Saugus when Ed, not a Catholic, gave to the Saugus Knights of Columbus land, on the shore of Lily (Prankers) Pond, where Shadowland Ballroom was once located, to be the site for their new home.

But of all the acts of thoughtfulness which I have learned of in the life of Mr. Gibbs, I was most moved by what he did for Ms. Janet Nicholson, a first grade teacher at the Armitage School. She was having a controversy with the school committee, the nature of which I do not know. Mr. Gibbs intervened and saved her job. Some years later when she died, without any surviving relatives, he made arrangements to have her buried in the Gibbs family plot in the Riverside Cemetery. This act of itself speaks eloquently of the principles which governed this man's life.

Ed Gibbs and family (Four sons, Edward, Berthier (Bert), Ralph and Charles served in the military service of the United States and returned home at the end of WW II.)

William H. Robinson

"Mr. Saugus"
Bill Robinson
Town Clerk

by
Barbara Robinson Couturier

For those of you who are younger than myself, I would like to tell you about my dad, Bill Robinson – "Mr. Saugus." The license plate on his car even read "Saugus."

Bill Robinson.

Bill Robinson gave 50 years of his life to the Town of Saugus. Known as "Mr. Saugus," Bill was a 50-year veteran of Saugus' often stormy political scene and recognized as one of the state's foremost authorities of parliamentary procedure and state statutes on voting procedures. He was born in Lynn in 1916 and moved to Saugus when he was only 17 months old. He was a product of the Saugus school system. Bill married Gladys Pickett. He had three children–Barbara, Brian and Dale and six grandchildren.

Before taking on the responsibility of Town Clerk in 1964, Bill worked as a supervisor at the GE in Lynn. He was raised on Ballard Street and later moved to Intervale Avenue when he married.

Over the years Bill had been a member of the Planning Board 1933-45 and 1947; Finance Committee 1942-1946; Board of Selectmen 1946 and 1948-1952. He was also a Town Meeting member and Town Moderator from 1962 until 1964. In 1964 he became Town Clerk and served in that capacity until his death in March of 1979.

Bill was Vice President of the North Shore City and Town Clerks Association and was one of nine members on the Executive Board of the Massachusetts Town Clerks Association.

Bill diligently worked on the renovation of the junior high. He was instrumental in the building of the Veterans Memorial School, which before its erection was a wooded area in front of his house with the rear facing Intervale Avenue. He was one of the original organizers of the Saugus Credit Union and was a Past Master of the William Sutton Lodge of Masons.

In 1952 he was a delegate to the Dwight D. Eisenhower Presidential Republican Convention. He wore one of those white brimmed hats with a blue and red ribbon around it. They still have those today. I will never forget how proud I felt of him. Being a child of 11, I wondered why he wasn't the president!

The Town Clerk's job was a curious blending of official duties and responsibilities as contained in the Chapters and Sections of the General Laws, and the Bylaws of the 351 towns and cities in the Commonwealth of Massachusetts. At the state level, Bill had duties and responsibilities which came under the jurisdiction of the Secretary of State, the Director of Accounts, the Attorney General, the Division of Fisheries and Game and the Public Works Division. Working for the town was Bill's life.

He was respected by political friend and foe. He maintained an even-handed approach to each issue which he faced. During his long political career, he achieved numerous successes and setbacks.

Bill Robinson at Town Hall.

Clayton Trefry Looking Back on His Life

by
Clayton W. Trefry

Clayton Wallace Trefry
Born: March 7, 1919, Everett, Massachusetts
Father: Wellsford Blake Trefry
Mother: Edna Renita Cameron

A sickly child, doctors recommended a move to the country. When only a few weeks old, we moved to Revere and then to Saugus, naturally, as mother was a Saugus native.

Started school at the Henry Waitt in North Revere. The school was named for one of the founders of the Waitt and Bond Tobacco Company. They manufactured Seven-Twenty-Four Cigars. "Get Back of a Seven-Twenty-Four."

We moved to Cliftondale from Revere when I was in the second grade and attended the Cliftondale School for about one year. Just before Christmas in 1926, we moved to Saugus Center. I was half way through the third grade and spent my remaining elementary years at the Roby School. In the fourth grade I remember Hazel McCarrier as my teacher, I believe a sister of George McCarrier, later a long-time School Committeeman. In the fifth and sixth grades my teacher was Elsie Anderson. Elsie was later married to Paul Haley. Paul was an author, *Lynn Item* reporter and Town Moderator under Chapter 17. He later became the principal speech writer for the Secretary of Labor in the Eisenhower Cabinet.

In junior and senior high school I was a good student and especially liked English and history. In high school, I first started attending Town Meeting, a life-long love affair.

After school I was employed by Lawrence Stone in a machine shop as an apprentice. We had one customer, Lynn Buckle Manufacturing Company, who made metal shoe buckles. Our job was to design and make dies to punch the buckles. Over the years, I made, quite literally, hundreds of buckle dies. With the advent of WW II, our world branched out and we did much in the war effort and I was deferred for some years.

Clayton Trefry.

In the year 1944 I was married to Barbara Newell Stone. In the summer I was drafted into the service. I spent one and one-half years in the navy, including about ten months overseas, mostly in the Philippines.

Barbara and I had two children, Susan Cameron Trefry and Jonathan Stone Trefry. We were married for 45 years. She had a long and losing battle with pancreatic cancer and died in 1989.

In June of 1991, I was married to my long-time and dear friend, Helen Grace Poole. We continued to live at Felton Court, in a house I built starting in 1954. In 2005 we sold the house and moved to an apartment.

Following high school, I attended briefly Suffolk Law School and studied at Lynn Night School, algebra and geometry. My real love was the law and I have often thought I should have pursued it.

My public life began when my children were in elementary school, and I first became involved in the Parent-Teacher Association. I quickly became the local president and then moved to the town-wide PTA Council. When the Town Meeting formed a 15-member School Advisory Committee, I was appointed to it by Moderator C. F. Nelson Pratt. This group made many far-reaching recommendations, the effects of which are still felt. Because of my background, in 1959 I ran for School Committee. With 17 candidates I ran a good solid ninth. Not good enough to be elected. I was, however, elected to the Town Meeting, and became very involved. Twice more I tried for School Committee in 1961 and 1963. I improved my vote, but not enough to be elected. In 1964 a vacancy on the Board of Selectmen came about and I decided to try. I had to convince some of my supporters, but they agreed. I was elected in a special election. In 1965 I was defeated by 13 votes. In 1967 I returned to the Board and stayed until 1977 when I decided not to run.

In 1966, when out of office, I spent a year on the Finance Committee. In 1978 I served as a member of the Board of Registrars. I also was the Veterans Agent in the '90s.

In 1980, after Town Moderator Augustine Gannon was named a judge, I was elected Moderator, a position I held for 15 years. In 1977 I decided to leave the Town Meeting and retire. My public service was over 40 years.

As a youngster, my parents sent me to Sunday school at the Cliftondale Congregational Church. When we moved to Saugus Center I continued at the First Congregational Church in the Center. I joined the church at age eleven and later taught Sunday school for about five years until Barbara and I were married. In the '50s, when she told me she planned to join the Cliftondale Congregation, I transferred my membership. I once told a candidate for pastor at our church that I had held every position except janitor and pastor and I felt I was still in line to be janitor. Among my happiest memories are the 12 years I taught fifth grade in Sunday school. I was also the Church Moderator for twenty years.

The Republican Party in Saugus has been a long and pleasant relationship for me. I first joined when I voted in the primary in 1946 for Bob Bradford for governor, I have been happy to be a member of the Saugus Republican Town Committee, serving several years as chairman and trying to breathe some life into it. I have attended several state conventions.

For about five of its last years I was active in the depression-born 4-Arts Club, a local dramatic club. It died with the advent of WW II.

I have been proud to be a member and active in the Saugus Lions Club since 1966, a local organization.

In 1977 I was honored to be selected as Saugus' Man of the Year.

Between us, Helen and I have four children, eight grandchildren and six great-grandchildren. We are happy to share them together.

Francis C. "Skip" Moorehouse

by
Clayton W. Trefry

Francis C. "Skip" Moorehouse, a former Saugus Town Manager, grew up in Saugus in a large family of six boys and one girl. He graduated from Saugus High School in 1941. As a youngster, he was especially close with his brother Joe, who was only one year older. Some will remember that in the '30s he and Joe were part of an operetta sponsored annually by the Universalist Church. Although the Moorehouse boys were Catholic, this was an ecumenical effort and all were welcome.

"Skip," a nickname he carried all his life, was married to Jane McCullough, from a prominent Saugus family, and they had one son, Michael. Following high school, he was employed by the General Electric Company in their apprentice course and graduated from Lowell Technological Institute. He also graduated from Northeastern University, majoring in Industrial Relations. With GE, he rose rapidly in management and eventually was part of the negotiating team. This was an experience that would be very important

to him in later years. An Army veteran of World War II, holding the rank of lieutenant, he later served in the National Guard, where he was a captain and company commander.

Skip Moorehouse.

Moorehouse was long active in town affairs. He was a veteran member of the Planning Board, a member of the Pranker's Pond Committee and the Industrial Development Commission. He was a Boy Scout leader and worked with the Saugus American Little League. He served as Saugus Town Manager from 1970 to 1973. A born leader, the job seemed made for him and he approached it with vigor. He was everywhere and made himself known to all. "Skip" was always happy to share his leadership with the Selectmen and invited them to take part. His presence at meetings of the Finance Committee was taken for granted and his position on all questions was made clear. Moorehouse's return to the General Electric was a personal decision, and he left with the regret of the Selectmen. He was tendered a public testimonial dinner upon his departure and a scholarship was established in his and his wife's honor.

He is probably best remembered for his historic proposal to "sewer" the town. Public sewers are taken for granted now, but when he proposed it, the norm was to appropriate $300,000 to $400,000 annually. "Skip" suggested $8 million (about $25 million now). It was enthusiastically supported by the Selectmen and some citizens, who had never anticipated receiving such services, were elated to see sewers come down their streets.

The death of Francis C. "Skip" Moorehouse at the age of 58 in 1982 was a significant loss to the town.

Norm Hanson

by
Clayton Trefry

Norman B. Hanson, born in 1924, is a native of Berlin, New Hampshire. He is a Marine veteran of World War II. Norman was one of the leading political figures of Saugus during the last third of the twentieth century. In 1947 he was married to Evelyn Pratt, one of the four daughters of C.F. Nelson Pratt, the celebrated Saugus political activist. They have four children, a daughter and three sons. One son is a Saugus firefighter and another is the Sealer of Weights and Measures in Saugus.

Norm attended Burdett College and worked for about four years for a CPA firm before spending many years with the General Electric in Lynn as an accountant. He is an active member of the VFW.

His political future may have been initiated by his father-in-law when he appointed him to the Saugus Finance Committee. In 1959 he was appointed to the Saugus Town Meeting where he served for six years, the last two as Moderator, before being elected to the Board of Selectmen, eventually becoming their chairman.

During his years as a selectman, he was instrumental in appointing Francis "Skip" Moorehouse as Town Manager. This turned out to be a stroke of genius, as "Skip" proved to be an energetic, creative leader.

After six years on the Board of Selectman, Hanson was appointed Town Accountant, a position he held for fifteen years. In that role he served as a close advisor to several Town Managers, as a trusted assistant on many occasions, and served on several occasions as temporary Town Manager.

Later Hanson served as Saugus Town Manager from 1981 until his retirement in 1986.

Although he owns property in southern Maine, he continues to live in Saugus and to take an active interest in town affairs. He was named Saugus Man of the Year in 2003, in recognition of his 40 years of excellent service for the Town of Saugus.

Edward J. Collins

by
John Burns
(Largely borrowed from an article by Lisa Guerriero in the *Saugus Advertiser* at the time of the retirement of Ed Collins from his position as Town Manager in 1996)

Ed Collins is the Hyde Park native who moved to Saugus after his marriage to Gail, who grew up in Kittery, Maine. "We decided to move halfway between the in-laws," Ed explained. "To the day she died, my mother thought Saugus was next to Montreal. She never crossed the bridge."

Ed attended Boston College and received a degree in finance and accounting. He remained at Boston College to attend law school, with a concentration on studies in taxation.

He began his career with the State Department of Revenue, eventually rising to the rank of Deputy Commissioner. In that office he gained valuable insights into financial aspects of community management.

"I had the job of overseeing all of municipal government, making sure towns were in compliance with state law," Ed said then.

Eventually, he decided that he wanted to involve himself in municipal government. He served one term as a Saugus Town Meeting member, and then, on November 8, 1977, was elected to the Saugus Board of Selectmen. While serving on that board, he was advised that holding that office while working in his state position might represent a conflict of interest, prompting him to resign as Selectman before his term was over.

His interest in his town's well-being did not, however, diminish, and later, after serving as chairman on the Board of Appeals for ten years, he applied for the position of Saugus Town Manager in 1991.

"I wanted to see if I could walk the walk as I was talking it," Ed said. "I was telling officials across the state how to do things. I wanted to see if I could implement them myself."

He was hired by the Board of Selectmen, and from the beginning his financial schooling and experience served him well in the management of the town.

"The finances were in tough shape," Ed recalled. "They didn't have any reserves built up. As soon as we took control, we established reserves."

While keeping a sharp watch on town funds, he was well aware that his office demanded that he give attention as well to preserving and bettering Saugus. To that end he created the town's first Community Development Department and hired Jean Johnson Delios to run it.

With the help of Delios and Richard Cardillo, Personnel and Finance Coordinator, Ed started to move on his Capital Improvement Plan early in his term in office. He saw the vast needs of the town in all branches of service. "No more Band-Aids" was his slogan. In 1995 he announced to the people of Saugus:

"Our Capital Improvement Program, embarked on four years ago, is finally taking shape. As these plans came together, they have formed a vision of what we can do with imagination, with thought, with concerted action and above all with adequate resources to move toward a wonderful future for Saugus. The vision has been lacking, the means to take it from the dream stage to reality.

"Then a unique, once-in-a-lifetime opportunity to move from dream to reality came our way with the opening of the Square One Mall, and with the favorable settlement we were able to strike in our tax dispute with RESCO, our largest single taxpayer, these events allowed us to put aside money in anticipation of our Capital Improvement Program.

"There is a clear, even urgent need for the major overhaul which is spelled out in our Capital Improvement Program. Our Town Hall and other municipal buildings, our schools, and our public safety facilities (fire and police), our library, our Senior Center and our recreational facilities show obvious signs of years of neglect. There is a desperate need for extensive repairs and, in some instances, new construction. The cost of doing nothing, or to resort to Band-Aid,

emergency repairs, will in the long run yield us far less and cost us far more."

With additional state grants, the Program was underway. "Once I knew I had the money, spending the money was easy," Ed said.

The Program, completed after Ed's retirement, will serve for years to come as a monument to his magnificent contribution to our town – a product of what he brought to the office, his financial astuteness, his intelligence, his courage, and above all, his vision.

After leaving office, Ed received an offer from Mayor Thomas Menino of Boston to serve as his chief financial officer. After serving several years in that position, he suffered a stroke, recovered and went back to work for a time, and then retired.

In retirement, he has said there are many aspects of political life he won't miss, but he reflected on his career with fondness. "It's nice to manage something and see it come to fruition," he said. For us in Saugus, we are mindful of and grateful for what his efforts caused to come to fruition in our town – the Capital Improvement Program.

Charles G. Aftosmes

by
Robert Long

In the Saugus Town Meeting form of government, the importance of the Finance Committee's role can not be overlooked nor understated. It is charged with the responsibility of holding public hearings on all town meeting articles that could have a financial impact on the town's resources. At the conclusion of the hearings, the Finance Committee votes its recommendations to the Town Meeting. These recommendations will become the main motion and subject to debate once the Annual or Special Town Meeting commences.

To maintain the credibility of the appointed Finance Committee, the appointing authority, in this case the Town Moderator, must search out and find honest, fair and open-minded people of integrity. In 1966, Richard Barry, Town Moderator, found such a person in Charles G. Aftosmes, more fondly to become known as Charlie. His tenure would extend through five different Town Moderators until he declared his retirement from public service in February, 2000.

His thirty-four years of continuous membership on the Finance Committee, of which the last thirty years were spent as chairman, clearly demonstrated how highly regarded Charlie was by his fellow committee and town meeting members.

Charles Aftosmes, at the podium, Town Meeting.

Like many Saugonians who have contributed so much to our community, Charlie Aftosmes was not born and raised in Saugus but chose our town as the place where he and his wife would raise their family. So, his circuitous route began with his birth on September 8, 1922, in Somerville, MA. Shortly thereafter, his family moved to Dorchester where he attended public schools until his graduation from the prestigious Boston Latin High School in 1940. His education continued at Boston University until he was drafted into the U.S. Army in January, 1943.

After completing basic training and courses at the Army Radio School, Charlie was transferred to the University of Nebraska for testing to see if he had the necessary qualifications for a newly created "Army Specialized Program" for foreign areas studies. You see, what many of us never knew about Charlie was that he was multi-lingual, with a background in French, Greek, Latin and Spanish.

Charlie's next service career stop was at the University of Missouri, to study Italian. From there, he was sent on to Fort Warren, Wyoming, and Fort Knox, Kentucky, as an interpreter working with Italian prisoners of war. With the end of hostilities, he sailed to Naples, Italy, with soldiers that were being repatriated back to their homeland. After which, he was discharged in March, 1946.

The return to civilian life presented an opportunity for several events to occur in Charlie's life. During a September, 1946, visit to his aunt's house, he met his soon-to-be-wife, Poppy. They were married in June, 1947, and shared nearly 58 years of togetherness. This happy marriage lead to the birth of their two lovely daughters, Maria and Catherine, and the family's eventual move to Saugus in 1960.

Concurrent with his family life, Charlie's professional career was also developing in a rapid fashion. After graduating from Boston University in 1948, he went to work for General Electric as a Cost Accountant. With the passing of time, his responsibilities increased until his retirement in 1985 as Manager of Finance for the G.E.'s Development Assembly and Test Department. As with many dedicated people, Charlie still found time to blend a number of interests into a busy schedule. While being a husband, father, working professional and finance committee member and chairman, he also served as president of the Community Credit Union in Lynn. Later, Charlie was Vice Chairman of the credit union's governing committee and involved in numerous church and social groups.

The tall, bespectacled chairman was dignified in manner and his finance committee meeting were run in a most polite and orderly fashion with everyone having a chance to be heard. However, should the discussion display signs of disorder, Charlie's booming voice would quickly restore civility and decorum. And, what a voice it was! During conversations, his normal speaking voice would be much like anyone else's. In fact, I have even known him to speak in a whisper. But, his public speaking voice could sometimes sound like it was coming from "On High." There was one particular town meeting when Charlie took the podium to give the committee's report. As he was about to speak, the sound system failed and the Town Moderator asked Charlie if he need to wait for repairs. To the laughter of the entire audience he replied, "I think everyone will hear me." And, they did.

One event that clearly demonstrates his commitment to follow personal beliefs goes back to the passage of Proposition $2\frac{1}{2}$ in the early 1980s. This law would limit the ability of local communities to raise revenues by rapidly increasing property taxes. Charlie knew that should the voters support the restriction, the teaching career of one of his young daughters would be short-circuited through layoffs in the ensuing local cost reeducations. Despite that, he strongly believed the property taxes were becoming too great a burden for the average homeowner to handle. He voted for the law and his daughter was laid off, but that was the man living with his convictions and conscience.

In recognition for his years of service to the town, Charles G. Aftosmes was named "Saugus Man of the Year" for 2000.

Mary T. Burke

by
her daughters
Linda, Carol, and Judy

Mary's dedication to the Town of Saugus is not to be forgotten. When she moved to Saugus over 50 years ago, she began working at Sub-Villa and waitressing at Augustine's Restaurant on Route 1. She soon realized, as a single mother of three, that inspiring her daughters meant being involved with youth programs in Saugus.

Our mother started as a Campfire Girl leader and Camp Counselor, which sparked her interest in child safety and lead her to become the first female school crossing guard for the town. She could be found any school day, dressed in full uniform and wearing a bright orange vest safely crossing children to the Evans School.

Mary T. Burke

Not stopping there, she became a Town Meeting member for several years before taking a job dispatching for the Saugus Fire Department where she was employed for 15 years. During this time, Mary was quoted as saying, "I've learned so much about fire prevention and safety that it has inspired me to go into the schools and share this knowledge with the youth." Shortly after, she became the Safety Chairman for the "Stop, Drop and Roll" program that she and Captain Charlie Thomas taught at local schools during Fire Safety Week.

Throughout her involvement at the schools, Mary became fond of working with the children, which soon led her to run for a seat on the Saugus School Committee. Being voted in with overwhelming results she served as a dedicated member for 14 years and performed remarkably as Vice Chairman for several of those years. Throughout her career on the School Committee, Mary was truly devoted, and she had a great relationship with the teachers and students and took pride in her work. Continuing her involvement in ongoing safety campaigns, Mary headed a statewide study for child passenger safety to have seatbelts installed on all public school buses and lead a fingerprinting program with the Saugus Police Department for over 4,000 children.

Known as Mrs. Burke, she could always be found at every school program, such as Flag Day, Earth Day, Graduation Day, band concerts, sporting events or just having lunch in the cafeteria with the students. Mary and her patriotism made sure all of the Saugus schools had new American flags which she had arranged to be donated by the VFW Post 2346 Ladies Auxiliary where she was a life member and served as President for two years. She was also District 10 Past President, Youth Activity Chairman as well as State Safety Chairperson, Publicity Chairperson and Color Bearer in the Ladies Auxiliary. Mary was also involved with many fundraisers such as Heart Fund, Cancer Fund, Cystic Fibrosis Fund, Telethon Chairman of the Saugus Fire Department Muscular Dystrophy Fund, Danny Thomas/St Jude, March of Dimes, Chapter 766 Special Needs Sub-Committee, the "Say No to Drugs" campaign and a leader for SADD (Students against Drunk Driving). She was also a member of the 350th Founders' Day and Hammersmith Stroll Committees.

Mary's dedication and love for her work rarely went unnoticed. She was widely recognized throughout the town, winning numerous awards year after year. One of Mary's proudest moments was being honored for her service to the community and being awarded the first "Person of the Year" award by the Saugus Boosters Club. Currently, each year, a scholarship in her name is given to a SHS graduate.

Even after reaching retirement age, Mary continued with her love for the town and became active in the town Recreation Department and loved her volunteer work at the Saugus Parks Summer Program, where she was an arts and crafts instructor as well as counselor. Throughout the summer, Mary could be found handing out snacks and ice cream or helping out at a cookout with food donated by her favorite local restaurant, Hammersmith Inn.

Wanting to help seniors enjoy life, Mary became a member of the Saugus Senior Citizens Association and a member and President of Heritage Heights Tenants Association where she lived and conducted arts and crafts classes, had cookouts, and ran monthly Bingo trips to Foxwoods. Mary's favorite time was the Friday Night Bingo she ran at the community hall at Laurel Gardens. When anyone needed support, Mary was always available to listen and help if she could. She was a great asset to the town of Saugus and for those of you who had the pleasure of knowing her, you can honestly say she was "The Heart of Saugus."

Florence Chandler

by
Janet Leuci

Town Manager, Town Counsel, standard supporter of the ERA and advocate for women's rights, selectman, volunteer, instructor, student, devoted mother, grandmother, sister, loyal friend. Florence Chandler has been all of these and much more. She is truly an inspiration to women everywhere, not only because of extraordinary accomplishments in the face of adversity, but because, even now, although retired, she continues to contribute to women's issues, her community, and causes in which she believes.

Florence has always believed that women should become involved in politics at all levels, that women see things differently than men and offer a balanced point of view. That at the age of 74 she traveled by bus to Washington, D.C. in April 2004 to participate in the National Organization of Women's March for Women's Lives and "would go again tomorrow" does not surprise those of us who admire her boundless energy and passion for women's rights.

Faced with supporting three teenagers after a divorce in 1976, Florence worked full-time as a bookkeeper for the Saugus School Department. She soon recognized, however, that in order to advance in the work world, it would be necessary to further her education. She enrolled in the Salem State College evening program and two years later in 1978 graduated, magna cum laude, with a degree in government and history.

While at Salem State a professor encouraged her to pursue a career in law, and Florence applied and was accepted to New England School of Law. She worked days as a full-time secretary at Harvard University where, as a university employee, she was allowed to take courses at Harvard Law School gratis. Although she was a full-time student at New England School of Law evenings, she was allowed to transfer twenty-four credits from Harvard Law School toward her law degree. She graduated from New England School of Law, cum laude, in 1981 at the age of 50 and passed the Massachusetts bar.

In 1982 while serving as assistant chief in the Division of Local Services of the Massachusetts Department of Revenue, Florence was one of thirty women appointed by Governor Michael Dukakis to the Governor's Advisory Committee on Women's Issues. She served for four years, advocating statewide for women's issues, recommending legislation, budgets, jobs, and policy, testifying before the Legislature, serving on committees on Comparable Worth and Elderly Abuse Prevention and in 1986 as the editor of *Womenspeak*.

From 1986-1989 Florence served as Town Counsel for both the towns of Southbridge and Sturbridge. But of all her accomplishments, Florence is most proud of having been the only woman town manager of her time. In 1989 while other women served as secretaries or administrators, Florence, as chief executive officer of the town of Southbridge, Massachusetts, was overseeing a community of 17,000 and a budget of 22 million dollars. She was respon-

sible for all the town's operations, including its airport, wastewater treatment plant, water distribution system, personnel policies, labor negotiations, preparation of the annual budget and capital program, coordination of all town departments, contract administration and governmental relations.

Securing a federal accounting facility for the town of Southbridge was certainly one of the most remarkable achievements of her tenure as town manager, although Florence is quick to credit Senator Edward Kennedy as "the real workhorse of the whole proposal who really went all out for that small town." The competition among cities and towns was intense, but those who know Florence, also know that she would never give up, no matter how dismal the outlook. After frequently shuttling to Washington, D.C. to meet with the entire Massachusetts delegation, who were also the recipients of a town wide letter writing campaign, Southbridge was one of the communities chosen. Thanks to Florence's dedication, hard work, and tenacity, the residents of Southbridge, a relatively poor community, benefited from an increase in tax base and an increase in jobs. "It's fun to remember those days," recalls Florence, "although I don't know what kept me going – just sheer determination and cussedness, I guess. I still hate to lose."

While most people who winter in Florida spend their time basking in the sun on the beach or by a pool, Florence remains active volunteering at a shelter for abused women and children. She also volunteers for the American Association of University Women, helping to provide financial aid and scholarships for women who want to return to school. Referring to a passage from *A Streetcar Named Desire*, Florence says that she believes "in the goodness of strangers." In the course of a lifetime many are helped by strangers, but what distinguishes Florence, is her unselfish drive to give back.

Florence's contributions to her own community of Saugus are amazing. She was elected to the Board of Selectmen for two terms from 1987-1991, served as a representative to the Essex County Advisory Board, as a member of the Saugus Finance Committee, the Master Plan Committee, an elected town meeting member, president of the Saugus League of Women Voters from 1978-1980, and President of SAVE. In 2003 Saugus showed its gratitude for her devoted commitment to the Town by naming her "Woman of the Year."

Florence cares deeply about Saugus and its future. Who can ever forget the evening, when Florence, as a selectman, after a controversial vote on a golf driving range issue, was verbally attacked by an opponent. Florence stood up, started off the selectmen's platform after the gentleman, shouting, "Don't you talk to me that way!" The rest is history. As we all now know she was right. That particular business which she opposed, now defunct, was nothing but trouble for the town and for the abutters.

Civil Servants

Without recognition she has helped countless individuals, organizations, and neighborhoods. This writer recalls the evening that Florence, exhausted from her duties in South-bridge, drove two hours to Saugus to attend an important hearing before the Zoning Board of Appeals to help a neighborhood at risk only to find that the hearing had been postponed. Such was and is the commitment of Florence Chandler to the Town of Saugus.

In 2001 she gave countless hours trying to convince voters, businesses, and other community groups of the benefits of passing the Community Preservation Act so that the Town could receive matching funds from the State to secure open space, historical preservation, and affordable housing. Day after day she walked neighborhoods distributing literature.

Florence says that she believes in giving back. When it comes to Saugus, the town she loves, she has never stopped. Intelligent, tenacious, feisty, compassionate, caring, Florence Chandler is truly one of the town's treasures.

Janet Leuci

by
Ellen Burns

It was nearly thirty years ago that I first met Janet Leuci, and remembering her distress at my actions on that occasion it's probably amazing that we shortly afterward became better acquainted and are now such close "political" and even personal friends.

At that time, Janet and her neighbors on or near Wilbur Avenue, off Essex Street near what is now the Square One Mall, had been upset considerably by the blasting being done by TriMount Bituminous, on Route 99, over the hill, and especially by that company's plans to extend their operation to residentially-zoned land adjacent to homes on Wilbur and other nearby streets. So a large group of these people had been encouraged to attend a hearing held by the Saugus Board of Selectmen on TriMount's request to expand even further.

Simultaneously, this writer, as League of Women Voters zoning chairman, had finally decided to do something about our Selectmen's continued refusal to follow state laws regarding newspaper notices before important zoning hearings, which plainly required two weekly ads starting at least two weeks beforehand. The Selectmen's clerk, who in those days - the mid-1970s - was also the Town Clerk (and in this case was also the father of the Selectmen's chairman!) had even told me that the town had its own laws and could and certainly would ignore the state's requirements! So after I addressed a formal complaint, in writing, about the matter

to the Saugus Town Counsel (carefully quoting from state laws), that official showed up at the Selectmen's TriMount hearing where he said plainly that their notice was indeed not legal, and that the Selectmen's hearing could not go on.

Not surprisingly, Janet and her many well-prepared neighbors were stunned by what happened, but they didn't just go home and sulk. They ultimately hired a lawyer who filed against the town, leading to an out-of-court settlement in 1976, which limited the expansion of the quarry, even by future owners, prohibited extension to any residentially-zoned land, and even set aside a 12-acre buffer zone. And at the forefront was Janet Leuci, who was then taking time out from teaching to raise a family.

Janet Quagenti Leuci was born in Revere, graduated from Revere High School, and went on to Boston College, where she received a Bachelor of Science degree in Secondary Education and Spanish. The following year she got a Master of Arts in Italian from Middlebury College. At Woburn High School, on her first teaching job, she met Bill Leuci, another teacher there. They were married in 1965 and moved to Saugus in 1969, after Janet had been a Spanish and Italian instructor at Boston College, and after Billy, the first of their four sons, was born. She then began teaching at night at Harvard's extension school, as well as night classes at Saugus High. In 1981, she went back to regular teaching at Malden Catholic, for five years, then in 1986 went to Revere High School to teach Spanish and Italian. In June, 2003, she retired from teaching, but her service to the Town of Saugus went on.

With a family of four sons, three of them married and adding new Leucis to the family tree; with a gourmet kitchen; and with membership on the pastoral council of her church, Janet's life would certainly seem full enough, after her retirement, even without two other very important factors.

The first of these factors is her continued involvement in Saugus town affairs, since that TriMount victory, eventually going far beyond her immediate neighborhood.

After the TriMount settlement and her return to teaching, Janet had joined the Saugus Action Volunteers for the Environment (SAVE) and served as the group's secretary. Then, in 1986, when another misguided Board of Selectmen voted to grant an outrageous earth removal permit to the owners of the New England Shopping Center as they prepared to start construction on what is now the Square One Mall, Janet got busy again. With SAVE members added to her active neighbors, an organization very effectively called NO-BLAST (Neighbors Opposed to Blasting Ledge and Stone Trucking) was formed, which elected Janet Leuci their president.

The mall owners (then FAM Realty Trust) turned out to be pleasant and reasonable, for nearly a year held many meetings with NO-BLAST, and in October, 1987, all parties signed an agreement, at the Leuci home, which said, in part: "The blasting …will now be limited to only 86,000 cubic yards, a reduction of 82 percent from the plan approved by four members of the Board of Selectmen on Sept. 15, 1986."

It was in the early 1990s that Janet and her neighbors began to have problems with York Ford, on Route 1, when the company was illegally using residentially-zoned land for parking more than one hundred cars, and at the time was even planning to build a body shop on residential land. Janet and her neighbors organized once more, held block parties, dinner dances and yard sales to raise money, and in July, 1995, the Saugus Board of Appeals, to whom the York case was remanded by the State Appeals Court, ordered the cars removed.

It is to the credit of Janet and her neighbors that they did not oppose York's request to rezone some of their residential land for a repair shop and some parking, at which time a two-acre buffer was set aside, to protect nearby residents.

Woman of the Year, Janet Leuci, 2005.

During this same time, Janet Leuci began for the first time to hold local appointive and elective offices, starting in 1989 when Town Manager Norman Hansen appointed her to the Saugus Planning Board, where she joined this writer who had been appointed the previous year. That Janet was not appointed to a second term, in 1994, when three members of a new Board of Selectmen refused to approve her naming by another manager, Edward J. Collins, tells you how "political" the board had become just five years after my own "maybe best ever" Board of Selectmen had so heartily approved Janet's appointment!

But by that time Janet was already a very effective force in Saugus Town Meeting, to which she was first elected in 1991 with Precinct 4's highest vote, which she continued to get, with just one exception, through the most recent town election.

During recent years, she had continued to speak up about things which come in her neighborhood – like the proposed change of zoning in the Collins Avenue area – and elsewhere in town, and she has served on the town's Growth Study and Hillside Protection committees.

But, remember, all that is just one of "two important factors" in Janet Leuci's life.

The other concerns her own health. During the NO-BLAST campaign, in 1987, Janet had a cancerous kidney removed at the New England Deaconess Hospital. In 2001, she had colon cancer surgery, followed by chemotherapy, and in 2003, further surgery. In 2004, as this is being written, she has regular tests, and her most recent results are optimistic.

How does she do it all, including a lot of time spent with her grandchildren? All of us who know her well and admire her so much continue to wonder! That she's been a constant effective force for the good of Saugus and its residents is certain, and we all hope she'll be around forever.

In 2005, Janet was honored as Saugus' Woman of the Year.

Ellen Burns

by
Nora Shaughnessy

When I was first approached to write a "thing" on Ellen Burns, I felt a mixture of emotions. First, of course, I was flattered, but then I was perplexed by a mixture of perspectives. Ellen is hard to know, sometimes difficult to like, impossible to dislike. We've had our differences, but I was always struck by her energy and empathy, and willingness to learn, not only from people, but from her own errors. It's challenging enough for anyone to do, but far harder for someone as intelligent and disciplined as Ellen. Nevertheless, her own honesty and insistence on fairness demand that. Ellen Burns is harder on herself than anyone else could hope to be, and it tends to make her harder on the rest of us, as well.

When I first met Ellen, she reminded me of my mother, and I can't think of a better compliment. Like my mother, I found Ellen impressive and more than a little imposing. She didn't look to me like other women of her age or place, which I mistakenly took to be Saugus. She didn't look like anyone else's mother, but I knew she was. Her son, David, was a year behind me at Saugus High, and her husband, a retiring, soft-spoken man, was Chairman of the English Department.

I found my instinct to be correct: Ellen Burns is extraordinary, and though she makes Saugus her own place, she comes from everywhere. But first, she comes from Ohio by way of Kansas City, Missouri, where she earned a Bachelor's Degree in English and Education at Missouri University in 1936. She's pleased to tell you that Eleanor Roosevelt spoke to her company when she was commissioned as an ensign in the United States Navy at Smith College in 1943, where she completed training.

Ellen met John in the Navy, just after WWII, when she was a WAVE communications officer in Boston, where he was sent after serving in the Pacific aboard a destroyer escort. She joined when her brother did, to serve the country both loved during WWII, and she was sent east for training and to study codes. She's still serving her country, but now it's her fellow Saugonians, and her various "families" here.

Woman of the Year, Ellen Burns, 2004.

After she and John married, they lived in Cambridge, but then returned to his hometown of Saugus, where she was at first bored, but then as involved as Ellen always will be where ever she is. Her determination to affect change is served by her enthusiasm for making things better than she finds them, and this lends her discipline further strength.

I am not sure if the discipline came first, or the Navy set it into place, but Ellen can find a warrant from seven years ago, and tell you who spoke for or against an article in that Town Meeting. I can barely find my behind with both hands, and am constantly awed by her meticulous memory, and the largely self-imposed file system that supports it.

She is something of an intellectual: a thinker, well-informed, and always ready for battle, but with the requisite number of blind spots. Mr. Burns, John, is a fine match. His quiet, gentle exterior hides a mask of wit and humor, tempered by kindness and patience, but firm and equally resourceful.

You'd have to be patient to be married to Ellen. The word we're supposed to use now is "assertive," but Ellen is as bossy as my mother was. She knows quite well which is the best road to take, and has little tolerance for those of us who can't quite make the grade. In fact, our fellow Town Meeting member, Elly Rosenberg, says Ellen's strong ideals and positive approach to problem-solving is what makes her so admirable.

Ellen has been in Town Meeting since 1977. She was a member of The Charter Commission, disagreeing with the majority on Saugus's becoming a city. "Fortunately," she says, "it was defeated at the polls!" She's been an appointed member of the Zoning Board of Appeals, the Planning Board and the Library Board of Trustees, and numerous Town Meeting-created committees. She has authored several changes to the town charter and zoning by-laws, made many — too many to count — amendments to Town Meeting Warrant Articles, and written many Articles themselves.

And Ellen has those wonderful blind spots: like the one that causes her to look askance at computers, preferring her own old typewriter and paper files to an artificial contrivance like a screen with some intelligence and a lot of unfathomable space. Ellen is ultimately taken by fact, and by what she can touch, rather than by preposterous ideas. It makes her the ultimate realist, and may well be the basis for her ability to see with more clarity than I often do.

Another Town Meeting member, and friend for whom both Ellen and I have a great deal of respect, Janet Leuci, says this:

"No other Town Meeting member commands as much respect as Ellen. When she walks to the podium in long, resolute strides with elbows pointed, everyone takes notice and listens."

Janet Leuci thinks that one of Ellen's finest moments at Town Meeting came when a local attorney got a court injunction preventing the Planning Board from meeting to make a recommendation on a rezoning issue. "Town Meeting would have had to reconvene for that one article, but Ellen made a motion to adjourn *sine die*, and the article was killed. Her quick thinking forced the necessity of the company involved to negotiate with the neighbors."

I can easily agree with what Janet says that Ellen is a fighter, willing to fight Town Hall, and find the best way to do what's fair for the people involved. She influenced my mother the same way, though both my mother's parents were in Town Meeting at one time or another.

Janet Leuci goes on, "So many of us have depended on her over the years. She has great instincts and insight. I do not know what we would do without her. She is invaluable to the Town."

Janice Jarosz, former Selectman, writer, and editor of *The Saugonian*, for which Ellen wrote a column intermittently, says it a bit differently. "Ellen," she says, "made a statement to me years ago that I shall remember forever. It was 'don't brood.' Wow! To me this was so powerful yet so simple. Ellen not only spoke those words but lived them... I remember one campaign we worked on at the state level that we lost quite handily. I just about threw in the towel but Ellen was up the next day on the phone chatting about another positive endeavor she was working on with not a hint of regret."

Both Janet and Janice agree on Ellen's knowledge and understanding of zoning law. Janice says she even dubbed her the "Queen of Zoning."

My own real introduction to Ellen, prior to my election to Town Meeting, was when I joined SAVE (Saugus Action Volunteers for the Environment), an organization founded by Ellen and a few others, with the plan "to promote a better quality of life in Saugus through environmental concern and action." This group is responsible, in part, for curbside recycling in town; for the Saugus Tree Farm, which will make trees available in neighborhoods far more inexpensively than they would be commercially, as well as for preserving town trees from unnecessary removal; for preserving Prankers Pond, and a large part of Vinegar Hill from development or pollution; and of course, for preventing further development of the RESCO incinerators and landfill on the Saugus marshes.

It is for all these reasons that Ellen was made Saugus's Woman of the Year this year, 2004, and she deserved it long ago. When I commented to David Burns that she looked uncomfortable up there, on the podium, the day she received this accolade, he answered, "but poised, always poised."

My sorrow is that Pat Annis, Ellen's friend and colleague in all this, could not be here to see that, or to read this.

Janice Jarosz says, "Despite all her family responsibilities, Ellen has been able to mix her love of politics and environmental vision while keeping a balance. I do not know if it's her strong German heritage or those 300 stairs she climbs in and out of her home. Whatever it is, it works for her."

It works for all of us, and Ellen isn't finished.

E.L. Masters has Lucinda Matlock saying:

> What is this I hear of sorrow and weariness?
> Anger, discontent and drooping hopes?
> Degenerate sons and daughters,

> Life is too strong for you—
> It takes life to love Life.

Dr. Frederick J. Wagner

by
Carol Wagner

Dr. Fred Wagner.

It was in 1952 when Dr. Frederick J. Wagner, having recently moved to Saugus with his young family and busy with his Boston optometric practice, was encouraged to enter town politics. Fifty years later and 90 years of age, Dr. Wagner still feels it is important in his life to "give back to the community." Dr. Wagner has traveled a long political road. In Saugus, he served first as a member of the town Youth Commission and then became a Saugus Town Meeting member, an elected Selectman for eight years, and acting Town Manager for four different intervals. For the past twenty-five years he had held the position as Chairman of the Board of Assessors. He has always had time for Saugus. In 2002, Saugus honored him as "Man of the Year."

His political career began when a new friend, Frederick Willis, Attorney to the House of Representatives, encouraged Dr. Wagner to seek a seat on the Board of Selectmen. A controversial issue regarding the granting of a liquor license in proximity to Boy Scout Camp Nihan had arisen against the desires of the citizens. Dr. Wagner won that election, and his first act was to recall the license.

It was also during this time that he was serving as President of the Boston Society of Optometrists and had recently been appointed by Governor Foster Furculo as a member of the State Board of Registration of Optometry to oversee the licensure and activities of members. For the next 25 years he was reappointed by Governors Endicott Peabody, Francis Sargeant, and Edward King. Balancing his position of practicing optometry with the responsibilities of local and state politics has always been a serious but enjoyable challenge.

Since those days in the 1950s, Dr. Wagner has involved himself continually in his professional affairs while also finding the time to be involved in the affairs of the Town of Saugus. He was voted an honorary member of the Massachusetts Chiefs of Police Association while also serving as a member of the Metropolitan Bay Transportation Authority and the Metropolitan Area Planning Council for the Commonwealth. President Nixon appointed him to be a member of the Selective Service Board for the 9th District. Adding to all of these activities he had time to be Director of the Saugus Bank and Trust and an active member of the American Optometric Association.

Dr. Wagner has taken a great satisfaction over the last fifty years watching Saugus grow from a town with inadequate facilities and serious environmental problems to a burgeoning town government. During his first three years as a selectman, he was involved in the building of three school facilities (Belmonte, Oaklandvale, and Lynnhurst). The town installed more than five miles of main sewer lines, ten miles of paved highways, a mile of new water mains, nearly a mile of concrete curbing, and two miles of storm drainage systems. A sub-fire station was built and more police officers and firemen were added. He is proud of the fact that in 1964 while serving as a member of the Board of Selectmen the *Boston Globe* published this statement, "The year 1964 will go down in history as the greatest year of civic improvement and achievement since the Town of Saugus was incorporated in 1815."

While continuing to practice his profession at age 90, Saugus residents can also find Dr. Wagner every Monday night at Town Hall trying to resolve people's tax problems. Today, Dr. Wagner still enjoys the challenge of balancing his professional responsibilities with his political responsibilities.

State Department Service

The difference between stupid and intelligent people – and this is true whether or not they are well-educated – is that intelligent people can handle subtlety.

— Neal Stephenson

James Franklin Jeffrey

Saugus Man Answers Call to be Ambassador to Albania

by
Chris Stevens
(*The Daily Item* October 18, 2002)

Saugus native James Franklin Jeffrey has made a career out of living in tenuous places at the beck and call of the United States Government – first in the military, then as a diplomat, and now as the newest ambassador to Albania.

Sworn in on Tuesday afternoon, October 15, by Deputy Secretary of State, Richard Armitage, Jeffrey, a career member of the Senior Foreign Services, was given the formal title of minister-counselor to be ambassador extraordinaire and plenipotentiary of the United States of America to the Republic of Albania.

"Albania will be a challenging area," Jeffrey said Tuesday night by phone from Washington. "For many years it has been rocked by conflict, but now, thanks to America's aid, they have fragile peace."

"It is a peace Albanians are critical of," Jeffrey added, saying "it will take a sensitive and experienced hand to maintain."

That is something the 1964 Saugus High School graduate (who was named "Most Likely to Succeed") has experience with, after serving in Kuwait when the country was still reeling from the Gulf War. Throughout his diplomatic career, Jeffrey also spent time in Tunis, Sofia, Munich, Adana and Ankara.

"It's a combination of playing poker and doing brain surgery," he said.

When asked how one trains for such a position, Jeffrey said, "Like anything else – experience and practice."

Currently, Albania, which is slightly smaller than the state of Maryland, is working toward integration with Europe. The country has calmed down since the civil unrest with neighboring Kosovo and Serbia and is moving steadily toward the direction of the European Union, while also trying to establish normal relations with neighboring Slavic countries and remaining as neutral as possible in the ethnic conflicts in Kosovo and Macedonia.

Experience and Practice

- Career member of the Senior Foreign Service, Class of Minister-Counselor

- Married to Gudrun Melitta Jeffrey, two children – Julia and Jahn

- Born in Melrose, Massachusetts, now a resident of Herndon, Virginia

Education

- Sorbonne University Overseas Language Program, 1978-1979, Certificate in French Language

- Boston University European Program, 1975-1977

- Master of Science in Business Administration, North-eastern University, 1964-1969, Bachelor of Arts

Military Service

- United States Army, 1969-1977 – Second and First Lieutenant, Captain. Stationed, in addition to the United States, in Vietnam and Germany. Received Department of Defense Meritorious Service Medal, 1976; Department of Defense Joint Service Commendation Ribbon, 1973; Department of Defense Bronze Star, 1973; Department of Defense Vietnam Service Ribbon, 1973; United States Army Ranger Tab, 1970; United States Army Airborne Badge, 1969.

A Statement of James Franklin Jeffrey, Ambassador Designate to the Republic of Albania

To The Committee on Senate Foreign Relations

June 25, 2002

Mr. Chairman and Members of the Committee, it is a great honor for me to appear before this Committee to review my nomination to be Ambassador of the United States to Albania. I am deeply moved by the faith and trust which the President and Secretary Powell have demonstrated by nominating me. If confirmed by the Senate, I promise to coordinate and cooperate closely with this Committee and with your colleagues in the Senate and House of Representatives, in support of American goals in Albania and the larger region.

I am delighted to have by my side here my wife Gudrun, and my daughter, Julia. Gudrun, my companion for thirty years, is as enthused as I am about the possibility of living in Tirana and promoting bilateral friendship. My son Jahn, a dual citizen of Germany and America, could not be here as he was drafted into military service in Germany and has volunteered for a German unit on order to Kabul. Julia will serve as an intern this summer in this very institution.

My children are following in a family tradition. I served in the United States Army from 1969 to 1976, volunteered for Vietnam, and served there in 1972. My father, Herbert Jeffery, a disabled veteran, enlisted in the Massachusetts National Guard, was called up in 1940, and served on active duty for five years, including on Guadalcanal. My mother Helen, waiting for her fiancé for years as he passed from the South Pacific to hospitals in the United States, set an equally shining example. I deeply regret that my parents are no longer with us.

I have devoted my twenty-five years of service as a Foreign Service Officer to crisis management, conflict prevention, and when necessary, supporting military action, in Europe and the Middle East. I have worked in Balkan affairs as an embassy officer in Sofia, and as Greek Desk Officer, in the 1980s; in the 1990s, I was deeply involved in peacekeeping in Southeastern Europe, and later served in a senior position implementing the Dayton Accords. I have also worked on the Arab-Israeli issue, and for the past six years I have been active in our efforts, out of Turkey and Kuwait, to deal with both Iraq and Iran. In the past year, I have had the great honor to help my country, in a way, respond to September 11, as we in Turkey engaged that ally in a massive support and troop deployment effort culminating in Turkey's assumption of the International Security Force in Afghanistan. Over these past thirty-three years, in and out of uniform, I have tried to promote our values, and to ensure that diplomatic action and military options were fully balanced, coordinated, and complementary. I have every intention of deploying this knowledge and experience in Albania, if confirmed, to help preserve the triumph of diplomacy, which we, our allies, and the people of the region, working together, have achieved in the Balkans against the forces of oppression and aggression.

If you entrust me with this mission to Albania, my first priority, always, will be force protection – of those personnel assigned to me, their dependents, private American citizens in Albania, and all Americans under threat of any actions emanating in any way from Albania. That was my first duty during my tenure as Deputy Chief of Mission in Kuwait and Turkey, two countries under a fearsome terrorist threat, and I intend to bring the same focus to Tirana. Simultaneously, I pledge to prosecute any and all responsibilities related to the Global War on Terrorism with utmost vigor. Another vital priority for me will be facilitating the further integration of Albania into Western institutions, promoting reform, and opening that country up to trade, including with the United States. Leadership of all our mission staff, maintaining high morale, and protecting classified information will all have a top priority. I deeply believe in the mission which I hope to be given, and will devote all my energy to it if confirmed. In so doing, I will build on the work of our former Ambassador, Joseph Limprecht, who died tragically just a few short weeks ago.

United States relations with Albania are excellent; the level of cooperation and friendship we enjoy there is hard to match anywhere in the world. This stems from the great admiration a succession of Albanian governments, as well as the Albanian people, have for the United States and everything it stands for. It is also a reflection of the strong and positive engagement – along with our European Allies – that we have sustained in Southeast Europe over the past nearly ten years. If confirmed, I intend to build on this excellent relationship and use it to further United States goals in Albania and in the region.

Jim Jeffrey and wife Gudrun.

Continued close cooperation in the war against terrorism will be my first goal, as I have said. Fostering a continuation of Albania's helpful approach to problems in the region will also be at the top of my agenda. Albania's relations with its neighbors are good, and the government gives no rhetorical or physical comfort to those outside Albania who seek, through violence, to destabilize the region. It cannot always control what comes and goes across its borders, however. Strengthening Albania's borders, a United States goal for some time, continues to be of critical importance, both as a contribution to regional stability, but also to help restrict the insidious illegal trafficking in drugs, arms, and people. The latter problem is a signal issue for the Albanians, one where they recognize their insitutions' shortfall in restricting the illegal trafficking but have yet to get a handle on the problem. We should continue to help them do so, both through our assistance and by urging the government to take the tough decisions necessary, and exert maximum political will on law enforcement organs.

Albania very definitely and appropriately sees its future in Europe. Pending continued political stability and progress on the reform agenda, the European Union recently announced plans to open negotiations with Albania on a Stabilization and Association Agreement, a development that will put Albania on the path for future membership. Albania is also a NATO aspirant, and is working closely with us to make progress on its Membership Action Plan to ready its armed forces and its political institutions for membership in the Alliance. A Europe whole, free and at peace needs a stable and integrated Balkans region. Working closely with European partners, the United States is assisting Albania integrate into European, Euro-Atlantic and world institutions. If confirmed, I will help lead that effort in Tirana.

Lastly, although Albania had made great strides since overthrowing communism in 1991, and since the upheaval of 1997, its transformation to a fully functioning democracy and prosperous market economy is very much a work in progress.

Transparent commercial law, fully functioning independent courts, well-developed NGOs, free movement of capital, and a society largely free of corruption are still only goals. But progress is being made in many areas, including privatization, free media, and electoral reforms.

I thank you for the opportunity today to discuss these issues, both in terms of current United States policy and my own background and vision of how I might carry out the duties entrusted to me if confirmed. Albania's tragic history of repression and isolation, and its very geography, have challenged its people fundamentally. Through robust engagement with Albania and the region, we have a chance to help bring Albanian people into the Euro-Atlantic community, and to strengthen the growing stability and peace in the region. I look forward to the opportunity to be a part of that effort by representing my country in Tirana.

The State Department Hills

by
Betsy Nelson Hatfield
(With many thanks to the Hills, who provided facts, anecdotes, and perspective)

Robert B. Hill (1920-1999) was in high school, so it would have been the late 1930s when a Saugus High School teacher took her class to a foreign affairs event in Boston. According to Bob's wife, my sister-in-law Constance Silver Hill (1920-2005), another Saugus native, it was a lecture he heard that day that inspired his interest in the U.S. Foreign Service. The functions of the economic and political officers were not quite as neatly divided during the years of his service as they are today, and Bob served with distinction through a wide range of assignments abroad and in Washington, DC.

Bob attended Bowdoin College in Brunswick, Maine, graduating with honors in 1942. After three years in the Army Air Corps, he passed the foreign-service entrance exam and embarked upon his 33-year career.

His first overseas assignment, in 1946, was in Antwerp, Belgium. Then, in 1949, Connie and Bob were married; they had known each other since they were four years old and living next door to each other in East Saugus. Bob's parents were Frank and Evelyn Hill. Connie's were Dr. John and Katherine Silver.

Bob and Connie traveled directly to Bob's - although, given the important role of the foreign service spouse, it may be fairer to say "their" – new post in Budapest. (In 2000, when Connie and I went to Poland and Hungary to visit their diplomat sons Chris and Nick and their families, we stopped to see the handsome house in Budapest where Connie and Bob lived in as newlyweds.) Two subsequent assignments were also in continental European capitals: Paris, from 1951 to 1954, and Belgrade, from 1958 to 1961.

Several tours of duty brought the family back to the States: opportunities for graduate study at both the Fletcher School of Law and Diplomacy at Tufts University and the Naval War College in Newport, Rhode Island, and several assignments in Washington. Bob also served as Diplomat in Residence at his alma mater, Bowdoin College, during the 1975–76 academic year.

Foreign service is a family business. It is a life rich in rewards for a family, paramount among them, of course, getting to know many cultures and their interesting people at first hand. Some experiences are exotic. In late 1967, after leaving the two oldest of their five children in schools in Rhode Island, the family traveled by ship from New York City to Naples, Italy, and then on to Istanbul, Turkey, where they spent several days sightseeing before boarding a train for Bob's next post at the U.S. Embassy in Ankara. Three other trips, to and from Turkey, involved traveling on the Orient Express between Istanbul and Paris, where the Hills were able to spend several days in between transatlantic flights.

Because of the many moves, the repeated re-establishing of oneself in new communities and schools, it is a way of family life that demands flexibility and cooperation - and then some. The Hills, I discovered, could move into a house at noon and eat in a dining room with pictures on the wall the same evening! Sacrifices are called for. Frequently, older children are in school in the states while their parents are thousands of miles away.

There can also be danger. The Hills were in Haiti during part of the rebel Ton Ton Macoute era. Following a hold-up by armed rebels of a car that was taking Bob to the U.S. embassy during one nighttime emergency in late 1963, Connie and the children were speedily evacuated to their house in Rhode Island. Bob remained behind for several months in those pre-cell phone, pre-instant news days.

Bob and Connie's five children, Prudence, Christopher, Elizabeth, Nicholas, and Jonathan, have keen and happy memories of growing up well informed in a home where U.S. and world events were everyday topics. Four of the five were, in fact, born overseas. Evenings before dinner, Bob and the children sat in the living room for an hour's discussion of current events and politics, with Bob some-times playing the devil's advocate, to the children's conster-nation. All five of the children remain avidly interested in world affairs and two have made foreign service their career.

Chris and Nick Hill followed their father into the State Department, where they also are serving with distinction. Chris, age 53, the immediate past U.S. Ambassador to South Korea, is the Assistant Secretary of State for East Asia Pacific and chief U.S. negotiator in the talks with North Korea.[1] In 2005, Nick, age 46, earned a Master's degree (his second) at the National War College of the National Defense University in Washington and is Chief of the U.S. Embassy's Trade Policy Unit in Tokyo, Japan. Both have received accolades for their distinguished service on behalf of the United States.

---

1. On September 19, 2005, in *CompuServe News*, Asso-ciated Press reporter Burt Herman wrote, "North Korea on Monday agreed to stop building nuclear weapons and allow international inspections in exchange for energy aid, economic cooperation and security assurances, in a first step toward disarma-ment after two years of six-nation talks." Chris Hill characterized the agreement as a "win-win situation," while cautioning, "We have to see what comes in the days and weeks ahead." The talks continue as of this writing.

Evocative Names

In the beginning, there was Chaos. Chaos nurtures Progress. Progress enhances Order. Order tries to defy Chaos at all cost. But my friend, if and when Order wins the final battle against Chaos, I will mourn, 'cause Progress will be dead.

— Anonymous

Evocative Pages for Saugonians

by

Thomas Sheehan and John Burns

A twist that we come thus to this,
remember the face and not the kiss,
which names beget and names beguile,
which took their turn and gave us style.
People and places, here are some
that've brought us to the millennium.

Gladys Fox John Mullen Abraham Pinciss John Leahy Pearl Belonga George Drew Adventure Car-Hop Braid's Market Franklin Pike Googie Amory Hoffman's Hardware Randy Popp Father Francis Hardiman Butler's Drug Store Wesley Gage Miss Chase / Hurll John A.W. Pearce Stanley Day Sr. Stanley Day Jr. Norm Hanson Miss Dorr Miss Bannon Mrs. Gibson Donald Hammond Leon Young The London Sisters Fred Forni Edward Gibbs Red Milano Jerry McCarthy Edie Noretsky Maple Farm Dairy Nicholson Dairy Stillings Farm Dairy Peter O'Grady Jack Fahey Albert Moylan Bill Bright Bill Weld Edjo Wozny Jimmy Boyle Bazooka Bob Burns Walter Blossom Butch Batchelder All The Nagles On The Hill George McCarrier C. Carrol Cunningham Charles Flynn William Rockhill The Economy Store Walter O'Grady Harry Bamford Eddie Smiledge Roy and Willard Buckless Don Ryder Saugus Drive-In Theater State Theater Dream Theater Ludwig's Cleaners Rev. Clay Rev. Bee Vin Pendleton Porter's Donuts Steve Agneta Eastern Industrial Oil Vortexol Heinkel Burke's Variety Store Lt. George Hull Eddie Higgins Tony Flammia Slink Mike Maruzzi Gustafson & Warren Florists The Meadow Glen The Wigwam Young's Market Unity Camp Mike Tanen Dot Runge Kay Spencer Ken Fabrizio William Kelley John Burns Bill Doyle Father William Culhane Dr. Carp Mildred Salsman Tom Gecoya George Moriello Tom Connors Mike Harrington and Eddie Shipulski Bomar's Gas Station Don Moses Ma Corbett Kimball's Market Hollis Hogle Marcie Caruthers Charlie Bilton Jim Allen Frank DeMaso The Bidwell Sisters Eddie LeBlanc George Beckford Fred Landry Earl Dudman John's Gas Station & Bar Broadway Club George Eaton James Shurtleff Robert Hagopian Hazel Marison Pioneer Store Carl's Duck Farm Augustine's Dick & Jim & Ada Dow Norman LeBlanc John Busdriver Taatjes Bob Kodzis Harry & Gloria Hashem Harry Mazman Don Trainor Doug Waybright Penney's Orchards Bertha Morrison Elizabeth Taylor Marleah Graves Miss Goss The Music Teacher Siaglo's Piggery Fred Rippon's Mushroom Plant The Pit Rumney's Marsh Walter Neal Paul F. Neal Gus Belmonte Harold Vitale The Bel Air Diner Myra Beckman Paul Gibbs Fred Willis Alfred Woodward Art Spinney

Matt Russo Joe D. Evelyn Rodgers Lennie and George Flaherty Tom Skahan Joe Laura Charlie Sellick Jimmy Maher James Sullivan Jimbo & Brother Bentley Roy Bacon The Surabian Brothers All The Ludwigs (Sammy Jimmy Wilbur Herbie Frankie Barbara) Marc Fauci Virginia Means Dotty Hatch Jimmy Fauci Lorraine Bousineau Evie Jones Doctor Roos Fiore Sacco Ellie Devine Billie The Cheerleader McCarthy Eldon Sweezey Dr. Edward Faulkner Louie Sherman Walter DeFranzo Bennie Wolfe Jim MacGillvary Red Parrott Georgie Miles Dave Lucey Hank Tosczilowski Buzz Harvey Mad Anthony Morandes Porky Bernier Bennie Rice Warnie's Cafe Herb White's Diner The Slop Shop Joe Sanborn Marshie Berrett The Felton The Sweetser The Armitage The Mansfield Orin Bentley The North Saugus The Emerson Raymond Love Sam Parker Lon Green Herb & Alice Wills Janice & Ron Jarosz Fred and Betty Quinlan Freddie Crafts Donkey Field Indian Slide Indian Rock Lily Pond The Dam at Lily Pond The Canal Rooms at The Tash's Artie Tash the Fisherman Bud DeMaci Fred Brooks Walter LeBlanc's Gas Station Jimmy Meter Reader Griffin Joe George & Sis Laskey Bill & Steve Peach Chris Serino Belden Bly Tom O'Hearn Buddy Murphy Art & Don Stead Dick & Edson & Frank Evans Bruce Waybright All The Fortis on Lincoln Ave Coach Bobby Gaudet Nick and Sue Capecci Parsons Oil Co. Benny Fullerton Welcome McCullough Mr Mansur Helen Moses DesChene Nick Vanagel Dick Barry Jimmy MacDougall Frank Pyszko John Gould Louise Solomita Tony Cogliano Bob Kane Ormy Brooks Gilbert Bradbury Fr. William Carey Fr. James Piersoll Janette Fasano Dennie Cronin Frank Parkie Parkinson Bill Maloney Soupy Campbell Brownie Muckles Beaver Jake Sinagna Dropkick 39 Stone Dottie Pike George Pike Dick Rubin Prof. Don Junkins Eddie McCarthy Grayce Chapman Hugh Menzies Bobby Braid Louie Gordon Herb Upton Red and Dick and Jane and Dan and Darren McCullough Msrs. Morrison and Butler Rev Walter Smith Carl Maynard Carl Matson Ted Brierly Tim & Graham Churchard Brian Cunningham Sanborn News Capt Joe & Judy Burns Charlie Hecht Mrs. Woodbury Jean Sherman Stan & Tootie Green Jack & Martha Warren George Nicholson Vernon Evans Bill and Margie Calhoun Bruce Wallace Jim Burns Doc Carter Edna Winslow Scott Brazis Malcolm Bisbee Lil Pittard Neil Howland Tommy Atkins Skip Moorehouse Larry Daniels Heavenly Gates Paul Ciccarelli Dr Silver Tony DeMatteo Carmine Moschella Bill Falasca Paul O'Brien Charlie Comfort Bob Fawcett Paul Huggins Sherman's Market Ray & Jeanette Maes Rexall Drug Store Kennie At The Gas Station In Saugus Center The Old Library The New Library The Stanleys on The Pike Chief Bo Parrott Eddie Cafarella Chief Stuart Del Godding Roy Bucchiere John Bucchiere Virginia Oliver The Prentice Brothers The Cinder Path down to Smith Road Ted Jaquith Vin Murray Hack Wilson Jim Patch Lou Finocchioro Kevin Wortman Paul Bund Arthur Strout Paul Kinnaly John Scarborough John Janusas Hazel Fiske Jerry Mitchell Dr Chadsey Dr

Clark Dr Beckman Mrs Louise Hawkes Donovan Florists Graham's Market   Don and Art Stead   Art Statuto and Mim Sophie Melewski Anthony Scire Norm Downs Al Powers Dick Provenzano Bob Wentworth Basil Parker Tommy Atkins Eddie Ayers Bill McKinney Tommy Carr Jimmy Driscoll C.F.Nelson Pratt Helen Sharp   James Butterworth Ernest Merrithew Fiske's and Sawyer's and Monteith's Ice Houses   Hart Bus Lines   James Conway Charles Flynn   Bill Rockhill George Quarmby Tony and Dick Serino Anna Parker Chief Thompson Frank Sloan Frank Bennett Ronnie Carlton Jim Marano Dan Sharp Charlie Woodell   Arthur Williams   Henry Peckham Lawrence Morse Lucey Mears Norris   Harold Dodge Eddie Ayers Art Rowe Mellon Joy   Mildred Dinsmore Ray Costey George Hull Wally Woods Eric Brown Danny Neville Henry Wheaton Bill and Florence Peach Jimmy Quinlan Jim Harrington Sandra Whyte Chris Whyte Anna Hastings Old Pioneer Store Benson Shapiro Jack Shapiro Cogliano's Market Baker Hill Standpipe Board of Trade 39 Stone Bob Belyea Ruth Belyea Bucker Holmes Joe Siaglo Russ and Alice Babcock   Hal Huff   Ed Gaudet Harry Woodward Bailey Mason   John Stinson Frank Green James Shurtleff   Pat Cusick Hank Waitt Dan McLean Dean Sacca Buddy Tottingham Ernie Salsman Billie Callahan Eddie Hayes Les Woodbury Phil Barbanti David Lee Wilson Brian Guinta   Myron Manoogian Samuel Gillespie Welcome Goss   Brian Andreottola Tommy and Jimmy Morse Gen. Tom Courant   Ben McGlashin Joseph Kerwin Leo and Richie Kane Brian Robinson   Janet Leuci Jesse Lambert Jesse Morgan Rhoden Eddy Keith Manville Isabel Hallin Annie Hallin Paul Haley Ashton Davis Lorraine Davis Austin Griffin Joe and Charlie and Dottie Cox   Alfred Woodward Paul Boucher John Kennedy   Don Halpin Johnny Hancock Elmer Watson Kellie Reehill Fred Brussard Bobby Parley Art Michelson George Longfellow Tom Spencer Tommy Hashem   Dutchland Farms Ice Cream Dickie Mallar Howard Johnsons   Dick Rubin Larry Senfleben Lloyd Reynolds June Reynolds John Lumsden Johnny Knights Charlie Tordiglioni Delores Hiltz Peter Scully Bobby Foster Raphael Zammitt Katherine Griffin Dora Parasco Edith Bateman Nonda Anganis Louie Vient Dave Hurwitz Jim Currier Mary & Betty Brougham   Mickey Dygert Lloyd and Grover and Eleanor Parsons Joe & Richie & Alice & Kay & Bill & John Burke Bob Osgood Jackie Burton Ellen Burns Joe Borghetti Ozzie Gregson Florent Daniels Larry Daniels Tessie Woods Lyla Kush Brother Parker Charlie Davis Eileen Hayes Domey Charlie and Edie McKenna Rev. John Mulloy Buster Courtis Red Jenkins   Kenny Buck Jones Edith Forward Del Pitman Lorne and Kenny and Stanley and Mike and Don Green Hank and Stan and Frank Wladkowski Lois Pye Eunice Harrington   Henry McKeever Lenny Cook   Ballard Gardens Chickland Barbeque Roma Gardens The Blue Star Oak Knoll Eddie Koschei Bob Connell Ben Belonga Nick Baressi Dick Allen Charlie Cooper Harold Rice Fred Willis Vera Jean York George Fyfe Keystone Battery

Ernie Light   Nicoli Cafe Butchie's Salem Street Auto and Tony also   Dennie Cronin Lumber   Graham's Market Edwin Earl The Wigwam The Aero Club Happy Valley Cabins   Cal's Social Club Ace Welding Tom Trainor George Hussey Don Trainor Harry Mazman Ada Aucella Roy Pearson Bennie Fullerton Harold and Warren Igoe Matt and Jamie and Betsy Stanley Konczal Betty Konczal Tom Hennessey Don Grimes John and Eddie Falasca Edgar and Al DeSteuben Stewart Atkins Natalie MacAdoo Stuart Kidder William Legrow Robert Vatcher Lloyd Farrin Robert Lord Andy Britt Fred Neale Frank Bond George Cronin Larry Cronin David Anderson Grace St. Cyr Bill and Kay McCarthy Fred Fischer Bernie and Paul and Clarence Noyes Jim Amero Walter Butler Peter and Jim Hanlon Tom & Tim & Laurie Sheehan Vickie Gregson Tony Borghetti   John O'Neil Tom and Helen Dow Ralph Fiske Jim Lovejoy Archie Amirault Dorothy Gibbs Mal Comfort Rocco and James and Christy and Mike Ciampa Newhall's Package Store Jesse Brown Roger Howland International Clam House Pugach Furniture Bob & Fred's Grill Ethel Blundell Joe Markowski Allenhurst Riding Academy John C. Harris Joe Kiley Peter Wishnewsky Dimi and Jimmy Nicolo Edward Quinn Jake Tucker David Penny H. Joseph Berrett Steve and Don Pettito George and Leo Philpot Shirley Sproul Eddie Fritz Harlan Searles John Fahey   Gordy Sheppard   Jim and Phyl MacDonald Coach Ted Galligan Gene and Charlie and Joe Decareau Bob and Judy Hoffman Steve Carlson Robert Leland Joe and Matt Gerniglia Rail Anstrice Kellog Ina Jalava Charlie Donovan Emilio Maestranzi Bob Christiano Fiore Sacco Dick Murphy Charlie Thomas LJ McKanas Charles Glebus Wilfred Edmands Jimmy's Auto Parts Ryman's Garage Joseph Kellner William Hobbs Gerald Brazis Harriett Vatcher Rodney Bamford The Wozny Brothers Bob and Dave and Marcia Hughey Jackie Henderson from the Ozarks Bob Waitt Guy Collins Bill Cahill George Bickford Walt & Terry Ruszkowski Bob Phillips Darren Brown Chuckie and Karen and Jay Shipulski Ada & John Anderson   Richard Kasabuski   Mike Ferrera Bob Nickerson John and Dan and Tom Heaney   Chet Gay The Esserys   Edson & Patty Eisan Billy Horne Ginnie & Bimper Gigger Sinagna Jake Mushawee Beaver Red Sid Rory Joseph Meacom Arthur Williams Jessie Lambert Lucy Mears Norris   Dick Fritz Pam Thornton Red Meagher Danny Laskey Frank Foster Louie Roveto Itzy Noretsky Johnny Nelson Husky Walsh Eddie O'Neil Donna Stanton's Novel Ideas Linda Farley Husky Gronski Ted Wheeler Yvonne Bourque Paul Waugh Bill Moffat Saugus 5&10-$1 Nelson's Service Station State Candy Shoppe Lincoln Cafe Butch's Place-Squash Sq-Tel.1003 Charlie and Tom Gaeta   Morell's Barber Shop Washington Square Delicatessen Jack Burton J H Brown R L Sweezey Screens & Shades-Tel. 1306 Michael Russo Paul J Hayes George Wheaton's Pioneer Food Store-Tel. 955 Charlie O'Connor's Barber Shop Wesolowski Brothers Printing Chester Francis E Bishop Vogt's Service Station Brown's Shoe Repairing   C H Stocker Co. Fred P. Taylor C.W.

Kennerson's Sunnyside Market-Tel.952 Dahlen's Store SHS Pres. Ed Patterson   Herman G. Bunker-Tel. 1111 Sherwood's Dutchland Jim NJ Smith Don Jones Green's Landing Fred England Allen Sawyer Lynwood Riding Academy   Joan Barnes Kathy Cargill Babe Emberley Diane Bena Davis Home Circle Store Carol Banks Dixon Terry & Anne Dancewicz   S.J. Cronin Shoe Repairing Mary Canfield Luke Terry George Anganis Johhny & Babe & Jennie & Penelope Gabriel   MaryLee Plummer Viola G. Wilson Rogers Shoe Store Jim Harrington and another Jim Harrington Harold E. Dodge Bob Holbrook's Saugus Center Service Station Tel. 1000 Britt Brothers J.B. Allen Washington L. Bryer Sailor Tom's On The Pike F.C. Fearns Dexter & Dahlberg Kiyak & Duckboats Tel. 301-M Jeff Fiorvanti Viola Brown George & Carolyn Brown Katie McCormack Nicholson's Farm Milk Tel. 886-J Felice Napolitano Jimmy & Bernie McLaughlin Mrs. Gavin Steve Spinney Marlene Monto Dick and Mouse Marshall Jackie Marshall Val Cassella The Saugus Pine Cabins Walt Merrithew The Evans Ensemble (Shirley / Violin, Edson / Piano, Richard / Drums, and Frank / Trumpet)   Chickland Barbecue –"Where Chickens Are Graduated With A Degree In Taste" Maureen Glynn-Cook Jack MacDougall Mary Gaudet Helen Parent Barbara Lovett Pat Stickney Virginia Marino Uncle George Lovett Bill Merrithew Rita Burns Jeannie Foster Alexa Pagliarulo Jasper "Jeep" Sheehan All the Heffernans, Bob Clayton Trefry Paul Heffernan Mal Comfort Bob Smith Paul Galvin Mike Soper Walter Wadjo Wozny Nat Diamond Janice and Tommy Grillo Nate Murphy Maureen and John Cardinal Lance Penney John M. Penney Frank / Bud / Carl / Conrad / Helen Berthold John Waugh Bob Sacco Adrien & Nelida LeBlanc George and Debbie Lovett Mom Diamond Gary Doak Marge and Howie Spoffard Doug and Patty Lennan Doug Lockwood Frank / Marylou Manning Tony and Debbie Cerulo Jackie / Bob Girard Louie Goldberg Greg / Cheryl Natalucci Lou Deveau Barbara Deveau Alex Winn Peter Scully Bobby Gullidge Ray and Barb Exel Lennie Nadeau Omar Nadeau Bill Diotte John Diotte Matthew Ouellette The Saugus Herald The Town Crier Vincent Brogna Nancy & Art & Walt & Dave and Paul and Mom Neal Lennie Fauci Steve Fauci Ed / Helen Parent The Stead Girls Claire McTighe Jim Smith the letterwriter Terry Spillane Eric and Tony Lennan Neil Olson Buck Murray (Pilot) Mrs. Peckham Miss Ney Eliz. Nelson Tom Tringale Leo Dow Jule Geddes Effie Stanhope Joey & Danny Burns Mike Phillips Giggles Pezullo Johnny Hatch Gus Hanson Jack Ulban Ron & Terry Doucette The Browns The Husseys Across the River Bill / Lorraine / David Sanborn Manny Macedo Mike Macedo Jeff LeBlanc Raoul Wyler Nora Shaughnessy Bernie Friberg Bernie Lucey Ed McKenney Miriam Kochakian   Mike Donovan Bill McKay Buddy McKay Bart Brady-Ciampa Woody Dill Walter Dill Lennie Dill Joe Pace Mary and Kay Reehill Midgie South Bob Salsman Napolean DeMars Butch Barbanti Tom Raisch Eddie Roy Lila Kusch Ernie Kusch Toby Hamilton Frank

Forti George Hamilton Thelma Burton Frank and Sis Tangredi John Fauci Glen McKay Russ Murray The McLaughlins (Mick and Mac) Doctor Clark Norman Yeo Andy Britt Joseph Moynihan Morris J. Fisher Jacqueline McLaughlin Al Gosselin Bernie / Paul / Clarence Noyes Herbert Mason Jim Amero Wilfred Edmands Capt Ralph Fiske John Stuart Charlie Popp Joseph Kellner Eddie Quinn Roland Junkins Ray Howland Cal Vatcher Clayton Foote Joe D'Amico Milton Hazel Frances Banks Capt. James Conrad Frank Tabor Jr. George Day Cpl. Warren Spence Helen Inch Porky Moore Harry Lyman, Chess Giant the old and new names the old and new places The New High School   The Old High School   the quiet commands the pulling tell of interests the found selves the dark varnish on the floors the long echoes the dash the class the elan lasting into the new millennium, these memories.

Education

Treat the Earth well: it was not given to you by your parents, it was loaned to you by your children. We do not inherit the Earth from our ancestors, we borrow it from our children.

— Native American Proverb

Ellery Emerson Metcalf

by
his children

This is the story of the life of Ellery Emerson Metcalf, derived from the best recollections of his children.

Ellery was born on June 28, 1895, in his parents' home on Howard Street in Saugus. He attended the Saugus Public Schools. According to a report card from the Roby School, Grade 7, he was an A-B student, with his worst subject being drawing, according to his teacher Mary Wall. He graduated from Amherst College.

He taught for 47 years at the Essex County Agricultural School, retiring when he reached the age of 70. During his service there he taught many subjects including government, mathematics, and a variety of subjects related to farming.

In his summers with school not in session, he would wheel out his motorcycle and visit his students working on farming projects at area farms, nurseries, and other farm-related activities.

In his public life he served on the Saugus School Committee and the Saugus Board of Selectmen. Often when he rose to speak on the two boards, he would tease his friend, the eloquent, booming-voiced orator, Nelson Pratt, by borrowing his standard opening remark, "As unaccustomed as I am to public speaking…"

He was a moving force in the Victory Garden in Saugus during World War II, and later initiated the Victory Garden on the Lynn City Commons.

In September of 1943, he served with his friend, Paul Corson, as business manager of a hugely successful Big Victory Harvest Fair held at two sites, the Town Hall and the High School auditorium.

At the 32nd annual conference of the Massachusetts Association of Agricultural Teachers and Directors, he was awarded a gold watch in recognition of his outstanding services.

He was selected as an advisor to the Essex County Chapter of Future Farmers of America. Our family has received frequent letters from former FFA members expressing their appreciation for the help they received from our father.

During his teaching years until his retirement, he served as secretary of the Essex County Agricultural Society, which sponsored the annual Topsfield Fair.

His dedication to his chosen field and his innovative contributions in agricultural husbandry brought him country-wide recognition through the years.

He was frequently called to serve as a consultant by gardening firms like Jackson Perkins, whose roses graced our garden. Among his papers we have found a study of the Catshell Strawberry, dated 1934. The sight of two quarts of these berries, now, 70 years later, comes off the page and makes me drool.

He was the originator of two breeds of chickens, the White American and the White Ace, recognized nationally as producers of white chicken breast meat. The White Ace won first prize in the Eastern Massachusetts "Chicken of Tomorrow" two years in succession. Eggs from these chickens were shipped to the Vatican, India and various countries in Europe.

His passion for wildflowers grew during the 1950s. This passion was noted by Ralph Pearson in an article in the Boston Herald, July 1, 1963, in which he was hailed as a "purist." The article stated he had 125 varieties of wild flowers. Whenever we went for a ride with Dad, he made sure to have baskets, lined with burlap, and a spade in the trunk of the car. He was always on the lookout for new wild flowers. There were frequent visitors who came to our garden to view these specimens. It left us with a life-long love of gardening and curiosity about wild flowers.

My Life After Saugus

by
Richard Rohrbacher

Before I can talk about my life after Saugus, I often wonder, why Saugus? I was born in Malden Hospital on March 16, 1940 and lived in Medford where my mother and father, Leola and Albert Rohrbacher, Sr., and my older brother, Albert Jr., shared a second floor apartment with my grandmother, Hazel Fleming. The house was just out of Medford Square on Mystic Avenue and was a typical late 19th century two-story, two-family structure.

At that time the Mystic River ran through our backyard and in the early 1940s my dad worked on boats as a second job. Today the house is gone and the river has had its course radically changed and it does not now flow as near to Medford Square.

We lived in Medford until 1943 when my dad decided to move the family to a more suburban country environment. My dad had a choice of literally dozens of fine suburban and rural communities to relocate to, so I have often thought why Saugus? Why not Billerica, Hopkinton, Wakefield, or Middleton?

As I recall my father had an uncle, my great uncle, by the name of Will Rodgers, who owned a farm in Saugus at the foot of Appleton Street where it meets Central Street. As a little child I remember the family driving to Saugus in my dad's Model A Ford with my brother and me in the rumble seat to visit Guy Rodgers' Farm, as my dad would refer to it. Sometimes Guy would milk a goat and we would drink the milk warm. Also he did something called "witching for water," which seems mysterious to me to this day.

Dad also had another distant relative at the other end of Appleton Street by the name of Ruth Gove. George and Ruth Gove lived at the corner of Appleton Street and Cliff Road and I believe the house may still be standing. I remember they had a daughter, Jeanne, whom my brother dated in high school.

The result of all these connections to Saugus had a strong influence on my dad's decision to move our family out of Medford Square and into Saugus. 1943 was not a time when people were flocking out of the cities. My dad was often accused of being a bit crazy to even think of this relocation. Banks, however, were cooperative in those days for people, who like my dad, wanted to relocate to the suburbs.

The bank offered my dad a $4400.00 mortgage on a new home being built on Juliette Road just a few hundred yards from the Rodgers Farm. Nine Juliette Road was one of the first half-dozen homes being built in that development and it would be our home for many years. I believe the interest rate was somewhere around one percent and Dad was given the option of buying 11 Juliette Road, when built, for $2200.00. Unfortunately all Dad could afford to purchase at that time was 9 Juliette Road.

My dad did not want his children to grow up in the city and Saugus seemed to him at the time to be a great spot for his family to live. He could not have been more correct in his judgment. Saugus was a fabulous, wonderful, and mysterious place in the '40s and '50s for a child to grow up in and play out their fantasies. The apple farm on Appleton Street, Somerby's I believe it was called, Lily Pond, the ice house, the dam, the grove, the Saugus River, the swamp, Appleton's Pulpit, and yes, even the Old Iron Works, which at that time was still mostly under the ground, were ideal places for children to play and mature.

U.S. Steel purchased the Old Iron Works sometime in the early 1950s and immediately erected a fence around what used to be a favorite play area for neighborhood children. Many of the homes around the Iron Works, especially homes with children who played there, had collections of artifacts, which we kids picked up on and around the grounds surrounding the Old Iron Master's House. I

remember an official from U.S. Steel coming to our house and offering to buy back the artifacts which consisted of coins, metal cups, and other pieces of iron fashioned by the old forge and operated by the early settlers of Saugus or Hammersmith as it was known by at that early time. The official made it clear to us that if we did not accept his offer U.S. Steel could go to court and have the artifacts seized. Whether he was correct or not, Dad accepted $5.00 for the miscellaneous artifacts, which are now on display at the current restored Iron Works, or at least they were back then.

I graduated from Saugus High School with the class of 1958 and promptly departed for college having been accepted for appointment to the United States Military Academy with entrance on July 1, 1958. Nine years later I briefly returned to Saugus and stayed only long enough to earn some advanced degrees in education from Boston University. In 1973 I departed Saugus for the last time never to return for more than an occasional nostalgic visit 30 years later.

I have lived in many different locations throughout the continental United States from Massachusetts to Nevada and places in between. I am sure many departed Saugonians have shared the same if not more exciting experiences, which life in this great country of ours provides. There are however nine years of my life spent in the Great State of Alaska (1995-2004), which I wish to share with you. Eight of those wonderful years were spent in rural or bush Alaska where my wife, Elizabeth, and I lived with Eskimo people in four small isolated villages in Western Alaska along Bristol Bay and the Bering Sea.

Alaska is truly the last frontier. It is two and one-half times the land area of Texas; however, due to its odd shape, the distances within the state often exceed 1,000 miles. If one were to remove the mercurial projection from our globe maps and superimpose a true map of Alaska onto a map of the lower 48 states, Juneau would be about where Miami, Florida, is located, while Barrow would be where Minneapolis, Minnesota, is located and the western tip of the Aleutian Islands would be somewhere in California, near

Los Angeles. Added to this is the fact that over 90% of Alaska has absolutely no surface transportation system. There are no highways or roads linking remote Alaskan villages. The only way to travel is in small single engine planes seating two to six passengers and equipped to land on rather short dirt runways. Rivers and waterways are another method of travel. The Yukon River winds its way from the west coast of Alaska for over one thousand miles to the Yukon Territory in northern Canada. I might mention the rivers have to be ice free to be of use as transportation, but they are not most of the year.

Rural or bush Alaska has earned its title as it is more rural than I could ever have imagined without experiencing its vastness for myself. In rough figures, Alaska has approximately 600,000 square miles of land or about one square mile per person. It's interesting to consider that approximately 400,000 people live in Anchorage and many of the remaining 200,000 people live in the other three cities which most people are familiar with, namely, Juneau, Nome and Fairbanks. Did I tell you there are no highways or roads in which one can drive to Juneau or Nome? Think about this: approximately 90% of the population of Alaska live on less than 50,000 square miles. This leaves rural Alaska with 550,000 square miles which is over fifteen square miles per person. If you want solitude, space, and no crowds, bush Alaska is the place to go.

More than half of this vast wilderness is treeless tundra or huge glaciers. One of the glaciers, the Mendenhall Glacier, is larger than the State of Rhode Island. There are 10,000 lakes in Alaska and 3,000 rivers. There are over 10,000 miles of coastline, exceeding the coastlines of both the East and West coasts of the lower 48 states. Everything in Alaska is larger than anything I had ever thought existed while I was growing up in Saugus, especially the fish and wildlife. Who would think of releasing a 25 pound salmon because it was too small. Fifteen pound rainbow trout and northern pike are commonplace. I believe there is a stuffed king (Chinook) salmon in Anchorage Airport, which was a record 100 pounds caught with a rod and fish hook. Huge brown grizzly bears, some of which stand nine feet tall on their hind legs and weigh over 1,000 pounds, and enormous moose are a quick reminder of just how dangerous a wild animal can be.

You might be asking, who would want to live in the rugged, cold, and at times cruel land? Rural Alaska is where most of the Native Alaskan people live and subsist on land that their ancestors settled on when they came over on the land bridge that joined North America with Russia some 10,000 years ago. Yupit and Inupiat Eskimos, Athabascan Indians, Tlinkets, Aleuts, and Haidas have settled and subsisted for many thousands of years on this land, long before Western Europeans thought of moving westward.

During the eight years Elizabeth and I were in the bush we lived and worked with Yupik Eskimos. The Eskimo people generally settled on the north and west coasts of Alaska. Inupiat Eskimos settled the northern and westernmost reaches of the Alaskan coast, while Yupik Eskimos settled the western and southwestern coast. Some Eskimo people moved inland and established villages on major rivers such as the Yukon River and the Nushagak River. Yupik Eskimos were known as Coastal Yupik or Riverine Yupik Eskimos depending on where they lived. During our eight years with them we lived and worked in both Coastal and Riverine Yupik schools.

For thousands of years Yupik Eskimo people lived as semi-nomadic hunter-gatherers, moving back and forth along the coast or up and down river valleys with the natural rhythm of the seasons and animal migrations. The climate was harsh with snow in September, ice break-up in late May and temperatures of 30 or even 50° below zero. All their energy and ingenuity went into perfecting a technology of survival. Education for boys meant learning to hunt, travel, and make tools; girls learned to sew skins, cook and store food, and raise families. All their needs came from the land.

They spoke a language that was elegant and precise, and kept a rich oral tradition of myths, tales, family histories, and exploits. There was, however, no written language, or the need for one. Shamans, healers, and expert storytellers in each clan served as living archives, passing along all they knew to apprentices. The rest of the world was so remote that the name Eskimo People gave themselves, i.e. Yupit and Inupiat means: "The Real People," or simply, "The People." To them there were no others.

Elizabeth and I relocated to Alaska seeking an adventure and a change. However, we had no idea of what we would find. I will never forget the look on her face or the question she asked me upon landing at our first village assignment. The village was Togiak, Alaska, a large, Yupik Eskimo village of 500 people, located on the Bering Sea in Western Alaska north of Bristol Bay, the salmon capital of the world. As she stood on the short dirt runway, a light rain and wind blowing in her face, she quietly asked, "What have you gotten us into this time?"

As the drone of the small Cessna single engine airplane died out and the plane disappeared on the horizon, we were engulfed in silence. There were no buildings save a few storage sheds, and no people or facilities anywhere to be found. We were two exhausted teachers who had traveled all day to reach a village 400 miles west of Anchorage and here we stood, completely alone on a wind swept dirt runway with a soft summer rain blowing in our faces. We were to discover that wind and rain are normal weather for the Bering Sea coastline and it seemed the only things out of place were the two of us and our dampening baggage. For the first time in my life I could not address her question as I did not know what I had gotten us into.

We would have begun walking; however, we did not know which way to go. Soon we heard the drone of another engine, this time coming from a small four-wheel ATV pulling an even smaller trailer with wooden side panels. These small four-wheel vehicles, used in the lower 48 for recreational purposes, have largely replaced the dog-sled as a primary means of travel allowing the Eskimo hunters to cover a larger hunting area and greatly simplifying their lives. The driver pulled up, introduced himself as Ox. He instructed us to put our baggage into the small trailer and sit on the fenders of his four-wheeler. Eskimo people are generally smaller than Westerners; however, Ox, who later turned out to be a good friend, was aptly named due to his immense size.

There are no speed limits in the bush and most Eskimos know only one speed, pedal to the metal, so our one mile trip to the village was comparable to a scary ride at an amusement park. If you have never sat on the fender side-saddle of an ATV going full throttle down a bumpy dirt road you have missed an adrenaline rush. The ATV rapidly came to a halt at Togiak School, a single story building made up of modular buildings, many of which were barged in from Attu Island near the tip of the Aleutians and fitted together in one long series.

The school was but one small building in 1950 and as the village grew more buildings were barged in and connected to the original buildings. Then in 1972, after oil was discovered on Native land at Prudoe Bay and the United States Government negotiated the Native Claims Settlement Act giving the State of Alaska control of the oil fields, hundreds of new schools were built in the bush for the Native children. All of these new schools were similar, with classrooms, a wood / metal shop, a gymnasium with one basketball court and a kitchen attached to the gym that doubled as a cafeteria during lunch time. Togiak did not receive a new school in the 1970s; however, a new gymnasium and a wood / metal shop were attached to the long line of existing buildings at that time.

Teacher housing was either attached to the school or within 50 feet of the school. Ox had let us off at Quarters #3, which was approximately 30 feet from the school. We quickly regained our balance and set about to find the key to our new home, which was, as the principal had told us, on a ledge over the door. As the sound of Ox's 4-wheeler diminished and disappeared, we entered what was to be our new home for the next fourteen weeks. It was comfortably furnished and because we were itinerant teachers we were provided sheets, towels, pots and pans, a television and a VCR. Since there was no TV reception the VCR became our only entertainment, that is, after we acquired some video tapes.

I think it was at this point in time we both suddenly realized that here we were, in the Yupik Eskimo Village of Togiak, with only the few damp suitcases of personal belongings, no food nor any way to acquire food, and it was quiet, eerily quiet. We later learned two things: that one can order dry goods or can goods from Anchorage and hope they get to you in three to four weeks – that was little consolation to us at this moment – and that in the summer, most Eskimo families go fishing or to fish camps where the men fish salmon while the women cut and dry the fish on fish racks for the coming winter. People in remote villages seem to know who is visiting their village and Togiak was no exception. Even with the population reduced, the remaining people knew who we were and what we were doing in their village. It was not long before we heard a knock at the door. Upon opening the door I was greeted by an Eskimo named Dan who asked me if I wanted any fish or caribou. When I said yes, he produced a hind leg of a caribou he had shot only a few hours before. The leg still had the fur and hoof on it and was covered with blood. In addition he produced three of the largest salmon I had ever seen. He smiled and departed as rapidly as he had appeared. This was our first exposure to a culture where the richest person in the village is the one who gives the most away. Eskimo people not only honor older people; they share everything.

Elizabeth looked at the meat and fish piled on the porch and quickly told me she did not clean fish. From that day on, I cleaned the fish and she cut up the meat. She possessed much more skill than I as she knew how to separate the sinews and produced meat roasts rather than cut up meat since we had to freeze most of it. An inspection of the kitchen revealed canned vegetables and dry goods left by previous occupants and soon we had a feast of baked salmon. Salmon soon became a staple of our diet. Elizabeth purchased a cook book entitled, *101 Ways to Prepare Salmon*, and it wasn't long before she had tried all of the recipes. She then had me go through the book and check off the ten or so favorites and they became regular meals for me for the next eight years.

Did I tell you about the four seasons in Alaska? There is a summer, although it is only about two months long and it remains light for most or all of the days during this season. The summer is followed by *almost winter* which replaces our autumn. *Almost winter* season can be cold, raw, and the snow begins anytime after September 1st. The next season is *winter* which begins in October and is the longest season imaginable. It begins anytime after October 1st and can last through April, a period of seven months. December and January are particularly rough months because it remains dark for most or all of the day. Winter is followed by *still winter*, which can last through May and into June. Then summer just kind of happens without notice only now the sun never sets and sleep patterns can be severely interrupted. *Summer, Almost Winter, Winter,* and *Still Winter* are what you can expect in most of Alaska.

Teaching and living in these conditions, hundreds of miles from the nearest road that led anywhere, with two hours of subzero twilight in December and January, wasn't for everyone. During our years of living with the Eskimo people we saw many unsuspecting prospects come from the Lower 48, lured by a salary scale that topped out at over 60,000 dollars. We heard of some teachers who got out of the Cessna that had flown them in, took one look, and climbed back on the plane. Others lasted a few months and fled, amid rumors of breakdowns and/or weird behavior. You can now understand why my wife and I, because we stayed and stayed for eight years, were totally accepted by the Eskimo people. For the first few years they would say to us as we departed to go to another village, "Will you be coming back soon?" After we had returned for the second or third time, they would now ask us upon our departure, "When are you coming home?" It was then we knew we had been accepted into their culture.

Dick Rohrbacher's "Catch of the Day."

We moved nine times in three years between four different Eskimo villages. Two of these villages, Togiak and Manokotak, were on the Bering coast and were predominantly of the Moravian faith. The other two, New Stuyahok and Koliganek, were inland on the Nushagak River and were of the Russian Orthodox faith. We then settled down to four years in Togiak, the largest of the nine villages in our school district, as permanent teachers. My last year with the district was spent in Koliganek, the smallest of our K-12 schools, where I was the only permanent high school

teacher and had 18 students, 16 females and two males, grades 9 through 12.

As schoolteachers, and I, as a basketball and cross country coach, Elizabeth, a music and art teacher who could sew and bead like a Native, we slowly became part of Eskimo village life. We taught the Yupik children as they taught us; we learned the musical patois called village English, and how to say "yes" by raising our eyebrows. The parents and grandparents laughed at our comical first efforts at speaking their language, then showed us what they knew. Elizabeth introduced the elementary school children to the violin with four inexpensive instruments she purchased on the internet. Over time, the principal and district superintendent saw the enthusiasm in the children's faces and her program received the support it needed to accommodate over fifty children from kindergarten to fifth grade. Soon there were Saturday recitals and before we left Togiak, the school boasted of the only stringed orchestra in the bush. The orchestra had a bass, two cellos, and violas in addition to many violins. One time a visiting physician at the health clinic observed the children leaving school at the end of the day and could not believe what she saw. Over 40 children carrying violin cases was a sight she had never witnessed in any of the villages she had been to and she had been caring for remote inhabitants of Alaska for many years. To satisfy her curiosity she went out of the clinic and stopped one of the children and asked her to open her violin case. She could not believe that in such a remote place so many children would be playing the violin. Before we departed Togiak for the last time, many of the children were becoming skilled musicians.

It was customary in bush schools, and in some cases required, that teachers allow one hour a day for cultural activities. This could be anything from native beading, cooking, or sewing to listening to an Elder speak about the Native ways. I will never forget the first time I invited an Elder to speak with my high school students. The Elder's name was Dan Nanalook, Sr. and he was the most respected Elder in the village. His ability to communicate the Native ways to new generations was legendary and because he rarely spoke in public I was excited when he agreed to speak with my class.

It is difficult for Westerners to fully understand the power that Elders possess in the Eskimo culture. Up until 100 years ago they were the shamans, healers, and expert storytellers, and without a written language, the responsibility of passing on the culture to future generations fell on them. The Elders have been predicting global warming for a century now, long before the Western world had coined the term. Two centuries ago they predicted the arrival of the paled-skinned strangers as riding out of the east, traveling in swift boats and fired powered chairs in the sky. Elders told of these pale-skinned strangers bringing wonders to The People: thin birch bark to write on, a way to contain fire inside houses, and the ability to speak across great distances. Perhaps the most important prediction they made was that Light will come in the form of the word - one of the many obvious references to Christianity, which arrived with the missionaries in the late 1890s.

The day of the presentation finally arrived. I had allotted one hour for the talk and had incorporated it into my social studies curriculum so the students would not think they were having an hour off. At the designated time Dan Nanalook Sr. knocked on the door of the classroom. I welcomed him to the class and ushered him to a comfortable chair set in front of the classroom with the students' chairs in a semi-circle. He sat down and quietly inspected the room, glancing from student to student, and not saying a word. Keep in mind that in the Eskimo culture it is an insult to look a person in the eye, which frustrates many new teachers. Though this norm was not universally practiced, it was commonplace enough to experience it, especially when speaking with older people. Mr. Nanalook silently stared above the heads of the students and the students silently stared anywhere but at him. After approximately five minutes of deadly silence I realized something was terribly wrong. I broke the silence by inquiring whether he needed anything such as a glass of water which he quickly waived off. The silence went on for another 55 minutes at which time he got up, smiled and nodded to me and left the classroom without ever uttering a single word.

I did not know how to react in front of the students so we went on with the lesson without a single reference to the hour of silence. After school I spoke with his daughter, a middle-aged woman active in village politics, and told her what had transpired. She knew what had happened and apologized for her father's behavior. I told her I was the one apologizing and only wanted to ascertain what it was that we could do to have him return and this time speak with the students. She explained that he fully intended to speak with the students; however, when he arrived, the sight of Eskimo high school children dressed in NBA and NFL logo shirts, Nikes and jeans made him feel these young people were not worthy to hear, did not deserve, nor had they earned the privilege of hearing the knowledge he wanted to impart to them. This was the first of many clashes of cultural beliefs with the modern times these young Eskimo students live in. To the Elders, male school children should be learning survival techniques such as hunting, fishing, and trapping after school and females should be learning to sew, bead, cook, and operate the Eskimo household. Basketball has no place with the Elders and is referred to as the devil's game.

You might think I am crazy, but I again requested his presence in my classroom and this time I told him the students would be ready to hear what he had to say to them. On the day he returned the students wore plain clothes and other footwear. He again knocked on the door and was escorted to his chair. There was an uncomfortable moment of silence when I had deja vu of the last visit; however, he quickly broke the silence and began speaking in a soft yet authoritative voice. He spoke for the next hour and a half and when he finished he quietly smiled and departed the room. All of us in the room agreed we could have listened to his stories forever and not been bored. Elders teach by telling one long, continuous story where each episode in the story has a lesson to be learned. The listener has to interpret what the lesson or moral of the story is so each person may have a different outcome. I learned more from this talk and other talks like this about life and the Eskimo people than any book or course could have ever accomplished.

Yes, this is Togiak School. So much for the one-room log cabin with a wood stove, the rows of fur-clad children reciting the alphabet. Although 90-odd percent of Alaska is still a roadless wilderness of tiny villages adrift on an ocean of land, the trappings of today's technology and education arrived a little over a decade ago and are here to stay – computers, standardized tests, and the latest instructional buzzwords.

But outside there's that sled load of caribou going by, and you'd discover scores of incongruities in a walk around Togiak, or any other village in the region. Satellite dishes next to cabins chinked with moss; racks of meat, fish, and drying animal skins by trim prefabricated government subsidized houses; sled dogs and the latest high-tech snowmobiles, VCRs and outhouses; a tiny video arcade with a woodstove. It's as if you're viewing the aftermath of a violent collision between the past and present.

That image isn't far from the truth. The modern age didn't so much advance on the Eskimo People of Alaska as it exploded over their heads like a dazzling firework. They've known schools for less than a century. The willingness of the Eskimo people to be shaped into something else is surprising, even disconcerting. Although they had their own unique culture firmly in place, they obviously wanted what the missionaries offered. One can only speculate whether knowledge, spiritual enlightenment, medical care, or trade was most important. Schools, though, were certainly a major attraction.

Student achievement has climbed steadily, if not dramatically, perhaps as a result of acculturation and more effective instruction. Standardized test scores now average ten points higher than a decade ago – though that average still ranks under the 50th percentile nationally – and the number of students performing at top levels has soared. Eskimo schools have begun earning a few statewide academic awards to go along with their athletic titles; some students are at last finding success in college. Several have returned to become teachers, and there is the promise of more to come.

In spite of all the advances staggering problems remain – some educational, some social. Money is tighter than ever; students are still at a cultural disadvantage; teacher turnover is still high, alcohol abuse affects a majority of households. The future can only promise more difficulties, some as yet unseen. Perhaps the greatest challenge is, to quote a wise Elder, to "walk in two worlds with one spirit" – to hunt caribou and then sit down at a computer, or sew mukluks and later balance a checkbook – to remain Yupik in a world of modern technology. The odds against striking such a balance are steep; but then, thousands of Arctic winters have bred into The People a talent for survival. They may just pull it off.

As Elizabeth and I look back on our adventure in Alaska we are filled with dozens of fond memories of a kind, generous, and gentle people known as Eskimos. There is not a day goes by without one of us receiving a collect call, or letter or homemade card, or emails from our past students. At least a dozen young girls who are now young ladies constantly remind Elizabeth that she was like a mother to them and they miss her. My ex-high school students are all for the most part doing something positive with their lives. Many went on to the University of Alaska in Anchorage or Fairbanks. Some were training to be teachers so they can return and teach in their own village. Some went into the service and are currently serving in Iraq while others went to Job Corps in Wasilla, Alaska, to learn a trade. And some got married and settled down in the village to begin raising their own families in the Native traditions. Our students and their parents continually thank us for opening their eyes to the possibilities that lie before them, when all along it was they who opened our eyes to a side of life that seems to be waning in America today and to the possibilities that lie before us.

Vernon Wynne Evans

(Material from the *Lynn Daily Evening Item*, January 1975)

Vernon Evans was a Saugus civic and political leader for half a century as a Selectman, School Committeeman, Principal of Saugus High, Superintendent of Saugus Public Schools and a State Representative.

A native of Saugus, he served as submaster and a teacher of history at Saugus High for twelve years, then three years as the principal (1930-33), followed by eighteen years as Superintendent of Schools (1933-51).

One of the state's outstanding minds on parliamentary procedure, he served two terms as a State Representative (1920-24), and was defeated by a narrow margin in his bid for a senate seat in 1924.

President of the Saugus High class of 1913, he was captain of the baseball team and known to those of his period as one of the best fielders and batters the school ever had.

He graduated from Boston University College of Liberal Arts with honors in 1917 and immediately enlisted in the US Army for service in World War I.

While serving in France with Battery A, 319th Field Artillery, 82nd Division, as a sergeant, he was chosen to attend officers' training school and in three months was commissioned as second lieutenant.

Following the war, he served in the Reserve Officers Training Corps for many years with the rank of captain.

On returning to this country, he was chosen as a library trustee at the age of 21 and then served as selectman in 1928 and 1929, resigning to assume the principalship of Saugus High.

For many years, Saugus High graduates were awarded diplomas which Mr. Evans personally signed in his unique calligraphy, copies of which are still cherished in hundreds of Saugus homes.

He was Chairman of the Saugus Republican Town Committee for many years, largely during the years when that party maintained a 10-1 majority of the voter support. The town has since become Democratic by a 2-1 margin.

The Board of Selectmen in 1965.
Seated (l-r): Chairman Vernon Evans and Frank Berthold.
Standing (l-r): Dr. Herbert Upton, Dr. Fred Wagner, and Atty. Richard Reynolds.

Mr. Evans resigned as Superintendent of Schools in 1951 for health reasons. After a short period of rest, he again ran for selectman and was subsequently elected to office for seven consecutive terms (1955-69), most of the time serving as Board Chairman.

He was defeated for reelection in 1969, after which he maintained only limited contact with the political scene.

An ardent supporter of the Saugus Police Department, he championed appropriations for the department. Requiring little sleep, he spent many evenings and nights riding in police cruisers observing, firsthand, auto accidents, arrests, major fires and manifold events of the town in the past half century.

Immediately after completing service in the first World War, Mr. Evans taught English at Swampscott High for a year.

Shortly thereafter, he married Gladys Wyatt Evans, a Saugus concert soloist of that era. They were divorced in 1929.

He later married Mrs. Annie M. Thomas of Lynn, a nurse. She died in 1964. In 1971, Mr. Evans married Mrs. Evelyn Billingsley of Saugus, who was mother-in-law of Selectman Benjamin A. MacGlashin.

Mr. Evans died on January 4, 1975, three days before his 80th birthday, in Saugus General Hospital after a lengthy illness.

At the time of his death he was survived by two sons, Vernon W. Evans, Jr., a circuit court judge in Tampa, Florida; and Glenn R. Evans of Saugus; a step-daughter Mrs. Marjorie Timanus of Miami, Florida, and a brother Percy G. Evans, a retired professor from DePaul University.

A Warm Remembrance

by
Bob Wentworth

Vern's friends recall his presence at social gatherings as creating an uplifting atmosphere. His gift as a raconteur, his sense of humor, an infectious laugh, and his optimistic view of life made him a welcome guest at any event.

He was a delightful conversationalist, with a keen sense of history, and was well informed on current events. When he spoke, whether to groups or individually, his remarks were presented with dignity, never condescendingly.

Vern was a prolific letter writer. He would write substantial letters commemorating the spirit of an occasion in the lives of his many friends and acquaintances. All of his letters were written in his laboriously hand printed style. The following is a fine example of his unique penmanship.

A sample of Vernon Evan's handwriting (including a partial signature).

Lest We Forget

by
Judy Virnelli

We became good friends, but it didn't happen in the beginning. I was a fifteen-year-old junior at Saugus High School in 1951 and was assigned to "Mr. Moylan" for English. He was a graduate of Saugus High School and Harvard University. I really don't remember much about the class. We all had assigned seats and my teacher was a rather slight, yet stern-looking man, dressed in Brooks Brothers clothes, whose face would turn red and whose eyes would get large when he became upset with you. This didn't happen too often; we all behaved pretty well in that class and did in fact respect him. But I was a daydreamer and I remember that there was a wonderful large maple tree outside the classroom window which I was drawn to… bright red and yellow leaves in the fall, barren limbs in the winter and sprouting buds in the spring. This lack of attention on my part invariably upset him. His face would get red, his eyes would get very large, and he would stop everything, "Miss Cochrane, pay attention!" This is what I remember about my junior year with Mr. Moylan.

In 1957, I returned to Saugus High School as a ninth grade English teacher. Mr. Moylan was no longer Mr. Moylan, but Al Moylan. I really can't say when we became such good friends. He was now the school librarian and I probably met him in the teachers' lounge or helped with study hall when it was held in the library. I looked forward to seeing him. He always had something interesting to say and was always planning trips abroad and attending symphony and plays in Boston. I also discovered that he had a great sense of humor. He loved a good time as much as he liked good music, good books and good food. Frequently, the teachers would have parties and he was always there enjoying himself, often one of the last to leave. He also loved to give a party, which was usually held in the spring before the school year ended. He would most carefully plan the menu, selecting only the finest wines and beer and other spirits. His mother, a quiet Irish lady who lived with him, was always out in the kitchen, preferring not to be part of the party. He cared a great deal for any kid in school who was having a difficult time. This is what I liked about him the most…he liked all kinds of people. Didn't matter if you were a rogue or a saint. In fact I think he might have found the rogue more interesting. The last time I saw him was in the middle sixties. My husband was stationed in the Navy in Argentia, Newfoundland, and I was home visiting with my children. I always looked forward to seeing Al. We went out for a drink together. I think it was at the Ship in Lynnfield. It was there that he told me that he was having serious health problems. That was the last time I saw him.

Such a good friend and good man. I still miss him.

Albert J. Moylan

Time and A Man to Remember Memorable Saugus High School Teacher and Librarian

by
Tom Sheehan

Swiftly the years have shot past edges of my eyes as if time, in one quick breath expelled, never knew the labor of minutes. And in minutes I read of his dying: in a second, an instant of pain as though a rusty lance had found the deep core of heart I sometimes think is made of rock, his name leaped from a page of print.

An *obituary* of Albert Moylan. Standing in his place, behind his desk or in front of the blackboard, nerves on occasion sweeping his body, diminutive, yet heroic, eyes deep and forehead high, his shadow cast, he remains these sixty long years running.

He seemed smaller than me, smaller than teammates hulked deep in the back of his class, smaller than systems, peoples, and peers, smaller than the act of life itself. But he had hidden depths that fooled me.

I owe this man something I rue was never paid. Even now, when I know the haunting of a stumbling boy, his words, as if they'll beat forever, echo: The words will come! The words will come!

He seemed so sure, as if he knew he had reached the tenderest flank of an adolescent brain not wholly rock, not made with gears of granite, not tuned to a time of glory when I was athletic and vibrantly young. He seemed so sure, yet I doubted the coming of myself and the words, as if the music of them would never meet.

Now I am tested! His words leap before me. His face turns as if a moon of him reveals another side I am afraid to see, and I dig for the rock of my heart, to break it open, lay self bare. In the stony silence I wear, in the cavern caused by the sound of his voice poised from the podium, the echo wails: The words will come! The words will come!

How did he know?

How did this man see the long road, make such an oath?

We gave him trouble, not knowing the pains flanking his heart, pains that he carried home from World War II as an Army officer. No! I lie! I gave him trouble he had a ton of room for, a sponge for my smart replies, yet a crucible for all our promises.

And today, still framed against a disappeared but powdered blackboard crested by crumbling chalk in a school that no longer exists, he looks past the knowledge of my eyes and says: The words will come! The words will come!

I mean them for him.

The Eighth Grade

by
Chris Danahy

My family moved to Saugus in 1953 when I was just three years old, and I went through grades one through twelve in Saugus. I have wonderful memories of all of those years, but when I think back about my years in Saugus, it's my time in the eighth grade that comes to mind first.

I grew up on Second Street, so my elementary school days were spent in Cliftondale Square, the first four at the Cliftondale School and then two at the Sweetser School. It wasn't until autumn of 1962, when I entered junior high school, that I could spread my wings and move about the whole town. The junior high school stood at the intersection of Winter Street and Central Street as you enter Saugus Center. I had always been intrigued by Saugus Center but I didn't spend much time there while I was in elementary school. It was just a little too far from home for a young boy to spend his spare time, and all of my friends lived on the Cliftondale side of town.

Education

The only time that I walked through the center up to that point was when I was going to watch a high school game at Stackpole Field, which I thought was the greatest place on earth. The mandatory stop when I walked through the center was Sanborn's News. Sanborn's was a great penny candy store so it was a popular place for the kids who lived in Saugus. I knew everyone from the Cliftondale area, and I was looking forward to meeting the kids my age from the rest of the town when I got to junior high.

I spent my first year of junior high meeting as many of the kids in my class as I possibly could. That was fairly easy because there were different kids in every one of my classes and we changed classrooms every hour, whereas in elementary school we spent the whole day with the same class. I didn't get to meet many of the eighth graders because not too many classes had a mixture of seventh and eighth graders. Eighth graders didn't mix much with seventh graders in those days anyway. It was as if they were the seniors and we were the freshmen even though we were only a year apart in age. I figure that I'd meet the kids from the class of 1967 when I got to high school but I was excited as I entered the eighth grade. I really enjoyed the sixth grade, when my class was the oldest in the school, and I was looking forward to it again as an eighth grader. The following year I'd be a freshman again and it would three years to work my way to the top of the heap again as a senior.

I had just finished a great summer, spending most if it at King's Beach in Swampscott with my friends from Second Street, but I was looking forward to going back to school for the first time that I can remember. I took the bus from Cliftondale Square to King's Beach almost every day that summer with all of my friends from Second Street but I knew that when school started I'd be spending more of my time in Saugus Center and not spending as much time with my childhood friends. I had met Kevin Carroll in the seventh grade and I spent a fair amount of time with him on weekends, taking the bus to Boston and going to Fenway Park to watch the Red Sox play. You could walk up to the gate on the day of the game and buy good seats in those days and there were scheduled doubleheaders on Sundays for which you only had to pay admission once. The bus line that serviced Saugus made it possible for someone my age to easily get around the Boston area and I took full advantage of that. I knew my neighborhood like the back of my hand and it was time to explore the rest of Saugus.

When school started I was even more pleased to be there. I liked all of my teachers but there was one class that I couldn't wait to get to each day. Miss Leoshena was my English teacher and that very quickly became my favorite subject. Cathy Leoshena was not only a great teacher; she was also beautiful. She reminded me of a goddess and it wasn't long before she was known amongst the eighth grade boys as Miss Cleoshena or Cleo for short. I was repri-

manded by Mr. Bryant, who was another teacher, when he heard me call Miss Leoshena Cleo. Mr. Bryant didn't come down on me too hard because I think he realized that the nickname was in admiration of her, not at all to make fun of her.

Miss Leoshena's class was the quietest I'd ever been in. She never had to settle the class down at the beginning of the period because everyone just came into the room, sat down and waited for her to speak. Her beauty commanded the attention of both boys and girls. The girls watched Miss Leoshena's every move, hoping that someday they would be like her, while boys sat there mesmerized, dreaming that they would someday meet a woman like her. We also listened to what Miss Leoshena said so we learned even though that might not have been the primary goal when we first walked into her classroom. Miss Leoshena's primary goal was to teach us and she did a wonderful job at that. She made school fun!

The year started off smoothly as I enjoyed all of my classes and being a member of the eighth grade class. In early October I awoke one day to find that the junior high school was on fire. I ran to the school with my friends only to find that the school no longer existed. We sat around all day watching the fire department put the fire out but it was obvious from the moment we got there that there would be no more schools days at the junior high.

We had an unexpected one week vacation, while town authorities tried to figure out where we would be going to school now that there was no longer a junior high school. They decided to send us to the high school in afternoon sessions with the ninth grade, so after a month of being "king of the hill" at the junior high we became an orphan class without a school. We went to school from 12:30 to 5 P.M. and we were barely settled when the east wing of the high school was set on fire. The fire department was able to contain this fire but we had to miss another week of classes while the debris was cleaned up.

When we returned to class it was November so we had to walk home from school in the dark. It was a particularly dark walk home on November 22nd when President Kennedy was assassinated in Dallas, Texas. Like everyone else I remember exactly where I was when I heard the news. I was in class in the multi-purpose room at the high school. We were dismissed early so the sun was still up for the walk home but it was still a very dark walk. Even those of us who were only thirteen years old could sense that the world had changed as we sat glued to the television set that weekend. When we returned to school I wasn't the least bit surprised to learn that Miss Leoshena was in Washington. She was so affected by JFK's death that she drove down to Washington D.C. as soon as we were dismissed from school and stayed there all weekend. Miss Leoshena told us of the impact that the week would have on world history. She told us that she just felt that she had to be in Washington D.C. for the funeral so she drove down.

We weren't accomplishing much academically because we hadn't been in school too much during the first three months. In December we heard that the Veterans School on Hurd Avenue was being converted to the new junior high school. School officials wanted us to go to classes for a full day, not split sessions as we were doing, but we wouldn't start there until the beginning of February because adjustments had to be made to the Veterans School.

It was a somber Christmas in 1963 because nobody had recovered from the Kennedy assassination. About the only thing I remember that was somewhat joyous about Christmas of 1963 was that my family got its first color television set. The general mood of people was that nothing really mattered anymore. We needed something good to happen.

Not long after the assassination, Arnie Ginsberg of WMEX in Boston started playing a few songs by a group from England called the Beatles. This was before FM radio, so there weren't many radio stations, but WMEX was the station that all teenagers listened to. This band caught everyone's attention and before long they agreed to fly to the United States to appear on the Ed Sullivan Show in February.

The Beatles were fantastic and they opened the door for many other groups from Great Britain to come to America. The shroud that hung over America wasn't lifted by the Beatles' arrival, but they certainly gave us something to look forward to. They played on national television on a Sunday night in February right about the time that we started at the new junior high school. The Beatles started a stream of music from Great Britain that gave us something to look forward to each week. Miss Leoshena was young enough to enjoy this influx of new music with us as we settled into our new school and tried to salvage what we could out of that chaotic school year.

After only a month in the new school the arsonist struck again. The new wing of our school was set on fire in the middle of March and we missed another week of school while the mess was cleaned up. This time, however, the arsonist made the mistake of writing on a blackboard, "Of all the things in this school, it's Mr. Perry that I hate the most." That message told authorities that it was a student who was lighting the fires and they quickly traced the handwriting and arrested one of my classmates. The rest of the students weren't surprised at the arrest because we suspected that it was this kid who was lighting fires all along. What puzzled us was that Mr. Perry was singled out because he was a popular teacher and a very good one. That put an end to the fires and we spent the final two months of

the school year salvaging what we could out of that tumultuous year and got ready for high school.

That school year was tough on everyone but it had to be especially difficult on the teacher. We didn't go to school for more than a month without being disrupted by a fire or a tragedy but Miss Leoshena didn't seem to miss a beat and made the best out of a tough situation.

After graduating from junior high school I never saw Miss Leoshena again and I'm sorry that I never took the time to go back and visit her. The fact that I'm writing about the 1963-1964 school year 40 years later and finally realizing the impact that Miss Leoshena had on me exemplifies what a good teacher she was. Miss Leoshena later married Ken Fabrizio, who was another teacher

Mrs. Kenneth Fabrizio
(nee Cathy Leoshena.)

when I was in the eighth grade. She lost a battle to cancer a few years ago when she was still much too young. Only when I read about her passing did I realize how much she meant to me and I'm sure to the thousands of other students she taught through the years. I hope she and her husband enjoyed the years that they were given together because Cathy Leoshena deserved that much. I've always felt that teaching is one of the noblest professions and Miss Leoshena was one of the best.

An Extraordinary Teacher

by
Tom Sheehan

The header lead-in on an Internet magazine, *VerbSap*, says, *Verbum Sapienti Sat Est*. A word to the wise is sufficient. VerbSap. Concise prose. Enough said.

I bet John Burns has had that thought in his mind since he began to read, since his tastes formed those many years ago. VerbSap, John says, and delivers that message in all his messages.

So much has been said of him over the years, and examples are pulled and placed here for their exhibition, and for his testament:

From English teacher Judith Gaffney, whose only regret was that she grew up in Winthrop where she could not have John

176   Education

Burns as a teacher: "He is a man of joy, joy in life, joy in learning and joy in sharing his knowledge with others. Sadly we hear so much about teacher burnout." But at his retirement party, after six decades in the Saugus School system, clarified that about him, "It's wonderful to see a man who has taught so long with so much love. And I think he's truly loved. He's beloved by thousands. He is an honorable man with everything that word implies. He's generous of his time and knowledge, a staunch advocate for his friends and one of the finest men I have ever had the pleasure to know."

VerbSap!

From former School Superintendent William Doyle, when discussing Burns' retirement in 1999: "It will be a tremendous loss to the Saugus Public Schools. He's a very bright man. He's an outstanding individual. He treats everyone with kindness, understanding and compassion. There's one word that personifies John Burns – a gentleman."

VerbSap!

A Boston Globe reporter once said to me, "I understand that you can reduce John Burns to one word."

I said, "Unflappable."

VerbSap!

From Tim Churchard's poem, *Room 101, for John Burns:*

This Gaelic hawk glided from the rim
of Pranker's Pond into my life, tearing bits
off Frost, Steinbeck, Yeats, and Joyce
and hand-fed me until I was his.

I was lost and you found me. You lead me
to Shakespeare and Willie Loman.
You knocked me down with metaphor, dared me
to get up, and of course, gave me your hand.

Your passion still surrounds me.
You come back again and again in my classroom.
You speak to my students.
I am grateful.

VerbSap!

From a newspaper interview with Paul Heffernan, who had John Burns as both a sophomore and senior English teacher: "He encouraged you to buy the New York Times and read the magazine section or anything else you wanted. He wanted you to either agree or disagree with it... After leaving Saugus High, I attended a Catholic institution of higher learning and I thought I would be at a disadvantage because I figured the other students came from private schools. When the Freshman 101 English professor asked the students how many of them had to write a weekly critical essay in high school, my hand was the only one to go up."

VerbSap!

From an article, *A Tour through the New Saugus Library*, by Tom Sheehan:

How many rooms (of the new library) should be named? Name them all. For other generations of teachers of the new and old school, who follow each of us to this day, their echoes beating behind us, their words touching out to the eternity we stretch at.

Name the hallway. Name an alcove. Name the boiler room. Name them all. Pay tribute to those who linked us with words and ideas.

But save one room.

Save one room before it gets too late to name a room. Save one room for the teacher of whom I have heard countless graduates say was the best teacher they've ever had, who drilled on the words and word choices, who scratched at hidden brilliances like a diamond locked in loam, who parlayed rhyme and meter and unshaken beauty for the poetic form, who reveled in both our meager and our grand successes, who brought fever and fervor to its appropriate stance, who made thinking an art form and good literature a way of life, who is still a robust reader of words written the way the masters intended them to be written: alive, moving, full of magic.

Name one of the rooms *The John Burns Room.*

It will sing of itself.

VerbSap!

John Burns Revisited

by
Paul Heffernan

Summer 1964 faded into fall and Landslide Lyndon Johnson roared toward earning the sobriquet given him with scorn by Texans so many years before. Hemingway's *A Moveable Feast* was published posthumously. Saugus town meetings dragged on. Prankers Pond no longer hosted Saugonians, the dam on the river having been breached years before shattering a town jewel.

In September, Ellen Burns motored in the family Dodge Dart, brown with cream colored top, from 30 Cliff Road the mile or so to Saugus High. Passenger John Burns leaned over, bussed his bride, got out and entered at the office entrance for the start of what would have been his twenty-fifth year of teaching English, had not WWII service interrupted his vocation.

John walked down the ramp from the C Wing toward the last room on the right in the West Wing (was it W08 or W10?) with that slight bounce in his step. Preferring sports jackets to suits, he walked this opening day into his class with his favorite camel hair jacket. A brown brief case swung up onto a somewhat barren desk. The jacket was doffed. The short-sleeved white shirt paid homage to one of those brilliant warm early fall New England days.

With the dedication of the top right section of the front blackboard to bon mots du jour from students, John Burns invited all to stump the teacher. The only rule was that these words were not to be from the "zoo section" of the dictionary. Each day he would fend off most challenges to his vast vocabulary with ease. A student who succeeded in stumping him viewed a man who calmly rejoiced in a new word and who never had to apologize for not being omniscient.

Introduction to the New York Times Sunday edition followed. The legendary weekly assignment to write a critical essay seemed onerous at first. But students grew into taking a stand in writing on various issues. Discussions in class were lively. All students were allowed maximum leeway when opining. All views were to be respected and given a fair airing. Woe to him who attempted to demean another's views with the ad hominem, rather than attempting to carry the day with logic.

When a young man wandered from the topic at hand in a sidebar with another, JB would apply "the glance." If "the glance" failed and nose to earlobes blanched, order was restored with a "How much longer are we to be treated to this endless flow of drivel?"

In the classroom John Burns was always professional, interested in his students' reading, tough but fair. Teaching was not a job but a vocation.

He operated in arenas beyond Pearce Drive.

In the public square, he and his wife Ellen created the local environmental group, SAVE, that has continued to be a force for conservation in Saugus for some 25 years or more.

But his magnum opus in the world beyond teaching was his successful restoration of Prankers Pond. For years, indeed decades, he worked tirelessly to find a way to bring life back to "the pond." He was willing to work with all who showed an interest in coming together to recreate a recreation area for all. When others would have quit, when others would have abandoned the task due to political or financial roadblocks, JB found a way. Through toughness and perseverance he succeeded in creating a magnificent town resource enjoyed today by hundreds each year.

Friends never mentioned the "R" word, retirement, to John. After exiting the classroom, JB went on working for Superintendent Bill Doyle on grants and special projects. He kept on running writing contests for students and savoring their work.

Did he eschew retirement because he thought of it as the vestibule of the Grim Reaper's manse?

He told one fellow who called on the phone and who breached the unspoken topic, "a chacun à son goût." Amused, John told others that the fellow thought he was swearing at him and hung up the phone.

A former student saw JB simply as man engaged; a man of energy and action; a man of toughness that could not hide an unabashed kindness and sweetness:

- A call from a new widow whose husband was tragically killed in a car crash. She was concerned about her son's final English exam needed to graduate. The son and his teacher were not hitting it off. "Tell your son not to think about it again. I will take care of it."

- A noisy scene at a Saugus eatery years ago. JB, at one table with his group, is being pestered by the son of a prominent Saugonian, at a table behind him. He gets up, picks the fellow up with both hands and tosses him into the next booth.

- As a newly minted groom in the 1950s, he could still find time to have a cup of tea with his mother most days after school at the family home on Stone St.

- Himself distraught over his dear friend Bill Regan's death, he would appear for many days at the Regan home asking how he could help Bill's family.

When retirement did come, did this man sit around and wait for his appointment in Samarra? As this book shows and the one that preceded it showed, JB throws himself into new projects. And he entertains an occasional former student in the house on the cliff over the pond.

On one such occasion, a former student enthusiastically told him and Ellen about revisiting an Evelyn Waugh classic and how one paragraph early in Charles Ryder's story was simply magnificent writing to be savored. "Can you find it for us?" John asked. Ellen pulled the work from their expansive and organized library. The former student found the passage and it is reproduced here:

Education

How ungenerously in later life we disclaim the virtuous moods of our youth, living in retrospect long, summer days of unreflecting dissipation, Dresden figures of pastoral gaiety! Our wisdom, we prefer to think, is all of our own gathering, while, if the truth be told, it is, most of it, the last coin of a legacy that dwindles with time. There is no candor in a story of early manhood which leaves out of account the home-sickness for nursery morality, the regrets and resolutions of amendment, the black hours which, like zero on the roulette table, turn up with roughly calculable regularity. (*Brideshead Revisited*, Little Brown Co., New York, 1944.)

Who enjoyed the moment more: the student in his reading the above passage, or, the revered teacher in listening to a former student revel in great writing?

Summer 2005 fades into fall. George W. Bush fails to satisfy the Right or the Left at the start of his second term. The latest "Harry Potter" story hits the New York Times best seller list. Saugus still has endless town meetings.

And a street lamp burns on Cliff Road and that flame leads another generation of Saugonians to "the pond."

John Burns, English class, in the '40s.

More John Burns

by
Bob Wentworth

I've known of John Burns for close to seven decades (1938). Most of those years my knowledge of him was of a second-hand nature through long-time family friendships. During those years he had acquired a reputation of great renown:

professionally as an educator in the Saugus School system, and personally as an individual widely admired for his extraordinary intellect, character and decency.

It wasn't until 1999, while working with John in connection with the preparation and publication of the book, *A Gathering of Memories, Saugus 1900-2000*, that I really got to know him. His persona, at that time, moved from legend to reality. I witnessed the qualities that were obviously the basis for his stature… and were these attributes ever accurate!

Thus began my personal and treasured friendship.

His management of the *Memories* book project was masterful. He had a vision. Vague and wide-ranging it was to all of us (the committee) at first, but he gradually guided us through the maze associated with such a huge undertaking and brought it to a highly successful conclusion. The success, I believe, was in large part because the concept embodied John's personality.

In a sense, *A Gathering of Memories* is a reflection of John Burns.

I never had John as a teacher in a classroom setting. However, the last six years have been an enriching experience. For John is an educator in the broadest sense of the word, and in his presence, we are always learning.

It Happened in Essex County

by
Richard C. Howland
(The Essex County Genealogical Newsletter,
Signs of the Times: Saugus, 1937)

Historically, 1937 was the beginning of President Franklin D. Roosevelt's second term. Economically, it was slipping back to the worst year of the Depression, 1933. Prophetically, it was just hinting at our entering World War II.

But for me, age fourteen, it was just the end of the eighth grade and the beginning of Saugus High School with one big winning surprise, and for our town, one big tragedy.

Looking back then, I remembered Miss Pearl Belonga, my fifth grade teacher in the *old* Roby School, a small two-story four-room wooden building which still stands. She taught a fourth and fifth grade class in the same room at the same time. She would not allow labels of limitation and was intolerant only of a student's giving up on himself. Through all the subjects she taught and the classroom dynamic itself, we also learned about honesty, cause and effect, the practicality of manners and compassion for all.

Economically for me, the summer of '37 presented three opportunities to get out of the Depression. The first one was to sell and deliver the *Saturday Evening Post*. The result was in keeping with the national economy – poor.

The second proved a moderate but temporary step in the right direction. Friends and I walked from East Saugus to Saugus Center, and up Main Street to the west side of Route One and picked all the blueberries we could carry back. We knocked on doors on Main Street and sold all we had, two quarts for a quarter, before we hit the Center and cut our profits with ice cream sodas.

But number three was the big surprise–winning a big beautiful bicycle with balloon tires, headlight, horn, speedometer, carrier, rearview mirror, and chrome fenders. All the kids were playing a game called Hi-Li. It had its craze-days like Yo-Yo and Hula Hoop. It was played with a paddle, a rubber band and stapled ball. The old Waldorf Theater in Lynn sponsored a Hi-Li contest. The competition took place on three consecutive Saturday afternoons, the final on the stage. Even in those tough times I was a little older than most to get a bike. But its Cadillac appearance ended my Depression.

Selling magazines and blueberries, playing Hi-Li, listening to *Tom Mix*, *Jack Armstrong* and *Little Orphan Annie* on the radio were fading fast. Shining faster were choosing my high school course and looking forward to sports, plays, clubs, and the Big Band Era.

The summer of 1937, though, brought an incredible event involving a beautiful young woman who was not allowed to remain a teacher in Saugus High. At first, the episode was local and sad. Then it became national and tragic.

Her name was Isabel Hallin. She coached the 1937 Senior Class Play, *Seventeen*, reported as the most dramatically and financially successful school play ever. She was indeed very blonde and beautiful, stylishly dressed, and definitely a talented teacher and potential actress.

But Miss Hallin had the leading role in a true tragedy whose supporting and non-supporting cast went from townwide to nationwide. It began at a Senior Play rehearsal which was held in the basement of her home where her father had a family room, a bar, and bottles of wine. The whispered and written rumors shocked listeners and readers: Teacher Hallin offered and gave drinks to cast members.

Leading the attack against Miss Hallin was school committee member Myra Smith who had been principal of the Felton Elementary School. After investigations and discussion the committee met for its ultimate decision on a warm summer evening in the Superintendent's office in front of the old Saugus High, built in 1906 and destroyed by fire in 1963, on the corner of Central and Winter Streets.

On the lawn and pathways looking up at the office window was a big crowd including local and Boston reporters, students, parents, and passersby. Some were harassing the school committee by throwing words and eggs. Some were waiting to question them when they came out the front doors. Most attending the meeting behind closed doors, went back through the hallways leading to the Junior High School and out rear doors on to Denver Street.

Superintendent Vernon Evans recommended that Miss Hallin stay. Throughout his years in office, Evans was known and respected for his intelligence, common sense, leadership, and compassion. But Miss Smith got the committee's majority vote and Miss Hallin was dismissed.

The teacher did come back in the fall to a home football game at Stackpole Field. In a shining fur coat, she was elegant as ever and when the students saw her, there was a standing, spirited applause. She went to New York, was written up in national magazines, and had radio and screen tests.

The ultimate devastation following the ultimate decision came all too soon: suicide.

Now for those of us in the hot toddy – hot milk times of our lives, past and present memories alternate between becoming clearer and hazier.

One thing is certain. In those times such a trauma as the Hallin happening was rare, but decency and lovely lyrics and music were rampant.

Time to play a big band cassette.

Marleah Elizabeth Graves

by
Gretchen Davis Hammer

Marleah Elizabeth Graves was born at home on May 17, 1907. Her parents, Herbert Wilson Graves and Ethel Nourse Graves, and her two older sisters – Marian and Helen – were delighted with this new addition to their family and home. And home remained at 18 First Street, in the Cliftondale section of Saugus, for the remainder of Marleah's life.

Being the youngest in her family and learning from her older sisters, Marleah too decided to become a teacher.

After all, her older sister, Marian, attended Framingham State College and became a teacher of nutrition within the Medford School system, where she met her future husband, Stephen Mugar. Her other sister, Helen, graduated from the Posse-Nissen School to become a physical education teacher prior to her marriage to Laurence Davis. So, to follow suit, Marleah graduated from Saugus High School with the class of 1924, and matriculated to the North Adams Normal School (now North Adams State College) in western Massachusetts to become an elementary school teacher. Following receipt of her teaching certificate, she returned to Saugus and began her teaching career at the Mansfield School on Lincoln Avenue, having signed a contract with the Saugus School District to teach for approximately $1000 per year. After two years there, Miss Graves transferred to the Cliftondale School from which she retired in June 1975. She had devoted 49 years to teaching three generations of Saugus young people – and she loved every minute of it – but she wasn't done yet! Retirement for Miss Graves meant that she would now have time to tutor students in the subject nearest and dearest to her heart – reading. And this she did, for the next several years.

While teaching was a large part of Marleah's life, her family and home were her heart and soul. She loved her animals – her dogs and her cats. At Christmas time all her friends would receive a card with the latest picture of her cat and dog adorning it. During the winter, many folks around town housed the goldfish who resided in Marleah's two goldfish pools in the summer. Marleah took pride in her fishponds, which were adorned by beautiful pond lilies. One would find students and parents alike during the summer months feeding the fish or just watching them. One of the longest-lived residents of the pool was a goldfish which had been given to me on my sixth birthday. Cleo lived between there in the summer and eventually Anstrice Kellogg's huge aquarium in the winter for the next twelve years – growing to be about eight inches long and producing hundreds of offspring – before meeting his demise when Miss Kellogg's tanks froze when her furnace malfunctioned while she was away.

Gardening was another favorite pastime of Marleah's. She had several gardens around her home in Saugus and her summer place "up country" in Washington, New Hampshire. All the gardens were planted with the birds in mind, and bird houses brightly adorned the gardens as well. And Marleah, knowing the names of all the birds, would try to teach them to her nieces and nephews.

Marleah was often seen driving around town in her old model-T Ford, complete with a rumble seat, or – in later years – in her beloved two-seater Dodge. She loved to drive, and being a passenger in that rumble seat was a thrill of a lifetime for those of us who were so lucky!

Wanting to instill a love for reading in her nieces and nephews, Marleah put a *reading nook* in her attic, with puffy pillows and a bright rug on the floor in front of a bookcase full of *favorites*. I spent many happy hours curled up in that corner, wrapped up in the adventures of the Bobbsey Twins, the Hardy Boys, and Nancy Drew, while the rain or snow knocked on the window nearby. To me as a child, this was pure heaven!

Another very fond memory I have was being allowed to spend an afternoon visiting her classroom. I was about five years old, and second graders seemed very grown up to me. I rode to school with Aunt Marleah and walked up the huge steps of the school, anticipating what a wonderful time I was going to have. Fred England had volunteered to be my guide for the afternoon, pulling up a chair beside his desk, where I remained for the rest of the time. I watched him as he wrote, listened while he read, and went with him out to recess. To this day Fred remains my "knight in shining armor." What an afternoon I had!

During her lengthy and productive career Marleah received several awards and honors, including being named the Elementary School National Teacher of the Year in 1970. For her, however, no honor would ever compare to that of a former student returning to visit her classroom or write her a note to say "thank you" for her patience and devotion to him and – often as the years went by – to his children and grand-children as well. As her niece, it was fun to be somewhere with Aunt Marleah and have someone rush up happily just to say "hello" to Miss Graves.

Marleah died at the age of 86, leaving six nieces and nephews (and their families): The Reverend James Davis, Patricia Davis Hoffman, Franklin Davis, Gretchen Davis Hammer, David Mugar and Carolyn Mugar. This much-loved and highly respected aunt and teacher's legacy will live long within the Town of Saugus. An endowed scholar-ship in Marleah's name was established at Saugus High School, to be awarded each year to a student who is planning on becoming an elementary school teacher.

The Cliftondale School.

Carmine Moschella

by
John Burns

In his long life and career in Saugus, Carmine Moschella has made his presence felt in his own quiet way. As a teacher and school administrator he was widely respected for the skills he brought to these positions and for the sense of fair play he always displayed in his dealings with students, his colleagues and the public.

After his retirement he served the town as a town meeting member and as a member of the school committee. In both capacities he was governed by the same principles which he adhered to in his private life and to his life in the school, looking always for courses of action and decisions which looked to the future in his service to his constituency.

But no commentary on Carmine would be complete without paying heed to the wonders he can do with wood, to the elegance he bestows on wooden structures he undertakes, whatever its eventual utilitarian purpose might be.

We see them at the Pearce Drive entrance to Saugus High School and at the Town Hall; the beautiful Veterans Memorial on the lawn, the lobby trophy cases and, in the hall, the grand table used by the selectmen.

Academia

Why should a group of simple, stable compounds of carbon, hydrogen, oxygen and nitrogen struggle for billions of years to organize themselves into a professor of chemistry?

— Robert Pirsig

The Little Professor from Saugus

by
Norma Shapiro

Rose Shapiro, on her hands and knees, scrubbing the kitchen floor in preparation for the coming Jewish holiday, looked up to see what had cast a shadow across her work. It was six-year-old Benson, an escapee from the Roby school recess. Kindly Miss Fenner, his first grade teacher, gently persuaded the boy to come back to school. Who could have guessed that this potential six-year-old dropout would become a well-known academic?

He lived on Taylor Street, across from the police and fire station, and would rather have been playing among the big red fire engines. Best of all, he would have loved to play on the land that had been the old Shapiro farm at the northeast corner of Main Street and the Newburyport Turnpike. As a child he frequently climbed the heavily wooded ridge behind to play in the outcropped rocks, known as "the cave."

Ben's grandparents, Jacob and Lena Shapiro, and their children — who would eventually number ten, moved from Chelsea to Saugus in 1911. Jacob was a cattle trader familiar to farmers all over Essex County. Lena grew vegetables, and was known for her Sunday meals that fed up to 100 people on the food from the farm when World War I rationing made it difficult for many to eat as much as they needed.

By the time Ben was born, in August 1941, his father, Ernest, was out of cattle trading, and into selling insurance, mostly in Lynn. For 25 years, Ernie was on the Board of Library Trustees, and was one of the library's best customers. He shared his love of reading with all three of his children, Jack, Barbara, and Benson, and continued the Shapiro tradition of vegetable gardening to help feed the growing family.

As he grew older, Benson loved watching the Saugus Iron Works reconstruction just around the corner from his home, from which he developed a curiosity about the invention of technology, an excitement about the process of engineering, and an interest in the development of the business. Of course, at that age, he would just have said he was watching the heavy equipment at work!

As a member of that first class to spend all four years at the "new" high school on the Newburyport Turnpike, he remembers the intellectual challenges he found in English teacher John Burns' classroom. Asked to write Sunday New York Times articles from another point of view, Ben found his mind opening, and his interest in a broad range of ideas ignited.

At graduation, Ben was awarded the H. G. Josephson Scholarship, and as he stood to receive the award, he felt as if he continued to grow, taller and taller, beyond the 5'6" frame that contained both the little Shapiro boy from Saugus, and the internationally recognized professor and business consultant he would become.

Then, Ben, with his drive to understand the world and what made it tick, and to explore new horizons, headed west to Ann Arbor, to study chemical engineering at the University of Michigan. Experiencing the richness of a large university, Ben also developed a love of literature, theatre, and Michigan football! He excelled in his work, enjoyed research and writing, and was inducted into Tau Beta Pi, the national engineering honor society.

For several summers, Ben worked at Procter and Gamble. At first he loved being an engineer, and aspired to manage a large chemical factory. Then he discovered that the strategy of what to make and sell came from the marketing department and the top management team. So, following in his big brother's footsteps, he applied to Harvard Business School, where he would gain recognition as a Baker Scholar (top 5% of his class), and find a passion for helping business people to serve their customers well, and build their companies into economic engines of their societies.

"The Little Professor."

After a few years in industry, Ben returned to the Harvard Business School to get his doctorate, and then to join the marketing faculty. Today, Benson P. Shapiro is a well-known authority on marketing strategy and sales management with particular interests in pricing, product line planning, and marketing organization. He is also the Malcolm P. McNair Professor of Marketing Emeritus at the Harvard Business School where he taught full-time from 1970 to 1997. He continues to teach there in several executive programs including the CEO Program, Young President's Program, and Business Marketing Strategy, and currently chairs the Sustainable Marketing Leadership for Mid-Sized Firms Program. Since 1997, Professor Shapiro has concentrated his time on consulting, speeches, research and writing.

During his 27 years on the full-time Harvard faculty, he taught a wide variety of MBA courses including Industrial Marketing, Sales Management, Creative Marketing Strategy, Integrated Product Line Management, and participated in many executive programs. Professor Shapiro has also held various administrative positions including Senior Associate Dean for Publications, Research Director, Head of the Required MBA Marketing Course, and Faculty Chair for Strategic Marketing Management, a two-week program for senior marketing executives.

Ben has had over 3000 MBA students, many of whom have returned to visit and continue to seek his advice, and some who have become the leaders of major corporations and professional service firms. The former students often remember Ben's final class where he urged them to go out and make the system work — for employees, stockholders, and the economy — by honest dealing and serving the needs of the customer.

Professor Shapiro is the author, co-author or editor of fourteen books, and nineteen Harvard Business Review articles including "Leveraging to Beat the Odds: The New Marketing Mind-Set," "What the Hell is Market Oriented?", "Manage Customers for Profits, Not Just Sales" and "Staple Yourself to an Order." Two of his most recent books, both co-edited, are *Seeking Customers* and *Keeping Customers from the HBS Press*.

He has served as a consultant to over 300 companies including startups, medium-size firms, and large international corporations. And, he has participated in well over 160 executive education programs outside of Harvard for corporations and associations.

Ben Shapiro has an office located in Concord, Massachusetts, and he travels widely to speak and teach. In 2004, he received an honorary doctorate in Athens, Greece, and, in 2005 he spoke in Germany, Austria, Italy, Portugal, Spain, and Mexico.

Still, his heart is never far from Saugus. At least once each year, often in the spring, he walks the town center, revisiting the places that gave him his start, and remembering the people who played such seminal roles in his life.

It was this affection for his home town, and the lessons he learned there, especially from his father, that prompted Ben to endow the Ernest L. Shapiro Fund to support educators in the Saugus Public Schools to help maximize student learning, enhance educational programs, and promote staff development.

Ben Shapiro looks forward to the success of future generations of Saugus young people who will make their own special contributions to our world.

Some Words from Paul Hewitt on His Career

by
Paul Hewitt

I figured I was one of the lucky ones in Saugus High School in Massachusetts, for I knew exactly what I wanted to do with my life. I wanted to win the national amateur flyweight boxing championship and then get into a life of cartooning. This was reinforced by my school counselor who told me that because of my talent for art I wouldn't have to take the more academic courses in high school. That's right: "Wouldn't have to." When I wasn't sparring with my next door neighbor, Eddie McCarthy, a professional lightweight boxer, I was drawing comic strips. When Eddie went off to the Korean War, he left me under the wing of a local boxing hero, Kenny Isaacs. Kenny guided me along the New England Amateur Athletic Union's silver medal when I was sixteen, but a brain concussion suffered in a warm-up bout for the next year's try at the gold dampened my dreams of ring glory.

(Paul G. Hewitt was a Silver Medalist Flyweight Boxing Champion for New England States at the age of seventeen.)

I also put my comic strip plans on hold when I met cartoonist Ernie Brown and followed him into silk screen painting. Ernie turned out to be a life-long friend, and designs the cover lettering and title pages to all my textbooks. Eddie McCarthy was killed in Korea just before I was drafted into the army. As luck would have it, the Korean conflict came to an end the day I finished basic training. I never went to Korea. Instead I remained at Camp Carson in Colorado for my two-year stint. Upon discharge I remained in Colorado to prospect for uranium, a popular pursuit at the time. My brother Dave and Ernie Brown joined me, but both left after a half year with no success. Then, with another prospecting companion, Millie Luna, I found uranium, enough to keep me excited for some years, but not enough for commercial gain. What I did gain was marriage to Millie three years later in Miami, Florida.

I went to Florida with Ernie Brown to seek silk-screen printing employment. Instead, I found a job painting billboards for an outdoor advertising company. Once employed, Millie joined me and we were married. It was in Miami that I met sign painter Burl Grey, who inspired me toward a new path – the quest for scientific knowledge. Burl was an extraordinary guy, with whom I had lost contact until very recently. None of the painters wanted to paint with him because of his intellectual bent. Painting billboards was a two-person task, and conversations with Burl didn't involve the usual discourse about sports, cars, and sex – the fare of most painters. Rather than superficially

One of Paul Hewitt's physics cartoons.

discussing these topics, Burl preferred to ponder the hows and whys of the world about us and to query philosophical matters. He had no background in physics, probably missed an exposure to it in high school as I did, and he subsequently didn't know nature's rules. But he had an insatiable curiosity about the physical world.

I'll always remember one day when he called attention to the tension in the ropes that supported our weights and weight of the staging we were on. He twanged the rope nearest his end and beckoned me to do the same with mine. He was interested in the relative tensions in the ropes. If we stood systematically and each had the same weight, the

Academia

Another of Paul Hewitt's physics cartoons.

tensions should be the same in each rope. But Burl was heavier than I, and he wished to confirm that the tension in his rope ought to be greater than the tension in the rope nearest me. The twanging sounds confirmed his hypothesis. Together, we reasoned it should be so, because more of the load was supported by his rope.

Such conversations drove many other painters bats, but I was enthralled. When I walked toward Burl, he asked if the tension in his rope increased as a result. We agreed it would, for we reasoned that his rope was supporting even more of the load. Burl then asked if the tension in my rope would become less. And we agreed that it would, for it would be supporting less of the total load.

We went further and used exaggeration to form our reasoning. If we both stood at an extreme end of the staging and leaned outward, we would imagine the opposite end of the staging rising like the end of a see-saw, with the rope going limp. Then there would be no tension in the rope. From this we had an explanation for the case of my walking toward Burl. We reasoned the tension in my rope would gradually decrease as I walked away from it. It was fun posing such questions and seeing if we could answer them. I'd bring the most interesting of these questions home after work and Millie and I would have a go at them. One that none of us could answer was whether or not the tension lost in one rope due to my walking away from it would be exactly compensated by the tension gained in the other rope. For example, if one rope underwent a 50 pound loss, would the other rope gain 50 pounds? Like exactly 50 pounds? And, if so, would this be a grand coincidence? The answer to this wasn't known to me until more than a year later, when Burl's simulation resulted in my leaving a full-time commitment to painting signs and going full tilt into formal education.

I returned to Massachusetts and made an appointment with the admissions director at M.I.T. I wanted to be a scientist and contribute to making a better world. I was convinced that the problems of the world would best be solved by scientifically-educated people, and I wanted to be one of them. When the director learned I hadn't taken science and math classes in high school, he advised me to go first to prep school and make up high school deficiencies in math and science. By this time Millie's and my first child was born. When the director further learned that neither I nor my family had any money to speak of, and that I had to work part time to support my wife and child, he suggested I go to the "state supported M.I.T.," Lowell Tech, some 30 miles north. I took both of his suggestions.

It was at Newman Preparatory School in Boston that I learned about the rule that provided the answer to the rope tension problem! The rule was EF=0, which said that for any object in equilibrium, the sum of the forces (EF) acting on the object would equal zero. So on the staging, the upward tensions in the ropes would be exactly equal in magnitude to the downward forces, our weights and the weight of the staging. The upward forces, however they may have varied, would always add up to our weights and weight of the staging. So, yes, a 50-pound increase in one rope would be accompanied exactly by a 50-pound decrease in the other.

How different one's thinking is when one has or does not have a model to guide it. Burl was a technocrat of sorts, but if he had been mystical in his thinking, and guided me in that direction, we might have been more concerned with how each rope "knows" about the condition of the other. Such an approach, which intrigues many people with a nonscientific view of the world, could have led me to who knows what. I shudder to wonder if I could have become a pseudo-scientist of some sort had I been as greatly influenced by someone with flakier views than Burl's at this impressionable stage of my life. I owe a lot to Burl Grey.

So now I'm teaching others about what I didn't know when my thirst for scientific knowledge was whetted. It was exciting to discover that all the diverse phenomena of the world are tied together by a surprisingly small number of rules, and satisfying to share that excitement now. Everything is connected to everything else, and in a beautifully simple way. The rules of nature are what the study of physics is about. A knowledge of physics changes the way we see the world. There is sense to it all. And to point out this sense to my students is a very satisfying occupation – for me, much more stimulating than painting signs.

Paul Hewitt

Scientist, Philosopher, Teacher, Cartoonist, Pugilist

by
John Burns

While *The Gathering of Memories* was in production in 2000, I heard from numerous ex-Saugonians from all over the world. Many of them were former students of mine at Saugus High School.

Paul Hewitt was among them. It was welcome news indeed to hear from Paul, one of my favorite students of all time, after an absence of half a century.

I have vivid memories of Paul as a student in my classroom, and as a cartoonist and *student* advisor to me in the production of *The Focus*, our school magazine. His creativity was exceptional. His native tact and good humor gave great latitude to his frankness and enabled him "gently" to label an occasional idea of mine as "dorky," then cheerfully put the idea into sketch form with his "Hewitt Drewit". (Does "dorky" have any current standing?)

When in March, 2002, I heard from Paul, he sent me a copy of his most recent book, *Touch This! Conceptual Physics for Everyone*, used incidentally as a text at Saugus High

School. The book was a revelation! I am in awe of what this young man of such great promise has done with his life. His science book is truly one of a kind. It has a warm, inviting look. The author seems close at hand, anticipating the reader's needs. The lively, humorous illustrations help to convince the reader that science need not be intimidating, and is not an arcane matter reserved for the special few. He clarifies science in a light-handed manner.

After the passage of 50 years I have come to know what Paul Hewitt has done with his life. The Paul Hewitt I knew in the late '40s was a truly gifted cartoonist whose humor and insights gave his work a special impact. I did not know of the vast potential that lay beneath his lively, congenial exterior.

Through his book I caught up with a rich sampling of his life experiences.

It is compelling to look at the events of his life and to reflect on the influences that merged in the developing of this unusual man: his abundant gifts, his energy and determination, his appetite for life and his infinite fixation on all the "why's" that cross his path.

And what a magnificent teacher! What a unique approach to teaching, to learning!

From this book we learn so much of this multi-dimensional man who cannot resist a challenge and whose diversity of interests knows no limits.

His life and accomplishments give all Saugonians much to be proud of.

Some of Paul Hewitt's Thoughts on Science and Other Matters

Science, Art, and Religion

by
Paul Hewitt

The search for order and meaning in the world has taken different directions: one is science, another is art, and another is religion. These three domains differ from one another in important ways, although they often overlap. Science is principally engaged with discovering and recording natural phenomena; the arts are an expression of human experience as it pertains to the senses; and religion addresses the source, purpose, and meaning of it all.

Science and the arts are comparable. In art we find what is possible in human experience. We can learn about emotions ranging from anguish to love, even if we haven't experienced them. The arts do not necessarily give us those experiences, but describe them to us and suggest possibilities. A knowledge of science similarly tells us what is possible in nature. Scientific knowledge helps us predict possibilities in nature even before these possibilities have been experienced. It provides us with a way of connecting things, of seeing relationships between and among them, and of making sense of the myriad of natural events around us. Science broadens our perspective of the natural environment of which we are a part. A knowledge of both the arts and the sciences makes for a wholeness that affects the way we view the world and the decisions we make about it and ourselves. A truly educated person is knowledgeable in both the arts and the sciences.

Science and religion have similarities also, but they are basically different from one another – principally because their domains are different. Science is concerned with the physical realm; religion is concerned with the spiritual realm. Simply put, science addresses how, religion addresses why. The practices of science and religion are also different. Whereas scientists experiment to find nature's secrets, religious practitioners worship their God and work to build human community. In these respects, science and religion are as different as apples and oranges and do not contradict each other. Science and religion are two different yet complementary fields of human activity.

Later, when we investigate the nature of light, we'll treat light first as a wave and then as a particle. To the person who knows only a little about science, waves and particles are contradictory; light can be only one or the other, and we have to choose between them. But to the enlightened person, waves and particles complement each other and provide a deeper understanding of light. In a similar way, it is mainly people who are either uninformed or misinformed about the deeper natures of both science and religion who feel that they must choose between a belief in religion or a belief in science. Unless one has a shallow understanding of either or both, there is no contradiction in being religious and being scientific in one's thinking.

I vividly remember being approached by students, while I was a guest lecturer in Bible Belt states, who were painfully torn between "believing" in science which intrigued them, and believing in religion. They were enormously relieved when I told them that I thought people could embrace both science and religion without contradiction! When I cited the wave-particle example above, one student cried tears of joy, sobbing "Thank you" over and over. I went on to tell them that I was acquainted with scientists who didn't believe in a personal God, and scientists who were devoutly religious – and that both groups were generally happy citizens and first-rate scientists. And both groups included profoundly spiritual people. Einstein, who spelled God N-A-T-U-R-E and didn't believe in a personal God, put it well when he said "Science without religion is deaf; religion without science is blind." The religion and science he spoke of, of course, were deeper and more spiritual than the versions likely embraced by whoever was responsible for the pained confusion in the students mentioned above. How many young minds are stunted by those who indoctrinate under the guise of education?

My beloved sister, Marjorie Hewitt Suchocki, is a highly spiritual person and a prominent Christian theologian at a graduate school in Claremont in southern California. Like many contemporary theologians, she views God as a supreme presence permeating all space and time. Her questions about meaning are in a realm related to, but distinct from, the realm of science; they do not conflict with science.

Science provides answers to questions that primarily ask how. Religion deals with why – questions about our place in the universe that have stirred the inquisitive souls of humans for centuries. A variety of religious answers abound, which gives richness to human diversity. An important message of science, however, is that not knowing is okay. It's okay not to know – especially in this awesome time of exploding knowledge about who and where we are, when an open mind is better prepared to discover why we are.

The tragic part of our past is replete with the power of those who claimed attainment of absolute certainty. The bright part of our future will be devoid of their influence. And if we find that one of nature's rules is that absolute certainty will always elude us, so be it. Again, it's okay not to know. This personal attitude widened to all fields of knowledge leads to wisdom.

In Perspective

Only a few centuries ago, the most talented and most skilled artists, architects, and artisans of the world directed their genius and effort to the construction of great cathedrals, synagogues, temples, and mosques. Some of these architectural structures took centuries to build, which means that nobody witnessed both the beginning and the end of construction. Even the architects and early builders who lived to a ripe old age never saw the finished results of their labors. Entire lifetimes were spent in the shadows of construction that to them were without beginning or end. The enormous focus of human energy was inspired by a vision that went beyond worldly concerns – a vision of the cosmos. To the people of that time, the structures they erected were their spaceships of faith, firmly anchored, but pointing to the cosmos.

Today the efforts of many of our skilled scientists, engineers, artists, and artisans are directed to building the spaceships that already orbit the earth and others that will voyage beyond. The time required to build these spaceships is extremely brief compared to the time spent building the stone and marble structures of the past. Many people working on today's spaceships were alive before the first jetliner carried passengers. Where will younger lives lead in a comparable time?

We are at the dawn of a major change in human growth. This is not appreciated by those who benefit from the progressive uphill climb in health, nutrition, comfort, and human well-being over the past centuries. For too many, perception along the climb has been that advances have peaked – with only decline to come. Prophets of doom have never lacked public attention. Some welcome doom as fulfilling certain religious prophesies. But nevertheless, we advance. We are some fifteen million years from the Big Bang, with at least 100 billion more years to go. So, like a child, we have more future than past. Buckminster Fuller put it well when he likened us to chicken eggs about to be hatched. Inside the limited environment of the eggs are undeveloped chickens consuming and exhausting their inner-egg resources. It may seem to the chicks that doom is at hand, until in desperation the chicks break through their shells and hatch – entering a whole new range of possibilities. Similarly, the earth is our cradle and had served us well. But cradles, however comfortable, are one day outgrown. Like the chicks poking through the shell, we probe habitats beyond the earth. So with the inspiration that in many ways is similar to the inspiration of those who built the early cathedrals, synagogues, temples, and mosques, we aim for the cosmos.

We live in an exciting time!

Medical

Keep a watch also on the faults of the patients, which often make them lie about the taking of things prescribed.

— Hippocrates

Segmund Adam Wesolowski

by
Saugus Advertiser Staff
(*Saugus Advertiser*, August 12, 1993)

Sigmund Adam Wesolowski; class valedictorian of the class of 1941, Saugus High School, was recognized by his classmates as a man who would leave his mark on the world and in the remarkable life he led he did not let them down.

Outstanding among his accomplishments was the part he played in the development of the heart pump. He was a pioneer in arterial prosthesis for diseased arteries. He was widely acknowledged as one of the most knowledgeable, leading authorities in the treatment of intricate and complicated vascular heart diseases such as arteriosclerosis.

His educational experiences were extensive: he attended Harvard University, 1941-1944; M.D., Tufts University, 1948; Intern in Surgery, John Hopkins Hospital, 1948-1949; Charleton Research and Teaching Fields, Tufts University College of Medicine, 1949-1951; Tufts University, M.S., 1951; Resident in Surgery, Zeskind Surgical Research Laboratory, New England Medical Center of Boston 1949-1952; and Alliance College Institute SC. D., 1970.

Dr. Wesolowski finished his residency at Kings County Hospital, New York, 1954-1956; Registrar Thoracic Surgery, Griggs Hospital, London, England, 1956-1957; Clinical Professor of Surgery at State University of New York, Downstate Medical Center, 1964; Chairman of Surgery, Meadowbrook Hospital, East Meadow, New York, 1964-1966; Director LGH Cardiovascular Research Laboratory, Mercy Hospital, Rockville Center, New York, 1966-1978; Chief Thoracic Cardiovascular Surgery, Mercy Hospital, 1974-1978; Chairman Department of Surgery, St. Raphael Hospital, New Haven, Connecticut, 1978-1979; Chief Thoracic Surgeon, Veterans' Medical Center, Togus, Maine, 1980-1988.

He was a member of 54 national and international cardiovascular societies, the author of two books and 176 surgical publications.

He was the recipient of numerous awards, the last of which was the prestigious Jacob Markowitz Award, Boston, 1988.

His accomplishments are listed in *World Who's Who in Science*, *Who's Who in America*, and many other prestigious publications.

All his artifacts such as books, movies, publications and various other memorabilia have been donated to the Society for Biomaterials – of which he was a founding member –

and are housed at Clemson University, Clemson, South Carolina.

Despite the demands of his life in science and medicine, Dr. Wesolowski took time away from these activities to serve his country – as a Midshipman in the U.S. Navy in World War II and as a Captain in the U.S. Army Medical Corps in the Korean War.

Norma Robie Nadeau

A Memory of My Beloved Sister

by
Shirley Robie Caproni

Norma led a life of love, compassion, courage and dedication. She was the second born of six children of Ralph and Edith (Greek) Robie. She was the oldest daughter; this would have a strong impact on her life. The values that she embraced were embedded in the previous generations of both parents.

Henry Robie arrived in Boston in 1639 from Castle Donningham, England. He settled in Exeter, New Hampshire. He was a judge and one of the founders of Hampton, New Hampshire.

Ralph Robie, our father, was born in Plymouth, New Hampshire, in 1891. He was an only child as his mother died when he was three years old. In his early twenties, he moved to Boston seeking other opportunities.

Our mother, Edith, was born in a small fishing village in Blue Rocks, Nova Scotia. Her father was captain of a large vessel and spent months on the Grand Banks. Her mother raised nine children in a small house at the edge of the ocean. Mother was the second born. She and her older sister were expected to help raise the younger children.

As a young woman she moved to Boston to further her education. She became a nurse, and married Ralph Robie. Their first two children were born before the Depression. Father lost his auto dealership business because of it. They moved to Salem, then to Lynn where four other children were born. The oldest daughter, Norma, was expected to care for the younger children as there were no other family members available in this country.

In 1939, the family moved to Saugus Center into a large house off Central Street. It was up a dirt road beside the mill. Through the back woods you could reach Lily Pond and the dam. The canal ran along the side of the property.

One winter, a young girl fell through the ice on the canal and drowned. Her body was brought into our house in attempt to save her life, but their efforts were not successful. The following summer, my younger sister and I almost drowned in Lily Pond near the dam. Norma, as the oldest, was held responsible. This event was to lead to our move to Cliftondale in 1940. We lived on Lincoln Avenue. Norma graduated from high school in 1945. She went to work for a realtor in Cliftondale Square. This was fortunate as she was able to facilitate the purchase of a large, fourteen-room house on Chestnut Street in East Saugus. We moved in the summer of 1946.

On July 4, 1948, Norma married Robert Nadeau, also a Saugonian. They lived in Lynn, and then purchased a house in Woburn. They focused on raising their two children, Raymond and Linda. Norma and Bob were involved in their children's lives through school, church, and neighborhood activities. They were also involved in issues pertinent to the community problems.

She never forgot her family in Saugus and was always available when needed.

Norma Robie Nadeau.

In her mid-thirties, she was diagnosed with a disease known as scleraderma. She was told this was a rare disease; she was one in a million.

She was an intelligent woman who wanted answers so she researched her disease and discovered just how rare it was. This just heightened her fear. After many years, she wrote a letter to the chat line in a Boston newspaper asking if there were others out there with this disease. She was amazed at all the replies she received here, as well as around the country. With the support of her husband, Bob, she answered all the letters.

We have heard it said, "It is better to light a candle than to curse the darkness." My sister, Norma, did this and the candle became a torch of hope. It became clear to her that there needed to be more support available for victims and their families. She contacted the Arthritis Foundation in Boston to request their help in forming the Scleraderma Association.

In 1976, the Association was founded. She was president of the Association until her illness prohibited this. During her leadership she was on television many times doing public service announcements to bring about awareness about this disease. Her dedication to fellow sufferers and their families never wavered.

She was the recipient of the Arthritis Foundation's "Volunteer of the Year Award" in 1978. In 1980, she received a Special Service Award. She had also been nominated in 1982 for the prestigious Charles B. Harding Award for Distinguished Service. The Harding Award is the highest volunteer award presented by the National Chapter of the Arthritis Foundation. She and her husband served for two years on the executive committee of the Massachusetts Chapter of the Arthritis Foundation. She will always be remembered by the volunteers and the staff there for her courage and dedication.

As to her family and friends, her loss cannot be measured. She was an inspiration to all she touched. At her memorial service, her son, Raymond, captured the essence that was Norma, as follows:

In Memory of Norma E. Nadeau
9/26/27 – 7/30/82

Because grief shared is grief diminished, my father, my sister and I would like to thank you all for gathering here with us today. We are here to celebrate the life – and mourn the passing – of a remarkable woman, who flew the battle flag of bravery the last years of her life, while reaching out to give aid and comfort and education to those whose suffering she knew only too well. We are here to comfort ourselves because for most of us it is still difficult to understand why good, kind people must endure years of affliction, confronting daily the spectre of death.

For many of us here, my mother was an inspiration, living proof that faith, courage, and love are the necessary ingredients of a life well lived. For many more of us, she was friend, neighbor, confidante, mother-confessor, always ready to listen and to understand, and to impart her wisdom.

It is my family's hope that those of you who can, will remember a woman years before illness insidiously slowed her down, a vibrant woman whose involvement with her family, her friends, her community, and her church, filled her life. A woman who fought the good battles, with vigor and intelligence. A woman of robust physical stamina who could out-distance anyone in backyard badminton, who threw a bowling ball with the best of them….a woman who took to the dance floor as if born to dance, and who, partnered with her ever faithful and loving husband, could manifest for us the grace and harmony of two souls locked in a music of lasting love.

We ask that when you need to remember her, do so this way. Remember that the gift of her poor besieged body to medical science is the most precious and most generous legacy that anyone can bequeath. And when one feels the need to communicate with her giving spirit, as many of us will do, do so at the ocean, her ancestral home.

Stand forthright and feel her presence in the sea air, listen to her voice in the chatter of gulls. Remember her every time a sparrow perches on a sill, eager for the seeds you've generously placed there for its survival. Remember that she was a lover of life who took sustenance from the wondrous chaos around her.

Remember with pride her valiant effort to overcome, the power of her will to carry on and face head-on the most overwhelming obstacle any of us will every face. Remember what one writer said, "The sad thing is not death: the sad thing is the life's loss out of earth where the living survive."

The life of this woman is indeed over. But her spirit lives in those of us she touched, in those of us she comforted, listened to, and loved. For she was generous in her love. A true Christian, she found good in every place she looked. Another legacy we hope will be passed down to future generations.

We must remember that we cannot weep for those who have at last found peace and respite from their torment. We are grateful the agony is over. But that special place she filled in our hearts and in our lives can never be refilled. At a time like this, absence becomes the only horrible presence.

We grieve for ourselves in our sorrow and others grieve for us, but not so much for what we have lost, because some things we can never lose. But rather, for what has been taken away from us – too soon.

This heroic woman that we remember today has left a legacy we can all be proud of, a legacy in which we can all share, a legacy my family sincerely hopes is carried on with conviction and generosity.

Once again, and to close, it is my family's wish that you join us here in celebration of this exemplary life. For many of us it is impossible right now to honor her wish that we not mourn, for we do indeed mourn this loss; we must remember her directive that we carry on, with passion and commitment, and a view toward the future. No one person I have ever known has understood more fully the implications of looking to the future. For those of us left behind, there is a responsibility. I believe, along with my family, that it is a responsibility we can all assume. With the memory of my mother behind us, a task we must take on with courage and love.

Again, my father, my sister, and I thank you for all sharing with us our memories, and for sharing with us our loss.

> Do not stand at my grave and weep;
> I am not there. I do not sleep.
> I am a thousand winds that blow.
> I am the diamond glints on snow.
> I am the sunlight on ripened grain.
> I am the gentle autumn's rain.
>
> When you awaken in the morning's hush,
> I am the swift uplifting rush
> Of quiet birds in circled flight.
> I am the soft stars that shine at night.
> Do not stand at my grave and cry;
> I am not there. I did not die.
>
> — By Mary E. Frye

Volunteer Trips

by
Frank R. Virnelli

After completing my training in plastic surgery in 1971, I established a practice in Winchester, just a few miles from Saugus, where my wife, Judy Cochrane Virnelli, and I had grown up. I was very fortunate to be in an area that had been actively seeking a plastic surgeon and was busy almost immediately. I developed a practice that included a good balance of reconstructive and cosmetic patients and worked with an exceptional group of colleagues at Winchester Hospital. I was also able to join the faculty of the plastic surgery training program at Boston University and spent half a day each week working in Boston with residents. I was very happy with my practice but I was disappointed that I didn't have the opportunity to perform cleft lip and palate surgery. Correction of these challenging deformities had been a special interest of mine in my training, but in the Boston area almost all this type of surgery was done in two hospitals where I did not have privileges. Repair of cleft deformities had improved remarkably in the previous decades and I wanted to be able to do the surgery that had interested me most in my training.

Cleft lip and palate deformities affect a small percentage of Caucasians and an even smaller percentage of African-Americans. However, they are much more common in Asians and Native American populations including the indigenous populations of North and South America. Clefts can involve one side of the lip (unilateral) or, less commonly, both sides (bilateral). The unilateral cleft lip frequently involves a complete separation of the lip and extends entirely through the roof of the mouth (palate). In some patients the cleft is present only in the palate. Extreme forms of these deformities are among the greatest challenges facing a plastic surgeon.

Prior to 1950, most repairs of cleft lips left a severe residual deformity of both the lip and the nose. During the last years of the Korean War a young American plastic surgeon, Ralph Millard, was stationed in Korea and became very interested in treating the large numbers of Korean children with clefts. He was very unhappy with the results of reconstructive methods that were used at the time since they all left very obvious scars and permanent deformities.

He collected a large number of photos of children with unilateral clefts and had them displayed around his tent so that he could study them. One morning he woke and looked at the photos and realized that there was a way to rearrange the tissue so that scarring would be minimal and in most cases the residual deformity could be almost imperceptible. This rearrangement became known as the Millard rotation advancement repair and is now the gold standard for unilateral lip repair. Millard continued a lifelong study of cleft problems and, along with many other plastic surgeons, improved treatment methods for every type of cleft deformity including the associated nasal defects.

Today people often comment that they never see children with cleft lip scars because with proper repair the residual scar and deformity is often overlooked. In advanced nations cleft palate teams work with patients from birth, utilizing physicians, dentists, speech pathologists and support personnel in order to obtain the best possible results.

During the last fifty years a large number of volunteer organizations from advanced nations have sent teams to developing countries to provide medical care. Many of these groups have included plastic surgeons who have repaired a wide variety of deformities in children and adults.

In 1977 I decided that I would like to make a volunteer trip to a developing country, preferably with a plastic surgery *resident* from the Boston University program. Our national society published a pamphlet listing opportunities for volunteer work overseas and I wrote to all the organizations that offered trips of two weeks or less. Only one, the Christian Medical Society, would allow *residents* to accompany me. I immediately sent in an application and was notified that there would be a trip to Honduras in 1978 that would welcome a plastic surgeon.

I spent months collecting medical supplies from every source that I could think of and was very pleased with the enthusiastic response that I received from most of those contacted. An excellent *resident*, Bruce Baker, who was just completing his training, agreed to go with me and helped gather supplies. We soon realized that it would be very difficult to transport everything that we were collecting and had to concentrate on small items that would be of greatest value in a developing country.

In May of 1978 we joined a group of about 70 people from all over the US and traveled to San Pedro Sula, Honduras, the largest city in the country. The first night was spent in a local Bible college where we had to sleep on pieces of cardboard that were placed over some old bed springs. Without air conditioning we weren't very comfortable and very few of us got much sleep.

The following day we traveled several hours by bus to the town of Santa Rosa de Copan in the northeast corner of the country where there was a small hospital. The surgical team of twelve stayed in Santa Rosa. The rest of the group went several hours further into the country over terrible roads to stay at a primitive children's camp in order to supply medical care to remote communities in that area.

The surgical team really lucked out and we stayed in the homes of local physicians in Santa Rosa. Bruce and I stayed with one of the pediatricians. He always left the house before sunrise and after he left we would have breakfast with his wife. She spoke a little English and since we spoke no Spanish our initial conversations were pretty limited. After a while the three of us would use our dictionaries simultaneously in order to communicate. We often had tears running down our cheeks before we finished breakfast from laughing so hard as we struggled to be understood. This provided a wonderful stimulus to learn some Spanish and I have worked hard to acquire enough to communicate with Spanish speakers who are patient enough to speak very slowly and are willing to often repeat what they have said.

Our work in the hospital was some of the most satisfying that we had ever experienced. We were particularly interested in repairing cleft lips and palates and there seemed to be one or two new cases waiting for us at the hospital when we arrived every morning. We also treated a number of severely burned children who had contractures of their necks, arms and legs that were not only terrible cosmetic problems, but also significantly restricted their function. Burned children with these problems are extremely common throughout Latin America. Primitive stoves using kerosene or gasoline are found in houses in all the rural areas that I have visited because they are inexpensive. They are very dangerous when children come into contact with them and fires in houses are a very common problem. As a result of experience working in Latin America, treatment of burn contractures using a combination of large flaps and skin grafts has also become one of my special interests.

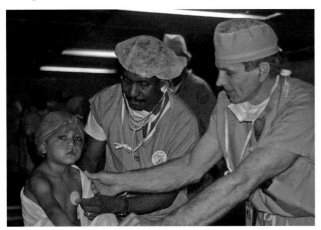
Dr. Frank Virnelli at work in Colombia.

There also was a remarkable assortment of congenital deformities of the face, hands and feet. Working with the general surgeon, we were able to help many of these unfortunate children. We also performed surgery on a number of adults who had never had access to plastic surgery. Of course, we weren't able to help all the patients who sought help and it was very difficult to see the disappointment of families when they were told that we would not be able to help their children.

After working well into the evening every day for the first week, we made a weekend trip to the Mayan city of Copan, located in northern Honduras near the Guatemalan border. Copan is a very special place that can be included with Machu Pichu on the short list of the most impressive archeological sites in the Western Hemisphere. The pyramids, stellae (large stones with carvings and hieroglyphics that document the history of the city) and the Mayan ball field are unsurpassed in the quality of the workmanship and wonderful state of preservation. It was a very welcome

break and we returned to Santa Rosa eager to return to work.

We continued our busy schedule and were extremely pleased with our results. The support of the local personnel and patients' families was wonderful and we made a lot of friends in a short time. We were particularly pleased with the absence of serious complications. We all hoped that the group could return the following year so that we could work together again and do additional surgery on some of the patients who required more work.

Eighteen months later I did return with another *resident* (who has continued to make trips to Honduras over the past 25 years). It was wonderful to renew friendships and continue the work. We saw a number of patients from the previous year, but I was very disappointed when most did not return for follow-up examination and possible additional surgery. Communication and transportation are overwhelming problems in all developing countries and we realized that most families never received word that our group was returning.

During this second trip, I met many Peace Corps workers who were concentrated in this corner of Honduras because they had been transferred from Guatemala and El Salvador, which were both in the middle of civil wars. I enjoyed spending time with these volunteers and was very interested in hearing about their experiences, most of which were extremely positive. A few workers were discouraged by how difficult it was to get people to accept new ideas or change to more efficient methods of farming (or in one case beekeeping).

The Christian Medical Society did not return to Santa Rosa after that trip and I subsequently traveled to the Dominican Republic, Mexico and Ecuador on projects that they sponsored. The wonderful patients, extremely supportive and appreciative families, poorly supplied hospitals, and severe poverty were remarkably similar in each country.

I subsequently have made trips with several other organizations traveling to Colombia, Guatemala, and Bolivia treating as many patients as possible regardless of the type of deformity. While each group has done its best to provide excellent care, the lack of key personnel would sometimes compromise the amount and quality of work that could be accomplished. The first four groups that I worked with lacked sufficient funding to pay for travel expenses for personnel who would be willing to donate their time but could not afford to pay their own expenses.

Two years ago I joined a team sponsored by Rotary International for a trip to Venezuela. Volunteer Rotarians had worked for months raising funds for the project and developed an excellent relationship with Venezuelan Rotarians who provided excellent housing and food throughout the project. The group is called Rotaplast and was formed in California about 15 years ago. The group is organized to treat cleft lips and palates although in special cases other problems are also treated.

It was my first experience (after fifteen earlier projects) with a complete team of pediatricians, anesthesiologists, dentists, operating room and recovery room nurses, interpreters and support personnel providing care comparable with that available anywhere. From the initial screening of large numbers of children the first day to the final follow-up clinic the day before we left, the support of local volunteers was the best that I have seen. I was able to perform more procedures than on earlier trips while working in a very efficient and safe environment. While it isn't possible to get long term follow-up on all patients, I am not aware of any significant complications on the Rotaplast trips that I have taken.

Teaching surgeons in developing countries is an important part of volunteer trips and I have always welcomed the opportunity to work closely with plastic surgeons in other countries. In 2004, while working in Venezuela, a plastic surgery resident from Bogotá made the long trip to the city where we were working and spent a day working with me. The following day the chief of plastic surgery of Bogotá's children's hospital worked with me. The exchange of ideas was very valuable and I was able to arrange to have excellent DVD's of the repair methods used by the world's best cleft surgeons. These are supplied free of charge by Smile Train, an excellent organization that specializes in teaching surgeons in developing countries how to repair clefts so that they would not be dependent upon volunteer groups to get this very important work done. In 2005, I worked with the chief of pediatric surgery at the military hospital in Guatemala City and had a similar excellent experience.

Many patients have been special on these trips but one boy really stands out in my memory. He came to our clinic in Colombia in 1995 after being turned away by an earlier group apparently because they already had more patients than they could treat. He had an untreated complete unilateral cleft and was seven years old. He appeared to be an excellent candidate for surgery, but our pediatrician noted a heart murmur on the screening exam. There was a cardiologist available in the hospital and he was referred for an evaluation to be sure he could tolerate anesthesia.

We were overwhelmed by the volume of surgery on the trip and the next time I heard about this boy it was the next to the last day of the project. The cardiologist had done a number of tests and determined that the murmur was insignificant. I put him on the schedule for the following morning to follow an infant that we wanted to do first.

During the first case that morning, we were informed that the boy had eaten some candy that his family had given him and we were told that he would have to be cancelled.

I had a long talk with the anesthesiologist, who was as good as any that I've ever worked with. She came from the largest pediatric hospital in Detroit and had an enormous experience working with children. She was reluctant to give him general anesthesia, so I said that I would do him with local anesthesia and sedation since I didn't want to see him turned away again. She finally agreed to give him anesthesia as long as we did him in the late afternoon at the end of the schedule.

When he finally arrived in the operating room, he was exceptionally cooperative and both the anesthesia and surgery were uneventful. I was working with an excellent resident who was completing her training in plastic surgery at Lahey Clinic and we were both very pleased with the result. I took Polaroid pictures before putting on the bandage and then we took the boy to the recovery room. On the way the anesthesiologist thanked me for talking her into doing the case.

In the recovery room we showed his father the photos taken before and after the repair and he told the resident, "Dios va a pagarle."

When I translated, "God will pay you," she started to cry.

This case and many similar ones on these projects have been the most satisfying of my career in plastic surgery. I hope that I will be able to make many more of these trips before I retire.

Cheryl Landry

Eye Doc with Heart

by
Carolyn Edy
(*Good Housekeeping*, March 2000)

Braving danger and bearing glasses, she helps the vulnerable survivors of a gruesome war.

Cheryl Landry has shone her penlight into the eyes of thousands of Bosnian children, but she doesn't let herself dwell on what they've seen. "If I had to stop and think about all the sad stories, I wouldn't be able to function," says Landry, 43.

An optometrist in Woonsocket, RI, Landry stumbled upon her overseas calling in April 1996. While reading through an optometry journal, she noticed a recruitment ad for medical professionals to treat refugees in Bosnia. When she called for information, Landry learned that the relief organization didn't have an established program. But, if she could pay her own travel expenses – and bring all the necessary equipment – the organization's volunteers would help her reach refugees once she got there.

When Landry told her parents and her husband, George Rouse, that she wanted to go, "it went over like a lead balloon." Rouse, a computer software consultant, says he wasn't surprised by his wife's plan. "But I was concerned about her safety," he notes.

Nonetheless, Landry forged ahead, launching a drive to collect used eyeglasses. Friends, strangers and eyeglass companies from Maine to Alaska ultimately donated 7,000 pairs. During the four days prior to her flight, Landry's family, patients, and colleagues worked around the clock in her living room to clean, label, and bag the lenses. "Those last few days were killers," she says.

Soon after she landed in Split, Croatia, Landry was stopped by soldiers on the Bosnian-Croatian border. All 18 boxes of eyeglasses that she'd brought were confiscated. Undaunted, Landry started examining patients at orphanages, asylums, and camps the next day, as planned. When her supplies were located several days into her trip, she returned to fill prescriptions.

"People were very grateful," says Landry. "You'd get kissed or they'd break out in huge smiles. It was really satisfying." But her accomplishments were bittersweet: In a region where a single pair of glasses costs a month's salary, Landry could meet only a fraction of the need. "When I tried to leave, people were running after me yelling, 'Doctor! Doctor! Please, please,'" she recalls.

To manage the overwhelming demand, Landry focused on the war's youngest survivors during her next three trips, which were sponsored by the Bosnian Children's Fund. Even though she saw up to 90 kids a day, a few stand out in her mind. There was the five-year-old girl whose severely crossed eyes straightened instantly with proper lenses. And the little boy she met at an orphanage who'd been found in a garbage can; he was farsighted, but had been wearing lenses designed for someone with severe nearsightedness.

Landry's husband has accompanied her on the last two trips, and the couple will travel to Kosovo this spring to provide lenses for the refugees there. "It's not that she's totally fearless or anything," says Rouse when asked about his wife's latest project. "But if she decides to do something... she'll do it."

Growing Up in Saugus
Part 4

Wasting one's youth is better than doing nothing at all with it.

— Georges Courteline

Growing Up in Lynnhurst

by
Paul Downing

When discussing Ray Bradbury's *Dandelion Wine* with my students, I commented often on Douglas's safe, secure and innocent growing up. I too had that kind of growing up, made possible by the relative isolation of where I lived, when I lived there, my family and the people in my neighborhood.

The Lynnhurst section of Saugus was bordered by woods, a large reservoir, woods, Elm Street, Walnut Street – and more woods and fields. A wooded section of Lynn abutted the area and so with few exceptions there was little interaction between the neighboring people from Saugus and Lynn.

Saugus Center was three miles away – two if you walked over the hill, through McCullough's farm and past the Saugus Iron Works to Central Street and the center of town. Actually, from ages ten to fourteen we often took this journey on Saturdays to go to the State Theater. Here, for 35 cents, we saw two movies, a cartoon, a newsreel, and perhaps an installment of the latest running serial. Three hours of magical enjoyment and penny candy, too.

The North Saugus, East Saugus and Cliftondale areas of town were too distant to be readily accessible, so until we went to the Central Junior High (1949) we knew little about these areas or their denizens.

Lynnhurst, then, was a kind of island, where we kids, maybe three dozen of us close in age, grew up together, with our elementary school, our local church, the neighbors, our friends and our families. You knew everyone, kids called many of the ladies "Auntie," you were welcome in most homes, and people of all ages achieved a togetherness that I've never seen since. We had our characters – interesting, humorous and odd – but they were few.

Dads worked hard, many at the General Electric plants in Lynn where my father worked for forty years. Mothers stayed home, tended children and visited across backyard fences. Kids and dogs roamed freely.

Our daily lives back then? Food and gasoline were rationed, we squeezed white margarine and orange powder together to make "butter," we listened to the radio for entertainment: *The Shadow*; *Amos and Andy*; *The Great Gildersleeve*; *Mr. Keene, Tracer of Lost Persons*; *Henry Aldrich*; *The Green Hornet*; boxing matches (Joe Louis was the champ); and of course the Red Sox, our boys of summer. Imagine sitting on the floor in front of a large floor-model radio (and that's what we had to do,) thrilling to the squealing-door opening

of *Inner Sanctum* and really getting into it. Different times? You bet. Good times? Right again.

The people in my neighborhood? I'd like to spend some time with them, going from house to house, street by street, with just my best memories added.

There were only a dozen or so streets, of which only four were of any length. Many were named after presidents or other important men.

My street, Fairmount Avenue, extending from the Lynn line down to Walnut Street, was the longest. On the Lynn end lived the Grays, my friend Donny, his parents and three siblings. Donny had this old house foundation in the woods near his house on which we built a "fort," a one room cabin about 10' by 10' complete with a door, some chairs and an old pot bellied stove. We spent a lot of time there one year, some of it preparing for an attack by the Melanson boys (a tribe from further into Lynn), which never did take place but which provided us with a lot of intrigue and suspense.

Old Man Mahan had a small dairy farm near the Grays and delivered his milk in glass bottles. The Lundskogs (and daughter Gloria) lived across from Mahan. Gloria was a big, older girl, who used to throw rocks at me when I teased her.

George South lived down the street a bit. He had blond, almost white hair and really big ears. He was my pal, along with his uncle, Ronnie, one year his junior.

Tommy McCann came next, a year older than I. We grew up together. Once he beat the hell out of me – my fresh mouth was to blame – but we went on to play high school football together and even attended a prom at Lynn English later, on a double date. Tommy married Janet Richard, his school sweetheart, and died young in his 40s.

The Stewarts lived next door to us: Bobby, Jimmy and Bruce. When I was twelve, they moved because their parents each fell for and switched partners with their best friends, the Baracloughs. It caused a minor sensation.

Years later I did hear from Jimmy, but never saw them again. Once, Patty Denham and I started a fire in the woods. When the firemen came, I blamed the Stewart boys, but they were at the movies. The truth came out and my butt was sore for a week!

Bo Madden and his wife Gerry bought Old Man Bartosh's house across the street. Mr. Bartosh, from middle Europe, had a small orchard and a massive grapevine from which he produced a very potent red wine. My father would visit him occasionally and come home a little unsteady on his feet. Sometimes we'd help ourselves to a handful of grapes if Mr. Bartosh wasn't home. Bo had four cute daughters: Carolyn, Debbie, Barbara and Joanie, all friends of my sister, and one son, Bobby, who later built a house on Cleveland Avenue, right behind his parents. They were a nice, caring family. Barbara, in fact, married Eddie Ciampollilo, the kid from across the street. Carolyn later taught Home Economics at the high school.

Across from us was a field, now occupied by four houses, where older boys played football and baseball. I watched them, learned from them and they'd let me get into the games, taking it easy on me, thank God. (Of course, I would be the one who'd have to chase any ball that found its way into Old Man Bartosh's yard next door.) Ray Maes, Donnie and Roland Junkins, Randy St. Pierre, the Frederickson boys, Ralph Roman, Jack Henderson – God, they were giants!

Walter Kyle and his wife, Aunt Bessie, lived next door to the Kenneys. Shirley, my age, was very much a part of our group and her brother Jackie was my sister's age. We kids interacted a lot with the Kyles. Another thing our family shared with the Kyles was the telephone service. We had a party line! Our number was SA 8-0677M. Kyle's was 0677I. Blood's was 0677G and I forgot the fourth one, but it was a four-party line. If you wanted to make a call, you might have to wait until one of the other people was "off the line," finished talking, and sometimes Aunt Bessie would talk interminably and someone listened in on OUR conversations occasionally; we could hear another person breathing. Who'd put up with the situation today? We'd mention to the person we were speaking with that "I can't tell you now 'cause someone's listening in," and then we'd hear a click, as the person hung up.

What a system!

Next to them were the Denhams – Patty, Joanie and Dickie were all about my age and Judy was younger. Joanie and Dickie played a big part in my younger life, both in elementary school and in church-related activities. Dickie and I played sandlot sports together until ages 14-15. Then we all kind of went our separate ways. Dickie moved back to the neighborhood recently. I plan to get together with him soon.

The Westmores, Nancy, Michael and Danny, all younger, lived across from the Denhams. Further on lived Phil Quinn and Johnny Limoges, Kenny St. Pierre's friends. And then, as Fairmount Avenue came to Walnut Street, we'd come upon Janice and Wayne Burpee (who became Lees when their mother remarried), Russell, Morris, Westby Rogers and Donnie (Mucka) Murray, all younger, and quiet Prescott Murray and the pool-playing, stogie-smoking Jimmy Mullins, a legend at the Rat Hole, a pool hall in Saugus Center.

Sterling Avenue ran off Fairmount in this area. Laura White (my first girlfriend – sixth grade) and her brother Steven lived on Sterling. The Whites had the first television in the neighborhood, and for a while a dozen of us early teenagers would hang out there in the afternoon watching cartoons and test patterns, until, of course, we all got our own TVs in 1950. Jack Henderson and his two beautiful sisters lived on Sterling as did Paul Goodwin and his brother, all smart kids, all older than me.

Fairchild Street was the last street off Fairmount, and it was loaded with kids: Artie Kenney, Ralph (Swede) Swenson and his twin Chandler (Channy), Gail Piper and his sister Susan, Valjean Hart (who later taught with me as Valjean Anderson) and the Deans: Julia, Donald, Marietta and Paul (the brat). Most of these kids were my age or slightly younger. I played high school football with Swede, and both he and Marietta were in our church group. Marietta married her high school sweetheart, Raoul Weyler, who died very young.

Parallel to Fairchild was Blueridge Avenue, where lived three kids I went all through school with and still see – Janice Nelson, Kenny Ballard and John Mullar. Kenny had a younger brother, Donny, best friends with Stevie White. John had an older brother, Dick, and sister, Hope. John, Kenny and I learned to read before first grade, and we used to read *Mother West Wind Stories* to the other first and second graders.

Kenny is probably the kid I did most with. We started school together, played high school football, were in all the same classes, hung out with the same groups, and later we played bridge (with Doc Graham and Freddie Case, two classmates) for thirty years.

The Paines lived across from the Ballards: Phil, Dottie, (our age) and June, another of my sister's pals. Behind the Paines was Fairchild Field, where, well before the new Lynnhurst Elementary School was built, we'd play pick-up games of softball, baseball and football, sometimes against kids from North Saugus, Saugus Center, and even Bristow Street. When a bat broke, we'd tape it together; when the cover got knocked off a baseball, we'd wrap it in black electric tape. We never had any adult supervision for baseball with four on a side (no catcher), or for football with two-to-six on a side. Whoever we could scare up would come to play. The only time we played organized ball was when our park instructor signed us up for a town-wide softball league when we were all about thirteen. We won the league title and all got little keychain softballs as trophies (I still have mine). We were the Lynnhurst Falcons – I played first base. It was a great season, and not one parent ever came to watch us!

Parallel to Fairmount and closer to Walnut, progressively, were Cleveland, Harrison, Garfield and Newcomb, with Washington, Edison, Jefferson and Oakcrest crossing these, running from Fairmount to Walnut.

At the upper (east) end of Cleveland lived the Hutchins family, whose kids included Thelma, and Joanie, both older, Martha Jane (our age), Norma, and finally boy Joey. Joanie babysat for us until I was twelve or thirteen. She loved to wrestle and would always lose! I often wondered how a twelve year old could so consistently "pin" a sixteen year old – did I miss something?

Next to the Hutchinses lived Charlie Blood, an innovative kid who spent time, as we all did, at a tiny pond that we called Wormy, located behind Mahan's farm. We'd cook out there, catch hornpout, slide on the ice in winter and just kick around.

Across from the Bloods were the Junkinses, another G.E. family like the Hutchinses, whose kids, older, were Roland, Donald and Betty, who married Howard Leck and lived for years on Fairmount. Roland became a minister and Donald a professor and poet.

A couple of houses down, past the Wormsteads and Hammerstroms, were the Fredericksons, Ralph (Buddy), Chet and Kent. Ralph hung out with Ray Maes and the older boys, Chet had polio as a child and had a little trouble getting around, and Kent was a quiet, really smart kid who, when I was four or five, would come to my house on Sundays to read me the Sunday "Funnies," and that's how I learned to read so early.

Across from the Fredericksons were the Sewells, Kippy, his wife and three daughters: Marilyn, Marcia and Barbara. This was a pretty straight family, due in part to the mother's being a teacher, but Marcia, the cutest and my favorite, was a rebel. Their nana, Mrs. Poola, was a custodian at our little school.

Further down were the Comeaus, Ray and Bobby (younger), and across from them the Browns. The parents were a little odd (I remember one time, on Halloween, we lit a bag of dog crap on fire, ringing their doorbell and hiding to watch them come out and stomp the fire out – Saugus amusement). Sammy Brown, the son, was one of our oldest friends.

Down from them lived Sonny Adrien, who had a physical "condition" and got around the area in cart pulled by a *goat*! He moved before I knew much about him, but I always remember the goat!

The Dodges moved into the Adrien house. They were a large earthy family whose kids included David and Maryanne (older), Susie (my age), and Corrine (Queenie), my sister's best friend. The neighborhood kids would constantly be at the Dodges', grabbing cookies or whatever.

The Maeses lived down next to the school. Charlie, Ray, Dick and Mariette, all older, were very much a part of the fabric of the neighborhood – Charlie, the soldier who died so young; Ray, who even as a teenager ruled our universe; Dick, the sailor who married and had six to eight kids; and Mariette, the valedictorian (along with Kent Frederickson), who moved to Australia in 1956 and never returned.

Living in the Maes house were two other kids, Philip and Delores (Dee Dee) DeVlaminck, both about our age and very much a part of our group. Philip and I did a lot together when we were twelve to sixteen. He was shot and killed at age twenty while working at the Merit Gas Station on Route One. I felt really bad about this because he never really had a lot and I had so much. Dee Dee, a cute, really nice girl, whom I teased unmercifully, married Donny Reardon, had three beautiful children and became a widow at age 45.

The school bus stop was right in front of the Maeses'! We began our mornings there during grades seven through twelve, right across from the empty lot where the older boys (Maes, Fredrickson, etc.) put in two horseshoe courts. Going there to play horseshoes was a regular summer after-supper activity. We'd often have to wait our turn to "play the winners," but enjoyed watching while we waited. One time while playing against Dickie Denham (who also sleep-walked around the neighborhood and almost drowned diving to the bottom of a not-so-shallow pond – we pulled him out and had to resuscitate him), I threw a double ringer, and wouldn't you know it, he "topped" me, throwing one of his own! Curses! Good thing I liked him (despite his being a Boston Braves fan, who kept throwing the 1948 Red Sox playoff loss to the Cleveland Indians in my face).

Next came our school, the Lynnhurst Elementary, a three room school with a small, closet-sized library, which the community shared. We had two grades in each room. Miss Reynolds taught grades one and two on the first floor, Miss Brigham, the principal, taught grades five and six above her, and in the large main room, probably the original building, Miss Cronin taught third and fourth.

Mr. Bradbury, a high school science teacher, came to show us movies occasionally, Miss Grillo would come as our music teacher and Miss Griffin came once a week to play games (physical education). We'd play dodge ball or "red rover" outside on the unpaved gravel playground in the spring and fall, and "Wonder Ball" inside in the winter or on rainy days.

We'd hang out at the school steps after supper – people would just show up – and we'd talk for hours on summer nights and sometimes we'd sing!

We all came out of that school ready to do a good job and we did just so. We missed the old school (it's torn down now), for there we learned our numbers, letters, hand-writing, geography and began to learn about ourselves. (The bathrooms were in the basement. The boys lined up to get into school a little early each day, hopefully to be the first in the bathroom to "write our names" on the dry slate wall of the urinal.)

There was no lunchroom at the school so we had an hour for lunch, walking home and back, which was easy for me – living four houses away – but hard for kids who lived a mile away.

A little further down Cleveland were the Daveys, whose kids included Fran and Eddie (older), Janice (our age), and Susan (younger, who later married Sammy Brown). They were a quiet, serious family. Hicksie lived across the street from them, next to the McLernon, an old Scottish family, pillars of our church.

Hicksie, Thomas Wilbur Hicks, was, and is, one of my favorite people and also one of my chief rivals (although the rivalry was greater in *his* mind). We liked the same girls (only me first), had the same paper route (only me first) – get the picture? Tommy's father was very demanding: Tom would have to do chores, usually for us, at the most inopportune times. When we'd have a game against another group of kids and we needed him to play, sometimes we'd help him finish mowing the lawn or whatever, but usually we'd just go play and he'd have to stay behind.

Tommy and I did a lot of stuff together. We even went to ballroom dancing school when we were fourteen! When he moved to Lynn in the tenth grade, I really missed him, even though quite often we'd still get together. I was his best man and then gave the same toast at his son's wedding that I made at Tom and Martha's. We had a lot of parties at his house when we were young married people. He lives in Maine now, and when I think of him it could be in reference to the time when we were thirteen and got the giggles in church. We had to leave, in disgrace, but laughed our asses off running down the street. We still see each other every year or so and have a great time. Last year it was with Kenny and Marilyn Ballard, too.

Down the street from the Hickses, past the hunchback lady's house, was the local dump. Can you believe it, our own dump! Right next to Jimmy Weir's house. (Most people didn't actually dump stuff there; I'm not sure who did. Most of us burned our trash in the backyard behind a rock or whatever.) Before World War II was over we kids would go down there, with the scouts or the school, and peel the tinfoil off cigarette packages to make into softball-sized balls of tinfoil to aid the "war effort." Picking through trash, although nasty in retrospect, isn't half bad when you're a kid.

As I'm writing this, I'm amazed at the freedom we had. When we were ten to fourteen, an average summer day would begin when we laced up our new, black high-top Ked sneakers, wolfed down our cereal, grabbed our bikes, met with "the kids," swam in the reservoir, played some kind of ball, maybe hitch-hiked to Reading or wherever, played war games in the woods, searched the dump for treasures, and then after a quick sandwich for lunch (and usually listening to the latest fifteen minute installment of *Our Gal Sunday* or *The Romance of Helen Trent*) we'd go back out until supper to continue, freely and innocently, our day of fun. Parents didn't question us, except to inquire how our day went. No one bothered us and very little "sinning" went on. Today's kids will never experience what we had. And weren't we lucky.

Getting back to our neighborhood, Edison Street ran from Fairmount to Walnut, passing the ends of Cleveland and Newcomb. Joe Sullivan, who later married Shirley Kyle, lived there. Joe introduced me to the gathering of maple tree sap to boil down to thin but delicious syrup, and he had the first "crystal" radio I'd seen. He played centerfield on our softball team and was very strong. Once he punched me in the mouth, but I never held it against him; I had teased him too much.

"Chubby" Thompson lived four houses down from Joe. "Chubby" (real name Howard) was a good athlete and played a lot of ball with us. He was a good looking blond boy who couldn't avoid getting into trouble. I'll always remember the time the pond warden, old Bob, came down the path, whistling to warn us to get out of the forbidden reservoir before he got to us. As we were hopping down the path, trying to get dressed, "Chubby" stuck a quarter up his nostril so he wouldn't lose it. When we got to Mr. Leger's store he couldn't get it out of his nose; we had to get pliers!

The "Rezzy" was great – our own private pond where we'd swim for hours. The pine forest dropped a pine needle carpet, which softened our footfalls and provided a cushion to relax on as we, after swimming, would lie and talk and suck on popsicles that we'd buy for a nickel at Mr. Leger's store. We'd collect returnable bottles at two cents each and turn them in at Leger's for candy, gum, or popsicles. (I have to admit that we'd occasionally leave the store with an extra unpaid-for goody.) Sometimes Jimmy Baldasare, a younger kid who always had some money and who used to hang out with us, could be pressured into treating all of us to a popsicle. We could be shameless.

Mr. Leger lived past 100. Just before he died, he made the papers by thwarting a robber at his store. He attacked the would-be robber! We were so proud of him – and at his age!

Parallel with Cleveland was Harrison Avenue. Ray Maes lives there now with his wife, Jeanette. Hicksie and I used to lift weights in his basement when we were fifteen or sixteen. Ray's buddy, Ralphie Roman, grew up right across the street. Sometime Ray should write something like this – he'd have some stories to tell.

Harold Everett still lives on Harrison and had three kids: Elliott, who died at 50, Pauline and Cynthia. For a while Harold was a chemistry teacher at Saugus High (where Pauline also taught for a few years) and an elder at our church. He also had two huge gardens on both sides of Harrison, running 50-75 yards along the road. We never raided his gardens. Beans? Squash? Pansies?

It was a big deal every fall when Harold killed the pig he'd spent the year fattening up. How he dispatched it will go unsaid, but eventually it wound up suspended, to be dunked head first into a barrel of boiling water, emerging pink and steamy ready for the hair to be scraped off prior to it being dismembered and prepared as ham and chops and bacon for the Everetts' winter treats. Growing up, we never missed this spectacular event.

At one end of Harold's garden lived the Rippons. Al, his wife (Harold's sister), and their three kids, Donny, Norma and Carl. Donny was frail, but could pitch a softball like crazy. Carl stepped on a board, which flipped up, had a nail at the end and destroyed his left eye and Norma had a mild neurological disorder that made her movements shaky (she outgrew this). Despite their troubles they fitted in well with the other kids.

Barbara Tetrault lived a few houses down, a happy, vivacious girl who was very attractive to me when I was fourteen or fifteen. The attraction was intense but short-lived and when it was over, guess who came calling at the Tetrault's house? Yup-Hicksie!

Down at the end of Harrison lived the Whitcombs, another G.E. Family. Johnny, our age, was kind of a blond, Elvis – looking kid. He was part of our group.

The aforementioned Dena family lived originally in the only two-family houses in the neighborhood, situated next door to our church, the Dorr Memorial Methodist, one of our prime meeting spots. Sunday school pageants. May Day celebrations, the solemn elders, the choir (my mother sang in it and Kenny Ballard's father Bob often accompanied the choir with his trumpet), and most important to us, the Methodist Youth Fellowship, the "M.Y.F.," begun when we were in our early teens. Part of the activities revolved around religious instruction, but kids of all faiths could enjoy the social part- dances, parties, Sunday afternoon meetings, etc. Also Kenny Ballard, Swede and I went to Rolling Ridge, a Methodist youth camp in Andover for a week in the summer of 1953 and 1954. Meeting kids from all over the state was quite an experience. Interacting with them socially (with, of course, a little religious instruction thrown in) was unforgettable. Such a beautiful place and our church even paid the $35.00 that it cost each of us to attend.

Further down Garfield and including Newcomb were the Broughtons (three kids younger) who had a huge garage where we had several parties. Bobby "Monday" Munroe lived across the street (but in Lynn) with his older siblings, Eddie and Ginny. "Monday" was a popular member of our church group.

The Weirs, Sadie and Al, whose daughter Jan (Donald Junkins' true love) was a true beauty, were fixtures in the 'hood, along with Wilson "Willie" Laverne (our age) and his younger sister Dawn. Arthur Keefe, Jimmy, "Jake" Weir and his sister Betty, Arthur "Skippy" Potter and his sister Ann – all lived on Newcomb. Jake and Skip were an integral part of our social, school and athletic life. We had a few "tree houses," but the best was a TWO story job in a tree next to Jake's house where we spent a lot of time during one summer (1951?). Skip, a year older, was kind of my counterpart, in that he and I would usually "captain" our respective sides in sandlot play. He would always choose Chubby and David Richards and I'd choose Kenny, Hicksie and Jake. We had some intense competition, but few arguments, believe it or not.

I had a paper route for two years, delivering daily and Sunday papers. Most customers took the Lynn Item, but I had a few Boston Globes and Travelers, and one Christian Science Monitor (Mr. Everett). Eighty customers, and I made five dollars a week for the first year. Then I *bought* the route and made fifteen dollars a week, decent money then for a fourteen year old kid. Among other things, I bought my own bicycle and portable radio. Each customer owed 52 cents a week; I'd usually get tipped three cents from each house and made a nickel per paper from the distributor. At Christmas I'd make an extra $40-$50! Phil DeVlaminck or Hicksie (who later took over the route, of course) would fill in for me when needed.

Whom have I missed? Joe Syms, Otto Persson, "Chick" Case, Jimmy Schier, Chink Deveau, Bobby Zarba, Dotty Bergstrom – all were a part of our lives, too.

Because we learned who we were, and, despite our parochialism, the transition to junior high wasn't difficult. We were a bit shy, but we all found our niche in different aspects of school society and academia. Although many of our bonds remained strong, other friendships began, and sadly some of us drifted apart, moved, or just lost touch. (Susie Dodge did plan two reunions, one in the '70s and one in the '80s. Both were well attended, with 20-25 of us returning – they were fun).

So that's what growing up in Lynnhurst in the 1940s and 1950s was like: with the memories that delight, amuse and haunt; with people smiling back through the years, a twinkle in their eyes acknowledging that they were there, and they too remember. Isn't that just the best!

Variable Sites

I watch the ripples change their size
But never leave the stream
Of warm impermanence

So the days float through my eyes
But still the days seem the same

— from "Changes," by David Bowie

The Three Faces
of Five Locations

by
John Burns and Eric W. Brown
(using material from Norm Downs' slide show)

Following you'll find five different Saugus locations each
with pictures from three different periods of time.

Site One

The first is the North Saugus School site (now the North
Saugus Professional Building). It is at the corner of Water
and Walnut Streets.

I. Early North Saugus School.

II. Later North Saugus School.

III. North Saugus Professional Building.

Site Two

The second site has seen even more significant change over
the past century. It is in Cliftondale Square adjacent to
where the rotary is today.

I. The Hatch Home.

II. Hanson's Garage.

III. The Cliftondale Mobil Station.

III. The Pythian Office Building;
home of the Chamber of Commerce.

Site Three

The third is fairly easy to recognize in all three of its forms. It is in Saugus Center.

I. The Pythian Building.

Site Four

This next location (also in Saugus Center) has undergone some more dramatic changes. It is at the corner of Jasper Street.

J. S. Meacom.

II. The remodeled Pythian Building;
home of the "Rathole."

II. Murray's Seafood.

Variable Sites

III. The Saugus Center Professional Building.

III. The Sweetser Corner Housing Complex.

Site Five

This final location (in Cliftondale Square) looks extremely different in each view.

The Lincoln School.

The Sweetser School.

Social Notes

The human race will begin solving its problems on the day that it ceases taking itself so seriously.

— Malaclypse the Younger

Saugus' First Bikinis

by
Janice Jarosz

Recently, on the *Today Show*, a question was asked about the debut of the bikini bathing suit, specifically the year in which it was introduced to the fashion world. Only one guest in the audience knew the answer.

But back in Saugus, MA, another viewer was watching the show and she also knew the answer – only on a more personal level. Sis Laskey was watching that day and the question brought back fond memories of a time long ago when she and her friends wore the first bikinis in Saugus. It was 1946 when the country enjoyed its first year of peace after World War II.

Ms. Gladys Dole, a resident of Lily Pond Avenue and neighbor of the George Prideaux family, had a flair for fashion design and she loved to sew. She subscribed to all the latest magazines and knew what was "in" and what was "out" before anyone else. Marion Prideaux, "Sis" Laskey as we know her today, grew up in the Lily Pond area with her two best friends, Ruth Stead and Regina Hurley, and lived two doors down from Mrs. Dole.

The girls were inseparable, especially during the summer months when days were spent swimming at Lily Pond. The area surrounding Lily Pond in those post-war days was made up of single family homes spread out through the wooded meadows and waterfront property. It was a quiet and peaceful place full of fresh air, quiet afternoons, and leisurely swims. The threesome would leave their homes early in the summer mornings returning only for lunch and supper – which were sometimes annoying breaks as they took away from their free and unscheduled days.

It was during the summer of '46 that Mrs. Doyle first laid eyes on the new bathing suit look sweeping the country – the bikini. She wanted to design one herself and she knew just the girls that could and would wear them. Always wanting to be the first to make a fashion statement, she quickly made some mental notes when the girls visited her one day and purchased enough grain bags, which cost 25¢ a piece, from Charlie Comfort's store, to make three new bathing suits.

The material was dotted with pink flowers. There was no pattern needed - she just went by the sizes of the girls and proceeded to whip up the first three bikini bathing suits to hit the quiet little town of Saugus.

The suits were two-piece with lace at both sides and the top was lined and decorated with a bow in the middle. "Sis," Regina, and Ruth loved them and all agreed that the best part was that they all could look alike. They wore them for at least two seasons. Sometimes, when they felt a little daring, they would pull the lacing along the sides a little tighter to reveal just a bit more.

"Do you think Marion should go out in public with that suit on," was the remark her father made to her mother. "Oh George," she replied, "she looks beautiful."

To this day, over 50 years later, the girls still share a close friendship with one another. And sometimes when they get together they love to wander back in time to those carefree and innocent moments of chumming around together, swimming, cooking potatoes over a campfire, dreaming of what their futures would hold, laughing, sharing secrets, and wearing those beautiful bathing suits.

Ballroom Classes

by Janice Jarosz

After living in Melrose for several years, my family moved back to Saugus when our new home on Howard Street was finally built. Little did I know that not only was it wonderful moving into a brand new home, but also I would again have the opportunity to take dancing lessons from Miss Virginia Austin.

Looking back now, many of us who were lucky to take ballroom lessons from Miss Austin realized that her classes were way ahead of their time. As her students, we were able to create and develop our own dancing style, and in the process, learn how to dance as a couple.

Miss Austin's ballroom classes were taught long before Justine was dancing on *American Bandstand*, or *Saturday Night Fever* was ever thought of.

The interaction with the opposite sex at thirteen and fourteen also created a multitude of mixed emotions. We couldn't wait for dance night to arrive, but dreaded the confrontation at the same time. Some of us still cringe when we remember sitting on the wooden benches, hoping someone would ask us to dance, and when no one did, we found ourselves pretending we really didn't care but also secretly praying the dance would soon be over.

The classes were held at the Pythian Building on Central Street Wednesday evenings, from 7 – 8 PM. The fee of 25 cents covered the dance instruction by Miss Austin backed up with Miss Hattie Strout at the piano. Mr. Thomas Hawkins, a drummer, would sometimes accompany Miss Strout.

The boys had to wear ties and the girls, dresses. If a boy wanted to ask a girl to dance, he would have to walk across the dance floor, bow to the prospective partner and say, "May I have this dance?" The girl had only two responses: "Yes, you may," or, "No, you may not!"

Sometimes to break the ice and help with the mingling, Miss Austin would have the boys form an inner circle around the dance floor and the girls would form an outer circle. On the count of "three" each circle would move around the floor in opposite directions. When the counting stopped, the circles stopped and you would now be facing your dance partner.

Dance Recital, 1950
l-r: Carol Bouve, Barbara Ulban, Janice Penney, Pamela Burnham, Sandra Bouve, Shirley Ulban, unknown, Ann Sano

There were never enough boys to "go around" so the leftover girls would have to dance together. The lucky boys never had to do this.

Russ Cutter, who is still taking dance lessons to this day, would make it a point to seek out short partners. "They had to be shorter than me which left a narrow margin," laughed Russ. "I still prefer short girls."

Lynn (Rattigan) Walsh bragged about the fact that she learned how to waltz and polka better than anyone else in the class. It wasn't that she was any smarter – it was just that being the shortest made her the most popular choice.

Billy Shubert's mother signed up her thirteen-year-old in the hopes that he would develop socially. He agreed to take the ballroom lessons only when he heard from his friend, Freddie Sylvia, that Miss Austin passed out candy bars. After two weeks of lessons and no candy bars, both he and Freddie quit. Billy still can't waltz but he did become more outgoing with only two weeks of lessons.

The lessons always began with Miss Austin leading the group with a demonstration of the steps. We were then supposed to find a partner and somehow walk through it. After several practice steps the music would start up and we would finally be on our own. Miss Austin would then walk through the class checking for the correct steps that we took. I don't think she ever found many of us doing the dance right but when she did, that couple was rewarded with Necco candy wafers. I don't remember anyone doing it, but if couples were caught dancing too close, she would click her clicker in their ears as a warning.

At the end of each season Miss Austin would hold a Ballroom Banquet at which the girls were allowed to wear their very special party dresses. Tresses would be pulled back with ribbons and flowers, and for some of us, like Roberta Surrette, it was the first time we wore lipstick – only a pale pink and not too much!

Roberta didn't want to talk too much at the banquet because she wanted to make sure the lipstick stayed on her lips until school time so her classmates could see it. Wearing lipstick in public meant you were truly grown up.

Miss Austin held those wonderful dance classes for almost a decade. But then Elvis started swiveling his hips and the Beatles arrived from London and all too soon dancing together as a couple went out of style.

But for those of us who had the opportunity to have been a part of that time of innocence in our growing years, we look back with warm and happy memories – memories of our soon-to-be forgotten youth.

The Art of Teaching Dance

by
Janice Jarosz

Virginia Austin was born October 6, 1929, in Medford, and spent most of her growing-up years there. Her mother, Florence, enrolled her beautiful young daughter in a dance class with Janet Putnam, also of Medford, who was a professional dancer in her early years and now an instructor. Virginia was a most promising student who could have continued in her very successful professional career had she not had such a strong yearning to become a dance instructor.

Not to intrude on the following of her former, well-loved and respected teacher, Miss Austin chose to open her dance studio in Lynn. It didn't take long for the dance business to grow, and in 1946 Miss Austin rented the Pythian Building on Central Street in Saugus, and the Austin School of the Dance officially opened its doors that fall.

Like everything else in a small town, word spread quickly that a brand new dance studio was about to open for business. Excited mothers brought their aspiring daughters to registration day with high hopes that possibly a star was in the making!

Most mothers secretly felt that they just might have another Shirley Temple in the making and dance lessons would be the "first step" in launching their daughter's career despite the fact that very few families had the wherewithal to subsidize such dreams.

I remember the day my mother dressed my sister Karen and me up and walked us down to the Pythian Building to sign up for classes. I was five and Karen was three. All the young girls in our neighborhood were doing the same and I could feel the urgency and excitement of the day.

Registration day meant many things – a young girl's career was on the line. Miss Austin would interview you and, in her professional opinion, would decide on what type of classes, if any, you were suited for.

As soon as I saw Miss Austin for the first time, I knew right then and there that I wanted to become a professional dancer. I can still remember that first glimpse of her. She was wearing black tights and a leotard with a wide, silver belt around her very tiny waist. I had never before seen anyone so glamorous. She held her head erect and her chin high and moved with controlled motion along the dance floor. When she stopped and spoke to me for the first time, I saw her sparkling eyes.

"Janice and Karen, please come to the middle of the floor," she said and I did. Karen, on the other hand, refused to leave my mother and I knew then that her career was over. "Perhaps Karen is a little too young right now – maybe next year will be better," Miss Austin said. I could see my sister's look of relief and she never did go back.

Virginia Austin may have been interviewing me, but I also was deciding on my own career as well. I knew that from that day forward I was going to be a famous toe dancer. My dream went awry when I was assigned to a ballet class instead and before anyone consulted me I was signed on to a beginner's ballet class and in September of 1949 I became a student of Miss Austin's School of the Dance.

Miss Austin insisted on, quietly demanded, and never settled for anything less than perfection. Each dance step was reviewed and gone over religiously; heads were always held high, hair had to be done a certain way and leotards had to match and underwear was never to show through the costume and makeup had to receive the blessings of Miss Austin. Nothing was worn on recital night unless it was approved by the teacher.

Miss Austin held her dancing techniques and her students to very high standards but not without kindness. She never made us feel that we were personally responsible for the flaws in our appearance or performances. We knew she was always on our side, guiding us and always encouraging us to do better. We, her students, gratefully accepted all of her advice and suggestions.

Sad to say, my promising career as a dancer came to a sudden and tragic end when, after two years of lessons, my family moved to Melrose and it was too far to attend any more classes. I never did get to wear a pair of toe shoes, which I regret to this day. On a happier note though, once my father introduced me to the nuns at my new school, I knew right then and there that at age seven, I now truly wanted to become a nun.

Anna Bergh on left and Murial Bryant, 1952.

Another Friday Night at the Drive-in

by
Janice Jarosz

It was 1939 – the country was at peace, Franklin D. Roosevelt was president and, in Saugus, a brand new open-air theater opened at what is now the Marshall's Shopping Center at the junction of Route One and Lynn Fells Parkway.

Saugus was full of "things to do" in those days despite the fact that automobiles were at a premium. In Cliftondale, there was an indoor movie house, in Saugus Center, there was a pool hall and the State Theater, and on the Pike, there was a golf range behind Russo's Candy House, and another golf driving range where the present Square One Mall sits.

Several churches held dances on weekends and opened their gyms for weekly basketball games. Oh yes, there was plenty to do in Saugus in 1939.

At a time before home television and video games, the drive-in theater was a welcomed addition for teenagers and young families to enjoy an evening of entertainment. Very few families owned automobiles, and teenagers would take the trash out and make their beds all throughout the week in the hopes of being allowed to borrow the family car for a date at the drive-in.

Dick Eastman finally got up enough courage to ask his father for the car to take Carolyn to the movies. They had a great time, but when it was time to leave, Dick forgot to disengage the speaker that was on the window. It was not easy to face his father in the morning and come up with a good reason as to why the back window was missing.

Richard Boudette patronized the theater quite often himself. He told me the story of how the ushers knew who had the kids in the trunk of the cars and who didn't. The price was at a per person rate so some very ingenious patrons would pack their friends in the trunk, then let them out when they got past the ticket taker.

Mr. Boudette explained that all the usher had to do was see the level of the back of the vehicle. The cars, with 'extra passengers' in the trunks, were generally tipped to the rear, almost dragging the tail pipes on the street. Some kids just couldn't figure that out – but Dick did.

Norman and Gail Peach often took their three young children with them for a much-needed Friday night out. In those days, babysitters were not easy to find or, better still, even affordable. It was generally one or the other; you didn't have the extra money or you couldn't find anyone willing to care for three kids at a time, even in the immediate family as they, no doubt, had families of their own.

Eddie Murray remembers the greasy egg rolls that were available at the refreshment stand – this was long before any of us knew about fat grams. One could even purchase a mosquito coil that could be lit and placed on the dashboard to keep the bugs away during the show.

Harry Cakounes was the real celebrity back in the '60s. Because of his family connections he was given a yearly pass to take in any and all movies throughout the year. Naturally, Harry was always very popular come the weekend – his friends didn't have to use the trunk to get in to the show - he went first class all the time. Now, about those foggy windows, Harry…

Harry still has the last pass he was given before the drive-in closed in 1974 and it's one of his treasures. He also has

many of the programs that were given out weekly starting in 1939.

The drive-in theater business survived throughout the war years by selling war bonds on the side and practicing the dim out. Special reduced rates were given to those supporting the war effort. However, competition became keen when the Revere Drive-in opened on its present site and, a short while later, the Lynn Drive-in opened on the Lynnway, in Lynn. Despite the fog that always rolled in around 10 p.m. at the Lynn spot, the newer theaters offered some real high tech stuff, enticing customers from the Saugus operation.

Today the screen, the poles and the refreshment stand have all been torn down, taking away all the memories and mementoes of a happier time in our lives growing up in Saugus.

The Dreadnought Social Club

by
Janice K. Jarosz

In honor of "Women's History Month," I chose to write about "The Dreadnought Social Club" that was first organized in the town of Saugus on October 15, 1910, by twenty very young Catholic women. Miss Ethel Garra, who served as one of the founders, named the group. While the photograph spells Dreadnaught with an "a," all other newspaper accounts spell the word with an "o."

In my research, the only reference I could find was HMS *Dreadnought* built by the British in 1906. This ship was considered the most powerful battleship of its type, and other countries soon started building them also, including the United States. The interpretation of the word Dreadnought, as it appears in the books of the club, states: "The Dreadnought is considered the strongest and best ship in the U.S. Navy, built to defend the rights of the USA and **her** people." Little did any of those founders realize how significant their choice of name would turn out to be.

The Dreadnought Social Club quickly became one of the most popular social groups in town. The young ladies of the club included Miss Agnes Smith, president; Miss Blanche Donnelly, vice president; Miss Katherine Brady (mother of Betty Quinlan), secretary; Miss Jennie Donnelly, treasurer; and among its members: Misses Julia and Etta Dunn, Mabel and Louise Booth, Lena and Eva Ouimet, Margaret Donnelly, Mary Murray, Anna Deloughrey, Madeline Walsh, Regina Vernazza, Tillie Colella, and Alice Williams.

Dreadnaught Club on stage, 1913.

From all accounts, the girls hosted wonderful parties and dances throughout the several years the club was active. An "April Fool" party and dance was held April 1, 1913 at the Odd Fellows Hall that attracted a crowd of more than 200 people. In the press release, the club stated that, "A number of novelty Germans were features of the program of dancing which began at 8 o'clock and continued until midnight."

I cannot for the life of me learn what a "novelty German" was or what it meant. "Little Germans" or "novelty Germans" were always a feature of widely popular dances and parties, according to the articles I read, but nowhere does it enlighten the reader as to its meaning. Mrs. Quinlan doesn't know either!

Miss Garra must have known what she was doing when she named the club, as an attack on the organization was lodged by the Reverend Timothy J. Holland, from the pulpit of the Church of the Blessed Sacrament on Sunday, July 13, 1913. (It must have been after he saw all the smiles on their faces at the Saugus Musical, March 17, 1913).

It was while Reverend Holland was urging the people of the church to cooperate in making a picnic and field day to be held soon that he opened his attack on the Dreadnought girls.

"I want everybody to join right in and help and not be like this club of girls who call themselves the Dreadnoughts. Where they got that name I don't know, but whoever named it ought to be ashamed of themselves. They went on an outing a short time ago and disgraced themselves and their town by acting like lunatics; and the older persons who went with them; well, I don't know what to say about them.

"I don't want any girl in this parish to join this society and I won't have it! The girls never sought my advice when organizing this club and I never sanctioned it. I'll make this club disband or know the reason why. They have a treasury but never do anything for charity, and all they think about is enjoying themselves." (What's wrong with that?)

The priest was referring to the time the girls went on a July 4th outing to the farmhouse of E.W. Schofield of Dracut. They were at the farmhouse from Thursday evening, July 3, until Sunday evening, July 6.

Mrs. Smith, one of the chaperones, claimed that the girls were very well behaved, in bed every night at a reasonable hour, and fulfilled their duty as Catholics by attending mass on Sunday, July 6.

She approached Father Holland after the mass for the purpose of defending the girls. "You did not have any business saying what you did about the girls when you have no proof of any wrongdoing."

"I don't want to hear anything more about it," replied the irate rector, and he then ordered Mrs. Smith from the church. Mrs. Smith refused to leave saying, "I paid to get in here and I will speak my mind!"

Several days later, a letter was received from E.W. Schofield, the Dracut farmer and host, stating that the girls conducted themselves like ladies and were welcomed back next year. He closed the letter by stating that they were the finest body of girls he had ever entertained at his farm!

More evidence surfaced in defense of the club when it was learned that the Dreadnought Girls sponsored the May Carnival, netting close to $72 that was promptly turned over to the church. Furthermore, each girl also pledged one dollar for the mission and donated five dollars for the shrine of the Blessed Virgin in the spring of 1913.

It was also revealed that, while on this outing, several of the girls saved a woman who was floating in a rowboat without oars on Long Pond. They located another boat with oars and rowed out to save her. The woman declared that the girls deserved a medal.

Whether or not Rev. Holland retracted his statements, only the Dreadnoughts know, and they're not talking.

Restaurants

Coffee should be black as Hell, strong as death, and sweet as love.

— Turkish Proverb

Where Everybody Knows Your Name

by
Janice Jarosz

I wonder how many Saugonians remember what restaurant advertised this bill of fare! John Burns couldn't, and neither could Charlotte (Rupright) Line. Imagine being able to order a baked ham dinner, choice of vegetables, dessert, beverage, plus the local news, all for 75¢.

Co-owners Herb White and Marion Foley first worked together at the A.B. Madison Company of Revere. With the war finally over, opportunities and money became more available. Both Herb and Marion thought the time was right for a new venture.

The location they picked was the building block on Central Street then belonging to the Simon Shoe Company of Lynn. Included in the block was a 5-and-10-cent store, Bob's Shoe Box, a fish market and Charlie Burnham's Hardware Store. Being good business people, they saw the potential breakfast and lunch crowd.

So, in 1947, after signing a few papers, Herb and Marion got busy outfitting the first restaurant in the Saugus Center area. The final touch came when the proud owners placed a large blackened iron pot over the front entrance. This pot became a hallmark for the newly established "Iron Pot Restaurant."

Herb Whyte's Iron Pot menu of the day.

"Herb was the whip and I did the grill work," said Marion Foley. Eugene Newell, Gert Lancaster, and Grace Driscoll were a few of the many employees who worked there. Other workers would come down from the Dog Cart and Ridings Grille, the only other restaurants in the town of

Saugus in 1947, according to a reliable source. (There were a few places located on the Newburyport Turnpike, but you needed a car to get there.)

The Dog Cart was located where the Tumble Inn is now, and Ridings Grille was located in the Butler Building on the corner of Jackson and Essex Streets. Some old timers remember the afternoon at the Grille (Bea Crabtree Meader was the waitress and witness) when John Mancini told Charlie Thomas that he would pay for the squash pie if Charlie would throw it at the fan. Charlie took the bet, picked up the pie and threw it dead center into the fan. The squash and its crust splattered all over the walls with complete abandon, covering poor Irving Hoffman in the process. Mr. Hoffman's only reply was, "Charlie, I always thought you to be a quiet young man!"

"Things like that never happened at the Iron Pot." Herb White would not allow it, Ms. Foley stated quite emphatically.

During the late '40s and most of the '50s, the restaurant was open all day and night and business was brisk with the locals. There was a horseshoe-shaped counter and overstuffed booths aptly named "the family pews," along the sides. Friends and neighbors would come in, have their lunch or supper and stay all evening, talking and visiting with one another.

The Saugus Police Department also played an integral role in the success of the "meeting place." Two policemen walked the beat each day and night and would always stop in to check the coffee and the guests, exchanging pleasantries. After a few years, many officers and townsfolk were lucky enough to be on a first name basis with one another. The restaurant even fed the prisoners at the station on orders from the police chief.

Lt. Roland Mansfield would stop in before his shift for coffee, carrying his lunch brought from home. On one of these visits, Marion had one of the workers sneak his lunch bag into the back room without his knowledge. While back there, she slipped a piece of cardboard in place of the meat in his sandwiches. He never knew who did it, but Marion finally confessed to his widow several years after his death. They both enjoyed a good laugh over the prank.

The spirit of friendship, the chance meeting of fellow Saugonians, and the central location seemed to be just as good a reason to visit there as the food and service. This was also a time in history when people either had more time for one another or took more time for one another, and for the next ten to fifteen years, the business thrived.

The Iron Pot stayed the same for many years, but everything else around it changed. There were more automobiles, more jobs elsewhere and policemen no longer walked the neighborhood beat. Customers could now drive to other places and strangers from out of town now patronized the restaurant. Some of the regulars found their way to the Tumble Inn, but for the most part, the blending of good cooking and time spent together gave way to fast food chains and delivered pizza.

Before Route One, There Was Butch's Place

by
Janice Jarosz

Dr. Lillian Salsman, late of Marblehead, MA, wrote a family history on the Salsman family of Saugus entitled *Homeland, Volume II*. The book was published in 1986. In it, she traces the history of her family back to Berlin, Germany, and the war between France and Germany in 1809, which caused the imprisonment of two ancestral brothers. The young Germans were captured and wound up impressed on a French frigate bound for Canada. Casper Salpzman (original spelling) and his brother eventually jumped ship near Lunenberg County, Nova Scotia, and swam three very cold and dangerous miles to freedom.

Three descendants of those brave lads, Elmer, Percy and William, now spelled Salsman, settled in Saugus in the early 1900s where they built the row of small homes on Howard Street directly across the street from where Butch's Place would be.

Percy, nicknamed Butch for obvious reasons, was a strong lad who became a professional boxer in the Boston/Chelsea area. During the years 1915-17, Butch made it to the semi-finals and his fans watched many a fight at the Mechanics Building in Boston. The Prudential Building rests on that site today. During his career, he went from a lightweight contender to the welterweight category, and among his closest friends at that time were the Jacks – Dempsey and Sharkey.

During his boxing years, Butch matched talent with some of the best. Competition was keen, as the sport was extremely popular with both the male and female population, but as the years went by, and his strength was not what it used to be, Butch turned his eyes and energy to Squash Square.

Taking advantage of the repeal of Prohibition in 1933, Percy purchased one of the first liquor licenses in town and opened up a bar called Butch's Place on the site where the Jiffy Mart now stands. Being the only bar for miles around, as the surrounding communities of Melrose, Stoneham, Wake-field, and Winchester were all dry, the business was an overnight success.

It was not long before the bar expanded to the two-family house that was and still is behind the Jiffy Mart. Ernie Salsman, a nephew, remembers the dumbwaiter that was installed to keep up with the customers. Butch gave away free steamed clams every Friday night and, to make sure he always came out on top, he soaked the clams in salt water all day to insure thirsty customers.

John Kohler remembers walking down Main Street from his home in Wakefield to enjoy some of those free clams. On any given Friday night, automobiles would be lined up all the way to Staples Farm hoping to get a parking space.

The bar was located on the first floor and stocked with enough bologna sandwiches to cover the liquor license rules. Cards and entertainment were on the second floor, which was the reason for the dumbwaiter.

Live entertainment was brought in, ranging from vocalists to violinists. Doris McArthur, a well-known singer in her day, made beautiful music at the club accompanied by a snappy piano player. Rumor had it that they made beautiful music offstage as well.

Pitchers of beer went for five, ten, and twenty-five cents each and whiskey was $12 a case.

Herbie Barber remembers the place and Elmer Salsman's beer drinking pony. Elmer would lead the animal into the bar and serve him a beer. Herb also remember the time when a poor drunk fell asleep at the bar and woke up dressed as a female.

Mike Mancuso, who lived near Butch's Place, told me that, as a teenager, he would try to sneak out his family's back door for a chance to visit Butch's, but would always get caught by his watchful father.

The business thrived for several years and serious money was made. Unfortunately, Butch passed away in 1937 from pneumonia and his brother Elmer took over. The war clouds were gathering and those clouds were everywhere, even at Butch's Place.

Located in such a remote area of Saugus, most would-be patrons reached Butch's Place by auto. However, when the war broke out, gasoline was rationed and could be used only to travel back and forth to work. Uncle Sam did not make any allowances for petrol to make visits to Butch's and routine visits by government officials prevented any motorists from claiming they worked there.

In 1942, the business, and the era, closed forever.

The Tumble Inn

The Window Seat

by
Stanley Green

Without intending a plug for the Tumble Inn, a long-time family-friendly restaurant in Cliftondale, one facet of the establishment is worthy of note.

That facet is the four-seat table looking out to the busy sidewalk and the passersby.

The table history, dating back to shortly after the end of World War II, is noteworthy for its long-term occupants, including a couple dozen or so characters, authorities in sports, politics, and broadly speaking, on any subject common to western civilization.

Among the first steady occupants were Doctors Herb Upton and Ted Golan, soon to be joined by Dave Lucey, for years a football coach, and later a businessman, town official, and Registrar of Motor Vehicles.

At the same time another strong character, vying with Lucey for the final and correct verdict on any subject, was Fred Surabian, a certified expert on all Saugus High sports with a strong well-documented opinion on any matters relating to that subject.

Over the years many many other well-informed gentlemen swelled the ranks of the group crowding the table. Among the regular occupants were John O'Brien, Captain with the MDC, "Iron Mike" Harrington, Herb Connors, Stan Hartigan, and Dave Nagle, a local homebuilder and state political heavyweight. Others were Art Spinney, a football star at Saugus High, Boston College, and the Baltimore Colts, Ned Cerasuolo of the florist family, Freddie Quinlan, then with the Department of Weights and Measures, Art Statuto, football player with Saugus High, Notre Dame, the Buffalo Bills and the Los Angeles Rams, Ralph Bean, a convivial companion, Charlie Flynn, a well-known local attorney, and myself, often cast into the role of referee.

Arguments flourished daily, based around local sports and all-time stars, and local politics with the constant inference that unnamed and influential forces were somehow at work.

Political discussion came into sharp focus when our own Dave Nagle was appointed as Appointment Secretary to the soon to be elected governor, Frank Sargent.

Sargent's election opened a trove of positions to be filled in the time honored tradition of rewarding faithful supporters who got the vote out. Dave Lucey was named to the prestigious post of Registrar of Motor Vehicles, Ned Cerasuolo was named to a spot on the Mass. Pike, where his hard-earned and genuine knowledge fitted in so well. Charlie Flynn was named to the Lynn Court as a magistrate, where his Syracuse University background and law school prepared him to serve well for many years.

Every day, then and now, the corner enjoyed the occasional drop-in, including Jack Vater, long a member of the Saugus Department of Public Works, and now a resident of Beverly and Florida, along with Dom Russo, so close to the family-owned design shop and beauty salon, and Frank Matarano, the "Iron Messiah."

Some of us, in less demanding positions, were destined to serve as arbiters and referees and peacemakers, for arguments were seldom clearly won or lost, but merely continued.

Tumble Inn goes upscale at Salem Country Club.
Dave Lucey Jr., Charlie Flynn, Tom Nolan, Ned Cerasuolo, Dave Lucey Sr., John O'Brien, Jack McLain, Fred Surabian, and Dave Nagle.

At present the table is usually occupied by Dave Nagle, Ned Cerasuolo, myself, and "Doc" Wagner, for many years Chairman of the Board of Assessors, many times temporary Town Manager between appointments, and a choice as Saugus Man Of The Year in 2001.

As a fitting close to this vignette of our Town, I recall an episode in which the chair members were informed that a female passerby, of substantial age and size, made the statement that several members had "ogled" her. The dictionary meaning of "ogle" is "to keep looking boldly" or "to make eyes at." I'm sure that at some time an occupant of one of the chairs may have paid an unspoken and respectful compliment to a female passerby, but to "ogle," never!

Kane's Donuts

1955 - Present

by
Bob Wentworth

This year, 2005, marks the 50th anniversary of this Saugus landmark, an establishment of lasting pleasure for what it serves and the setting in which it serves.

Through two ownerships it has not deviated from its high standards and its character.

Currently Kane's Donuts is family owned and operated by the Delios family, with Peter and Kay Delios becoming the proprietors in 1988.

Peter's experience in the donut business dates back to 1959 when he and his brother opened a shop, Tony's Spa, in Chelsea. Later in 1969, the Delios family purchased Mrs. Foster Donuts on Chestnut Street, in Lynn, near the site of Manning Bowl, continuing there until they sold it in 1986. By 1988 becoming impatient after this brief hiatus, and at the urging of second son Paul, they purchased Kane's Donuts.

Paul, who hastened this idea, has since moved on to own and operate two restaurants in Charlestown: Paulo's Trattoria and Mez.

Peter Jr. assumed the management role at Kane's in 2001 after his father retired from daily involvement in the business. He is assisted by brother Stephen and sister Maria, both working as head bakers. Grandchildren Peter and Elena help staff the busy customer counter which is also anchored by Mrs. Florence McKenna, a 25-year associate with the business.

Rounding out the Delios family is daughter Catherine, a registered nurse in the Cardiac Care Unit at Lynn's Union Hospital.

Truly a family business with the matriarch Kay continuing an active daily role in overseeing the front end of the operation.

Kane's Donuts was founded in 1955 by Bob and June Kane and they operated this business until 1985.

After his discharge from the U.S. Navy, Bob began his bakery experience at the old New York Model Bakery on Summer Street in Lynn in 1947.

During these learning years, the idea of having their own business began to evolve. The thought, however, of a full-line bakery was a bit overwhelming as an initial step. Fortunately, New York Model opened a separate donut operation across the street from its main bakery. Although Bob didn't work in the new location, it did give him the chance to closely observe the process. He soon realized that this was a more appropriate and manageable undertaking for a start-up venture. After eight years at New York Model, in 1955, Bob and June embarked on the entrepreneurial phase of their life.

Evening at Kane's Donuts.

Living in Lynn, but having been raised in Saugus and educated in Saugus schools (Bob being a prominent member of the Sachem backfield in the 1944 undefeated State Class B football champions) and with family still in Saugus, they decided to return and start their business in their home town. They purchased the property at 120 Lincoln Avenue, the present site of the shop, which consisted of an apartment on the upper floor and what was then Buzza's Variety Store at street level.

Bob and June, with son Doug and daughter Judy, moved into the upstairs apartment, and Bob, with friend Kenny Buckless, completely renovated the downstairs, converting it into the donut shop, the configuration of which remains much the same today, 50 years later.

Four years later the Kane family moved to a home on Guild Road, a short walk from the shop, where Bob could handily maintain his early morning hours and long work days.

Finally, in 1985, after 30 years of six and seven-day work weeks, and having developed "Kane's Donuts" to the preeminent status that it still retains, Bob and June made the decision to sell and start enjoying a life of leisure with more time for family, golf and travel.

Kane's Donuts: Passageway To A Bygone Era

by
Tim Alperen
(*Saugus Advocate*, November 12, 2004)

Kane's Donuts is like Cheers: it's a place where everybody knows your name.

A local institution since 1955, Kane's has served old fashioned, homemade hand cut donuts and pastries to Saugus residents and in that time has become a veritable landmark. As a matter of fact, the neon sign that bears the establishments name is registered with the Saugus Historical Society.

But it's more than kitschy nostalgia that makes Kane's such a special place. Certainly, nostalgia plays a part, as Kane's harkens back to a disappearing culture that centered around community and family. Mom and Pop operations like Kane's used to be ubiquitous in American towns and cities. These were the places where you could go and know the proprietors or owners on a personal and first name basis.

It was a time when the staff knew your order by rote. And it was a time when you seemed to know everybody else in the place and those out on the street.

In that sense, time stands still in Kane's and it is what in these days of chain establishments makes Kane's an anomaly.

Difference isn't always celebrated in today's society. More often than not, it is eschewed. But Kane's persists and thrives because there, the more things change, the more they stay the same. In other words, they are different not because they refuse to change with the times, but because they preserve a sense of a different time.

Kane's offers a unique experience that you can't get in most of today's eating and drinking establishments. Kane's offers a sense of place, a sense of community–a sense of home.

Kane's is unique, not just for Saugus; it is a unique entity in today's mass produced culture. Its thriving persistence in the face of the national chains and generic alternatives is testament to the fact that there is something special about Kane's that will probably see it still serving its monstrous coffee cakes and homemade donuts, with a smile and a hello, well into the next fifty years.

Arts & the Theater

No generation is interested in art in quite the same way as any other; each generation, like each individual, brings to the contemplation of art its own categories of appreciation, makes its own demands upon art, and has its own uses for art.

— T. S. Eliot

Louis Malcolm MacKeil and Wallace Nutting

by
Stephen P. Carlson

The name Wallace Nutting is familiar to many Saugonians. That of Louis MacKeil is not. Yet, they are forever linked, as Louis became one of the foremost experts on the life and work of the noted antiquarian.

Wallace Nutting (1861-1941) was a Congregational minister who gained fame in the early twentieth century as an author, photographer, and entrepreneur. He became involved in Saugus when he was convinced by William Sumner Appleton, an early preservationist and founder of the Society for the Preservation of New England Antiquities (now known more simply as Historic New England) to acquire and restore the Iron Works House in the 1910s. In addition to restoring what he called "Broadhearth" to his vision of its colonial appearance, he acquired the nearby Scott Mill. There he established a factory to colorize his photographs of New England and to manufacture reproduction colonial furniture. He also built a blacksmith shop next to the Iron Works House and began to produce reproduction colonial ironwork.

While Nutting spent less than ten years in Saugus before transferring his operations to his home town of Framingham, there are many families in the town whose members worked for him as colorists or in other capacities. Through his various business endeavors, Nutting became a well-known and respected figure nationally in the study of American colonial culture. As Thomas Andrew Denenberg points out in his recent biography of Nutting (*Wallace Nutting and the Invention of America*, Yale University Press in association with the Wadsworth Atheneum Museum of Art, 2003):

> …[Nutting] played an important role in the development of a colonial revival aesthetic and ideology. He collected, reproduced, and marketed colonial artifacts, and the goods and experiences he offered his middle-class customers promoted his idealized notion of a time and place that he called "Old America." … Nutting's interrelated endeavors, from his varied writings (including Furniture of the Pilgrim Century and the monumental three-volume Furniture Treasury) to his photography (both amateur and professional), chain of restored museum houses, renowned collection of seventeenth-century furniture, reproduction colonial furniture business, and advertising program … [created him as] an

influential cultural critic who deftly combined myth and materialism, contributing significantly to both the growth of consumerism and the development of an antimodern worldview in the twentieth-century United States.

So how did Louis MacKeil become interested in Nutting to the point that he would become recognized as one of the leading authorities on the man's work, especially his extensive photographic output? In a booklet Louis MacKeil wrote about Nutting for the Saugus Historical Society (1984), he described his only encounters with the man, when he was a child of about twelve:

> Around the year 1912 he came to my grandmother's house in Natick at least a half dozen times when I was there. He was interested in buying some of the antiques in the house, in particular a large grandfather clock. Nutting had a reputation of not liking children, so I wasn't noticed; he was interested in the clock. He sort of pestered my grandmother to sell it, and eventually she did for $300. Many years later, when I saw the clock in one of his photographs, it reminded me of this incident and sparked my interest in finding out more about this man.

Louis MacKeil was born on April 15, 1900, in Natick, Mass.. He served in the U.S. Navy, on board the cruiser USS Raleigh, from 1923 to 1927. He then worked for the Boston Navy Yard for about a month. Ten years later, in March, 1937, he returned to the yard, where he worked as an electrician until retiring in February 1969. He moved to Saugus shortly after the end of World War II.

One of the more interesting aspects of his career occurred during World War II, when women began to enter the Navy Yard workforce. While most people think of women as "Rosie the Riveter," they performed all sorts of work that had traditionally been the preserve of men. In a July, 1980, interview with a National Park Service historian, Louis recalled his experiences with women workers in the Navy Yard. At the time, he was serving as a leadingman, or foreman, in the yard's Electrical Shop:

> Well, the first day they hired the girls, I was down at Pier 10, working on the DEs [escort vessels] down there. And they came down to the [Shop] 51 [Electrical Shop] shack on Pier 10. The guy walked in and said, "I have eighteen girls for you." And I said, "What?" He said, "Eighteen girls." I said, "What am I supposed to do with eighteen girls?" He said, "Put them to work. That's what they came down here for." I said, "You're

kidding!" "No," he said. "Look, I'm doing what I'm told. I was told to bring eighteen girls down here. There's the eighteen girls; I'll see you later. Goodbye. Put them to work." So I picked out some of my best mechanics, and they all kicked. "I'll quit before I'll take any women." I said, "Look, I'm not doing it. It's from upside [management]. I can't help it!" So I had eighteen the first day; the next day it got down to probably fourteen. Of course, the ships are noisy, you know? The next day it would probably go down to twelve; the next day eight. I finally wound up with five. And I selected two, and put them … wiring up the switchboards. And the mechanic down there said, "I don't want any women down here with me. I'll quit before." I said, "Look, I have got to do it! You can quit if you want, but if you quit, somebody else is coming down to take your place. So if you want to quit, quit!" … So I told them [the men], "Look, put them to work. Have them form off the cables." … And they did that, and not one error! Those girls formed those things up, and we had no errors on that job. They were very dedicated and very good. I kept them for quite a while. I used to have trouble. Fellows came down to see the girls, try to date them and all that. And I would go down there and say, "Get out of there." … But that was the biggest trouble, the fellows coming down and bothering the girls. And those girls were really in there to work. And they wanted to do the work! … They were really sincere about coming in to help out. … [The men] accepted them after a while. And some of them then said, "Gee, these girls are doing fine!" And they would pitch in and help them, any way they could. But at first, they weren't accepted at all. Even I didn't want to accept them! I was told what to do, so I said I might as well make the most of it.

Following his retirement, Louis began a quest for knowledge about Wallace Nutting that would last for the rest of his life. As former Saugus Historical Society President Mary Borg wrote:

> He was not content to accept "facts" as gathered by others. For many years Louis searched for truths. He corresponded with people who knew Nutting, and followed up on known sources of information, traveled great distances when necessary, sometimes just to copy a paper, and kept volumes of notes.

Louis recalled both Nutting and his own work in an interview with Richard Provenzano in 1975, quoted here with his permission:

> After I retired, my wife had passed away so I again took an interest in his [Nutting's] pictures, especially the country scenes. I prefer Nutting's outside pictures over his interior shots because you can't find that kind of scene today—the country roads and the birches. You can still take interior shots in old houses with a woman dressed in old-fashioned clothes. You can reproduce the interior shots but you can't reproduce the countryside. That's the way I look at it—the countryside is lost but there are still a lot of old houses around.
>
> He [Nutting] came to Saugus around 1916 and started the restoration of the Ironmaster's House then. Of course, he had the red brick building [Scott's Mill] near the Ironmaster's House, and he had his furniture business and his picture business there also. He used the Scott house in front of the red brick building. That was used by the colorists also because I understand he didn't have enough room inside the factory for his colorists. I have been told that he had about a hundred of them working for him in Saugus.
>
> I've talked with several people who have worked with Wallace Nutting. There were two women who worked for him. I've talked with Beatrice Julien and Florence McCarrier. I've also spoken to Lewis Husson who worked at the Saugus Iron Works for Nutting as a picture framer. He also made the trays that Wallace Nutting put out. In fact he made one for his wife as a gift before they were married. I also talked to Del Goding and his brother Lowell. Del was a chauffeur for Wallace Nutting while he was in Saugus and Del's father also worked for him in the furniture department. One time in Framingham when Del was acting as chauffeur, Wallace Nutting told him to help Mrs. Nutting with her very large garden and Del refused. Del pulled out his license—I guess those days chauffeurs had special licenses—and he said, "See there? The license says chauffeur. I'm not working in any garden—I'm not a gardener." That ended that.
>
> I've also talked with Everett Nutting, a relative of Wallace Nutting who still lives in Augusta, Maine. He worked in Framingham

for Nutting when he was sixteen — that was in 1911. He wasn't sure what relation he was to Wallace Nutting — probably a second cousin. His mother died when he was young and his grandfather brought him up. He was interested in photography and got his first camera when he was fifteen. His grandmother told him that since he was interested in photography so much he should go to Framingham to work for him. Everett got there and the studio was still being built out of a garage. This was in Framingham at a place Nutting called Nuttingholm. Everett hung around a few days and watched the carpenters until the place was ready and until Nutting came around and spoke to him and gave him a job. He took him down to a boardinghouse run by a Mrs. Doty. She is now dead but I understand that her daughter or daughters are still living in Framingham. Her place was where the colorists, or at least some of them, roomed. A couple of her daughters were colorists also. Everett Nutting stayed there six months and didn't like it. Nutting found out that he could type so he put him to work in the office. He asked Nutting if he could take some pictures and paints home and Nutting replied that he might as well go right to work in the coloring section with the women, but that only lasted a short while.

Everett Nutting also told me how he ate with Nutting's family on Sundays and how during the meal there was no conversation—they just ate. At his own home, everyone talked and laughed and enjoyed themselves but that's not the way it was at Wallace Nutting's. One time he dropped his fork and went to pick it up and Nutting said "Tut tut!" and called the maid in to pick it up and get a clean one. Everett Nutting wasn't happy there at all. After Sunday dinner, they'd go out for a drive. Wallace Nutting had a seven-passenger Stevens-Duryea—that was a touring car. Wallace Nutting drove and had a chauffeur sit with Everett in back while his wife sat with him in the front seat. They would drive around the countryside and that's when Nutting took his pictures—at least some of them. One funny thing was when they'd come to a place with water. If Nutting wanted to take a picture with birches or whatever and wanted ripples in the water, he'd have Everett Nutting toss pebbles in the water to make ripples for the photograph.

I once talked with a man from Penn State who is writing a book about Wallace Nutting. This man got interested in Nutting because he was fascinated that the man was into so many areas and did so well in all of them. Of course there any many things said pro and con about Wallace Nutting, but there isn't any doubt that the man had a great deal of ability.

Mary Gage is a person remembered by everyone interested in Wallace Nutting. She was the head colorist in both Framingham and Saugus. Wallace Nutting would take pictures in black and white and then designate what colors he wanted. They could vary according to the time of year he was trying to show. He could use the same photo for both a summer or fall scene by using different colors. He'd say what colors he wanted on a chart and give it to the head colorist who would color a picture and give it to Wallace Nutting for his approval and then the picture would be put on display to be copied. The other colorists would then paint pictures using that one for a model. Each colorist had a sheet of small pictures. They'd do one color, say the blue in the sky, and then when that dried, they'd do another color. I understand the colorists only got three cents apiece for the small pictures, but the larger ones of course were not done in sheets and earned them more. Each colorist would do the entire picture she was working on. As far as I know, they didn't paint the pictures on an assembly line basis. If Nutting didn't like the way a picture looked, he'd reject it. The head colorist would be in charge of the painting of all of the girls under her. I understand that Wallace Nutting had about one hundred women coloring at Saugus and the same number coloring at Framingham.

Yes, he really did use platinum paper. Everett Nutting speaks of trimming the photographic paper off the pictures and saving the strips to redeem the platinum. The paper used made it a very expensive process for those days.

All of the former colorists that I've talked to apparently enjoyed their work—they didn't seem to feel that they were underpaid or anything like that. They rarely saw Nutting himself, however. Usually it was someone else who directed them on a day-to-day basis.

I've always thought of Wallace Nutting as being a shrewd Yankee. He came from an old Yankee family on both sides—the Fifields in Maine and the Nuttings who settled in Groton, Massachusetts, in the late 1600s. Yes, I guess you could say he was a tight-fisted Yankee. This fellow Goding, his chauffeur, went with him out west—Illinois or somewhere—and Nutting got sixty dollars for a lecture and chuckled about it. "What do you know about that?" Nutting said. "I got sixty dollars for advertising my own material." That's the way he looked at things.

He always tried to be a perfectionist—that's my opinion. I think when he was a preacher, he always tried for the perfect sermon and never could reach it and it bothered him to the point of sickness. He didn't lack friends, however. Believe it or not, he had a list of his favorite people—those he liked—perhaps twenty-five in all.

A good example of his standards is the way he made reproduction furniture. He'd get a piece of old furniture, take it apart, and measure each piece of it and then draw it or have it drawn. From these drawings, he'd make reproductions. I can understand why his reproductions are worth so much. A comb-back Windsor chair of his sells for six hundred dollars today because the work in it is better than what would be found in the original. I think that explains the kind of man he was as well as anything.

In 1984, Louis was persuaded to share his knowledge of Nutting through the writing of a biographical booklet about him for the Saugus Historical Society. This writer recalls spending many afternoons at the table in the kitchen of his home on upper Main Street helping to shape his efforts. These visits usually ended in his basement, where his large collection of Wallace Nutting prints was on display.

And once the booklet was published, Louis became the consummate salesman. He brought copies with him as he made the circuit of antique dealers and attended meetings of the Wallace Nutting Collectors Club. And his dedication to his work was entirely selfless. All of his royalty checks were endorsed back to the Historical Society. His death on January 24, 1987, was a loss to all who had the privilege of knowing a man who, as Mary Borg said, was "a down-to-earth individual… with good old-fashion horse sense and Yankee ingenuity."

The Four Arts Club

by
Peter Roy

The Four Arts Club was founded in the fall of 1932 by Walter Roy and his wife, Phyllis (Parsons). For the next ten years, it was to be an opportunity for drama hobbyists in and around Saugus to be a part of an amateur theater production group without having had years of training and or experience. As was said years later by a former member, Clayton Trefry, of his recollections of the Club, "It was a challenge to belong and participate; they strived for perfection."

Walter and Phyllis lived at 1 East Denver Street at the corner of Central Street, across from what was then Young's Market. As part of their property, there was a 20' x 40' one-room, vintage cottage facing Central Street, soon dubbed the Clubhouse. It was here that the Club held its business meetings, rehearsals and social events throughout the ten years of its existence. That portion of the lot was sold in 1963, the Clubhouse demolished and a ranch style home built there.

Co-founder Walter Roy.
His wife Phyllis (Parsons) was the other co-founder

The Club members met on the first (business) and third (social) Tuesdays of the nine month season for approximately two hours. Following each of the meetings preceding a production, casting and rehearsals were held. The members also gathered socially in the off-season for weenie roasts and for field trips to take in plays put on by groups such as the Barnstormers in Tamworth, New Hampshire. A trip of this sort took three hours and involved costs such as contributions for the driver's gas (25¢), tickets (83¢) and the cost of an overnight cabin ($1).

Throughout the year, the Club held music appreciation nights, went caroling on Beacon Hill at Christmas, attended museums and Esplanade concerts, went on sleigh rides, to the beach or to a bowling alley, met at the clubhouse for

Halloween costume parties or to just play ping pong or board games. These were among the ways the members stayed close. They also gathered to build scenery and to maintain the Clubhouse by making repairs, painting, splitting firewood, or just dusting and washing windows and ashtrays. There was a strict Club rule that there was to be no liquor at any official Club functions.

The membership was "capped" at forty during the early years and annual dues were three dollars. If there wasn't a waiting list, they were involved in a membership drive. In order to even out these ups and downs, the Club adopted associate membership, which could be elevated to full membership when vacancies occurred. This was somewhat successful. After the bills were paid the treasury balance was nearly always in the range of $30 to $50 which was quite an accomplishment at that time.

As part of the preparation for each production, all of the members pitched in with various tasks. Stage models were built to be used as patterns for scenery builders. Programs, tickets, posters, press releases, bumper stickers, matchbooks and postcards had to be designed, produced and distributed throughout the town to promote every upcoming production. The scenery had to be built if sets stored in the backroom of a Cliftondale store couldn't be modified. Arrangements for props, makeup and scripts were made and costumes had to be rented for those plays which required something that wouldn't otherwise be found among the members' existing wardrobes.

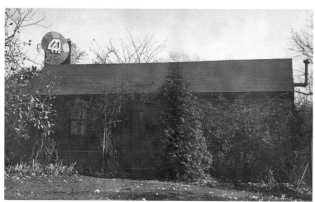

The Clubhouse.

Ads for the programs were sold to such businesses as Ships Haven, Butler's Drug Store, Keystone Storage Battery, Saugus Bowling Alleys, Park Card Shoppe, Cal's Lunch, Lynn Daily Item, Parsons' Fuel, Center Beauty Shoppe, Eulalie's Beauty Shop, Billy Garet & his Orchestra, Wilson's Variety, Vogt's Sinclair, Saugus Pharmacy, Adlington Hardware, Sunnyside Market, Russell Box Company, The Saugus Herald, Dutchland Farms, Chickland, Fullerton's Funeral Home, Howard Johnson's, Lynn Gas & Electric, Young's Market, Dennis Cronin Lumber, Carl's Duck Farm, G. Frank Newhall, Hart Bus Lines,

Saugus Credit Union, Sterling Diner, Gibbs Oil Co., and McCarrier's Package Store.

Tickets were distributed to the members for them to sell and patrons and patronesses were recruited. Among these names were those who were sponsors during the 1939-40 season: Addison, Adlington, Bennett, Bucchiere, Cheever, Davis, Flockton, Foster, Fuller, Fullerton, Furbush, Gibbs, Hill, Kelley, Mason, Merrithew, Nigro, Parsons, Peckham, Perkins, Rice, Robinson, Russell, Silver, Sullivan, Weiner, Wentworth, Wilkins and Willis.

Walter with a bevy of beauties.

There was talk in 1939 of a new high school with a large auditorium, though it was seventeen years premature. Also, some spoke at that time of a 1000-seat theater coming to Cliftondale. But, the fact remained that the Town Hall was one of the only places where a play could be staged in town at that time, although at least one production was put on at the Sweetser School auditorium. The Hall had to be booked for two performance nights as well as dress rehearsals when the Club's lighting and sound equipment could be set up and tested while the cast got their lines, places and timing down. Police and janitorial details were required.

The Club was also a good neighbor. Each year it gathered food and clothing for holiday baskets distributed to needy families in the area, sent cards and flowers to members and friends who were injured or ill. In 1937, the "CCC Boys" were invited to attend a performance; benefit performances were put on for the 4H Club, the Riverside Club, the Cambridge Masonic Lodge and Everett Kiwanis at various times. In 1938, the Major Gordon VFW Post was given permission to use the Clubhouse after their hall in East Saugus was condemned.

Remembering the period to be one of austerity and ingenuity born of the Depression, the camaraderie and excitement over joining with others to put on plays was understandable. In addition, opportunities arose for plays to be selected by the members not just to entertain, but also to provoke thought. Such was the case when, in 1937, after spirited debate among the membership, Irwin Shaw's 1936 one-act, anti-war drama, "Bury the Dead," was selected to be presented by the Club. Given the turmoil in Europe and strong public sentiment in this country, both for and against our involvement, it must have sparked some heated conversation. Twenty-seven parts were cast while others in the Club worked behind the scenes for three performances in town, two in other towns and two radio broadcasts and achieved the highest level of "professionalism."

Such success was what so many of the Club's members worked so hard for, but along the way there were the mundane aspects of any group's existence over a period of time. The Club presented three to four plays each year and there was a need for off-stage esprit de corps, as well; however, the costs of arrangements for all of this meant that the topics of money and meeting attendance were discussed frequently. There seemed to be no easy solution to distributing tickets for each member to sell and getting all of the monies back in a timely fashion; but, since bills were accrued and had to be paid, there was constantly the unpleasant need to "remind" members of their deficiencies. From time to time, there was need to refocus on the fact the Club had been founded for enjoyment, but needed to pay its way.

In 1938, the Club initiated the Four Arts Club Cup Tournament. That year, fourteen other theater groups vied for the award. Five judges from among the Four Arts Club membership attended each contesting show and an engraved cup was presented to the eventual winning group: the Concord Players for their presentation of "French Without Tears." The Four Arts Club was subsequently lauded in an editorial in the Lynn Item for its "progressiveness" in establishing the competition.

In September of 1941, there was talk of doing a show to benefit the British War Relief. A notation in the Governing Board Meeting minutes dated December 7, 1941, said that a fifteen minute recess was declared in the midst of the meeting to "listen to Walter Winchell's report on the war." As was the case with many other activities at this time, the Club was dealt a heavy blow as many of its members, male and female, went off to war. The Club was eventually disbanded, but the friendships continued throughout the lives of those with whom I was acquainted and the spirit of goodwill and group accomplishment enriched all their lives.

The following is a partial list of those who participated in the Four Arts Club during the ten years of its existence:

Doris Abdou, Ernest Allen, Nelson Ashby, Thelma Ashby, Ruth Baker, Gratia Batchelder, Kenneth Bean, Ernest Beliveau, Roger Bouve, Frederic Bowler, Miriam Boyle, Albert Burgess, Harriet Burton, Margaret Cameron, Miriam Cameron, Marvin Cann, George Carter, Dorothy Chatterton, Lloyd Cheney, Edward Colby, Vivian Copp, Wes Cromwell, Meryl Daniels, Ralph Dockendorf, Mickey Donahue, Harold Doran, Patricia Drake, Ruth Eyre, Albert Fava, Elva Fava, Al Fernald, Andrew Fleuriel, Bernie Gaylor, Elma Godfrey, Shirley Gordon , Robert Greeley, Fred Green, Eleanor Hatch , Gertrude Hazel, Marjorie Hentschel, Arthur Holbrook, Rose Holbrook, Bill Hubbard, Bob Humphries, Anna Husler, Betty Iarrobino, Tony

Iarrobino, Anna Jarvis, Veronica Kazikonis, Prudence Kelley, Emily Lattimer, Dana Lewis, Norma Manuel, Melvin March, Clarence Martin, Gordon Martin, June Martin, Harriet Mason, William Mason, Robert McGowan, Elizabeth Mead, Madeline Merrill, Richard Merrill, Edna Miller, Helen Monahan, Robert Munroe, Paul Murray, Nellie Nay, Paul Neal, Harrison Nourse, Catherine O'Connor, Ella Ogilvie, Katherine Ogilvie, Humphrey Owen, Frances Page, Gladys Pickett, Mickey Provenzano, Ellen Quint, Stewart Quint, Francis Rich, Kenneth Richardson, Geraldine Ring, Sally Roberts, L. Dix Robbins, George Robinson, Gladys Robinson, William Robinson, Mildred Rogers, Helen Rounds, Lottie Rounds, Phyllis Roy, Walter Roy, Edward Sampson, Loretta Sanborn, Elwin Shaw, Clarence Stacy, Jay Steadman, Clayton Trefry, Jack Trick, Mary Louise Tyrrell, Albert Wade, Gwendolyn Walters, Hazel Walton, Sidonia Weiner, Marion Wheaton, Chan Widell, Sumner Widell, Arthur Wilkins, Dotti Wilkins, Kay Wilkins, Viola Wilson, and George Young

Dotti Wilkins (Sanborn), Phyllis Roy,
Gladys Robinson, and Harriet (Pat) Mason.

Elizabeth Bishop

Pulitzer Prize Poet with Saugus Roots

by
Michael Hood[1]

The Saugus Setting: 20 Sunnyside Avenue

One consideration in regard to Elizabeth Bishop's Saugus experience is the pleasant physical setting which surrounded Bishop during her residence at 20 Sunnyside Avenue (in 1925 and 1926). Although one might suggest that a positive landscape environment does not guarantee a positive living experience, no information has yet come forth to suggest that Bishop's Saugus experience, via the landscape environment surrounding her while she lived with the Shepherdson family at that address, was anything but pleasant.

When Bishop and the Shepherdsons initially resided at 20 Sunnyside Avenue in 1925, their house was the last one on the north side. After 20 Sunnyside Avenue, the land was open, or open to woodlands. And too, east of houses at #21 and #23, the last two houses on the south side of Sunnyside Avenue, Bishop and the Shepherdsons were afforded additional open land, or open with woodland, and to boot, at given points on the south side, a view of seascape. It should be noted that it is common knowledge among Bishop followers that she had a lifetime attraction to the sea and for elevated residences affording landscape/seascape views. Her 20 Sunnyside residence afforded her both of these interests.

Once again, Bishop's Saugus experience appears to have been positive. It should be added that I.S. (an anonymity choice), a Saugus resident since the 1930s who only recently moved to Maine, pointed out that at the time during which Elizabeth Bishop lived at 20 Sunnyside Avenue, the surrounding area was pleasant. I.S. stated, "Up in the area now called 'A Street,' there was a wonderful pond, 'Cranberry Pond.' I don't remember if there were any cranberries or not, but that's what we called it. The street was an unpaved road/trail that led to the pond, and it had a wonderful little waterfall." Another Saugus resident living in the vicinity of Sunnyside Avenue, but during a later time frame than I.S., and here identified as O.S., stated that the

area referred to as Cranberry Pond was really a "land depression created out of a snow melt where kids skated in winter."

Whether one adheres to I.S. or O.S., it is clear that the landscape environment nearby where Bishop and the Shepherdsons resided afforded Bishop a positive experience.

Elizabeth Bishop,
Pulitzer Prize Poet.

One biographer of Bishop, Brett Millier, in mentioning the Shepherdsons moving from Revere to Saugus says, "Later, the family moved to slightly better, yet less memorable, circumstances in Cliftondale, a section of the town of Saugus." Although Revere possibly was more "memorable" than Saugus in that it was given direct attention, for example, in Bishop's unpublished story, "Mrs. Sullivan Downstairs," the Saugus landscape environment where Bishop held residence was uplifting: it afforded Bishop an opportunity to take in her neighborhood natural environment as a positive experience.

Furthermore, "slightly better" would imply/suggest a slight improvement. However, there is no evidence that Bishop's household/living experience at 20 Sunnyside Avenue, Saugus was uncomfortable in any manner, shape, or form, nor that neighborhood residents might have been a negative factor in the life of Bishop.

If, as Millier states, the Saugus "circumstances" were only "slightly better" than those experienced by the Shepherdsons in Revere, why would that be the case, how were they different, and also, what in fact might have been the implied troubled/uncomfortable "circumstances?" Millier's statement would seem to warrant explication.

Then there is the question as to why Bishop did not write about her Saugus experience. Perhaps she did, and perhaps she didn't. Merely because nothing has yet to definitively show itself as a Bishop-Saugus poem, or as a Bishop-Saugus prose piece, doesn't mean that either or both don't have a direct and/or indirect yet-to-be discovered existence, even if they be non-complete. And too, maybe Saugus simply afforded her a sanctuary wherein words had no place, or would have violated a good thing in her life: an emotional and mental memory space of spiritual privacy, which she chose not to share, consciously or unconsciously. And too, why should she have had to write about her Saugus experience? She may have written more from out of her Saugus experience than about her Saugus experience.[2]

---

1. Note: This entry is extracted from an in-depth article written and published by Michael Hood, of Uxbridge, MA, tracing the roots of renowned Pulitzer Prize poet Elizabeth Bishop, who some purists call the best American poet of the first half of the 20th century, and who studied at Saugus High School for her freshman year

We found, in our and Hood's musings and wanderings and research, that poet Elizabeth Bishop had lived at 20 Sunnyside Avenue for at least two years and had spent her freshman year at SHS. We had seen her report card, a signal of things to come, and found in her poems places that surely must have been parts of Saugus urging her roots at poetry.

On a follow-up note to Michael Hood's article, "The Atlantic Monthly" had an entry earlier this year, a poem from the unpublished work of Elizabeth Bishop. The poem was titled "Just North of Boston," written presumably just before Bishop's death in 1979, and refers to some Route 1 landmarks in Saugus where she had just paid a visit to the place she once lived.

The old Ship's Haven Restaurant appears again in italics... *But look-an 18th-century man-of-war has run aground: She's struggling there against the rocks, her lights still lit, directing rescue operations. No- it's worse: it's half a man-of-war.* (Oh, The Ship, now empty, now asea in a rental plea).

Then came a look at Wedding Gowns, Inc., once with full window displays and most recently leveled... *Now come the wedding clothes for rent: six brides are standing in a row, dresses agleam like glare-ice; next, their grooms, with ruffled shirt-fronts, pink or blue, all on a brilliant stage, on stilts. How can they meet? When will they marry?* (That building was recently torn down where the bridal shop once stood and before that it was a lawn mower repair shop and a tool rental shop and, way back, way way back, Ryman's Garage, when the Main Street overpass was constructed.)

A bit later, on the hill, a now defunct Chinese restaurant, Weylu's, brings itself back in her words... *Gold!* **Gold.** *A Burmese temple? Balinese? An oriental-something roof, with grinning dragons.*

Then, on the road but a few hundred yards away, leaps up the old Carvel Ice Cream shop... *Just beyond, an ice-cream cone a gratte-ciel outlined in glowing yellow, glowing rose on top-the ice cream-strawberry.*

---

2. Michael Hood's full biographical study of Elizabeth Bishop has appeared in The Worcester Review (Vol. XXI, Numbers 1&2) Worcester, MA, Worcester County Poetry Association, 2000. The article was later presented at Case Western Reserve University (Ohio) in 2000 as one of a series of scholarly papers celebrating poet Elizabeth Bishop. In this updated version of the initial article: the Bishop-Saugus experience, the general and/or critical reader is afforded new Saugus-related material to consider in regard to Pulitzer Prize poet, Elizabeth Bishop.

And finally, southbound on Route 1, the world-famous steak house, The Hilltop, with the huge cactus sign and the... *Twelve Hereford steer, three Hereford calves of sturdy plaster are deployed.* And was not one once rustled and mounted atop a building by capricious and ingenious MIT students?

Some members of the MIT community may still remember *Ferdi*, the fiberglass cow that *somehow* made its way to the top of the Great Dome in 1981. Now those who don't can visit the cow at the MIT Museum's Hall of Hacks.

What did the then-owner of The Hilltop think of the joke, the theft? "At first, the restaurant's owner was upset about it," Hilltop Steakhouse's vice president of operations told the AP. "But then we got so much publicity about it. We were inundated with people who came to see the place where it was missing. I've been here 24 years, and that incident still comes up often."

So many things gone down the river, but still afloat.

Civil War Battlefields Revisited

Artist from Lynn Gaining Attention with His Scenics

by
John Laidler
(*Boston Globe*, October 5, 2003)

Jeff Fioravanti has two passions: creating pastel paintings and delving into the rich history of the Civil War.

Now the Lynn resident has found a way to combine the two.

For the last two years, Fioravanti, 45, has been painting landscapes of Civil War battlefields.

While not the first artist to take up the subject of the Civil War, Fioravanti has taken a different tack than most. His works do not feature battle scenes, but depict how the battle sites look today–minus monuments and telephone poles.

Recently, Fioravanti has been gaining recognition within the community of Civil War history enthusiasts.

During November and December, 30 of Fioravanti's paintings, together with print and note card reproductions of those works, will be shown at the National Museum of Civil War Medicine in Frederick, MD.

Some of Fioravanti's paintings portray makeshift hospitals used during the war, and he is scheduled to appear at a Civil War medicine symposium in West Virginia sponsored by the museum October 25-26.

He also will be the featured attraction at the Gettysburg National Military Park's bookstore in Pennsylvania on October 11-12.

Closer to home, Fioravanti last fall donated a framed print to the Civil War Roundtable of the North Shore, a group of Civil War buffs that meets each month at the Grand Army of the Republic Hall in Lynn.

Fioravanti, who works part-time as a graphic and Web designer, is thrilled by the attention his art has received. He said it is helping him move toward his goal of becoming a full-time artist, and also to contribute to keeping alive the memory of an important American episode.

"It's what defines our country today," he said of the Civil War.

But his paintings are designed to allow viewers–both those steeped in history and those who are not–to reflect on those times in their own terms.

I'm not trying to depict the way the battle was," he said, but instead to show "what we see when we walk the fields."

"I'm trying to let people attach their own emotions. I'm giving them the scene. The painting is not completed until they attach what is meaningful to them."

"His work is very evocative," said Nadine Mironchuk of Chelsea, secretary and a board member of the Civil War Roundtable. "It's a simple pastoral scene. But he will pick a site and . . . a time of day and a mood that will just bring you right back to the battlefield. It's almost as if you are peering through the mist into the past."

"Among Civil War battlefield painters, he has made a difference in that genre," said George Wunderlich, executive director of the National Museum of Civil War Medicine.

Most of those artists, he said, focus on "what they think a battle may have looked like during the course of the conflict. What Jeff has done is give these places a life of their own. He's saying the battlefield is a beautiful place both because of the history and because it's a physically beautiful place. He's given us these very realistic views in art of these places that a lot of Americans hold a very near and dear place in their hearts. But he's done it in a way that allows not only the memory of what's happened there in the past affect the viewer, but allows the viewer to put their own memories into it."

Fioravanti, who grew up in Saugus, came back to art recently. While working as a production materials planner in 1987, he was inspired to think about art after an aunt posed as a model for a Gloucester artist. For about two years, he took pastel painting lessons and even sold some paintings. But busy with family duties, he stopped doing artwork.

It was not until 1996, after being laid off, that he "picked up my pastels again."

Since then, his career has grown steadily.

He has donated a painting of the Gettysburg battlefield to the Gettysburg Battlefield Preservation Association and was featured this past April in the annual art show, "History Meets the Art," held in Gettysburg. Fioravanti was sponsored by a local gallery, Gallery 30, to take part in the invitation-only show.

In addition to Gallery 30, his works, which also include seascapes and other New England scenes, are exhibited at A.R.A. Gallery and Art 3 Gallery in Manchester, NH. He has also exhibited in national and international juried and invitation-only shows, winning some honors.

Fioravanti, who with his wife, Cathy, has an eight-year-old daughter, Nicole, said he has always had an interest in the Civil War. But it deepened about 10 years ago after his wife gave him a history book on the war, and later when they visited Gettysburg and other battle sites.

That led him to more reading on the subject, and to become active with reenactment and preservation groups.

"Combining artistic and historic interests has been exciting. I'm trying to give people an attachment to our nation's soul, to our heritage," he said. "And I'm trying to put it together in such a manner that you don't have to be a history fan to appreciate it."

Addenda

Subsequent to this article, Mr. Fioravanti was scheduled to appear at the 10th Annual Association of Mid-Atlantic Civil War Roundtable's (AMART) Civil War Symposium in November of 2004, at Princeton University. The theme of this Symposium was "The Battle of Gettysburg."

Sponsored by the Camp Olden Civil War Roundtable, the 2004 Symposium featured some of the most recognizable and respected authors, historians, and authorities on the American Civil War known today, including Nobel Prize

Winner, Dr. James M. McPherson, who received the award for his highly acclaimed, *Battle Cry of Freedom*, a one-volume work on the American Civil War.

In addition to Dr. McPherson, other notables scheduled to appear and offer programs include: Dr. David Martin, Jeffrey Wert, Troy Harman, Patrick Falci, George Wunderlich, Jane C. Peters Estes, Stanley Saperstein, Joe Bilby, Craig Caba, and the African-American performance group, "Seven Quilts for Seven Sisters."

Mr. Fioravanti is a member of several preservation organizations throughout the United States. He also holds membership in six national and local art associations, including advance standing or signature membership in the Pastel Society of America (New York, NY), Connecticut Pastel Society (Meriden, CT), and the Pastel Painters Society of Cape Cod (Barnstable, MA). He is also listed in Marquis' *Who's Who in America*.

His work can be viewed at:
      http://www.fioravanti-fineart.com/
and a small sampling is available in the second color section on page P.

Harry Stead

by
Chicki Hollett

Harry Stead left Yorkshire County in England arriving at Ellis Island sometime around 1907. He thankfully landed in Saugus where he spent his remaining fifty-five years.

He attended the Roby School where he was continually cornered and coerced into entertaining his peers with his cockney accent which eventually disappeared and became true Saugonian.

He married Catherine Roche from Peabody in 1929 and lived at 64 Central Street before moving to 19 Lake Circle in 1938 in order to accommodate their growing family. Their union increased the population of Saugus by eight children.

Harry worked as a sign painter and graphic designer for General Electric in Lynn. He started home art classes with the Famous Artists Method where the assignments would be mailed to the school to be critiqued by artists such as Norman Rockwell. His works were primarily in charcoal and oils. He was offered a teaching position in Nebraska but chose to remain in the Lily Pond area. In its day it was a great place to raise children, as Lily Pond offered an atmosphere of pure enjoyment that only nature could provide...

ice skating, swimming, boating, fishing, sandlot football and baseball, etc.

The "Taming of the Mare" pen and ink is one of Harry's few remaining works that have stayed with the family.

Harry's creative gifts continue to manifest themselves in various forms among his entire legacy.

Samplings of the Stead family artwork can be found in the second color section on page L.

A History of the Theatre Company of Saugus

by
Rosemary DeGregorio

Founded in 1968 as the Saugus Towncriers, the Theatre Company of Saugus, Inc. has thrived over the past 38 years and has garnered a large, appreciative audience. For many years costumes, props and major pieces of scenery were stored in the homes and garages of individual members. Rehearsals were often held in members' homes and in rented halls when funds allowed. Performances were held at the local schools when the thespians could be wedged into their calendars. Today, the Theatre Company has found a temporary home at the "Little Theatre" hall in St. John's Episcopal Church in Saugus, where many of the productions take place, and the company rents public storage space for its theatrical necessities.

Brian Dion as Tevye in *Fiddler on the Roof.*

The Theatre Company of Saugus came into existence when, in the spring of 1968, Mrs. Betty Boucher, wife of the Town Manager, approached Leo Nickole, Professor of Theatre Arts at Emerson College, to help establish a community theatre in Saugus. A committee worked through the summer writing a constitution and establishing a board of directors. Their first production, *Never Too Late*, followed shortly thereafter, directed by Professor Nickole. In 1990, the group became incorporated as a non-profit theatre company, and changed its name from the Saugus Town-criers to the Theatre Company of Saugus, Inc. (TCS).

Theatre Company of Saugus, Inc. Officers (l-r): Board Member Jacqueline DiGenio, Vice President Leo Nickole, President Rosemary DeGregorio, and Board Member Carolina Lanney.

In addition to at least three shows now produced annually, TCS also has a community outreach program, and has produced shows to raise funds for the Fine Arts Department of the Saugus schools, and the Saugus Public Library Foundation. The Company assists local organizations with their shows, offers theatre workshops to the members of the community, and grants a yearly scholarship to a high school student who wants to pursue a career in the theatre arts.

TCS also periodically competes with other community theatre groups around the state, and in 2003, the cast and crew of a winning play was invited to participate in an international theatre festival in Belgium, becoming the first American group to earn such an honor.

TCS has worked hard to remain faithful to its mission statement, "to foster and promote an appreciation of the theatre arts and to stimulate production of living theatre for the entertainment and cultural enrichment of the Saugus community."

William J. Maloney

by

Tom Sheehan

William J. Maloney, a professional artist and retired Art Director of Raytheon Company, has been painting for over 40 years. He is a graduate of Massachusetts College of Art with a B.F.A. degree in painting. He has studied under

nationally known marine painter Don Stone. Mr. Maloney, formerly a long-time resident of Saugus and painter of the cover of *A Gathering of Memories*, is currently teaching painting on Cape Cod.

He has won innumerable oil painting prizes, is affiliated with many painters' societies and has had many one-man exhibits of his paintings.

His website is at:
    http://www.maloneystudios.com/
and a selection of his work can be found in the second color section on page N.

Bill Maloney, our cover artist, at work.

Robert Maloney

by

Tom Sheehan

Robert Maloney earned a B.F.A. from the Massachusetts College of Art. At Mass Art Robert put a great deal of focus on fine art (painting & collage) and graphic design. He has shown at numerous galleries including "Maloney and Sons," an exhibition with his father William and brother Paul. His 2D and 3D constructions incorporate elements of the urban landscape, typography, topography and architecture. Many of his pieces straddle the line between a structure being torn down and a structure being erected. Lately the computer is as important a tool as brush or saw. With digital camera skills, he layers images and textures together seamlessly and prints the work on archival paper with archival ink. He incorporates these images into 3D by printing them out in reverse, which are transferred onto gessoed Masonite with acrylic medium.

A few of his images can be seen in the second color section on page O.

Debra Spencer Vitkosky

by
Tom Sheehan

Debra Vitkosky graduated from Saugus High School in 1971. She attended Massachusetts College of Art for two years and transferred to San Francisco Art Institute, receiving a B.F.A. in painting in 1974. She continued her education in interior design and for 28 years has combined painting and interior design, often commissioned to paint fine art pieces. She taught at Endicott College and North Shore Community College, receiving a Masters Degree in Education in Arts and Learning in 2003. In 2004 she studied oil painting restoration working on pieces from the Uffizi Gallery in Florence, Italy. A member of The American Institute for Conservation of Historic and Artistic Works, she has restored paintings for private collections, antique dealers and framers. At Endicott College she designed a large fountain in front of Tupper Hall, including symbolic elements, scale, and materials to be used in the creation of the Fountain at Water's Edge. Currently she works out of her studio in Rowley, Massachusetts, on oil painting commissions, personal painting, interior design and color consulting.

The Endicott College Fountain at Water's Edge.

Janet Kierstead

by
Tom Sheehan

Janet Kierstead received an M.A. in Art Psychology from Leslie College in 1982. Her interests brought membership in the Copley Society of Boston (Copley Artist, 1991),

Rockport Art Association (three one artist exhibitions), North Shore Arts Association, and the Massachusetts Center for Native American Awareness, which explores and reveals her Native American heritage. Selected exhibits and collections have been at Museum of Fine Arts (Boston), Seneca Historical Society (Brant, NY), Catherine Lorrilard Wolfe Exhibit and the Salmagundi Club (NYC), Foxhall Gallery (DC), Pease Gallery (Edgartown), MA College of Art, and the Kierstead Gallery (Rockport).

Her website is at:
    http://www.janetkierstead.com/
and some of her paintings can be seen on page K in the second color section.

Pauline Healey

by
Tom Sheehan

Pauline Healey was raised in Saugus and became a permanent Florida resident in 1998, after snowbird years from 1986. Originally painting in oils, she has been painting in watercolors since discovering its magic and beauty after joining the Fort Myers Beach Art Association. She has taken watercolor workshops with many famous artists and her work has been accepted in Juried Shows in the Art Leagues of Marco Island, Cape Coral, Bonita Spring, Fort Myers, Sanibel-Captiva; and the Art Associations of Naples and Fort Myers. She has won many awards and has been featured in Watercolor Magazine (2000).

Her website is at:
    http://www.paulinehealey.com/
and a few of her works can be seen in the second color section on page J.

Donna Rossetti-Bailey

by
Tom Sheehan

Donna Rossetti-Bailey graduated from Boston University School of Fine Arts in 1974 with a B.F.A. in Art Education and taught a winning award program for 23 years in Rockland Public Schools and now teaches pastel and drawing classes at the South Shore Art Center in Cohasset. She has won innumerable awards and honors for her work and her memberships include Connecticut Pastel Society, Pastel Society of Cape Cod, American Artist's Professional League, Cape Cod Art Association, Allied Artists of

Sophie Melewski admires Edith Carrigan's untitled oil painting
at the Rotary Arts and Crafts Show at the Senior Center, May 1990.

America, National Association of Women Artists, North River Art Association, Gallery Artist at South Shore Art center and the Pastel Society of America, among others. She has lived on the South Shore for over thirty years.

Three of her paintings can be seen on page I in the second color section.

Rotary Arts and Crafts Exhibition

by
John Burns

From my first glance I found this picture very appealing. There is a genuine air to it, a warm, natural moment caught by a perceptive camera man. It is easy to share in Edith Carrigan's obvious pleasure in seeing her painting the subject of attention, and likely admiration.

Sophie's study of the picture strikes me as a study in itself: the leaning of her body attentively toward the picture, the reflection in her facial set of respect, curiosity, and, I'm influenced to think, more to speculate about.

A great picture!

Donald A. Mosher

by
Tom Sheehan

Don Mosher began his art career after winning his first award at age eight and has since won hundreds of awards for his work. A 1968 graduate of Vesper George School of Art, Don has been a painting instructor and demonstrator and has been featured in several national publications including *Yankee* and *American Art Magazine*. His paintings hang in the permanent collections of large corporations, institutions, and private homes in America and abroad, including the Peabody Museum, Portland Art Museum and the State House in Boston. Don is a member of twelve art organizations from Boston to New York and he was the first inductee into Saugus High School Fine Arts Hall of Fame for Visual Arts in 2003. Don resides in Rockport, MA and his web site is at:

http://www.rockportusa.com/mosher/

and some of his works can be found on page M of the second color section.

Dana Cameron

by

John Burns

Like her mystery series protagonist, Dana Cameron is a professional archeologist. She graduated from Saugus High School in 1983, and in addition to her B.A. from Boston University, she has an A.M. and a PhD from the University of Pennsylvania. She's worked on Old and New World Sites dating from prehistoric times to the nineteenth century. An alumna of the Breadloaf Writers Conference, Dana began her mystery writing career with the publication of *Site Unseen* in 2002, the first novel featuring New England archeologist Emma Fielding; Aaron Elkins called it "a rip-snorting good mystery." This was followed by *Grave Consequences* (2002), *Past Malice* (2003), *A Fugitive Truth* (2004), *More Bitter than Death* (2005), and in 2006, *Ashes and Bones* (all from Avon). The *South Florida Sun-Sentinel* described *More Bitter than Death* as having "a unique, surprise-filled plot that's enhanced by mature, intelligent characters." An IMBA bestselling author, Dana is a member of the American Crime Writers League, The Femmes Fatales, Mystery Writers of America, and Sisters in Crime (she is past president of the New England Chapter); you can learn more about her at

http://www.danacameron.com/

Music

If music could be translated into human speech, it would no longer need to exist.

— Ned Rorem

Donald C. Hammond

Musician, Teacher, Friend, Saugonian – 1915-1998

by

Frank L. Perry

The first news of Don's passing came in a Lynn Item obituary on July 30, 1998. It read in part, "Services will be held in Port Richey, Florida for Donald C. Hammond, age 83. He lived in Port Richey for 22 years and is survived by a daughter Donna of Deerfield, Illinois, and a son David of Middleton, MA."

Don was born April 28, 1915, in Lynn to Clinton and Mary Vickery Hammond, both of whom came from Marblehead. They were lured to Lynn by employment at GE. When Don was only three, his family bought a home at 9 Richard Street, East Saugus where he lived until 1954.

The following are some joyful memories that he wrote to his children:

- I remember walking with my mother, drawing my small red wagon, as we went down Newhall Street to do our grocery shopping at Charles and Gosselin's Market in East Saugus. Also going to the grain mill at the railroad tracks in the same area.

- Sitting on our cellar bulkhead on Richard Street as I crudely attempted to make a violin. It obviously marked the beginning of things to come.

- Walking home each day from the Mansfield School and going past Dr. Gales's home with the beautiful chestnut tree in front. Remembering Dr. Gale, a Civil War veteran, who annually gave a talk at school for Memorial Day.

- My parents giving me my first violin on Christmas Day 1924 and Paul Neal coming across the street to play "Pop Goes the Weasel." The violin was purchased from Mr. Cyre, a violin maker on Monroe Street, Lynn.

- Going to Russell Peterson's on the hill in Cliftondale to take lessons.

- Getting my first Boy Scout uniform in the meeting room over the firehouse in East Saugus. Remembering the firehouse where horses were used to draw the fire-wagon.

- Playing in the elementary school orchestra with Miss Cram as director and being released early from the Ballard School once a week to walk to the Felton School for rehearsal.

- Helping my mother sell candy and ice cream at the Central Junior High School when she first began that adventure.

- Seeing her advance until she founded and was in charge of the high school cafeteria.

- Remembering the respect my mother always received from the school staff and how I frequently was reminded that I should always appreciate all she did for me. As I look back I realize that she did so much more than she had to.

- Enjoying many of my school musical activities: the school orchestra, performing for the *Pirates of Penzance* operetta, under the direction of Ethel Edwards; performing at the All State Orchestra Festival at Symphony Hall under the direction of Dr. Howard Hanson; as a very young man, participating in the All Eastern National Festival at Syracuse, NY, under the direction of Francis Findley, it traveling to Syracuse with Vinnie Pelrine and his lovely parents via the Mohawk Trail with snow banked on the highway.

- Going to the Strand Theater on Union Street and hearing the fine theater orchestra which performed every day under the direction of Byron Ricker.

- Studying with Byron Ricker and becoming a member of his fine Greater Lynn Symphony Orchestra. Making many performances throughout the Greater Lynn area.

- Ethel Edwards, music supervisor, visiting my parents and convincing them to send me to the New England Conservatory of Music as a high school student. It also was through her advice and assistance that I commenced the study of the trombone.

- Studying with Roland Reasoner and Louis Kloephel at the Conservatory and with Eddie and Aaron Harris in Lynn.

- My mother driving with me into the Conservatory every Friday night to perform in Louis Kloephel's brass ensemble. It was a rare privilege.

- Going to the Rev. Allison Gifford's rectory home of the East Saugus Church to be a part of his family orchestra with John, Natalie, Hamilton, Gordon, and Ruth Eyre. A joyful experience! One of our favorite pieces was "Songs My Mother Taught Me."

- Organizing a semi-professional orchestra for the purpose of presenting a Sunday evening concert at the East Saugus Church.

- Recalling that I organized a Saugus High School assembly program including organizing orchestra and arranging to present the program at an assembly at Marblehead High School. The performers had the morning off from classes and were transported by Vernon Evans, principal, and Carroll Cunningham, English teacher. In those days it was a big event.

- Having my own dance orchestra and hiring the Saugus Town Hall to sponsor my own successful dance.

- Performing a violin solo at graduation with Evelyn Smith, a fine senior pianist as accompanist.

- Going with Dana Lewis to Revere Beach to enjoy an all night battle of music between Guy Lombardo and his Royal Canadians and Glenn Gray's Casa Loma Band.

- Dana and I getting the job of having our band play on Saturday nights at Fred Willis and Duke Cunningham's White House Nightclub on the Pike. At that time Fred was on the Saugus School Committee and Duke was my English teacher. Later Fred became Speaker of the Massachusetts House of Representatives and Duke the judge of the Saugus Court.

- Studying violin with Truman Carew, a famous orchestra leader at the Spanish Gables Ballroom at Revere Beach.

- Recalling that I drove as a chauffeur for the Rev. Walker of Saugus who was a cripple. He was a lecturer who gave a weekly broadcast as a commentator from radio station WEEI, and I would drive a 1931 front-wheel drive Cord which was a most unusual car. I remember well that it was not easy to stop on the icy Boston streets.

- Getting the opportunity to play in Truman Carew's second band at the Relay House in Nahant and eventually joining his first band and playing a summer season at the Frolics at Salisbury Beach.

Don married the love of his life, Ruth Steubesand, in 1940. Ruth lived at the top of Bailey's Hill. Their parents were close friends but Ruth and Don saw little of each other until 1935 when she passed by him in Cliftondale. He called for a date that very night and as they say, "the rest is history." They remained totally devoted until her passing in 1998.

In 1936, at the age of 21, Don founded the Saugus High School Band, a position he held for ten years. Since this was only a part-time position he also led the Marblehead High School Band. In 1946, his efforts earned him the full-time post as Band Director of Swampscott High, where he organized the town's first performing band for the football games.

I was honored to be Don's neighbor for many years. This friendship continued through his life in Florida. He never forgot that he was a Saugonian.

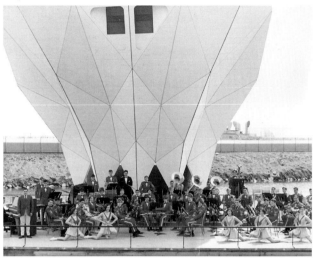

SHS Band at Expo '67, Montreal, Canada.

Donald C. Hammond

by
Robert "Bud" Courtis

In 1936 at the age of 21 Don was appointed to form a band at Saugus High School, and served as its director for ten years.

It was a happy time for such a venture, a wonderful opportunity for this young man to exert his energy, his musical talent, and his gift for inspiring young people in a common cause.

The band prospered in a setting that displayed small town, America, at its best. The whole community joined Don in the successful launching of the Saugus High School Band. Scores of parents were the prime moving force, with their suppers, their tags days, and their countless other creative money-raising efforts which helped to supply uniforms for this newly formed band. School committees, selectmen, and town meetings lent their assistance. Police, and fire and other town departments pitched in. Service clubs lent willing assistance. Industries like Eastern Tool were very supportive. And leaving their mark on this community effort were community leaders like Harry Dodge, Town Treasurer; and civic leaders, Henry and Pauline Peckham and Edward Gibbs.

It was a tribute to the town and these times that such things as these could come to be.

Another happy circumstance for the growing band was that success was joined with the wonderful football teams of that era, in providing for the town thrilling, memorable Saturdays as the band marched down Summer Street, under the beautiful autumn maples, heading for crowded Stackpole Field.

During those ten years from 1936 to 1946, many honors came to Don and the band for their participation in holiday parades and band competitions in this area and around New England, bringing great pride to our whole town.

A Letter from Don Hammond to His Friends in Saugus

This letter is being sent to three people who mean very much to me. All three men, two of whom presently are 68 years of age with one 65 were students of mine at Saugus High School in the late '30s.

An immeasurable joy to me is that fact that all of us are in contact with one another. This letter is intended to provide convincing evidence that at this stage of my life, your devotion and love form a sustaining force for which I am most grateful. Who would have thought 53 years ago that I would be sending you such a letter during the Christmas season of 1992.

As I refer to you in alphabetical order, let me relate that Bud Courtis and I have been close friends down through the years. This relationship has been enhanced partly because of an ongoing friendship with his parents, commencing when the band was organized in 1936. His mother, Dot, at age 88, is the most senior member of the Band Parents Association and I remember his late dad, Leonard, for his many contributions to the band. I recall so well when he built the Band Parents concession stand at Stackpole Field, when he welded together a huge metal carrier for the bass drum that was given to the band and which required that it be drawn on wheels while being played. None of us, I am sure, will ever forget the lights for the band hats which he designed and provided.

These were used for night games and made a big hit especially at the Lynn Manning Bowl. My Ruth, who was secretary to the manager of the General Electric Lamp Works in Boston, even arranged to have the bulbs colored red, white and blue when the band spelled USA.

It is indeed a most special treat, 50 years later, when Bud and his mother called us without fail every Sunday morning precisely at nine o'clock.

In a recent letter to each of you I mentioned that it was a very special privilege for me to receive a sort of autobiographical letter from Ludwig Hahn following the 50th reunion of the class of 1942. As a young boy, Ludwig and his dear mother meant much to me and reading, after all these years, the many events of his life stimulate deep thoughts, and make for an awareness that the years have been slipping by. I am so grateful for the thoughts and descriptions that Ludwig has expressed revealing so definitely the warmth and love of a very sensitive man. This does not surprise me; it is a perfect reminder of the good things that a love and interest in music can generate. Now, at the stage of life, Luke, as he likes to be called, is a member of the Mount Washington Valley Band, giving two weekly concerts during the summer and, as I understand it, he also has a brass quartet that brings much cheer to people during the Christmas season.

Roger Noble indeed worked hard to become reacquainted with me. He moved to California in 1965 and about three years ago commenced making unfulfilled inquiries as to my whereabouts until, I believe, he reached Bud Courtis. One day my phone rang and the caller stated he was trying to locate a Donald Hammond, the man who many years ago had been the director of the Saugus High School Band. After informing him of his success, I could not believe it was Roger Noble and especially when he said he was calling from California to thank me for what I had done for him when he was in grade school. It was a much greater shock when he enlightened me with the knowledge that he was 65, had seven children and then the most unbelievable announcement that the little, curly headed, cute kid that I loved so much was rather a big fellow, weighing in the vicinity of what an average pro-football tackle carries. We had a wonderful reunion by phone and he now calls me every month or two. Roger was special and needed help as a little fellow. I don't know if he ever was aware of it, but God bless the members of the Saugus Rotary Club because it was they who provided his first cornet.

He has continued his interest in music and presently is most active than ever. He plays in a large concert band and takes a very serious interest in the 175 piece high school band in his area. He recently followed the band to a competition at a distance of 130 miles and was delighted when the band won first place. His delight was mild, however, compared to how he felt when the director called for him to come to the field to accept a plaque in recognition of his having attended every performance of the band for the past season. Roger called me to relate the experience and obviously was very moved by the unusual and thoughtful gesture.

I trust you will not find this material boring and I hope as Adam so well stated that "it will stimulate a flood of memories." Let us keep in mind that we share over 50 years of history that truly can be considered precious.

A Merry Christmas from the year 1940.

The growth of the band was the crowning achievement of his career. It gave early signs of what it was to become. Names associated with these early days are baton instructor Ollie O'Hearn and memorable twirlers like Ginnie Means, the Means twins and Ruth Hatch, models for all future twirlers to emulate. The band was becoming an exciting entity in town, the band itself with the colorful presence of the twirlers, the Sachemaires and the flag squads.

SHS Band at the State House (Saugus's 350th Anniversary) Jerry Mitchell and Governor King.

Jerry Mitchell

by
John Burns
with materials from Marilyn Carlson

The career of Jerry Mitchell began very quietly in 1949 when he was appointed as Director of the Saugus High School Band on a part-time basis. In the same year, when he was selected to be the full-time Director of Music Education in the Saugus Public Schools, there was no hint of what the years ahead were to bring to music in our schools for four decades under the direction of Jerry Mitchell, "The Music Man of Saugus."

Jerry Mitchell's SHS Band at Disneyland.

The position and the man were made for each other.

His temperament, his talents, his energy, his instincts and his sense of theater created and nourished a remarkable era of music in Saugus.

He set high standards for himself and for all those he enlisted in his program. Merely to be "good" was not enough. The term would goad him and challenge him to seek the next level on the path to excellence.

As a realist he knew that visionaries go nowhere with their dreams unless they recognize hard work as an essential part of the process, their hard work and that of those they enlist in their causes.

He inspired those he brought into his program, who understood the goals he sought and witnessed the determination he brought to the task. They came to share his enthusiasm and his work ethic.

He was both an educator and a showman, and the mixture was reflected in the music program he devised, vocal and instrumental, at all grade levels. He brought substance and excitement to the classroom, to the concert stage and to the playing field.

His program expanded in many directions and in many forms. He welcomed variety, movement and new ideas. Out of this grew the exchange concerts which flourished throughout New England from 1955 to 1972, his Christmas concerts and his musical offerings like *Little Abner*, *Guys and Dolls*, and *South Pacific*.

The band continued to grow in size, in musical skill and in dramatic flair. It was an ensemble appealing to the ear and appealing to the eye. There came a point when awareness of the band, stimulated by the energy and salesmanship of Mr. Mitchell, became national. The evidence of this could not be denied.

Starting in the 1950s invitations to visit them were coming in from state capitals, from national entertainment centers and from special event historic celebrations.

Band members will have lasting memories of their visit to the Polo Grounds in New York to play at half time of a game between the New York Giants and the Philadelphia Eagles, of their playing at our national capital where they were awarded citations by Speaker of the House John W. McCormick and Representative Torby MacDonald,

Jerry Mitchell.

of their being selected to be the Massachusetts representative at the Canadian World Exhibit in Quebec and Montreal, of their several visits to Disney World, of their visit to Saugus, California, as an aspect of our celebration of our 350th anniversary in 1979, and of the visit to San Antonio, Texas where they marched in the "American Festival Parade" before 100,000 people along the parade route.

A distinct individual honor came to Mr. Mitchell in 1979 when he was invited to be a guest conductor of the Boston "Pops" Orchestra in Boston Symphony Hall on July 10,

1979, in conjunction with the 350th Anniversary of the Town of Saugus.

Jerry Mitchell directing the Boston Pops.

Further honors came to him in the year of his retirement: his induction into the newly formed Saugus High Fine Arts Hall of Fame, and his having conferred in his name the Jerome Mitchell Scholarship, established by a committee consisting of Dr. Edward Glinski, Mrs. Karen (McNeely) Cammarato, Mrs. Janice (Carter) Long, Russell Carter, and Mrs. Cathy (Cargill) Paccetti.

Memories of "The Maestro."

by
Ted Brierley Jr.

Jerry, teaching performing art, had to supply a vision of one way to play it, do it, march it and get back home in one piece so that every band member was on the same page. Too much interpretation could lead to someone playing out of place or marching off in the wrong direction. He did this by clearly laying out his program and then building everyone's self-esteem.

He worked with a diverse group of boys and girls from all classes every year and made every one of them feel like they were an important part of the whole. He always tried to set an example of professionalism based on his own experience that the kids could relate to and emulate. He worked methodically and diligently and got us where we were going in a step-by-step method. He was firm but patient about what he wanted to accomplish with the band, and everyone felt that if they did their part they would all share in the success. He made us stay focused and drilled us with the simple method of practice, practice, practice...

While doing this, he treated every one with dignity and respect and expected the same. He set the bar high and told everyone they could do it. I believe that he played the role of *maestro* for his own personal reasons and for his students so they could see what it takes and maybe someday be the *maestro* themselves. That's where the line of ego blurs and, in the end, doesn't much matter because both teacher and students were winners.

Strike up the Band

by
Ted Brierley, Jr.

Ted Brierley Sr., SHS Class of 1936, enjoyed many passions in life which included his friendships, sports, words, music and songwriting. Ted brought all of his passions together when he wrote his original school spirit fight song. "Saugus High" is a toe tapping tribute which captures the high flying spirit of the school, its students and all of its supporters.

Ted Brierley.

Born in 1919, Ted was a child of the jazz age. It was one year after the Red Sox won the 1918 World Series led by a young Babe Ruth. As a young boy he met his hero The Babe and as an aging man, he ultimately saw the Red Sox win it all in 2004. He maintained a strong singing voice and continued to write songs throughout all of his 86 years. He sang with church choirs, 1940s dance bands and wherever a piano could be found. He wrote many songs and even pitched his songs live to the likes of Nat King Cole and Louis Armstrong.

Ted played on the first Saugus High basketball team and loved to recall the flat footed, two handed set shot, underhand free throws and a jump ball after every basket scored. He loved football and one of his best friends and classmates, Robert Burns, was one of the greatest running backs in Saugus history.

As a band singer, he loved the tunes and melodies that could captivate an audience one moment with spellbinding grace and then turn them loose on the hard wood floor with the rhythms and driving beats that make dancers jump with joy.

Ted envisioned his "fight" song being sung by the students in the stands at Saugus High sporting events while the band played on. When he was well into his 80s, Ted put the finishing touches on his song and pursued his dream by presenting the song to the Center for the Arts in Saugus. The committee, led by Kathryn "Chicki" Hollett voted unanimously to endorse the song. The cause was taken up by John Macero, the Director of Fine Arts, and Amanda Shelley, the Director of the High School and Middle School bands.

On Sunday, May 16, 2004, at the Second Annual Fine Arts Hall of Fame Pops Concert, Amanda Shelley's arrangement of Ted's song was introduced as the official Saugus High School Fight Song. Amanda, along with Nancy LeMoine, the Director of the High School Chorus, led the premiere performance by the band and chorus. Ted was thrilled by this event and by the professionalism of the students. It was one of the proudest moments of his creative life. After hearing his song live that day, he looked forward to going to a football game and hearing the band play "Saugus High" and singing along with them.

Ted Brierley, "The Candy Man," had a "sweet" lifelong career in the candy business, which he loved. Having his song accepted by his beloved alma mater, then beautifully sung and played by the students, was the sweetest moment of all.

Ted kept his word to remember his friends and classmates after graduation and honored them by dedicating his song to the Class of 1936. And the band played on. Saugus High, Saugus High, Saugus High...

Saugus High

Dedicated to the class of 1936

Words and Music by Ted Brierley

Growing Up in Saugus
Part 5

The strongest principle of growth lies in human choice.

— George Eliot

Growing Up in Saugus Center

by
Betsy Nelson Hatfield

I haven't lived in Saugus for over thirty-five years, but its landmarks, influences, and smiles are woven into my skin. It is Saugus whose obituaries I turn to in the *Globe*, whose 2003 Little League fever and celebration I joined in, whose storied political history and the politicians who wrote it appall and tickle me to this day. Saugus is where I'm ***from***.

We had lived at 15 Parker Street for about four years when, in 1942, my father's work took our family briefly to Providence, Rhode Island. My parents rented the house for the year and on our return I entered the second grade at the Roby School. For a number of reasons, including my grandfather's death and my own unhealthy separation anxiety, not to mention a baby brother who was drawing some attention away from me, I cried a lot at first. Fred Brooks quietly befriended me. One day, he brought a little ball to Miss Chase's (later Mrs. [Margaret] Hurll's) room and, when I indicated by my waif's moue that I wanted it, he gave it to me. I have a special place in my heart for Fred.

During elementary school years, I was allowed to visit the homes of classmates like Janie Churchill, who lived on Highland Avenue, but otherwise I didn't stray far from Parker Street. There weren't the adventures with the gang of the kind my brother Jay so joyously recounts; my adventures, as well as much of my take on human behavior, would come from books, starting with *Heidi*.

Yet it wasn't an unusually narrow life and it wasn't solitary. It was one kind of girl's life in the '40s. I was sheltered. I played dolls and board games with Mary Lou MacMillan, Donna Julien, and later Allie Watson. I always had a cat (I played dolls with them, too. Got the claw marks).

Beginning in the mid-forties, my widowed maternal grandmother, who doted on Jay and me, came every day from her house in West Lynn to take care of us so that my mother could return to teaching. Grammy Gillespie made tuna sandwiches for lunch, baked chocolate cakes, played cards and games with Jay, read to me, told me stories about growing up in Scotland, and, wisely, never overruled or ever challenged our parents' decisions.

Sometimes after school I sat at our kitchen table with my mother and grandmother and one or two of my mother's fellow teachers while they drank tea and ate cake and told anecdotes. They included me, asked me what I thought about things - they were teachers, after all - and I felt privileged and grown up.

Our house was full of music. Both my parents played the piano, my mother, who had perfect pitch, particularly well. After dinner, we and any friends who were around sang standards. "Embraceable You" was the house song. As I implied, I read a lot: non-fiction and fiction, often set in other countries, *Photoplay* and *Modern Screen*, bread wrappers. A family treat I loved was going to the double feature at the Waldorf Theater in Lynn almost every Friday night. On Sundays, I visited my paternal grandparents with my father and ate home-made Swedish cakes.

I didn't like to sweat (some things never change). In the warm weather, exercise meant a walk to Sanborn's or the Saugus Pharmacy, a bike ride once around Prospect Street, a game of hopscotch under the trees in front of my house, the squares traced by a rock on the sidewalk, or a rhythmic game of jump rope chanting "A my name is Alice..." For a change of pace, I played marbles or jacks with my friends - in the shade, of course. After supper we might play tag or hidey-go-seek (I had to run, but by then the sun was down). Sometimes, my father took me to Flax Pond for a swim when he came home from work. In those days before polio vaccines, I was meant to stay near home, away from crowds.

Except for Pearl Harbor, World War II was almost an abstraction to me. There was the occasional air raid drill, but it was more exciting than frightening. My father, a tinkerer, had put up blackout curtains in our kitchen, so when the siren sounded we drew the curtains, closed the kitchen doors, and listened to the radio playing softly until the all-clear sounded. I remember once standing outside in the dark with my family and a sprinkling of neighbors, following the arcs of the searchlights, thrilled by the possibility of danger, secure among people I knew. We used oleo instead of butter. My grandmother squeezed and kneaded yellow-orange pellets into the pasty blobs, but nobody was fooled. I did think, over and over, about the warning sign on the buses that ran between Saugus and Lynn, "Loose lips sink ships." It may be why, to this day, I have a horror of betraying confidences.

My parents' approval always mattered more to me than popularity with my peers (trust me, there's a price to be paid for that). Their pleasure when I did well meant that I tried very hard in school. Even so, I was apprehensive about the first day of seventh grade. *Yes*, I sweat and, to my mortification, the soaking wet back of my pink dress stuck to the skin between my shoulder blades.

Central Junior High School, which was a whole neighborhood away, meant a new cadre of classmates, several teachers where formerly there was one, and eating lunch in the cafeteria. I worried about how well I would do and about how I would fit in with the new kids from other parts of town. But on the alphabetical seating plans that determined our location, and to some extent our destinies, in the classroom, O'Brien followed Nelson, and the smart, irrepressible Pat O'Brien Barnett became my new, then life-long, great friend. At my son Dan Silver's rehearsal dinner, Pat and I sang songs from Parker Street days and my mother accompanied us on the piano.

It was in junior high school that I learned the concept, although not the particulars, of being "cheap." I didn't like to walk past the Rat Hole because those boys who sat on the steps smoking or stood by the door might call out to me and that might mean I was cheap. One early evening I walked past when no one was out there, so I crouched down to look through the window. I still can visualize a pool table, a few boys, and not much else, not even laughing or shoving. Where was the danger? What a bust!

My most vivid memories are of Saugus High School. I liked it a lot. It was less regulated, less orderly, than elementary and junior high school. I had more personal freedom. There were more possibilities. There were more boys. It was the early '50s and I and other girls walked along with the high school band after Saturday football games, kicking up leaves, and walked to and back home from dances at the high school on Saturday nights. Some early evenings, we walked from Saugus Center to Cliftondale, hoping to run into boys to talk to and flirt with. We dated, went to movies, parties, and dances. Eventually, we smoked, but I didn't know of much drinking.. As for marijuana, that was for jazz drummers.

(l-r) Pat O'Brien Barnett, Marilyn Sarno (dec), Betsy Nelson Hatfield.

When I was sixteen, I got a job as candy girl at the State Theater. Richard Rubin owned the State; Edie Noretsky sold tickets, and Mr. Durgin collected them and maintained law and order on the right hand aisle, two-thirds of the way down, where the noisy high school boys sat. Jerry Pinciss and Fred Eicholzer were ushers. Of course, we got to see the movie that was showing. What an introduction to the world of work! I have never shed my nostalgia for the gangster films I associate with the State, starting with *Mildred Pierce* when I was about nine, and am finally writing a crime story of my own.

Saugus High School gave me opportunities: subjects, except for math, and teachers, including math teachers, that I liked. John Burns was my favorite. I still regard him as the best teacher I ever had; it was in his class that I learned to love the language. I was editor of *Focus* in my senior year, I had plays to act in, and I had a couple of wins in essay contests. Those opportunities gave me confidence when it came to apply to colleges.

I do wish we had women's team sports in high school. It would have been useful to learn the ins and outs of teamwork and winning and losing, a big advantage for men in the traditional workplace I would finally crack in 1979. Not that I can guarantee that I would have participated, given my preference for sitting.

I was also very involved in the Universalist Church. It was a liberal, activist congregation. I received a lesson in courage and integrity when one of our ministers signed an anti-Joseph McCarthy letter, or perhaps a petition, at the height of the dark power of the junior senator from Wisconsin.

At the time that I was writing essays about democracy and brotherhood at school, I was being urged, at church and at the church youth camps and conventions I attended, to stand against racism and anti-Semitism. That combination of influences led to activism: the League of Women Voters, the Committee for the Equality of Women at Harvard, and in 2004, the co-chairmanship of Massachusetts Seniors for Kerry-Edwards, my stab at setting right the growing gap between the haves and have-nots that is so frighteningly reminiscent of the injustice I saw in Latin America as a calling officer for Bank Boston in the 1980s.

Saugus felt like a one-class town in the '40s and '50s. I don't remember any overt social striving or even conversations with other kids about who had money. There was no country club set. Some neighborhoods were nicer than others, but there were no exclusive neighborhoods of the kind I saw "out"on Marblehead Neck or imagined existing in Brookline and Wellesley from reading the *Globe* society column. Those people were different, like the GE executives who lived close to the ocean, sailed, and belonged to clubs along with doctors from the Lynn Hospital staff. In Saugus, we, of course, had our handful of prosperous families, but they seemed few in number. Some kids, including Jay, went to private schools. A number of people had cottages in New Hampshire. Most mothers didn't work, although mine did, and she loved her teaching job whole-heartedly, setting an example of a committed, contented working woman for me to follow. On the other hand, if I had cast my developing gimlet eye for injustice nearer home, as I wish I had, I would have seen that some people in our town were struggling - poor health, money troubles, alcohol. I sensed it there in the middle distance, but I was too caught up in my own life and trajectory to internalize the sufferings of others.

In the wider world, sexism pervaded women's lives, although most of us were years away from labeling it, let alone confronting it. Magazines were full of "how to please a man" articles. Job opportunities for women meant teaching, social work, nursing, and office work, but the sheer absurdity of such limitations would not come home for more than a decade. In high school, I accepted as gospel that girls generally didn't take physics or the highest levels of math because they didn't become engineers.

I recall no sexist put-downs, however. Quite the contrary. Certainly in elementary and junior high school, girls were expected to outperform boys. We spoke up in class. In about the tenth grade, however, the norms changed some-what. I figured out that many (most?) boys preferred girls who didn't compete with them, but, with my parents in the driver's seat where my school performance was concerned, I just lived with that.

Take-aways

The lessons from my girlhood are always near at hand, like my eyeglasses, although not so easily consigned to a night table at the end of the day.

Tackle the tough ones (a lesson I am still processing). I was part of a clique in high school, and I didn't even realize it until the day an angry classmate made his accusation. I can't speak for anyone else, but I regret very much my igno-rance and insensitivity. Seen from fifty years out, cliques are defensive bunkers and pretty pathetic, but that is small consolation to people on the outside.

I also remember the night a blackball was cast against a prospective member of a society I belonged to. I was shocked by the pettiness and cruelty, but, except for letting a few other members and my family know how I felt, I regis-tered no protest and was, thereby, complicit in the percep-tion of that hateful form of elitism.

Or at least speak plain English (it's never too late). Several weeks ago at lunch, a friend described her son's wedding to the others of us at the table. "He married a woman of substance, I guess you could say." What she meant by "substance" was clear. "I don't know quite how else to say it," she continued with a smile. Saugus, I asked myself, (where did that come from) are you really going to sit still for this? "Why don't you just say 'he married a rich woman?'" I suggested, and we shared a laugh. Substance is something else.

Patronize your public library. My mother chose the house on Parker Street, she told me, because of its proximity to the Saugus Public Library. I can still visualize myself as a little girl rummaging around for children's books in what I remember as a big long bind, a deep bottom shelf, edged by a long bench, in the basement. I also recalled "graduating" to the upstairs adult section. What a thrill! My parents placed absolutely no restrictions on what I could read. Dream! Aspire! Borrowed books are cheap and they shape lives by opening up possibilities. In the summer after the sixth grade, I spent three days lying on my bed in the thrall of *Gone with the Wind*. My mother, I believe, thought it was good way to expose me to adult romantic love. It was.

Drive second hand cars. Like my own, the families I was surrounded by in Saugus lived within their means, which meant they lived modestly. Credit cards? No such thing. Home equity loans? Likewise. Closets were small because wardrobes were small: skirts and blouses and a few sweaters, shorts in the summer, a couple of pairs of slacks in the winter. School clothes were exchanged for play clothes at the end of the school day. Children got the clothing they needed either throughout the year or at Christmas, but not both. I had one or two dolls, a bike, roller skates, some jacks, some marbles, a game of checkers, and not too much else. Meals were cooked and eaten at home. My father liked to say he and my mother paid Jay's and my college tuitions by driving second hand cars, but there was more. They always put us before themselves. Jay and I were very lucky.

Families of the Town

The happiest moments of my life have been the few which I have passed at home in the bosom of my family.

— Thomas Jefferson

The Peckhams

compiled by
Bob Wentworth

Henry Amos-Bliss Peckham
1865-1951

Henry was born in Danielson, Connecticut, on July 4, 1865. He graduated from Holy Cross College in Quebec, Canada, and returned to Western Massachusetts working as a book-keeper in the Manchaug (MA) Mills, and as Assistant Post-master in Sutton, Massachusetts. He met Pauline in Sutton.

Shortly after his move to Saugus, he began a career in the insurance business, working as a cashier with John Hancock Insurance Company of Boston. In succeeding years he was associated with the Boston Mutual Life Insurance Company, serving in several positions before being promoted to Secretary. In 1910, he joined the Empire Life Insurance Company of Seattle, Washington, where he was appointed Secretary. He also became Treasurer of the Boston Casualty Company.

From 1914 to 1919 he was an Internal Revenue agent. In 1919 he began his own tax consulting service in Boston, which he maintained until the late 1940s.

Henry was widely knows throughout Greater Lynn for his civic and philanthropic activities. A 1941 *Saugus Advertiser* stated that, "No important civic, town or philanthropic enterprise has been undertaken for several decades that hasn't found his name and active support topping the list."

This was evidenced by his association with innumerable local and area community organizations, who sought his credibility and prominence by appointing him to committee leadership roles.

His work as a pioneer in the Boy Scout movement in the Bay Shore Council, and development of Camp Nihan, and his affiliation with the development of the First Iron Works Association of Saugus were two of his most treasured endeavors.

He served on many boards and committees within the Boy Scout movement, and headed the Bay Shore Council as president for ten years. He was honored for outstanding service with prestigious awards from both the local and regional chapters of the Boy Scouts of America. He was also instrumental in the development of the local Sea Scout organization, and continued in an advisory capacity for many years thereafter.

He was the Vice President of the First Iron Works Association, and was one of the first financial backers of the Association in its early days.

Henry was a soft-spoken, gentle-mannered person with a sparkling sense of humor. He was characterized in memorials published after his death thusly:

"His friendly attitude, his cheerful greeting, his ready-made smile, made him outstanding in any group of which he was a part." (Executive Board, Bay Shore Council, November 1951.)

"His strong mentality, his untiring energy, his sense of civic obligation and his wholesale philosophy of business and of life made him a most outstanding citizen."

"He had the gift of leadership that inspired confidence in others."

"He carried himself with vigor and unconscious dignity that gave the impression of bigness. No worthy movement failed to arouse his interest or appealed to him in vain." (First Iron Works Association, Charles Tapley, June 1952).

Pauline Rebecca (Adams) Peckham
1868-1943

Pauline Peckham, a native of Sutton, Massachusetts, lived in Saugus for 47 years, became widely known as a grammar school teacher/principal, owner and director of the Peckham School of Dancing, and coach of many dramatic productions.

Prior to her marriage, she sang and danced professionally, conducted one of the first women's orchestras in the country on Boom's Theatrical Circuit in New York State, and was one of the first women to tour the country in that capacity.

A school teacher for 32 years, she began her Saugus teaching career at the Emerson School in 1908, and became principal in 1911. Ensuing transfers placed her in principal-ships at the Ballard school in 1924, and the Roby school in 1932. She retired in 1938 at age 70.

Her dancing school for young people of all ages was one of the finest in the area. Classes were held in the Odd Fellows hall in Cliftondale. Each year the activities culminated in a magnificent May Ball, involving grand costumes and custom-made floats to augment the pupils' performance. Mrs. Peckham also sponsored adult Saturday evening ballroom dances at this same Odd Fellows hall which featured a live orchestra.

Pauline was extremely fond and proud of the Saugus High School band, under the then direction of Donald Hammond, and became one of the band's active and faithful boosters.

She was Director of the First Parish Church Choir until 1910. This church for years had been the music center of the town, and a very splendid choir was always the pride of the church membership.

She won great success as a dramatic coach. Scores of amateur dramatic productions for various charitable causes were coached by her. She handled some of the best amateur shows ever seen in town at the time. She coached operettas and dramatic shows for Saugus High School, Saugus Teachers' Association and the Annual Saugus Lions Club show.

In 1913, she was appointed Household Inspector by the Saugus Board of Health. She conducted inspections of homes throughout the town where people were thought to be living under unhealthy conditions, reporting all unsanitary households to the Board of Health.

Pauline was a very authoritative person, albeit a loving and caring human being. She was an excellent model for the, "Tough-love" school of discipline. She was clearly the dominant member of the family, and usually of any group with whom she was associated.

Mrs. Peckham acquired a reputation as a fierce disciplinarian during her teaching years.

Neil G. Howland, in writing for *A Gathering of Memories*, described his memory of his days at the Roby School under Mrs Peckham's principalship as follows:

"The prefect here (prefect having more heft than does principal) was Mrs. Peckham. She exuded, despite her diminutive stature, absolute authority to rule. Her word was law– total, complete, unquestioned and as a result, the school days hummed along with metronomic simplicity and usefulness."

A most accurate portrayal.

The Peckhams married in 1886 in Pomfort, Connecticut, and moved to Saugus in 1896 where they remained lifelong, proud, devoted and involved residents. They observed 57 years of marriage until the death of Pauline in 1943.

They became one of the town's best known couples, active in all kinds of civic endeavors. A 1941 *Saugus Advertiser* offered this characterization, "The Peckhams might well have been called Saugus' 'first family,' since both were very active in numerous civic, charitable, fraternal and social organizations with the town for close to half a century."

They had one daughter, Leila Bliss (Peckham) Wentworth.

Together they shared a passion, and took great pride in the development of their property in Saugus Center and their summer estate in Little Nahant, so that others might share their pleasure with the beautification of these settings.

Their Saugus Center residence became a hallmark during the 1920s and '30s. More than four acres were devoted to well tended lawns, sunken rock gardens and shrubbery replete with colored flowers and foliage arranged so that flowers were in bloom at all times. These gardens were opened for public visits periodically.

During the 1920s the Peckhams were the first to do any outdoor Christmas illumination of their property. Their display peaked in 1929-30 with some 25,000 lights illuminating the trees, shrubs and grape arbor in their sunken gardens.

Special trains were scheduled, departing from Boston's North Station direct to Saugus Center, where they remained for sufficient time for passengers to tour the property before returning to Boston. During these years the Christmas gardens attracted thousands from all parts of Massachusetts. Saugus became notable in these years because of these Christmas lights where displays of the Peckhams and Frank B. Sloans (Essex Street) dominated. *The Saugus Herald*, circa 1928-29, estimated, "At least one million persons have visited the lighting effects during the week of Peckham's and Sloan's residences."

The Longfellows

by
Jean (Longfellow) Raymond

Though the name Longfellow was echoed in Saugus for several generations, only one offspring resides in Saugus at this time, namely, Alan Merritt, son of Charlotte (Longfellow) and Harold Merritt.

The first Longfellow came to America from England in the late 1600s. With his wife and children he settled in Newbury, Massachusetts. He was a seaman and was later lost at sea. His wife and family later moved to Maine near Palermo where the family grew up, and pursued their individual lives. Most of our ancestors are buried in the Palermo cemetery. Our relationship to the poet, Henry Wadsworth Longfellow, was fifth cousin. We are directly descended from Nathan Longfellow. His brother, Stephen Longfellow, was Henry's great great grandfather.

In the 1800s, Isaiah Longfellow (my great-grandfather) heard of the fine soil further south, perfect for farming, so Isaiah traveled to Massachusetts and found a choice piece of land and farmhouse on Main Street in Saugus next to the Wakefield line. There Isaiah settled down with his wife and two sons, Ernest and Eugene. When retirement time came for Isaiah, his son Ernest purchased the property. Ernest married Jennie Mae Rich whose parents had also migrated to Saugus from Maine. Ernest and Jennie Mae had two children, Walter Whitcomb Longfellow and Gertrude Longfellow. While growing up, Walter (my father) had a pet pig who helped him while away the hours. The little pig followed him wherever he went. Ernest farmed his land with success and when his produce was ready, he took his goods by horse and wagon to the Melrose marketplace and sold them there.

When my father, Walter, went to high school, the distance was great so his parents bought him an automobile. As Walter drove to school, he noticed a boy walking the stretch from the turnpike each day. With winter approaching, it only made sense to stop and pick up this boy. This became a daily routine. The boy's name was Barney Shapiro. He and Walter became good friends over their school years. Barney never forgot my father's kindness and I remember as a young girl that Barney, a young Jewish man, appeared on our doorstep every Christmas Eve with a wheel of cheese and a bottle of wine for my father, and candy for us children. My father had won his heart just as he had many others over the years. Walter was a kind, moderate, compassionate man and all spoke well of him.

Ernest retired from farming in the 1930s. He was offered the fabulous sum of $32,000 for the farmhouse, barn and land by a neighboring business which added the property to their quarry. The site of the farmhouse remained idle and the farmhouse was eventually burned down by vandals. Following the sale of the farm, Ernest and Jenny Mae bought a comfortable home on Lynn Fells Parkway. Ernest's brother Eugene had one son, Clayton Longfellow, who moved from Saugus to Florida. Jenny Mae had one brother, Walter Rich. Walter and his wife, Ethel, had two children, Francis Rich and Leona Rich. Francis and his wife, Irene, had two children, Stephen Rich and Jennifer Rich. Stephen is presently the Town Architect.

When Gertrude Longfellow married, she moved to Melrose but Walter remained in Saugus. Gertrude married Roderick Hoag, a Melrose attorney and inventor. Walter married Ruth (Nourse) Longfellow from East Saugus. They bought a home in Cliftondale and raised their five children there during the Depression years. Their names were: George, Charlotte, Jean, Herbert and Charles. Walter, a General Electric apprentice course graduate, furthered his education and worked his way up at General Electric to the position of General Foreman of two West Lynn buildings. He retired as Assistant Superintendent at age 63 and died one year after

retirement. George was a World War II veteran and Herbert and Charles were likewise servicemen. Herbert embarked in business in Ohio and was later joined in the business by both George and Charles. Herbert died at age 51 and George died at age 60. The business was reorganized by Herbert's son, William, with most of the original employees.

Though the Longfellows are no longer a part of current Saugus history, the name of Longfellow was prominent for most of the 20th century.

A Brief History of the Hatch Family of Saugus

by
Michelle Michela

The Hatch Family of Saugus descended from William Hatch, a merchant who emigrated to Scituate, Massachusetts from Sandwich, England, in 1634 on the ship The Hercules. One of the descendants of William A. Hatch, Anthony A. Hatch (born in 1785 in Marshfield), moved from Marshfield to Medford sometime between 1810 and 1820. The Hatch family was involved in the shipbuilding industry in Marshfield so this move was perhaps due to the lucrative, growing shipbuilding industry in the Medford area during this period. Anthony A. Hatch and his wife, Betsy Blanchard, both died young in the year 1826 leaving seven children, including a son, Anthony Hatch.

Anthony Hatch.

Anthony Hatch, son of Anthony A. Hatch, was born in 1812. He was fourteen years old at the time of the death of both parents. He was known to be employed as a ship's carpenter in Charlestown in the 1840s. Anthony Hatch was married and widowed without children two times (married Laura Conant in 1834 and Mary Currier in 1839), before he married a woman from Somerville by the name of Keziah Russell in 1842. It was this Anthony Hatch who soon after his marriage to Keziah moved to Saugus and became a farmer, beginning the line of Hatches in Saugus.

The tale of how Anthony Hatch came to purchase the land in Saugus was recorded on the back of a photograph of the Hatch Farm by Anstrice Carter Kellogg, former Art Supervisor of the Saugus Public Schools (daughter of Emma Hatch Carter, who was one of the children of Anthony Hatch and wife Keziah). The tale goes as follows:

> Previous to the War of 1812, John Stocker owned this farm and built the house. Later the house was owned by Captain John Bickford. Captain Isaac Carlton then purchased the property from Captain Bickford and lived here for several years. He was a well-to-do sea captain, and once before sailing his square rigger commanded his wife to build a new house on the same location. He left sufficient funds for this purpose and expected the building to be completed when he returned. Instead of carrying out the captain's wishes, she renovated the home extensively and expended less money than he had expected. When Captain Carlton returned, he was so infuriated he would not even live in the house. At this time, there was a young ship's carpenter by the name of Anthony Hatch who was working in the Charlestown shipyard. Young Anthony heard of the captain's plight and decided to purchase the property. He managed the large farm that extended along Lincoln Avenue as far west as the railroad and as far south as the Revere line.

The Hatch Family Farm was located in Cliftondale Square where the monument stands now. The farm encompassed most of Cliftondale at the time.

Anthony Hatch and wife Keziah had four children (Addie, Emma, Anthony Hatch, Jr., and James) between the years of 1850 and 1860 while living on the farm. Anthony was very proud of his farm and animals, but he put too much confidence in one of his bulls. He was gored by this bull and died of wounds caused by the animal's horns in November of 1879 at the age of 67.

A Hatch milk truck comes a cropper
at Lincoln Ave. and Fairview.

Anthony Hatch, Jr., took over after the death of his father. He married Susan Prescott of Charlestown and had five children of his own including Elinor Wilmot, Anthony, George Prescott, Ernest Maxwell and Lester Clark. Anthony Hatch, Jr., started a milk company on the farm. The farm house was moved from Cliftondale Square to the Lincoln Avenue/Revere line area by train in the early 1900s. After the death of Anthony Hatch in the early 1920s, son Ernest continued on with the milk business.

Hatch Farm at the end of Laurel Street.

Generations of the Hatch Family lived for years in Saugus and enjoyed many happy memories there. The grandchildren of Lester have retold countless wonderful stories of living in their home at 121 Main Street with their father, Anthony Edward Hatch. Alice Hatch Vail, daughter of Ernest Hatch, lived in Saugus and gave many hours of her time to volunteer efforts in the town before her recent death. Although many of the Hatch descendants have moved from the town of Saugus their love for Saugus was carried with them wherever they have gone.

Einar Savolainen & Selma M. Luomala

My North Saugus Grandparents

by
Ray Exel

Einar Savolainen came from Finland sometime after the turn of the century (1900). He took the name John so that people could pronounce his first name. Selma M. Luomala arrived in America in the year 1906. They both lived in Boston, MA and met there. They courted and were married in 1909. They lived in Boston until the "Teens" and moved to North Saugus after they bought land on Ila Road and a house at 125 Broadway (Route 1) at the corner of Hawkes Street. While living in Saugus, John worked at L. B. Evans Co., a shoe manufacturer in Wakefield. John used to walk to work and home because there was no transportation and he had no vehicle.

House on Route 1 that became John's Café.

In the late '20s or early '30s, John's Café was opened. The porch of the house was framed in and that was the start of the café. In the back he had sixteen cabins built, three doubles and twelve singles. Both of these events happened around the same time. He was still working for L. B. Evans and running the bar. Selma ran the cabins and worked in the kitchen of the bar. Major changes took place in the gas station. A lift was installed on the right side. Later that was framed in so work could be done inside, out of the weather. They changed from the Tydol company to ESSO for their gas supplier.

Same house with John's gas station.

John built a take-out fried food place, in North Reading on Route 28, across the street from a large restaurant called Sailor Tom's. He sold this place in the late '30s. They went to Florida in the winter and stayed at Juno Beach with other Finnish people who had come to America. Their two sons ran the businesses at this time. Around September of 1941 John had a heart attack. The doctors told him to rest. This is

something he never did, so off to Florida they went. I think it was the fifth of December he died. At this time they had a winter home south of Juno.

Clarence ran the gas station and later built a golf course in Topsfield. Elmer ran the café and went into the army in World War II. He had three daughters and all became nurses. Martha and Laura ran the café while Elmer was in the service. After the end of the war, Laura Exel and Elmer bought the bar and Clarence bought the gas station.

Ray Exel's grandparents,
Mr. & Mrs. Einar (John) Savolainen..

John was one of the first to open these types of businesses on Route 1.

John was my grandfather.

The Dirty UPS Boxes

by
Janice Jarosz

UPS delivered a large package to my door one day several years ago. It came from Florida and was sent to me by my cousin, Virginia Junkins Steeves. Her mother, my great aunt, Alice (Penney) Junkins, had passed away and Virginia thought I might like some of the family memorabilia her mother had treasured.

I went through the items in a rather indifferent way; I had never really known Aunt Alice personally and the only thing I ever heard of her was that she was married to Ray Junkins and she never allowed him to smoke his pipe in the house.

After I looked at the family bibles, the pictures and the wedding dress of my great grandmother, I packed them all away in the cellar without another thought, or so I thought. It seemed that every time I went down cellar to do laundry, something was different. I could sense something watching me as I put bleach into a white wash. As time went on, I could almost feel someone watching me, calling on me in that lonely cellar.

I know what you are thinking right now – I must be somewhat crazy. However, after several years of ignoring the "calls" of my relative, I decided to revisit my relatives in those dusty UPS boxes.

It took a lot of time – going through letters, notes in family bibles, wedding pictures, hair bracelets and family heir-looms. The experience was overwhelming and it took months for me to comprehend the family history. When I did, suddenly everything that ever happened in the family made some sort of sense.

I learned that my great grandfather, Martin Luther Penney, left his home in Maine after a family argument and settled in Saugus. Here, he met Emma Josephine Parker, fifteen years younger than he, beautiful, educated and wealthy. The family home is still standing at 280 Central Street.

Obviously, the Parker family, one of the most prestigious in town, was not happy with the union though they did give the couple 96 acres of property on Howard Street, but in the process, cut them off and more or less disowned them.

They built a home on Howard Street and were the parents of ten children, four of whom died before the age of ten from black diphtheria. My grandfather, Henry Justin, who was the youngest, worked all his life on the farm. I remember him telling me how he got a brand new milk pail for Christmas when he was ten years old. He eventually suffered the same fate as his father. He met a German Catholic girl at a bakery in Melrose; they fell in love but her family disowned her and she was banished from her family because she married a Yankee Baptist.

Up until my UPS relatives "visited" me, none of us knew very much of either extended family and very little communication existed. Except for a few weddings and wakes, there were few family gatherings of any kind. Frankly the

Penneys of Howard Street were alone in the world. Both families lost so much joy and happiness in the process, as there was so much richness in accomplishments, in service to their town and country, and personalities full of courage and craziness that could have been shared.

In 1992, I penned *Dear Relatives*, a story about my great aunt, as a starting point, and tried to make the relatives more than just pictures and dates; I tried to introduce the long forgotten relatives to the present ones hoping to bring about a better understanding among our family members.

Once the book was published, I placed a few copies in the UPS box that holds the family memorabilia. Now when I go down cellar to do laundry, I sense a sort of peace – a feeling of contentment in the air within those archives – a peace that was so long overdue.

That experience taught me a deep appreciation of history and its importance in the world today. I continue to write about events and the people of Saugus in the hope of bringing those who have gone before us back to life through my words.

CNN Had Nothing on Grammy's Paper

by
Janice K. Jarosz

My grandmother could not begin her day until she read her newspaper and the ritual was the same each morning. After breakfast, and after the dishes were placed in the sink to soak, she would open the front door, retrieve her *Post* and retire to the living room where no one would dare disturb her until she read her paper.

It was an unspoken law in the house that no one even touched the paper until Grammy read it. And when one did finally get the opportunity, the newspaper had to be refolded back to its original condition and returned to the exact spot one found it – next to her chair. Those were the rules.

When *The Post* shut down its presses back when I was just a kid, it was as if there had been a death in the family. It took literally months for her to adjust to *The Herald* and finding the old favorite Jumble as a feature in *The Herald*, aided her in the healing process.

Newspapers were held in high esteem in most households years ago when I was growing up. But, with the advent of TV, and CNN News, the power of the printed word was somewhat diminished. In a now fast-paced lifestyle, it was easier and less time-consuming for most of us to turn on the radio or TV, rather than taking the time to sit and read a paper.

Recently I had the opportunity to read some old newspaper articles from *The Saugus Herald*. I was so impressed with the style and detail. Without the benefit of other means of communication, reports had to paint a clear picture of the event in a short and concise presentation. The following two stories are quite simple and probably quite irrelevant today as opposed to the present standards, but they convey to the reader, to me anyway, a genuine style and grace lost among the many facts and statistics of today.

Salsman Waiting At Dock For Bride To Be

"Waiting – Patiently Waiting" This is the song that Lieutenant William R. Salsman, of Combination 1, Saugus Fire Department, who is in New York, patiently waiting for the Steamship Carminia to dock, is singing.

There is a reason for his patience. On the boat is Miss Nell Kennah, of Dingle, England, who is soon to be his bride. It was a war romance. Salsman was an engineer in Uncle Sam's Expeditionary forces and, while in England, was attracted to the charms of the beautiful English miss. All will run smoothly if the immigration authorities at New York offer no objections as to Miss Kennah landing. Lt. Salsman and his English bride are expected to arrive in Saugus soon after their marriage and a fitting reception will be given the couple.

Thinking I found a wonderful story about their parents, I contacted the two children of Mr. Salsman, who were both now in their middle ages. "That's not my mother," stated Fran (Salsman) Penney. Richard Salsman, a son, also told me the same thing. "Our mother's name was Vesella Gould, of North Saugus, and our parents were married in 1922," exclaimed Mr. Salsman.

Despite the fact that the article made front page, none of Chief Salsman's family knew of the so-called "bride" from England or whatever happened to the romance. Lt. Salsman went on to become Fire Chief in 1936 and remained Chief until his untimely death at the age of 46. Evidently, the bride from England was never a passenger on the Carminia.

This next article needs no further explanation:

Sudden Death

While engaged in finishing her Saturday afternoon household duties, Mrs. Marguerite Azelia Davis, of Johnston Terrace, was suddenly prostrated with valvular disease of the heart and within one hour, at 5:45 PM, her death occurred. Mrs. Davis had suffered from visitations of this disease during the past four years.

The deceased was born in Peru, VT, 29 years ago last June. She came to Saugus with her husband, Edward R. Davis, seven years ago. Last August, they bought their new home on Johnson Terrace. In addition to her husband, Mrs. Davis leaves a little son, Ashton, aged six years.

— *Saugus Herald*, Page 5, February 6, 1913

Little Ashton Davis went on to graduate from Saugus High School in 1924, Harvard College in 1930, and Harvard Graduate School of Education in 1940. He began his teaching in Saugus in 1930 and became head of the English Department, principal of the Junior High School and eventually, principal of Saugus High School. His career spanned over 38 years.

Mr. Davis was a favorite among many and in 1968, a testimonial dinner was given in his honor. He passed away in February 1974, after suffering a heart attack in his home, just as his mother did so many years ago.

My poor grandmother must have left town on Friday, October 5, 1934 when the following story appeared on the front page of *The Saugus Advertiser*:

Town Almost Loses Its Roller, And Mr. Penney Now Seeks A Trespasser

Fences in Equipment on his Property and Defies Officials to Get it, but Henry Loses the Decision on a Subterfuge

The Saugus Public Works Department almost lost its steamroller Wednesday, to say nothing of a tractor and road scraper, and yesterday, Henry Penney of Howard Street was looking for somebody to arrest for trespassing.

Mr. Penney had temporary possession of the department's biggest piece of rolling stock, which he found parked on his property and to which he took a great liking. In fact, he treasured it so much that he built a fence around it.

It seems that Mr. Penney, earlier this year, gave his consent to public works to dump some gravel and loam from the new Golden Hills Road on his land through which the road runs.

Evidently perturbed because the truck men had succeeded in removing several loads before he discovered them, Mr. Penney sought retaliatory measures. Each night before the town workers left the job of grading the new road, they customarily parked the scraper, tractor and steamroller at the side of the road, on Mr. Penney's land. Wednesday morning, when they reported for work, they discovered that Mr. Penney had arisen very early in the morning and erected a neat little fence around each piece of equipment.

Henry was guarding his newly acquired property, and challenged the employees to step on his land to get the machinery. The foreman called Superintendent [of Public Works] Dexter G. Pratt, and Mr. Pratt, bewildered as anybody, called the police. What Mr. Penney planned to do with the roller is a matter of conjecture, but he was adamant about allowing anybody on his land. The patrolman called to the scene, argued earnestly [but in vain] because the aggrieved Mr. Penney was well within his rights.

Slowly the patrolman sauntered away from the imprisoned equipment, with Henry at his heels strongly emphasizing each point in his argument. The two disappeared over a knoll, and presto – the silent-watching crew of laborers jumped into action. The fence came down, chains were attached to the roller, scraper and tractor, and town trucks towed the rolling stock back onto the road.

When Mr. Penney returned, the fences were neatly replaced and members of the busy crew were happily whistling at their work.

Yesterday, Mr. Penney was seeking a warrant for somebody on a charge of trespassing, but according to the latest reports, he is having trouble finding a witness who saw anyone on his property. The boys' minds have suddenly gone blank.

Soup Versus Politics

Another example of contrasts between writing styles and news items of yesteryear, two generous paragraphs were given to the Tennis and Canoe Club on the front page of *The Herald* in 1921, praising the annual meeting of the club and the fine turtle soup that was served. The article also noted that the turtles were caught by members of the club fresh from the Saugus River.

Just under that gem of a story was a one-liner stating that, "Selectman so-and so Resigned from Office this Week." That was it – just a one-liner on the politics of the day. It appears that in those days, the political "pot" was not nearly as important as a tureen full of turtle soup!

Granted, no one will argue the point that our world has become much smaller since the days of my grandmother. The emphasis on better communication and networking has connected all of us; our fingers are constantly on the pulse of current events. We are subjected daily to broadcasts through all forms of media, of cold, hard, factual articles, up-to-the minute news events breaking all around our world, not to mention the constant roller coaster ride of our country's financial stability or instability, whether the case.

But I think my grandmother was right. Every once in a while it's nice to read simple, yet touching newspaper stories of people who not only touch your hands but also your hearts.

Tom Quinlan – True Saugonian

by
Betty Kudera Quinlan

In 1934, Tom and Julia Quinlan moved to Saugus from Malden. With three growing boys, Thomas, John and Fred, they felt the "country" would be a good place to bring up their family. A daughter, Florence, was born not long after the move to 103 Basswood Avenue.

An MDC employee and an avid baseball player, Tom organized and was the manager of the MDC Police baseball team. He also was involved with Saugus VFW baseball. There was no Little League, no Pop Warner, no Youth Hockey. Tom's sons were anxiously waiting to play on a team. He wanted to do something so he organized a "pick up" team called the Bly Club. Belden Bly, the well known teacher, coach, lawyer and state representative, sponsored the team. The Bly Club made a name for the community and put Saugus baseball in a positive direction.

During the Forties, when refrigerators were difficult to purchase, Tom had an ice business. He used his ice truck to transport the players to their games in other communities. Many of the players have stories to tell about the trips on the ice truck and incidents at the ball game. One recalled that Tom used a signal for stealing base – it was folding his arms across his chest. This being a non-baseball habit of Tom's, needless to say, there were many players running... even when they shouldn't have been! The boys also became involved in CYO baseball and yes, they used the ice truck for transportation. These organized baseball teams prepared the players for baseball at the high school level. When there was a high school baseball or football game, Tom was always there with his sons. He quickly became involved in the Boosters' Club to help support high school sports. He served as Chairman of the Playground Commission and was instrumental in the development of Anna Parker Playground. He was elected a Town Meeting member for many years, serving in Precinct Two. Tom's community spirit and love of sports has been carried on through the years by his extended family.

When World War II broke out, Thomas, the oldest in the family, wanted to join the Navy as soon as he was able. He graduated in 1942 from Saugus High with an early diploma so he could enlist. Love of our country was instilled in all the boys by their dad who served on the U.S.S. *Texas* during World War I. Thomas became a gunner / machinist on a Navy PBM and spent most of his enlistment in the South Pacific. Returning to Saugus after the war, Thomas married and settled in the community. He had three boys, Tommy, Stephan and Gary – all graduates of Saugus High. The boys all played Little League baseball and Pop Warner football. Tommy played baseball in high school and settled in Woburn where his son, Tommy, Jr., carried on the Quinlan baseball tradition at Woburn High. Stephan, with his wife Coleen, lives in Saugus. Their twin girls will be ninth graders at Saugus High in the fall of 2005. The girls have been actively involved in Saugus Youth Soccer, Town Basketball and Pop Warner Cheerleading . . . looking forward to perhaps being part of the high school cheerleading squad. Gary excelled as a football player and was an outstanding baseball player at Saugus High. He was also a member of the track team, setting many records. Graduating in 1980, Gary went on to play football and baseball and was a track star at Holy Cross. He was chosen to the Saugus Hall of Fame. He now coaches Pop Warner and Little League in Merrimack, New Hampshire, where he lives with his wife Diane and two children – Michael and Ciara. Michael plays Little League baseball and both children are involved in Pop Warner, Michael as a player and Ciara as a cheerleader.

Tom's son John graduated from Saugus High in 1946. He played baseball and is known in football as one of the best linemen to play at Saugus High. Coached in football by Dave Lucey, John was a member of the 1944 Class B State Championship team. He has been elected to the Saugus High Hall of Fame. Leaving Saugus High, John brought his talent to the football team at Boston College. After graduating from B.C., he started his career as a math teacher in the Saugus school system. He coached football at the high school and for many years was the Playground Director of the summer program. Following in his dad's footsteps, John managed a CYO baseball team and was involved in the development of Little League and Peanut Hockey in Saugus. He married a Saugus High graduate, Cynthia Robertson, and they are the parents of four girls – Pamela, Laura, Barbara and Tara – grandparents of eight and great-grandparents of two. John retired from teaching and there are many students that speak highly of him. They recognize John for his dedication to the youth in Saugus and his unique way of teaching. He always strived to have his student-athletes work hard and get the most out of their abilities.

The youngest son, Fred, graduated in 1950 from Saugus High. Carrying on his dad's love of sports, Fred was an outstanding baseball player and a running back on the 1949 Exchange Bowl Championship team. He was known to run like a deer. Belden Bly, Athletic Director in 1947, often tells the story about how Fred broke his collar bone at football practice. Belden brought him home. His mother, seeing the shoulder all bandaged up, chased Belden with a broom all the way up the hill. How dare someone hurt her son!... (typical Irish mom... no one hurts her boys!). Fred played CYO baseball and was the catcher for the Bly Club. He coached Pop Warner football and was elected to the Saugus Hall of Fame in 1995. He married Betty Kudera, a graduate of Saugus High and a member of the cheerleading squad. They have six children – Freddy, Lori, Karen, Ann, Kelly and Jimmy.

Freddy played Little League baseball, Pop Warner football and was a guard on the high school football team. He went on to Plymouth State and was chosen to the Little All-American football team. His daughters Kristen, Courtney, Carly and Bethany were all cheerleaders at Saugus High and son Patrick played football. Patrick is Captain of the 2005 football team at Plymouth State. His youngest daughters, Riley and Ella, plan to follow in the family's love of sports. They live with their mom Kali and dad in New Hampshire. Lori was a cheerleader at the high school, and married another Saugus High graduate, Tom Glew. They have a daughter Julia, who is a member of the Color Guard at her high school in Newport, N. C. Karen, although not involved in athletics, is carrying on the family's teaching tradition. She is a speech pathologist in the Swampscott public schools. She resides in Peabody with her daughter Briana. Kelly marched with the Saugus High School band as a baton twirler. She has a daughter Jaymie who plays soccer and basketball. Kelly, her husband Joe and children, Jaymie and John, live in Swampscott. Jim, the youngest of Fred's family, married Ann Dunn, another Saugus graduate. Jim followed in his dad's footsteps, playing as a catcher in Little League. He played Pop Warner football and two years of football in high school. His love of hockey from Youth Hockey on made him devote all of his energy to hockey. He was Co-Captain of the 1982 hockey team, but is probably more noted for his six-year reign as Saugus High Varsity Hockey Coach. He amassed a sensational 106-26-11 record, winning two state titles and four NEC Championships. Jim's son Eric was part of his dad's two state titles and championships. Eric's personal statistics in hockey at Saugus High are more than impressive. Besides Youth Hockey, Eric played Little League baseball and two years of high school baseball. After a year at Avon Old Farms he headed to Merrimack College. Jim's daughter Erin is a budding three sport athlete at Austin Prep and youngest daughter Emily plays Saugus soccer, softball and basketball. Jim won't be straying too far from the hockey program as he plans to establish a Saugus High Hockey Organization to continue to help the program grow on and off the ice.

Tom's only daughter, Florence, married Saugus High graduate Bill Peach. Florence was a member of the cheerleading squad while at Saugus High. They had three children – Billy, Steve and Katie. As their sons became involved in sports, Florence and Bill joined the Boosters Club. Now, nearly thirty years later, Florence is still helping the youth in Saugus by serving as Treasurer of the Boosters Club. As soon as they were old enough, Billy and Steve played Pop Warner football and Little League baseball. Steve was a natural at quarterback, and Billy was always there to catch his brother's passes. When they reached high school, the "Peaches" were the ones to watch. Billy and Steve excelled in three sports, football, baseball and basketball. Their natural talent and accomplishments, especially in football, brought much excitement to the community. After high school, Billy played for the University of New Hampshire. Steve played one year at Syracuse and then transferred to Boston College. Billy and his wife Michelle live in Hamilton with their two young children, a daughter Samantha and a son Cameron. Steve coached Pop Warner football, and his son Drew is already displaying his dad's athletic ability. Steve resides in Dartmouth with his wife Kim and children Drew and Bailey. Steve and Billy are members of the Saugus High School Hall of Fame. Their sister Katie lives in Saugus with her husband Tom Kaminski and sons, Kirt and Kreg. Kirt and Kreg play soccer and football at St. John's Prep.

Tom Quinlan, a fun loving man, was always thankful his family was given the opportunity to grow up in Saugus. He loved the community and was instrumental in the growth of organized sports in the town. Unfortunately, Tom passed away in 1969 and was unable to watch many of his grand-

children and great-grandchildren's games... but, according to some family members, they could feel his presence, his support... they just knew he was there with them... we all know Grandpa Tom wouldn't miss a game at Saugus High. Seventy-one years later, even though Saugus can no longer be called a place for country living, it will always be "*Someplace Special*" for Tom's children, grandchildren and great-grandchildren.

The Evans Circus at 305 Lincoln Avenue

by
Alwin Evans

There is a history of circus in my family. My name is Alwin Evans and, because I was the youngest of six children, I had plenty of opportunity to listen and to observe. It all began with my grandfather, Frank Evans. He began performing the circus acts back in the good old days when he was young, somewhere around the turn of the century. I remember my grandfather's circus photographs, which graced the walls of our home on Lincoln Avenue in Saugus.

In a barrel balanced on the high wire.

My grandfather could walk both the high tight wire and the slack wire. Grandfather Evans would thrill his audience by performing the most amazing feats including: walking across the tight wire, tumbling while on the high wire, crossing the tight wire in a wooden barrel, and playing a violin while riding a unicycle across the tight wire.

My grandfather lived a very colorful and exciting life working in the circus. Some of the people my grandfather worked with in the circus went on to great fame, including Joe E. Brown and Keenan Wynn.

With all that circus excitement in the family, naturally all the Evans children wanted to see whether they had inherited their grandfather's skill, agility and daring. My brother Edson borrowed grandfather's circus equipment and we all began to try our skills at walking the tight wire, riding the unicycle, and, of course, tumbling.

Edson, or as we usually called him, Ed, became the most proficient of our family in developing circus skills; I guess he must have inherited the Frank Evans circus gene or perhaps he was just bitten by the same circus bug. Ed used to walk the tight wire, placed four feet from the ground, at my mother's insistence. Ed also rode unicycle, both the low rider and the high rider. The seat on the high rider unicycle was six feet from the ground. Ed would cause quite a stir riding the high rider down Lincoln Avenue in Saugus. Ed would lean the unicycle against a telephone pole and climb up along the side in order to get onto the seat and then hold onto it until he gained his balance. Then off he would go, parading down Lincoln Avenue. It was an unbelievably funny sight to see Ed ride along on a unicycle, with drivers of passing cars poking their heads out their car windows, not quite willing to believe that their minds were not playing tricks on them.

Ed went to school at Florida State University. There he joined the Florida University Circus where he competed in tumbling and on the high rings. Floor tumbling was by far Ed's favorite sport. He also did tumbling while on a trampoline. It was really exciting; there was always some form of entertainment going on in our back yard. My father, Frank Evans Jr., once built a pair of stilts that he used in this amazing back yard. The steps on the stilts were seven feet high. Dad would sit on the edge of the garage roof to mount these gigantic stilts and then he would walk all around the yard on them. Unfortunately, however, that perilous experience came to a rather abrupt end when he fell and broke his foot. That did turn out to be the end of the stilts.

All this exuberant energy and enthusiasm did not always go without incident; there was the time when Ed, my brother Dick, Cal Vatcher, and Bobo Parrott were all working for Comfort's Hay and Grain. While they were on the truck making the rounds delivering hay and grain, Ed was doing

handstands on the back of the truck when he fell off and broke his left elbow in three places. Ouch!

Riding a special unicycle on the high wire.

Ed went on to become a teacher at Saugus High School. There he taught science and tumbling to students who showed an interest. The science was mandatory, but the tumbling was voluntary, and it turned out to be great fun for all who participated. Ed demonstrated his circus act at the Saugus High School Auditorium. There he entertained the audience with floor tumbling and riding the unicycle. He wowed the crowd by having a student perched atop his shoulders while riding the unicycle, a once in a lifetime event at Saugus High School.

Ed went on and taught at Buffalo State University. One time there was an incident in which he escaped from three university students whom he had failed and who had vengeance in their heart. The three students hoped to intimidate Ed at the very least. The three of them blocked his exit from the school building. Undaunted, Ed put his bag inside his office door. He then began to tumble his way past them. The three of them just stood there with their mouths gaping open as he tumbled along past them and out the front door. I am certain that they never had another teacher so immune to their intimidation.

Riding a conventional unicycle on the high wire.

The Maxwell Family of Saugus

Five Generations

by
Sam Maxwell

The Maxwell family is in its fifth generation as Saugonians. The family originated in Scotland, then moved to Ireland, and later emigrated to New Brunswick in 1839. My grandfather, Samuel Leonard Maxwell, married Helen Malcolm Cook Caie, also from New Brunswick, in Boston, in 1904. They moved to Everett, Massachusetts, following their marriage. They had six children, Mildred, William, Leonard, Helen, Garfield and Bayard, and in 1920 packed up for their last move, to Adams Avenue in Saugus. It was a close family and stayed nearby until after World War II.

During World War II, Grammy was proud to display her service flag with three stars in her front window. Two sons, Garfield and Bayard, and son-in-law Al Ahman all served in the Navy, and all three attained the rank of Chief Petty Officer.

After World War II, three of the children moved elsewhere in New England. Three remained in Saugus. One of them, my father William, married Cornelia Stevens of Nova Scotia and moved into a home on Endicott Street where I was brought up. My father eventually bought out C. F. Hallin, an automotive repair business in Market Square, Lynn. Mr. Hallin was a long-time resident of Saugus, also living on Adams Avenue. He raised Dalmatians as a hobby and one of his pups was my first dog, Rowdy. Many of my schoolmates at the Felton and Sweetser schools would remember the big black and white dog that walked me to and from school and showed up at recess to mooch scraps of lunches and play with us.

My cousin, Ernie Huber, Jr., had an interesting hobby that became an astounding success. He spent his spare time building and designing radio controlled airplanes. He eventually began experimenting with helicopters. Large scale models were used in several movies, and the helicopters seen in *The Towering Inferno* were designed by Ernie.

We also had a large extended family on my mother's side, consisting of three sisters and a cousin, all living in Saugus. We really grew up with a huge family in the greater Boston area though the largest and closest were in Saugus.

Growing up I was part of the Cliftondale Crowd and sometimes with the Baker Hill Bunch. My friends and classmates, Class of 1950, grew up during the war. It was a different kind of world then. Most adults were off to war and a lot of household tasks fell on the boys of all ages. Few criminals, more doors left unlocked and we always seemed to have more to do than we had time. There were scrub football and baseball games put together with neighborhood kids of all ages at the drop of a hat and played in the street. There were few autos to worry about then. We played tackle football in an empty lot on Endicott Street, or tag in the street with Lennie and Ronnie Hart, Ray Foss, and drafted anyone else that had the misfortune to walk by. Mooched a piece of ice from the iceman in the summer and played endless games of tag and dodge ball. The latter was usually set up on Morton Avenue near the corner of Lincoln. Benny Rice's kids were the catalyst for that game. I remember when Barbara Rice broke a tooth in our game. One among the many injuries. Benny was not only a Saugus High School algebra teacher, but a coach, attorney and good friend. Our group also included another good friend, Bobby Chiabrandy.

Some of the current relatives and younger relatives do not realize how rural Saugus was in the '30s and '40s. There were many horse-drawn vehicles around. Mitt Stocker and his honeywagon took care of the septic tanks since there were no sewers. Lenny Hart's dad delivered Hood's milk in Lynn with a horse and wagon. We drove the route with him once. I think the horse was named Pudgy. We had ours delivered by horse also, by Mr. Nicholson. Of course, we had farms galore, especially dairy farms. When I visit Saugus it remains much like it did then except the farms are gone. Route 1 was mostly farms and when it was a divided highway there were few businesses there. Today it's the grungiest stretch of highway anywhere and terrible to drive. I make a point of using Walnut Street and Essex Street to avoid it. Talk about unabated urban sprawl. We had our coal delivered by the Randazzos, who hauled it to a coal chute into the basement in large canvas sacks over their shoulders. I ran the furnace from a very young age, including hauling out the ash barrels. There even was a ragman that came around, and the knife sharpener with his push cart and bell tinkling away. The phones were primitive by today's standards. Just dial "0" and an operator came on. It quite frequently was Claire Smith from across the street. She would say, "Hi, Sammy, who do you need?" Just give her four digits and she connected you.

On the domestic front, when I was a little younger, I took great delight in riding the trolley from Endicott and Lincoln Avenue to Lynn to shop with my mother. Then I went through a stage of raising pigeons with my friend Tony Provenzano. We would walk to Cliftondale, take the bus to Malden, then another bus to meet the El and on into Haymarket Square where we bought homing pigeons from a man that raised them on the top of a building. They cost a whopping $1 each. Once in a while we'd have to retrieve a bird that still considered Boston home. Would that be of interest to a kid today?

Maxwell family gathering, Sam at upper left.

There weren't many Maxwell kids my age to horse around with, except the Hubers, and they were in Beverly. That changed dramatically when we reached 16 and could drive. I, and my contemporaries, went everywhere on bicycles as well. My favorite was a trip to Breakheart Reservation to visit with the military stationed there and get some hot cocoa and cookies. Seems to me they had a POW compound there, but I'm told not so, but I recall hearing men talking in German and Italian. It wasn't a prison as such, but the soldiers told us they were "babysitting" as the prisoners were content to be out of the war. Hmmm. They

did have an anti-aircraft battery as I remember. We also spent a lot of time camping with the Boy Scouts on the reservation. There was another battery atop Baker Hill next to the water standpipe. They had painted out the huge white Saugus for security reasons. That was easier to get to. From my backyard we could go through the woods we played in endlessly, to the top of the hill and there the battery members were always happy to see us and to tell us tall tales, but one time we saw a lot of activity by fighter aircraft off toward Nahant and were told a mini submarine heading to the Saugus River to hit the GE was sunk. I didn't know if it was another tale, but people in the neighborhood thought it was true. Ought to get Richie Provenzano to look into that.

Baker Hill was also the best site I've ever seen for flying kites. My father and Henry Davis used to make immense kites from newspaper glued into sheets and attached to a wood framework then take them up the hill. They had large reels of heavy twine and would reel them out over the marsh toward the GE. They never could retrieve one as the twine wouldn't take the strain of reeling in against the wind. It would break and we'd watch them head to sea with their long rag tail trailing behind. Another ride was down the marsh road at the foot of Morton Avenue through the Sim Carnation Company onto the dirt road (Saugus Avenue?) that led to the old racetrack. We could watch them testing Bren Gun Carriers near the Revere Airport (now the Northgate Shopping Mall). They had huge mounds of dirt they would run them up and over.

Of course my bicycle was used frequently to visit Grammy on Adams Avenue. The ride down Central Street was the neat part until I tried to pass a parked Lincoln and a driver going by thought otherwise and ran me into the Lincoln's rear at high speed. It didn't bother the Lincoln but my bicycle and I came home in pretty bad shape. I spent a lot of time at Grammy's when our uncles, especially Al, were home on leave. He would bring me things from the Pacific like seashells and such and talk to me for a long time. The Laviskas lived around the corner and we were like family. Charlie and I were great friends and later John had an upstairs loft in my sister Nancy's home on Bayfield Road. He was a former Saugus fireman and I gave him a gold plated chief's badge I found in Las Vegas. Never did find out who had worn it. Dated back to the early '30s. On my frequent visits to Saugus in the '80s and '90s John would chauffeur me around and he knew where everyone lived or did live and who they married and were related to. He was a walking encyclopedia. Another of my friends in that neighborhood was Billy McGinnis, who lived on the corner of Hill Street and his house looked down on the railroad tracks. We thought it great fun to hear the train coming and run down to put a penny on the track.

In the winter, the bikes were in the basement, and out came the sleds and skis. We would sled or ski from after school

Families of the Town

'til dark, sometimes later. Those of us that lived in the Baker Hill area had it so good! Clifton Avenue and the long run down Baker Hill into the Sweetser School yard were pure ecstasy. Even faced with the burden of climbing back up the hill. And even when I was hit by a large Flexible Flyer and ended up with a broken leg.

My family worshiped at the Cliftondale Methodist church to the thundering sermons of Reverend H. Newton Clay. He left a huge impression on me and things were never quite the same after he moved on. My grandmother and Aunt Helen were very involved in the church women's clubs. Grammy was President of the Women's Relief Corp No. 46 (Auxiliary to the Grand Army of the Republic) at the time of the 50th Anniversary in 1935. She was a member of the Rebekah Lodge and the Ungungun Club. Most of the Maxwell kids went to Sunday school there. In fact, my cousin, Joe Crocker, was my teacher and went into the ministry himself. My aunt, Grace Swan, was also a teacher. She also housed British sailors on leave in the US during WW II. Her husband Charlie was from Scotland and it was no surprise that the majority of sailors I met were Scottish. I was very disappointed to hear the church had been sold as it is one of the foundations Cliftondale was built on. I believe both my sisters, Nancy and Ruth, were married there as were Norman and Gail Peach. I was sorry also to see that the little Catholic Church at the juncture of Adams Avenue and Central Street was now a day care and youth center. It was a neat little church and I hope it is retained for posterity. I won't dwell too much on Cliftondale since Russ Blood did such a great job describing it in *A Gathering of Memories*. I remember it well and enjoyed his descriptions immensely.

I delivered newspapers in the Jackson Street, Mountain Avenue route. My good friends George Emberley, Tommie Graham, Billy McAdoo, Frank Dudman and Charlie Long-fellow all lived in the area of my route. My haircuts were at Charlie O'Connor's shop in the Square. He would call out back and my grandfather would come in and chat. He was a linotype setter for *The Saugus Herald* newspaper owned by Ernest Light and worked in a shop near O'Connor's shop or attached to it. Later, on Lincoln Avenue, but on the opposite side of the square, I had my haircut by Joe Laura, Jr. He later bought a farm in Vermont and my brother-in-law to be and I went deer hunting there. When older I would always stop at the Cliftondale diner and have a cup of coffee and a piece of pie on my way home from a date.

Much to everyone's surprise I did go out for football. The then coach and I had an immediate dislike for each other and I decided to eliminate his problem and leave. I did get on well with Coach Scarborough and he tried to get me to come out a year or so later, but I had discovered girls were much more fun. Even more so when I could drive and we had submarines to watch. I had an occupational license to drive a delivery truck for my dad at fourteen but could only drive in daylight and for him. I drove a 1929 Plymouth with

a rumble seat converted to a small pickup which we called the "jeep." Others in the family did go out for football and hockey and are in the Sports Hall of Fame. I count several players as good friends. Freddie Quinlan, Frank Dudman, Richie and Sal Nicolo, Bernie Lancaster and Bobby Harrie come to mind. I never missed a game during high school.

There is one mystery surrounding the house on Adams Avenue. My father, a devout car nut, as are most of the Maxwells, told me that when a Tin Lizzie (Model T) died it was dismantled and buried in the back yard. His brothers swore to it and cousin Gail said they told her too. The lot in those days had a vacant lot next door and was very deep. So we don't know exactly where it might be and it remains a mystery to this day. My Uncle Garfield had a 1939 Ford when I was about seven or eight. The first car I bought was a 1939 Ford Phaeton 4-door convertible with leather interior from Bobby Druid's older brother, Hank, for the princely sum of $200. I was in the Navy and that car sure got a workout and many engine changes. I had number plates in the trunk from New York, New Jersey, Rhode Island, Virginia and Massachusetts. When we accumulated too many tickets on our overnight runs home we would change plates for awhile. Massachusetts Department of Motor Vehicles came to the house and confiscated theirs. My sister "borrowed" it while I was at sea and backed it into Jimmy Smith's large elm tree. Only dent it ever had. My first auto was actually my dad's 1941 Plymouth. Very few of us had access to autos in the '40s and it came with a price. Homework suffered and no matter where I went, a phone call would alert my mother. Too many relatives around town. One night I was in the "Rat Hole" playing pool. I carefully hid the Plymouth around the feed store near the railway station. When I came out, very late, the car was gone. I called my dad and told him it was gone and I had the keys. He said, "So do I," and hung up. Needless to say I walked home and was grounded.

The younger generations are doing well and a number of them are still in Saugus. I live in Washington State, my sister Nancy now lives in Peabody near her extended family in Danvers and Hamilton. Ruth is living in New Hampshire near her daughter Stacia and granddaughter, Natasha, the latter getting ready for college this year. Gail Ahman Peach and husband Norman are still on Adams Avenue. Bruce Maxwell, his family and his mother, Betty, are in Saugus as well. I normally visit every year in the fall and make the rounds of friends and family. It's still a great historic town and there are no better people than those in Saugus.

The Flynns

Three Generations with a Common Thread

by
Peggy Flynn

Memories of Charlie Flynn include recollections of his father and grandfather. Charlie loved to tell how his grandfather, Daniel Flynn, came alone to this country from County Clare, Ireland, in 1884 at the age of 14. He settled in Saugus and worked at Gillis Counter Company, a shoe factory in Lynn. The company was situated near what is now North Shore Community College. After a few years, Mr. Gillis made Daniel a partner and, eventually, Daniel bought him out and continued to run the company under that name. Charlie's father, Charles, Sr., was the oldest of his four children - Charles, John, Ann (Howard) and Mary (McLaughlin). Daniel built a large two-family house at 8 Smith Road in Cliftondale. He was an avid reader, with a fondness for Charles Dickens. He memorized long passages and Charlie remembers him reciting his favorites. He put Charles through Bowdoin and Harvard Law, John through UNH and Ann through Simmons, quite an accomplishment in the early 1900s. He instilled in his children a love of learning.

Charlie's father Charles, Sr., born in 1896, was brought up on Smith Road and, when Charlie was born in 1929, they lived in a house across the street from his grandfather, Daniel. Soon they moved to 38 Jackson Street, still in Cliftondale Square. Charlie remembers his father's stories of the first attempts at aviation down on the marsh. When Charles Sr. was a youngster, he was part of a group of boys who were asked to help the local aspiring aviators launch their planes. They were to grasp ropes on each side of the contraption and, at a signal, run like crazy pulling the plane along in an attempt to get it off the ground. The boys would laugh at the efforts, thinking what fools these men were. But, as fate would have it, Charles, Sr. enrolled as a Naval Aviator in 1917 and was sent to Pensacola Naval Air Base in Florida. His tales of his experiences were greatly entertaining. One favorite story of Charlie's was when his father flew into a cloud for the first time and came out upside down! On a visit to Pensacola Naval Air Museum, Charlie looked up his father's profile. Along with the description of his service record was a quote from his father: "My Navy experience taught me to keep going when the going is labored, to keep my head under all circumstances, to delegate authority but insist on good performance, to trust others while keeping my eyes wide open, and not talk too much!"

Charles, Sr. began to practice law and became active in local civic associations and town affairs, serving as Saugus Town Counsel and as a member of the Sewer Commission. Along with Bill Rockhill and Jim Conway, he owned and operated the Rapid Transit Bus Company, which ran to Winthrop and Orient Heights. The garage was located on Woodbury Avenue. He was appointed judge, presiding over the Trial Court that was located in Saugus Center. He then practiced law in Boston, at the firm of Flynn, Esdaile, Morris and Barrett. A man of many interests, he could go out to get milk at the store or gas for the car and return with wonderful stories told to him by the people he ran into. He was a man who listened to what other people had to say. He passed that trait on to his son.

Charles Flynn,
third generation.

Charlie, after graduating from law school, moved back to Saugus and set up a law practice in Cliftondale Square. Charlie also became active in local organizations, as well as serving on the Board of Assessors. One of his proudest achievements when his children were young was receiving a national award from Camp Fire Girls for his service on the Board of Directors. Four of his daughters had involved him in the organization and he delighted in his participation. After serving as counsel for the Department of Labor Relations, he was appointed Clerk/Magistrate at the Lynn District Court in 1972.

To remember Charlie is to remember his compassion, patience and sense of humor. He had the wisdom to listen. He was an unusually patient man. His patience with the people who came before him in his role as Clerk/Magistrate for 28 years at the Lynn District Court is legendary. Those who worked with him remember how he would listen to both sides, let people tell their story and think carefully before he spoke. Anyone who knew Charlie knew that, if you were going to ask for advice, he would think long and hard about it. But then, after a sufficient pause, he would give you good advice, ideas and plenty of thought. His sense of humor was unique. If a group was pontificating on an issue, during a lull in the conversation Charlie would sum it all up with a one-liner that would have everyone in stitches. Or, if an argument was escalating, he would step in with a remark that would diffuse the anger, put everything in perspective and leave everyone laughing. He was a night owl. When he had to go out in the middle of the night to set bail or issue search warrants at the various police stations in the district, he loved to listen to the guys on the night shift, never worrying about the time. He loved golf. There wasn't a book, video or gadget out there that he didn't try in an effort to improve his game. There are still nicks in the ceiling from his inability to control his swing as he practiced in front of the TV. There are probably still golf balls behind the couch due to an errant putt. If he couldn't be out on the course, he could still practice, searching for that elusive Perfect Game!

There is a common thread running through the three Flynn generations: Daniel Flynn loved literature and put great value on education. Charles, Sr. expanded that love of knowledge and education and with it developed the ability to listen and learn from people from all walks of life. Charlie, like his father and grandfather, was a good listener, a thinker and a man of great patience. His seven children treasure the stories he passed down and the love he gave them was filled with strength, compassion and humor.

The Neals of Saugus

by
Nora Shaughnessy

It seems that I am the last of the Neals in Saugus, and I'm not even a Neal, since my mother married a Shaughnessy, but Neals have a way of showing up. My memories, both first and second-hand, seem thus far to be in the mainstay of the story of the Saugus Neals. It is good to see them where they can be accessed by others.

My mother, Nancy Neal Shaughnessy, was born in 1928, to Walter Frederick Neal and Ruth Alice Cohane. He was a Saugus boy, she a Salem girl, and both were high school graduates.

Nancy at Kilkenny Castle, 1985.

My grandfather, whom I called Dad, born in 1903, was the oldest of four children, and the Neals lived on Richard Street. His younger sister, Aunt Thelma, remembered when the Ballard School was being built. She'd ride on the loads of bricks being driven down to the site on sledges, drawn by horses. There were few houses down in the marsh area back then, and the Neal kids, both then and later, learned to swim in the Saugus River.

Olive was next oldest to Dad, and she knew Nana when both were in nurses' training at the same time, and that's how Nana and Dad met.

The youngest member of the family was Paul, and he worked during the Depression and war years for the *Lynn Telegram*, and later, the *Lynn Item*. I remember being told that during the Depression, he and my grandmother's sister were the only ones in the family homes to have work. Paul went on to be a radio newsman, and then Regional Information Office for the Feds in Boston until he retired.

He was special to me in so many ways. He never married and he took a kind of shine to me because of my interest in reading and music. He sent my mother and me to Symphony more than once and, in later years, I drove him to the opera, where he paid for my ticket. As a graduate student with no money, it was a wonderful opportunity for me, and we attended several seasons together until he died.

As a young man, he belonged to the Saugus Four Arts Club, acting and playing with the likes of Clayton Trefry on the Town Hall stage when it was also used for entertainment.

Nana came from a large Irish family in Salem. Her grandparents were from Ireland and they arrived here during the Famine, and the American Civil War. Like so many Irish, they were a political bunch, and her father had all ten kids reading the newspaper each morning. Her grandfather was from Cork, and he arrived in this country just in time to join the Union Army out of Salem. He had no money, of course, but he was attached to the cavalry because he was a farrier by trade. He was at most major battles, and took some wounds, one through the right hand. It festered, and they had all but decided to amputate when someone suggested that maggots be introduced to the wound. It healed and he mustered out, his livelihood intact. All the Cohanes were Catholic.

My grandfather's family, on the other hand, was a house divided by religion. His mother was part Irish and Catholic. My grandfather, who went to the East Saugus Methodist Church, like his father, converted when he married Nana. I remember him as a truly devout man, so honest and straightforward that he often seemed lacking in humor. And yet, he was good-humored and generous to a fault.

He was at first an apprenticed cabinet maker, but then couldn't make his living that way since the times were so difficult, and people could not afford to have fine work done in their homes. So, in 1930 or so, with one child already and another on the way, he got an appointment to the police in town for special duty. By the time World War II actually started for the U.S. he was a full time police officer with four children. When he wanted to "join up," my grandmother gave him holy hell and said, "You're not leaving me with these kids!"

For part of their first years together, he stayed in his parents' house in Saugus, while my grandmother stayed in Salem with her folks, and her children. It was then that Uncle Paul and Aunt Nora were the only ones with full-time jobs. Dad took a long walk two or three evenings a week to visit his wife and kids in Salem. He didn't have money for a street car, and his beat, along the Marsh Road, was a long, cold one that prepared him for walking virtually anywhere.

Great-Grandma Neal died first, and the wake was held at home on Richard Street, and my grandmother was feeling relieved and giddy. She and my great-grandmother didn't get along well, but she took care of my great-grandmother for most of the time the old girl was dying. Great-Grandma was tight with a buck, and cozy about her privacy. Even Nan was better than some stranger, but Great-Grandma still kept her purse hanging from the bedpost.

When the time came to go to the funeral in someone's big car, another guest – a Mrs. Feelin – was the butt of one of Nana's inanities when she said, "How ya feelin', Mrs. Feelin?" Another guest in the car later tried to total the number of mourners in the car that day, and he repeatedly came up one short. He reportedly started out each time with "...and the two O'Reillys was one..." sending everyone else into bursts of giggles, much to Dad's disgust.

It was still Depression time when they finally put a down payment on a house; he was a full-time officer, though he continued to do odd jobs when he could, and they bought a house on Jasper Street in Saugus Center. My mother, Nancy, an escape artist as a child, could manage to unlock the screen-door magically and "run away" to the old police station, where she was sure to get an ice cream while she waited for her father to come to escort her home. She must have been a tall five-year-old, and she never tired of telling me the story, but they lost that house, and then moved to another one on Baker Hill, where they lived across the way from the MacNeills: a group of brothers who, my grandmother used to say, "never used a door when they could use a window." One of the MacNeills went on to be a popular teacher at Saugus High while I was there.

It was during one of Dad's odd jobs that he acquired Butch, the springer spaniel, who was with them for many years. The fellow with him on some job had Butch along, and impatiently struck Butch on the head with a hammer. Outraged, Dad, took the hammer out of his hand, threw it aside, and "let the bastard have it." He came home with Butch, who was spoiled in no time like every other pet we ever had in the family. Once Nana heard Butch whimpering in the kitchen and went to the doorway to see why.... There was Butch, watching a mouse eat his food while he cried.

But my grandfather wasn't always paid for his little jobs. I don't know how many neighbors' stairs were built by my grandfather, and he wouldn't take money from a neighbor, even when they were hard up, much to Nana's frustration. But he was proud of his skills, and he was cheerful in his generosity.

In those days, police officers in Saugus couldn't serve in Town Meeting, so Dad talked my long-suffering grandmother into running. I suspect she only served one term but she always spoke of it as such fun that I couldn't understand why she didn't stay in. Speaker of the Massachusetts House, Fred Willis, a Saugus Republican, appointed my grandfather to be an Officer of the Great and General Court of Massachusetts House of Representatives and then Dad could run himself. He made it, and served several terms.

Prior to his service, just before the war ended, they moved into the house I still live in on Hood Street, in West Cliftondale. My mother was then in high school, from which she graduated in 1946, the same year as Patricia Ballard Annis, with whom she served in Town Meeting. After my mother died, I continued to serve with Pat, until she died. We became good friends. The Neals have a tendency to be community-minded.

My grandfather, whom I called "Dad," since my own father disappeared when I was a baby, had a sharp tongue, but not as sharp as Nana's. He had no meanness in him, just a temper, usually righteous. Nana, on the other hand, was self-absorbed and excessively fond of having her own way. She wanted all of us to be *just so*, and a good reflection on her. She cared very much about how things looked, rather than how they actually were, and tried to mold us into what pleased her.

Good luck turning me into a Barbie Doll! I was more interested in climbing a tree with a book in my pocket. So we were at odds from the beginning, and she was quite unpleasant to me. I knew at an early age that she only loved me if I acted the way she wanted, but that wasn't a good enough reason to subvert my own personality, and I grew up angry and determined to be different. I made the choices that I knew would please my mother, who was my dearest friend, and my comrade in fighting off the ordinary.

Dad was sympathetic, and took me everywhere he went, which made me happy. I loved him very much, and admired him, too.

One second-hand story I heard as a child was of one of his visits to Thelma after she had married James, a ne'er-do-well, who was occasionally missing from home for odd periods of time. Dad's educated "take" on these disappearances was that James was in jail for one or another of his dubious undertakings. During this particular visit to Thelma, she absented herself when the phone rang, and took the call in a closet. Of course, she was making book for the again missing James, and Dad recognized the signs quite easily, and with helpless dismay.

Walter Neal with his family.

One story I always loved was about him and his cronies. It seemed they were having a conversation about Saugus families and names. One pal said his full name was Howard Pranker Berrett, and my grandfather looked at him proudly and said, "I'm related to the Howard, the Prankers and the Berretts." Indeed, his great grandfather married a Howard - Mary Eliza - and her father, Grandsire Howard, gave them half the Howard cemetery lot at Riverside. Both my grandparents and Uncle Paul are buried there, along with two other Neal men from the previous generation. One generation before that, they came from Lynn, but in 1630, it was a Captain Walter Neal who landed near Portsmouth, New Hampshire, having been given a grant for war service to the Crown.

When Dad died of lung cancer in February of 1964, I'm told the funeral was quite something, with representatives from both sides of the aisle, someone from the governor's office, the secretary of state's office, a huge cast of family, friends, and hoodlums. Despite living with him at home while he was dying, learning at age five to give him oxygen, or brandy and soda to sooth his throat, I wasn't allowed to see the funeral, to see the regard he was held in. I knew what death meant by then; John Kennedy had been killed three months before and it was the only time I saw my Republican grandfather cry.

Of the next generation, my mother was the oldest and she was the only girl. I have always been exceptionally proud of her, because in a time when women were routinely passed over for promotions they deserved, she kept plugging, taking civil service exams, slowly, determinedly moving up, with only a high school education.

A feminist, she quietly (and sometime not so quietly) strove for what every worker deserves: equal pay and equal consideration. She was told by one boss, "Yes, well, but-so-and-so's son needs the job. After all, he has a family to support."

"So have I," she said, "and I'll go to the union over this."

When she retired, she was the Assistant Registrar of Vital Statistics for the Commonwealth of Massachusetts. Not bad for someone with no college degree, eh?

Her brother, Walter (Jr.), now lives with his wife in Florida, close to several of his children and grandchildren.

Arthur, like my mother, is dead. He often said he fought in the coldest GD war we were ever in and the hottest GD war we were ever in and we lost both of them.

Arthur Neal.

His childhood was quite tragic, too: he and some pals, all around eight years old, jimmied open the closet where my grandfather's service revolver was kept. One of the boys was killed. The story of this horror comes down to me from a few sources, not all agreeing. One thing I know is that a happy, impish kid became as much a victim as the poor child who died. The dead boy's mother called Art a murderer; the other kids taunted him, and called him worse; and Art simply forgot what he'd learned about reading.

My grandparents, frantic that he might be traumatized even more, scraped the money together to send him to a Catholic school for boys. There he met a Brother, who listened, and finally taught him to read again using comic books. The problem was that Arthur felt ostracized now, not only by his peers, but by his family as well.

From the boys' school, he went to Essex Aggie, and from there into the U.S. Navy, only to ultimately become a weapons expert and fight in Korea and then Vietnam. Except when he was home on leave, he never came home again, until he retired after twenty years and after adventures as fabulous as those from Kipling.

He never got so that he could spell properly, but the letters he sent me were full of fascinating information! By third grade, I knew the difference between the Peloponnesus and Polynesia, between the fiords of Norway and the firths of Scotland, Guyana and Ghana, Ecuador and Equatorial Guinea, and all thanks to Arthur's letters to me, all written on the back of map stationery.

David, the youngest of my mother's siblings, now lives in Florida, and is semi-retired. His son, my cousin, has a son – the only one so far, but there are so many Neals that you just never know.

Always Chasing Rainbows

by
Dick Howland
(*Gloucester Daily Times*, March 11, 1993)

As I wrote in this column one year ago, I saw my father only three times in my life: once when I was five, again when I was twenty-five, and finally when I was thirty. The total time we spent together was less than five hours. But we almost met just after my twelfth birthday in the summer of 1935. Had it happened then, I believe we'd have truly become father and son.

My parents separated when I was four. My father moved to New York City in 1927 and lived there until he died in 1954.

By the mid-1920s, father had become a nationally and internationally known show biz personality. He was a singer, actor, vaudevillian from a chorus part in the original production of Victor Herbert's *The Red Mill* to *Irene* to a headliner in an act that toured 46 of our then 48 states, Canada, and England. He sang at the Brown Derby and the Hippodrome in New York City. But he left his family in Lynn.

Over time, singers and songs have propelled each other. From 1918 through the early '20s one singer was William Howland and the song was "I'm Always Chasing Rainbows." The melody was based on the second theme from Chopin's piano piece, "Fantasy-Impromptu." The lyrics were written in 1918 by a Tin Pan Alley music man, Joseph McCarthy. My mother said this song was written for my father to introduce. He did and the results were mutually momentous.

By the summer of 1935, vaudeville and the economy hadn't seen good times for years, nor had I seen my father. But I had been writing him for months and he had always replied. Late in June I asked if I could visit him. The answer was yes. The family was stunned but scraped together the money for my trip.

On a beautiful August morning I took a bus to Haymarket Square in Boston, walked to South Station and boarded the train to Grand Central Station.

Looking out the train window for hours, I remembered the last time we had met he took me to breakfast at the nifty old Huntt's restaurant in Central Square, Lynn. I thought this time we'd eat in Times Square, New York, since my father now lived in a one-room apartment not far from 42nd Street. I just hoped I could help myself again to all kinds of fresh fruit sitting in shallow bowls, white with red borders, themselves sitting in little drifts of crushed ice. Besides, maybe this time he'd sing for me.

In late afternoon we pulled into Grand Central. The train-car I was in seemed a football field away from the nearest station entrance, so I ran all the way. Just inside I stopped and started to look around this multi-storied, horizon-filled maxi-mall. I saw offices, restaurants, stores, shoe-shine spots, and a theater.

Halfway through this panorama, a man came up to me and asked, "Are you Dickie Howland?" When I answered he said, "I'm Mr. Kenneally, a friend of your father's. He got your letter too late to cancel an important appointment. He's sorry but he won't be able to see you this time."

He shook my hand and was lost in a crowd moving away and I was lost again in a father moving away.

What to do? I wandered all around the first floor of Grand Central until I spotted a small office with a sign in the window: Travelers Aid Society. Immediately they became my home away from home and saved my one-day trip to the wilderness.

The Travelers Aid Society representatives cared for me like older sisters. They told me my next train home would be leaving early the next morning. They gave me money for supper in a station restaurant and a ticket to see a movie in the station theater. They told me to sleep on a big nearby oak bench where they would watch out for me all night and they gave me a big pillow.

Now I found out that the Travelers Aid Society began in St. Louis, MO, in 1849 to respond to people in desperate need as they journeyed across America to the California Gold Rush. The mayor of St. Louis left all his money to the Society, which became nationwide. The Boston office opened in 1867. Now there are sites at Logan Airport and on East Street across from South Station. The Grand Central Station site is gone but the Society has offices in Times Square and the Kennedy International Airport.

I'm still chasing rainbows but, unlike the lyrics, my chasing has not been in vain. I've caught up with a lot of rainbows, beginning with the Travelers Aid Society.

Before I boarded the train to take me back home 58 years ago, I stopped at the Society's office and thanked them.

But I've never thanked my father.

The Burns Family at 39 Stone Street

by

John Burns

When the Burns family piled out of our car at our new home in Saugus in 1926, at 14 Stone Street, later to be 39 Stone Street, fresh from the gritty streets of Cambridge, I was giddy with excitement at what I was witnessing. A new world! I was mesmerized with the woods that surrounded our house with Giant Rock looming up in the middle of it, birds serenading us, and Kenwood across the way, also known as *The Bluff*," towering over Hurd Avenue, its skyward rise foreign to my urban eyes.

The first impressions of the rest of my family I can only wonder about: our parents, Ellen and John E.; my brother Bob, a first grader; and my sister Rita, an infant. Brother Jim was to be born years later.

There lay ahead of us a wonderful life in our new town. In those years there were numerous families like ours in Saugus, presided over by immigrant parents, excited by the prospects of what this country offered them and, above all, their children.

As I reflect on my life, my schooling, my four years in the navy, my family life with Ellen and my son, David, my involvement in town affairs and my six decades in the Saugus School System, they have indeed been happy years.

Then recently I came across the words of a friend who in speaking at a class reunion said, "Life must be lived forward…, even though it can only be understood backward."

I have found looking backward a rewarding experience, offering me a new perspective on the lives of me and my siblings, but eye-opening insights on the lives of my immigrant parents.

The love and respect I felt for them took on a new dimension as I thought of them and the fullness of their lives, beside which their children's lives seem pale and ordained. Theirs as immigrants, founded on courage and vision, were adventures without fanfare. Unassuming and unselfish, they were the inspirational underpinnings of our family.

Robert

My brother Bob, next in age to me, from infancy had an active approach to life. Urban Cambridge where we lived was fertile territory. He liked to wander, to investigate the environs. Even as a toddler he had good moves, knew how to slip away.

He was in his glory, one day, when my mother tracked him down and found him at the corner drugstore. He was up on the counter, a pre-schooler, with a cigar in his mouth, doing an awkward dance routine for a group of amused customers.

On another, later, occasion, she found him at the railroad end of Porter Street, sitting five feet from a seemingly endless freight train, pitching coal at the train as it passed. Time to move to Saugus!

Years later in Saugus he found his action on the football field. Known as "Trigger Bob" or "Bazooka Bob," he was a scoring machine in his high school career, but the touchdown best remembered was the one he scored in 1938 against Melrose, the first touchdown scored in the new Stackpole Field. He was an early Saugus High School Hall of Fame selection, and was a true representative of the golden age of Saugus football.

His reputation as a crushing fullback and his All-Scholastic selection by *The Boston Globe* and *The Boston Herald* drew Frank Leahy, football coach at Boston College (and later coach at Notre Dame) to 39 Stone Street on a recruiting visit. After a year at Seton Hall Prep in New Jersey, where he won All Metropolitan Team honors as a fullback, Bob enrolled at Boston College where he played on the football team until he enlisted in the Coast Guard in World War II

The Burns Gymnasium at Saugus High School is named in his honor.

His career was spent as a sales representative for H. Childs Company. He was Sales Manager for New England and upper New York State. He died in 1972, leaving his wife Ginny and his son, Robert Jr.

A memory of Robert which I cherish:

A follower of Saugus High football, 12 year old Herbie Upton (well known later as Dr. Herb Upton) had a portion of a leg removed as a result of a sporting accident. Hearing of the tragic event and that he was Herbie's "hero," Robert paid him a visit with an autographed football. It was the first of his many visits as their friendship grew.

Rita

Rita was only 18 months old when we moved to Saugus. In time she came to share the excitement I felt about the beautiful setting of our home, reminding her of Frost's words… so "lovely, dark, and deep."

She remembers the single, twisting, rising path to the beauty and mysteries of these woods. The path to Giant Rock, where the boys and girls of the neighborhood held their May parties, to the high bush blueberries which our mother did wonders with, to all the wild flowers including the lady slippers, so coveted that the law protected them from plucking. She remembers the rabbits, so numerous then, and wonders where the fireflies have gone that used to light up the nights.

She is sad to see the beauty that we had in our neighborhood and in all of Saugus leave us a little bit at a time.

Another side of Rita, her cosmopolitan side, came into being when she went to work for Liberty Mutual in Boston, a career that she retired from in 1995 as Senior Litigation Information Specialist.

A lover of nature and of gardening, she loves as well what the city has to offer, the diversity of personalities she met at work and the theater, opera, museums and sporting events to be found in Boston.

Like our mother, Rita is an independent spirit. She has a disposition to tell things as they are, and the verbal gifts to say it right. She has a hearty appetite for politics and for the unique language employed by its practitioners in masking where they are on given issues or where they are heading.

A life-long Democrat she wonders if this had its origin at a pre-school party, when given a choice between Al Smith and Herbert Hoover lollypops, she chose the Al Smith lollypop.

In retirement she keeps up her life-long interests, keeps in touch with her old friends, and makes new ones. This comes natural to her. She is a generous, imaginative hostess and a lively companion.

She has a special place in her heart for her nephews, Robert Jr. and my son, David, who have a mutual feeling toward her and spend many happy hours in her company.

Jim

Jim, a gentle giant, many years younger than I, was my mentor as often as I was his. He spent some time in college classrooms, but not nearly enough to account for the knowledge he possessed and the wisdom he had acquired. In conversation he was equally at ease with Count Basie or Beethoven, with Frost or Yeats. Politics appealed to him, particularly as it related to the foibles and shortcoming of those engaged in it. The Nixon era fascinated him.

He played high school football, basketball, and baseball, and as a hitter at Stackpole Field launched a few rockets well beyond the boundaries of the field into the vicinity of Fiske Road. He maintained his interest in football, basketball and baseball in his adult life and discovered horses as well. From time to time he and his friends would visit Saratoga, there to lean on the railings to study and evaluate the world's best horseflesh.

Intellectually he deplored T.V., yet somehow he found The Three Stooges irresistible.

He won friends easily and was loyal to them. They loved him for his wit, his nimble mind and the generosity of his spirit. Conversation tended not to be sober or grim in his presence. His disposition was to be playful, never frivolous. Their meeting never ended on a sour note.

He seemed always to be the center of their gatherings, and when he died, these gatherings and the bridge club he was part of died too. I am always happy when I meet his friends and witness the lasting nature of their loving memory of him.

In both his personal and professional life, he fought for the underdog. Those who worked for him revered him for his unfailing good humor, his sense of fair play and the fun he was to be with.

My most lasting memory of Jim, I think because it was so typical of his caring nature under trying circumstances, occurred at the front door of his house as we were leaving for one of his last visits to the hospital. His heart must have been heavy as he thought of what he might be facing in the days ahead. As we started toward my car, he became aware that Rita's cat was following us. He turned back. Gently, and without comment, he lured the cat back, saw her back to the safety of the house, stroking her back, talking cat talk. He closed the door on her and we moved on to my car.

Aunt Mamie

Aunt Mamie – Mary Josephine Regan – was my mother's younger sister and the only one in her family to join her in this country. No record of our family would be complete without including our Aunt Mamie. She was a beautiful woman with sparkling blue eyes, always registering merriment with a touch of mischief, her skin a perfect mix of pink and white. Her grooming was always immaculate.

For a number of years she came to our house each Sunday by public transportation with a box of chocolates in her hand. Her arrival was always looked forward to; each visit was a celebration.

She never, or rarely, stayed overnight. As a city girl, totally at ease on the tough streets of Cambridge, day or night, she was intimidated by the peaceful streets of Saugus after dark. "The crickets would not let me get to sleep if I stayed overnight," she said, "and the damned chirping birds would have me up at dawn." Ironically in Cambridge she lived next to a firehouse.

We cherished every moment she spent with us, in our house, or on trips we took with her, to the movies, to Charlie Hecht's afterwards for ice cream, to Nantasket Beach and – lucky Rita, the trip she took with her to the World's Fair.

Her outer grace and beauty were more than matched by her inner goodness and generosity. No present she ever gave us seemed casual, but always a thoughtful, inspired choice for a very special person. The love she felt for us and we for her was so abundant that as children we were not rivals for her affection. There was enough love to go around.

Dear Aunt Mamie – she is in Riverside now with other members of our family.

The Oak Table

These days, Rita, ever a gracious hostess, makes frequent use of this oak table around which to gather her family or her friends to entertain them on holiday occasion or other festive events.

This round oak table, predating World War I, was for a time splay-legged, tilted, and missing critical hardware. Eventually this handsome sturdy piece, the Burns dining room table, was restored to the classic state it deserved through the skillful and generous services of our neighbor, Roy Moore.

And then, for a number of happy years, it took on an added function as the centerpiece, the gathering place for a think tank body of pundits, who convened there on weekend mornings to give weighty thought, not to be left to lesser minds, to a variety of critical matters: sports, political shenanigans, and random social events.

These ranks evolved over the years, blending friends of Robert, of Jim and of mine. During these years there were present such friends as Ray Kelly, Ted Brierley, Angie Nicketakis, Bud Murphy, Mike Harrington, Bob Wentworth, Danny Sharp, George Witham, Jim Blunt, Ron Carlton and numerous others.

The assemblage thinned out after our mother died in 1972 and closed down completely when Jim died in 1988.

Mother

My mother, Ellen Regan, came to America alone at the age of twelve to live with cousins in Cambridge. I think of the courage it took to do that! At that age, what had she heard about America to move her to come here looking for a new life? In leaving Ireland, however, she still brought a lot of Ireland with her. And in the end there wasn't much she missed of what this country had to offer. She was in line to vote when in 1920 the 19th Amendment granted her that right.

She spoke up for any cause she believed in and tangled with any politicians whose actions in her opinion jeopardized her neighborhood. They listened to her and seemed to like her, or at least professed to.

We were all grateful that she was very much at home in the kitchen. It was exciting to us all as we climbed the stairs to our house to catch the aroma of her abundant loaves of bread on baking day.

She loved sports. Football captivated her; she never missed a game when Robert and Jim were playing and continued to attend when their playing days were over.

At sporting events, she took in the whole scene. As a Red Sox fan, returning from a World Series game with the St. Louis Cardinals, in her summation of the highlights of the day, she gave a glowing picture of the Boston Mounted police and their handsome horses present at the game.

One night at a Boston Celtics game with Jim she found herself sitting next to a Chinese fan who spoke no English, a challenge to her will to communicate. By game's end, she and the Cantonese gentleman were somehow communicating freely about their beloved Celtics.

Her high moral standards occasionally ran counter to her compassionate nature. She detested alcohol, but had a warm spot in her heart for the victims of it. When an errant uncle arrived at our house after tippling, she persuaded him not to leave before sleeping it off. Shortly a fire broke out in his room. She found her way through the thick smoke and modest flames to bring him to safety. She readily accepted his explanation that the bed was on fire when he got into it.

Her children doted on her, were her constant companions at games, meals out, and all sorts of social events. In her later years, her eyesight failing, Rita daily read the papers to her, for while her vision was declining, her interest in the events of the day was not.

I have warm memories of the very numerous occasions when I would drop in and have a cup of coffee with her after a day at school. She was getting older, but these were not sick room visits, just the meeting of a mother and son who enjoyed each other's company. Our conversations were free flowing, but there was a common topic which kept popping up, dealing with Saugonians in the public eye, conspicuous for their ego, for their pretentiousness and for their craving for the limelight. It was always fun revising the cast of characters as worthy newcomers came to the fore.

When my mother died, the memories of these meetings softened a little the grief I felt at her passing.

Father

My father came over from Ireland as a young man with a verse in his pocket, bidding goodbye to Ireland and a dream in his heart of what he would seek and find in America.

I have only the haziest recollection of him in the years we lived in Cambridge before moving to Saugus in 1926.

He was a private man, to be known by his actions, not by his words.

Like the rest of us he loved Saugus, but he didn't talk about it. Despite a five and a half day work week, he spent hours in our yard, planting fruit trees, grape vines and vegetables. He was a generous provider and gave us a good life with his hard work and sacrifice.

At Christmas, an exuberance, which normally he kept well hidden, emerged in his elaborate preparations for making Christmas a joyous occasion for his family. It started with the Christmas tree, tilted and precariously sitting in a bucket of coal in our living room. He was scarcely able to control his excitement when he awakened us on Christmas morning to announce that we had just missed Santa Claus.

As we, his children, grew up, he didn't talk much about it, but we were aware that he was proud of us and what we were doing.

He had his own style of expressing the affection he felt for all his children. One gift I could never forget I received from him when my ship was anchored at a Pacific Island in World War II: a bag of apples from a Stone Street tree, in a brown paper bag, open on arrival, addressed to me in the care of my ship, the USS *Carlson*. The journey of that bag defies explanation.

I am sorry we didn't talk more about our lives together and to know earlier the full dimensions of our father and to know that the good things that happened in our lives didn't just happen.

I see better now the sense of responsibility which governed my father's life, the role he played as the oldest of 11 siblings, the devotion he had for his parents who lived in Lynn, the $10 dollar bill he slipped into his mother's prayer book in each visit, his loyalty to his church and his active work on many charities, delivering food to the needy, and the dedication he gave to his job as manager of two office buildings in the shoe district in Boston. He rose at 5 A.M. to prepare for his trip to Boston. Blizzards would not keep him from his work, as on one occasion when he walked through the blizzard to East Boston to find transportation to downtown Boston and his work.

I found it touching that my sister Rita, who as a child found him too strict and perhaps distant, learned by degrees the full worth and warmth of our father.

It has been rewarding to me to look backward, to understand that our parents were more than providers and observers of our lives, to see the part they played in shaping our lives with plans and dreams we never heard of, without any lectures that I can recall.

But what pleases me most about reflecting on this is that they were aware, as maybe I was not, of the fullness of their lives and of the fact that as immigrants they had found in their lives what they had been looking for in America.

The Rossetti Family

Four Generations in Saugus

by
John Burns

On my arrival in Saugus in 1925 as a fourth-grader fresh from the gritty streets of North Cambridge, I was over-whelmed by the rustic beauty of my new home town. I had an insatiable appetite to know more about Saugus and to know more about those who lived here.

At some hazy interval after my arrival, I became aware of an intriguing figure whom I would see in Cliftondale Square, a woman dressed in black, who came down from Baker Hill each day to attend morning mass at St. Margaret's Church.

I never met this woman, but eventually came to know that she was Mrs. Tomasina Rossetti, wife of Angelo Rossetti. They had moved here from East Boston to take up residence at 12 Summit Avenue, on the top of Baker Hill, in a house built by Angelo and a group of his friends.

Angelo and Tomasina arrived in Saugus with three children, Joseph, Louis and John, who in the years ahead were joined by six more siblings: Mary (whom I knew as Mary Lunt), Peter, Anthony, Patrick, Alexander (Sandy), and Emanuella (who preferred to be called Catherine and came to be called Kay). The second generation of Saugus Rossettis!

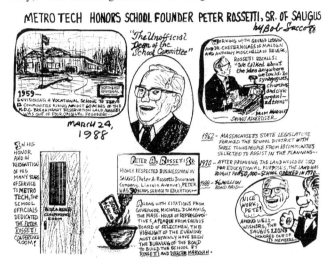

The offspring from this second generation of Saugus Rossettis are numerous. To illustrate, my modest research has led me to learn that my friend, Patrick, and his wife have 11 children. And not just Patrick. This extended family is truly extended.

Reality, in light of this, dictates that in writing this account of the Rossetti family I should focus on those family members whom I know or know of best: Peter Sr., Peter Jr., Louise, Patrick, Anthony, Joe (The Mayor of Cliftondale), Mary Lunt and her daughter Marie.

Peter Rossetti, Sr.

Peter and I graduated from Saugus High School in 1934. I was a "bookworm," and I'd guess he was too, and he had numerous after school jobs gathering money in for college expenses. In any event I can't recall our rubbing elbows much, if at all, prior to his heading off to Boston University and my heading off to Boston College to prepare for our careers.

In the early stage of his career Peter worked as an accountant for W. B. Hastings and for Fred England at the Standard Insurance Company. He was biding his time.

He saw what he thought was an opportunity to start his own business, this at a site on the Post Office side of Lincoln Avenue. To his disappointment, promises which had been made to him were broken and the plan dissolved. But Peter persisted and adjusted to the circumstances.

His next plan was more extensive and was successful. When the site of what was Braid's Market became available, Peter, as a Director of the Credit Union, obtained it and expanded the space and operation of the Credit Union.

The family home of Fire Chief Tom Nolan then became available. Peter bought it, razed it and established the Rossetti Insurance Agency at this site, a landmark in Cliftondale Square to this day.

In the years that followed, despite the growing demands of business upon his time and energy, he assigned a substantial portion of his life to the service of his community as a member and chairman of the Saugus School Committee, as a member of the Town Meeting, as a member of the Board of Appeals and as a supporter of youth activities. His service always had the stamp of service on it, never a hint of *climbing the political ladder.*

I think it would be commonly acknowledged that the crowning achievement of his life was the part he played in the establishment and success of the Northeast Metropolitan Regional Vocational Technical School. The hundreds of young people who leave that school and build substantial careers based on what they learned there are, and will be, living testimony to the vision and work he gave to make that possible.

Chief Nolan's house making way for the Rossetti office.

He was on the original committee planning this school and was chairperson of the committee in their second year of operation, and was still a member of the committee until his death.

By nature there is a built-in resistance to a Vocational School budget as it comes to a local town meeting for approval. Until his death in 1993, Peter fought this fight annually, diligently and successfully.

Peter Rossetti, Jr.

Peter Jr. was appointed to succeed his father upon his death in 1993 and has continued to hold the position in subsequent elections. In this, and in other aspects of his dedicated service to the community, and in his stature as a businessman, there is a remarkable parallel in evidence between father and son. It is not slavish imitation at work in the life style of Peter Jr., but rather the natural emergence of the energy, character and civic conscience common to them both.

Louise Rossetti and son Peter.

Louise Rossetti

Louise, widow of Peter Sr., and mother of Donna, Suzanne and Peter Jr. She is a strong, spirited woman with a very healthy view of life. She enjoys explaining that Louise Bernazani Rossetti before her marriage **wasn't**, for a brief time, a Bernazani. Going to work for Ryerson Steel Company after her graduation from Burdett College and before the era of political correctness, she was, in the interest of brevity and clarity, given the name of Burns by her company. Her friend, Lucyna Nowosielski, became

Lucy Nowell, and another friend, Sophie Monkewicz, became Sophie Monson. I think she found it amusing, devoid of any ethnic sensitivities. She would be bad company for those who enjoy making mountains out of molehills. To see her delightful lighthearted nature, just get her started on Italian food vs. non-Italian food, Northern Italian food vs. Southern Italian food, or talk to her about her long distance running, which she seems to look on as fun, a hobby, not an obsession.

Patrick and Anthony Rossetti

Patrick and Anthony I remember fondly. It was always for me a nice moment in a day to run into Pat in the vicinity of Essex and Felton Streets, and Anthony in the Center near Jasper Street. It has not occurred lately, but I do remember their warm smiles and the impression they would leave with me that these brief meetings were pleasant to them too.

Joe Rossetti, The Mayor of Cliftondale

Joe Rossetti, father of Joseph Jr. and John, was the oldest of the nine children of Angelo and Tomasino. He became an influential figure in his adopted town, and eventually being acclaimed as The Mayor of Cliftondale.

He was, in his time, the first president of The Baker Hill Improvement Association, a member of the Saugus Town Meeting and of the Board of Appeals. He was, for years, a volunteer fireman and volunteer policeman.

His base of operations was the Back Diamond Cigar Company office which he maintained in what was then known as the International Block, later to be the site of Hanson Chevrolet, and now the site of the Mobil Gas Station across from the Cliftondale Rotary.

He owned the first Ford in Saugus, on the top of which he displayed a huge cigar as an ad for his business. He reveled in the hours he spent making the rounds of "his square," greeting his friends and dropping in to the Tumble Inn for coffee with Dave Lucey, Dave Nagle and their crowd.

He had a gift and appetite for politics and skillfully ran campaigns for his brother, Peter Sr., and Father John Creed, both seeking School Committee positions.

He was a magnet for countless political figures, from inside town and statewide, who enjoyed spending time with *The Mayor*, men like Tip O'Neill, Tom McGee, Sr., Nelson Pratt, Dave Lucey, Belden Bly, John Curry, Herb Upton, and Dr. Golan.

These were colorful days for Joe Rossetti and for Cliftondale Square.

Mary (Rossetti) Lunt and Marie

A stop at Mary Lunt's card shop in Cliftondale Square was always a pleasant experience for me. Surrounded by Hallmark cards, she was sufficient of herself to say the right thing, the gracious thing for every occasion.

In 1979, Christmas season, a student of mine, her daughter, Marie Lunt, later Marie (Lunt) Sweetland, gave me a gift book by J. Bronowski, *The Ascent of Man*. It is not a book you read once and put down. It is a challenging, thought-provoking book, which I took as a compliment that her assessment of me was that it was my kind of book, that I would be up to the challenge. Thank you, Marie.

The Browns

by
Eric W. Brown

There are of course many unrelated Brown families in Saugus. The one I'll discuss here originally hails from the Damariscotta region of Maine and is currently in its fifth Saugus generation.

My grandparents, Norman and Virginia (Stratton) Brown, were both briefly mentioned in *A Gathering of Memories* and thus I will not say too much about them here. They moved into Saugus in 1938, and had four children: Eleanor, George, William, and Norma; Norman's mother Signe (Ericsen) also lived in Saugus for a brief period in her later years.

The eldest child of Norman and Virginia, Eleanor, married Andy Mullaney and had three children: Drew, Donna, and Laurie. They didn't stay in Saugus all that long, although Donna has since moved back into town.

George, the second child of Norman and Virginia, married Carolyn (Butler) and they currently live on Central Street in an area that some consider Lynnhurst and others consider North Saugus. They have five children: Eric (me), Darren, Heather, Ryan, and Christopher. It should be noted that there's at least one other unrelated George Brown in town.

My father is one of those people that everyone just seems to naturally like. He has a very direct and honest personality, and an unerring ability to remember names. He's renowned for his cooking and he generously shares the fruits of his skills with not just friends, family, and neighbors, but also anyone he discovers is particularly in need.

It's difficult to list all the ways in which he has helped the town, so I'll only touch on a few here. Besides representing Precinct 5 multiple terms on Town Meeting, he served over a decade each on both the Zoning Board of Appcals and the Building Committee, and volunteered countless hours at Lobstermans' Landing getting it ready for use. He was instrumental in producing the first Historic Saugus Calendar, and has singlehandedly raised enough money to make it happen on several occasions since. He was one of the organizers of the big 375th Saugus anniversary celebration held in Cliftondale, and

Carolyn and George Brown.

he was likewise one of the key figures in organizing the Cliftondale Merchants' Association Customer Appreciation Day celebrations in following years. He has sat on numerous committees, helped draft several by-laws, and assisted many local organizations. At different times he's been especially active in the Saugus Chamber of Commerce, the Saugus Business Partnership, and the Saugus Historical Society. He even helped to build a foot bridge in Prankers Pond.

George went to Essex Aggie after junior high, perhaps inspired by Norman's well-known skills with plants. Only a year away from graduation, he dropped out, but after a year away from school went to Saugus High and earned his diploma there.

It was during this period that his mother was hit by a car. To make matters worse, his father Norman was temporarily hospitalized, his health and well-being both being deeply affected by his wife's trauma. George had to grow up quickly when a neighbor tried to get the government to take away the much younger William and Norma; he completed an apprenticeship as a machinist, and negotiated with his employer what would later become known as mothers' hours in order to keep his family together and his younger siblings out of an orphanage.

He worked at a couple of Saugus machine shops including Precise Metals and Arco before founding Saugus Engineering. The story of Saugus Engineering's fate is interesting: one day a regular customer walked into the shop and asked my father how much he wanted to sell the business. My father, taken by surprise and half thinking it was a joke, offered a number that he thought was a little high. The customer immediately accepted and wrote out a check as a down payment. It turns out that this particular customer had on paper been doing contract work for the military, but had in practice been subcontracting out everything. They needed to acquire a manufacturing facility fast in order to stay in business. My father stayed on with them long enough to help transfer the business (which they ultimately moved out of town).

He did some contract work for Litton Medical Systems and it eventually grew into a full-time national position as a service engineer. From that point on most of the rest of his career was in the medical industry, with just an occasional period away.

During one of those periods he bought Allan's Hardware in Cliftondale Square and renamed it Saugus Hardware. He didn't stay away from medical engineering long, though, and before long sold the hardware store (which became a True Value affiliate) and started working for Toshiba Medical as a national field service engineer, a position he held for many years.

During his years in the medical industry he had observed two key facts: the first was that hospitals had long periods of downtime when they upgraded oncology simulators, and the second was that one particular model of oncology simulator could be mounted on a regular floor without specially prepared troughs. He came up with the unique business idea of renting out interim simulators that would be able to service patients while their regular simulator was being replaced, and GBA, Inc. was born. We (my brothers and I often helped on these jobs) would install an interim simulator over a weekend, and the hospital would find it ready for inspection on Monday morning. GBA has since expanded to provide mobile simulators that permanently ride around in trailers; these get hauled to hospitals by semis and require less work to set-up and tear down.

GBA (and my father along with it) is still active today.

He's had some interesting experiences throughout his years in the oncology business. He's worked in all 48 continental states plus most of the Canadian provinces.

It was an interesting, but tough, career. At one point his office was literally on the other side of the continent, and he'd be flying to California almost weekly (the weeks he didn't go there he'd be sent someplace else) and spending lots of time on airplanes.

My mother's family moved from East Boston to Stoneham while she was still quite young. She moved to Saugus after marrying my father; first they lived on Old County Road and then later on Central Street. Her brother Donnie and his family also eventually moved to Saugus.

My mother has generally avoided local politics, getting enough of a sampling from my father. She has been involved with lots of local organizations including the Saugus Historical Society, Saugus Youth Soccer, and Waybright PTO. She's done lots of volunteer work for both the Waybright and Belmonte libraries, and she works most Saugus elections as either a clerk or inspector, largely depending upon her mood, and she taught CCD classes at St. Margaret's. She's also helped out manning the Saugus.net phone lines on innumerable occasions.

In addition to facing the challenge of raising five children with a husband whose job required that he travel all the time, she's worked at various places as a bookkeeper.

Bill was the third child of Norman and Virginia. He married lifelong Saugonian Cheryl Orifice. They live just outside Cliftondale Square and have one son, Alex, who's still in school. Bill has been active in Saugus Town Meeting and the local 201 union.

I'm the oldest child of George & Carolyn. I'm married to Nhung (Pham) and we have one young child, Ariana.

Locally I'm known primarily for founding and operating Saugus.net, but I've also served on the Planning Board (I was the first associate member after the position was first created, and actually at that time the youngest appointed official in Saugus history), been a Precinct 9 Town Meeting member for multiple terms, held positions in numerous committees, and have been active in many organizations in town. I've been both a soccer coach and referee, and am probably one of just a handful of people who've voted on a school budget in addition to having been both a student and teacher in the Saugus school system.

Prior to founding Saugus.net I worked at a series of medical software houses including both Siemens and HP. Much of the actual work is pretty hard to explain to people outside the field, but there's a good chance that you (or someone you know) have seen my work first hand.

Siemens used lots of high-end computers. The IT people there used to keep me informed about when they were getting rid of older machines, either by auction or free giveaway. The first five Saugus.net computers had actually all served at Siemens in their prior lives.

Nhung is a native of Vietnam. She lived in East Boston for nearly a decade before I met her. Like me, she has multiple degrees; in fact, we met at Boston University (where I was teaching and she was attending).

Nhung runs a booth at Founders' Day every year, and she's a member of the Hammersmith Quilters Guild.

Families of the Town

Darren is the second child of George & Carolyn. He served as a Precinct 5 Town Meeting member for a couple of terms, and has been (and still is as of this writing) a member of the Historical Commission for several years. He is also currently the president of the Saugus Historical Society, a position he's held since 2000. Prior to being president, he served as vice president for a term. He also has a degree in historical preservation and has loads of experience working on various historical sites ranging from the Longfellow House to the Jeremiah Lee Mansion, so he's the ideal candidate for both his positions.

The Brown "kids," when some of them still were.

His wife Stacey (Breda) is a native of Melrose. She moved to Saugus after marrying Darren.

Heather is the middle child of George & Carolyn. She married Paul Cole, and they now have a baby daughter Sarah. They've since lived in Louisiana, Kentucky, and Danvers in addition to Saugus; in fact, they've not spent too much of their adult lives in town.

Heather went to Quinnipiac College in Connecticut right after high school, and now holds a degree in exercise physiology.

Paul attended high school and graduated in Saugus. His father's job in the National Park Service required lots of moving from place to place, and Paul happened to land in Saugus when his father was assigned to the Iron Works. After high school Paul went to West Point, where he earned a degree in military history, and is now a captain in the army.

Paul was always interested in music and performance. During high school, he was both active in the theatre group and was part of a local band. In more recent times he's gotten to sing in Fenway Park for the Red Sox *twice*.

Ryan is the fourth child of George & Carolyn. He married Marblehead native Danielle (Lemieux), and they now have a baby daughter Rebecca.

Ryan is one of those rare people who knew what he wanted to do in life while still a very young child, and as an adult achieved his goal. He always wanted to be a firefighter. He became an EMT and got a degree in fire sciences along the way, and today he's a firefighter.

Prior to becoming a firefighter, Ryan worked for the Saugus DPW for a number of years and served on the Saugus Traffic Study Committee and as a Saugus Town Meeting Member.

Christopher is the youngest child of George & Carolyn. He worked for awhile at *The Saugonian*, both supplying some writing and handling all its layout needs. He has been active in local organizations in town like the Saugus Historical Society, and he's helped out more than once distributing prizes for the annual Saugus.net Ghost Story Contest.

He is currently in a band called The 8mm Fuzz. Bandmates include Saugonians Steve Swallow and Joe Pelosi[1], and Medway native Vicky Lariccia. It has gotten a lot of local media attention lately; in fact, a recent article in *The Boston Herald* stated that the Boston musical scene may go national like the Seattle one did back in the '90s, and if so that The 8mm Fuzz will be one of the key bands responsible.

The Patriarch of the Surabian Family

by
Harry Surabian, Jr.

One of the successful examples of one immigrating to this country after the turn of the century is the patriarch of the Surabian Family, my father, Harry Mugar Surabian.

During this time the Ottoman Turks were starting their genocide of the Christian minority in Turkey. It has been estimated that, of the 3 million Armenian people living there, between 800,000 to 1.5 million Armenians died between the years of 1915 and 1918 in the first genocide of the 20th Century. This is the background that brought my

1. A photograph of all three Saugus members of the 8mm Fuzz is actually in *A Gathering of Memories* on page 217; it's something of a coincidence since at that time they weren't in a band together.

father, and shortly thereafter, my mother, who was soon to be his wife, to the United States of America.

In his youth my father received schooling in a Congregational Church School in Turkey and therefore had knowledge of English before migrating here. He realized even then that the United States was the land of opportunity, and, as had his three brothers before him, came to Medford, Massachusetts.

Many Armenians at that time in Turkey fled to other countries in the Near East, Europe and North and South America. In my many travels abroad I met some of them and noticed how well they assimilated and adapted to their new countries.

After my father and mother married they had two children, Carl and Fred, while living in Medford. The family then moved to Saugus, which is where Carl and Fred started their public school education. My father purchased the present property located at 1-15 Essex Street in Cliftondale Square sometime in the 1920s and went into a business known as the Cliftondale Market. The store was highly respected by his customers for the quality of the meats and produce that he carried.

As time went by during this period known as the Great Depression, my father had to close up shop because he couldn't afford to continue giving credit to his many customers which they couldn't repay in return. At this time my father had previously invested in a great deal of properties on the North Shore with his partners, and as a result of the poor times, all of this was lost. It was during this difficult time that I, Harry Surabian, Jr., was born.

Zaruhe and Harry Mugar Surabian.

A turning point in our family fortune now came into view. During the Depression an act of Congress repealed Prohibition in 1923. The Saugus Town Hall had four full liquor licenses available prompting my mother to suggest to my father that he apply for one of them. He did apply and was

granted a license. The Cliftondale Market now became the Cliftondale Liquor Exchange. My father operated the liquor store from that time and through the years of World War II until my brothers and I returned from our military service. Our father went into retirement and turned over the management of the business and the building to his sons. Retirement was temporary because he and my mother purchased and operated a seasonal cabin and cottage business in the White Mountains of Lincoln, New Hampshire.

Fred Surabian.

It was now becoming clear that the first generation of the Surabians was to be centered in this building in Cliftondale Square. My oldest brother, Carl, not only worked over the years in the liquor store, but also divided his time when he established Surabian Realty. I recall the time when an individual approached me, not knowing who I was, and said, "Look at the office window. They don't know how to spell Suburban Realty!" I replied that I would tell the owner of their "mistake" when I next saw them. During this period Carl's company, with which I was associated, acquired several extensive plots of land in town, including the land eventually occupied by Weylu's Restaurant for a period of time, and a portion of the land occupied by the current high school.

Carl who was very active in the Saugus Rotary, serving one term as its president, passed away in 1986.

Fred was active in the daily operation of Cliftondale Liquor Exchange. He spent time as a coach for Babe Ruth baseball and was a former town meeting member. His fondness, although he wouldn't admit it, was meeting every morning for coffee with a group known as the "Corner Booth" in the early '70s at the Tumble Inn Restaurant which still operates today in Cliftondale Square. I recall he met with local Saugus residents including Ned Cerasuollo, Edward Hartigan, Stan Green, Mike Harrington, Dave Lucey, John O'Brien, Dave Nagle, Dr. Fred Wagner, and Frank Matarano, also known as the "Iron Messiah." Some members of this group still meet there as of this printing. Fred passed away in 1998.

I, Harry Surabian, Jr., went on to teach social studies at Saugus Junior High School and after several years became a guidance counselor until I retired from the school system in 1990. My present avocation is being a musician in three concert bands.

The second generation of the family consists of Carl Jr. and Ronald, sons of Carl, and they presently occupy offices in the building. Carl is celebrating his 20th year as owner and operator of his residential real estate business, the Essex Appraisal Associates; Ronald is currently owner of the Elder Law Center and previously operated Video Waves at the same location. Time will tell what the third generation will do in this historic building.

Many of the readers may recall various tenants over the years. A partial list includes: Ludwig Cleaners, Bob and Fred's Restaurant, followed by Riding's Grill, Paul Woo's Laundry, Kitchens by Hastings, Nick DiVito's Shoe Repair, followed by Jerry Belmonte's Shoe Repair, Braid's Grocery, Surabian Realty, and, of course, Butler Drug Store.

Margaret Daniels and Her Family

by

Edward Moore

Margaret Harrington was born in Charlestown, MA, on October 13, 1881 and she died on December 25, 1982. Her mother died when she was thirteen and her father died when she was fourteen years old. She brought up her three brothers, Frank, John and William, along with her sister, Ruth, who died in her late teens.

She later married William Daniels, who was born in Boothbay, Maine in 1880. He died in 1945. He was a horse trader and carpenter.

Margaret Daniels.

Margaret and William were burned out in the 1908 Chelsea fire and moved into a house on Collins Avenue in Saugus. Sometime later, they moved down the hill and bought a house and store on the lot where the Blue Star was located. This store was the first gas station on the Newburyport Turnpike, then a dirt road. It had a one-gallon gas pump.

They later moved to 211 Essex Street, where they lived for many years. Margaret was also a Town Meeting member.

John and William Harrington lived with their sister, Margaret, until they married. Frank lived with her, a bachelor who was often at sea. Frank Harrington was with Black Jack Pershing, stationed in Brownsville, Texas, when they chased Pancho Villa back into Mexico. He also served with Pershing during WWI in France, as did his brother, William.

Frank, a Corporal in the 3rd Cavalry, was born in 1886 and died in 1953.

Margaret and William had eleven children.

Frank Daniels was born in 1906 and died in 1963. He was married to Natalie Farrell of Saugus.

Alice Daniels was born in 1907 and died in 1964. She was married to Roderick Moore of Everett, a World War II Navy Veteran. Roderick is now 91 years old.

Carolyn was born in 1910 and died in 1997. She was married to Frederick Hohmann, who died in 1961.

Mildred Daniels was born in 1909 and died around 1972. She was married to Joseph Morse of Everett.

William Daniels was born in 1912 and died in 1987. He was a Tech 5 in the Army and saw action at Lingayen Gulf and New Guinea during World War II.

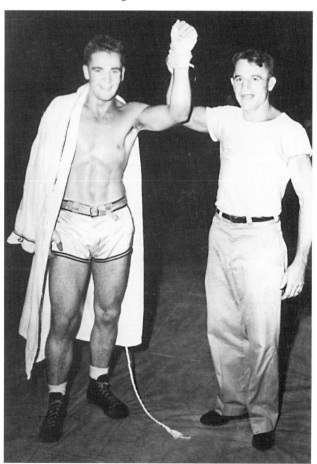
U.S. Navy Heavyweight champion, Laurence Daniels, 1944, with trainer.

Charles Daniels was a Navy diver during World War II. He died in 1985. He was married to Gertrude Fahey of Everett.

John Daniels was born in 1913 and died in 1977. He was a Tech 5 in the Army during World War II.

Walter Daniels was born in 1916 and died in 1977. He was a Major in the Army Air Corps. He flew 100 missions in a P-40 over China with the 75th Fighter Squadron of the Flying Tigers. He was awarded the Distinguished Flying Cross twice, an Air Medal, and a Purple Heart. He was an MDC policeman, Town of Saugus building inspector and State building inspector. He was married to Virginia Linehan of Woburn. Virginia still lives in Saugus.

Gertrude Daniels was born in 1918 and died in 1997. She was active in Democratic town politics.

Dorothy Daniels was born in 1920 and died in 2001. She was married to John Murphy of Winthrop. John was a World War II Navy Veteran (subs).

Laurence Daniels was born in 1924 and died in 1944. He was nineteen years old and a Lieutenant in the Marines, who died in a midair collision during a training flight in Florida. He also won the heavyweight championship of the Navy in 1944.

Margaret's brother, John Harrington, was the father of John (Iron Mike) Harrington, who played football for Saugus High with his cousin Laurence Daniels.

Margaret and William have died, as have their eleven children. Virginia Daniels, Walter's wife, survives, as does Roderick Moore, Alice's husband.

Neighborhoods

"How long since I was here?"

"You've been away as long as you think you have."

— Ace and the Seventh Doctor, discussing Ace's hometown

The Negro in Saugus Past and Present (1970)

Prepared for Confrontation for Racial Understanding Saugus, Massachusetts

by
Marion L. Starkey

That "no man is an island entire unto itself" applies to the communities of men. Until 1815 Saugus history is blended with that of Lynn, which originally took the name of "Saugust." In modern times the largest and liveliest community of black Saugonians spills over into Malden and Revere.

The South's "peculiar institution" never took root in New England, where farms were too small to profit by gangs of forced labor. In pre-Revolutionary times, white indentured servants, subject to a kind of temporary slavery, outnumbered men and women imported from Africa and sold for life. Some documents reflect confusion between the two forms of servitude. In 1716 the will of James Taylor lists four servants valued from L5 and L10, sums which might apply to unexpired terms of indenture, though one servant is identified as "an old infirm Negro man." Such terms were obviously on the mind of Mrs. Joshua Cheever in 1756 when she persuaded her husband to Free Gift on the grounds that no slave should be held beyond the age of 25.

One slave worked overtime for years to buy freedom for himself and his family. This was Hannibal, brought from Africa as a boy to enter the service of John Lewis. In 1769 he married Ebenezer Hawkes' servant Phebe, and began on the long task of buying freedom for her and their children. He had liberated the first three when the price of Phebe was upped to L40. At last the whole family became free, three sons, six daughters, and enjoyed the well-earned respect of the community.

When the Revolution broke out there were 26 slaves in the Lynn-Saugus area. That figure does not include the freedmen, and the days of slavery were numbered. In 1776 John Basset freed Samson "because all nations are made of one blood." The Bill of Rights in the Massachusetts Constitution of 1780 ended slavery conclusively, though it took the Quock Walker case in 1783 to prove it.

Saugus had one African celebrity, the famous King Pompey. Born on the banks of the Gambia, and therefore a Manding, in America he entered the service of Daniel Mansfield, who lived in the master's house at the Ironworks. In 1757 Mansfield's will not only freed Pompey but gave him two acres

close to a fine stand of white pine near Vinegar Hill on the Saugus River. There Pompey Mansfield as he was now called, lived in a stone house which still stood in 1907.

Legend has it that he had been a king in Gambia. Once a year all Saugus slaves, and some from Lynn, Salem and Boston were given a holiday to visit Pompey "and crown him again with song and dance...Each youth gathered leaves and flowers...and these formed the crown they placed on Pompey's head." In 1915 when Saugus celebrated its first hundred years of independence from Lynn, this tradition was reenacted as Episode IV in the Saugus Centennial Pageant written by Esther Willard Bates.

Did Pompey marry and raise a family? One would like to know more. There are no black Mansfields in Saugus today.

Saugus was surely represented in the Essex County Anti-Slavery Society, which gathered in Lynn to hear the famous English abolitionist, George Thompson. Feelings ran high and divided the community as they were to split the nation apart. On Thompson's second visit in 1835 to speak in the First Methodist Meeting House, the place was mobbed and stones thrown through the windows. The speaker had to be taken through a rear exit to the safety of a neighboring house.

On August 1 in the same year opponents of slavery gathered in Lynn Woods to celebrate the anniversary of the abolition of slavery in the British West Indies. In 1850 meetings were held to denounce the Fugitive Slavery Act. In 1857 Lynn got is first African Meeting House on Hacker Street, and chose August 1 for its dedication. On Friday, December 2, 1859, when John Brown was executed, church bells were tolled at sunrise, noon and sunset throughout the area.

The Civil War and the Emancipation Proclamation ended the efforts of the abolitionists. The problem of helping the Negro adjust to his new freedom was not, however, forgotten. Churches and missionary societies raised funds and sent teachers to the South to educate the freedmen. But the great drama has passed its climax. More conspicuous in the North were the new ethnic groups pouring into America, the Irish, Italians, Poles. These had their own problems, and when they finally surmounted them, some had a way of looking at blacks still struggling for an equal opportunity and saying, "Well, we made it, and it wasn't easy. What's the matter with you?"

If Saugus historians seem to ignore the blacks once they ceased to be mentioned in wills it is because they were so few. The 1960 census and the 1965 interim report both place the number at 73, the 1970 census may raise it to 80-odd, a small fraction of one percent of the total population of about 25,000. This is no cause for congratulation; Saugus had the reputation of being a "closed town."

After World War I an opportunity was made available for Negroes wanting to remove from the inner city to the suburbs by opening of the "old Miller farm" for real estate development. It was then that the clustering of Negro families began in the West Cliftondale section; between highways U.S. 1 and C1. Somewhat later, white families were also encouraged to buy and build in the community. This somewhat reduced the opportunity for black families, but did result in an integrated neighborhood, at least in the geographical sense.

The section has some peculiarities. One resident votes in Saugus, has a Malden phone number, a North Revere postal address, and pays taxes to all three jurisdictions. Roads are not improved; "they accept our taxes but not our streets," says a resident. Homes have to make do with cesspools and septic tanks for want of sewerage. Yet the place by no means reflects a ghetto desolation. Most residents own their homes and take pride in their upkeep. The rough dirt roads wind through woodlands where in spring pussy willows bloom and birds fill the air with song.

A natural community center is the First Baptist Church. Not that everyone belongs; some residents have church affiliations elsewhere, some take no interest in religion. Its membership draws from not only West Cliftondale, but Lynn, Malden, Revere and Boston; its pastor, Deacon Isaac Mitchell, lives in Billerica, where he plied his trade as a machinist.

In the early 1920s the church, then known as a "gathering" met in a "loft" or large room of a home on Broadway to listen to the preaching of the Reverend A. Herman. A white man, Mr. Herman had a little shoe shop in Cliftondale Square. In 1926 complaints from neighbors that the meetings were noisy caused a removal five blocks away. In 1929, when the congregation became the First Baptist Church, a meetinghouse was built close to the present Chateau de Ville. [Editor's note: formerly the Palace.]

The congregation has played an active part in improving race relations. At one time the entire adult membership belonged to the NAACP, thanks to the leadership of the Sunday school superintendent, Mrs. Pearl Backnall, who was also an active member of the Saugus Camp Fire District Committee and a community relations group. Since her death this participation has diminished, but leaders like Deacon Peacock and his wife Virginia are active in SCORE and in promoting exchanges between other Saugus churches.

Ecumenical meetings have been held with several denominations, but the most interesting relationship has been with the Methodists. Thrice the First Baptist congregation has met with the Cliftondale Methodists, and in March the entire congregation traveled in cavalcade to the Dorr Memorial Church in Lynnhurst. Deacon Mitchell

conducted a rousing service and the choir, which had been practicing from the Methodist hymnal, provided the music. Later there was fellowship over coffee and donuts. Dorr Memorial returned the visit in April.

Occupations in this section include truck driving, clerking, accounting, several kinds of skilled labor, and blacksmithing. The blacksmith, M.C. Brown, now retired, was employed for years at the Charlestown Navy Yard where he took pride in forging links for the anchor chains of U.S. war craft. After retirement he served Saugus for a time as a special policeman. Mrs. Peacock's brother, no longer a resident, took degrees at Michigan State and Clark, went into medical research and is now on the Boston University faculty. The only two Negro teachers in the Saugus schools live elsewhere in town.

Are social relations improving? Mrs. Peacock thinks so on the basis of the experience of her two children. As a child she attended school in Revere, where relations with her schoolmasters, pleasant enough during class time, ended abruptly when the dismissal bell rang. "I was lonely. Without my music I would have been lost." Her children get invited to parties, are asked to join the fun around private swimming pools. And her daughter Doreen Hopkins was very much a star in the Saugus High School play, *Into the Woods*, and had a role in a drama presented by the Unitarian-Universalist Church in Lynn, *The Man Nobody Saw*.

There is a scattering of Negro residents in other sections. East Saugus has several families in the areas of Bristow and Ballard Streets, though the owners of a lovely home and garden on the latter street recently died. A few live on upper Central Street; off Hamilton Street; and in apartment houses in the Center. Old time residents are accepted as a matter of course, but some newcomers have their troubles.

When St. John's Episcopal Church hired a Negro curate, the Reverend Robert Mayo, in 1962, it was lucky to have a home for his family on church property. The congregation did not at first make the Mayos unanimously welcome, and a few members even signified their displeasure by leaving the church. However, when Mr. Mayo proved very popular, especially with the young, most of them returned. Though a few unpleasant incidents occasionally marred their stay, they were eventually warmly accepted in parish and community, and many lasting friendships were formed. Mrs. Mayo served on the town's Camp Fire District Committee and was elected to be its chairman. They left Saugus in 1964 only because a particular challenging job was offered Mr. Mayo by the Council of Churches in St. Louis. He is now rector of a church in an all-white community on Cape Cod, where Saugus friends sometimes visit the family.

Very discouraging was the experience of Mr. and Mrs. Richard Janey when they looked for a house and plot of their own. At first they had been pleasantly settled in an apartment house in Saugus Center, but as their family grew they contacted realtors for roomier quarters. They were promptly steered to West Cliftondale. "I won't bring up young children between two major highways!" protested Mrs. Janey, and the search went on.

When at last they moved into a house on Sussex Street at the edge of the Lynn Marshes, in East Saugus, their troubles began. The neighbors didn't exactly send out a welcome wagon. One of them promptly put up a spite fence and had to be restrained by litigation from putting up another, six inches from the Janey doorstep. Neighborhood children were forbidden to play with Janey children; with one exception, a friendly eighteen-year old lad, the only recognition they got from their neighbors was the sight of curtains cautiously parted as they passed by. Active members of a North Shore society dedicated to providing equal opportunity, the Janeys stuck it out, hoping somehow to convert Saugus to an open town. They moved out last fall, not in disgust at their failure, but because Mr. Janey's job has been transferred out of state.

Consolation to the Janeys: two Saugus families have recently adopted interracial children who should open up neighborhoods. Then, too, a new organization was formed in Saugus in the particular interest of black Americans, in the spring of 1968, following the death of Martin Luther King and the publication of "The Report of the President's Committee on Civil Disorders." Called the Saugus Council on Racial Equality (SCORE), its purposes were the education of its members and the community about white racism, and the uncovering and eradication of racially prejudiced attitudes and practices which deprive any person of their freedom to participate fully in American life. Its members included clergymen and social action representatives from local churches, educators, and business and professional people, laboring people, housewives, students and many members of the League of Women Voters. In the months since its organization, SCORE has been instrumental in having Saugus Public Schools make a survey of its curriculum to determine the extent to which racial understanding is promoted; it succeeded in having a course in Black History added to the adult night school curriculum; it conducted a Black Identity Contest for all 5th and 6th grade students during national Negro History Week in 1969; its members distributed Fair Housing regulations to local realtors; it set up a Fair Housing Committee which would function independently in cooperation with Fair Housing, Inc. of Roxbury to encourage black people to move to Saugus; and it participated in a Fair Housing Open House where community attitudes were discussed with public officials and other citizens.

It was through the efforts of SCORE, with the cooperation of the League of Women Voters of Saugus and the Saugus Council of Churches, that the Confrontation for Racial Understanding was undertaken.

Stone Street Neighborhood

A Cauldron of Community Pride and Responsibility

by
Bob Wentworth

The residents of this small piece of Precinct Six–Birch, Catalpa, Dreeme and Stone Streets, and Hillside and Intervale Avenues–have been infected with a spirit that demonstrates an extraordinary sense of civic conscience.

Outwardly this neighborhood resembles any other within the town, but its history reveals an energy that percolates just below the surface.

These citizens, who at some time in their lives had roots in this neighborhood, stepped forward to dedicate substantial time and effort in service to their hometown.

Anthony, Earl – Birch Street
    Town Meeting, Conservation Comm. (1960-70s)

Blunt, Erving – Dreeme Street
    Town Meeting, Welfare Bd. (1930-40s)

Blunt, James – Dreeme Street
    Town Meeting, Assessor, Chief Clerk Bd. of Assessors, Playground Comm., CATV Cable Comm. (1952-90)

Bourque, William – Stone Street
    Fire Dept. (1967-99)

Bowley, Erwin (Gus) – Dreeme Street
    Custodian, High School (1940s)

Brady, John – Birch Street
    Town Meeting, Candidate for Selectman (1915)

Burns, John – Stone Street
    Educator, Language Arts Coordinator K-12. (1938-99), Chairman Prankers Pond Comm.

Chadbourne "Jo" – Stone Street
    Educator, Elementary School (1960s-90s)

Chapman, Carl – Dreeme Street
Supt. Public Works, Town Accountant, Town Manager (Temp). (1943-50)

Currier, James – Stone Street
School Comm., Bd. of Assessors. (1946-73)

DeFronzo, Ralph – Intervale Avenue
Building Dept. (1950s-60s)

Dinsmore, Mildred – Birch Street
School Comm. (1927-28)

Dodge, Harold – Birch Street
Town Accountant, Selectman, Treasurer, School Comm., Town Meeting. (1921-33)

Stone Street from Central Street.

Dodge, Phyllis – Birch Street
Town Treasurer. (1950s)

Down, Ted – Birch Street
Town Meeting. (1950s)

Dwyer, David – Birch Street
Selectman, Town Meeting. (1970s-80s)

Dwyer, Ted – Birch Street
Finance Comm., Town Meeting. (1970s)

Eaves, Joanne – Catalpa Street
Town Hall Retirement Office. (1990s-Present)

Espindle, Elaine – Intervale Avenue
Educator, Middle School, (1970s-90s). School Comm. Presently Supt. of Dracut Public Schools

Griner, Charles – Birch Street
Postmaster. (Early 1940s)

Keefe, Joseph – Intervale Avenue
Public Works. (1950s-60s)

Kochakian, Miriam – Stone Street
Educator, High School (1960s-90s)

Light, Charles – Stone Street
Bd. Health, Supt. Cemetery, Welfare League, Truant Officer. (1912-32)

Lucey, David – Intervale Avenue
Football Coach, Educator, High School, Selectman, School Comm., Bd. of Assessors. (1945-55)

Manoogian, Myron – Hillside Avenue
Educator, Vice Principal High School, Oaklandvale Principal. (1970s-2000).

Manoogian, Peter – Hillside Avenue
Educator, Coordinator of Social Studies, Town Meeting, Selectman, Finance Comm. (mid 1970s-Present) Presently with Winthrop School System.

Moore, Milton (Roy) – Stone Street
Forestry and Parks Dept., Cemetery Supt. (1953-89)

Moschella, Carmine – Hillside Avenue
Educator, Vice Principal High School. (1970-2000)

O'Neil, Edward – Birch Street
Draft Board. (1940-50)

O'Neil, Grace – Birch Street
Tax Collector's Office. (1940-60)

O'Neil, Jessie – Birch Street
Health Nurse. (1940-50)

O'Neil, Morris – Birch Street
Custodian, High School and Sweetser School. (1930-40)

Birch Street from Lincoln Avenue.

Pitman, John (Jack) – Stone Street
Selectman. (1928-50)

Rockwood, Sally – Birch Street
Town Clerk. (1980)

Robinson, Brian – Intervale Avenue
  Selectman, Town Meeting. (1975-77)

Robinson, Dale – Intervale Avenue
  Town Meeting. (1970s)

Robinson, William –Intervale Avenue
  Selectman, Moderator, Town Clerk, Finance Comm.,
  Planning Bd., Town Meeting. (1933-79)

Sherman, Jean – Stone Street
  School Comm. (1961-69)

Smith, David – Stone Street
  Selectman. (1977 - 81)

Tibbetts, Robert – Intervale Avenue
  Educator, High School. (Circa mid-1960s-2000)

Veetch, Donald – Intervale Avenue
  Educator, Middle School. (1970s-90)

Welch, Daryll – Intervale Avenue
  Educator, Elementary School (1965-2005)

What caused this phenomenon? Was it the water, a healthy ozone layer, or simply an abundance of old-fashioned pride and devotion to a beloved town?

Whatever it was, this record of involvement must be unparalleled in this community.

Is there any other Saugus neighborhood that can match this record?

Editor's Note:

Material for this story was compiled with the enthusiastic participation of many long time Saugus residents. The list kept growing and facts changing as our thoughts, at first fuzzy, gradually became focused. This process may have resulted in names being overlooked and with some imprecise data.

If so, it was a situation, solely, of frayed memories for which I express my regrets.

Reminiscences of an Early Life

A thank you note from Ralph Allan, Irvine, California, Saugus High School Class of 1953, to Gini Pariseau and *The Saugonian.*

by
Mr. Allan
(*The Saugonian*, June 16, 2005)

Spencer Avenue

Thank you, Gini, and *The Saugonian* – the article resulted in many hours of reflections, memories and, of course, deep thinking about the events and people of Spencer Avenue and some remembrances that as long and as hard as I concentrated, I was not able to retrieve – however, what is so very interesting about the preparation of this letter are the many remembrances that I was able to recollect about my childhood days on Spencer Avenue.

— Yours truly,
Ralph Allan
Irvine, California

... I was born in Saugus and arrived at 14 Spencer Avenue in 1935 (d.o.b.) and left (gradually) between the years 1953-1958 to attend Northeastern University and finally left for the West in 1958 to begin my career in Oregon. I have returned during the years, initially by myself, from Oregon and then from Ohio, and more recently with my wife from our home in Irvine, California, and, over the last 30 years, with my wife and sons for Allan family events and occasional vacations. On very rare occasions when my career activities brought me to New England, I would try to make a detour through Saugus for some very short drives through the town, some Heck Allen clams – maybe a lobster roll – and a drive down Spencer Avenue.

I was the fifth and youngest of the five Allan boys – in order of age: John (Jack), Robert (Bob), Carlton (Carl), Harry and me (Ralph) – sons of William (Bill) and Florence (Flossie, Floss) Allan. An estimated arrival date for my parents moving into 14 Spencer Avenue is around 1920-1925. Between Jack and me, there was a 21-year age difference. He was marrying Edna Amero, a SHS classmate, in 1935, about the time my mother was declaring that she was pregnant and I was on the way! All of the brothers, but me, and, of course, my parents, have passed on – but many memories, certainly, remain. Also, all the brothers, but me, served in WWII and are listed in the new WWII Memorial at the old SHS site at the corner of Central and Winter Streets. Bob, a P-38 pilot, was listed as MIA when his plane was hit and shot down during an attack on enemy facilities in Naples, Italy, on August 23, 1943. Placing a Gold Star Flag in the window of our home was certainly a sad time for the Allans as well as all the Spencer Avenue residents.

My dad, who was a pressman at the GE, had arrived in this country from Scotland, sometime around 1910 – he was so proud of his sons and their military service. When we received word of Bob's M.I.A. status, he was determined to go and find him, but, probably as a result of the anxiety caused by Bob's loss, suffered a heart attack and passed away not too many months after receiving the notice of my brother's last flight. Subsequently, we have learned that Bob is buried in a military cemetery in Naples.

The Robert F. Allan Square at the corner of Dudley and Ballard Streets honors the sacrifice he made to maintain the freedom and integrity of our country – something that Dad truly cherished as a first generation Scottish immigrant. My visits to Saugus always included a stop at the Square, where I was always pleased that it remained as a token of remembrance of Bob's ultimate sacrifice for our country. I was regularly pleased by the maintenance of the Square – and only learned recently that cousin Ron Blaisdell, a resident of Dustin Street and the only Allan family member remaining in Saugus, shepherds the maintenance of my brother's remembrance and neighborhood memorial. Ron's mother Gladys was a sister of my father and, I believe, arrived in the U.S. from Scotland around the same time as my father.

I also remember December 7, 1941. I was six years old. Bob was at Hickam Field in Honolulu and survived the attack without injury. All other members of the family were in Saugus, but soon after the attack, Jack (deep sea diver), then Carl (torpedo man) and finally, just before the war ended, Harry (a paratrooper) went off to war. My recollection, as a six-years old, of family stories of those days, included a first hand report, by letter, from Bob in Honolulu, that the pilots could not get the planes into the air to defend the Japanese attack – meanwhile, at home, there was the burning, in effigy, of Tojo – in the field between Meagher's house and our house.

I estimate that I was about ten years older than Gini Pariseau's childhood years (a great age difference when considering children and their peer group). I roamed the environs of the street, as well – but a little differently – there was so much space – we played football between Meagher's and our house and baseball on the other side of our house – with open space, on that side of the street, for almost as far as the eye could see. In fact the Doucette home, very close to the end of Houston Avenue, was the next structure that one could see on the right side of Spencer Avenue, except for the Brooks and Columbus residences on the left side of

Spencer as I peered down Spencer Avenue from #14. Esther Columbus is a cousin of mine and the daughter of my mother's sister, Lila. Esther presently resides in New Hampshire. In my day, probably because of the scarcity of homes, our playing area went from up and down the open spaces of Spencer Avenue and across the open spaces to Houston and Harvard Streets – an expansive playground, indeed, interrupted only by an old orchard located on the opposite side of Spencer Avenue from the Brooks family home – where any baseball hit that far from home base near the corner of our property at #14 was a home run, for sure!

Many of Gini's remembrances were mine as well: Veronica's Store, Mrs. Wiggins and the Ballard School – the warm spots – I have mentioned them so often when relating childhood remembrances! — the warm zones (of comfort?) when swimming in the river during the summertime – also, during the winter, a similar rather non-conventional, and rather unhealthy, play activity was sliding on Meagher's frozen (overflowing) cesspool and, as well, skating on the ice at the dump at the end of Ballard Street at "the Marsh Road." Another winter activity was that of "buckeying," i.e., jumping from one floating ice patch to another as the ice made its way (up or down depending on the tide) along the Saugus River. I generally avoided this more adventuresome feat and stayed very close to land, but was a keen observer as some neighborhood friends took more risk with the ice floe challenge – but only once do I recall a fire department rescue – right, Tom? My wife Vicki says, "It's a wonder we lived through all that!"

The neighborhood community, at that time, in addition to the families mentioned by Gini, included the Woodwards – a single father (very unusual for the times) and his two sons, Robert and Warren, who lived at the very end of Spencer where you could see for miles in almost any direction. On Houston Avenue, the Moshers – another home located at the very end of the street, where one could, again, see for miles! The Healeys' home was a little further up the street on Houston Avenue where Chuck Healey, the president of my SHS class and co-captain of the football team, and his younger brother David lived. The Adams home was still further up Houston Avenue, very near the boatyard. Adie, my age, was very friendly, easy going and, as a result, very popular. Next to the Adams residence was the Green residence, a two-girl family, both about my age. Further up Houston, near Veronicas (our local variety store) was the Smith family where it always seemed there was something going on – an active and busy home. It seemed that the kids there were, however, older than I. The Kasabuskis, who were new to our neighborhood when I was young, moved in right in back of us – older couple, very quiet, really good neighbors. I enjoyed watching a very much younger Kasabuski – I believe he is a descendant of our neighbor of the 1940s – play baseball for the Saugus Little League in the recent Little League World Series games. The Deons, a French-speaking fisherman family with twin boys a couple of years younger than I, lived near the intersection of Harvard and Houston where their home backed up to the boatyard, which also was a fun place to roam as a youngster. The Collettes were located right at the end of Harvard Avenue, and immediately next to the Saugus River. Paul, a longtime Saugus police officer, was a good friend of brother Carl. About mid-way up Harvard lived the Jenkinses right between the Mitchells (who were good friends of my mother) and the Erringtons. Sonny Jenkins was a year or two older than I; he was small but very fast and very hard to catch and tackle in the neighborhood football games. Mr. Twisden, who lived on the opposite side of the street from the Jenkinses and Erringtons on Harvard Avenue, was regularly provoked by blackberry-picking trespassers in his berry patch. He carried a big stick – literally! Ron Errington, a classmate of mine and close childhood friend, was very entrepreneurial; he ran a department at a 10-cent store in Lynn when he was still in high school; I remember working for him during one summer. It was indeed impressive! Further up Harvard lived the Fisher family; David and Ralph were especially good friends of my brother Harry. David went to the University of Chicago when Harry was there and they both spent a summer at a job in the Texas oil fields. I shared an apartment for a short time with David in Portland, Oregon during the early years of my career.

Again the Spencer Avenue article brought back many memories – the opportunity to rethink the early years and travel through the neighborhood of yesteryear, the goods and the bads – it was an interesting and thought-provoking trip, indeed!

Denver Street – Just Behind Young's Market

by
Alan Moeers

In 1940, my family, Mom, Dad, four boys and our little sister, moved into #3 Denver Street, just behind Young's Market. It became our home, our haven and our playground. Across the street lived the Rand family, with three boys the same ages as my brothers, Don, Jack, and myself. Roger, Melvin, and Donny became our first friends in the new neighborhood. We had our ups and downs, feuds and fights, but on the whole we got along pretty well. It was the Rand boys who introduced us to the wonders of The Woods. Behind the Rands' house was a veritable forest of trees sloping up to open fields with towering rocks, with pines and oaks surrounding them. Up at the top of the first path leading to the fields was the crumbling foundation of what had once been a part of a site called Unity Camp. No one seemed to know just what Unity Camp was all about, but it

became a stagecoach for us when we became cowboys being attacked by Indians, or a tank if we were attacking the Nazis during the war years.

Further up, past the open fields, above the upper treeline, was a long stone wall with a large rock strewn field sloping gently back down toward Denver Street. Off to the left and ahead of us was a steep hill, also covered with rocks, heading down to a large meadow. This became our ski area when winter settled in. We would build ski jumps over the rocks, piling the snow high so the skis wouldn't come in contact with them, and then constantly rebuilding them as the day wore on. There were long paths leading down close to the back of the Rands' house for sledding and just plain horseplay.

We met more neighbors as the years moved on through the 40s: the Popps next door, the Getchels, the Lawrences, the Wilsons, and the Decareaus around the corner. There was Bob Parlee from down the street past the railroad tracks and Bobby Waite from over on Central Street.

When World War II started, things changed, even if you were just a nine or ten year old kid. Donny Rand and I became Junior Commandos, pulling our red carts all over the neighborhood and beyond, picking up scrap metal and anything else that would contribute to the war effort. The older boys (and some of the girls) went off to war. Our brother Bob joined the Navy and went straight to New London and became a submariner. We saw the blue stars in the windows of the homes where sons and daughters were off to war and we saw them replaced with gold stars, and we knew what that meant.

These are just memories; some good and some not so good. But I cherish them all. And when people ask me where I'm from. I don't say "Massachusetts" or "Boston"; I tell them "I'm from Saugus, the nicest town any kid could grow up in."

Memories of Saugus, Massachusetts Denver Street Area

by
Philip J. Reiniger

On the far corner of Denver and Talbot Streets, where the convex rock formation stands exposed still, a blacksmith shop was located, evidenced by many pieces of mica found there. An old mansion stood atop the hill where the modern apartments are today. Atop the mansion was built an old tower for viewing in all directions. One could easily locate the trains proceeding from East Saugus then to Cliftondale by the smoke puffs from the steam engines.

Where the freight cars were plentiful on the Denver Street sidings, they held much intrigue for the young men and boys, especially on weekends. A treacherous game of tag was actively played atop the string of freight cars by the local youths. At least one fellow fell off. Some men were stowaways in the freight cars venturing off to cities west and south as the freight trains moved out.

Where the houses and red brick apartments stand today was a quarry that often flooded and was a local skating area in the 1930s. The face of the cliff near the crossing, where purple stone was quarried above ground level, still shows prevalent marks of stone activity from a past age when rods were driven into the cliff to break rock sections apart to be hauled by the donkey carts to the stone crusher.

A blizzard struck on St. Valentines Day one year. The next two days were spent digging out. It was necessary for men to shovel from the crossing, the full length of the siding, to reach the coal trucks at the far coal sheds. The coal chute conveyors often ran for days at a time to unload the precious coal from very large coal cars. The storage bins were over 25' high and repeatedly filled to capacity.

The action of World War II and Korea and beyond was the legacy of the men and boys of Saugus High from the 1930s and 1940s. Many are today resting in Riverside Cemetery nearby where their school stood. Many students from these years gave their lives for their country. The grave markers read like the school yearbooks to surviving class members. All are remembered for their unselfish efforts, answering the call to duty for their country in time of need. I cite the case of only one of many Saugus men, Frank Stanley Howard, a Saugus High graduate, class of 1935, who gave, when the prominent medium was radio, several radio addresses. One address in 1937, in the depression days, actively aided the spirit of recovery by stating facts as they were. He was known as the Voice of Youth. Soon the conscription for the Armed Forces became the major happening, and Stan promptly answered the call. He served in the army, first in North Africa where he was present at the visits of FDR and other dignitaries. Then he went on to Sicily where he received a Bronze Star and again was decorated with the Purple Heart. After the campaigns in Europe, he made a career of the army and served in Korea where he received a second Bronze Star. His service record was six plus years of combat. After returning to civilian life he was wholeheartedly quiet and unassuming, and only felt that he had performed his duty for his country.

There are many such accounts that show the character of the men and the families from which they came, the profile of

Saugus. Thus, Memorial Day each year has many lasting memories to the people of that generation.

Our Town, Our Neighborhoods, Our Villages

by
John Burns

The Saugus I knew when I moved here in the second quarter of the Twentieth Century consisted of three main sections: Cliftondale, Saugus Center and East Saugus. Central to these population centers was Kenwood with its lofty "Bluff," bounded by Hurd Avenue, Central Street and Winter Street, John Lindquist's old neighborhood, which he affectionately described in *A Gathering of Memories.*

In all these central areas we had our own neighborhoods, their boundaries well-defined, their characters self-honed. My neighborhood consisted of Stone Street, Intervale Avenue, Dreeme Street and Birch Street. Hundreds of memories linger, including that of Jackie, a sturdy Airedale whose Basque French owners, the Englehardts, would not admit him to their house until he had wiped his four pads clean on the pad outside their front door.

Saugus was an ideal place to grow up in, blessed as it was with the diversity of its terrain: its woodlands, its lakes and ponds, its rivers, the marsh and the ocean. Open fields were there for seasonal games, caves were there to be investigated, wildlife to be observed, tracked or hunted, and winter ice on the river riding the "buckeys."

Safety never seemed to be an issue; parental supervision seemed largely non-existent.

Reveling in the richness of our environment, during our early years, we were largely unaware of what lived and breathed on our outskirts, what life was like for those of our age whom we would not come to know until we reached junior high --- the kids from Lynnhurst, North Saugus, Oaklandvale and Golden Hills, from the "black" district on the outer edge of West Cliftondale where all the streets were named after birds (we came to find out later) and also to "Mosquito Ridge" on our northern limits bounded by Lynn and Route 1.

What all these places, these "villages," had in common in those days in the middle of the Twentieth Century was their isolation.

They were otherwise as distinct from one another as were the neighborhoods and sections "downtown." Each "village" had a singular character. They had their own racial or ethnic mix, their own occupational preferences. They had their own teams, their own school, their own church in most cases, their clubs, their "causes" and their culture.

But the isolation common to all these "villages" was a powerful presence in the "growing up" of the young in these sections and a healthy influence. Distance and limited transportation set their stage, defined their activities and determined their friends, and they never felt deprived. They came out of it with strong values, independence of spirit and friendships that have lasted through the years.

Words from Paul Downing to this book confirm my impressions about these "villages" when he speaks of his Lynnhurst:

> When discussing Ray Bradbury's *Dandelion Wine* with my students, I commented often on Douglas's safe, secure and innocent growing up. I too had that kind of growing up, made possible by the relative isolation of where I lived, when I lived there, my family and the people in my neighborhood. The Lynnhurst section of Saugus was bordered by woods, a large reservoir, woods, woods, and more woods…
>
> Saugus Center was three miles away – two if you walked over the hill through McCullough's farm and past the Iron Works to Central Street and the center of town. Actually, from age 10-14 we often took this journey…
>
> The North Saugus, East Saugus and Cliftondale areas of town were too distant to be readily accessible, so until we went to junior high (1949) we knew little about these areas or their denizens.
>
> Lynnhurst, then, was a kind of island where we kids, maybe three dozen of us, close in age, grew up together, with our own elementary school, our local church, the neighbors, our friends and our families (our "village").

In *A Gathering of Memories*, Frank Virnelli remembers fondly the unique experience that was his childhood and early adolescence growing up in and exploring the hundreds of acres which surrounded his home and over which he and his brother over time felt a sense of ownership in the outer limits of North Saugus.

We were "isolated from the rest of the town," he said. "While the isolation severely limited opportunities to play organized sports, the location offered a wonderful resource.

Uninhabited woodlands filled with hills, streams, mysterious cellar holes, and a maze of neglected old roads spread over an extensive area on both sides of Water Street. This provided a unique playground in which we spent wonderful days hiking, camping, building huts and log cabins, and learning to love the outdoors."

Later he returned to "his" island within "his" forest with a friend and their eight-year old sons and remembered that "no other campsite measured up to the island."

Their experiences forthcoming from their growing up in their "villages" need telling as we give ourselves to this goal of portraying a full-bodied picture of the century.

As I conjure up an image of young Frank and his brother Jim, pausing in the heavy work of gathering material for a camp fire or building a log cabin, to stir their imaginations to help explain those abandoned roads, those cellar holes, those...

Kenwood's "Bluff."

Loose Ends

I have great faith in fools; my friends call it self-confidence.

— Edgar Allen Poe

Looking Back at Old Saugus

by

Richard Provenzano with Robert South

On May 9, 1893, William Moulton Marston was born in Cliftondale, Saugus, and grew up to become one of the town's most unusual residents. To my great chagrin I must admit that until a few months ago, I knew nothing about the man, his wife and the very interesting things the two of them accomplished.

William Marston married Elizabeth Holloway and the two of them must have been unusually brilliant. According to an article by Marguerite Lamb in the Boston University magazine, *Bostonia*, Elizabeth earned three degrees, with an A.B. in Psychology from Mount Holyoke College. When she was turned down at Harvard Law School, she decided to go to Boston University. She had to earn money on her own apparently because her father didn't believe in higher education for women. She eventually got an L.L.B. degree in 1918 from law school and a Radcliffe Master's Degree in 1921.

William Marston eventually acquired three degrees from Harvard and also wrote several books. He also invented an early polygraph or lie detector in the same year that he got a Ph.D. from Harvard. His research assistant, Olive Bryne, (who wrote under the name Olive Richard) moved in with William and Elizabeth. William became the father of four children – two with each woman. The three adults and their children apparently all got along very well.

William Marston wrote an historical novel in 1932, *Venus With Us*, which dealt with Julius Caesar's private life. The book was loaded with acts of bondage and female dominance and has been described as "an erotic romp." According to one writer, Williams believed that "women could and would use sexual enslavement to achieve dominance over men." Many believe that his Wonder Woman stories furthered this concept.

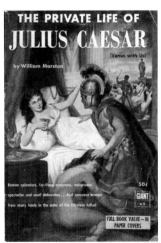

The cover of *The Private Life of Julius Caesar*.

During the Depression William Marston had trouble getting enough work to support his family. Even though he taught for a while at Radcliffe, Columbia, the University of South Carolina, Tufts, and the New York University, he apparently didn't stay long enough in any one place to obtain tenure.

Elizabeth, however, found a job as assistant to the chief executive of the Metropolitan Life Insurance Company in New York. William, Olive and the four children moved to his parents' home in Cliftondale, since William's economic situation was bleak, although he did make suggestions at Universal Pictures and had considerable influence in Hollywood in the Thirties.

William Moulton Marston became an educational consultant in 1940 for DC Comics which had superheroes like Batman, Superman and Green Lantern. Working under the pen name of Charles Moulton, William Marston created the first super heroine, Wonder Woman. A writer using a 1943 article in *The American Scholar* quotes Marston's comment regarding his creation:

> Not even girls want to be girls so long as our feminine archetype lacks force, strength, and power. Not wanting to be girls, they don't want to be tender, submissive, peace-loving as women are. Women's strong qualities have become despised because of their weakness. The obvious remedy is to create a feminine character with the strength of Superman plus all of the allure of a good and beautiful woman.

Wonder Woman was originally one of a group of Amazons living on an uncharted Paradise Island. She was the daughter of Hippolyte, Queen of the Amazons. When a Captain Trevor of United States Military Intelligence crashes on the island, the Amazons nurse him to health and Diana, Hippolyte's daughter, is chosen to return Trevor to the outside world. By doing this, she forfeits her right to eternal life and travels to the United States where she fights against the Axis Powers threatening civilization. Assuming the identity of nurse Diana Prince, she "leads the invincible youth of America against the threatening forces of treachery, death, and destruction!"

In 1942 Olive Richard, writing for *Family Circle*, discussed an interview with William Marston in which he expressed some of his ideas concerning his character and some of the theories she represented.

Richard revealed that her old Arab "protective" bracelets which she had worn for years were the inspiration for those worn by Wonder Woman. They allowed the heroine to block bullets shot at her by many Axis enemies. Olive Richard was the apparent real-life character on which Wonder Woman was at least partly based.

Marston was quoted as saying that his character Wonder Woman "satisfied the subconscious, elaborately disguised desire of males to be mastered by a woman who loves them." Marston went on to say that women "are nature-endowed soldiers of Aphrodite, goddess of love and beauty,

296

Loose Ends

and theirs is the only conquering army to which men will permanently submit – not only without resentment or resistance or secret desires for revenge, but also with positive willingness and joy!"

As the popularity of comic books soared in the 1940s, critics began attacking them as unhealthy influences on the young. Most of the charges against Wonder Woman and other characters were what one writer called "hogwash," but Jim Harmon writing a chapter in the book *All In Color For a Dime* (1970) continued to say:

> But when it came to Wonder Woman, the original Wonder Woman I mean, not the drastically different version currently published, it would be hard to deny the charge.

> Wonder Woman and her friends were constantly being whipped, trapped, chained, and tortured with lovingly delineated leather harnesses, bonds, and restraint devices… and in each encounter men were portrayed as either hulking hairy beasts… or totally ineffectual weaklings.

How much of this originated in Marston's beliefs in male-female relationships can only be guessed at by the criticism of comics in general and Wonder Woman in particular which reached a climax when an accomplished psychiatrist, Dr. Frederic Wertham, produced a book, *Seduction of the Innocent* (1954) which attacked the comic book industry with such vigor that comic book enthusiasts have never forgiven or forgotten it. In writing of Wonder Woman, Wertham wrote that she was always a horror type, was physically very powerful, tortured men, had her own following, and was a cruel, "phallic" woman – frightening for boys and an undesirable ideal for girls. While Wertham overstated his case on the evils of the comics, the book did scare some publishers out of business and while Wertham never advocated it, the Comics Magazine Association of America was soon formed and more violent and blood comics disappeared from the scene. Wonder Woman continued her adventure, however, and has remained in print ever since.

In 1998, DC Comics, a division of Warner Brothers, produced a hardcover book *Wonder Woman Archives, Volume 1*. It contained a foreword by Judy Collins, a social activist as well as a songwriter. The book contains ten stories from 1941 and 1942 featuring the earliest Wonder Woman stories. Miss Collins in her foreword writes that the heroine gave young girls a model and young boys a different way of looking at girls. "Wonder Woman taught us we could fly."

When Gloria Steinem started *Ms.* in 1972, she put Wonder Woman on the cover! A *Wonder Woman* television series in

the 1970s starring Linda Carter also increased interest in the character and plans were made to keep the comic franchise going.

A sample cover of a Wonder Woman comic.

In the year 2000, *Wonder Woman: The Complete History* by Les Daniels appeared, published by Chronicle Books of San Francisco. Loaded with color drawings and photographs, this work is a gold mine of information on the Wonder Woman phenomenon. In it can be found detailed information on William Marston, the origins of the Wonder Woman character, the Linda Carter television Series of the 1970s, a detailed discussion of Wonder Woman collectibles and a discussion of the Wonder Woman character of today.

What about William Marston and his family? They had been living in Rye, New York, since 1942, with Elizabeth working to support the family. William died in 1947. Olive, as near as I can tell, died in the early 1980s, but Elizabeth didn't die until 1983 when she was a hundred years young. Current Wonder Woman comics, still carry the words "Wonder Woman – Created by William Moulton Marston."

If We Had the Time

A Saugus High School senior shares a view of the world she is about to enter with her class.

by
Alma Nourse
(*The Saugonian*, February 24, 2005)

If we had the time! What more common phrase than this can be heard in these days of breakneck speed? In the great newspaper of life, we might read, printed plainly in large, black letters: "Wanted – TIME! by the Americans of the Twentieth Century!" The spirit of haste had indeed seized all classes – the college student, the businessman, the lawyer, the society leader, the housewife – everyone in fact. In this day, the world is ruled by the Great God Hustle, who alone watches placidly as his minions rush hither and thither, their faces lined with worry and care – some in stern reality in the pursuit of the nimble dollar – others dragged onward irresistibly in the eddying whirlpool of Humanity.

Where can time fly more rapidly than in our great cities? As one prominent stockbroker of New York remarked: "We live with a ticker-tape in one hand, a timetable in the other and a newspaper constantly before our eyes." Have you ever stood in the subway or elevated station of some large city and watched the great jostling crowds that wait impatiently for the coming train? When the latter arrives, with a great rush, they are upon it and sometimes one narrow, little door is invaded by a surging mob of men, women and children. Another train might arrive in a few moments, but even those who have time enough to spare, perhaps, must rush along with their speedy neighbors. Why wait a few moments for another train, when, with a little hurry and pushing, you may squeeze into the already crowded one before you.

If, as we are told, the age we live in makes such great demands upon us, both physically and mentally, not the least of these demands is made upon our brains and the system over which they preside. From this source, arise the many nervous ailments of our generation. The man or woman of today, overwhelmed by the manifold duties of life, is called a *neurotic* subject. But by this, I would not imply that we are invalids – Oh no! merely that as a race, we are much more addicted to nervous ills than were our grandparents in the slow, peaceful existence of long ago. As a result of this mental strain appears the demand for holidays and certain periods of relaxation, not necessarily rest, for the bow, stretched taut for too long an interval, at last snaps in twain.

There are many illustrations of the mischief which this deplorable lack of time has caused. Take, for instance, the ever-increasing amount of picture postcards. You have all heard of the friend who received, in place of those anticipated long letters from the traveler in Europe, a mere piece of pasteboard, a gayly colored part of France or Germany, perhaps, with the enlightening message – "We are here for the day." Can we wonder that, on the receipt of this lengthy epistle, the friend attributes his disappointment to the traveler, and not to his lack of time?

Another fact bewailed by so many literary artists of today is that the portrayal of Shakespearian plays and other classic dramas is slowly disappearing and giving place to light operas and musical extravaganzas. These critics speak, of course, from an American standpoint, and in particular of New York, but who can blame the man, who, after a fatiguing day in the Stock Exchange or law court, prefers a light, amusing play to one which might make further demands upon his already overworked brain? This is one more complaint to be laid against the door of Time.

Ex-President Roosevelt in his views on the strenuous life, counsels the public to spend their lives for worthy objects and not in the mad pursuit of trifles. "Give the guidance of your affairs to Habit."

The old adage that there should be a place for everything and everything in its place, might be changed for our generation to "Have a way of doing everything and do everything in that way." Everyone has the same amount of time to use in his own way. As one wise old teacher used to remark: "Don't say you have not time – you have all the time in the world." But since there are so many and great demands upon our time, we must choose between our tasks and our recreations.

Not one of the least lessons might we learn from the life of Abraham Lincoln. One of his most excellent qualities was patience, the art of waiting. Indeed, many have thought that in this very quality lay the secret of his success. "Lincoln," says one of his eulogists, "knew how to bide his time." Ah, if only more of us could cultivate the wisdom of waiting! Could we but realize, as did Lincoln, our loftiest aims and ambitions, the world would be the richer in no small degree! But to most of us, this dearest wish must be denied and with a sigh, we mingle our voices in the despairing complaint of myriads:

We could not offer you the profound wisdom of Plato mingled with the sparkling humor of Mark Twain. Not yet do the chronicles of our little class approach the dignity of a great nation's history. But, when our school days have been left forever, we dare to hope that some day, if you have the time, you will think with pleasure of these, our last and best efforts.

Classmates, in the toil and labor of your future life, although perhaps the Hall of Fame will remain a shadowy dream, yet, may you strive to remember "to give to the world the best you have, and the best will come back to you." We can no longer put off our inevitable parting, we must say farewell. Yet, in this world there is too great a measure of sadness. It is in these times of separation that our language appears inadequate, and to me, the auf-wiedersehen of the Germans–farewell until we meet again, seems the most beautiful expression of love, hope and cheerfulness–all in one.

Editor's Note:

This essay was not delivered in June 2005.

This was not the 2005 Saugus High School Valedictorian, Erin Cronin.

This was 1910, and Alma Nourse, First Honors student, addressing her 1910 Saugus

High School graduating class – **95 years ago**.

This certainly gives credence to the old saying, "The more things change, the more they stay the same."

Observe the reference to President Roosevelt. This was not Franklin Delano; it was Theodore.

— Bob Wentworth

Vehicles

Drive offensively... the life you save may be your own!

— Old motto of the AADA

Getting Around Town

by
John Burns and Eric W. Brown
(with some material from Norm Downs'
slide show)

The way we travel has changed dramatically over just the past century. During this time period our roads, railways, rivers, and skies have seen vehicles powered by humans, animals, wind, steam, gas, and electricity (to name just the most important categories).

The following photographs show, in no particular order, a sampling of vehicles in Saugus, mostly from the early portion of the Twentieth Century.

Charles Bond in his Surrey.

350th Anniversary Parade,
with Helen Cutter in the back seat.

Fire pumper at work.

A mail wagon horse and postman taking a breather.

One of Frank Bosworth's Fleet of Smart Vehicles.

The Saugus Center Tennis Club
fashionably atired for a day of biking.

Mr. Edmunds in his ox-drawn carriage.

Roadside problem, Main Street near Vine.

A smiling girl in her elegant carriage.

Summer Street: Harriet and Harold Dodge in their carriage
with observers Harold and Arthur.

On Main Street, a custom-built carriage by Frank Bosworth.

Vehicles

An overloaded Hawkes wagon embarking on vacation.

Bisbee Vehicle – hearse / ambulance.

A Frank Bosworth vehicle in the building stage.

V. Filig's butcher wagon.

Grocer Lillibridge making a delivery.

Stocker Coal Wagon.

Vehicles

No longer in service.

Heavy traffic on the Saugus River.

A schooner sailing into the Saugus River.

A canoe at the Prankers Pond Day celebration.

Gull and boat at rest.

Random Recollections

There was a point to this narrative, but it has presently escaped the chronicler's mind.

— Douglas Adams

John Lumsden

Odd Jobster, Jack of All Trades, Perpetual Motion Machine

by
John Lumsden

Apparently I was put on this earth to work. Whether I did or not remains debatable. One of the first chores that I can recall was being one of the many "go-fers" for the workers at Cliftondale Woodworking and Conrad's Broom Factory on Denver Street. Often you would be sent for a board stretcher at the woodworking shop, to Chesley's store for a quart of pigeon milk, to Saugus Center to Adlington's Hardware for a rubber hammer and glass tacks. I don't admit succumbing to all of these deeds, but I know today that some wonderful men served our neighborhood in the old days.

A favorite stunt at the broom factory was for Charlie Damory, who operated the machine nearest the door, to ask one of us to "Go see Otto at the last machine and get me some strap oil."

Upon request, Otto would point to a tin can in the corner. Upon bending over to retrieve the can you'd feel a sharp sting on your posterior. Otto had quickly removed the strap used to hold the broomcorn on the broomstick and snapped it at the rear end of the unwary victim. After the laughter was over, you would immediately go looking for your best friend to get him to visit the broom factory and get your turn to join the laughter.

Somewhere in this era I recall riding on the tailgate of a Model T Ford truck selling and delivering fresh garden products on a house-to-house basis. This business was run by Bob Griffin, who lived on Appleton Street and had gardens in the area of what is now Juliette Road and Greystone Road. My pay was all I could eat, and I did quite well.

Again in the Cloverdale Store, which was located on Central Street at Webb Place (the train depot yard), I would work in the back room bagging pecks and half pecks of potatoes, that's 15 and $7^1/_2$ pounds to you newcomers. That same location housed Devine's Restaurant, Eddie Smiledge's Bar Room and then the London girls (Anne, Ida and Gertrude) opened a tearoom restaurant and were there for many years. They had had a candy variety store next to the State Theater, but were ousted when Dick Rubin remodeled the theater.

Nick Vanagels, the barber, had his shop on the right side of the theater entrance and he moved across the street beside Keystone Battery when he was required to move. Next I can remember pulling a four wheel cart loaded with bread and going door to door selling it for five cents a loaf. This was for Mr. Foley who managed the A&P store in Saugus Center, and had to meet a sales quota for his bosses. I also had a paper route that went down Winter Street, up the hill to Kenwood and Laconia Avenue, across to Clinton Avenue, back to Winter and all the side streets down to about 40 Winter Street. Mrs. Lynch had a small variety store there where one could get refreshed with a bottle of tonic and a Devil Dog. Papers at that time were 2¢ apiece or 12¢ a week. Some customers gave you an extra penny for delivery or 13¢; the good ones gave 15¢.

I had another route that took in Denver Street and Adams Avenue with all the side streets.

My dad died when I was eleven years old, Neva was twenty-one, Bob nineteen, Harry seventeen, Ken nine and Chet was seven. This was in 1931, at the worst of the Great Depression, and my mother had her hands full. Our one source of entertainment was to go to the State Theater for the Saturday matinee to see the western movies or serial films such as the *Perils of Pauline*. You could not miss a week for fear of never knowing how the heroine ever got off the railroad tracks where she'd been tied down. When I reached the age of twelve, the price of tickets went from 10¢ to 25¢. That apparently was the end of my movie days.

Not so! When ticket taker / custodian / police officer Tim Bannon found out that I was thin enough to go inside the boiler door and do some needed repairs, and clean the boiler tubes, I became an unpaid employee. Never again did I pay for a movie at the State Theater.

I went from cleaning the boiler to being there after each matinee, helping to fold up the seats and sweeping the floor. In those days men were obliged to do many things to hold onto their jobs. The projectionist's extra duty was to go out on Saturday morning and put posters of the coming week's movies in the windows of all of the variety stores or other businesses in the area. I would run into the store with the placards, replace the old ones in the window, and give the owner a couple of passes to the theater, while Ike Sanborn, the projectionist, drove the car. One Saturday the car needed gas and we pulled into a gas station to get a dollars worth of gas, usually about eight gallons. Nobody ever had enough money to "fill it up." After getting the gas Ike discovered he did not have any money with him. We solved that problem by leaving me as hostage. Ike went home and got the dollar and came back to ransom me.

When I turned sixteen I became an usher and worked 44 hours a week after school and evenings, for a salary of $7.00 a week, $5.00 of which went to my mother to help with the household. Sometime during my stint at the theater, I got a permit and worked as an assistant projectionist, which entailed loading the projectors with film and trimming and adjusting the carbon arc lights, rewinding and examining the reels of film, splicing the film found with defects. One incident that I recall came about when Rollin Hanson, another projectionist, came into work after being off for a couple of days. Usually a showing consisted of newsreels, one feature movie, one or more cartoons, previews of coming attractions and another full-length feature. It was necessary, as a projectionist, to sit on a stool and monitor the screen at all times in case the film broke or an arc failed. After watching the same movie so many times, it got boring so the antics of the cartoons were a relief. When Rollie's shift came on, a cartoon of Bugs Bunny type came on the screen. Although it was his first viewing, I had seen it several times. I knew it by heart, and as it progressed I recited the lines of the script just one second ahead of the screen charters. After a few minutes, Rollie chased me out of the booth so he could enjoy the rest of the film.

One of the features of the weekly program was "Bank Night." Every one that attended the theater could sign up in a numbered lined ledger with their name and address. Each Wednesday evening, at intermission time, a cart with a wire mesh drum would be rolled out on stage, and the manager-owner would have someone from the audience come up onto the stage to rotate the drum and pull out a numbered ticket. The manager would open the ledger and check the name against the number drawn. If the party whose name was drawn was present and could come forward "within a few minutes" they would be given the amount in the "Bank." If they were not there, the prize would go up 25 dollars for the next week. The theater had seats for about 500 people and when the "Bank" got to be over $250.00 all the seats were sold out. To make it fair, a loud speaker was installed outside the lobby area and people outside could listen to the drawing and claim the prize if present. Whenever the prize reached the $500.00 mark, the crowd outside would be big enough to block Central Street and create a traffic problem even though there were few cars on the road. Years later, when I was working elsewhere, I used to go back to the theater and run the "Bank Night" program when the owner was away.

Somewhere in this time frame, I worked at Lily Pond for Ike Merrithew. Ike had a canoe rental business on Lily Pond at the end of Summer Street, where the Knights of Columbus building is now. My brother Bob had worked for Ike for several years. His business consisted of a small 20 X 20 foot refreshment stand which sold candy and tonic and picnic items, located just inside the present gates to the K of C area. To the left and down the banking was Canoe House #1; Canoe House #2 was 40 yards farther along the shore of the pond. Each contained 25 to 30 canoes that had to be refurbished each spring (painted and patched), as well as a dozen rowboats that would be leased to fishermen.

Back to the Grove, Ike had a dance hall where the present K of C hall now stands. It was called Shadowland Ballroom. In good weather the sides of the hall were opened up for ventilation. It had been extensively used in prior years as a picnic area with crowds coming out from Boston and Chelsea on streetcars to hold picnics and rallies for various organizations. Lily Pond had two islands, one of which was connected to the main grove by a bridge. We as kids would go to the far end of this first island and swim across to the other island. We would rest on a large rock just off shore before swimming back to the main island. There was a camp on the other island and it was taboo to visit it.

When I finished high school in 1939, I enrolled in the Civilian Conservation Corps (CCC). I was sent to the camp located at Breakheart Reservation here in Saugus. At that time men were working, when they could get a job, for twelve dollars a week. The CCC paid 30 dollars a month, of which 25 dollars was sent to my mother to help maintain the household. I worked with road crews building roads, trails, and timber barriers along dangerous drop-off areas along the winding roads that were built throughout the reservation. We spent a lot of time building the parking lot at the upper pond. Off to the right side of the road there was a small valley between two knolls, which we filled in and graded. This consisted of the crew climbing into the back of an army truck, following the dump truck to the gravel pit, where with pick and shovel we loaded the dump truck. The truck would dump the load at the site and return for a refill. After several loads it would be back to the parking lot area where we loaded wheelbarrows and moved the gravel to needed locations. Once the area was filled in, and an exit built to the main road, it was necessary to build a creosoted log barrier at the end of the lot to prevent accidents. Other crews were doing gypsy moth work by cutting out and destroying the nest sites by painting them with a creosote mixture with a paintbrush tied to a long pole. After a while I was assigned to be a junior leader assigned to run the Dispensary, which gave me 36 dollars a month.

A few words here are needed to explain the chain of command at a CCC camp. The captain at Breakheart was an army captain, William Hooker Smith, who later became a general and was involved at the World War II Battle of the Bulge. He was assisted by several lieutenants serving as supply officers and mess officers, three state forestry men, a recreation director and a part-time doctor, Doctor McRobbie, who came each morning for sick call and then returned to his office in Swampscott. It was my responsibility to handle any and all injuries and sickness that might occur after he left.

The camp consisted of a horseshoe-shaped arrangement of a one-story army barracks, officers' quarters and offices, and several other out buildings, such as the garage and maintenance sheds and a building at the entrance area, which is now the location of the Kasabuski Skating Rink. On the right was a small radio building, which was a recreational short wave group's location. Next came the Canteen and small Recreational Hall and Barracks #1 and #2. Across the back end was Barracks #3 and on the left side were Barracks #4 and the Supply Office. The next building was the kitchen, dining room and Officers' Mess. The Dispensary was at the head of this horseshoe next to the road. On the left end of the building was a door going into a treatment room with chairs, treatment tables, a large pot-bellied stove and a large medical supply storage closet. Next were my quarters, which consisted of two cots, closet, table and chair. The "ward" room had another large stove, six hospital beds, tables, chairs and an adjoining bathroom. This room also had an entry-exit doorway.

One hundred feet up the hill the Officers' Quarters was located with accommodations for the officers and full-time civilian employees of the Forestry Department. My duties in the dispensary included being present when Doctor MacRobbie came for sick call, tending to anyone who might be confined to the dispensary, cleaning and making up cough syrup by the gallon and dispensing medication that the doctor might prescribe. At one time we had a flu epidemic and I had to take over one of the barracks and get additional help, as we had almost 50 people down with the flu. I remember "Red" Gorham ran such a fever with perspiration that it was necessary to change his bedding four times. Overnight he lost nine pounds in weight.

Since I gave the necessary shots and kept the records of the same, I was allowed certain "should we say" privileges in the kitchen. When they served chipped beef on toast, shrimp or crabmeat, which a lot of people didn't like, I had a heyday. In fact, I had a secret hiding place. It was in the main electrical fuse box located in the Officers' Mess area, and I could put eggs and bread and any extra pastry I came across in my hiding place. When I returned from town I was always able to have a bedtime snack. While I was there I attended courses in Boston at Wentworth Institute and I went to a welding school.

On February 14, 1940, the famous blizzard of Valentines Day occurred. That evening, when it first started, I was going into Boston to school and I walked through the woods, down along the shore of Lily Pond from Broadway to Appleton and Summer Street and then to Saugus Center. I still remember the vicious wind and sleet blowing in my face as I walked along. By this time I realized it was futile to attempt to go into Boston, so I called the camp and received permission to stay at my mother's house overnight. The next morning, when I returned to camp, I had a young man, "Red" Oteri, for sick call and no doctor available due to road conditions. After taking his history and temperature, I realized we had a case of appendicitis, which meant we had to transport him to the Army Hospital at Fort Banks in Winthrop. We loaded the army truck with a crew of men to shovel out the ambulance in case it got stuck or tied up on the way to Fort Banks. Off we went and upon reaching the causeway in the Beachmont section of Revere we found that the road was impassable due to heavy snow and high sea.

We backtracked to the highway and on to Winthrop via East Boston. We made it and needless to say the colonel at the hospital was very surprised to see us arrive. Another trip to Fort Banks was with a "walk in" from another camp who had a fever of 106. When we arrived at the hospital, he had pneumonia and we found out the next day they had to do an emergency appendectomy that evening.

Another time I got called to one of the barracks for a man having a seizure. I can remember running through the pitch-black night over rough terrain and swore my feet only touched the ground every other step. When I reached him he was cyanotic and had difficulty breathing. I was able to place a flat pack roll (army issue) of bandage between his teeth to open his airway and prevent him from further gnashing his tongue and gums. Another trip to Fort Banks. The army model ambulance that we had was equipped with folding D-ring stretchers and had a smooth metal floor. While loading the stretcher into the ambulance, I was at the head end and as we were setting it down my foot slipped and the stretcher landed across my legs pinning me in that position. I was in the position at his head I needed to be in, so I said, "Go ahead, I'm okay." About half way on the trip he started to come out of the seizure and complained of being nauseated and was going to throw up. With his head in my lap, I could not move too easily, so I had to do some fast talking to convince him that by deep breathing we could control that problem.

Another time I had an incident, which came out all right, but at the time I was not aware of the danger that existed. One of the kitchen help had a laceration, which the doctor stitched up and told me to bandage it and give him a tetanus shot. The doctor then went home. I gave the patient a small amount of the tetanus serum and waited an hour with no reaction. So I gave him the rest of the shot and sent him on his way. He came back again in about an hour and said, "I tink I got a cold." His sinus and nose area was all stuffed up and he was having some breathing difficulty. I watched him for a period of time and he broke out in a severe case of hives. We treated that with calamine lotion; it cleared up and he was okay. I had very little training at that time and did not recognize the danger of his reaction to the serum, which could have been fatal. One of the training courses was a Red Cross First Aid taught by Harold Atkinson of the Saugus Fire Department. I used to make up Browns Mixture Cough Syrup by the gallon and he would drop in to get enough to cure the whole fire department.

One incident that I recall was an unannounced inspection. Usually we had a little warning when the inspecting officer would arrive in the parking lot. It was a white glove inspection and when the expected time approached everything had to be ship shape. On one occasion I had a crew of goof balls assigned to paint white, the interior ceiling and open rafters, etc. The floors in the ward-room were varnished hard wood. When they got done, we had to get scatter rugs to cover up the paint spilt on the floors. The one surprise visit I had was when the inspecting major walked in and I had the place torn apart, with chairs on the beds and the floor still damp from washing and a pile of dust in middle of the treatment room. Instead of a white glove inspection, he took one look and said, "As long as you are busy, I won't need to bother you," and walked out. Whew!

In January of 1940 I was sent to Fort Devens to run the dispensary for the indoctrination program when doctors were examining new entries into the CCC program. We had to do the paper work and give the required shots. The only problem I can recall from there was I had a young fellow walk in one evening telling me that he was subject to epileptic seizures and thought one was imminent. We put him in a safe spot, loosened his clothing and he had his seizure, recovered in an hour and was on his way. His having an aura or warning sensation allowed him to get to a safe location and avoid the embarrassment of having a seizure in a public place.

While I was at Fort Devens the construction of the fort in preparation for World War II took place. The construction was done by two firms united for the contract, Coleman and Bowen. I found out there was no emergency care plan in operation, so I volunteered on my free time to go out on the construction site and supply first aid where needed. I can remember vividly going across the area and dodging huge Euclid trucks and Caterpillar tractors after dark, and I had never worked around heavy construction equipment. After a few days they set up an aid station with a doctor and nurses and I was no longer needed, but I had my foot in the door and I got a job in the comptroller's office. My boss was a Frank Curley, a nephew of James Michael Curley. This was 1940 and the country was just coming out of the depression. Jobs were scarce and 90% of the office staff had political connections. I still did some of the First Aid routine for the office staff, mostly "Alka-Seltzer Monday mornings."

In later years, reading the newspapers about Boston politics and state house actions, I recognized so many of those I worked with at that time. One, Mike Skerry, became Speaker of the House. I had an interesting experience of doing bookkeeping for a contract that was for 25 million dollars and soon went beyond that amount, and having to reconcile and close out the first contract. It was a cost plus program, and I once had a company car and driver take me into Boston with a 10¢ check to Brockway Smith to close those accounts for the first contract. I was in charge of writing out all the checks and getting them signed by an officer from each company, from Coleman & Bowen and the Comptroller. One Friday evening there was a check for New England Power Company, due Saturday, that I would deliver in Boston the next morning. On Friday evenings I would take a train into Boston from Ayer, from Boston to Malden Square on the Elevated Railroad, and then catch a bus to Saugus. It was my habit to get something to eat at the White Tower Restaurant. The owner Jimmy, a Greek, would always cash my paycheck ($40.00) for me. That evening I asked him to cash my check and he said "Sure." I handed him the check for New England Power made out for $60,000.00; he wanted me to hide under the counter because surely someone would kill me for that much money. I wasn't worried because I didn't know of anyone with the name of New England Power who could endorse the check.

I was in the position of being able to expedite the issuance of checks and could help a contractor get his check in a hurry if he needed it. I became very friendly with Sidney Grossman who was always anxious to get payment for lumber which they supplied to us. It was unbelievable; when we first started, our offices were in one of the newly built barracks with no interior finish, and while we were making up the pay envelopes with cash, before a check writing system was installed, we had money stacked on any horizontal construction piece that could be reached. We even had a carpenter cut pieces of 2"x4"s and put them between the studs so we could pile the cash closer to where we were working. I was paid 40 dollars a week and when we changed over the books I worked until late at night and never thought of anything but getting the job done. Getting 40 dollars a week after working at the CCC for 36 dollars a month, I was wealthy.

When the job at Fort Devens ended, I was asked to go to Colorado with Frank Curley for the construction of a plant for Remington Arms. At the same time I received a notice of a job available at the Charlestown Naval Shipyard. This was 1940, and I was 20.

Did I Ever Tell You I Had a Terrible Time in School?

I was supposed to go to *kindergarden*. They told my mother it hadn't been invented yet. I found out later they lied; we just spelled it wrong.

In the first grade, the teacher told my mother I would be a wonderful student if I would only keep my mind inside the window.

In the third grade my teacher took us to Lily Pond, ice skating. I fell down; they skated off into the horizon. Boy was I lucky that a Saint Bernard came along. Did I say "lucky" or "licky"? Some dog.

In the sixth grade the teacher called me "the Wandering Jew," just because I didn't stay in my seat. I wasn't sure whether she meant the plant or a character from literature. Apparently I was a character.

In the seventh or eighth grade I had developed a close friendship with Sub Master (Assistant Principal) Leon Young and would spend any spare time in his office shooting the breeze. In fact, I visited his daughter at his camp in Alton Bay about six years ago, and she invited me to use the camp.

Now the principal, John A.W. Pearce, he was another matter. When I went to him to complain about a teacher and I asked him, "Do you know what a wet hen is?" he appeared not to understand. The next year I was a member of the debating team, and when they held a general assembly for the debate, he introduced me as a young man that wanted to know if he knew what a wet hen was. Gee, was I embarrassed. He did it to me again at graduation. My middle name is Percy, and no one was going to find that out, so I requested that it be omitted from the graduation ceremony. Fine during rehearsals, when everybody with the name of Hester, Archibald, Luigi, etc., suffered through the revelation with their classmates. The night of graduation I became a little leery of his intentions. I went to another friend, Bill Braid, who was at the time Chairman of the School Committee, and told him of my suspicions. He assured me that it would not occur under such a formal affair. Well, John A.W. did call out "John PERCY Lumsden." Obviously the whole class was surprised, for there was terrible uproar of laughter. I think I may still have splinters in my butt from where I dropped through the floor.

My junior and senior years I was working 44 hours a week as usher in the State Theater. I was too busy to get into too much trouble. Although I did blow up the chemistry lab twice, but that's another story.

I look back at school and can remember every teacher; they were all wonderful. Some, because of my age, I did not appreciate at the time, even the wet hen.

Tomorrow I will be 83 and now they are telling me perhaps I had ADD.

A lot they know; I was good at multiplication, six children and nineteen grandchildren.

My Early Stomping Grounds

I will describe some of the locations that were my stomping grounds, yea, 60 or 70 years ago.

At that time, Route 1 was dual lane highway with farms and residential sites.

The Poor Farm property was on the east side of Route 1 where the present high school is located, and the west side of the turnpike covered the area from Main Street to Essex Street, except for a small area of residential property on Essex Street, which is now considered as the northwest exit ramp to Route 1.

There was a stream running through the property called Shute Brook. You could see the start of this section when you entered Saugus from Melrose. It ran along the right side of the road and then crossed under Essex Street at the foot of the grade. It was then joined by a flow from Stevens' Pond, crossing through the meadow until it reached the turnpike and went under it for about 100 yards. Today, most of this sector of the brook runs through a culvert under the Square One Shopping Mall. At that point it is joined by another sector that drains the area along the Bennett Highway, back to the Revere city line. The brook is again joined by a sector that feeds into it, starting at the low area along Hurd Ave., parallel with School Street, and continues along beside the railroad tracks and joins the main stream at Davis Court, and then runs along side of the present high school to Highland Avenue and Vine Street, where another stream joins in. The main stream continues flowing 100 yards to the rear of the dwellings on Main Street and at the end of Emory Street, turns south and again flows east passing under the railroad tracks through a culvert under the State Theater Building and Central Street until it empties into the basin of the Saugus River.

I give this information by trying to recall our many expeditions of exploring the source of the water flow. I may be wrong about some of the inlets, but we were restricted by the code of that time, respect for private property. Therefore, we did not trespass. Except maybe occasionally!

I mentioned Stevens' Pond, which at that time was named Quimby's Pond and was located in the area known as Cook's Woods, the wooded area west of the turnpike. We used to go up into the woods to fish at the pond for hornpout (catfish), with a leery eye open for "old man Quimby," who would chase us out. My children will remember Stevens' pond as the place that we released the canvasback ducks.

One day I had taken Janet to practice for the PAL Bugle and Drum Corps, at the VFW parking lot on Main St. While there, I noticed five tiny ducklings picking at cigarette butts at the edge of the parking lot. They seemed to be hungry, and I was able to pick all of them up in one hand. Apparently, the mother had been killed and they were on their own looking for food. I said I can't leave them there. I've got to do something! Okay, so I took them home, built a cage, and put an old wading pool inside the fence. Unfortunately, and too soon, one duck stood on top of another one and, alas, it drowned. Okay, one down. Next thing that happened was also an accident; Elizabeth wanted to see the ducks in the cage so she lifted the cover to examine them. At that time, one of the ducklings decided to explore the rest of the world and tried to jump out.

Elizabeth reacted by slamming the cover down. We gave it a decent burial.

Now we had three. You know what, as they get bigger, ducks get messier, and smell more. They are wild; they have to go back to nature. We headed for Stevens' Pond to release the three remaining ducks. At this time there was a Scottish gentleman living in what used to be Quimby's house. His name was John Shane and we soon became friends. John used to let me use his rowboat to go fishing.

We kept track of the ducks until late summer. I did not see Shane until the following spring. When I inquired as to the status of the ducks, he informed me that when winter came and the pond froze over, the ducks did not fly away, but stayed. His only recourse was to do the practical thing, so he wrung their necks, dressed them and put them in his freezer. Ninety-nine blue bottles sitting on the wall! There comes an end for all things.

The Lumsden family.

Today, most of the area has been divided into house lots, some with huge expensive houses and other areas with condominiums. They even tried to pass a bylaw restricting parking on the street. Now you don't even feel free to take a walk in your old stomping grounds.

Cook's Woods; I spent many days there as a firefighter on brush fires that burned over the area. As a boy with friends we went to an area of the woods about where the Stop and Shop is now located, and would catch large black snakes, four or five feet in length. In typical boyhood style we would "snap" them, much like a bullwhip, and amazingly we'd have a dead snake. One day we decided to tie a piece of twine around their necks and drag them along the Central Street sidewalk. Worked out fine, lots of ohs, ahs and eeks, plus the threat of calling the cops, so we departed.

Another episode from Cook's Woods; one day we discovered a hole in a hollow tree. "Lets explore," we said, so, using a dead branch, we poked in the hole. Hmm, something

soft in there, poked again and lo and behold a squirrel ran up the hollow portion inside the tree, must have been solid wood up higher because he stopped. There in front of us was a nice bushy tail. So we, Frankie Bruce or Forrest Fogg, can't recall, grabbed the tail and a tug of war ensued. One of us pulled while the other held the body, until we reached the nape of the neck and could control the direction of his teeth. We got him. I can remember at one stage of having a piece of fur from the end of his tail come off in my hand. So if you see a squirrel that has a blunt end on his tail say "hi" to it and tell him "I'm sorry."

Another time, I was in a canoe on Lily Pond (Prankers) and I saw a squirrel swimming between the islands. I paddled over, picked him out of the water, put him in the bottom of the canoe, covered him with a blanket and went to a dump site. I found a suitable box to put in him in, and then took him home to a cage. You know those critters never were social, prone to growl every time you fed them. I had three of them at different times and couldn't tame a one. Had to let them go. My friend Frankie Bruce had a pet crow and he was lots of fun, would steal anything loose and when you ran he would chase you, landing on your head or shoulders. Never tried it with a flying squirrel. I wonder?

Oh yeah, the third squirrel. This one happened in Donkey Field. So named because during the Civil War the army kept mules and donkey to haul the supplies corralled there. This area now has the Waybright School in one sector and Heritage Heights, the Senior Citizen housing, in another that used to be Veasey's farm pasture. In this area there were a few pine trees and a rocky terrain. We (I don't remember how many or who else was present) spotted a squirrel one time in a small tree. Tally ho! The hunt was on, and we chased the poor thing with sticks and stones from one tree to another. In desperation the squirrel dove into a crevasse between and under the rocks. Okay, so now we have him trapped. How do we get him out? Well, I went home and got a one-gallon empty mayonnaise jar. Back at the scene, we put the jar at the opening in the rocks, built a fire, smothered it with green boughs, and fanned the smoke into the burrow. Out came the squirrel into the jar. We snapped the lid on, and Frank Buck had nothing on us. I took it home, put it in the cage for a week or so, but it just kept on growling every time I went near, so we let it go. I think I probably should have put my energy into crow hunting.

Let Me Tell You a Story

Years ago the property that covers what is now Saugus High School and the land across the Newburyport Turnpike that has become Square One Mall, was the town Poor Farm. Highland Avenue continued out to the highway, which was then two-lane Route 1. The Tudor Mansion, the house used for the town Poor Farm, sat on the left of Highland Avenue with a work shed and storage area to the right. Across the street was a large barn that housed the livestock… cows, pigs and horses needed to operate a sustaining farm for the inhabitants of the Poor Farm.

I was twelve years old when word came that the barn had burned. So, off we went to inspect the damage. Upon arrival the sight that greeted us was an open pit with the carcasses of livestock that had died in the fire lying on the floor. Gruesome or gory at any rate. I don't recall our reaction. Now Chet, (I'll blame him) decided that since it was the height of the depression (1932-33) and food was not that plentiful, the only way to get more was to have someone else eat less. After, when we sat down to a meal, instead of saying grace, Chet, would say, "Did I tell you about the Poor Farm fire?" With that Neva would leave the table. Pretty good system I'd say!

A Fireman's Notes to A Grandchild

Thank you, *Breezey*, for asking me to give some information about my life as a *fire fighter*. (Take note, a *fireman* is one that shovels fuel into a boiler, usually on board a ship.) I noticed that you used the correct title, thank you.

I was proud to be a fire fighter. Every fire I have ever been involved with while on the Saugus Fire Department was like being on a championship football team that was out to win. It was dangerous; you had to rely on your fellow fighter, he backed you up and you watched for his safety. It always bothered me, when after a rigorous battle with a fire, somebody always commented that we "had saved another foundation."

My first fire involved a large barn on the corner of Essex Street and the Newburyport Turnpike (Route 1). It had been remodeled, using the first floor and loft area on a second floor as display areas for furniture. The attic area was an open storage space.

Sometimes fiasco occurs without intention or invitation. Unfortunately, the alarm for the fire sounded at about the same time as the dismissal of the Saugus High School. Several hundred students came out the doors of the school and saw the black smoke pouring out of the building. A hundred yard dash, and they arrived at the fire site. Helpful, you bet, pulling the hose out of the engine so it could be hooked up to the hydrant. Oops, not all of it. We had a pile of spaghetti on the ground with enough hose to reach the next county. Finding the connection at the end of a proper length of hose proved to be a chore. I had only been on the department a short time and had very little training. It is now almost 50 years ago and my memory has shrunk, but I can remember being up in the attic area with a hose line and hot tar from the melting roof coating dripping on me, saying

to myself, "What the heck are you doing up here?" The other idiot did not answer.

I've had ceilings fall on me, gone through floors, froze in below-zero weather, slipped on a roof and had my hair trimmed with a singe once or twice. Sorry, I have to go now.

Grandpa, or the Great Grumper John.

A Funny Thing Happened at the Firehouse

Some time about 1965 or 1966, fire fighter George Fyfe and I were assigned the job of painting the main doors to the old fire station behind the Town Hall. At that time, the doors were constructed of lumber about three inches thick, with inset glass on the top section, and panels on the base. The doors were about ten or eleven feet high, arched at the top and divided about four foot up in the style of "Dutch Doors." They were secured together at the top of the lower section with a slide bolt, so the top section could be opened separately from the bottom, as well as opening to the left and right sections.

In the course of our conversation George accused me of using an idiom that was in vogue apparently. It was from one of Shirley Temple's movies, who said it to show distress. It was "Oh, Lawdy," which was acceptable from a young lady. Of course, I denied it. I would never say "Oh, Lawdy."

We were using a folding fire ladder about nine feet tall. At the last door down, George put the ladder against the door, took his brush and bucket of cream paint and mounted the ladder. Unfortunately, someone who always does the wrong thing had not engaged the slide bolt that locked the two sections together. As George's weight applied more pressure against the door the higher he went, the door sprung open. Now Humpty Dumpty had a great fall, but he didn't have a bucket of cream paint and a nice shiny red fire engine for him to land upon. We spent the next hour wiping up paint from the engine and the floor. All the time, George was swearing me to secrecy.

Oh, yes, guess what I said as he was catapulting through the air? It was "Oh, Lawdy!"

Random Recollections of My Home Town, Saugus

by
James H. Davis

A Police Raid

When my father, Laurence F. (Mike) Davis, was a young man he was concerned with earning enough money for law school. His father, Ernest C. Davis, was a clerk in the general office building of the Boston and Maine at 150 Causeway Street, Boston, adjacent to North Station. The family lived on Taylor Street across from where the old fire and police stations were for many years.

At one point, Dad was a special policeman, on call whenever needed. Today's officers are rigorously trained; in those days training was informal and, possibly, inadequate as the incident I am relating to indicates.

There was word that some bootleggers were making illegal liquor in a barn in North Saugus. A raid was organized, which included my father among the officers. In charge was a Saugus police sergeant. When the officers approached, the bootleggers fled, except for one who scurried up a ladder into the loft of the barn.

The sergeant ordered my father to enter the barn with these words, "Officer Davis, we're right behind you!" With those encouraging words, my father entered. Ahead of him was the ladder to the loft. With the enthusiasm of youth he started up the ladder, then realized that might not be the best course of action. Too late, he found himself looking into the wrong end of a gun held by the man in the loft. Dad started talking to the man while working his legs around the ladder. When Dad dropped, the man fired. Dad said he felt the bullet pass by his ear. Now on the bottom of the barn, Dad drew his service revolver and fired. Dad said he really wasn't too particular about how close his shots came to the man above him in the loft. The man then threw down his gun and surrendered.

The police sergeant? He was later Saugus Police Chief John T. Stuart.

The bootlegger? No one is quite sure.

Dad took a safer job as a reporter for the Lynn Item where he met a young, attractive clerk who had just begun work at the Saugus Town Hall. She was Helen Graves, daughter of Herbert Wilson Graves and Ethel Nourse Graves. She later became his wife. After completing Boston University Law School, he opened an office in Central Square, Lynn. Dad later was elected to a term on the Saugus School Board and,

still later, served for a number of years as Town Meeting Moderator. I used to watch parliamentary procedure in action by sitting in the balcony at town meetings. I was the first of the four children born to the young lawyer and the former town hall clerk.

My Family and the Saugus Iron Works

In the late 1940s, the First Iron Works Association managed to save the old Ironmaster's House (as it was then called) from being dismantled and moved to Henry Ford's Greenfield Village in Michigan. As is well-known, the move to acquire the property was due in great measure to the dogged, single-minded energy of M. Louise Hawkes. Miss Hawkes was a longtime town hall employee, never married, who devoted herself to the DAR, preservation of the Iron Works, and the Universalist Church. After acquiring the property, the question arose as to what might lie under the slag piles (known locally as "the cinder banks"), across Central Street from the Ironmaster's House and possibly under Central Street.

The Association received a major impetus when the American Iron and Steel Association, a group of steel manufacturers, donated one million dollars to begin archeological excavations. Roland Wells Robbins, an able, self-taught archeologist who had earlier found the site of Henry David Thoreau's cabin on the shores of Walden Pond in Concord, was retained to direct the project. Mr. Robbins set up an office in an annex at the back of the historic house. Miss Hawkes devoted herself to showing visitors the house and trying to tell Mr. Robbins how to do his job. Mr. Robbins did not welcome instructions.

I saw some of this firsthand in the summer of 1952, between my first and second years in seminary, when I was hired as a guide while the excavations were in process. It was a long, hot summer. I did have the advantage of being able on occasion to go down where the laborers were working at uncovering artifacts previously concealed by the Saugus River mud. The museum where a selection of finds was displayed was a converted shed. The blast furnace had just been rebuilt and the charging bridge was under construction. A huge tree trunk had been shipped from Oregon to connect the principal waterwheel (seven would eventually be reconstructed), and the cams that would operate the large bellows for the blast furnace. I still remember the thrill of seeing the cam shaft first turn and listening to the noise of the cam operating the bellows.

A couple of years earlier, my father, hired to do the legal work for the Association, was heavily involved with the rerouting of Central Street so that the excavation could proceed. Much of this work Dad did at night, with our dining room covered with blueprints, surveys, and other documents. I think few were aware of the legal work which had to be done to facilitate the project.

Whenever Miss Hawkes had a question or, more than likely, a complaint, she would call my father. She could seldom reach him at his Lynn office, so she would call him at home. For some reason, she could seldom find him at home even when he was deeply engrossed with the papers on our dining room table.

Mother became the last clerk of the First Iron Works Association. She succeeded Miss Hawkes, who died just a few days after my father. I remember Miss Hawkes' sister talking with Ben Fullerton about Louise's funeral arrangements the day of my father's funeral at Saint John's Episcopal Church. The church was full (and quite large number of people had been at the funeral home calling hours) and I took the service with the kind assistance of Donald W. Noseworthy, rector of the parish.

When mother succeeded Miss Hawkes, following the transfer of the property to the National Park Service, she had quite a few records and other materials relating to the First Iron Works Association. Shortly, before moving to an assisted living facility, she turned these over to me with the understanding that I was to deliver them to the National Park Service. Consequently, after an exchange of correspondence, I drove down to Saugus and delivered these records to the NPS historian at the Iron Works. We went through the material together in some detail – the process took us several hours!

Somewhere along the way, we made an interesting discovery. Mother was a direct descendent of Joseph Graves, an early settler of Lynn. A member of that early family was one of the watermen who ferried bog ore from Nahant, up the Saugus River to the Iron Works! We are also descended from Alexander Gordon, one of the Scots prisoners, who were captured in battle and sent over to the colonies to work out their freedom as indentured servants. Some of these were sent to Saugus; it is known that Alexander Gordon eventually ended up in Exeter, New Hampshire, but whether he was first at Saugus is unclear.

The Iron Works is very much a part of Saugus's history; it is also part of mine as well.

Saint John's Episcopal Church

Saint John's was originally organized back in the mid-19th century. The present building, now much enlarged, was consecrated in the 1870s by the Right Reverend Benjamin Paddock, Bishop of Massachusetts. For many years, it was a mission congregation; that is, it was not financially self-supporting and part of the clergy stipend came from the mission funds of the Diocese.

My Davis grandparents were Episcopalians. I had heard that Grandpa Davis once wanted to become a priest, but family finances wouldn't allow it, so he ended up as a clerk with the B&M. At one time he was on the vestry. Dad, however, had never been confirmed. Dad came back to the Episcopal Church and Mother came into the Church when the Reverend Morris F. Arnold (known as Ben) came to Saugus in 1940.

Ben Arnold was an able pastor and the congregation grew markedly during his too-brief-tenure. He presented me for Confirmation in 1942 before he entered the Army Chaplains' Corps in World War II.

Not only were my parents parishioners, they became personal friends with the Arnolds to the extent that when, they went out of town, their children stayed with us. As a chaplain in World War II, Ben Arnold was injured when his jeep was blown up by a mine during the aftermath of the Normandy invasion. He carried a metal plate in his forehead when he returned. Although there were those who hoped he would return to Saugus, he ended up as rector of Grace Church in Medford, MA, went from there to Christ Church in Cincinnati, Ohio, where he remained for some years. He was nominated for Bishop of California, an election won by the controversial Bishop James A. Pike. At the end of his active ministry he was back in Massachusetts as Suffragan Bishop.

He was succeeded by the Reverend Frank E. Greene, Jr., who had served on the staff of Trinity Church, Copley Square, Boston. Saint John's was still a fairly small parish, though now self-supporting. The regular parishioners knew each other. I especially remember Frank. P. Bennett. Jr. and his wife. They always occupied the third pew from the front on the right side. Anyone who presumed to sit in that pew would be asked to move over so the Bennetts would have the aisle seats! Mr. Henry H. Calderwood was the longtime parish treasurer. James Ash was the elderly Church School superintendent who directed the children, marching in procession, to bow to the altar when entering the church for the service that preceded Sunday School.

Frank Green went to Saint Mary's, Uphams Corner, Dorchester, in 1947 to be succeeded by the Reverend Percy E. Johnson, who managed to clash with some of the parish power structure over some of his ceremonial changes in the celebration of the Eucharist which he tried to introduce. It was not a happy time either for the parish or for the rector. He died very suddenly in the spring of 1950. I remember it well, as Dad was Senior Warden at the time. So far as I can recall, the parish did not have a separate search committee; Dad did much of the interviewing himself. Sunday services were provided by a non-parochial priest from Rhode Island for some months, the Reverend R. O. Meader.

The Reverend Donald Noseworthy was the first of three clergy, all of whom had pastoral abilities and each of whom stayed for some time. During his tenure, the church and parish hall were enlarged and the parish grew markedly. Steve Austill was ordained to the Diaconate with me and ten others at Saint Paul's Cathedral, Boston, in June, 1954. The Reverend Roger Nelson was a gentle, loving, caring, and effective minister.

An Unusual Letter Carrier

Bob Terrill was a longtime Cliftondale letter carrier. When I met him he had been retired for some years, and was living alone in a small apartment in East Lynn, not far from Central Square. I met him because we shared an interest in local history. My Graves grandparents knew him from his days as a letter carrier.

We used to talk for hours at a time. Rather, Bob talked and I listened. Somewhere I have notes which I took during our conversations; it would have been better had I been able to tape record our sessions.

Among other things, I learned that Eustis Street (near the Cliftondale railroad station) was probably the best built street in Saugus. It was once the route of the Cliftondale Railway, a horsecar line which connected Cliftondale with Malden prior to the building of the Saugus Branch in the 1850s. The rails were laid on granite ties. For all I know, they may still be there.

Boston Street (in New England, streets are named for the places to which they run) was the earliest through road, running from West Lynn and crossing the Saugus River in East Saugus. At Cliftondale Square it headed down towards Franklin Park as Lincoln Avenue. It would go on to skirt the Saugus Marshes and enter Malden. This was the major land route connecting Boston with North Shore coastal communities. It could not run further toward the coast because it had to go around, rather than through, the vast area of marshland which is reputed to be one of the largest such areas in the world. When British troops marched up to Salem (as they did in an action preliminary to the Revolution), they came through Saugus; when the militia marched to Cambridge Common from the North Shore towns, they came through Saugus via Boston Street and Lincoln Avenue.

In East Saugus was a well-known tavern and inn, the Blew Anchor, whose proprietor was Landlord Jacob Newhall. His title is even to be found on his tombstone in the old burying ground in Saugus Center. There is a story (which I cannot verify) that when one militia unit was coming through Saugus on its way to Cambridge Commons (where militia units encamped prior to Bunker Hill), a couple of thirsty soldiers spent so much time at the bar of Blew

Anchor that they neglected to follow their comrades to Cambridge!

[Historical note: Paul Revere and others who gave the alarm did not yell "The British are coming!" in spite of the popular legend. After all, we were all British at that time. The alarm was "The Regulars are out" – the regular troops being the King's troops, in other words the troops of the regular British Army. The troops of the colonies were the militia units. It was these units that formed the basis for the American Army to be commanded by General George Washington.]

As time passed, there were other roads in addition to the original coastal road. One was the Newburyport Turnpike, which ran a few miles inland. A 1900-era photo shows a dirt road, somewhat rutted. A book of this era comments that "The Newburyport Turnpike is of little economic benefit to the Town of Saugus." One is tempted to wonder whether today's Saugus tax collector would hold that opinion of today's multilane highway with its endless commercial establishments.

September 21, 1938

For some long forgotten reason, Miss Casey, my fifth grade teacher at the Roby School, kept me after school that day. As I walked home through Saugus Center heading for Pearson Street where I lived, I noted the weird orange color of the sky. As I crossed Columbus Avenue (where my Davis grandparents lived) and passed the police call box, which kept the police station in touch with Patrolman Tom Spencer (a signal light on the pole would notify the officer that the station needed to talk with him; individual police radios were far in the future in 1938), I remember thinking I had never before seen the sky such a color.

I had not been home long before the storm hit. It was obviously more than an afternoon storm; the wind blew with a fury I still remember. Mother and I stood in the dining room and watched the wind rip our garage doors off (our old garage had doors which swung outwards). The trees on Pearson Street starting losing branches; we soon lost electric power and telephone service. The night was long and dark, with the noise of the storm. Dad was away, on a business trip to the midwest.

The next day, Saugus Center had a surreal appearance with trees and wires down everywhere.

We went out for a walk to see what we could see. I'm sure my three siblings came too, as Mother would not have left them home alone. I remember Summer Street, Prospect Street, Pleasant Street, and others, almost blocked with the remains of the lovely trees which had fallen during the storm. They sky was sunny, the storm had left us, but the damage remained.

The New England Hurricane of September 21, 1938 has been the yardstick against which later storms have been measured. So far, at least, none has quite measured up. Weather forecasting capabilities in 1938 were not what later capabilities were; thus the storm hit virtually without warning. It was known that a storm was coming up the coast, but it was expected to go harmlessly out to sea and not make landfall. That did not happen. The storm instead slammed into southern New England with the full fury of an unexpected hurricane, catching many people in precarious situations and causing over 600 fatalities, especially in Rhode Island and Connecticut. So far as I can remember, I do not believe there were any fatalities in Saugus despite the heavy damage to our wonderful shade trees. I believe we were without power for three days and there was no school for that time. There was a hurricane in September of 1944, and some in later years, but none with the fury of the unexpected guest on September 21, 1938.

Remembrance of Things Past

by
Ed Sproul

It's been more than 50 years since I lived in Saugus, from 1932 to 1950, the year I went off to college. Early memories become more fixed and I'm sure that most of us can recite the names of our grade school teachers but now have difficulty in remembering the names of people we worked with before retirement. Twenty-five or thirty years ago I drove through Saugus with my family – the house I had been born in and my elementary school had been torn down, my junior high school closed and my high school moved. Saugus had been a small town, with farms, a train service, and most of us walked to high school, except for those who lived in North Saugus and took a school bus. One of the early Howard Johnsons (the place to take your prom date) was on Route 1 and except for a Chinese restaurant, some notorious cabins, a few bars and some retail stores, there was very little development.

My first memories are of the house my parents rented on Trull Circle, just off of Cliftondale. I recently found a Shakespearian reference to trull, a term for harlot, strumpet, or any woman of questionable morals. I assume, however, that the street must have been named for a Trull family that lived there. An immediate neighbor was Dr. Furbush who had an office on Lincoln Avenue. He was our family doctor and his daughter Eleanor became a dear friend of my older

sister and still is. When he died in the late 1940s or early 1950s, Mrs. Furbush gave me his vintage brass microscope.

In 1936 my parents built a house on Intervale Ave (address #26, phone #523J). My cousins lived across the street and other neighbors were Warren, Doane, Pearson, Pendlebury, Dabney, Burns, and some I have trouble remembering now. We had no planned playtime activities but used the street for "kick the can" or played pickup scrub baseball at an empty field off Stone Street.

We all attended the Felton School on Central Street, named for a former president of Harvard who had come from Saugus. There were six rooms; grades one through three on the first floor and grades four through six on the second floor. The basement was divided into lavatories for girls on one side and boys on the other. This was also our "shelter" during the air raid drills that were routine during the war. Teachers were: Miss Sullivan, grade one; Miss Curtis, two; Miss Robey, three: Mrs. McCarrier, four; Miss Nason, five: and Miss Tomlinson, six (who became Mrs. Donoven during Christmas vacation). I wore corduroy knickers until the sixth grade when I finally prevailed upon my parents to buy me long pants.

Each school day started with the Lord's Prayer, salute to the flag, and singing of God Bless America. We celebrated holidays by making cutouts of Pilgrims and Indians, for Thanksgiving; Christmas decorations in December and other appropriate holiday decorations. Memorial Day exercises were held outside on the lawn. In May 1944, my sixth grade, I was assigned the recitation of a poem, "The Blue and The Gray." I am still awed with the sense of history and continuity as I recall that day and the very old man, seated, slightly hunched with his Civil War uniform hat on, almost 80 years after the war had ended.

Cliftondale was our shopping center. Groceries were bought at Walkey's Market or Sherman's where my mother would call in her grocery list before picking it up. Other stores were Butler's Drug (which also sold paperbacks of baseball history), Hoffman's Clothing, a five and dime store and a newspaper store. My barber was Charlie O'Connor who charged forty cents for a whiffle and would give me back one penny with the admonition, "Don't spend it but put it away and save it for a new Ford." Dr. Beckman was our dentist. Those were the days before painless dentistry and I always felt that he had the biggest thumbs in existence. His wife, I believe, was a school teacher. They had no children. Despite his gruff exterior, he was very thoughtful; took me on his boat in Gloucester and actually came to visit me in college. In later years when he was a widower he squired my widowed mother. He died in the early 1970s.

In junior high school years, dancing class was held on Friday nights at the Odd Fellows Hall. Typically all the boys would be on one side, the girls on the other. At a signal the boys would dash across the room to pick their first partner. I don't know if I benefited from the instruction but this weekly event became a great focal point for our early teenage social experience. Boy Scout Troop 64, with Scoutmaster "Bucker" Holmes, met on Tuesdays at the Cliftondale Congregational Church and summer camp was at Camp Pow Wow. "Bucker" had been in my father's class of 1922 at Saugus High School and was said to have been a star running back.

World War II was a memorable event for us all. I was too young to serve and there was no one in my family in the military, but all were involved in war related industry. The windows in our house were fitted with plywood inserts to block any interior light during the night. My father was a volunteer air raid warden and at the signal would don his white helmet, arm band and pick up his whistle and flashlight before inspecting the neighborhood to ensure that there were no visible lights. As pre-teens, we were junior commandos. Our charge was to collect scrap metal and balls of aluminum foil to deposit at the State Movie Theater on Saturday afternoons. I have learned since that these were never actually recycled but it was a program to instill in us a sense of participation in support of the war effort. At home our scrap metal and newspaper were sold to the junk dealer, Mr. Goldberg, who I think lived in East Saugus. He made house calls, weighed the goods with his hand-held scales and paid accordingly. I'm not sure whether these goods ever supported the war effort but these activities were a lead up to the recycling programs that are now mandatory in most communities.

I walked home for lunch while at the Felton School. The radio would be on, and my mother, teary eyed, listened to Kate Smith who closed her daily noontime broadcast with, "Remember if you don't write you're wrong" and I shall never forget lunchtime June 6, 1944, with the live broadcasts from the Normandy Beaches. During this period all of Saugus was "entertained" by the nighttime loud whistling noises emanating from GE. Considering the large work force there, it was a very well kept secret until it was revealed that this was the testing of the first jet engines.

Reflecting on growing up in Saugus in the 1930s and 1940s had a very positive impact on my life. We all tend to remember the pleasanter incidents. Critics of the art of Norman Rockwell, the great illustrator of *Saturday Evening Post* covers, accuse him of depicting life as he would liked it to have been and not as it was. I hope that I have not fallen into this trap.

All Aboard the Narrow Gauge

by
Richard C. Howland

Over time, trains have been the theme of songs, stories, and movies. No exception were the World War II years, beginning in 1941 with "Chattanooga Choo Choo" and "Take the 'A' Train" and ending in 1945 with "The Atchison, Topeka, and the Santa Fe."

The only day I ever skipped school from cherished ol' Saugus High was with classmate Rolly Wormstead, now of Lynnfield, in our senior year. We took off for Boston to see ice skater Sonja Henie, actor John Payne, and Glenn Miller and his orchestra in the movie *Sun Valley Serenade*. But also in the same theater that same day we saw in person Glenn Miller and his most popular orchestra with Tex Beneke and the Modernaires. In the movie and in person, they featured "Chattanooga Choo Choo," the song that ranked first in the Hit Parade for nine weeks.

In 1941, Duke Ellington, star jazz player, composer, and orchestra leader, also made the Hit Parade with "Take the 'A' Train," named, I read from Time-Life Music, "for the New York City subway to Harlem." Ellington's jazz is deservedly making it again in the Nineties.

I wish I could have written a Hit Parade song about the BRB&L, the (Boston, Revere Beach and Lynn) Narrow Gauge which began in 1875 and ended in January, 1940. But here now it's the subject of *The Essex Genealogist*. Besides, we don't need a Hit Parade. We're into nostalgia.

When did I start riding on the BRB&L? My mother began taking me in 1928 when I was five years old, and we traveled on it often until 1933 when we moved to Saugus. When we started, the cost, reflecting the prosperity of the Roaring Twenties, zoomed from a dime to fifteen cents. Just think though – today it would cost more for a parking meter.

Why did we go to Boston? We didn't go to buy clothes there. When you walked from City Hall down Market Street until you hit Broad Street and the Narrow Gauge Lynn Station, you could have shopped at four outstanding clothing stores: Goddard's, Magrane's, Kennedy's, and Besse Rolfe's.

We didn't go to Boston to see movies either because we had so many theaters in Lynn: Paramount, Warner, Capital, Comique, Olympia, Waldorf, and Uptown.

We went to see a cousin and her family, and the subway train that took us from Boston to her home in Brookline was unusually noisy, crowded and claustrophobic. The underground horizons were dark, cement walks, and the above ground horizons were crowded streets and jam-packed apartment and business buildings.

Why did we go on the Narrow Gauge rather than the even more historic and prospering Eastern Railroad which began in 1838 and became part of the Boston and Maine? There were the two known advantages. This station was generally less crowded than the decades-older Eastern Railroad Station at Central Square, and there was the expected pleasure of floating on the ferry from Crescent Beach to the wooden slip at Rowes Wharf.

My wife, Joanne, born and raised in Lynn, also was introduced to the BRB&L in the late Twenties. For a few years every time her family went to Boston, they took the Narrow Gauge. She remembers the seats of bright supportive straw like Lynn's electric trolley cars before the buses. She loved the ferry so much her mother had to keep pulling her back from the railing. There was only one annoying sight for her. As the ferry approached the slip, there were grapefruit and orange rinds and banana peels piled up.

What moved all generations – children, parents, grandparents that rode the train and ferry? What moved them when they took such a trip? What moved them even more, decades after such an excursion shut down? Perhaps before noting the still stimulating sights, know the primary significant construction factor: the Narrow Gauge track was laid between the Eastern Railroad Track and the sea.

What we saw, smelled, and still feel were the marshes, the Saugus River, the Atlantic Ocean, the Point of Pines, Rowes Wharf, and stretches of sand and sky.

For me the loveliest and most lasting aura from the old BRB&L railroad came on my last such ride on early evening in late July, 1940. From Rowes Wharf to our Market Street station, the east and west horizons, the setting sun, the warm salty southern wind mellow me still.

To go from Lynn to Revere Beach and Boston and back, to "swing and sway" in memory, we can take another "A" Train – our Narrow Gauge reminiscence – that will always stir our spirits.

Life on the Saugus Branch

by

James Herbert Davis

North Station, Boston, took on a life of its own as the holiday season neared in the 1940s. Decorations appeared and a platform was erected at the east end of the concourse upon which was placed a portable organ. Weekdays saw a fifteen-minute carol sing, which was broadcast over a Boston station. Sheets with the words of familiar carols were handed out. (Perhaps it is indicative of a more puritanical era that a line in the second verse of "Hark the herald angels sing" was changed from "Offspring of the Virgin's womb" to "Offspring of the blessed one.")

The large crowd filled that end of the then-large concourse, through which those who had to catch their train would edge their way. Boston commuters had much practice in getting through crowds at rush hour. On the platforms the wind was getting sharp with some flakes of snow in the air. Saugus Branch trains normally left from Track 2; Track 1 was used by express and mail cars. At this busy time of the year, passengers sometimes had to edge their way past baggage carts loaded with parcel post and express waiting to be loaded into late evening trains bound for Northern New England points.

Before the train was opened for passengers, Al Gardner, rear brakeman, placed the required kerosene lanterns on the brackets at the rear of the last car. He also carried a flagman's kit containing a flag and fuses and a portable kerosene lantern to be used in case of an unscheduled stop along the way. Saugus Branch trains still saw an occasional 4-4-0 engine (the 4-4-0 was to the railroads what the DC3 became to early airlines). More and more, 2-6-0's were seen on Branch passenger trains. The last American type engine (4-4-0) was seen on the Branch in January, 1947. The passenger cars were open-platform, left over from an earlier era, many were wooden, made by the Laconia Car Company, Laconia, New Hampshire, which built many for the lines of the early era. (An exception was a string of three steel open-platform cars purchased second-hand from the Lackawanna by the B&M and often run in one of the regular Saugus Branch trains. Those three steel cars plus the #1455, a 2-6-0 which was a regular Saugus Branch engine for a time, have been preserved and may be seen at the Danbury Railway Museum in Connecticut.)

The coaches were reasonably comfortable, usually clean and well-maintained. They were warm in winter, except when the doors had been opened at one of the many stations for too long. In the winter, the train crew in passing from one car to the next were careful to hold on to their uniform caps. The wind could be especially sharp when the train crossed a section of the marsh between Franklin Park and Linden. The cars could also be warm for the evening commute during the summer. It did not take experienced commuters long to sit on the right (east) side of the cars when boarding in North Station. The left (west) side could be at least undesirably warm – no, hot – after a day from sitting in the yards. A sideshow for homebound commuters was the train's passage near a swimming hole in the marshes; it was sometimes occupied by a group of males who did not bother with the formality of bathing trunks.

The regularly-assigned conductors were men who carried two stars on their uniform coat sleeve (each star represents 25 years' service – thus these were men of 50 years' seniority on the railroad. Horace Hiller and George Murdoch were two known to many Saugus Branch commuters. George was fairly reserved and quiet; Horace was gregarious with a booming voice. Early one morning, Horace Hiller came down to Lynn station to take out his train and abruptly dropped dead on the platform. Horace never got to enjoy the retirement earned by his more than 50 years' service on the railroad.

One memorable morning, my sister Pat and the train arrived at Saugus station at the same time. Pat showed the signs of hasty preparation with hair flying to the winds, open coat and no makeup. Horace saw this from his position on the open platform and called, in a voice loud enough for the amused commuters to hear without trouble, "Young lady, tomorrow morning I expect to see you down here in your nightgown!" Pat was not as amused as her friends in the crowd.

One bit of railroad humor used by Horace and Al Gardner was for one to announce from the front end of the car "PLEASANT HILL" and the other would call "HAPPY VALLEY" from the other end. Saugus was served by five stations, the first actually located in Revere, the last just over the line in West Lynn: Franklin Park, Cliftondale, Pleasant Hill, Saugus and East Saugus. In the 1940s only Cliftondale and Saugus had ticket agents. The Branch had an unusual number of grade crossings for its length; all-in-all there were 22 crossings requiring gate tenders. In an unsuccessful attempt to discontinue passenger service, the B&M released figures showing that ticket revenue just about paid for the many crossing tenders. However, the Branch had a large number of industries with freight service. The railroad declined to state its freight revenue from the Branch. A local freight took care of the necessary switching. As a young boy, I would watch it as it switched cars for Stocker's coal yard. My grandmother Graves' home in Cliftondale gave this young rail fan a good view of the tracks and the crew often waved to the kid who stood by the fence.

Leaving North Station, the Branch trains were included in the evening rush – of many trains going to a variety of destinations on various main and branch lines. Saugus Branch trains ran down the Eastern Route of the Portland Division to Essex Junction, where one could feel the change from the rock–ballasted main line to the Saugus Branch, which had ties laid directly on the ground. The first passenger car (often a combine) was a smoker; the others were smoke-free. Some passengers played cards (some games had continued for years!), many read evening papers, some dozed – (more than once I felt the conductor's hand on my shoulder just in time for Saugus Station.) The crew knew the regular passengers and would look out for them.

After Saugus, the trains would continue to East Saugus, Raddin and Lynn Common, returning to the Eastern Route main line at West Lynn. Lynn was the last stop. The train covered 13.5 miles from North Station to Lynn and made 14 or 15 stops (some trains did not stop at West Street, Everett).

The passengers saw rather little of the engine crew. At least one Branch engineer always had a pipe. I don't believe his train ever pulled into Saugus Station when he did not have it firmly clenched in his mouth. Passengers took the engine crew for granted unless an inexperienced or inept engineer made too many rough stops; the many stations on the Branch gave ample opportunity. My father told me of when he was much younger, about going into Boston with his uncle. Claude Davis was a hard-bitten old Yankee, a passenger engineer on the Central Vermont, running out of White River Junction. Uncle Claude prided himself on being an engineer who gave his passengers a smooth ride. That day, an inept engineer was more inept than usual, making several very rough stops. Dad said he could see Uncle Claude getting more and more irritated. On arriving at North Station, they saw the Branch engineer oiling around the engine. Uncle Claude made a great show of looking over the engine.

"Know something about engines?" the man asked. Uncle Claude nodded curtly, "Ayuh, reckon I do... But I see you don't know a damn thing 'bout lapping a brake valve!" (The original version of the story has Uncle Claude using a few more adjectives, which I will omit here.) Then he took the hand of his nephew and they walked off, leaving the man speechless.

Saugus Branch passenger service died not many years after Conductor Hiller's sudden death. Sunday trains were discontinued in the early 20th century, the lightly-patronized Saturday trains went in the late 1940s, the Monday-Friday trains were gradually whittled down as commuters left for the more flexible schedules offered by the automobile. At the end there were just two trains inbound in the morning and two outbound at the end of the workday.

Now the once well-kept roadbed is weed grown and one of the two tracks has been taken up, as have been the signals. Station buildings not demolished (as has Maplewood) have been converted to other uses. The crossing gates are gone. One can surmise that if the trains had continued but a few years more that they might have been incorporated into the "T" commuter rail network. Perhaps. The roadbed is still there; perhaps it may yet be revived. But for now the Saugus Branch, built some years before the Civil War, is quiet. The enjoyable life of a Saugus Branch commuter is a pleasant memory. At least several generations of my family commuted on the Branch. My grandfather Davis retired as chief clerk of the freight claims division and worked in the large B&M general office building at 150 Causeway Street, adjacent to North Station. Of course, he had a pass as an employee. My grandfather Graves (whose home provided my vantage point for train watching in Cliftondale) was a uniform salesman for Leopold Morse and Company, located in Adams Square, Boston. He walked from his home to Cliftondale Station and rode the early train inbound; I believe he also walked from North Station to Adams Square. His job took him to a number of places in downtown Boston to measure staff for uniforms – hotels and restaurants and even the Charles Street Jail. He died while I was too young to appreciate fully the extensive knowledge of the lore of the historic city he acquired in the course of his job. Both of my parents commuted to Boston to attend college; Mother to attend Posse Nissen (physical education college for women, later absorbed by Sargent College of Boston University) and Dad to attend Boston University College of Law.

Both of my sisters commuted for a time between college graduation and eventual marriage. Gretchen remembers how she and her cohorts would decorate their end of the car at Christmastime and even before a presidential election! It was all in the spirit of good fun and fellowship and enlivened the homeward ride at the end of the work day. As for me, if I had a test that day, I would do a last minute review of my notes on the morning trip. If there was no test, I would look to see if #302, the overnight train off the New Hampshire Division which carried Pullmans from Montreal was on time; if it was, it would be due in North Station near train #2110, the second of the three inbound trains from the Branch. The third train, #2112, was normally only two cars and carried the fewest commuters; it would be discontinued about 1950.

In my memory I wish I might yet hurry down to Saugus Station, green bookbag in hand, to catch #2110, arriving perhaps a minute or two early, in time to look down the tracks to East Saugus to see the engine puff as it leaves East Saugus station. The bell rings, the crossing tender lowers the gates, the train pulls in, perhaps with #1455 or even #939 (one of the very last 4-4-0 American types) on the point. The train stops with a squeal of brakes and a cloud of smoke and steam. Horace lowers himself to the platform, greets many of the passengers, signals the engineer while we are getting seated in the coach and getting our tickets ready to be collected by Horace or Al Gardner. George Murdoch was usually the conductor on the earlier train. We are on our way to Boston.

Commuting by bus or car was never so enjoyable or pleasant.

A view of the river (with ducks) on a snowy Hammersmith Stroll in 2003.

Gathering Time

by
Jim Gaines

First through empty chambers of the quick
warm North Shore night without speaking
I elder brother lead you younger fellow
apprentice sachems in a forest of cloud
pierced by early arrowheads through dense leaves
sun from Cape Ann's curled fingers
Indian pipes despair of this racing season
moss instantly forgers damp footprints
we reach our pond ours alone Duckfoot Island
dreaming on hills' shoulders we turn
I left you right searching our testaments
wind and fire told in weathered oak
driftwood rings too pure in nature
to sink with sallow perch and pout
at water margin log-heavy we share
steps back to Mosquito Ridge the tarpaper shed
later when January binds bristling drumlins
in holy robes of ice we crouch
by a Franklin stove equal born
painting our faces with ancient heat

We Remember

He: We met at nine.
She: We met at eight.
He: I was on time.
She: No, you were late.
He: Ah yes! I remember it well.

He: We dined with friends.
She: We dined alone.
He: A tenor sang.
She: A baritone.
He: Ah yes! I remember it well.

— from "I Remember It Well"
by Alan Jay Lerner & Frederick Loewe

Elsie Hatch Wadsworth

by
Clayton W. Trefry

Elsie Hatch Wadsworth, 1886-1962, was the daughter of Anthony Hatch who had a farm on Eustis Street which extended into North Revere. She was married to Leslie Wadsworth and they had three children–Phyllis (Amidon), Ruth Irene (Sullivan) and Leslie, who became a Congregational Minister. Mrs. Wadsworth graduated from Saugus High School in 1902 and from Boston University in 1908.

Having joined the Cliftondale Congregational Church in 1902, she remained a participant throughout her long life. However, church was not her only interest. She served as president of the Saugus Historical Society, as a member of the Cliftondale Womens Club and the Riverside Club. She worked hard for the League of Women Voters and the Women's Christian Temperance League during their infancy.

A familiar figure in Saugus, she is probably best remembered as part of the celebration in 1915 of Saugus as an independent town.

How Much Muckles Brown Roams, Laborer's Eclat

by
Tom Sheehan

Fifty years with your feet still,
your chest, and I can follow footprints of your memories wherever
horizons dig me Saugus. A hill holds
your voice, a trench your hands about
the shovel's spine, one off-color story
so yellow and purple I blushed, the boy
in me showing off again. Oh, Muckles,
there has not been another just like you,
robust, cracking where we could not see,
so much of earthquake, all the dying we'd
not know, yet you tremble now at Riverside,
stones shake, and call me back late hours,
the crow winging, and silent at last, but you're
never letting go.

John Cunningham

by
John Burns

In the early stages of our work on *Of Time and the River*, I contacted Charlie Sweeney, once of Saugus and now of Amesbury, two towns prominent in the lives of the Bannon family, for information about that family. Charlie, whose mother was Helen Bannon, and his wife, Betty, were generous in providing me with extensive material about this renowned family whose male members gravitated toward baseball diamonds. Two of them, from Amesbury, played in major league baseball at the turn of the last century, James for the Boston Nationals and his brother, Tom, for the New York Giants.

The "Bannon" I have chosen to represent the Bannon family in this book, the son of Catherine Bannon Cunningham, is John Cunningham, who graduated from Saugus High School in 1935.

The act of unparalleled heroism John displays in a drowning incident on the Saugus River on January 9, 1934, deserves to be recorded for future generations.

In the tragic unfolding of the events of that day, John was not the only hero.

The action of that other hero, a victim, the automatic impulse he obeyed in a terrible moment, leave us to look with awe upon the great sacrifices human beings, no matter how young, are capable of offering in times of crisis to serve those they love.

This is the story of that event as reported by *The Lynn Telegram – News* of January 9, 1934.

Boy Scout in River Plunge Rescues Two

John J. Cunningham, 16, Saugus High School Pupil, Saves Annette Farley, Aged 11, and Walter Butler, as Leo A. Farley, 10, Begging Him to Remember Annette, Sinks to Death

A move was under way today to obtain a Carnegie hero medal as well as a national citation from the Boy Scouts of America and medal for John J. Cunningham, 16-year-old Saugus High school student, and a Star Boy Scout, who risked his life yesterday afternoon when he dove through a hole in the ice at the Saugus River and rescued two children in an accident that claimed the life of one.

The victim of the tragedy was Leo A. Farley, Jr., aged ten, son of Mr. and Mrs. Leo Farley of 60 Hesper Street, East Saugus, who deliberately chose to die when he saw that Cunningham would be unable to rescue both him and his sister, Annette, aged eleven.

Cunningham had already rescued Walter Butler, aged ten, of 55 Hesper Street, Saugus, who had fallen into the water with the Farley children.

"Whatever comes, take care of my sister," Leo cried, as he broke away from Cunningham, allowing Cunningham to concentrate his full attention upon pushing Annette onto a stronger piece of ice.

Cunningham followed the boy's instruction, and after getting Annette to safety, he turned to look for Leo and found that the boy had disappeared beneath the water. He made several attempts to recover the body, but all were unsuccessful.

Pierce R. Parker, Scoutmaster of Troop 64 of Saugus, of which Cunningham is a member, stated today that the facts of the rescue would be laid before the National Council of the Boy Scouts of American and that he had no doubt but that Cunningham would be given a citation.

At the same time interested citizens of Saugus are planning to bring the story before officials in charge of the Carnegie Hero Medal award in the belief that they will take suitable action.

Forcible measures had to be taken by police and firemen at the scene of the tragedy yesterday when the grief crazed father of the victim, who had been notified of the accident, made several attempts to rush into the ice-filled water, in an effort to recover the body of his son.

The children were thrown in the water when the ice gave way as they were taking a short cut across the river on their way home from school.

Leo, a pupil at the Mansfield school, and the Butler boy and Annette Farley, both of whom attended the Ballard school, were crossing the river near the Masonic Hall in East Saugus, a hundred yards above the East Saugus Bridge. They had nearly reached the shore when the ice broke under Walter Butler and he went into the water.

The two Farley children jumped to the edge of the ice and reached for their playmate, when again the ice broke and they were thrown in the water.

The screams of their companions attracted the attention of young Cunningham, who was walking near the railroad tracks. He dashed for the water's edge and shouted for the children on the ice to call for help.

Without waiting to remove even his shoes, Cunningham dove into the water and made for the three children. He assisted the Butler boy to the shore and then returned for another child.

Annette Farley was the next to be saved and young Cunningham struggled to get her up on the surface of the ice, far enough back from the water's edge to insure against its breaking through again.

Again he returned to the spot where Leo had been struggling, but the boy had disappeared beneath the surface. Cunningham dove again and again, once grasping an arm of the drowning boy, but he was unable to keep his grip because of numbness from the cold.

He was finally forced to swim back to the edge of the ice and hold on to save himself until assistance arrived.

The Saugus Fire Department responded to the call for help, and ladders were scaled across the ice. Ropes were thrown to Annette Farley, whom Cunningham had cautioned not to move on the ice, lest it cave away and she was hauled to the ladder by Captain William R. Salsman, who with Chief Mellen R. Joy, Hoseman Albert Jervis, and Lt. Ralph Berrett, had answered the call.

Cunningham was the next to be brought to safety. The Butler boy, who had been pushed ashore first by Cunningham, was wrapped in blankets and taken to his home. Cunningham and Annette Farley were taken to the Lynn Hospital to guard against the effects of their exposure.

Saugus and Lynn Police arrived on the scene almost as soon as Saugus fire apparatus, and the father, Leo Farley, before his daughter and her rescuer had been taken from the ice.

The body of the boy was brought to the surface by Thomas Berrett, Saugus tree warden, with James Pike, who procured a boat on Ballard Street and dragged for the body.

Artificial respiration was used on the boy all the way to the hospital and for an hour after he was admitted, but proved fruitless. He was pronounced dead sometime after arrival.

Besides his parents and sister Annette, he leaves a brother Owen, and a sister Bernice.

The hero of the tragedy, young Cunningham, is the son of Mr. and Mrs. John C. Cunningham, 17 Appleton Street, Saugus Center. A junior in Saugus High and a member of Troop 64, Boy Scouts, he is an excellent swimmer, and actively interested in athletics.

Police and fire officials, in commending the heroic work of the schoolboy, marveled that he was able to do the valiant work he did in the frigid waters of the river.

Successful Rescue Ends in Ocean Tragedy
Search Continues For Heroic Saugus Youth

by
Ed Meaney
(*Lynn Item*, August 30, 1971).

We learn in this account of the heroism of two young men of Saugus and the death of one of them, a story which should not be forgotten.

Marblehead – The search continued today for the body of Dana H. Johnson, 18, 45 Elm Street, Saugus, who perished in the raging surf at the Marblehead end of Preston Beach Saturday afternoon after he joined a companion in the heroic rescue of two brothers.

The brothers, David Mattson, 8, and Daniel Mattson, 10, 2 Orchard Circle, Marblehead, have been released from North Shore Children's Hospital in Salem where they were taken by police after being snatched from death.

Police said that Johnson and a friend, Jerry F. DiSisto, 18, 10 Blue Ridge Avenue, Saugus, were walking along the beach near First Rocks at the end of Shuman Road when they observed the Mattson boys slip off the rocks into the pounding waves.

Johnson quickly went to the assistance of one of the boys, helping him safely onto the rocks. He was then swept out to sea by the surf.

The second Mattson boy was rescued by DiSisto, who swam to safety with the lad on his back.

With Johnson and DiSisto at the time of the rescue efforts were Ann M. Atherton, 14, 38 Blue Ridge Avenue, and Kerry A. Kerwin, 17, 30 Blue Ridge Avenue, both of Saugus.

Lieutenant Inspector Richard C. Fullerton and Lieutenant John R. Russell of the Police Department directed operations Sunday in an effort to locate the body, assisted by the Coast Guard, scuba divers from Logan Airport and local diving clubs.

Initial calls on the tragedy were received at police headquarters around 2:15 p.m. with Patrolmen James Elliot and Jack Percy hastening to the scene.

The two officers were directed by neighbors and witnesses to the drowning to the rocks at the end of Shuman Road where the surf was pounding angrily. They were told by witnesses that "a youth rescued two boys, then was pulled into the water and never came up."

Officer Percy said, "Young Johnson had already gone under the water. This was about 20 yards from the rocks where he was last seen."

The Fire Department sent Engines 1 and 3, and Ladder 2, along with its boat to aid in the search for the youth's body. Fire officials also put in a call for assistance from the Coast Guard at Point Alerton which dispatched a helicopter to the scene.

The Police Department's whaler, manned by officers Herman Nickerson and Richard Jodoin, also made a search of the area but to no avail.

Lieutenant Inspector Fullerton led additional police in the search operation, the detail including officers Peter Clark, Gerald Tucker and Kenneth King. Any hope that the body would be washed ashore before nightfall quickly vanished and arrangements were made for a continued search through the weekend.

Johnson, son of Mr. and Mrs. Richard Johnson, was born in Cambridge and was graduated from Saugus High last June. He was planning to enter Northeastern University next month.

A Firsthand Account of Old-Time Saugus from a Lady Who Knows

by
Richard G. Provenzano
(*Saugus Advertiser*, May 5, 1994)

Several weeks ago I interviewed Dorothy Comfort, a longtime resident of Saugus. Mrs. Comfort had many memories of old Saugus which she was happy to share. What appears below is in her own words and appears here with her permission.

Moving to Saugus

I spent my earliest years living in Jamaica Plain but we moved to Saugus when I was just seven years old. My parents bought a house on East Denver Street. It was a single family but we reconstructed it into a two-family house, and I have lived in Saugus ever since.

When I first moved to Saugus we used to have trolley cars to take us to Lynn; this was around 1909. I started the third grade at the Roby School in Saugus Center. I only went there for two or three years and then we moved to East Saugus, to a house on Newhall Street and I went to the Ballard School.

One of the things I remember from my childhood was Unity Camp, which was on a hill near the corner of Central and Denver Streets. There were many affairs there. Different groups from around Boston would come there every Saturday and have picnics. I was pretty young at the time, but I remember that my brother and I and some of the other kids used to go up there and hang around and see what was going on. There were always things going on. There was a path from the big round building going down the hill towards Denver Street where in a small building they served sandwiches and ice cream and light lunches. The dances were usually in the evening.

On Sundays they used to have spiritual meetings. My brother used to be a soloist at the Episcopal Church and when the spiritualists found out that he could sing (he was only about 11½) they had him sing on Sunday nights. They liked him so much that they had him for the whole season that year. They gave him only 50 cents a night, but that was a lot of money in those days!

They used to have the boys sing in the choir and pay them ten cents a Sunday, but they finally decided that they couldn't do that any more. So they stopped paying the boys, and naturally the boys didn't want to sing if they weren't going to get paid!

Frank T. Bennett, who was the Deacon in the church at the time, took my brother aside and told him that if he sang a solo every Sunday, he would give him a quarter, but he had to go to his house to collect it!

The Universalists were also very active in those days. Their church used to have a big fair every year. That's the Unitarian-Universalist Church now. Every year their affair would run for three days, Thursday, Friday, and Saturday. This would always be around February 21. They used to have an operetta and children all around the town would be in it and Amy Jones used to coach it.

One night at the operetta my brother and I sang, "When You and I Were Young, Maggie," and I was dressed up as an old lady, and my brother had a tall silk hat with a grey cotton suit that my mother made for the occasion. We really went over quite well.

I remember that when I went to the Roby School, the building next to it, called the Park Press Building now, had a post office on the right and a variety store on the left. As a kid I used to go in there and spent pennies on candy and things. One of my favorite candies was a sort of square molasses chewy candy and anytime I had the money, I'd go in there and buy one of those; they were wonderful!

Movies, Races, and World War I

Movie theaters? Oh yes, we used to walk over to Cliftondale and go to the Dream Theater. They used to have someone play the piano with the appropriate music for the silent films. They had a lot of westerns, as I remember. The Dream Theater was the only place to see movies in Saugus for many years. When I lived in East Saugus, however, we sometimes would walk across the frozen Saugus River in wintertime and go down to West Lynn to the theater in Houghton Square.

Another thing we would do would be to go over to the Franklin Park Race Track. On July 3 every year they used to have a bonfire. Another thing about the track that I'll never forget – one day my brother and I were out front of our house when we heard an airplane go down in Franklin Park, so my brother jumped on his bicycle and went over. He just couldn't get over it. He said there was a big hole in the ground where the airplane crashed, and of course, the pilot was killed.

On the Saugus Branch Train

I graduated from high school in 1920 and got a job right away at John Hancock in Boston and worked there for seven years. I used to go into Boston by train. That was the Saugus Branch train, and I'd get on at Saugus Center. I was living on East Denver Street at the time. Every morning I'd go down to the depot with our collie dog and buy *The Boston Globe* and put it in his mouth and he'd take it home. It created quite a bit of attention, as you can imagine.

There used to be a grocery store on the corner of Webb Place and Central Street where the J&M place is now, and there was a restaurant at the corner of Jasper and Central. On the corner of Pleasant Street and Central there was a store called Mitchell and Douglass and it sold groceries.

There was a tennis court across from St. John's Church near the Iron Works, and there was a path on the edge of the property that went down to the river. Before you got down the slope, there was a tennis court and I used to play tennis there quite often when I got out of work. Near the Saugus River there was a building where they used to have dances and parties and they had canoes you could rent.

Another thing I can remember from those days was taking the trolley car that went to Lynn. Just before you got to Springdale Avenue on Winter Street, there was a spring on the right hand side. The trolley car would stop so that the passengers could get a drink from the spring. My mother used to send us down there sometimes with jars just to get the water there to bring home. It was very good water, and I wish I could have some of it even now.

Saugus was a wonderful and interesting town in those days but much of it has changed in the years since!

Richard Howland

by
Neil Howland

Historically, 1937 was the beginning of President Franklin Delano Roosevelt's second term. Economically, it was slipping back to the worst year of the Depression – 1933. The world was shortly to fall into the turmoil created by Nazi Germany and the Second World War. But the summer of 1937 nonetheless proved to be an opportune time for Dick Howland, a Saugus eighth grader, age fourteen.

Along with the national craze of goldfish eating, the country was swept briefly, and particularly by teenagers, by a game called Hi-Li. It did not have the widespread craze effect that yoyos or later the hula-hoop did, but it seemed every time you turned around then somebody had a Hi-Li paddle, which was a small wooden paddle with a tiny ball stapled to the paddle on a long elastic string. Doesn't sound like much and it wasn't, but America and Saugus were wallowing in the depths of the Great Depression, so the simpler, the better. The idea was simple – keep the ball in the air by hitting it.

Dick proved as adept at playing Hi-Li as he was at most everything else, and he followed his dream of winning a big prize by whacking that little ball continuously non-stop for, lord knows, how many times. The *Lynn Item* newspaper was sponsoring a local competition to determine who the young champ would be. The Grand Prize was to be a brand new bicycle, with whatever accessories were then the rage. The finals were to be held at the Capital Theater in Central Square, Lynn, as part of the publicity campaign by the newspaper. The "Cappy" was kind of a grimy theater but it housed for many years live acts of vaudeville in conjunction with movies. Dick's father and my grandfather, William B. Howland, had appeared at the Capital in the past as a vaudeville star and now Dick was going to tread the same stage. Dick had survived a series of local competitions in round robin fashion and now was headed for the finals against a lad who many years subsequent became Lynn's Police

Chief. I no longer remember how many times consecutively Dick was able to whack that ball but he finally won out. A little old perhaps for a bicycle, but never too old for pride in accomplishment.

Richard C. Howland was born in Lynn and, as mentioned (see "Always Chasing Rainbows" on page 272), his father was a well-known celebrity, a singer who basically rejected the overtures of Hollywood to stay on the stage, and his mother, a Lynn woman, Blanche Roderick, had Lynn roots that went back to the Civil War era. But as a result of what essentially was desertion by his father, Dick and my grandmother were forced to live at an early age with my father and his family in Saugus, a not uncommon Depression Era experience, and I loved them both. Dick was filled with a lot of drive to succeed and he always had great success in school. He graduated in 1941 as the Salutatorian in his class. As with many young men, the looming chaos of the Second World War interfered temporarily with Dick's longer-term ambitions. Dick's first taste of the college experience was courtesy of the United States Government, when after being drafted into the Army he was sent to Carlisle Barracks, in Pennsylvania, where he was to become a commissioned officer. Because of the vicissitude of the current war effort, Dick's officer cadre was yanked out of school and was sent immediately overseas as infantrymen. He landed in Nyswiller, Holland, where he found shelter with a Dutch family with whom he maintained a lifelong and joyous relationship. Dick was soon injured in the Battle of the Bulge and on Valentine's Day he was sent back to the States and was subsequently discharged in the summer of 1944.

Dick pursued his dreams of education by matriculating, again with the help of the Government on the G.I. Bill, at Tufts University in Medford, and later he also received his Master's Degree from B.U.

How well I remember his first job, an English teaching assignment in Laconia, NH High School. At that time I was then commuting to college myself and I drove Dick, who didn't own a car, to the original preliminary interview. He taught English, and Laconia proved to be a happy experience for Dick and his new wife, Joanne Lapham, and they subsequently moved on to a number of teaching assignments and administrative roles at Dean Academy, Franklin, Massachusetts and as sub-principal at Newton High School for 13 years, where his children, my cousins, graduated from. His final assignment was as principal at Manchester-by-the-Sea High School, an assignment that both he and Joanne dearly loved. My Aunt Joanne had spent many happy summers in Gloucester and they both felt right at home in Manchester and later they owned a beautiful converted condo in West Gloucester, near where Jo had summered so many years before as a child.

Dick was very much engaged in school social life and the well-being of his students was of great importance to him. His stewardship of his school involved the usual pep rallies for the big football games as well as setting the course for the educational path of his young charges. He made national headlines by his adroit handling of a nasty bigotry situation, which the locals wanted to blow out of all proportion.

Dick had always been happy in his work as a principal and enjoyed the stimulation of school dynamics. He enjoyed his students and their affection for him was reciprocated.

Partly as a result of Aunt Jo's physical problems with cancer, Dick opted for early retirement. He not only busied himself around the condo with gardening and other chores, he remained a force in the community by virtue of a weekly column that appeared in the Gloucester Daily Times newspaper. Dick was also a frequent contributor to the Essex Genealogical Society magazine and on a random basis for the North Shore Sunday newspaper.

Frequently in these columns Dick would hint at the long-term impact psychologically on his life as a result of his experiences as a child living in hand to mouth fashion because of his father's abandonment. One of his most poignant columns occurred in March of 1993, entitled "Always Chasing Rainbows," when he referred perhaps in a cathartic way about his trip by train to Manhattan to visit his father, who then failed to show up. Dick was just 12 and alone in the Big Apple. Then there was the touching column of November 12, 1992, in which he described why he did not eat cold hot dogs for Thanksgiving as a result of his service experience in Europe.

After his retirement Dick and I spent literally hundreds of pleasurable hours together over casual lunches. In addition, in those late years of his life, he and I spoke together for hours at a time about unresolved episodes in both our lives, from which we were hoping to abstract meaning – a message from life. Some of it I think Dick and I got right, but his place in the family remained tantalizingly elusive to us. He was a hero to me, always with a sweet and generous nature. I love him now as much as then.

Although none of us answer fully all the questions about life, Dick remained ever thoughtful and contemplative of his odyssey. I think his understanding of himself grew as a result of our many and long conversations. I do not mean to make this sound too much like an instruction class because we had great, great fun.

The last year of his life was marred by the so-called Lou Gehrig's Disease, which killed him, despite the loving ministrations of his wife and three children, Rick, Ron, and Marsha. His grandson, a wonderful musician, played

"Amazing Grace" at his funeral as we bade him adieu. Amazing Grace indeed — he was filled with it.

The Milburys

by
Paul Heffernan

About 40 years ago, I walked into a small, dark, dirty corner store not far from Cliftondale Square in Saugus. As I came in the door, two balloons were being batted toward me by a young woman cursed with a severe mental handicap.

Her father, George Milbury, barked at her while chewing on a disgusting remnant of a stogie. Her mother, Alma Milbury, came toward me and led Marsha Milbury back behind the counter.

Forty years later, Alma died in her 90s in a nursing home where she had lived for only a year or so. She had been a fixture in Cliftondale for decades. She was never seen without Marsha on her arm... not once.

Her daughter Marsha, living with relatives, died shortly after her mother. I will risk being maudlin by saying one cannot conceive if Marsha could comprehend why her devoted mother was no longer her constant companion.

Now if heaven exists, and I say it does, Alma Milbury deserves the seat closest to the Eternal Light that guided her life for all those 90 years.

Al and Ethel: Reasons for Reunions

by
Dick Howland
(*Saugus Advertiser*, October 15, 1992)

How come a 51st, 52nd, 53rd reunion? Just after our Saugus High Class of 1941's 50th reunion, we decided to try a 51st. As a friend so sadly but aptly noted, such classes are "highly susceptible to a rapidly declining enrollment."

Our 51st was outdoors at King's Grant Inn, sparkling under an afternoon June sun. The attendance exceeded our goal. The gang was mellower than ever and so enthusiastic that before the party was over, we voted overwhelmingly to have a 52nd.

Every reunion makes nostalgic connections of the *Way We Were* with the *Way We Are*. At much earlier ones, part of the ritual was to compare physical and financial appearances. Now we finally see with our hearts, not with our fading eyes. Al and Ethel (Blundell) deSteuben are two moving, poignant examples. Al became a GE apprentice upon graduation from high school and volunteered for the service in 1943. Ethel became a bookkeeper for Sherman's Market in Cliftondale Square, then worked in the GE and joined the Navy in 1944.

Albert and Ethel deSteuben.

Al went from the infantry to the Army Specialized Training Program at Queen's College, then back to the 272nd Infantry Regiment, 69th Division. Sergeant deSteuben was horribly wounded in Germany in 1945.

Probably because his dog tags were missing, he was unconscious, and his surname was of German origin, Al was placed with German patient-prisoners. He was therefore operated on by a German surgeon who had to amputate his left leg above the knee. The American doctors were impressed with the German doctor's skill.

Al spent a year of rehabilitation in an Army hospital in New Jersey. Before his discharge in February 1946, he and Ethel met again during their visits home. They were married in August, 1949, after Ethel's naval service was over.

Al went back to the GE apprentice program, which included night classes at Lowell Institute under the auspices of M.I.T., but he didn't stop there. He kept taking a variety of courses "for the fun of it."

Then he enrolled in Harvard College Extension School, received an Associate of Arts Degree in 1975 and hit the heights with his Bachelor of Arts Degree from Harvard in 1981.

His life-time zest for education helped motivate their three daughters to study and succeed. Their eldest is a special education teacher, their next a visual coordinator, responsible for merchandise displays in nine Filene's stores, and their youngest is an attorney.

Al had a stroke in 1983. Ethel said, "It was caused by massive clots, the result of constant irritation of his prosthesis on his other leg. It was very difficult for us to accept this second major insult to his body, but we began to fight back."

The year after her husband's stroke, Ethel faced and overcame breast cancer and stress. On Christmas Eve, 1985, she brought Al back to their home still filled with love, courage, and determination. The deSteubens missed our 45th reunion, but helped enliven our 50th and 51st. Although Al couldn't talk, he said more with his smile then we did with our words.

Al and Ethel and every classmate are the reasons for our reunions and it's very encouraging to know that reunions are possible after we graduate from Earth. So our Class of '41 can look forward to our most fabulous one ever.

Where in Heaven, though, will we have it? No problem – we'll have both memorable indoor and outdoor locations. We'll reserve new creations of our old Assembly Hall, Stackpole Field and Lily Pond.

To tap it off, all our classmates will be able to attend. All our favorite teachers will be able to drop in to give them a deserved Coach MacPherson hug.

Oh, and thanks to our returning youth and Glenn Miller's availability, we'll be listening and dancing to the music of the Big Band Era.

And we'll be living in the eternal Big Spirit Era.

Ethel and Al.

Ethel and Albert celebrated their 50th wedding anniversary with a large group of family and friends in 1999. They attended the 60th reunion of their high school class in June 2001. Albert passed away shortly thereafter in August 2001; Ethel passed away in December 2002.

Doug Lockwood

Remembering a Quiet Benefactor

by

Neil Howland

Strange how little, ordinary incidents sometimes rattle around in our memory bank forever. Even stranger when the incident that arouses such long, lasting memories occurs to an eight year old. What happened was this: I had begun school at that wonderful old fortress, the Roby School, in the fall of 1935 – well, it was not so "old" then. But the powers that be in the Saugus School System concluded in the fall of 1937 that where I lived on Victoria Street, which seemed equidistant between the mile long walk to Roby School and the near similar distance to the Wendell Street school, the Mansfield, obliged my transfer. The Mansfield was a wonderful old neighborhood school that housed the first four grades only.

One fall morning in 1937, I was on my new daily stroll to Wendell Street. I planned to stop and holler for my pal, Jimmy Colpitts, whose house fronted on Winter Street, three doors down from the East Saugus Methodist Church, with its famous spire. I had been at the Mansfield School for a couple of weeks and knew most of my classmates by sight, if not by name. As Jimmy and I were jostling each other along the short walk from his house, we were caught up to by one of our schoolmates, Dougie Lockwood, who was one of the kids I knew by sight but not name, and he joined us en route. Doug lived on Stocker Street, just across from the hard scrabble patch of land along the River, which the Town tried to dignify by calling it the Stocker Street Playground. The Town finally brought in a slide, swings, and seesaws to make this inhospitable patch of land an attraction for neighborhood kids.

Doug was decked out in a 1930s school uniform, you know, consisting of bib overalls, a freshly pressed open collar white shirt and his best pair of sneakers (his only pair). He was gangly, with a bland expression, and had a tousle of undisciplined blond hair and seemed quiet and under control. We acknowledged each other as little kids always do with just a nod.

On our walk to school that morning, as Jimmy and I did our usual autopsy on classmates, teachers, the school, and anything else we could think of, Doug listened attentively but made no comments. So, I learned on our first day together that that quiet attentiveness was a hallmark of his, an imprint he carried all his life.

As with all kids of that age in school you made friends quickly, and the occasional enemy list was always shifting, with real or imagined hurts within a 24-hour period.

Following the fourth year at Mansfield School, Doug and I and many of our classmates shifted to the fifth and sixth grades at the nearby Ballard School. These youthful peregrinations gave rise to an anecdote fifty years later. It was about this time that Dougie, now my chum, and I increased the scope of our playtime activities and locale by riding our bikes all around town and into West Lynn.

Sometime in the early '90s, I had written a newspaper article that detailed some of my lifetime experiences with books that ran the gamut from comic books to law school and on into the balance of my adult life. In the opening paragraphs of that newspaper piece, I recounted how Doug and I had come on to the Saugus Library in Saugus Center while on a bike-riding jaunt around town. Neither of us had seen the Library before. Both of us were totally and forever engaged by that first experience, our imaginations captured by the possibilities. My article was published, was popular, and widely read. Shortly after its publication, Doug showed up at my law office one morning with his usual cheerful greeting and he showed me a photo of the two of us, age 10, standing beside our bikes, about to set off for parts unknown. When I expressed a sense of amazement to Doug that he would have kept that old photograph of almost 60 years ago, he looked at me with his usual direct, but offhand way, and said, "That's nothing, Neil, I still got the bike."

Well, you had to know Doug to know that that spoke volumes about his character and patterns of behavior. He was decidedly conservative and a saver of useful things, of memories and of relationships.

Doug and I were members of the Class of 1947 at Saugus High School and I have elsewhere recited how gratifying that experience was for me, growing up in that wonderful small town environment. I am sure Doug shared similar feelings of kinship with me and with his classmates, although he did not talk much about it. Doug was always a fixture at our class reunions and had an acute memory of what transpired in that formative period for us. I was a working member of the reunion committees and, as a result of Doug's contributing photographs and memorabilia about our class, I asked him to formally join us in our 50th Reunion efforts. As was always the case, Doug chose not to be involved in the front lines of the activities, passing up such participation with a dismissive attitude about what he could contribute. "Gee, Neil," he said to me, "you guys are doing a great job and I appreciate your thoughts, but no thanks."

Although Doug and I shared many classes in our high school years, our social moments were spent in different orbits entirely. Resolutely Doug retained his quiet but very solid focus on achieving educational excellence, while I became somewhat mesmerized by the pseudo glamour of "The Rat Hole" and my efforts to achieve "jock" stardom (I didn't). Thus, we were traveling on separate vectors for a while but always remained good, good friends – that was easy, Doug had no enemies!

Doug matriculated at Northeastern University while I was on to Harvard College after a year at prep school. As a result, our contacts with one another diminished to the vanishing point. But, as with all members of the Class of '47, we tried to keep track of other people's paths in the grown-up world out there. Doug was an honorable U.S. Army Veteran of the Korean War. During his working life he worked for the Department of the Navy at the Portsmouth Naval Shipyard and for NAVPRO at General Electric. It comes as no news that Dougie stayed with one employer through his life. He was an engineer and a darned good one.

Doug Lockwood.

Doug was an only child and remained unmarried throughout his life, but had many cousins, some of whom lived among us here in Saugus. I just don't know why Doug opted for the solitary life he led. As adults, busy with our own dreams and pursuits, we weren't close enough for either of us to confide in the other. I would be astonished if at this point in time some special someone now disclosed that Doug has unburdened himself at their weekly poker sessions of those secret fears and passions we each harbor. Doug lived his entire life on Stocker Street, a couple of hundred yards from the Mansfield School, where our long friendship began. Many of the quixotic vagaries of life, which have alternately terrified and tantalized me, seemed by remote observation not to have bedeviled Doug and his calm, unruffled disposition.

So what can we conclude about this psychologically elusive personality, unhappily now in hindsight?

He was an utterly devoted and loyal son of Saugus. If we were to indulge in word association games the following would certainly apply: intelligent, handsome, happy, purposeful, dedicated, unassuming, reserved, enigmatic, shy, taciturn, thrifty, industrious, generous, focused. I could go on but I think you've got the sense of where I'm headed.

Doug never wanted to be the center of attention, *ever*. At our class reunion function, which he never missed, I would look from my MC podium to the rear of the room and there was my old friend, Doug Lockwood, always at the last table by choice. The generous bequest to the Saugus Public Library could only be made posthumously by Doug – he couldn't even begin to contemplate the unnecessary fuss he would have to endure if the gift were made during his lifetime.

We shall remember Doug with gratitude and love – the quiet benefactor.

Doug Lockwood Remembers

by
Bob Wentworth

In an August 7, 1999 letter, Doug wrote to his high school classmate and good friend, Neil Howland, complimenting Neil on his interesting writings of the Saugus scene.

His reading of Neil's articles triggered a fond memory from his mid-1940s high school years that has remained with him ever since. He wanted to share this "piece of trivia," as he referred to it, with Neil.

In an excerpt from this letter he said:

> In Gladys Fox's class we used a prose and poetry book in which I first encountered the poem, *High Flight*, by John Gillespie Magee, Jr. It inspired me to want to learn to fly someday. Someday for me was 15 years later at the Revere Airport. It remains one of my favorite poems and I still fly out of Beverly Airport.

The poem, *High Flight*, that Doug refers to begins with the line:

Oh! I have slipped the surly bounds of Earth,

and ends with the line:

Put out my hand, and touched the face of God.

Herein lies a classic story of a teacher touching the life of a student, awakening an interest, and inspiring him to pursue that dream to become a lifelong recreational pilot.

Edward B. Noel, 88; Raised Pigs in Suburbs

by
Tom Long
(*Boston Globe*, circa 2003)

Edward B. Noel, one of the last farmers able to earn a living from land inside the crowded confines of Route 128, died apparently of a heart attack, Wednesday, at Lawrence General Hospital. He was 88.

A lifelong bachelor and Saugus resident, Mr. Noel operated a piggery and vegetable farm on 20 acres of hilltop near the Mount Hood Golf Course on the Saugus / Melrose line. He didn't own the property, nor did he give it a name. It was known simply as Ed's Farm.

The couple who owned the property once offered to leave it to him when they died.

"I don't need the place," Mr. Noel responded, according to his nephew, Andrew B. Noel, Jr., of York, Maine.

The couple willed the property to the Baptist Church with the stipulation that Mr. Noel be allowed to farm it until he died.

And that's exactly what he did. Until about two years ago, Mr. Noel was still growing strawberries and tomatoes.

For many years, Mr. Noel also raised pigs on the property, making his rounds to restaurants to collect garbage for animal feed.

A couple of decades ago, when a new law required that garbage be boiled before it was fed to the animals, he gave up the piggery. "It was too much bother," his nephew said.

In addition to growing vegetables and raising pigs, Mr. Noel kept work horses, which he entered in horse pull contests at the Deerfield and Topsfield fairs. He mowed hay on the Saugus marshes and conducted hay rides.

Decked out in green "Dickie" trousers and work shirt with a matching baseball cap, Mr. Noel was a familiar sight at the Tumble Inn, a breakfast and lunch shop in Saugus, where–if he was having a good day–he'd buy lunch for the regulars.

His occupation required that he spend a good deal of time outdoors in all kinds of weather. It taught him how to read nature's signs, his nephew said.

"It's going to be a tough winter this year," he once said. "How do you know?" his nephew asked.

"Because the squirrels are gathering their nuts early," Mr. Noel said.

He also plowed snow with a backloader. "He was in his glory during the Blizzard of '78," his nephew said.

During one northeaster, when Mr. Noel was plowing snow at the Red Coach Grill in Saugus, he phoned his nephew to ask for help. "Just go to the farm, get the tractor, and drive over," he said.

"I've never driven a tractor," his nephew replied.

"Well, how hard could it be?" asked Mr. Noel. "The keys are in it, just keep pushing levers until it moves."

The levers worked and he joined his uncle at the restaurant.

Several years ago, his nephew said, an IRS agent showed up at Mr. Noel's door and asked why he didn't report the income from his vegetable patch on his tax forms.

"Because I don't sell it," Mr. Noel said.

"What do you do with it?" asked the IRS man.

"I give it away to friends."

"Well, why don't you give me some then?" said the IRS man.

"Because you're not my friend," Mr. Noel said.

"He was a real character," his nephew said. "He was the only man I ever knew who could start an argument in an empty room."

Harold Everitt

by
Ray Maes

Harold Everitt was born on October 13, 1909, at 41 Harrison Avenue in Lynnhurst and lived his life next door at 51 Harrison Avenue.

In everything he undertook, over a diverse range of endeavors, there was a special Harold Everitt touch. His life was marked by giving – to the young, to the old, to his beloved Lynnhurst, to causes he believed in, to anyone who needed his help. It would be fitting to say of him that he was "one who loved his fellow man."

After graduating from Saugus High School and North-eastern University, he worked for United Car Fastener, General Electric, and then spent 30 years working for Esso, where he was a safety engineer when he retired.

A second career was waiting for Harold at Saugus High School where he spent ten years as a successful and highly regarded chemistry and science teacher.

He worked extensively with the Boy Scouts of America for 45 years, from 1927 to 1972. He served in various capacities: as cub master of Pack 35 and Pack 110, as scoutmaster, as committeeman, as explorer adviser, and as institutional representative.

Harold was an adult adviser when I joined Troop 35. He was a busy man providing us with slide shows on nature, giving us wildlife lectures and, as an able musician, skilled in clarinet, saxophone and flute, he was inspired to form a scout orchestra. Unfortunately, the talent pool, with me among them as a failed flutist, was not there to make his dream come true.

His camping trips with us were special, like one of a week's duration, well-stocked with non-perishable items, food from a local farm, and fish we caught from the ocean nearby. We were happy to share our bounty with our parents when they paid us a visit, putting before them farm produce, hake chowder, apples, and blueberries.

Harold and his wife Edna were hardworking and imaginative farmers / gardeners. Together they froze and preserved much of what they produced. They raised large hogs and were up to the challenge of slaughtering them. Without assistance, Harold moved a large henhouse more than 100 yards by block and tackle and well-positioned pivot stakes (or dead men as some call them), and by using his automobile as a source of power.

Their garden did not prosper by accident. To get good humus soil for the garden, Harold habitually went into the swamp behind Fairmount Avenue to drag out heavily loaded sacks of swamp soil to enrich their gardens.

At the rear of the vegetable garden were their attractive rock garden and the fish pond with its varieties of waterlife, goldfish, frogs, etc.

He loved nature and took many hiking trips to the Presidential Range in the White Mountains with his friend Charlie Nute.

The environment could always count on Harold. He was the founder of The Saugus River Watershed Association, a productive group in a worthwhile cause. He was an active member of an ad hoc committee in the early 1980s organized to acquire open space for the town in general, as well as for Lynnhurst. They were successful in claiming important parcels of land which were processed through the Town Meeting and placed in the hands of the Conservation Commission in a series of steps that turned out to be a losing fight to save Vinegar Hill.

Throughout the years Lynnhurst was served by an unusual group of civic-minded leaders, generous with their time, energy and sense of purpose. Harold was prominent among them. He founded the Lynnhurst Cooperative Society in 1937 and the Lynnhurst Improvement Association in 1940. He served several times as a Precinct 5 Town Meeting member in the 1940s and was an original member of The Council for the Aging, founded in 1968.

He was a prime mover in the creation of The Veterans Memorial Park when the boys came home from World War II. The project was sponsored by The Lynnhurst Men's Club. Frog Pond, between Cleveland, Newcomb, Jefferson and Edison Avenues, was filled in and given over to this park. The area was beautifully landscaped and featured a bronze plaque honoring the five Lynnhurst young men who had died in the service of their country.

The men honored were:

- Charles Maes
- Lawrence Mitchell
- Charles Peabody
- Roger Whipple
- Lawrence Slawenwhite

On the opening day of the park, the mechanism for raising the flag on the new flagpole didn't work and Harold had to shinny up the pole to raise our colors. In time, the land for Veterans Park went back to the town, and the bronze plaque, the last reminder of that park, is now located in the Lynnhurst School.

In summing up the account of the life of Harold Everitt, one single incident might best illustrate the kind of man he was and what kind of service he was prepared to offer to his fellow man. At a meeting of the Lynnhurst Men's Club, a prospective member was rejected by one blackball vote. Harold would not tolerate that.

That night he trudged through deep snow to contact club members to discuss the charter rule that had sanctioned their vote. He convinced them that the rule was undemocratic. The rule was rescinded and the rejected member was voted in.

Prescott N. Murray, Jr.

("Sonny" or "Press" To Some)

by
Ray Maes

No story about Lynnhurst and those who dwell there would be complete without some words about Prescott.

The Murray boys, Prescott and Donald, sons of Prescott N. "Pecky" and Vi were from early ages into things of nature and boyhood adventure – i.e., animals – wild and domestic – hunting, fishing, trapping, bee keeping and most all bucolic efforts.

In Sonny we see proof that the apple doesn't fall too far from the tree. Both Prescott Sr. and Jr. are master story tellers, and excellent singers as well, as demonstrated on many occasions at Lynnhurst Men's Minstrel Shows.

When Sonny was about thirteen years old, his dad decided that he needed a program to build up his physical strength. He called on my friend, Jack Henderson, to provide a program, which turned out to be very successful. Shortly, among other physical feats, Sonny became the arm wrestling champion among his peers.

Sonny loves nature. Once, observing a crow's nest high in a tall pine tree, he went out with a group of friends to investigate. After three attempts he reached the nest and brought down a young crow in a bag. After a period of training, the crow became his friend and a fixture on his shoulder.

His pet raccoon (or was it a woodchuck?) didn't fare so well: one time when I was visiting him the critter bit him and I still have a vision of the sorry critter flying through the corn stalks.

Jack Henderson and Prescott Murray, 2001.

He loves nature and lives close to nature. Once he raised three hogs to butchering size and later a bull that got too big for his shed. Plenty of rabbits and chickens in his yard. Almost all the heat in his home was from firewood.

One time after some salt water fishing, he stopped by to ask Harold Everitt if he would like some mackerel. Harold said yes and Sonny said, "A bushel all right?" Harold and his family had many meals of fish from that.

When visiting Sonny's place and garden, just take the tour and try not to be too hard on yourself when you see how Mr. Murray's garden flourishes. Sometime in the 1970s I gave him a coffee can of shallots that came from Belgium and each year his harvest was in the bushels. Lynnhurst has had some great gardeners. To name some: Harold Everitt, Frank Bond, grandfather Erick Persson, John Bartosh, John (Jan) Van Bastelaer, Chester Fairchild, Leander Maes (my dad), Nelson Jewell, the Wormsteads, Gene Leighton and some others I am sure I have missed, but Prescott N. Murray, Jr. is "King of the Garden!"

It has been said, "Prescott is a real piece of work"... A-yuh!

Hawk Watch at Pranker's Pond

by
Tom Sheehan

Up gray stairs cut against the heart of earth,
taller than promise, shade given over
to hail evening's climb and gray-ridden rocks,
we mount to the everlasting station
where your scrutiny lingers on this pond.

When I was a boy I fished these rocks
flushed out of this shore, like a miner's earth
tossed by shovel to make an edge of pond,
here, below you, topography's station,
charred granite edges, time rolling over

from a long-dead fire, Ice Age hunting earth
and plush haven to put down Pranker's Pond,
to slam it meteoric among rocks
as if, in hindsight, no other station
could accept tumbling over and over.

One animate god gave you this pond,
watch guard from Christmas Eve to Passover,
all ends of the track up to the station,
all shore, all watering, and sculptured rocks,
all good ministries of this piece of earth;

where big-mouth bass, and pickerel under rocks,
and carp, gathered in flotilla's station
like dark submarines, lingering at earth,
once lined up in Le Havre, New London's pond,
waiting for silence to come, and over

their grayed and lichened surfaces the pond
accepts what peace comes, absolute station,
accepting, if by chance, peace under rocks
and all the dread world over, all over.
Nothing is so quiet as quiet earth,

nothing comes knifelike between earth and pond
like erosion, misdeeds, molestation
of waters, herbs, young saplings, Mother Earth,
pieces of Saugus, what you watch over
from that aerie on precipitous rocks.

Nothing moves you do not see, slate of pond,
duck, bluebird, cardinal calling out its mirth,
a dozen crows a starched pine gives over
to the fact of day, sad face of storm clocks,
clouds cascading down sweet immolation.

You, un-winged, un-feathered, are the hawks
who give their eyes to long-established bond,
who see seasons, under scan, recover
in part and whole, the essence of rebirth,
a cursed pond come back from profanation.

Honest Lawyer Belden Bly

by
Tom Sheehan

He claims cutthroat, pirate, dragoon
In long lineage, thus borne of wrecks,
Footpads, scoundrels in family's rune,
And some left hanging by their necks.

Oh such scoundrels he has known,
DNA'd deep down in his bones;
We see them caught up in his eye,
Those old rapscallions name of Bly.

This Bly did this and Bly did that
Today's newspapers oft proclaim,
Where Foxhill Bridge once was at
Now bearing up another's name.

This magistrate to them does gauge,
Full allegiance upheld by law,
For in his blood that hard lineage
's rampant yet and sort of raw.

He's a maverick still in bloom,
The oldest man in this here room,
We give him names, folk epithet,
And list all those we can't forget:

Master of the Rolls, defense dancer,
Barrister and mouthpiece of the day,
Honest lawyer, deft conveyancer,
And last not least, amicus curiae.

We see him in the old high school,
Deft warrior for the normal field;
Oh this Belden, not once the fool;
Lived he by wits, and sword and shield.

And then full half a century past
He set off, as our Legislator cast,
And carved 'neath the Golden Dome
A place that he can still call home.

But for all the names we endless send
From task varieties and titled jobs
In front of class or cheering mobs,
He's known best as our Saugus friend.

The Reverend Roger Nelson

by
Reverend John Mulloy

What a delight to receive the assignment to write a few words about The Reverend Roger Nelson. Like so many other Saugonians, I miss him dearly! Roger, as most people in town called him, was a precious part of the community for the thirty years he served as Rector of Saint John's Episcopal Church on Central Street.

It did not take me long, when I arrived in Saugus as a Johnny-come-lately in 1996, to notice that my fellow clergyman was a very special person. My own parishioners at Blessed Sacrament Catholic Church spoke of him with a warm reverence I had never heard before. His quietly powerful presence in Saugus for almost a third of a century greatly helped Saugus to be "someplace special."

Roger, a 33 year old priest, arrived at St. John's in 1973. Born in Braintree, schooled there, graduating from Trinity College with a major in history, and doing a one-year fellowship in history at Brown was not enough for Roger. He followed through on a life-long thought in his head to accept a call to the ministry. Doing this assignment helped me to learn the story of a high school senior on his way to the graduation ceremony at Braintree High School, going into the local Episcopal Church and sitting there all alone with His God. It was there that the man who was to have such a great effect on the Saugus community said the "yes" deep inside himself.

Now it was 1973 and the recently ordained and recently married and soon-to-be-a-father arrived in Saugus. He brought to Saint John's and the community his gift of being able to offer sincere and powerful prayer. While at Episcopal Divinity School in Cambridge, one of his classmates, Jonathan Daniels, had been killed while working the civil rights movement in the South. This painful experience caused Roger to bring a strong commitment to preaching and working for social justice. No community need was ever off his agenda. I often stood in awe

Rev. Roger Nelson at his last Holy Communion service, March 2003, with Shelby DiFiore.

that such a gentle person would speak with such depth and strength. Through my years I have met many a clergyman who fought angrily for the rights of others. Roger did it with warmth, love, kindness, and conviction. You could not say no to his invitation to do something about an injustice.

What really fired up Reverend Nelson, though, was ecumenism. When he arrived in town there was a fine spirit of cooperation among the many Protestant churches. The "United Parish" movement was something that truly excited Roger. Over the years he saw many ups and downs of this movement as other clergy came and went. But through the '90s we all looked upon him as the guiding father figure of this movement. Under his guidance both Catholics and Protestants worked together, planned together, and prayed together. The Saugus Clergy Association, led by Roger, not only met and talked but carried out all kinds of activities. At his invitation the Town Hall was filled for the new millennium, it overflowed onto the streets for his call to prayer after the September 11th disaster, the people of many churches prayed together each Sunday night of Lent, and the road to the lake in Breakheart Reservation was filled with tableaus of the Passion. Roger even got a crowd to be at the Ironworks to pray and sing at six in the morning on Easter!

He did all this while he did all that challenging stuff that the pastor of a small Episcopal Church must do. He had to keep the parish family united while the Episcopal Church made many changes to its prayer books and decided to ordain women and meet challenges of the modern world. Roger may have been great in the pulpit but he also had to lock and

unlock the doors, keep the boiler going, and keep the roof from falling in. Raising the necessary funds, doing the funerals and weddings, preparing the Sunday message were all part of his job description. He always seemed so calm and collected to me as I watched in amazement. Bouts with ill health, though, told me that Roger was really putting himself out to get all this done so well.

Surely the people who knew him here miss The Reverend Roger Nelson. I'm sure he misses the people of Saugus whom he knew so well. This "retired" priest now enjoys the company of his wife Dotsie, and the trips out west to visit his son Craig, and the special part time and temporary assignments the Bishop gives him. Roger certainly will be remembered as a very special part of Saugus history.

John P. Creed

by
Peter Rossetti, Jr.

John Creed attended Marshfield High School from 1954 to 1957. In his year book, the quote was, "John has to make a choice of religion, sports or politics." I think he chose all three.

John attended Fairfield University in Fairfield, Connecticut, where he received his bachelor's degree in education. He attended from 1961 to 1962 at St. Philip Neri School for language study, and then 1962 to 1967 was spent at St. John's Seminary. He was ordained a Roman Catholic priest in 1967 in the Archdiocese of Boston. He served at St. Margaret's Parish in Saugus from 1968 until 1977. He remained with the archdiocese until 1981.

During John's time at St. Margaret, he was always colorful, which endeared him to the parish. His interests in sports, politics and the daily lives of the parishioners soon became his major concerns. While in Saugus, he chaired Listen, Inc., a program designed to help people with substance abuse. As a liberal in a conservative institution, he found himself at odds with his superiors and, after a long period of soul-searching, he chose to sever his connection with the Boston Archdiocese as a priest, but not as a Catholic.

From 1981 to the present day, there is a strong connection to one of his first loves, the World Champion Boston Celtics. He does wear a Celtics Championship ring, an honor very few non-players can boast about. I can remember the time he picked up a few young players at Logan Airport. It was late in the evening, and in those days, things closed early, so John brought them to my parents' home, because he knew there would always be food and good company for a visiting stranger.

John also had a passion for politics. He is the only person I know of who can boast of serving on three different school committees in three different towns. He has served on the Saugus School Committee, the Marshfield School Committee, and presently, on the Silver Lake School Committee. On the Marshfield committee, he was chairperson for six years and vice chair for two.

John Creed.

At the present time, John lives with his lovely wife, Nancy, in Kingston, Massachusetts. He is both a sports announcer and political analyst with Radio Station WATD in Marshfield. He presently works as a public relations consultant to several school districts, including Northeast Metropolitan Regional Vocational High School. He fondly remembers his time in Saugus and frequently visits. He still has his hand on the pulse of Beacon Hill concerning education issues.

Memories of Vincent Pelrine

by
Stephen P. Carlson

Many people remember Vincent Pelrine as a musician who performed on the vibes with local musical ensembles in the 1930s and 1940s. I remember him as a man who was interested in many of the same areas as my late father, Paul Carlson, including music and photography.

Vin Pelrine was a ham radio operator. This interest was what brought him and my dad together. Vin, who was ahead of Dad in Saugus High, came to buy parts for radios from my grandfather, Helge E. Carlson, who ran his own radio repair business out of his home on Lewis St. on the hill in East Saugus. They became friends, a friendship that lasted until Vin's untimely death in the early 1970s.

The two areas where Dad and Vin shared interests were organ music and photography. In the 1950s, both acquired Hammond organs. Dad was the inveterate tinkerer, constantly working to upgrade the instrument in one way or another. The fact that he constantly had the organ apart was one reason why my half-hearted attempts to practice organ lessons were stymied.

Almost every Saturday night, Vin would come up to the house. Our dog Mitzi could sense when he was coming, probably because he always had a treat for her. Vin and his mother, with whom he lived following his divorce from his wife Peg, loved dogs. Indeed, Mrs. P, as everyone knew her, took in neighborhood dogs, most memorably a basset hound named Reginald. Reginald spent as much time in their Prospect St. house as he did with his real owners on Fiske Road, if I recall it right.

On those Saturday nights, Dad or Vin would play the organ, then stop in time to watch Lawrence Welk on television. Alternately, they would disappear downstairs into the darkroom to do some photographic processing.

On Monday nights, Vin would join my parents to travel to Weston to attend pipe organ concerts in the home and studio of an organist whose name I believe was Woodworth. While I stayed home with my babysitter, my uncle, on those occasions, I did go with them to concerts with silent films at the Stoneham Town Hall and at the Hammond Castle in Gloucester.

I recall many times going to visit Vin at his house. Dad helped him build his own darkroom, with oversize sinks to accommodate large photographic processing trays. Or they would work on some electronic project, whether related to the organ or Vin's ham radio. Or we would all just sit in his living room and talk with him and his mother.

One thing that stands out in my memories is that he owned one of the first Thunderbird convertibles, something that was attractive to a kid whose family transport consisted of Plymouth station wagons. Always attracted to fancy cars, Vin later owned a Shelby Cobra, and expressed regret that he had sold his first Thunderbird, which, since he always kept his cars in mint condition, would have been worth a fortune as a collector's car.

Vin would often accompany us on Saturday or Sunday excursions where Dad and he would seek suitable targets for their cameras. On those trips, he was an inveterate joker. I still recall clearly one trip to Gloucester where he took delight in pointing out signs with the names of the King brothers on them—Nosmo and Nopar (No Smoking and No Parking).

One of the amusements I had during trips was keeping a count of the numbers of different brands of gas stations we saw. This was an era in the 1950s and early 1960s when there was a proliferation of small chains. Whoever first saw a station would call it out by name and I would duly record it in a column on papers I carried. Vin delighted in calling out brands such as "Flug," "Libom," and "Ocaxet," although "Cities Service" defied efforts to pronounce in reverse. To this day, I still find myself using Vin's unusual versions of brand names.

Because of his background in radio, Vin, in the late 1950s, found work as a technical writer with a number of the high-tech firms which sprouted up along the Route 128 corridor following the launch of Sputnik, including Avco in Wilmington. In those jobs, he traveled extensively. I recall Vin coming up one Saturday after such a business trip to say that he had flown to Los Angeles to go to Vandenberg Air Force Base and that the 707 out of Boston had one passenger — himself — until it made a stop en route.

Vincent Pelrine is definitely one Saugonian whom I will always remember fondly.

Remembering Jack Shapiro

by
Neil Howland

I first met Jack Shapiro when we were classmates in the close-knit redoubtable Saugus High Class of 1947. That early boyhood acquaintance blossomed into an enduring life-long friendship of high regard and loyalty. He escaped my vision in the lower grades, but that's normal I guess when relations at that age tend to be mercurial, transitory, or at least kind of skeedaddleish as you try out – and fall for – important things like what style of shoes your new idol wears.

As I have written so many times before, Saugus in the '30s and '40s was akin to Mark Twain's Hannibal, Missouri, as a warm spot where we tadpoles could learn to swim and be frisky, without getting hurt. World War II raised ever present and somber shadows in our lives, but couldn't dampen our youthful zest for experimentation, enjoying life – and just growing up.

How's the old song go – "You've got to be a football

Jack Shapiro.

hero to get along with the beautiful girls," and Jack desperately wanted to wow our vivacious classmate, Vickie Gregson, so Jack and I found ourselves as scrubs together briefly on the great State Championship football team of 1944. Jack was not well coordinated, nor even very athletic in truth, and he soon – wisely – opted out for those classroom pursuits at which he excelled. During off hours he worked as a soda fountain clerk for Saugus Center Pharmacy where for a short spell in his pre-college days he enjoyed a short, brilliant career – presiding over the soda fountain with a splash and a dash and his considerable charm that attracted to his counter a large, abiding following.

Jack entered BU along with neighbor and friend, and classmate of ours at Saugus, Reverend Jim Davis. His ambition then was to become Jack Shapiro, MD, but the science requirements in physics, chemistry and math proved too daunting and he gravitated to business management studies, which had a second nature to fit his skill set. On next to the world famous Harvard Business School, after college, where he honed his estimable talents even more so. I was then at Harvard Law School and occasionally we bumped into each other in Harvard Square for lunch on the run. After all, our respective schools worked us like 18th century Chinese coolies on the Union Pacific Railroad so there wasn't much time. But what the heck, we were making great strides in our education – now even spelling words like "linoleum." Not bad for a couple of Saugus kids.

As we happily graduated from our respective institutions, we each turned to the U.S. Navy to fulfill our great country's military obligation for us – after all, it was the mid-1950s, and like so many young men in that period we served with pride, Jack as an officer in a commissary unit and I as a "white hat" (enlisted man) in a land-based Helicopter Rescue Squadron. As we observed, lucky not to be bouncing around the Indian Ocean on some cruiser: "What the hey – they also serve who sit and type." Jack's duties fitted right in with his future plans, of course, while I handled all Captain's Mast chores, formal Courts Martial, and happily edited the monthly squadron newsletter and, occasionally, a cold beer. Sort of the line of work a newly minted eagle would go for. Anchors Aweigh and all that. Much of Jack's service in the Navy was as the Navy Exchange Officer at the Naval Air Station in Sanford, Florida. After returning from the Navy, he continued his career with Filene's and later other retailers throughout the country. Up until his death, just days before his 76th birthday, he maintained an active consulting practice serving retailers and manufacturers who sold to retailers, including the Ralph Lauren Company. Jack had many connections both in his high school class and in the town more broadly, for which he always had a great affection. Many of us remember his warm smile and friendly manner in whatever task he was at.

The Last Picture Show

Formal symbolic representation of qualitative entities is doomed to its rightful place of minor significance in a world where flowers and beautiful women abound.

— Albert Einstein

A Collection of Random Photographs from Around Saugus

by
the *Time and the River* Committee

Following is a potpourri of photographs taken around Saugus. It has been organized into a few basic categories.

Leaving Saugus Center toward Cliftondale Square.

Saugus Center

Monument Square, Saugus Center, circa 1900.

Cliftondale

Cliftondale Square.

Soldiers' Monument with
Teldeu's and Adlington's stores in the background.

Lincoln Avenue in Cliftondale Square.

Ærial view of Cliftondale Square.

Merchants' Row, Cliftondale Square.

Old Route One

The Route One Rotary.

Route One; the Tudor Mansion is on the right.

The White House on Route One.

Turning around on Route One,
looking north toward the Essex Street Overpass.

The Red Coach Grill – now the site of Kelly's Roast Beef.

Breakheart Reservation

Silver Lake, Breakheart Reservation.

Early Route One construction.

Hitching Farm House at Breakheart.

Breakheart Ranger Bill Dalton in Breakheart's hills.

Pearce Lake Beach, Breakheart Reservation.

The Iron Works

Cinder bank site of the Iron Works in 1900; the so-called Iron Works Mansion is in the background.

Johnson Camp near Bear Hill, Breakheart Reservation.

Iron Works house prior to the reconstruction.

The Last Picture Show

A water wheel at the Iron Works.

The Saugus River heading toward the Iron Works.

Celebrating the 50th Anniversary of the
Reconstruction of the Saugus Iron Works.

Boats on the Saugus River.

Saugus Historical Society President Darren Brown
at the Iron Works for its reconstruction's 50th anniversary..

A bend in the river.

The Saugus River with GE in the background.

Foxes in the Golden Hills.

Miscellany

Iroquois Mills on Central Street, taken during the 2002 "Trails and Sails" event.

Hotel at the race track on the marsh.

Wild turkeys in the Golden Hills.

1938 hurricane scene; Essex Street opposite Eustis.

Granite Court.

The Ghost Dog House.

Index of Authors

Q

R

S

T

U

V

W

Y

Index of Illustrators

Photography Credits Index

[While we made every effort to ensure that the proper credits have been made, many of the pictures we received were themselves reproductions, and even when we had the originals the photographers' names were often nigh impossible to read.]

A
Alabiso, Judy 332, 339

B
Blanchard, James 62
Bliss, G.S. 342, 345
Brierly, T. 247
Brown, B. 279
Brown, Eric W. 21, 22, 150, 305, 322, 346, 347, 348, 354
Burke, L. 147
Burns, J. 179

C
Caproni, Shirley 193
Cerasuolo, Ned 121, 122, 222
Chaves, Joe 26
Couturier, B. 141
Creed, J. 338

D
Dalton, Bill 344, 345, A
Davis, Gretchen 137, 138
Davis, R. 106, 107
Day, S. 23, 128, 129
DeFranzo, Ray 80
DeFronzo, Rose A. 4
deSteuben, Karla 330
Downs, Norm 62
Draper, Cynthia 136

E
Evans, A. 263, 264, 265
Exel, R. 258

F
Fabrizio, Ken 176
Flynn, Peggy 268
French, Sylvia 74, 289

G
Gibbs, E. 140

H
Harrington, Jim iii, viii, ix, 14, 15, 16, 17, 103, 104, 105, 223, 305, 342, 346, 347, A, B, C, D, E, F, G, H
Hatch Family 256, 257

Hatfield, B. 251
Hood, M. 232

J
Jarosz, Janice 3, 13, 14, 16, 51, 56, 84, 91, 120, 125, 151, 181, 213, 220, 305
Jarosz, Jarosz 214, 216

L
Laskey, Sis 101
Long, R. 146, 337
Lucey, Kathy 97
Lumsden, J. 313
Lynn Historical Society 345

M
Maes, Ray 335
Maher, Rich 52, 53
Maxwell, S. 266
Maxwell, Sam 342
Mitchell, Jerry 243, 245, 246
Moore, E. 82, 83, 283
Moorehouse, M. 143
Moriello, G. 44, 45
Mystic Seaport L.F. Herreshoff Collection 12, 13
Mystic Seaport Photography Collection 10, 11

N
Nicole, L. 235, 236
Norm Down Collection iii, 124, 125, 208, 209, 210, 302, 303, 304, 305, 342, 343, 344, 347

O
O'Leary, T. 90
O'Neill, B. 157

P
Pace, J. 91
Provenzano, Dick 289

R
Raymond, Jean 79
Rodenheiser, R. 15
Rohrbacher, R. 170
Rossetti, Louise 278
Roy, P. 229, 230, 231

S
Saugus Historical Society 106, 230, 236, 238, 277,

Sweetwater Street shut down due to flooding.